NEW SCHOOL

DASH SHAW

FANTAGRAPHICS BOOKS

DRAWN 2010 TO 2012
BED-STUY, BROOKLYN, NY

FANTAGRAPHICS BOOKS, INC.
Seattle, Washington, USA

Editor & Associate Publisher: Eric Reynolds
Book Design: Dash Shaw
Production: Dash Shaw & Paul Baresh
Publishers: Gary Groth & Kim Thompson

ISBN 978-1-60699-644-7

First Printing: April, 2013
Printed in China

PRELUDE

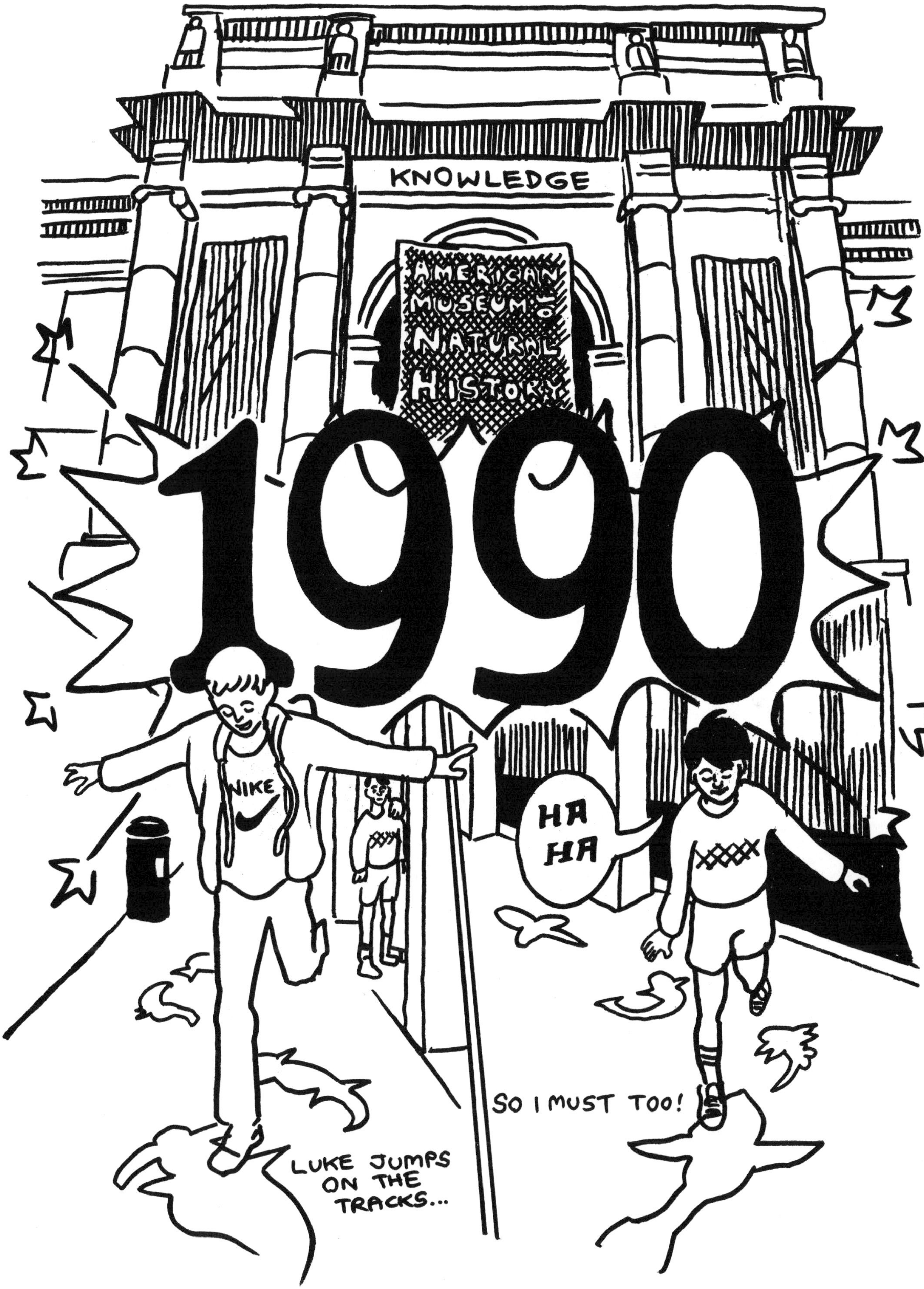
KNOWLEDGE
AMERICAN MUSEUM OF NATURAL HISTORY
1990
NIKE
HA HA
SO I MUST TOO!
LUKE JUMPS ON THE TRACKS...

LUKE TOUCHES THE ANCIENT TREE!

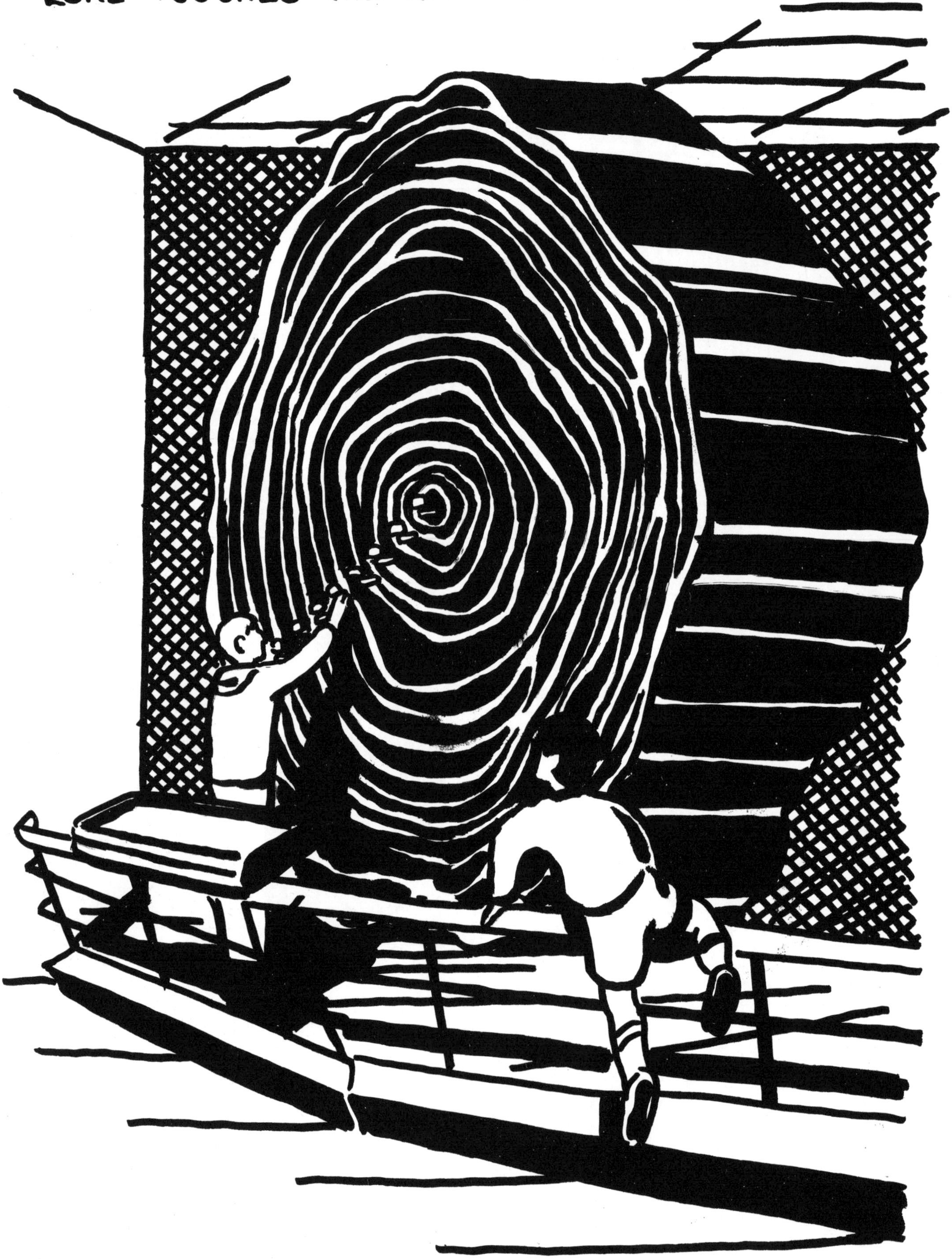

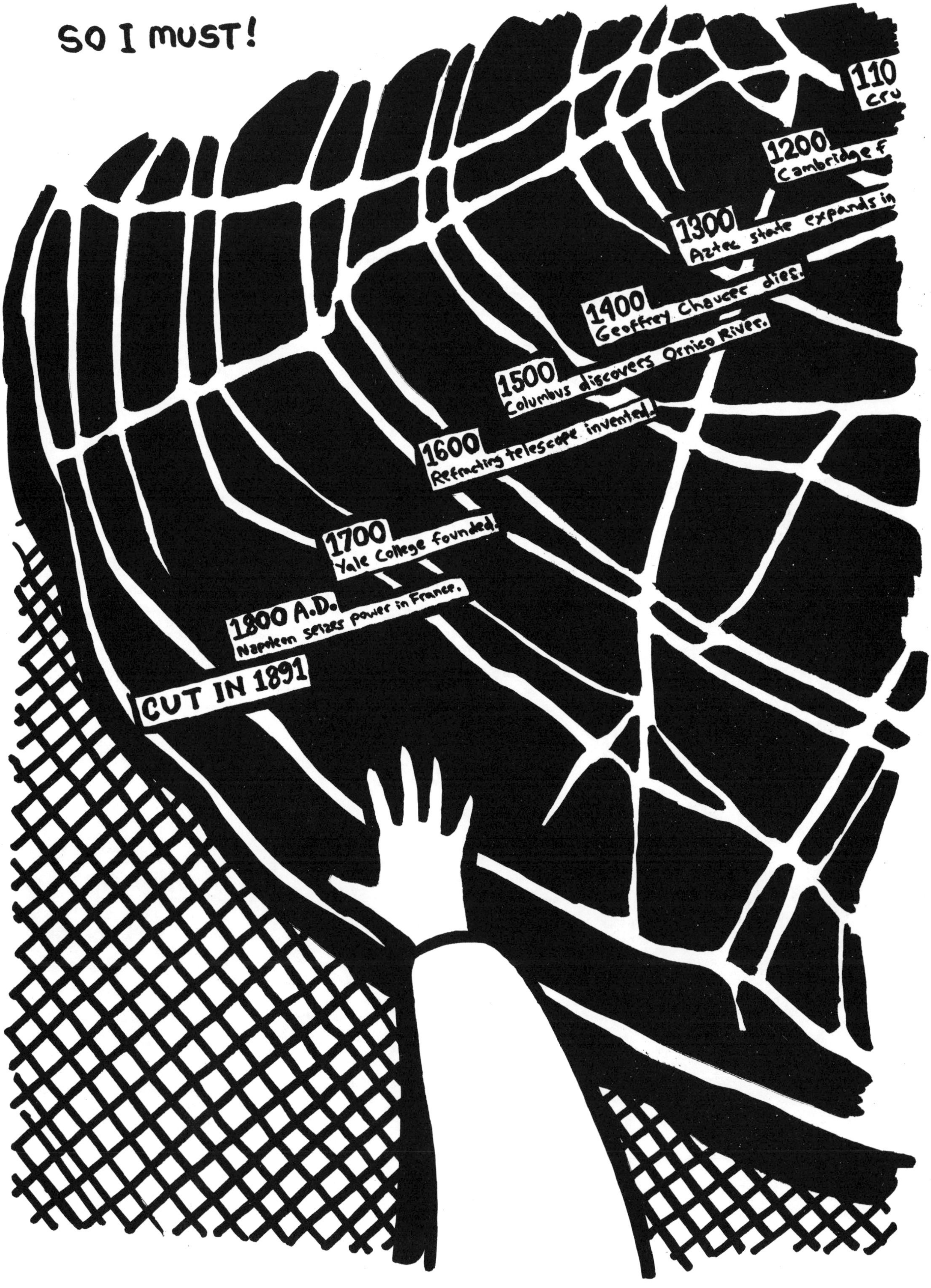
SO I MUST!
110
cru
1200
Cambridge f
1300
Aztec state expands in
1400
Geoffrey Chaucer dies.
1500
Columbus discovers Ornico River.
1600
Refracting telescope invented.
1700
Yale College founded.
1800 A.D.
Napoleon seizes power in France.
CUT IN 1891

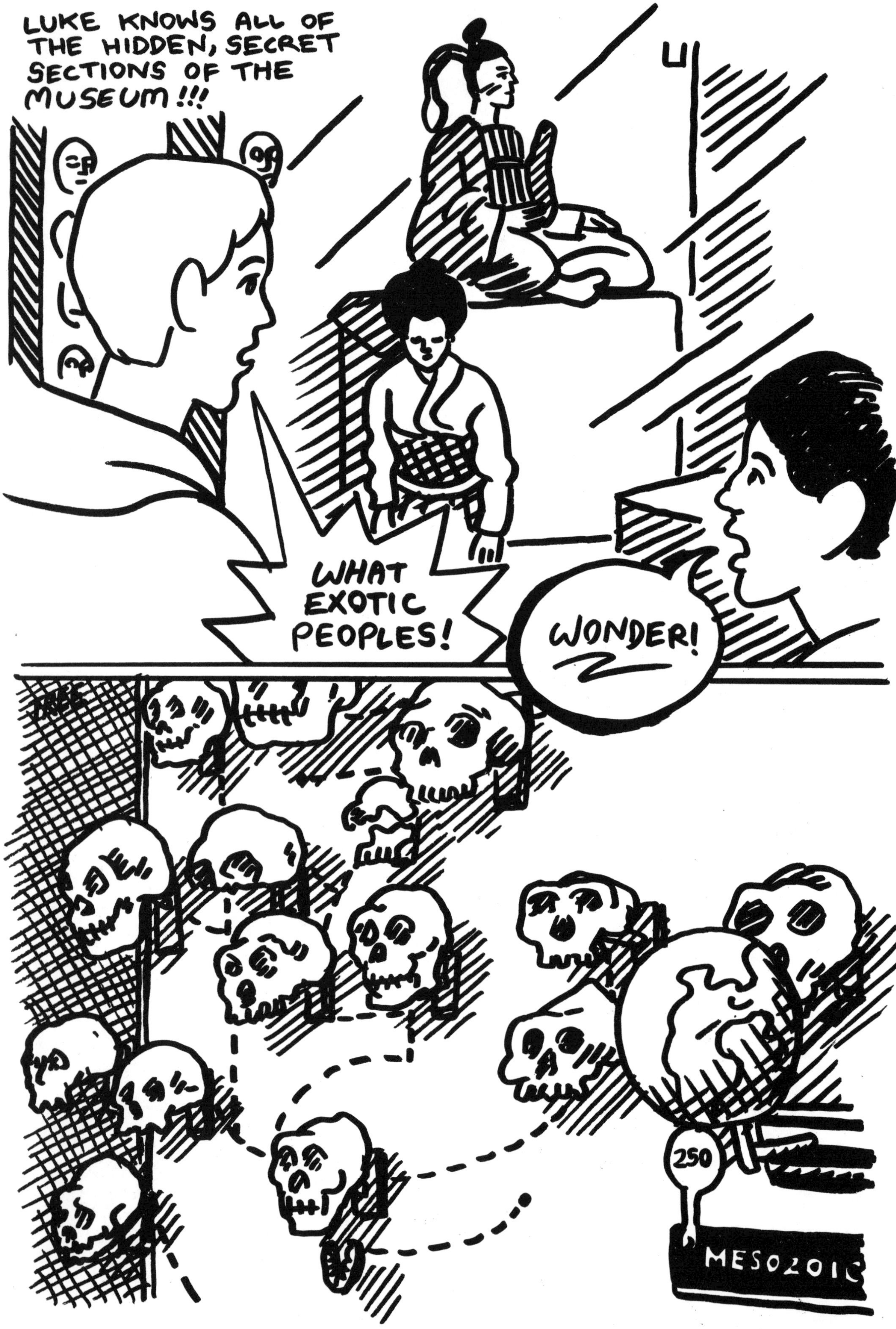
LUKE KNOWS ALL OF THE HIDDEN, SECRET SECTIONS OF THE MUSEUM!!!
WHAT EXOTIC PEOPLES!
WONDER!
250
MESO2010

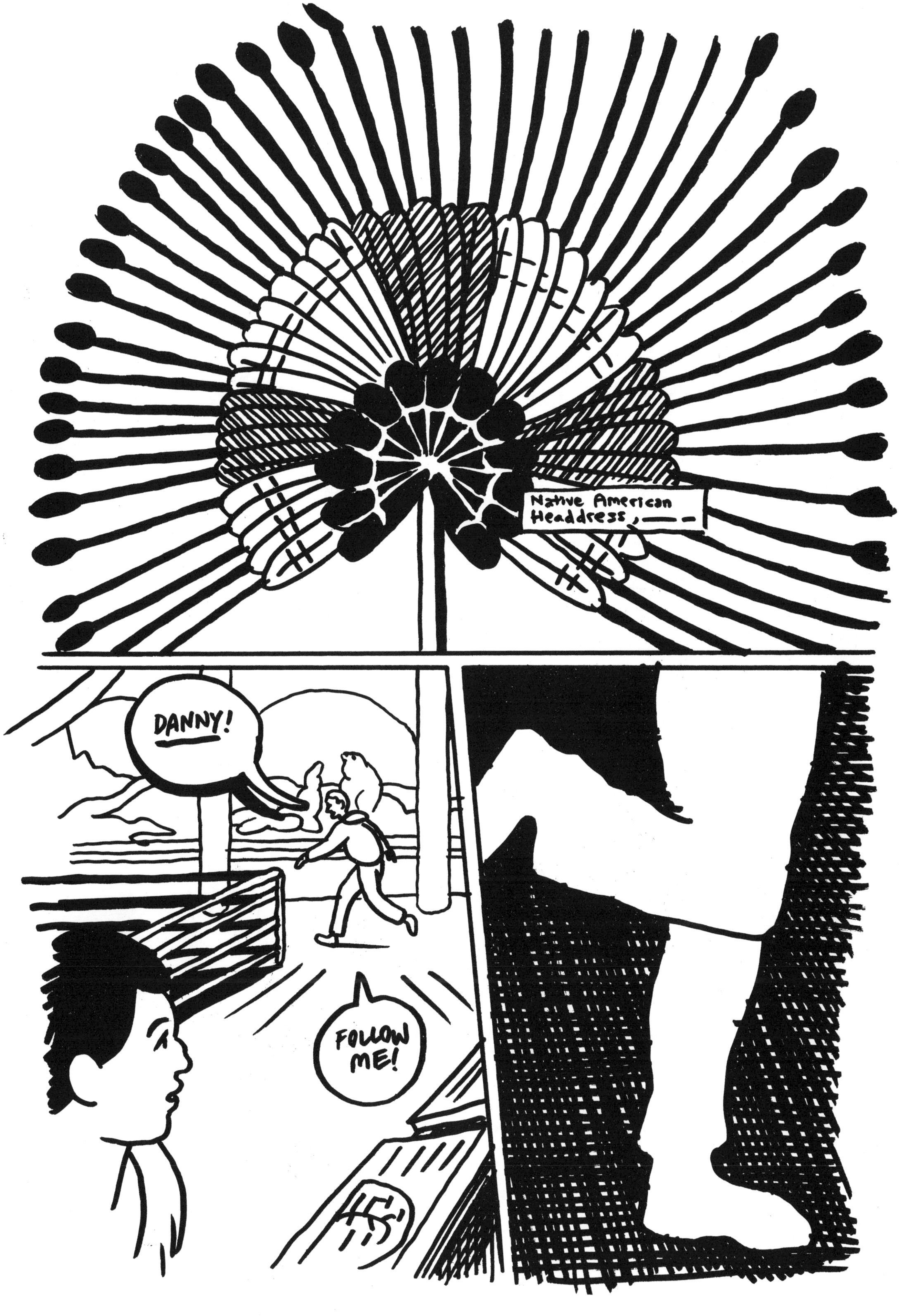
Native American Headdress, ____
DANNY!
FOLLOW ME!

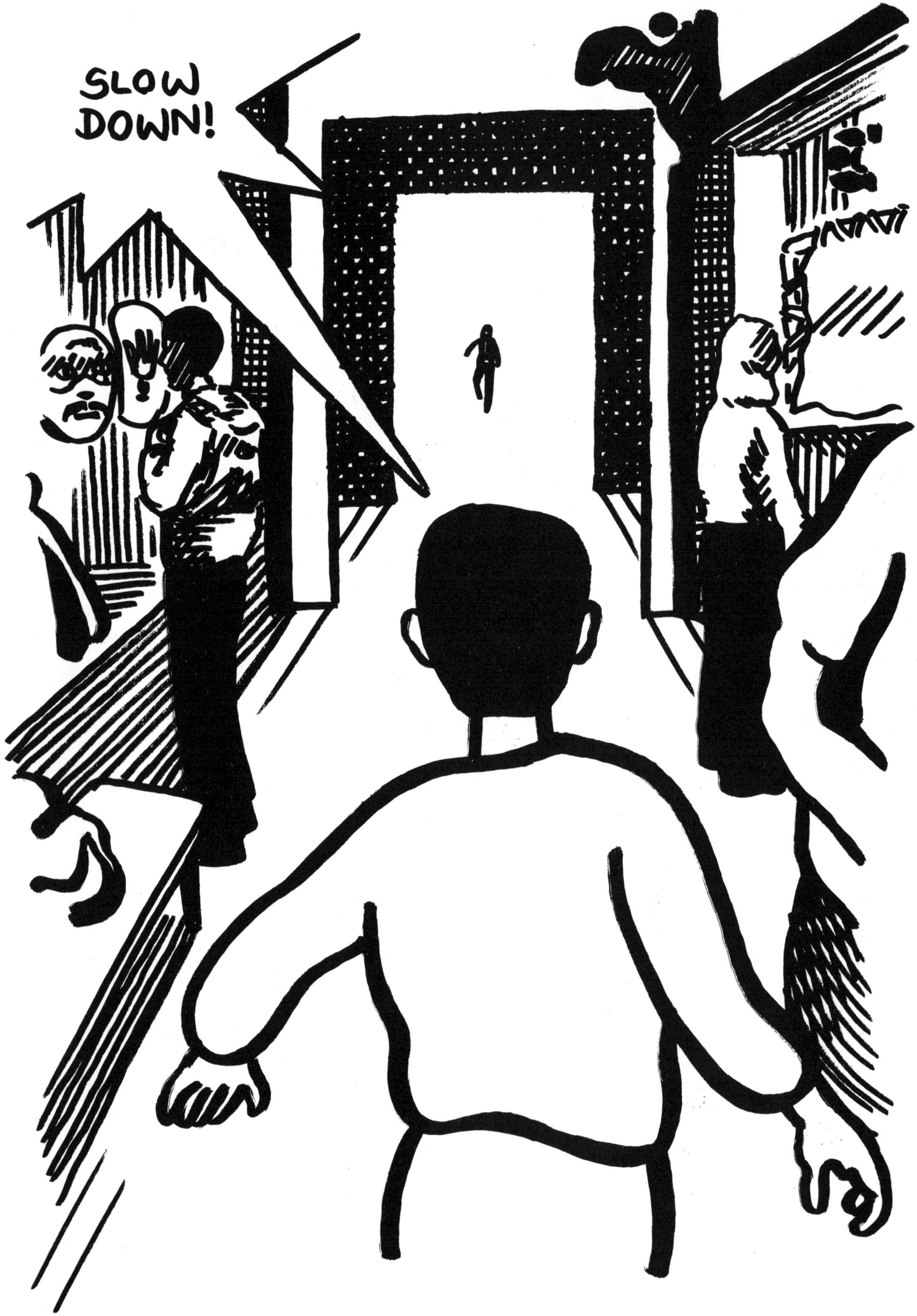
SLOW DOWN!

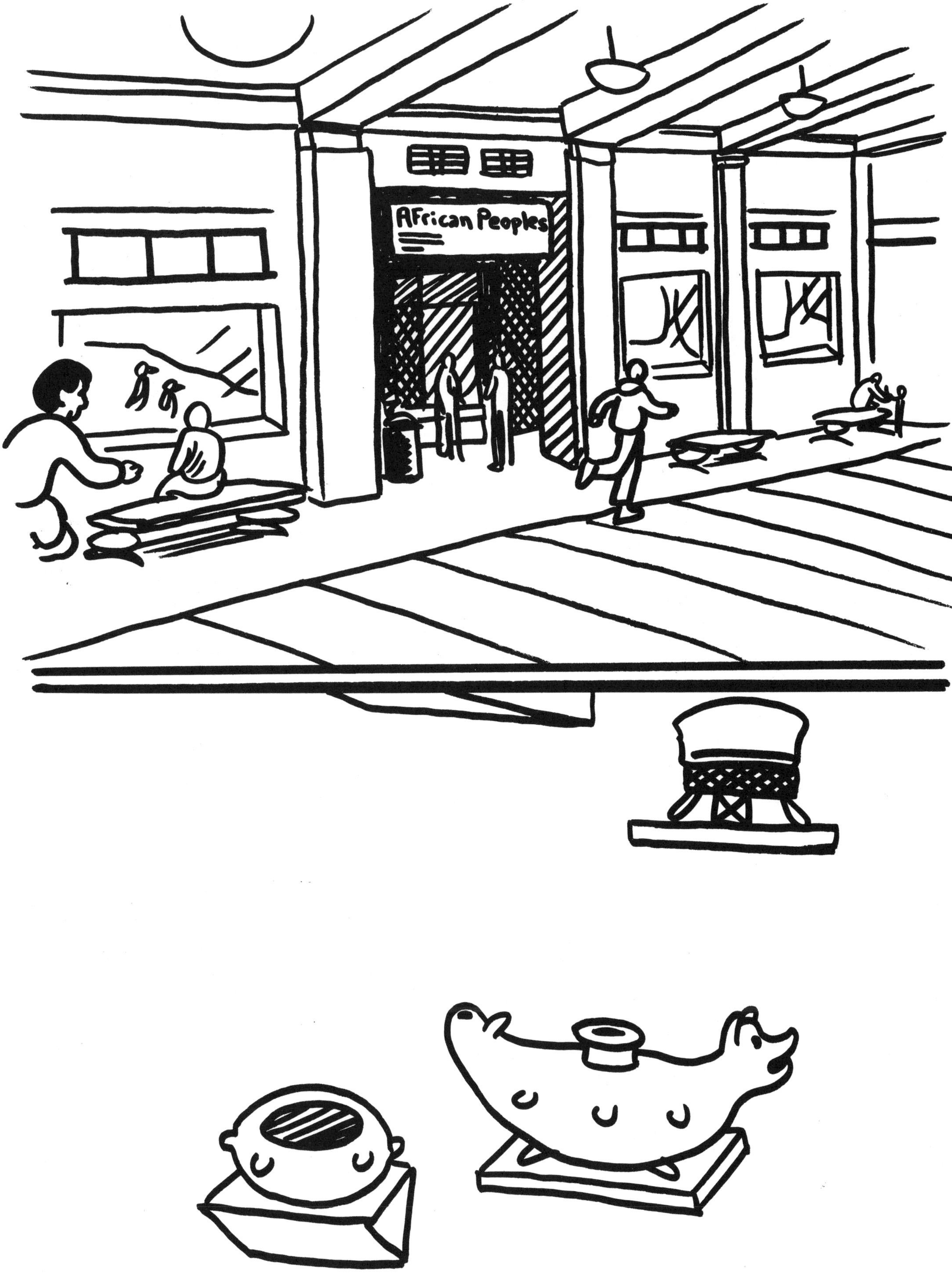
African Peoples

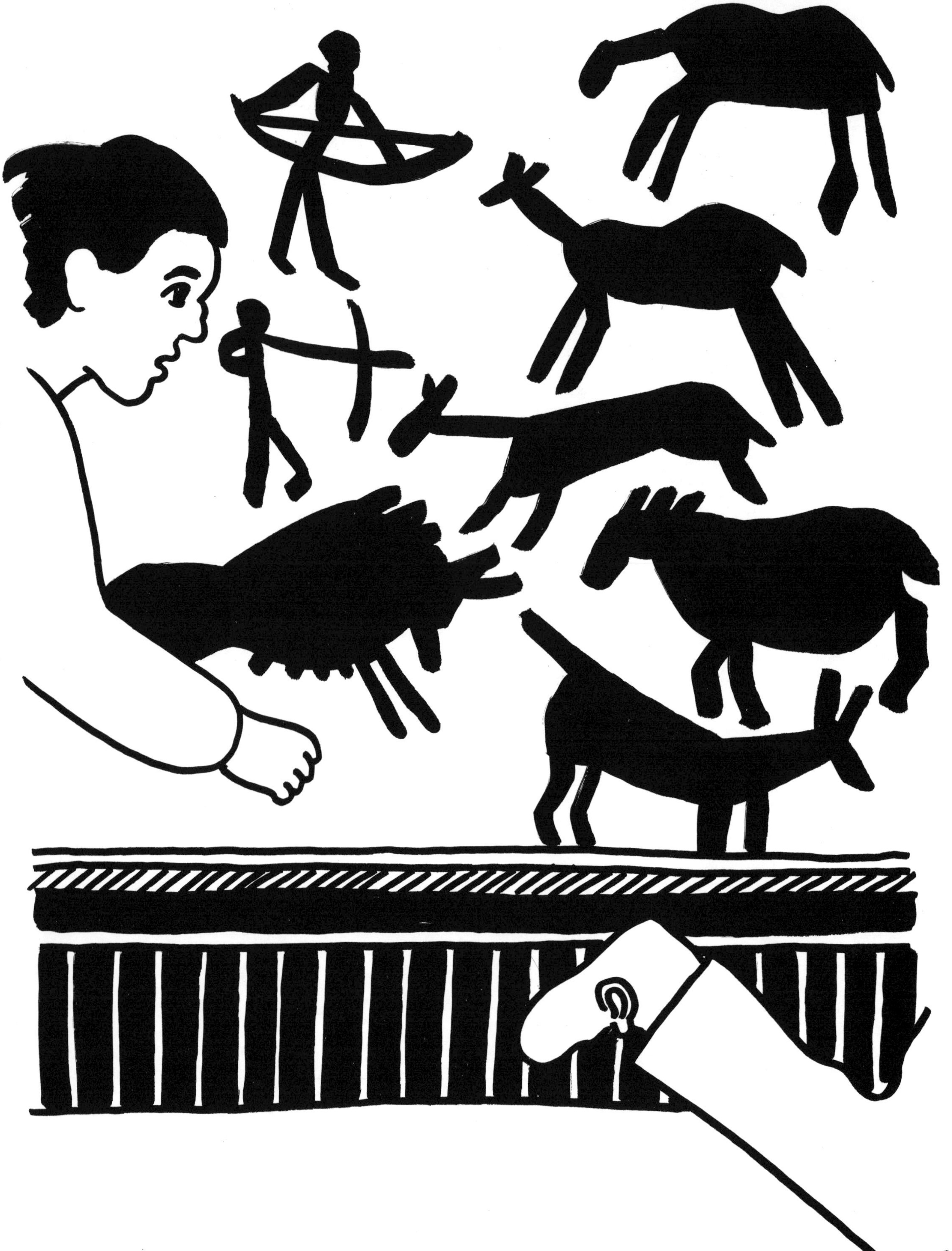

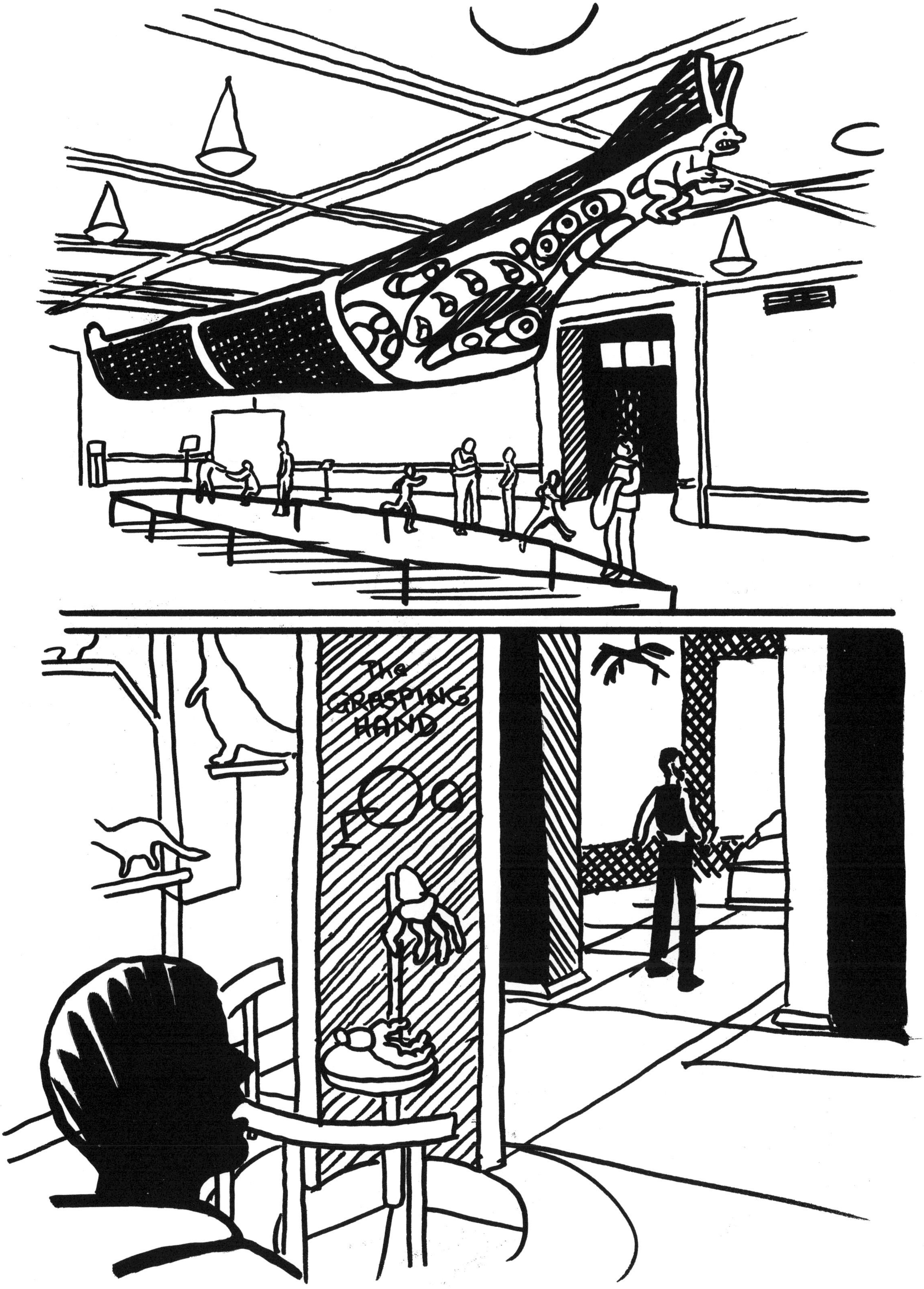
The GRASPING HAND

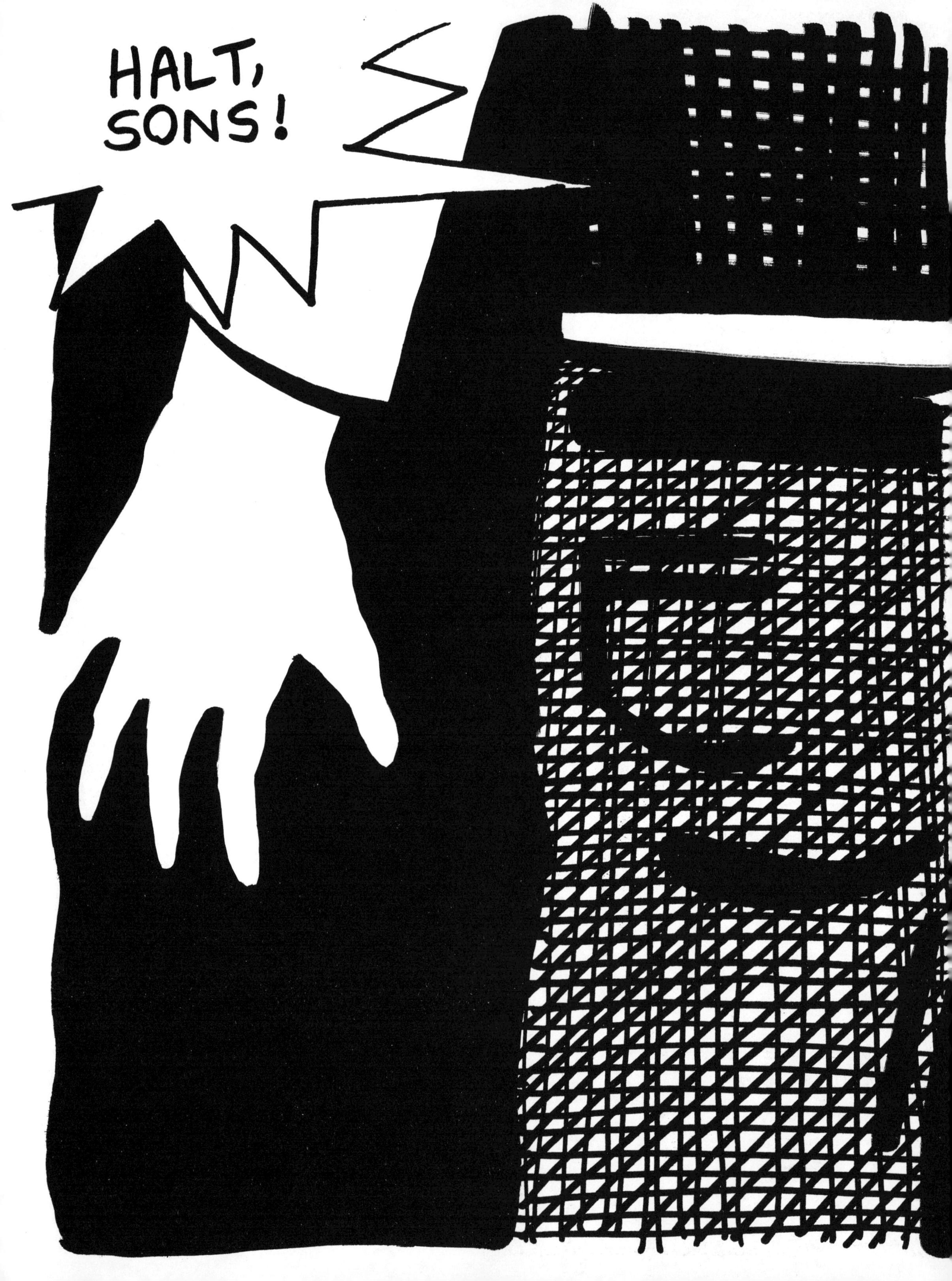
HALT, SONS!

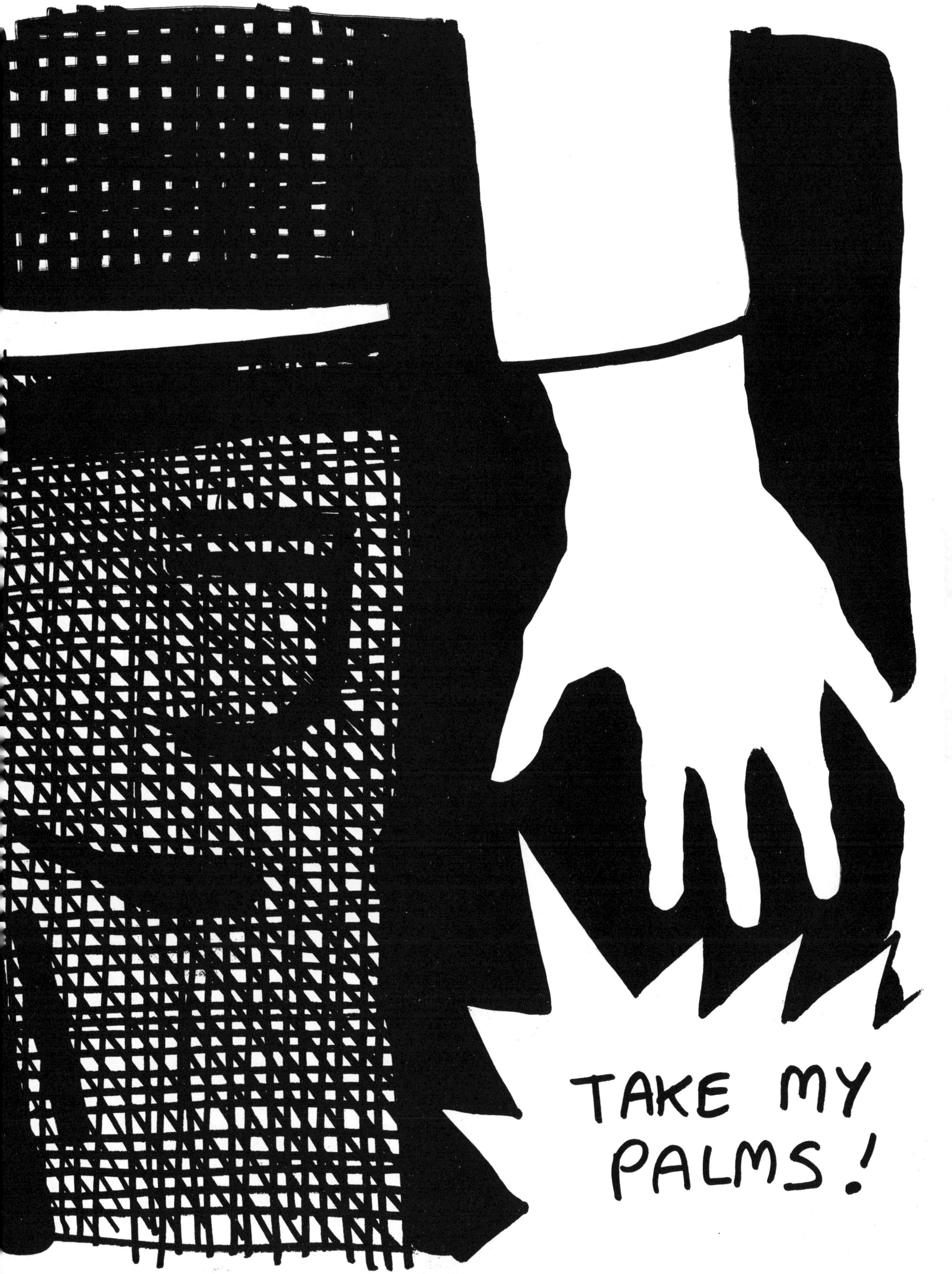
TAKE MY
PALMS!

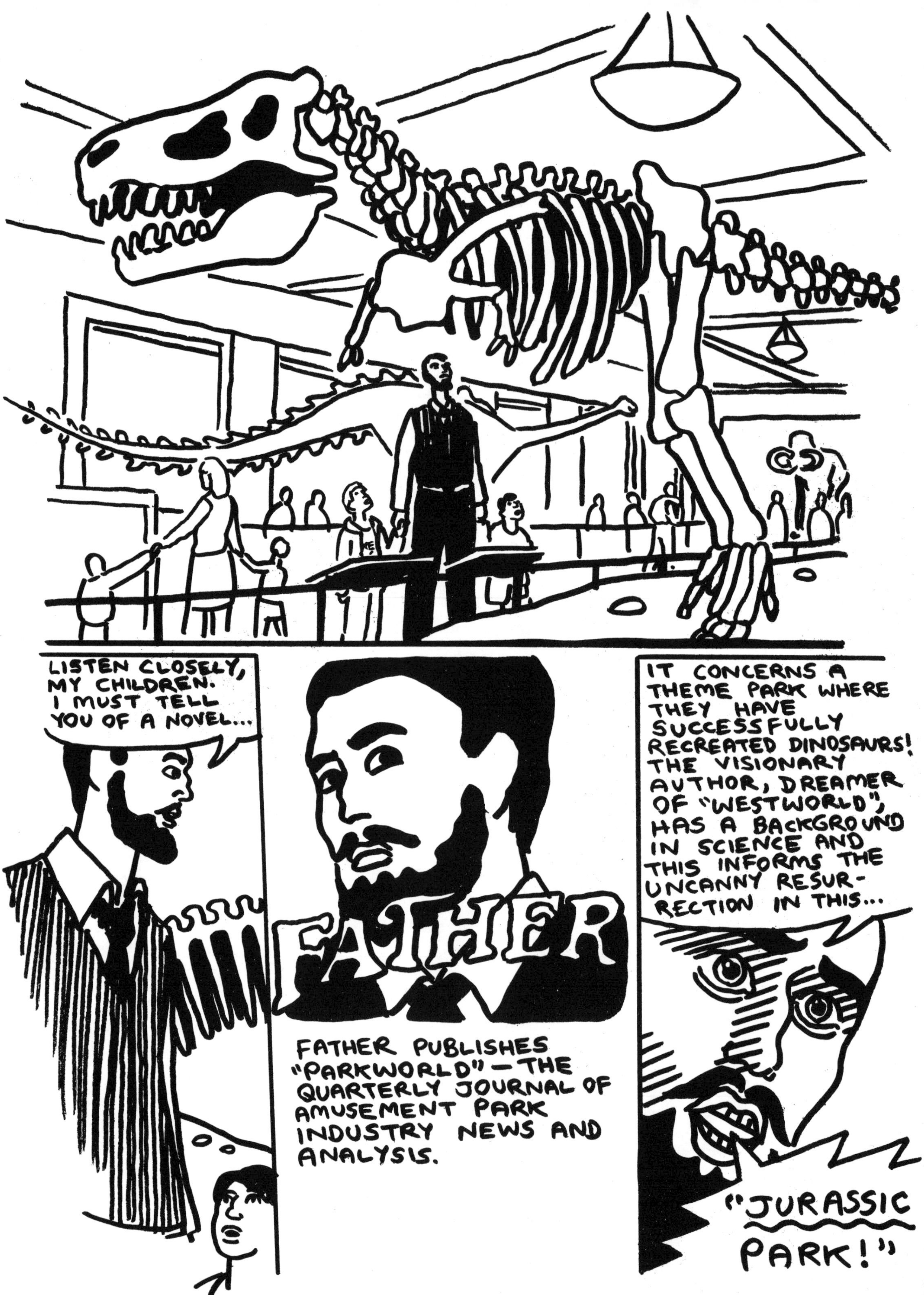

LISTEN CLOSELY, MY CHILDREN. I MUST TELL YOU OF A NOVEL...
FATHER
FATHER PUBLISHES "PARKWORLD" — THE QUARTERLY JOURNAL OF AMUSEMENT PARK INDUSTRY NEWS AND ANALYSIS.
IT CONCERNS A THEME PARK WHERE THEY HAVE SUCCESSFULLY RECREATED DINOSAURS! THE VISIONARY AUTHOR, DREAMER OF "WESTWORLD", HAS A BACKGROUND IN SCIENCE AND THIS INFORMS THE UNCANNY RESURRECTION IN THIS...
"JURASSIC PARK!"

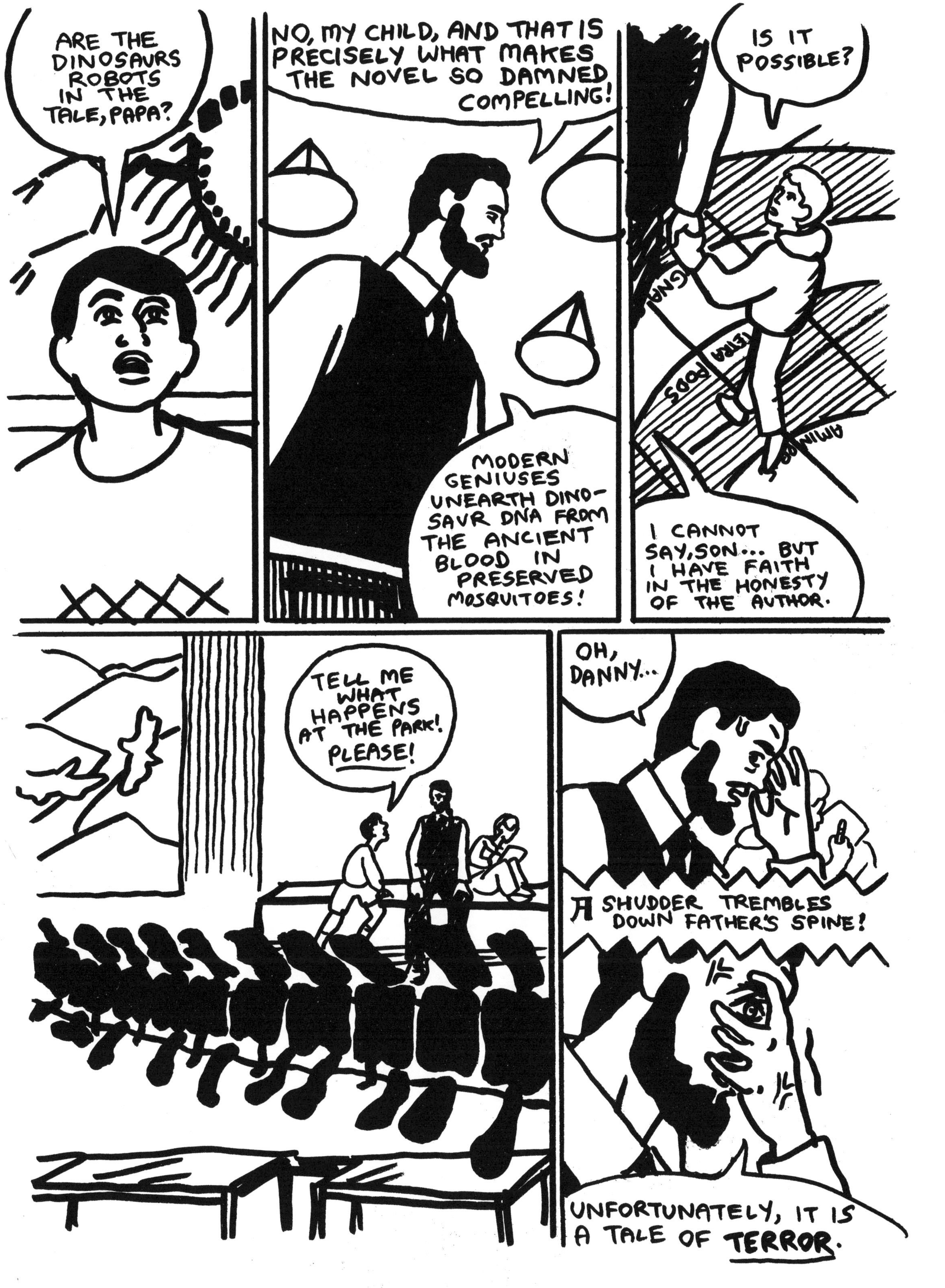
ARE THE DINOSAURS ROBOTS IN THE TALE, PAPA?
NO, MY CHILD, AND THAT IS PRECISELY WHAT MAKES THE NOVEL SO DAMNED COMPELLING!
MODERN GENIUSES UNEARTH DINO-SAUR DNA FROM THE ANCIENT BLOOD IN PRESERVED MOSQUITOES!
IS IT POSSIBLE?
I CANNOT SAY, SON... BUT I HAVE FAITH IN THE HONESTY OF THE AUTHOR.
TELL ME WHAT HAPPENS AT THE PARK! PLEASE!
OH, DANNY...
A SHUDDER TREMBLES DOWN FATHER'S SPINE!
UNFORTUNATELY, IT IS A TALE OF TERROR.

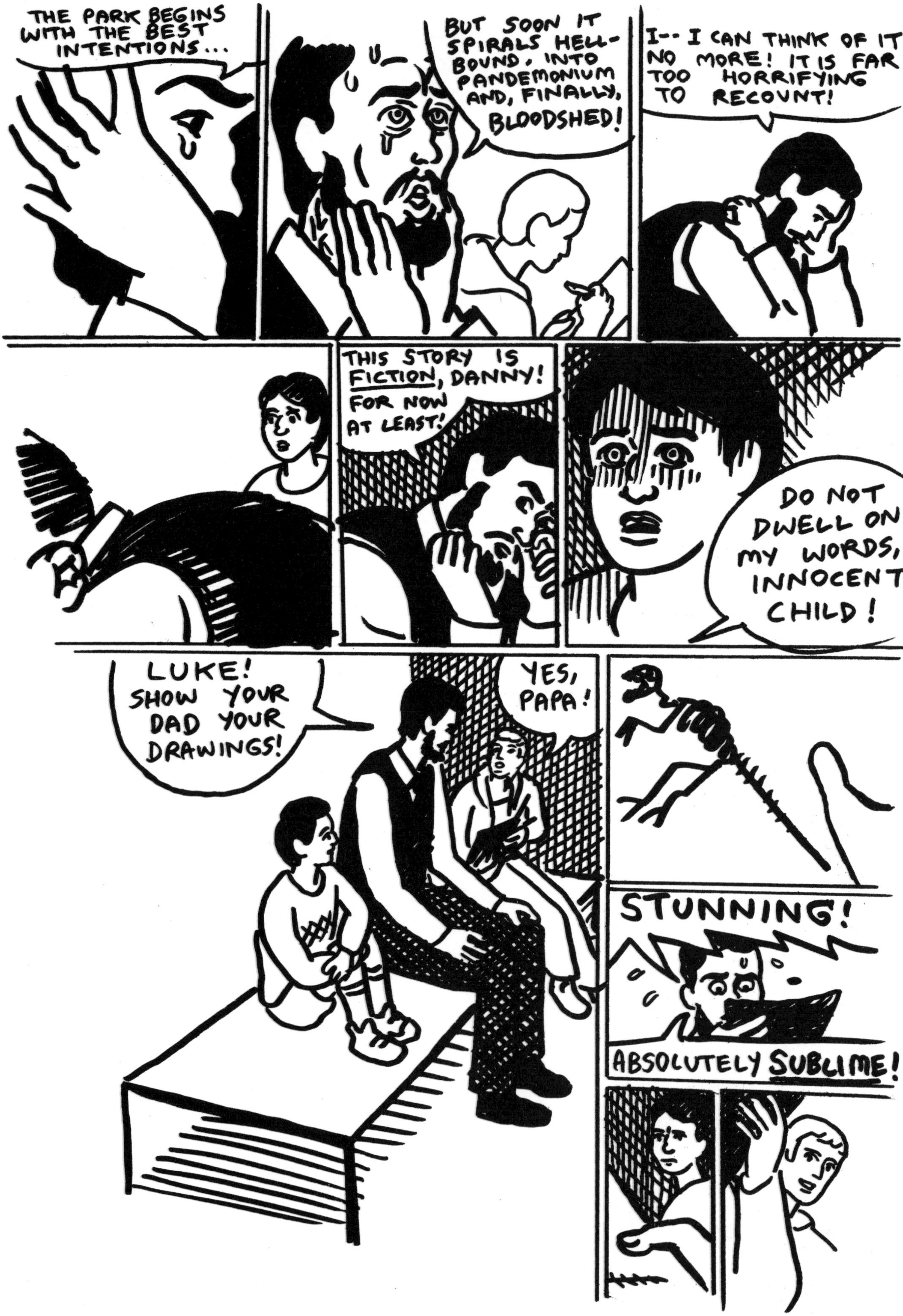
THE PARK BEGINS WITH THE BEST INTENTIONS...
BUT SOON IT SPIRALS HELL-BOUND, INTO PANDEMONIUM AND, FINALLY, BLOODSHED!
I-- I CAN THINK OF IT NO MORE! IT IS FAR TOO HORRIFYING TO RECOUNT!
THIS STORY IS FICTION, DANNY! FOR NOW AT LEAST!
DO NOT DWELL ON MY WORDS, INNOCENT CHILD!
LUKE! SHOW YOUR DAD YOUR DRAWINGS!
YES, PAPA!
STUNNING!
ABSOLUTELY SUBLIME!

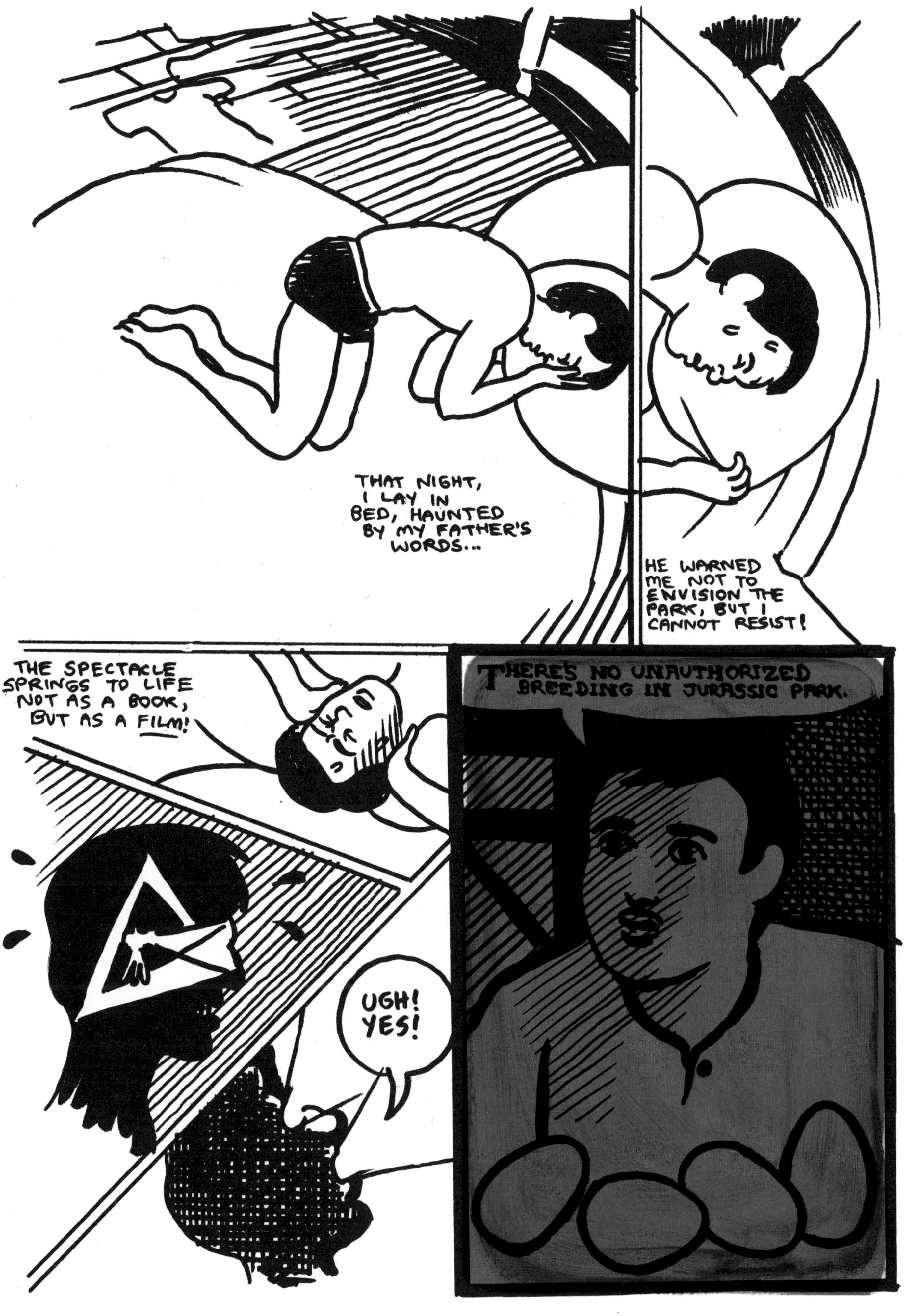
THAT NIGHT, I LAY IN BED, HAUNTED BY MY FATHER'S WORDS...
HE WARNED ME NOT TO ENVISION THE PARK, BUT I CANNOT RESIST!
THE SPECTACLE SPRINGS TO LIFE NOT AS A BOOK, BUT AS A FILM!
THERE'S NO UNAUTHORIZED BREEDING IN JURASSIC PARK.
UGH! YES!

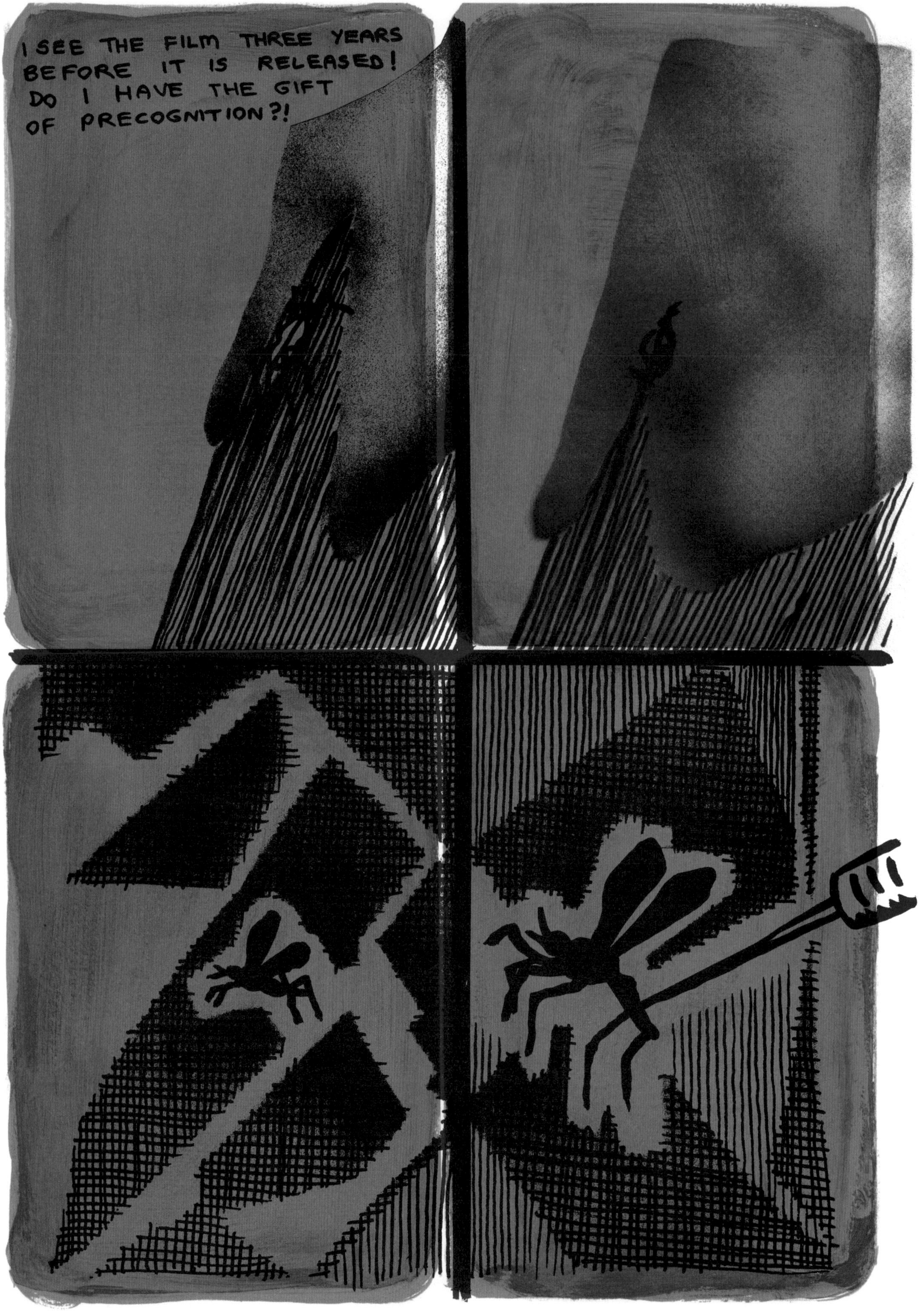
I SEE THE FILM THREE YEARS BEFORE IT IS RELEASED! DO I HAVE THE GIFT OF PRECOGNITION?!

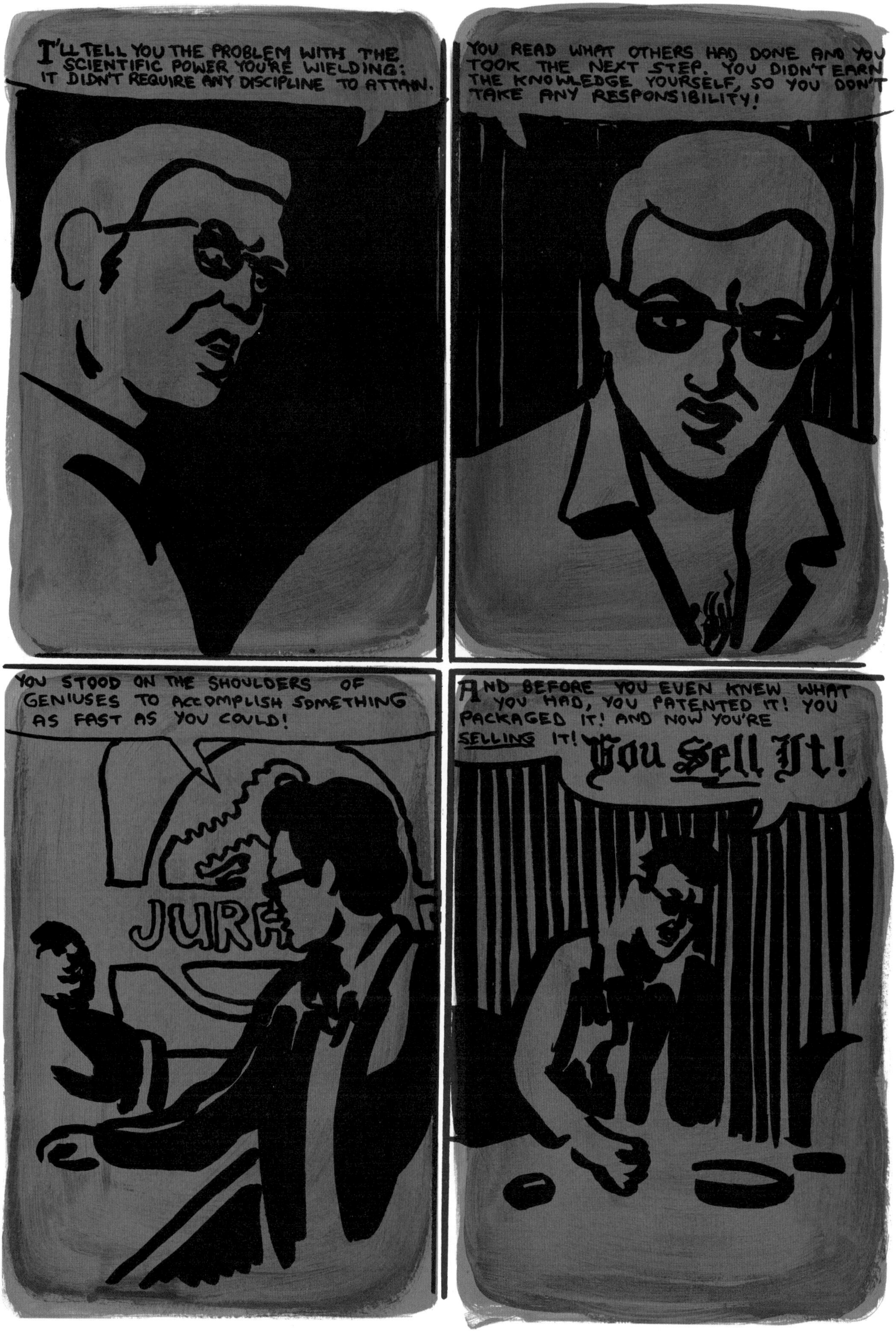
I'LL TELL YOU THE PROBLEM WITH THE SCIENTIFIC POWER YOU'RE WIELDING: IT DIDN'T REQUIRE ANY DISCIPLINE TO ATTAIN.
YOU READ WHAT OTHERS HAD DONE AND YOU TOOK THE NEXT STEP. YOU DIDN'T EARN THE KNOWLEDGE YOURSELF, SO YOU DON'T TAKE ANY RESPONSIBILITY!
YOU STOOD ON THE SHOULDERS OF GENIUSES TO ACCOMPLISH SOMETHING AS FAST AS YOU COULD!
JURA
AND BEFORE YOU EVEN KNEW WHAT YOU HAD, YOU PATENTED IT! YOU PACKAGED IT! AND NOW YOU'RE SELLING IT!
You Sell It!

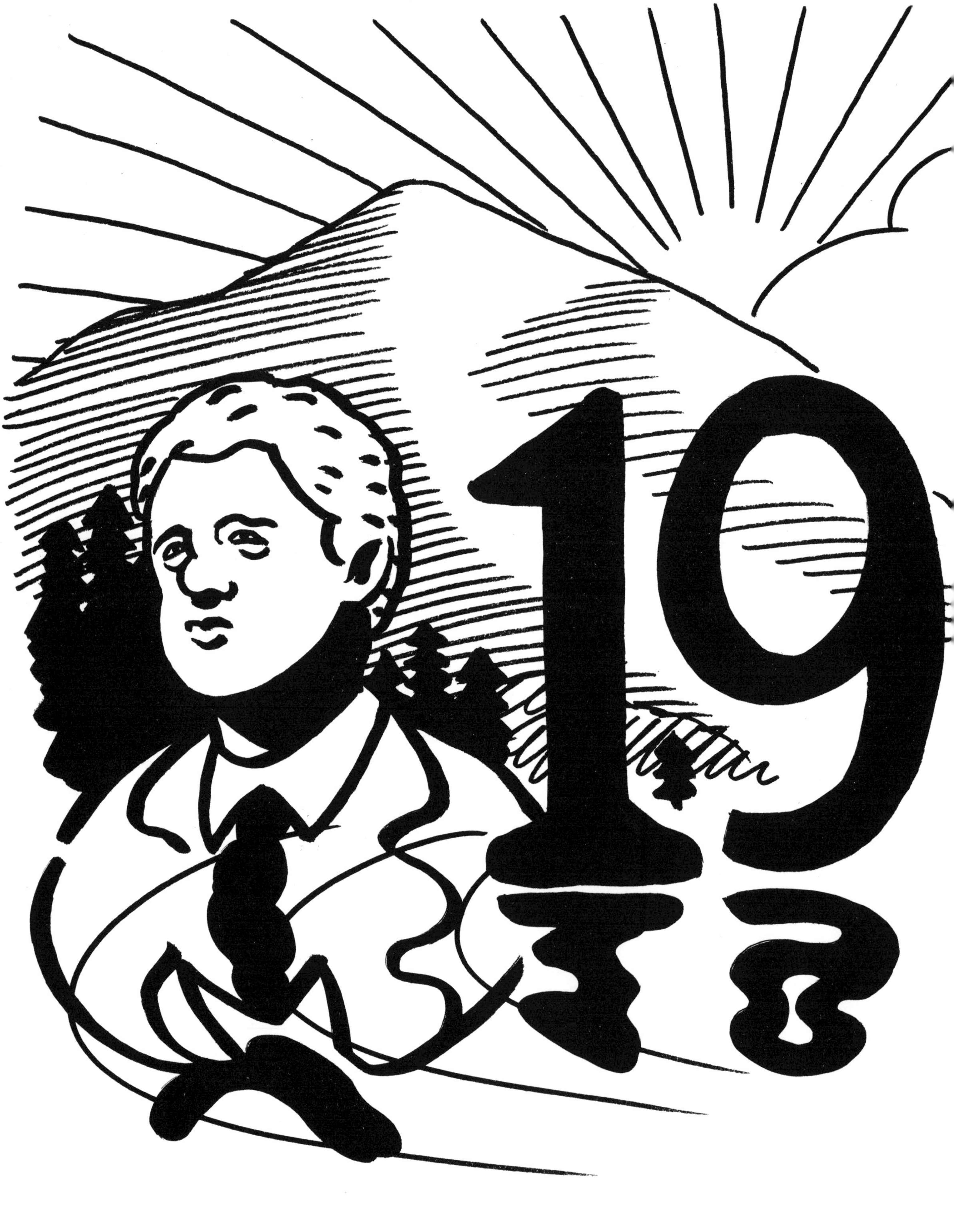
19

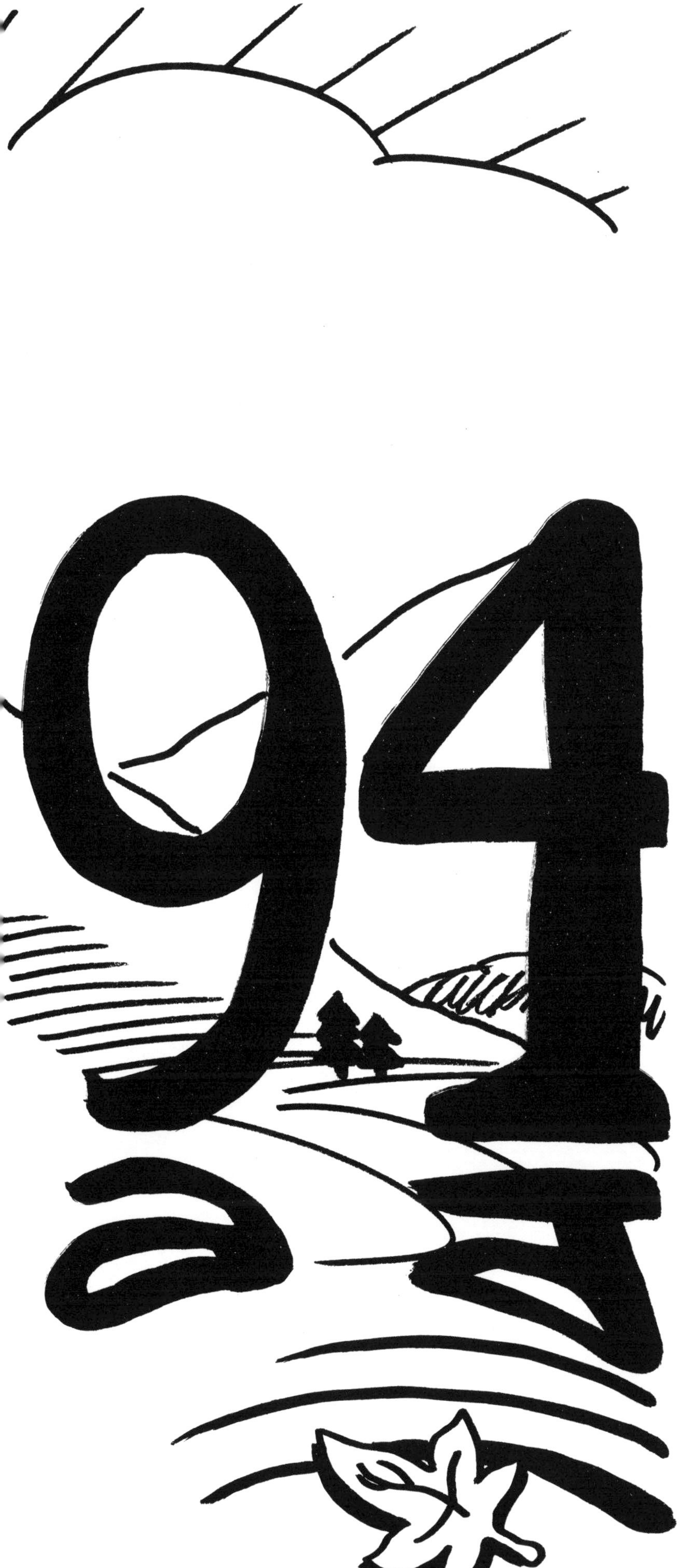
94

AT OUR BOY SCOUT EXPEDITION, LUKE DRAWS A VELOCIRAPTOR!

THE LINES ARE SO CONFIDENT! THE LEGS BEND WHERE GOD BENT THEM! IT IS ALL <u>TRUE</u>!

I TAKE HIS DRAWING AND HOLD IT UP TO FIRE-LIGHT -- THE GLOW RENDERS HIS PAGE TRANSPARENT, SO I <u>TRACE</u> IT!

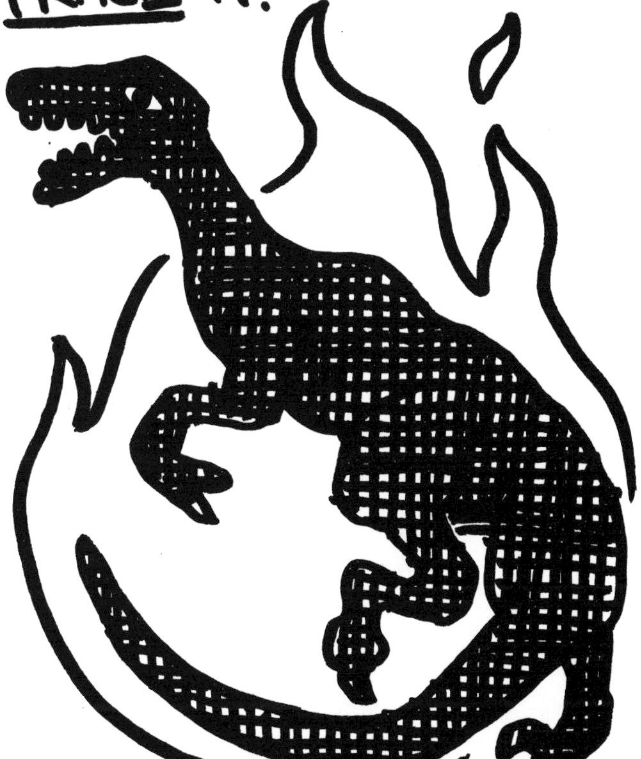

AFTER I DELINEATE IT, I FEEL I HAVE MADE IT MY OWN, SO I SHOW MY COMRADES IN THE TROOP...

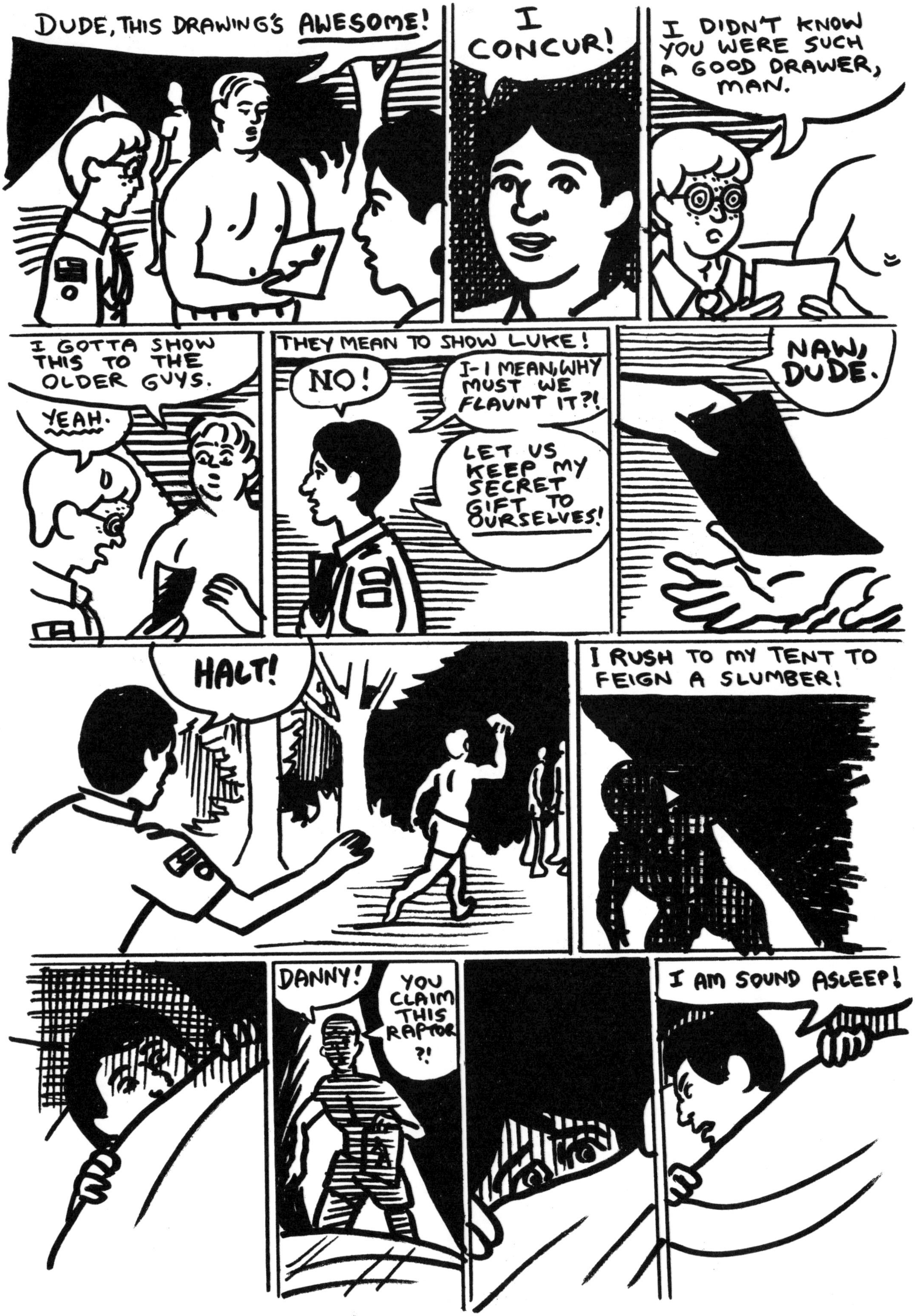
DUDE, THIS DRAWING'S AWESOME!
I CONCUR!
I DIDN'T KNOW YOU WERE SUCH A GOOD DRAWER, MAN.
I GOTTA SHOW THIS TO THE OLDER GUYS.
YEAH.
THEY MEAN TO SHOW LUKE!
NO!
I-I MEAN, WHY MUST WE FLAUNT IT?!
LET US KEEP MY SECRET GIFT TO OURSELVES!
NAW, DUDE.
HALT!
I RUSH TO MY TENT TO FEIGN A SLUMBER!
DANNY!
YOU CLAIM THIS RAPTOR ?!
I AM SOUND ASLEEP!

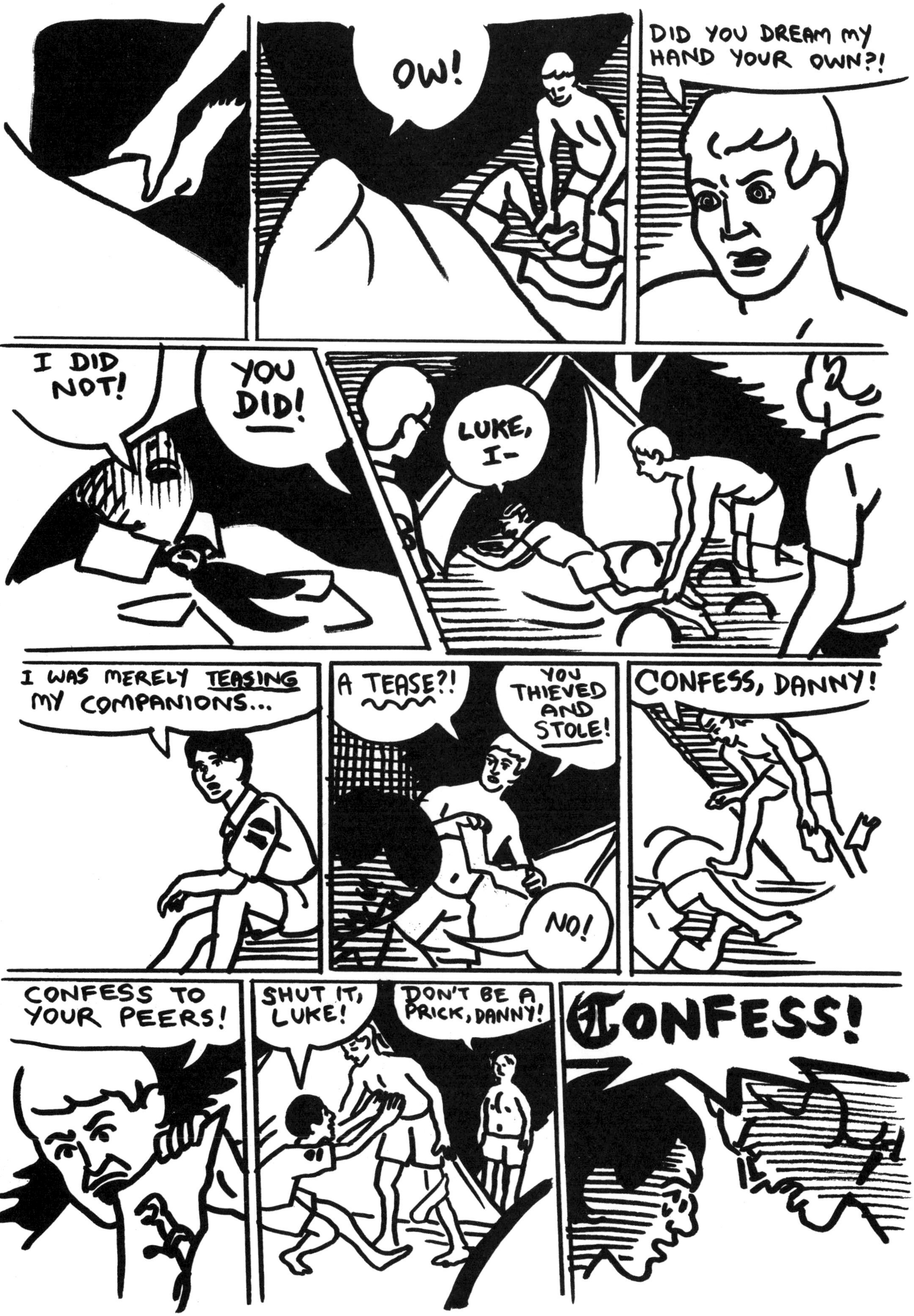
OW!
DID YOU DREAM MY HAND YOUR OWN?!
I DID NOT!
YOU DID!
LUKE, I-
I WAS MERELY TEASING MY COMPANIONS...
A TEASE?!
YOU THIEVED AND STOLE!
NO!
CONFESS, DANNY!
CONFESS TO YOUR PEERS!
SHUT IT, LUKE!
DON'T BE A PRICK, DANNY!
CONFESS!

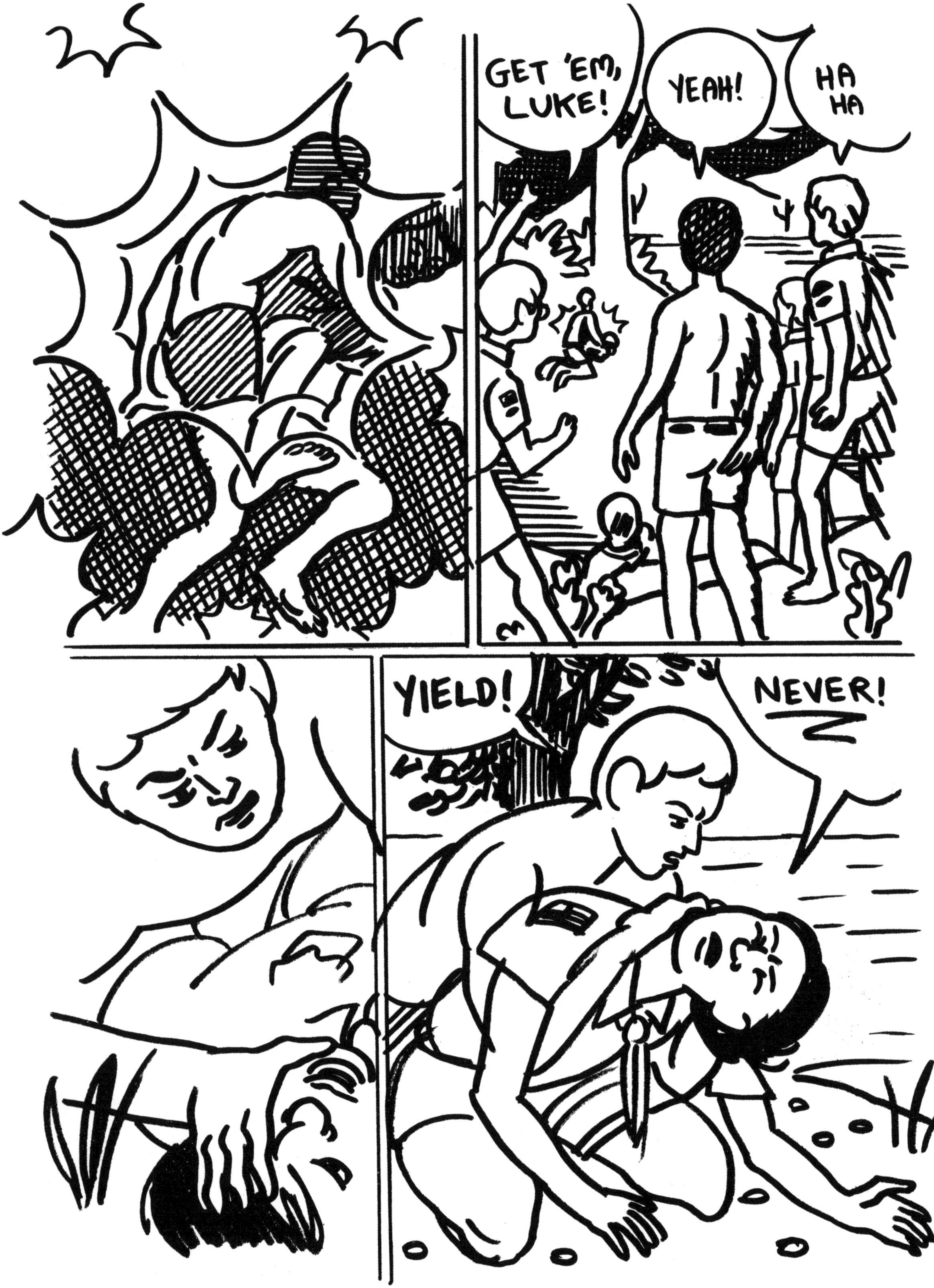
GET 'EM, LUKE!
YEAH!
HA HA
YIELD!
NEVER!

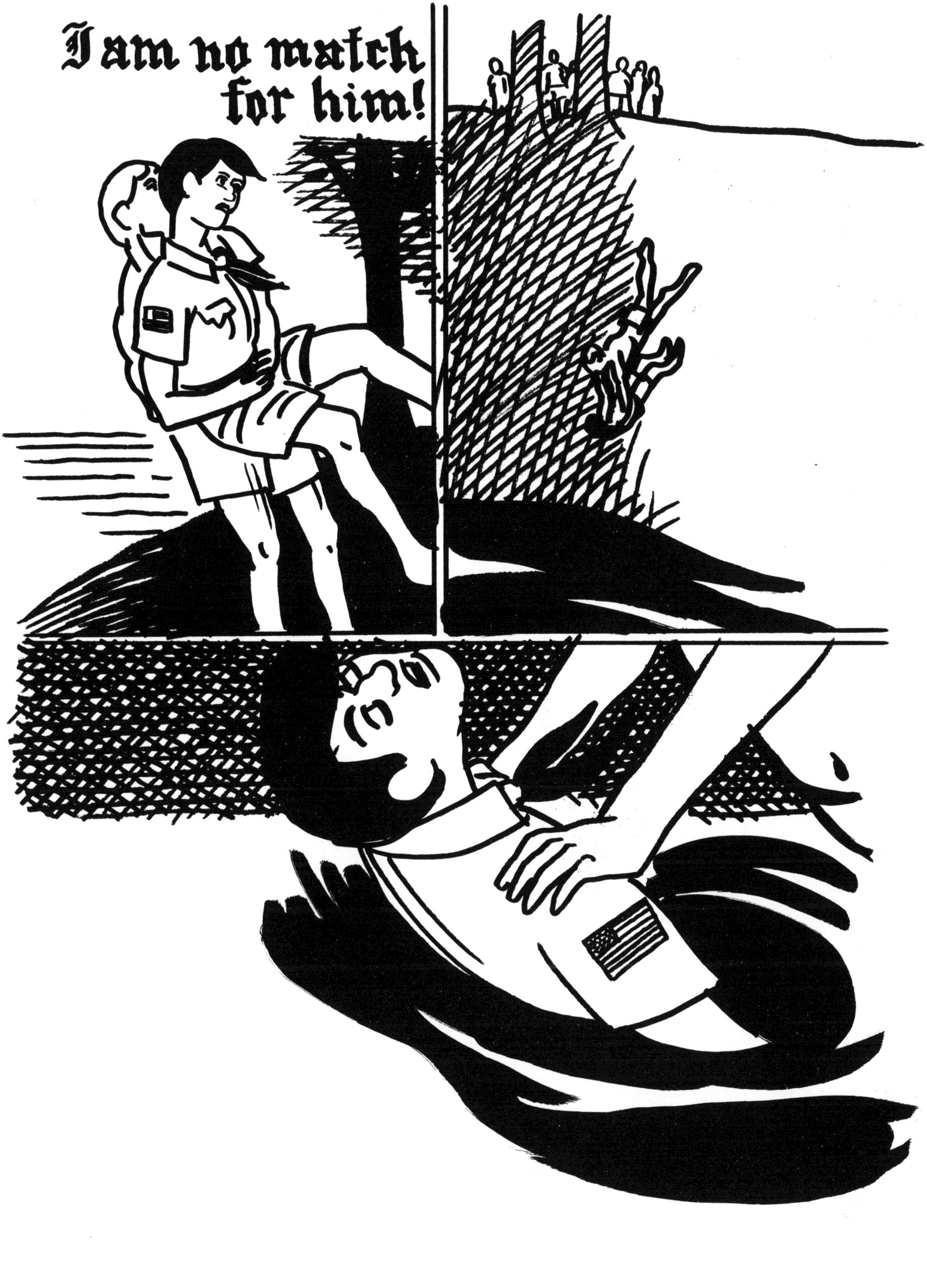
I am no match for him!

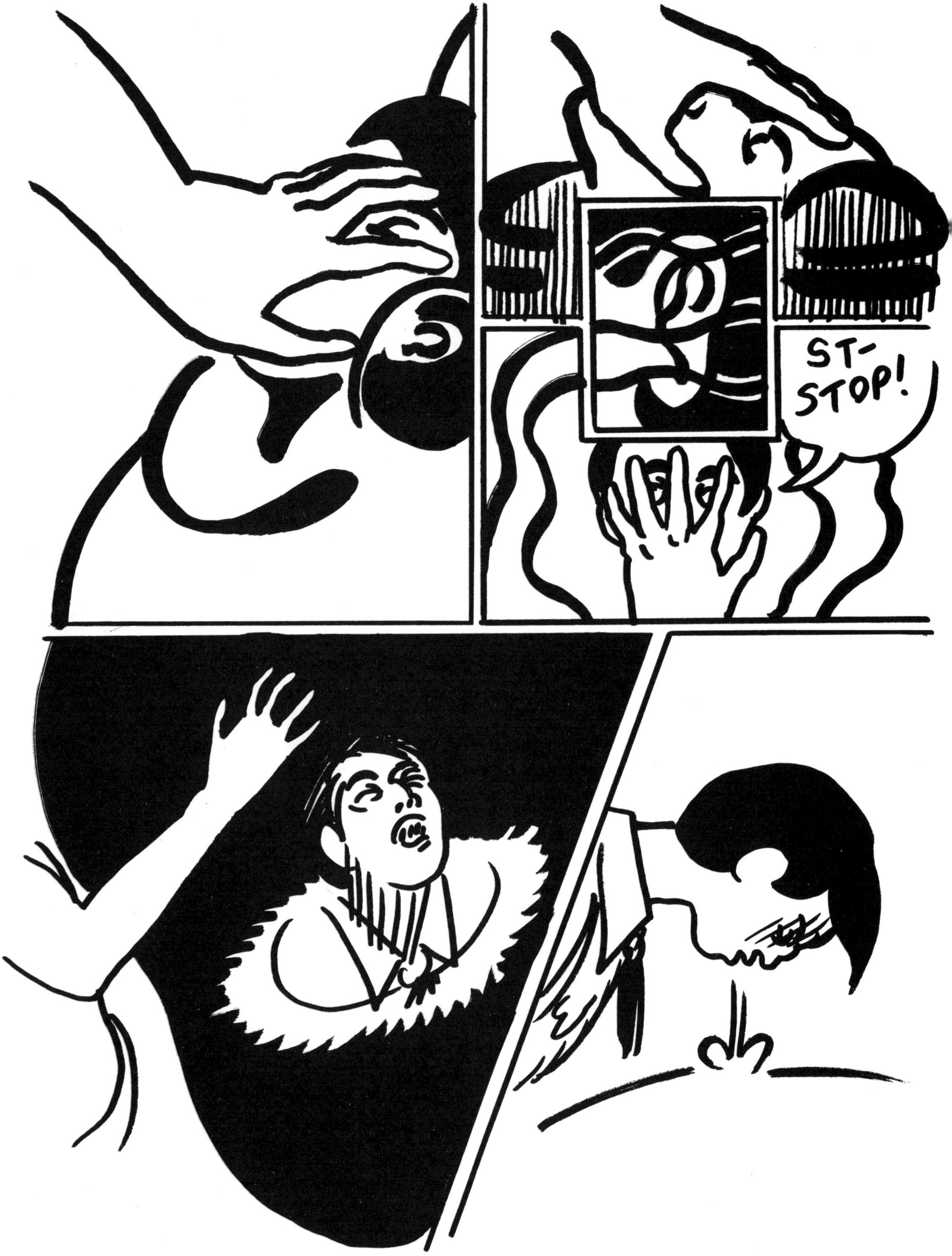
ST-
STOP!

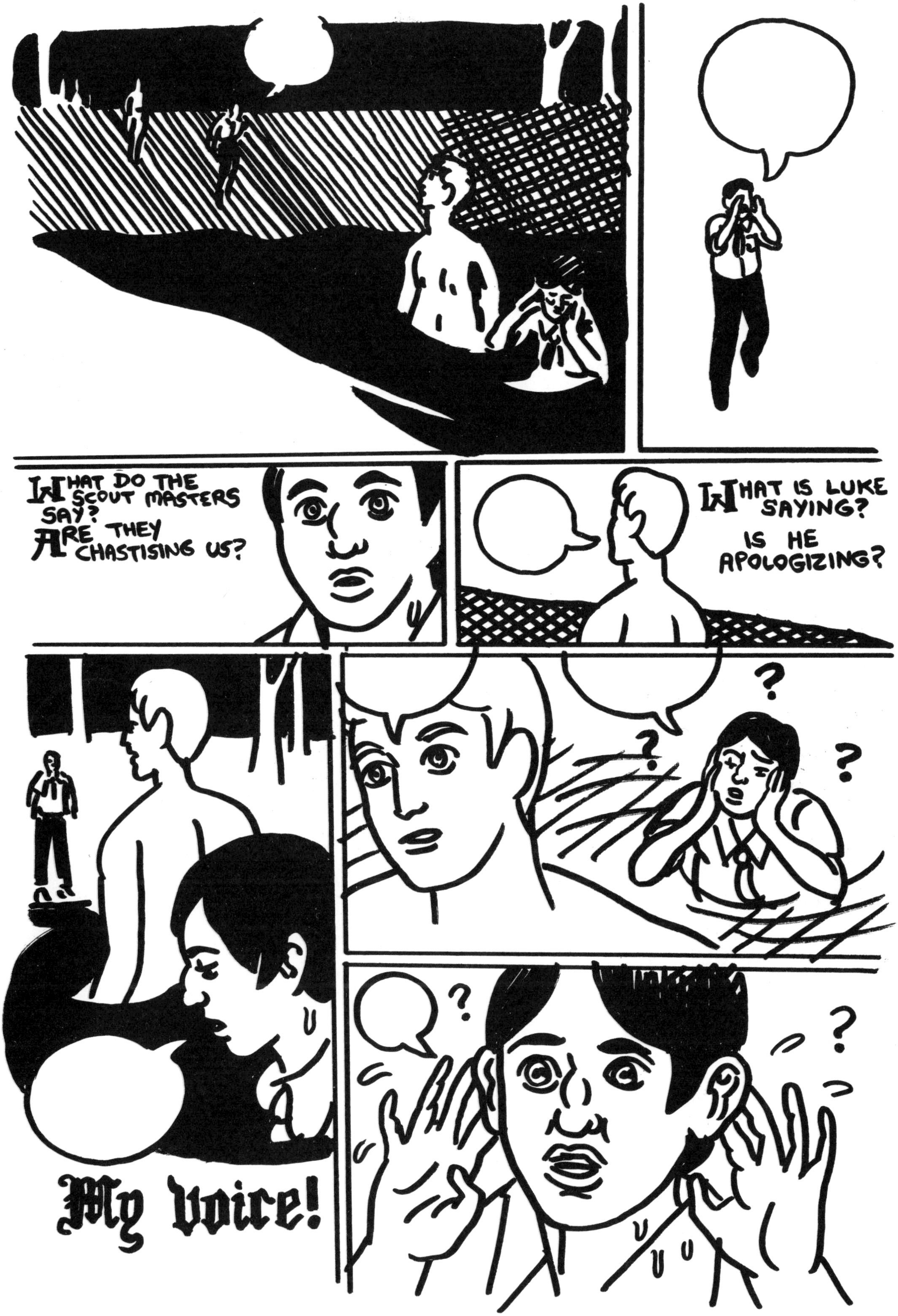
What do the scout masters say? Are they chastising us?
What is Luke saying? Is he apologizing?
?
?
?
?
?
My voice!

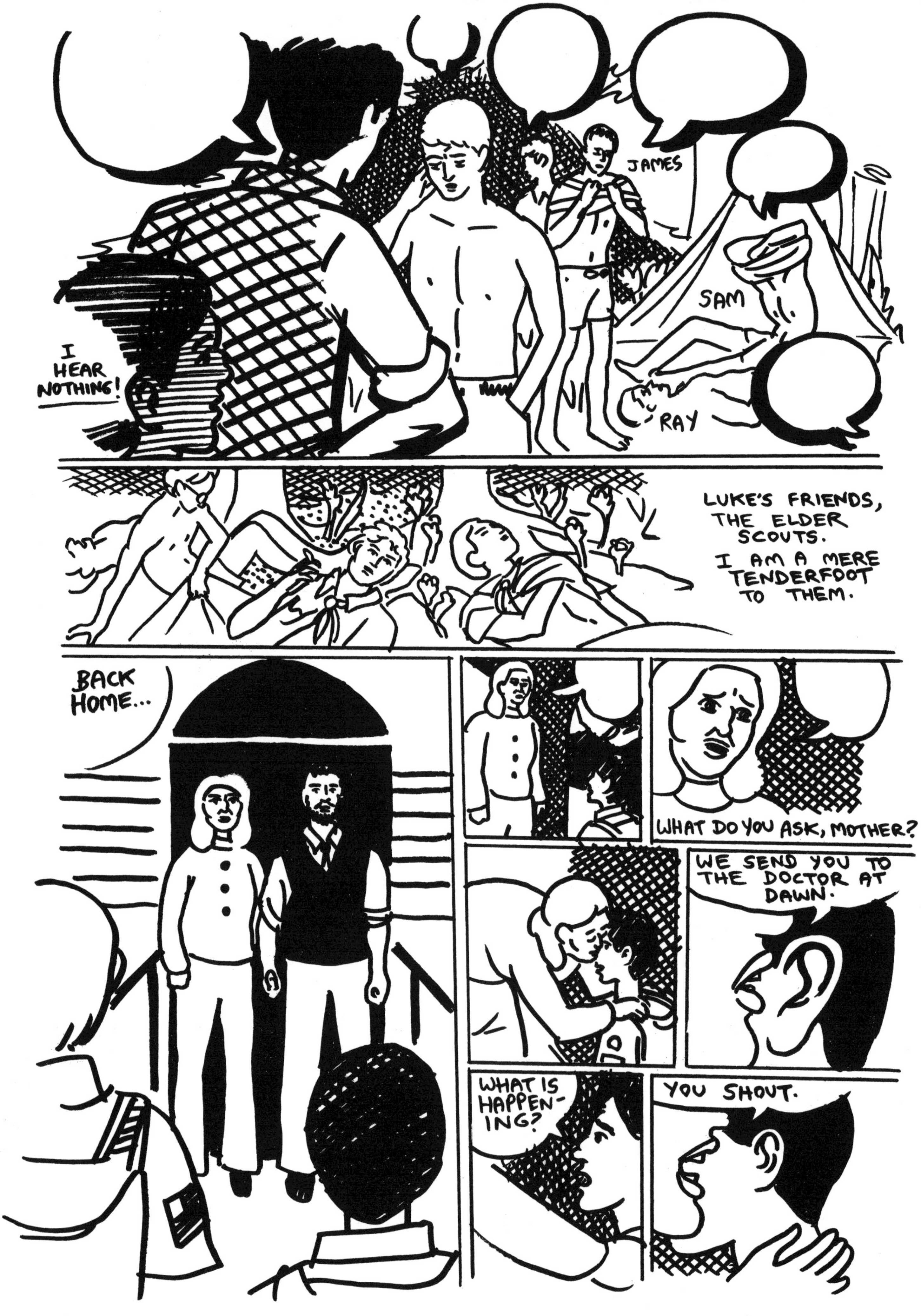
JAMES
SAM
RAY
I HEAR NOTHING!
LUKE'S FRIENDS, THE ELDER SCOUTS.
I AM A MERE TENDERFOOT TO THEM.
BACK HOME...
WHAT DO YOU ASK, MOTHER?
WE SEND YOU TO THE DOCTOR AT DAWN.
WHAT IS HAPPEN-ING?
YOU SHOUT.

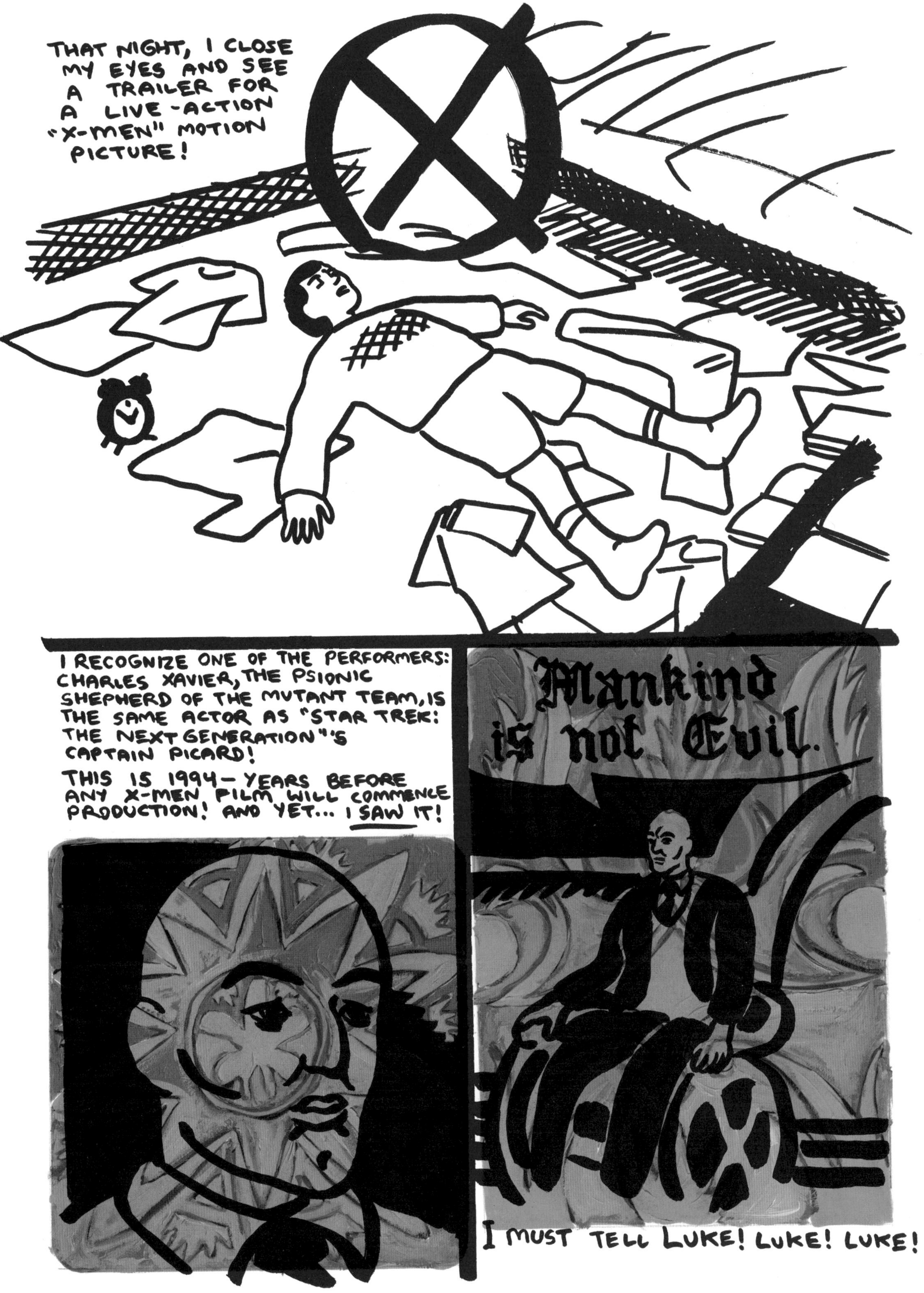
THAT NIGHT, I CLOSE MY EYES AND SEE A TRAILER FOR A LIVE-ACTION "X-MEN" MOTION PICTURE!
I RECOGNIZE ONE OF THE PERFORMERS: CHARLES XAVIER, THE PSIONIC SHEPHERD OF THE MUTANT TEAM, IS THE SAME ACTOR AS "STAR TREK: THE NEXT GENERATION"'S CAPTAIN PICARD!
THIS IS 1994— YEARS BEFORE ANY X-MEN FILM WILL COMMENCE PRODUCTION! AND YET... I SAW IT!
Mankind is not Evil.
I MUST TELL LUKE! LUKE! LUKE!

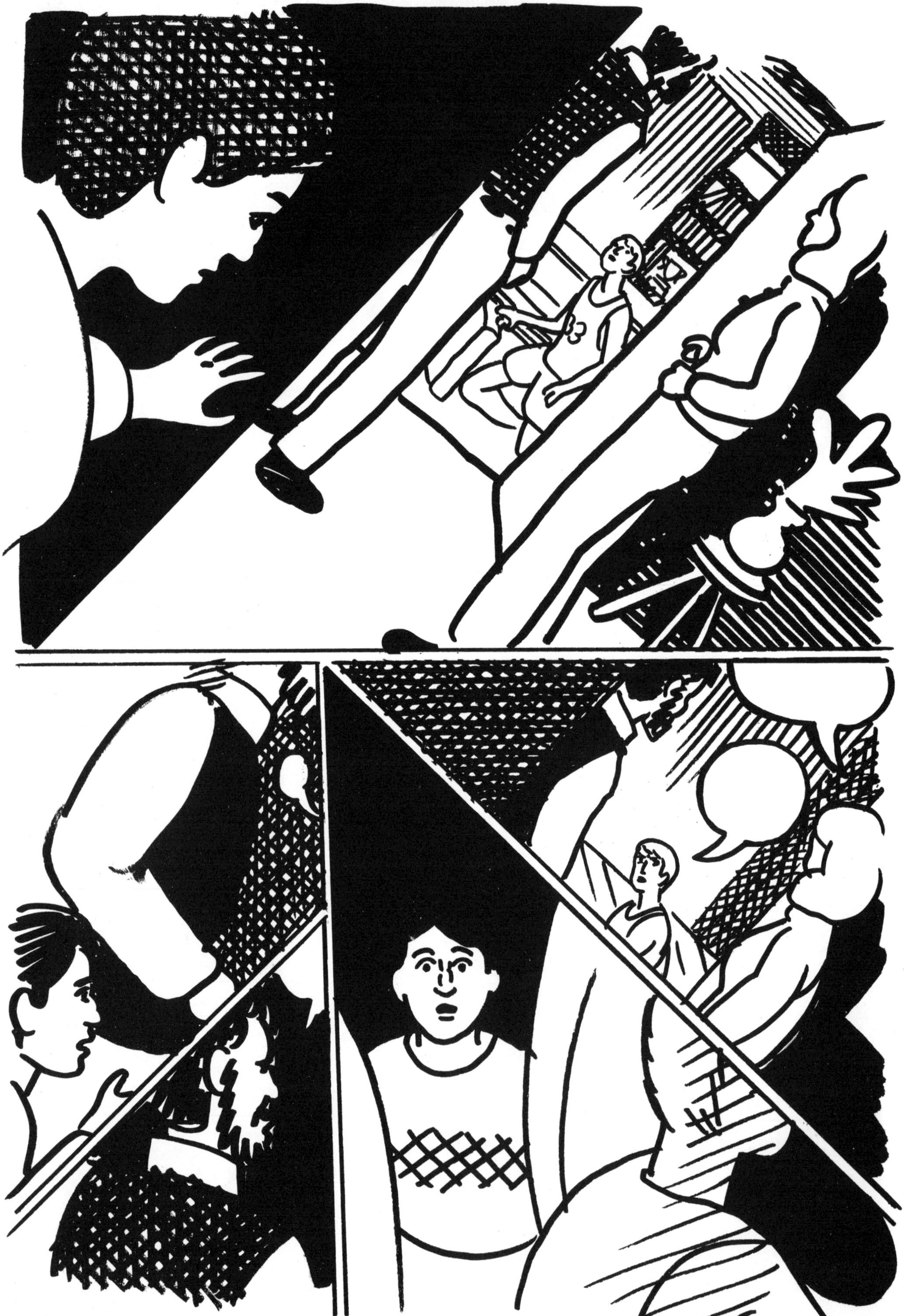

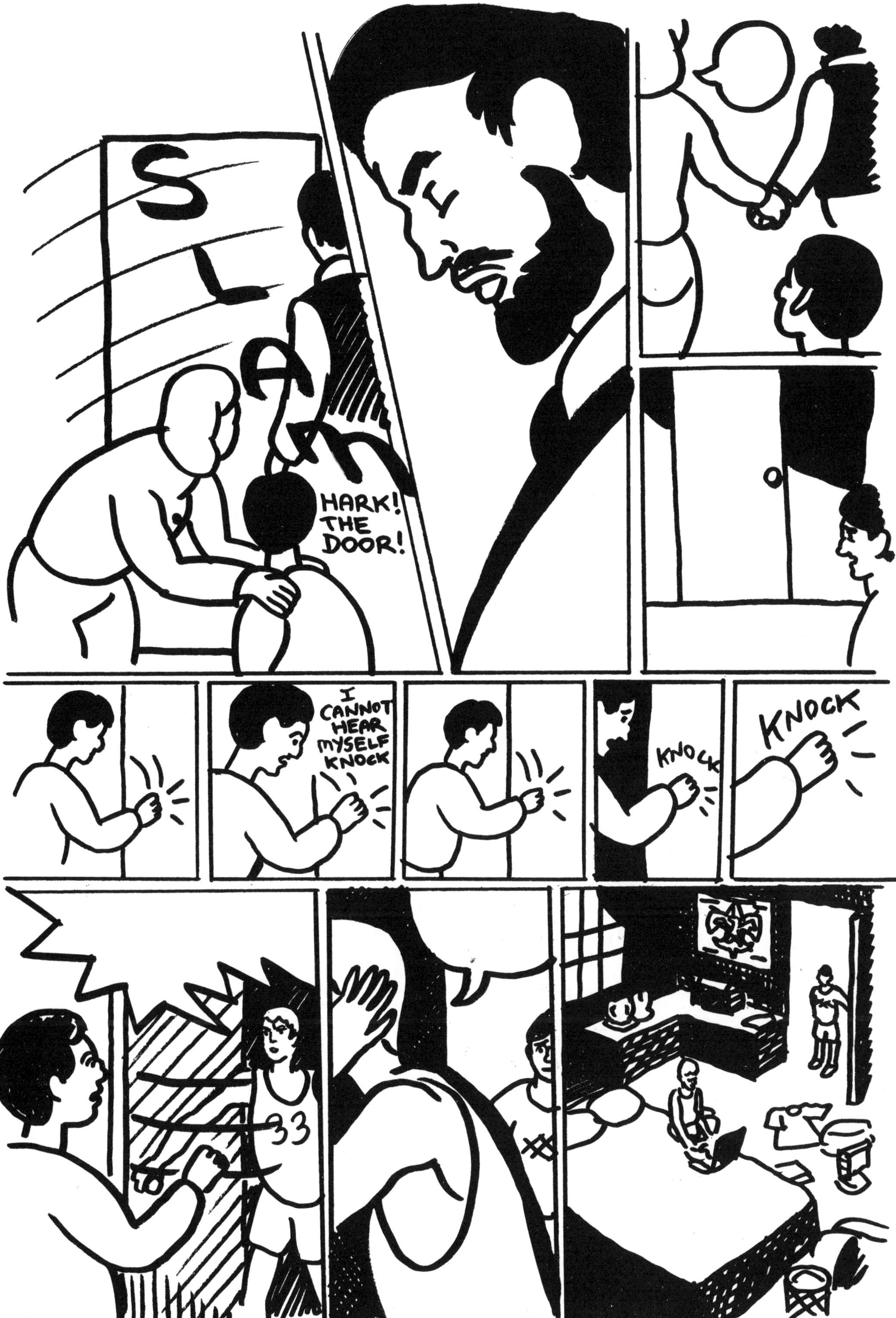
SLAM
HARK! THE DOOR!
I CANNOT HEAR MYSELF KNOCK
KNOCK
KNOCK
33

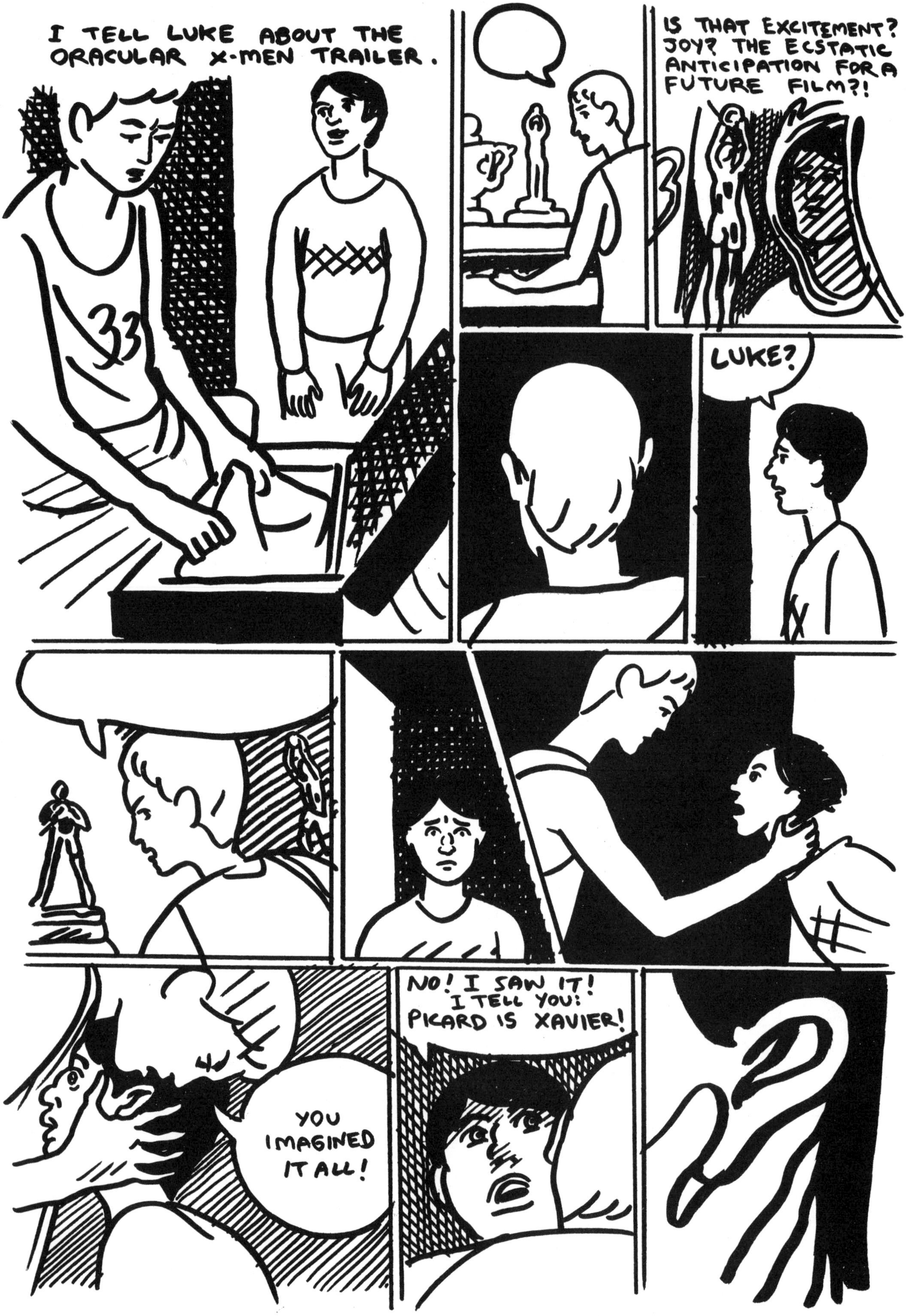
I TELL LUKE ABOUT THE ORACULAR X-MEN TRAILER.
IS THAT EXCITEMENT? JOY? THE ECSTATIC ANTICIPATION FOR A FUTURE FILM?!
LUKE?
NO! I SAW IT! I TELL YOU! PICARD IS XAVIER!
YOU IMAGINED IT ALL!

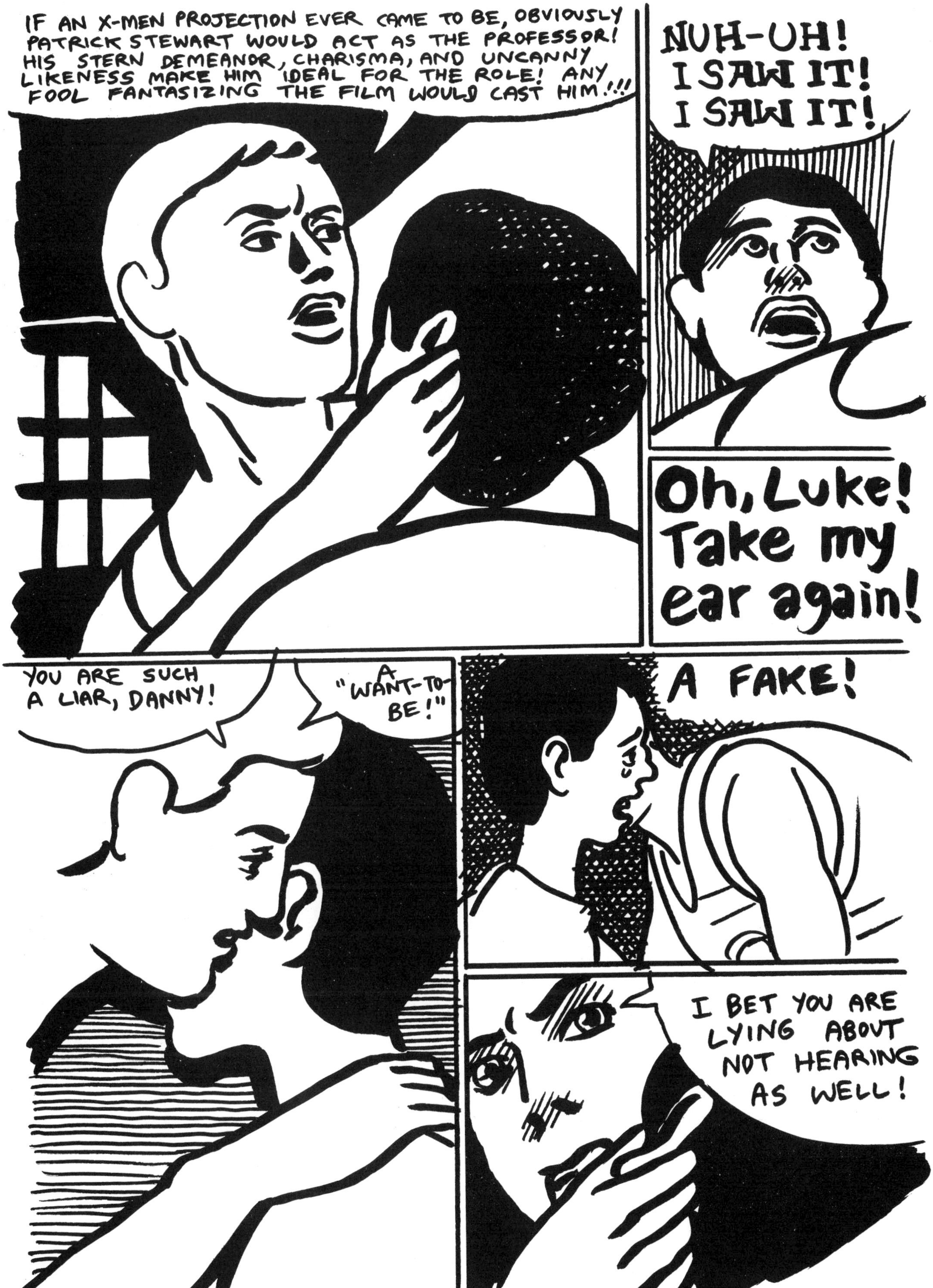
IF AN X-MEN PROJECTION EVER CAME TO BE, OBVIOUSLY PATRICK STEWART WOULD ACT AS THE PROFESSOR! HIS STERN DEMEANOR, CHARISMA, AND UNCANNY LIKENESS MAKE HIM IDEAL FOR THE ROLE! ANY FOOL FANTASIZING THE FILM WOULD CAST HIM!!!
NUH-UH! I SAW IT! I SAW IT!
Oh, Luke! Take my ear again!
YOU ARE SUCH A LIAR, DANNY!
A "WANT-TO-BE!"
A FAKE!
I BET YOU ARE LYING ABOUT NOT HEARING AS WELL!

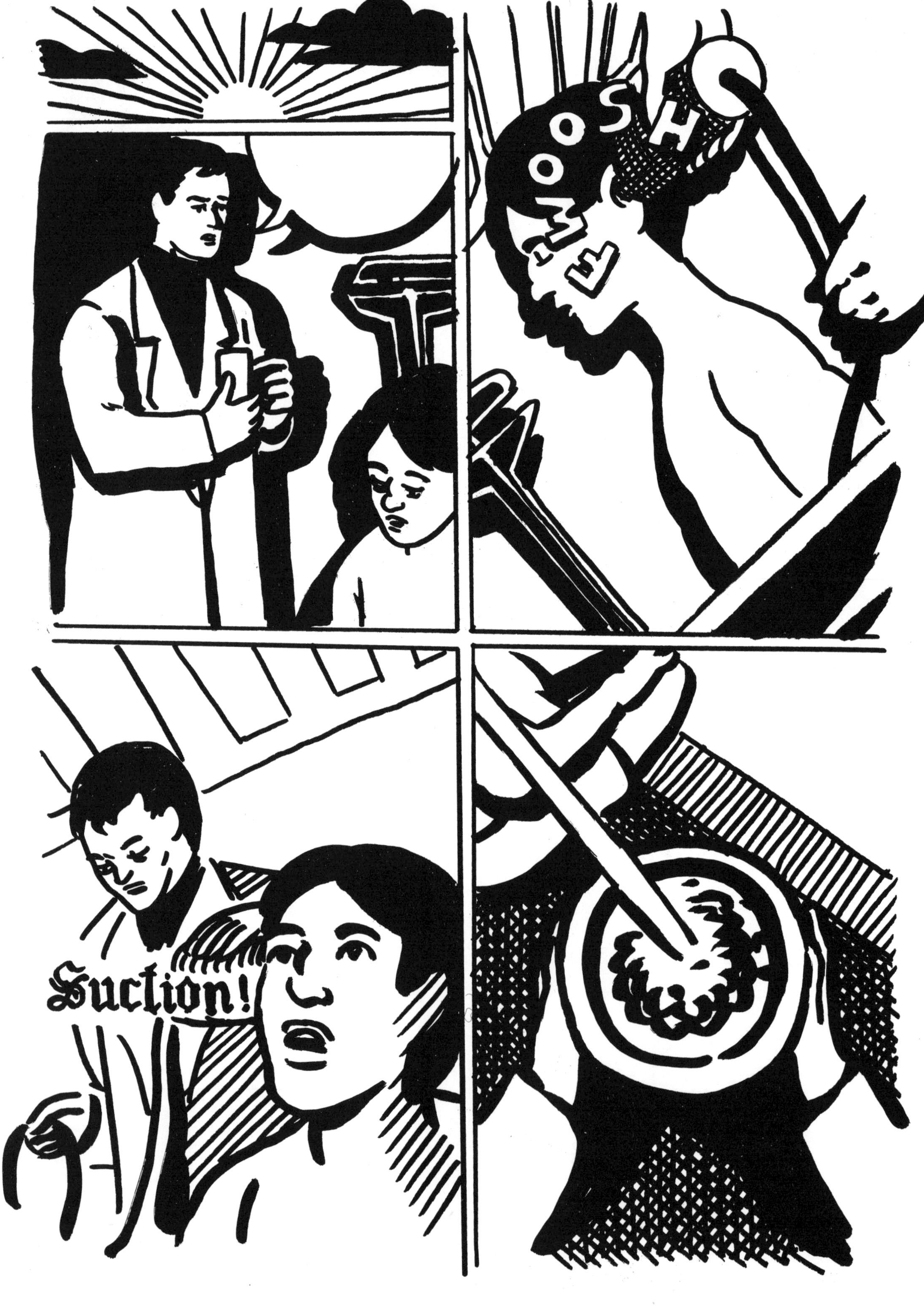
FWOOSH
Suction!

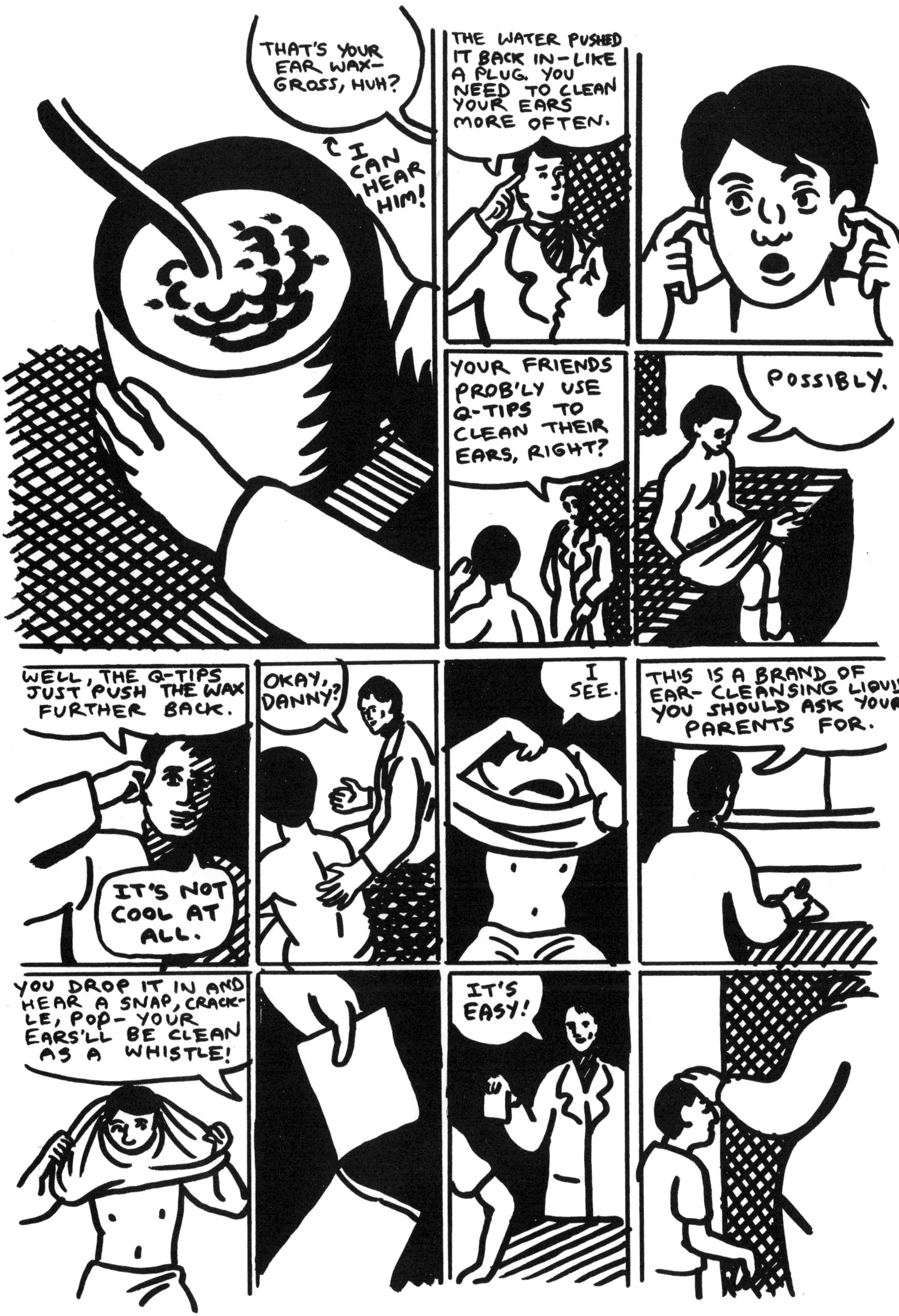
THAT'S YOUR EAR WAX- GROSS, HUH?
I CAN HEAR HIM!
THE WATER PUSHED IT BACK IN- LIKE A PLUG. YOU NEED TO CLEAN YOUR EARS MORE OFTEN.
YOUR FRIENDS PROB'LY USE Q-TIPS TO CLEAN THEIR EARS, RIGHT?
POSSIBLY.
WELL, THE Q-TIPS JUST PUSH THE WAX FURTHER BACK.
IT'S NOT COOL AT ALL.
OKAY, DANNY?
I SEE.
THIS IS A BRAND OF EAR- CLEANSING LIQUID YOU SHOULD ASK YOUR PARENTS FOR.
YOU DROP IT IN AND HEAR A SNAP, CRACK- LE, POP- YOUR EARS'LL BE CLEAN AS A WHISTLE!
IT'S EASY!

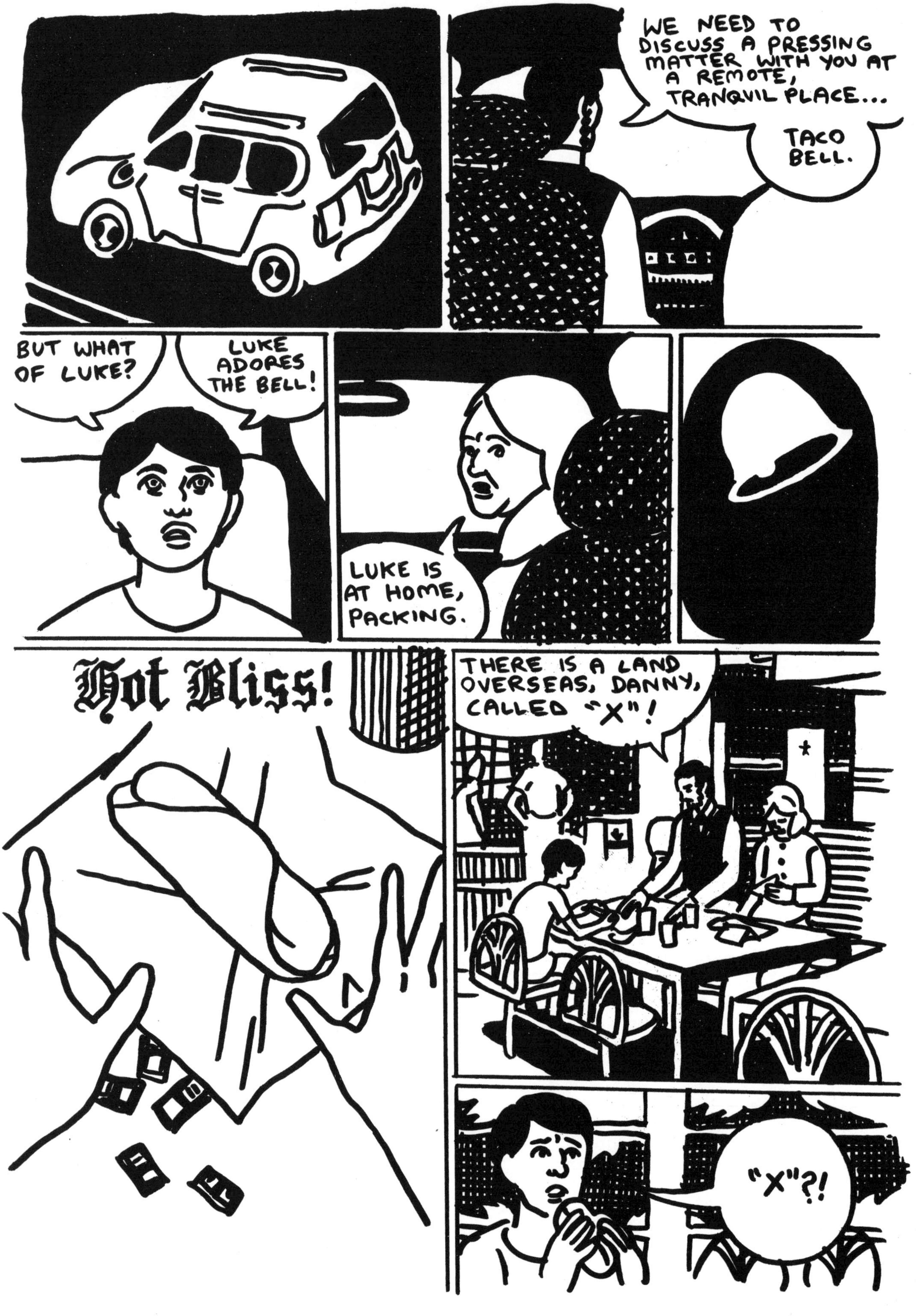
WE NEED TO DISCUSS A PRESSING MATTER WITH YOU AT A REMOTE, TRANQUIL PLACE...
TACO BELL.
BUT WHAT OF LUKE?
LUKE ADORES THE BELL!
LUKE IS AT HOME, PACKING.
Hot Bliss!
THERE IS A LAND OVERSEAS, DANNY, CALLED "X"!
"X"?!

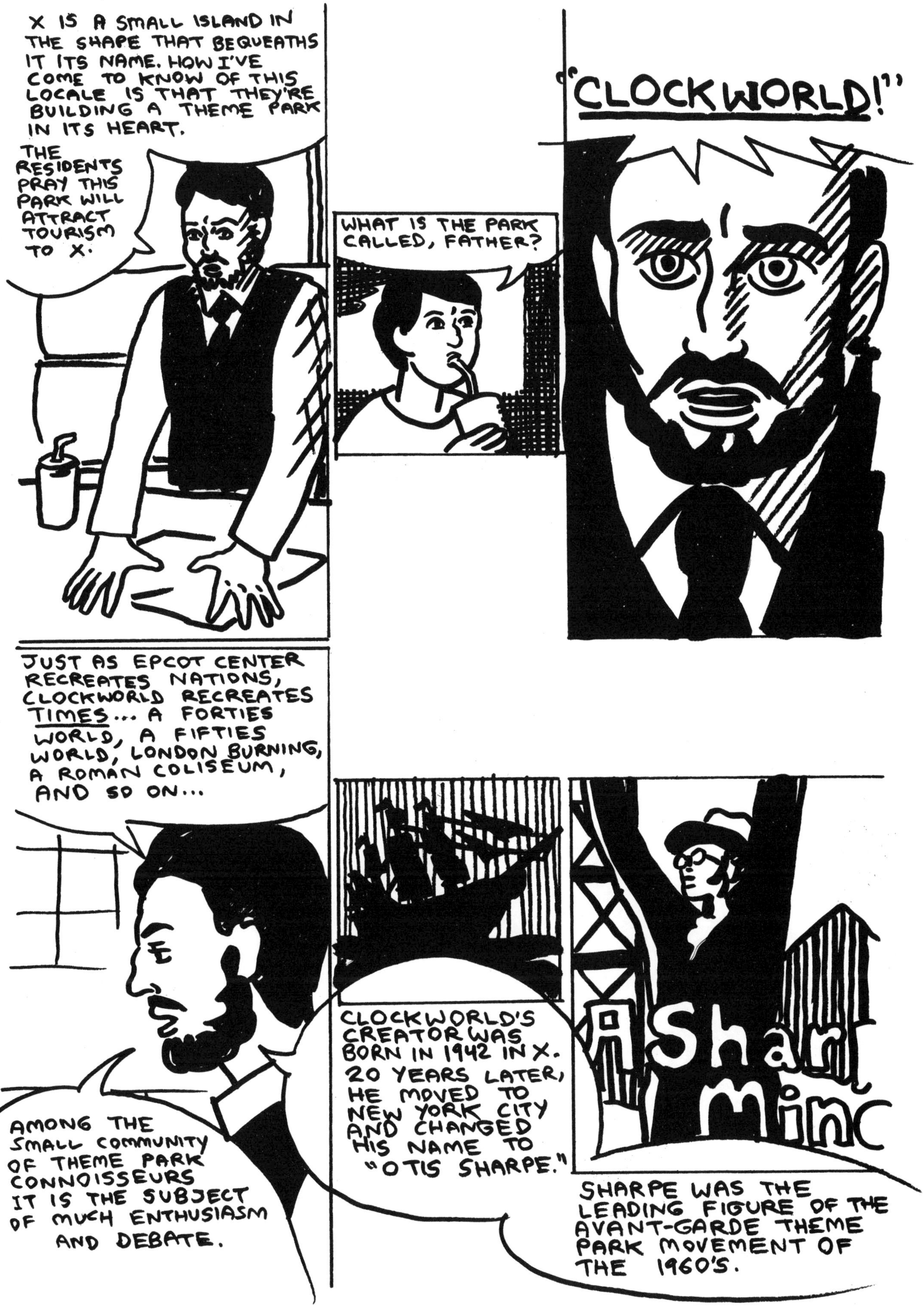
X IS A SMALL ISLAND IN THE SHAPE THAT BEQUEATHS IT ITS NAME. HOW I'VE COME TO KNOW OF THIS LOCALE IS THAT THEY'RE BUILDING A THEME PARK IN ITS HEART.
THE RESIDENTS PRAY THIS PARK WILL ATTRACT TOURISM TO X.
WHAT IS THE PARK CALLED, FATHER?
"CLOCKWORLD!"
JUST AS EPCOT CENTER RECREATES NATIONS, CLOCKWORLD RECREATES TIMES... A FORTIES WORLD, A FIFTIES WORLD, LONDON BURNING, A ROMAN COLISEUM, AND SO ON...
AMONG THE SMALL COMMUNITY OF THEME PARK CONNOISSEURS IT IS THE SUBJECT OF MUCH ENTHUSIASM AND DEBATE.
CLOCKWORLD'S CREATOR WAS BORN IN 1942 IN X. 20 YEARS LATER, HE MOVED TO NEW YORK CITY AND CHANGED HIS NAME TO "OTIS SHARPE."
A Sharp Minc
SHARPE WAS THE LEADING FIGURE OF THE AVANT-GARDE THEME PARK MOVEMENT OF THE 1960'S.

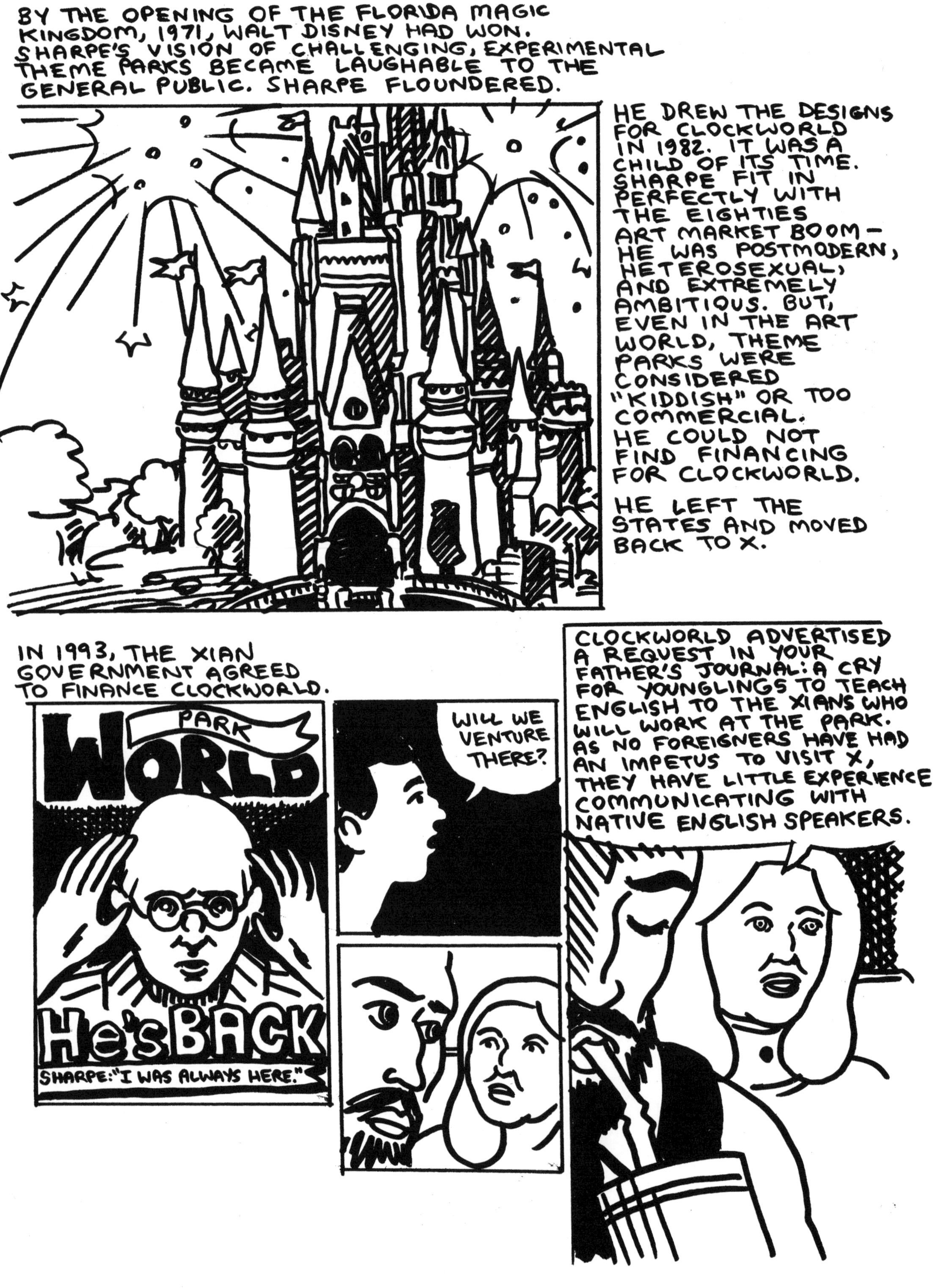
BY THE OPENING OF THE FLORIDA MAGIC KINGDOM, 1971, WALT DISNEY HAD WON. SHARPE'S VISION OF CHALLENGING, EXPERIMENTAL THEME PARKS BECAME LAUGHABLE TO THE GENERAL PUBLIC. SHARPE FLOUNDERED.
HE DREW THE DESIGNS FOR CLOCKWORLD IN 1982. IT WAS A CHILD OF ITS TIME. SHARPE FIT IN PERFECTLY WITH THE EIGHTIES ART MARKET BOOM— HE WAS POSTMODERN, HETEROSEXUAL, AND EXTREMELY AMBITIOUS. BUT, EVEN IN THE ART WORLD, THEME PARKS WERE CONSIDERED "KIDDISH" OR TOO COMMERCIAL. HE COULD NOT FIND FINANCING FOR CLOCKWORLD.
HE LEFT THE STATES AND MOVED BACK TO X.
IN 1993, THE XIAN GOVERNMENT AGREED TO FINANCE CLOCKWORLD.
PARK
WORLD
He's BACK
SHARPE: "I WAS ALWAYS HERE."
WILL WE VENTURE THERE?
CLOCKWORLD ADVERTISED A REQUEST IN YOUR FATHER'S JOURNAL: A CRY FOR YOUNGLINGS TO TEACH ENGLISH TO THE XIANS WHO WILL WORK AT THE PARK. AS NO FOREIGNERS HAVE HAD AN IMPETUS TO VISIT X, THEY HAVE LITTLE EXPERIENCE COMMUNICATING WITH NATIVE ENGLISH SPEAKERS.

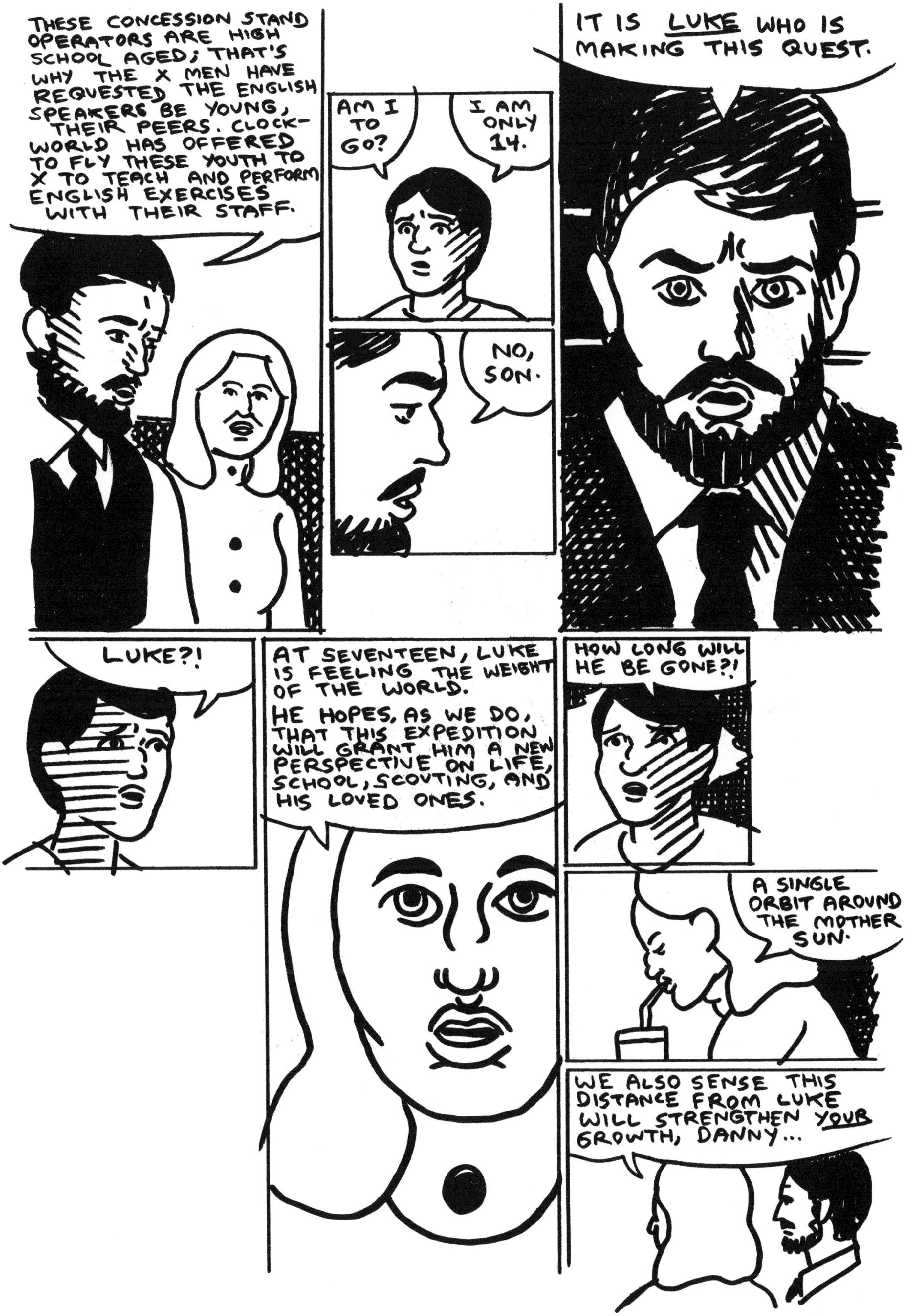
THESE CONCESSION STAND OPERATORS ARE HIGH SCHOOL AGED; THAT'S WHY THE X MEN HAVE REQUESTED THE ENGLISH SPEAKERS BE YOUNG, THEIR PEERS. CLOCK-WORLD HAS OFFERED TO FLY THESE YOUTH TO X TO TEACH AND PERFORM ENGLISH EXERCISES WITH THEIR STAFF.
AM I TO GO?
I AM ONLY 14.
NO, SON.
IT IS LUKE WHO IS MAKING THIS QUEST.
LUKE?!
AT SEVENTEEN, LUKE IS FEELING THE WEIGHT OF THE WORLD.
HE HOPES, AS WE DO, THAT THIS EXPEDITION WILL GRANT HIM A NEW PERSPECTIVE ON LIFE, SCHOOL, SCOUTING, AND HIS LOVED ONES.
HOW LONG WILL HE BE GONE?!
A SINGLE ORBIT AROUND THE MOTHER SUN.
WE ALSO SENSE THIS DISTANCE FROM LUKE WILL STRENGTHEN YOUR GROWTH, DANNY...

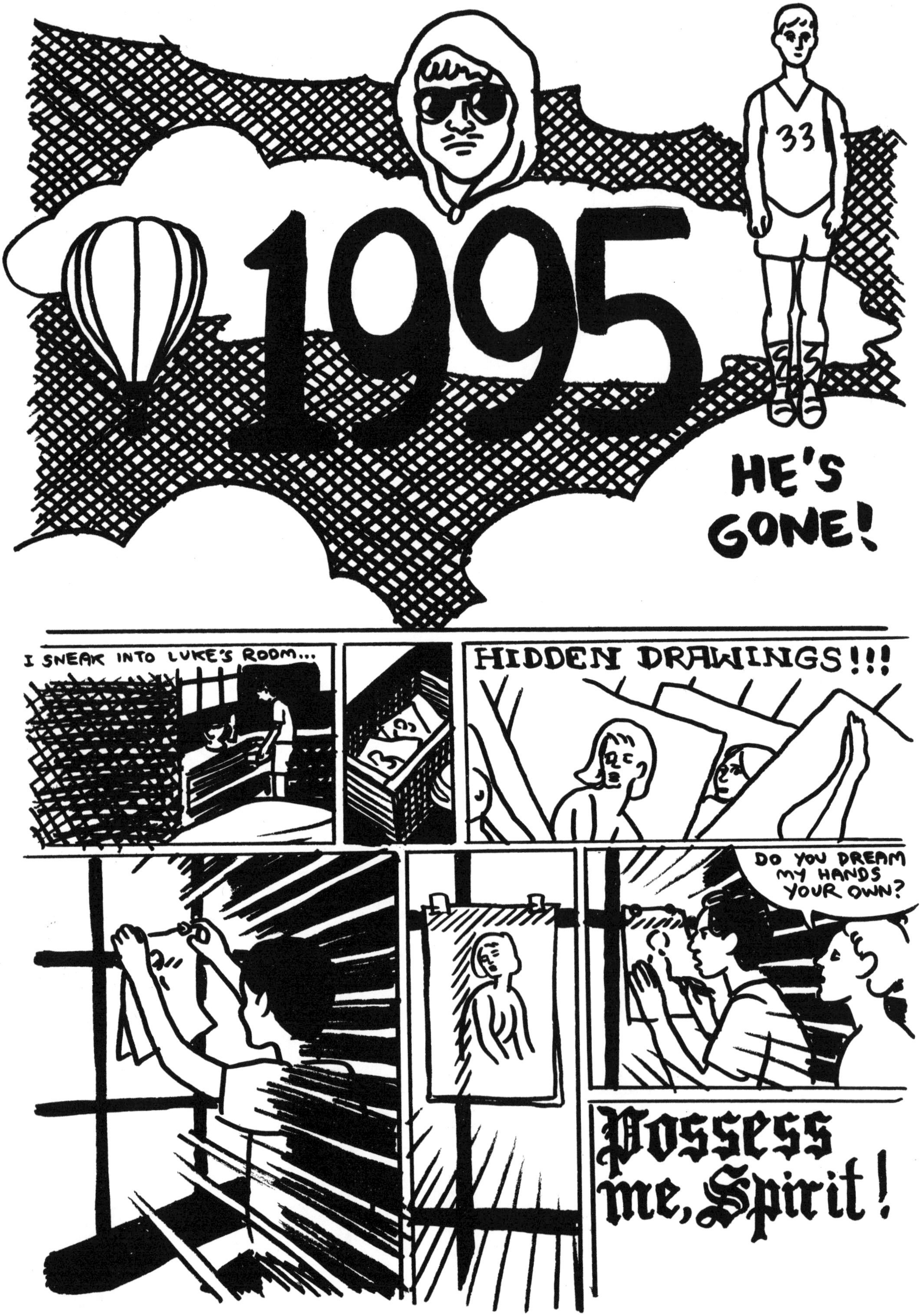
1995
33
HE'S GONE!
I SNEAK INTO LUKE'S ROOM...
HIDDEN DRAWINGS!!!
DO YOU DREAM MY HANDS YOUR OWN?
Possess me, Spirit!

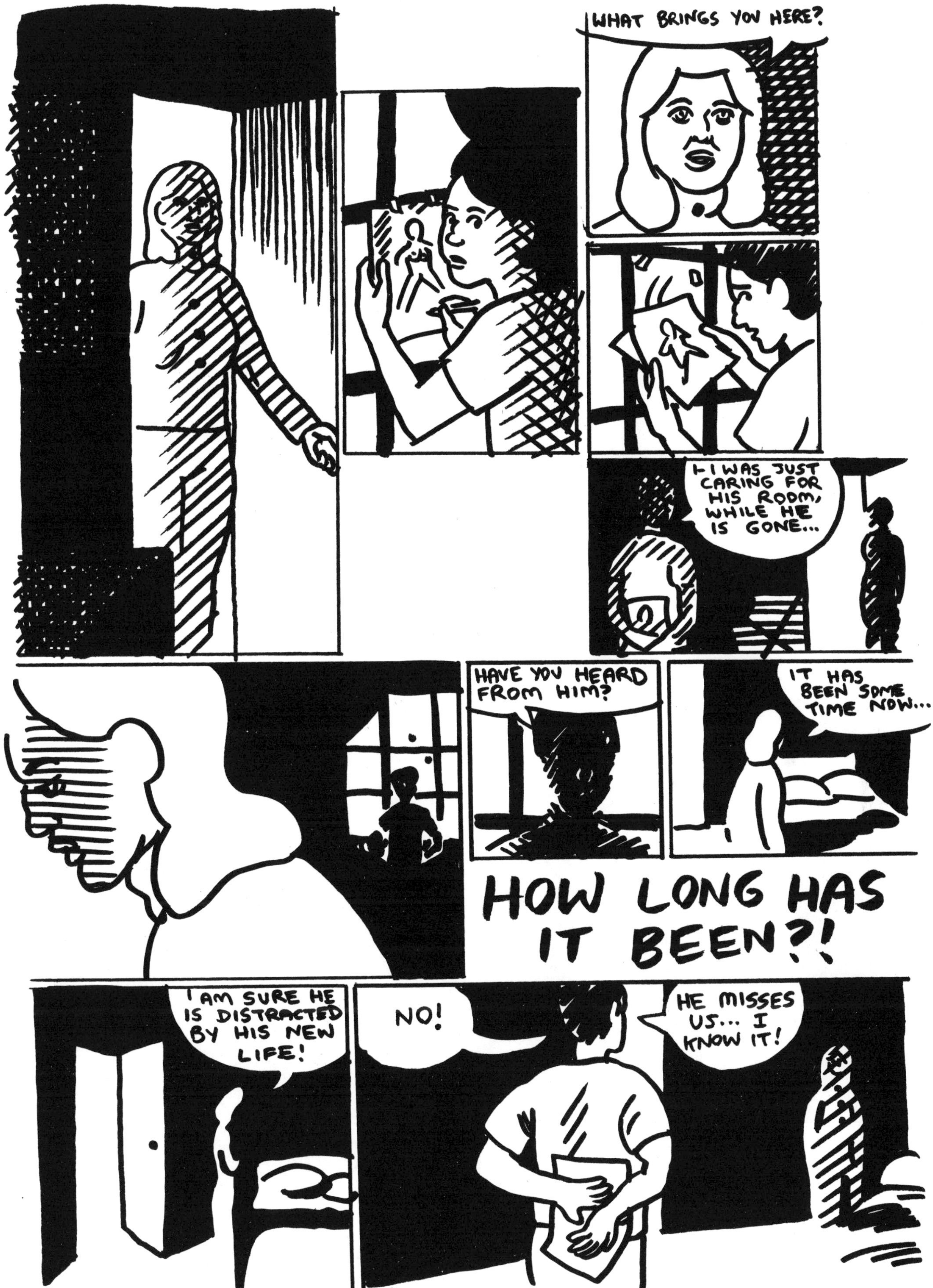
WHAT BRINGS YOU HERE?
I WAS JUST CARING FOR HIS ROOM, WHILE HE IS GONE...
HAVE YOU HEARD FROM HIM?
IT HAS BEEN SOME TIME NOW...
HOW LONG HAS IT BEEN?!
I AM SURE HE IS DISTRACTED BY HIS NEW LIFE!
NO!
HE MISSES US... I KNOW IT!

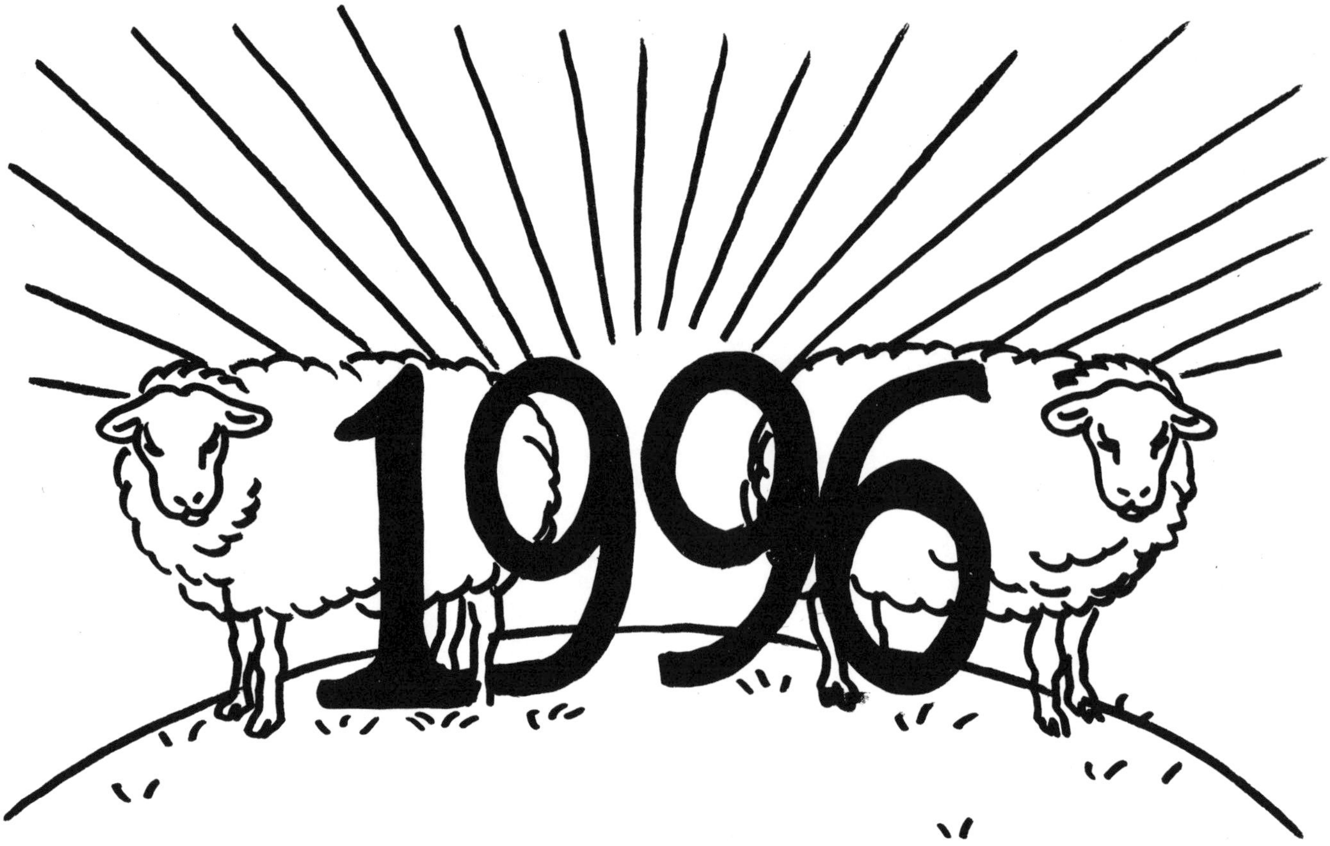
1996

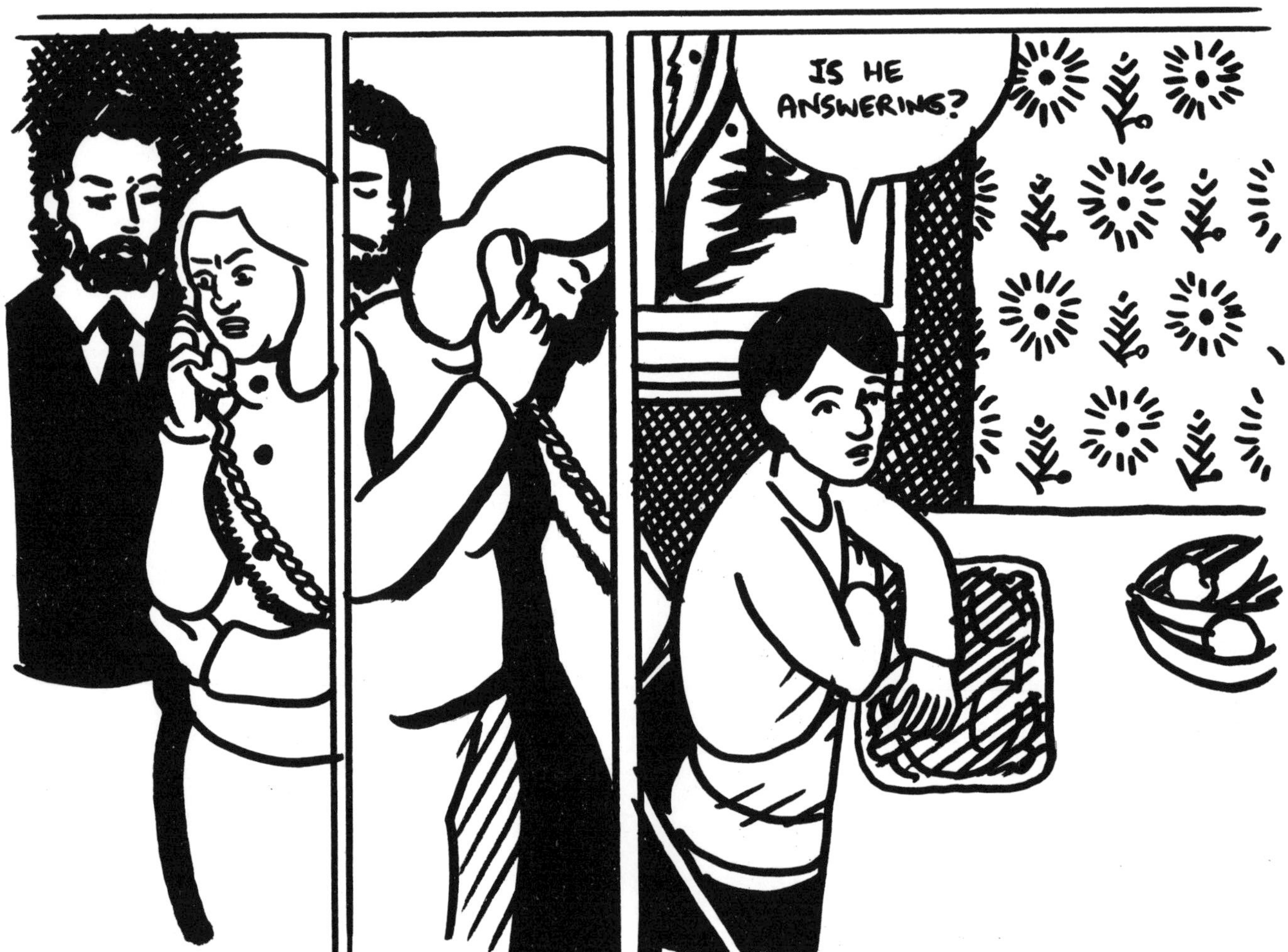
IS HE ANSWERING?

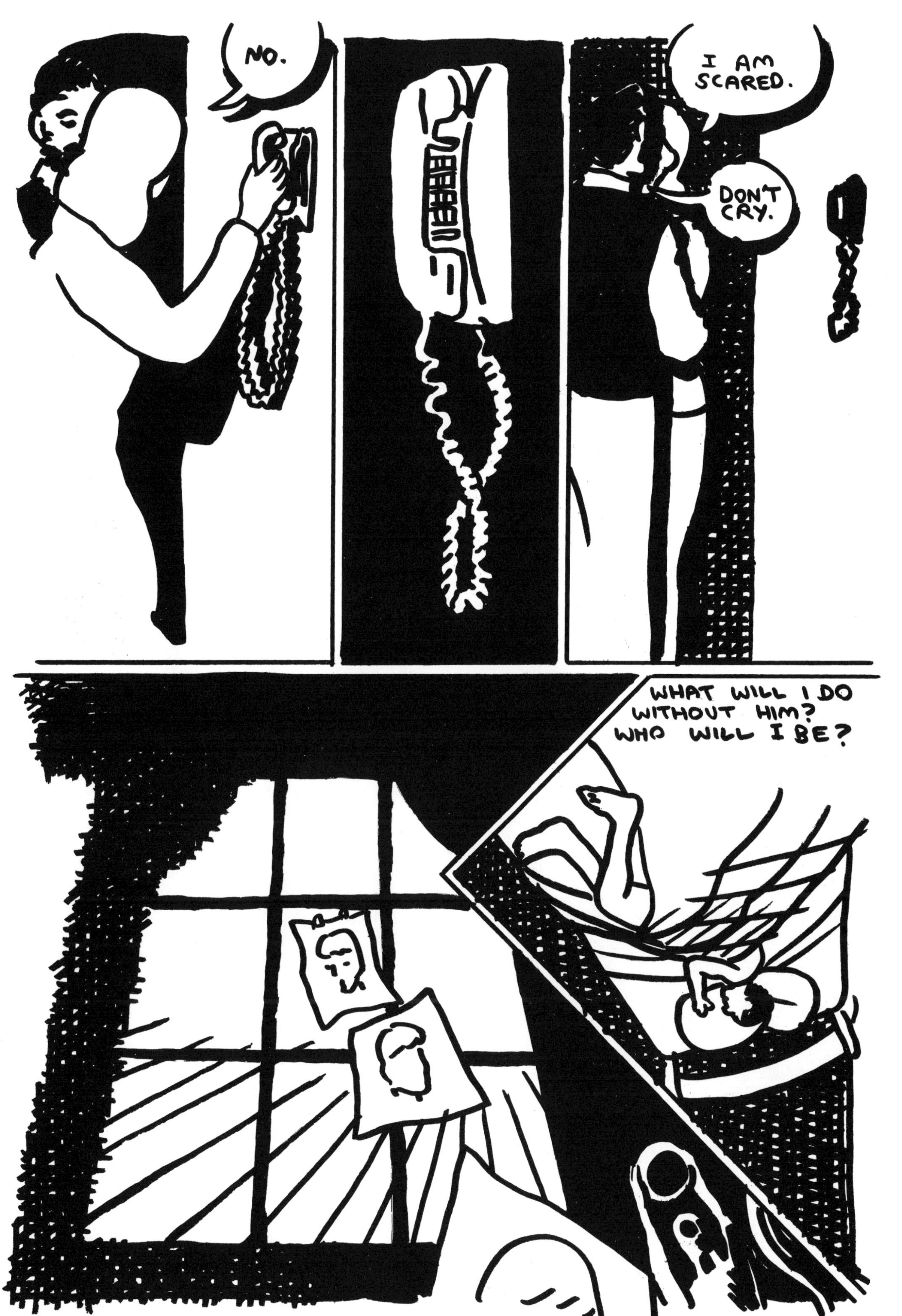
NO.
I AM SCARED.
DON'T CRY.
WHAT WILL I DO WITHOUT HIM? WHO WILL I BE?

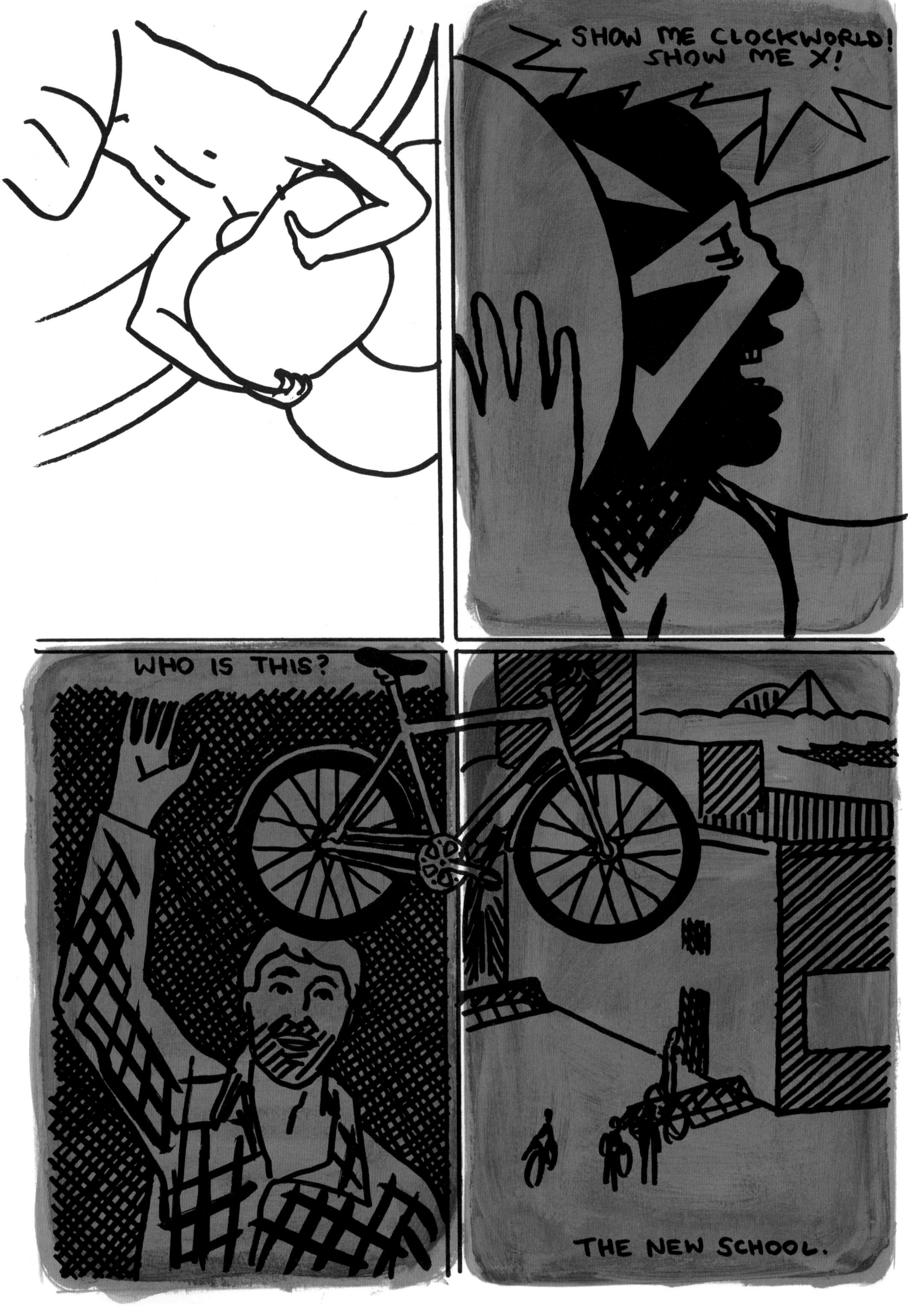
SHOW ME CLOCKWORLD! SHOW ME X!
WHO IS THIS?
THE NEW SCHOOL.

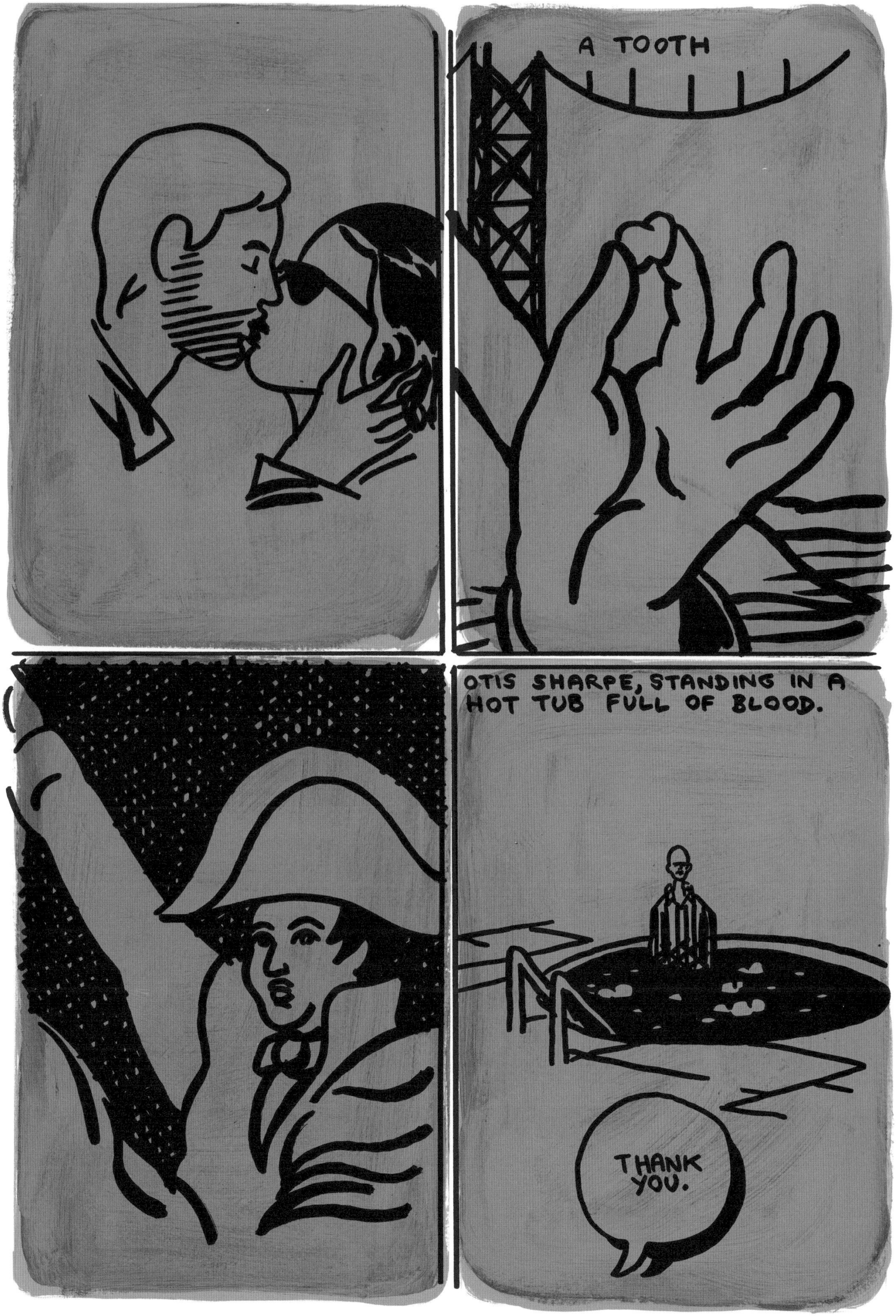
A TOOTH
OTIS SHARPE, STANDING IN A HOT TUB FULL OF BLOOD.
THANK YOU.

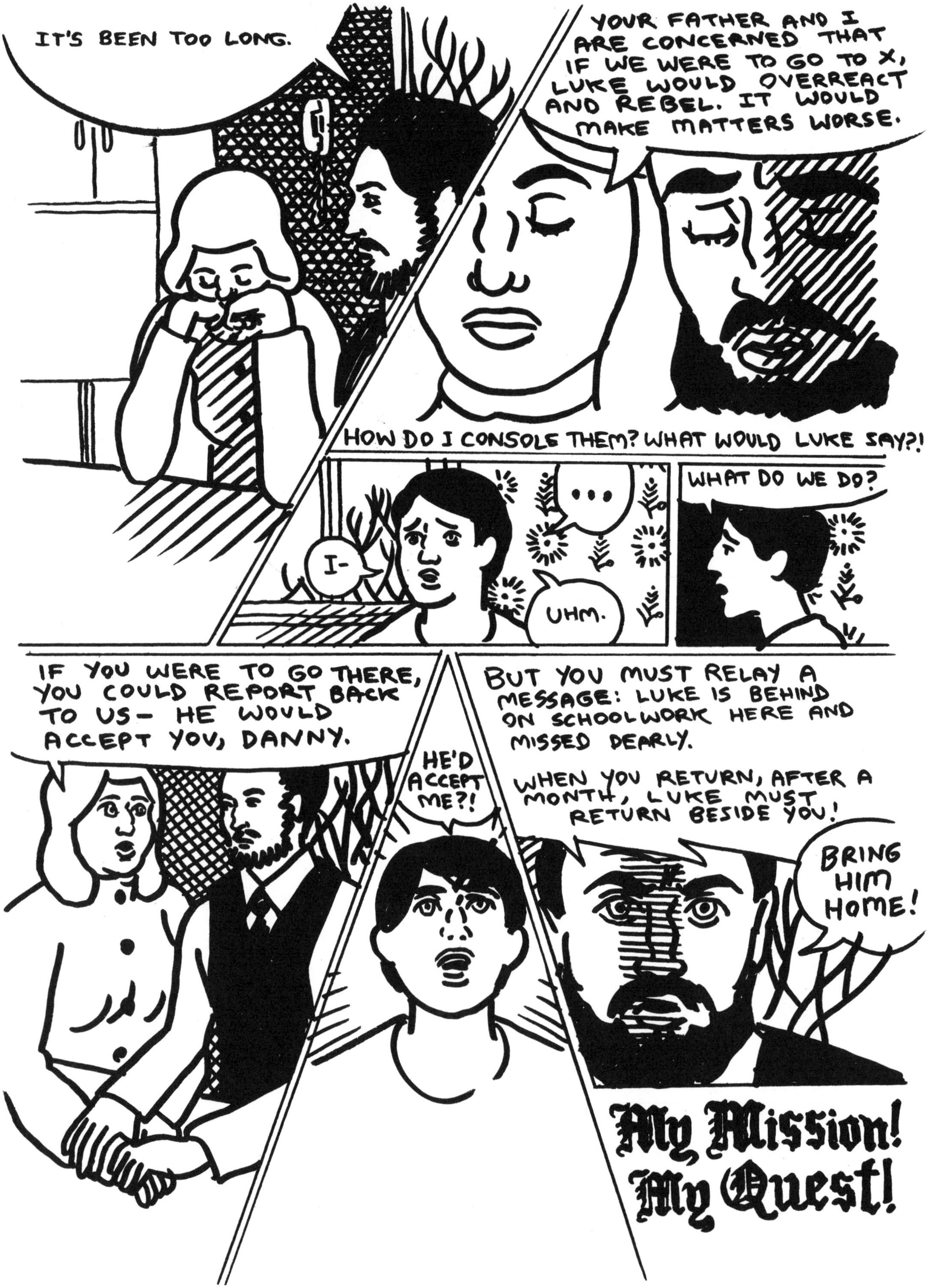
IT'S BEEN TOO LONG.
YOUR FATHER AND I ARE CONCERNED THAT IF WE WERE TO GO TO X, LUKE WOULD OVERREACT AND REBEL. IT WOULD MAKE MATTERS WORSE.
HOW DO I CONSOLE THEM? WHAT WOULD LUKE SAY?!
I-
...
UHM.
WHAT DO WE DO?
IF YOU WERE TO GO THERE, YOU COULD REPORT BACK TO US- HE WOULD ACCEPT YOU, DANNY.
HE'D ACCEPT ME?!
BUT YOU MUST RELAY A MESSAGE: LUKE IS BEHIND ON SCHOOLWORK HERE AND MISSED DEARLY.
WHEN YOU RETURN, AFTER A MONTH, LUKE MUST RETURN BESIDE YOU!
BRING HIM HOME!
My Mission! My Quest!

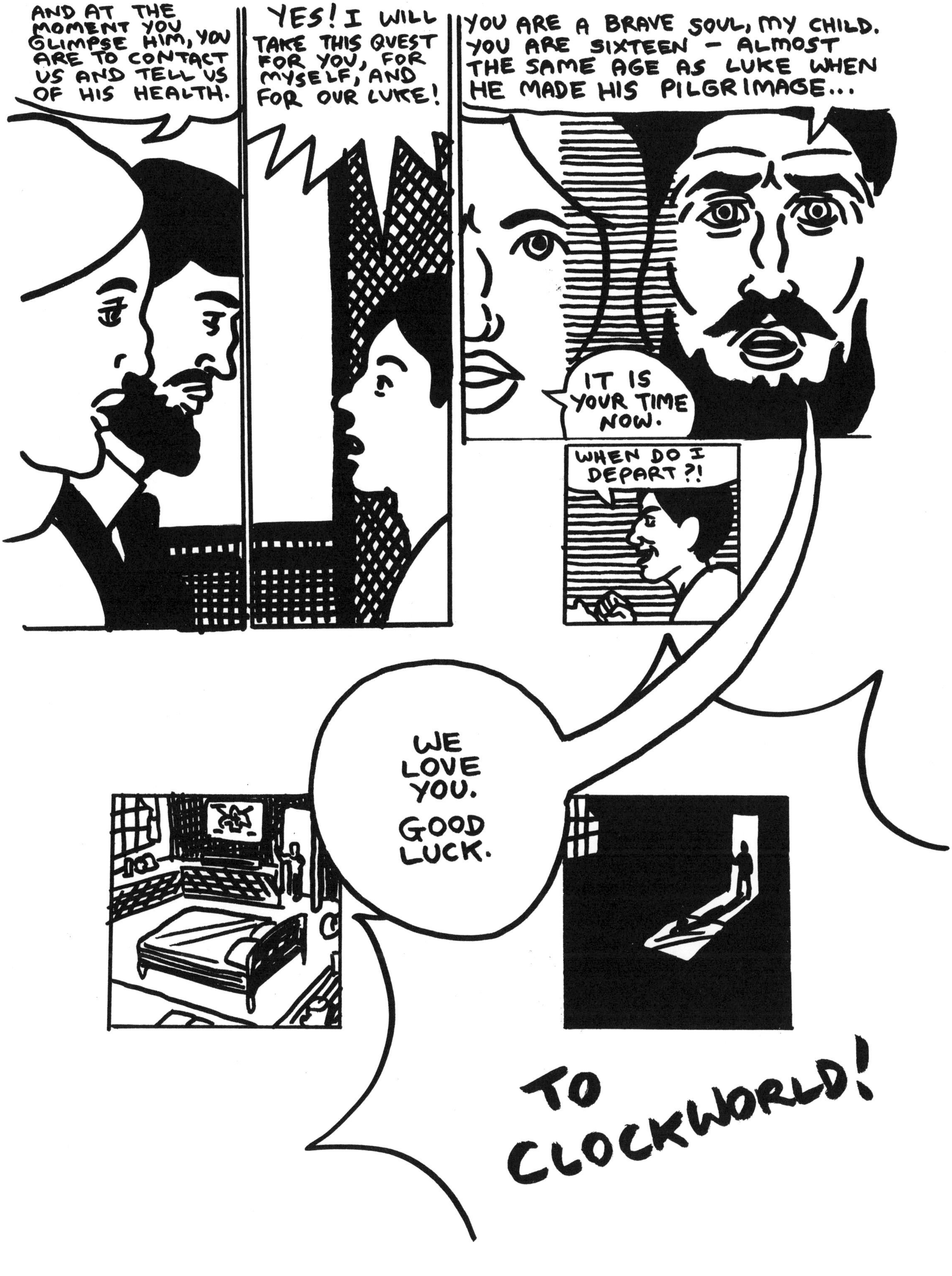

AND AT THE MOMENT YOU GLIMPSE HIM, YOU ARE TO CONTACT US AND TELL US OF HIS HEALTH.
YES! I WILL TAKE THIS QVEST FOR YOU, FOR MYSELF, AND FOR OUR LUKE!
YOU ARE A BRAVE SOUL, MY CHILD. YOU ARE SIXTEEN - ALMOST THE SAME AGE AS LUKE WHEN HE MADE HIS PILGRIMAGE...
IT IS YOUR TIME NOW.
WHEN DO I DEPART?!
WE LOVE YOU. GOOD LUCK.
TO CLOCKWORLD!

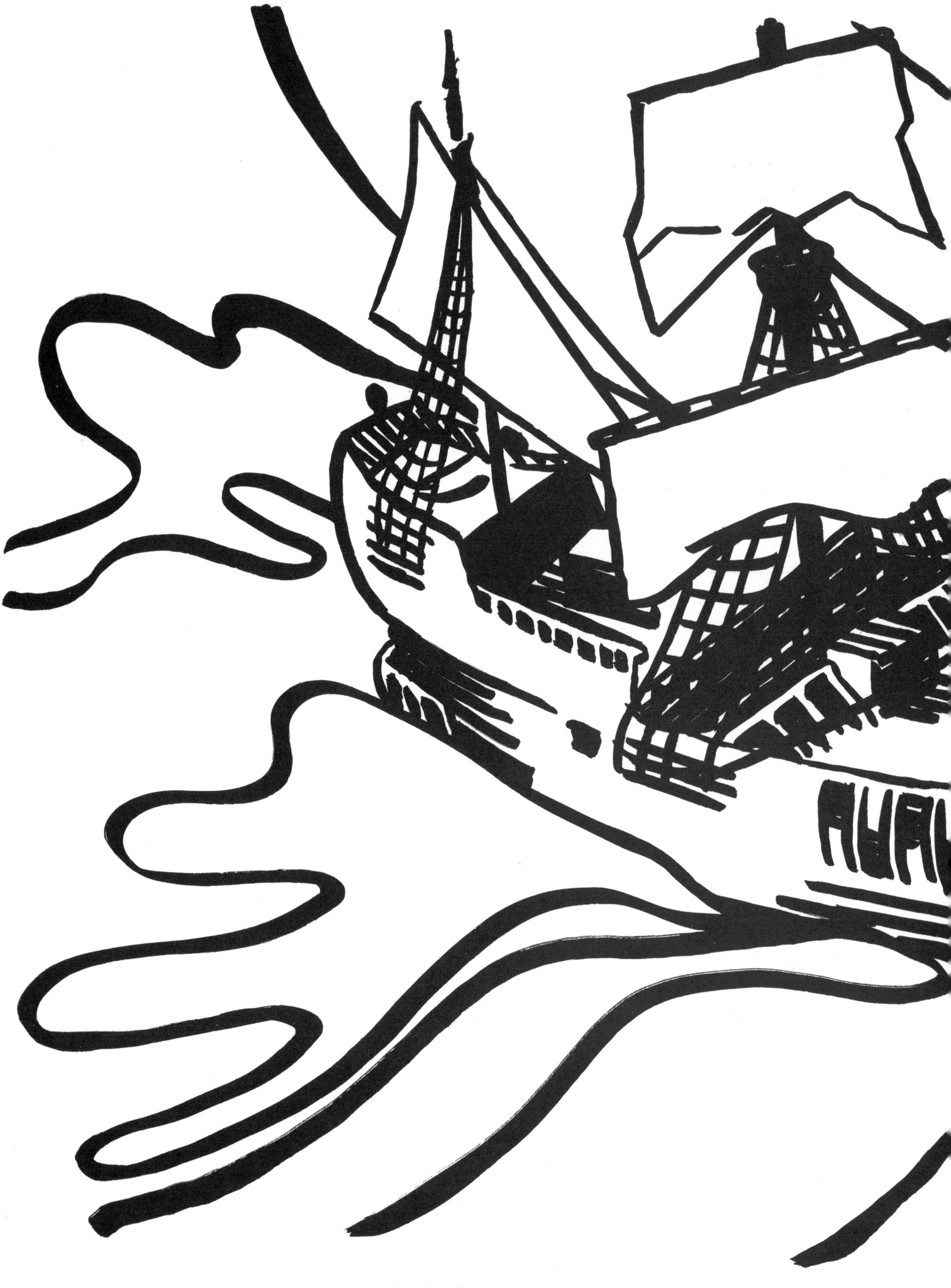

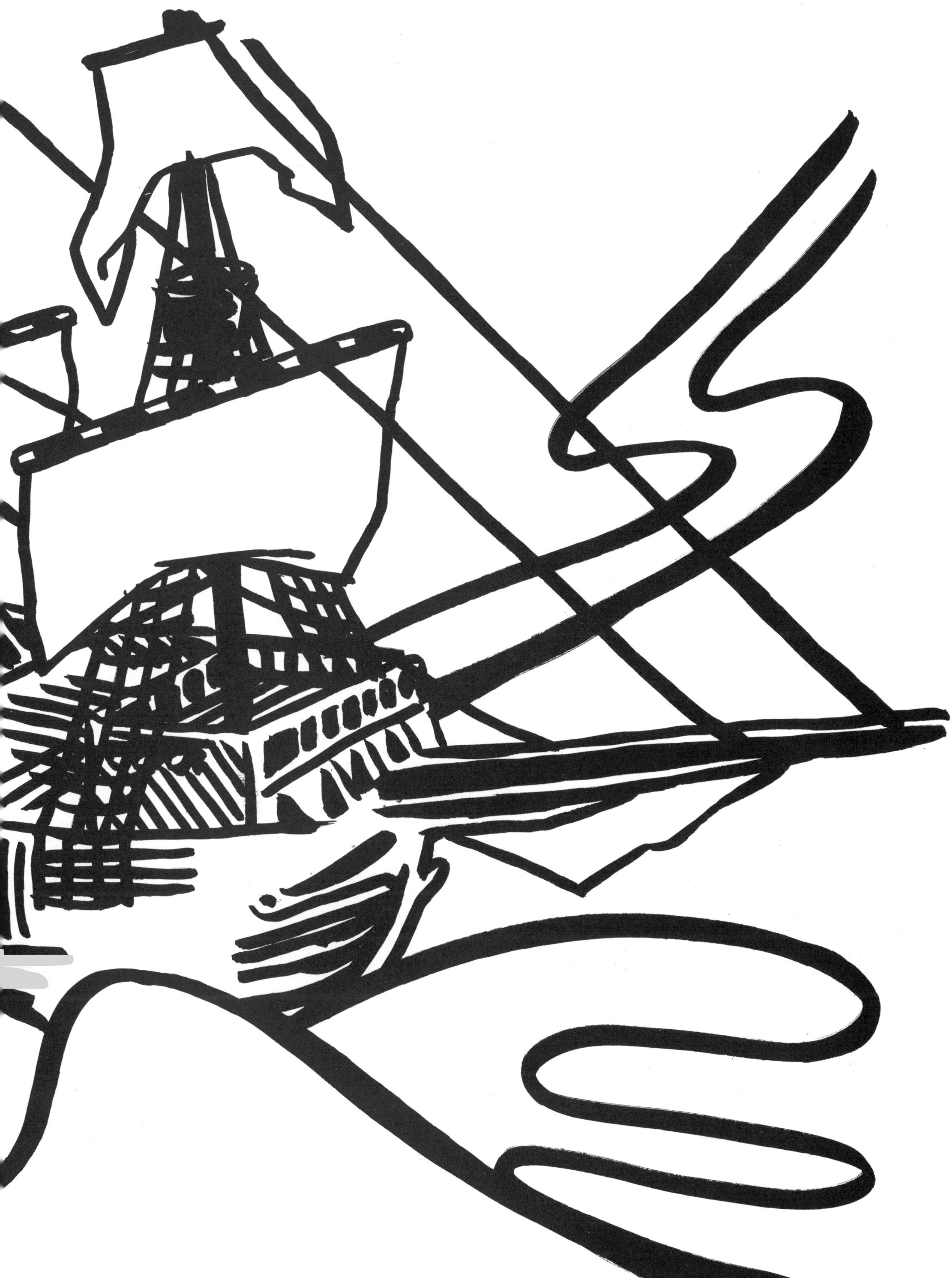

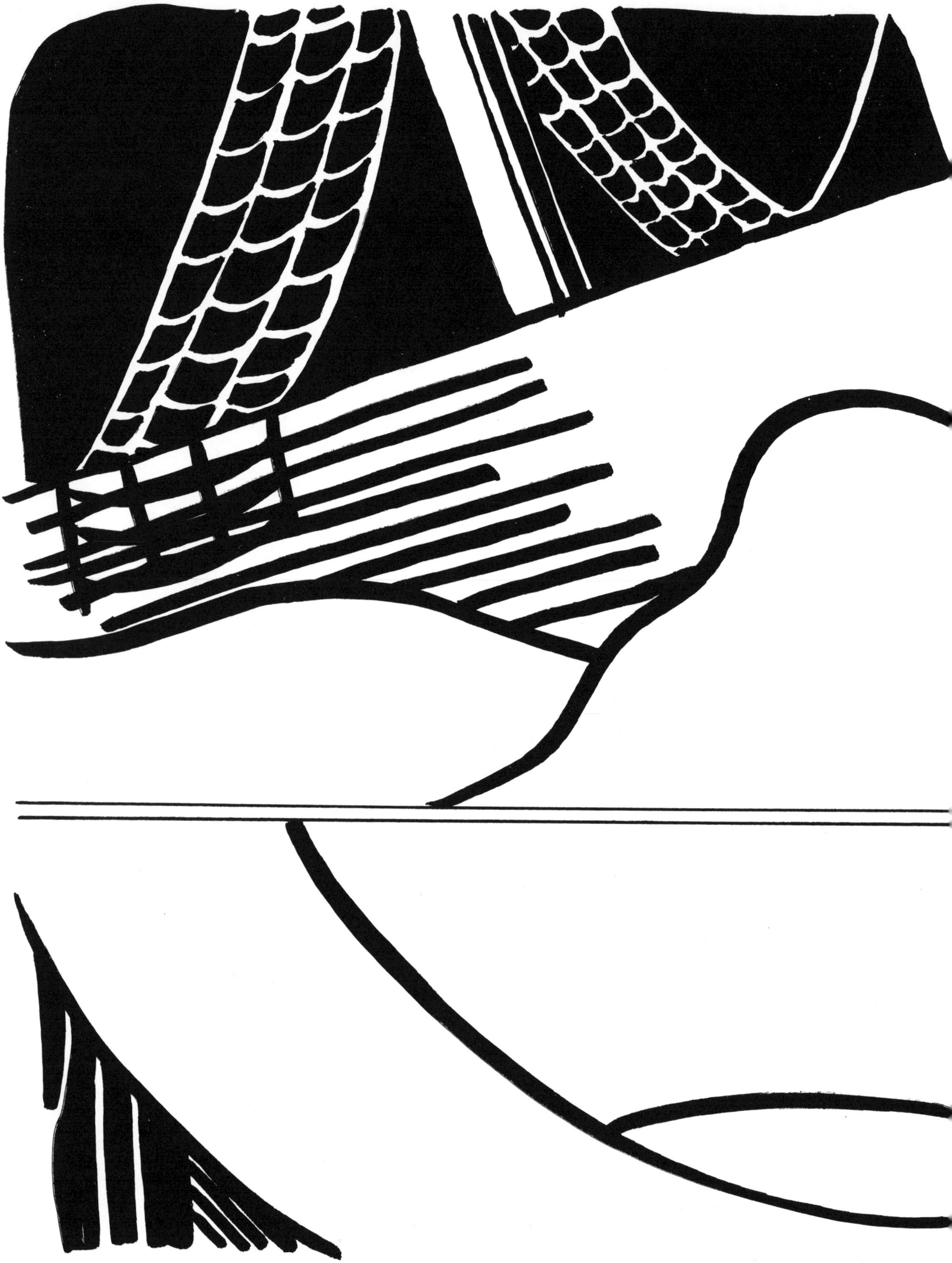

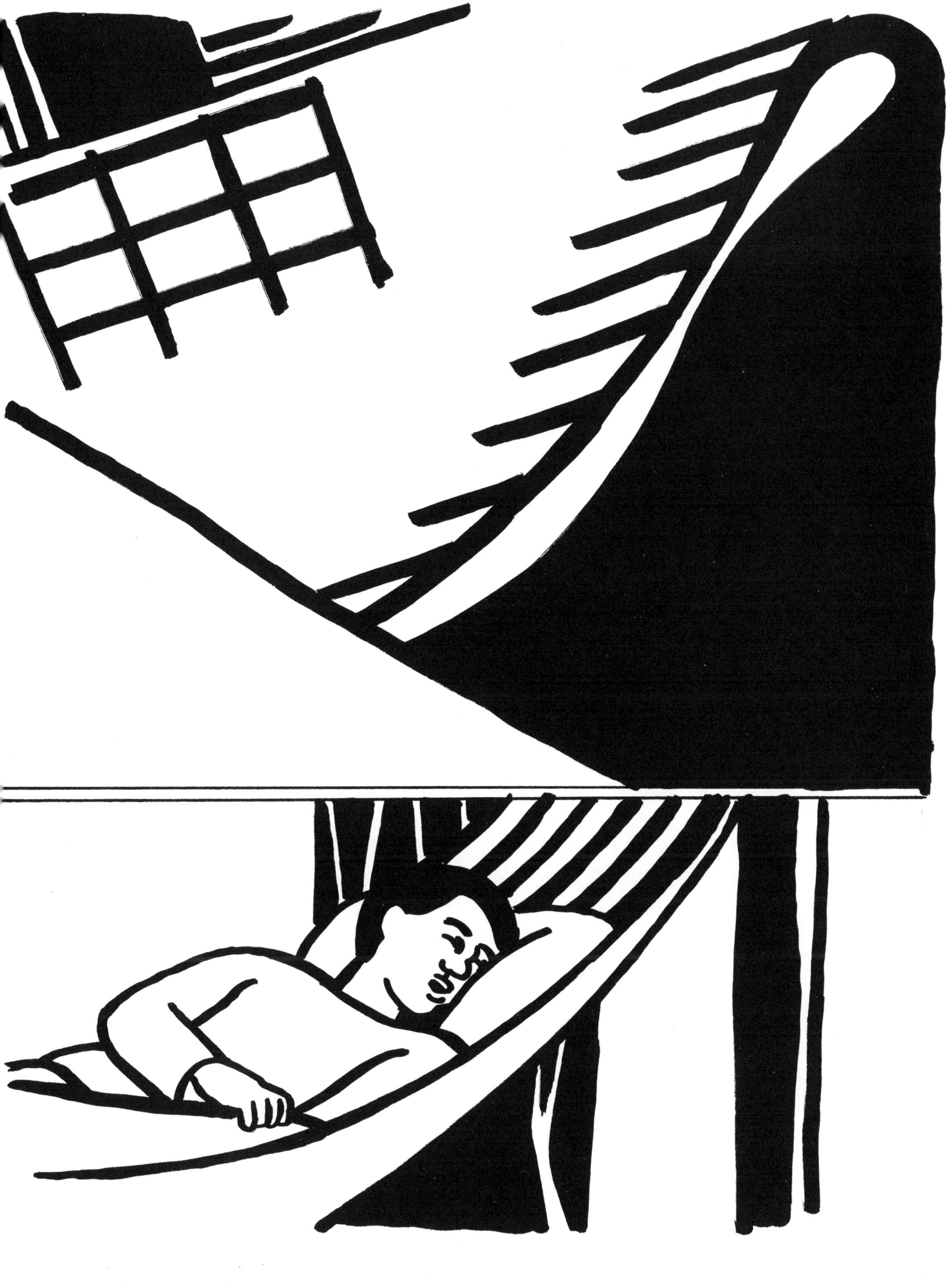

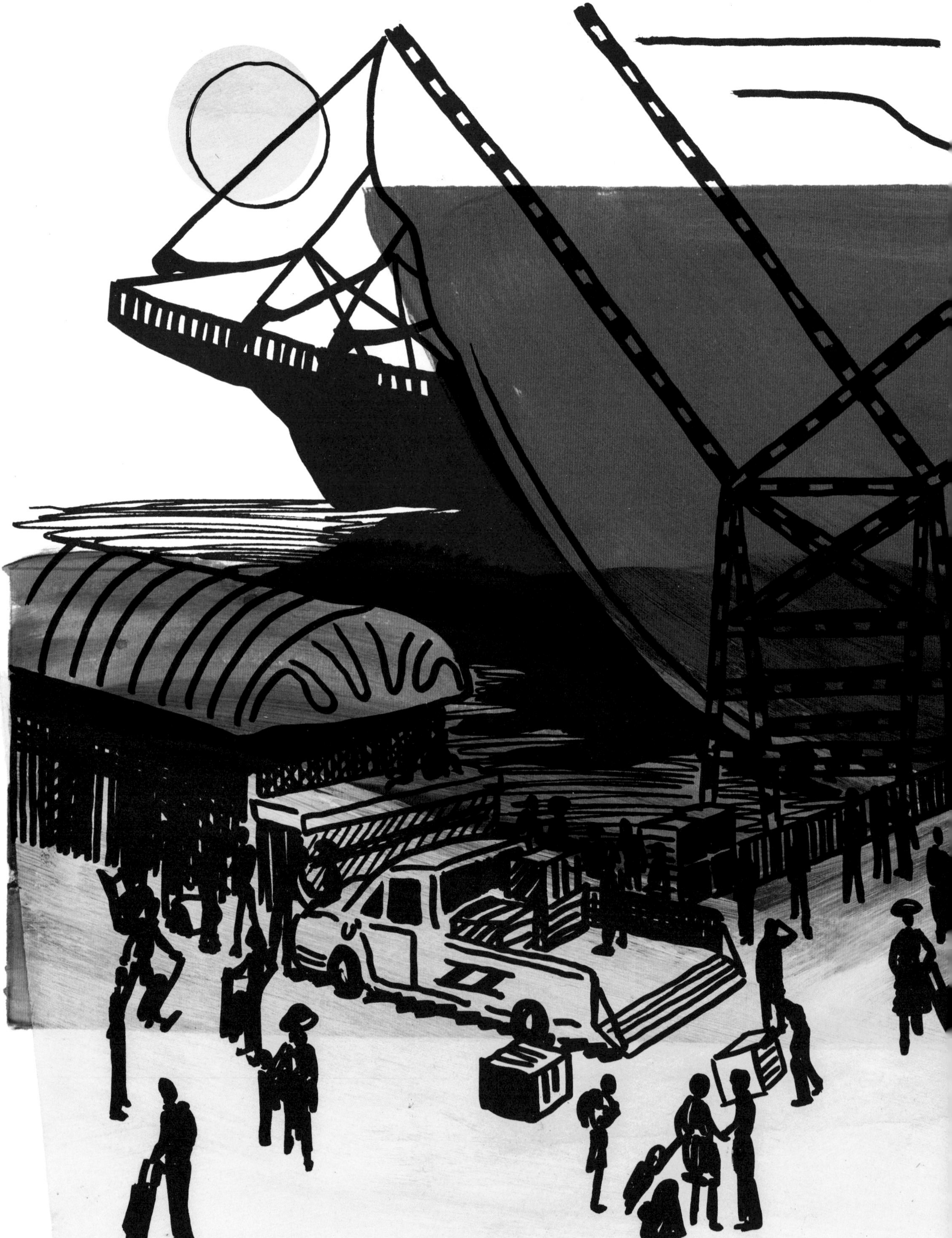

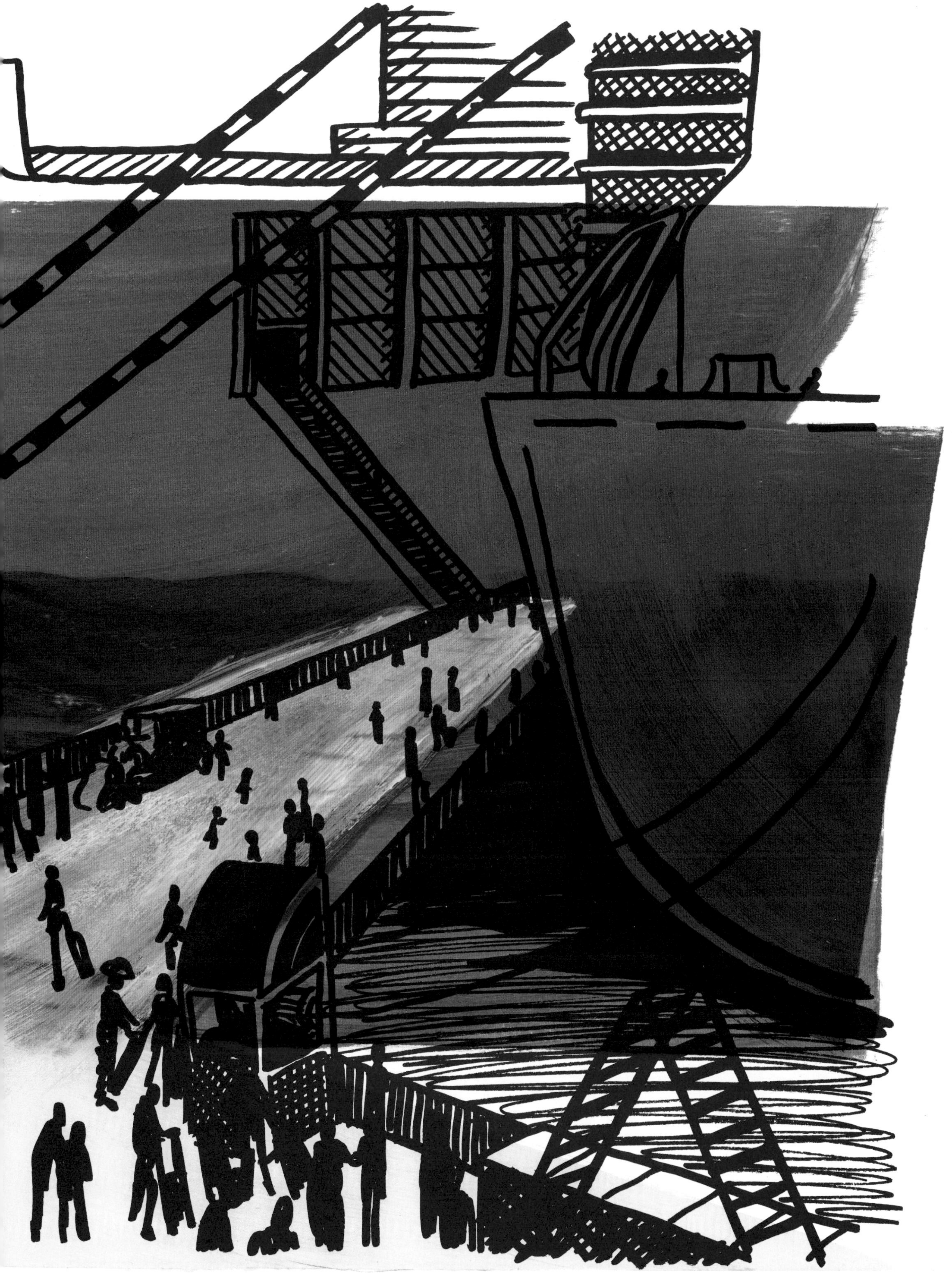

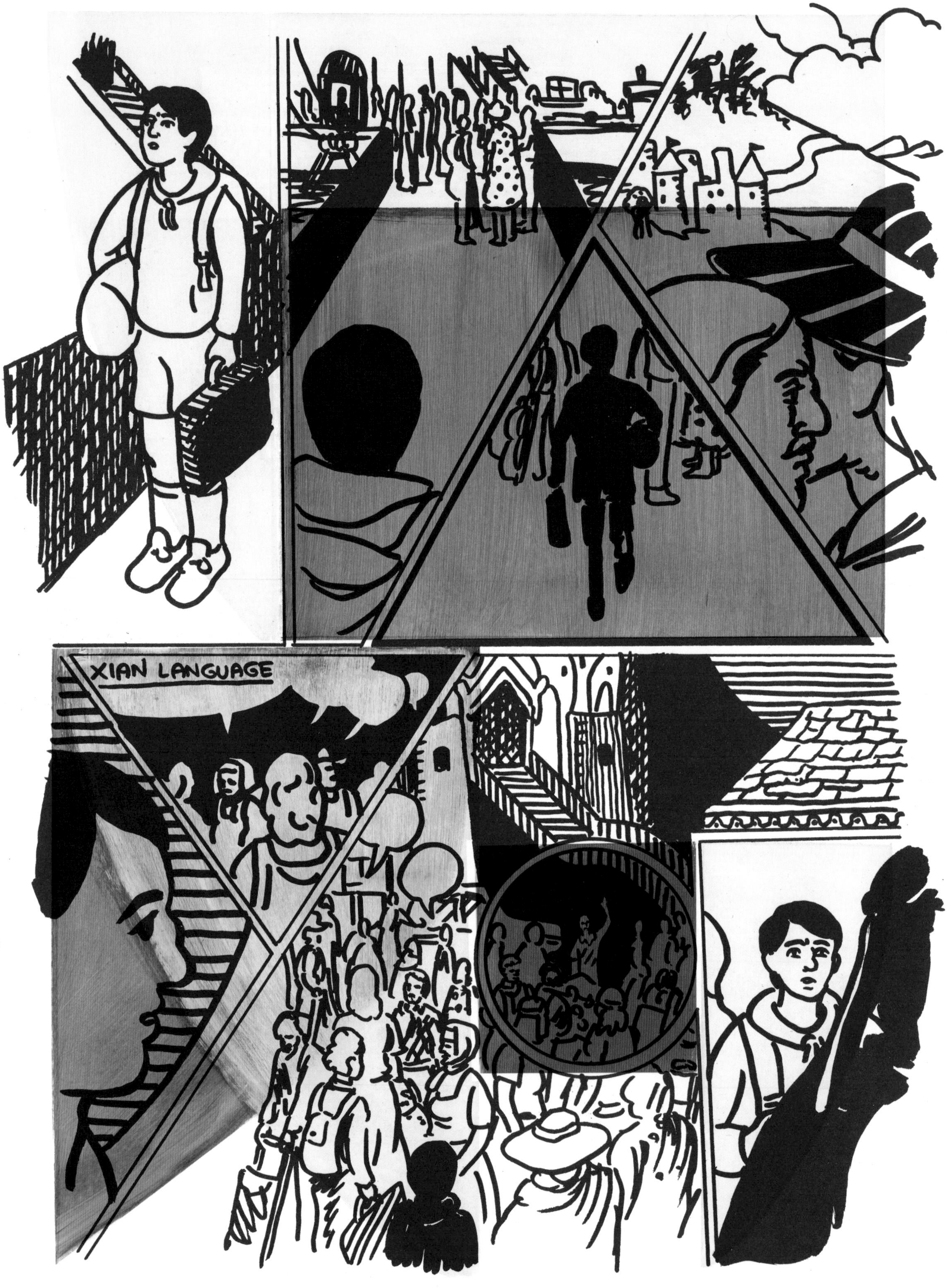
XIAN LANGUAGE

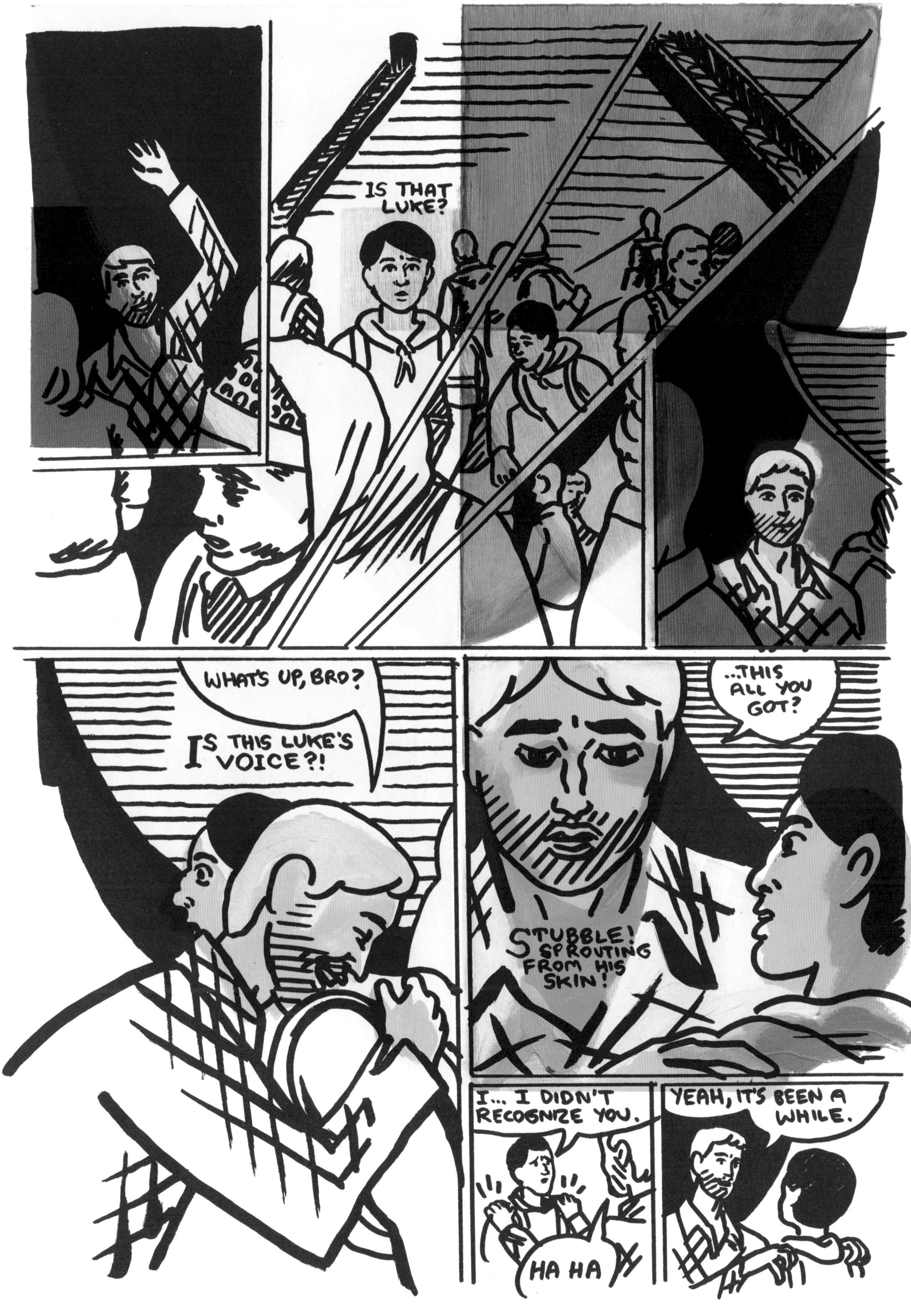
IS THAT LUKE?
WHAT'S UP, BRO?
IS THIS LUKE'S VOICE?!
...THIS ALL YOU GOT?
STUBBLE! SPROUTING FROM HIS SKIN!
I... I DIDN'T RECOGNIZE YOU.
HA HA
YEAH, IT'S BEEN A WHILE.

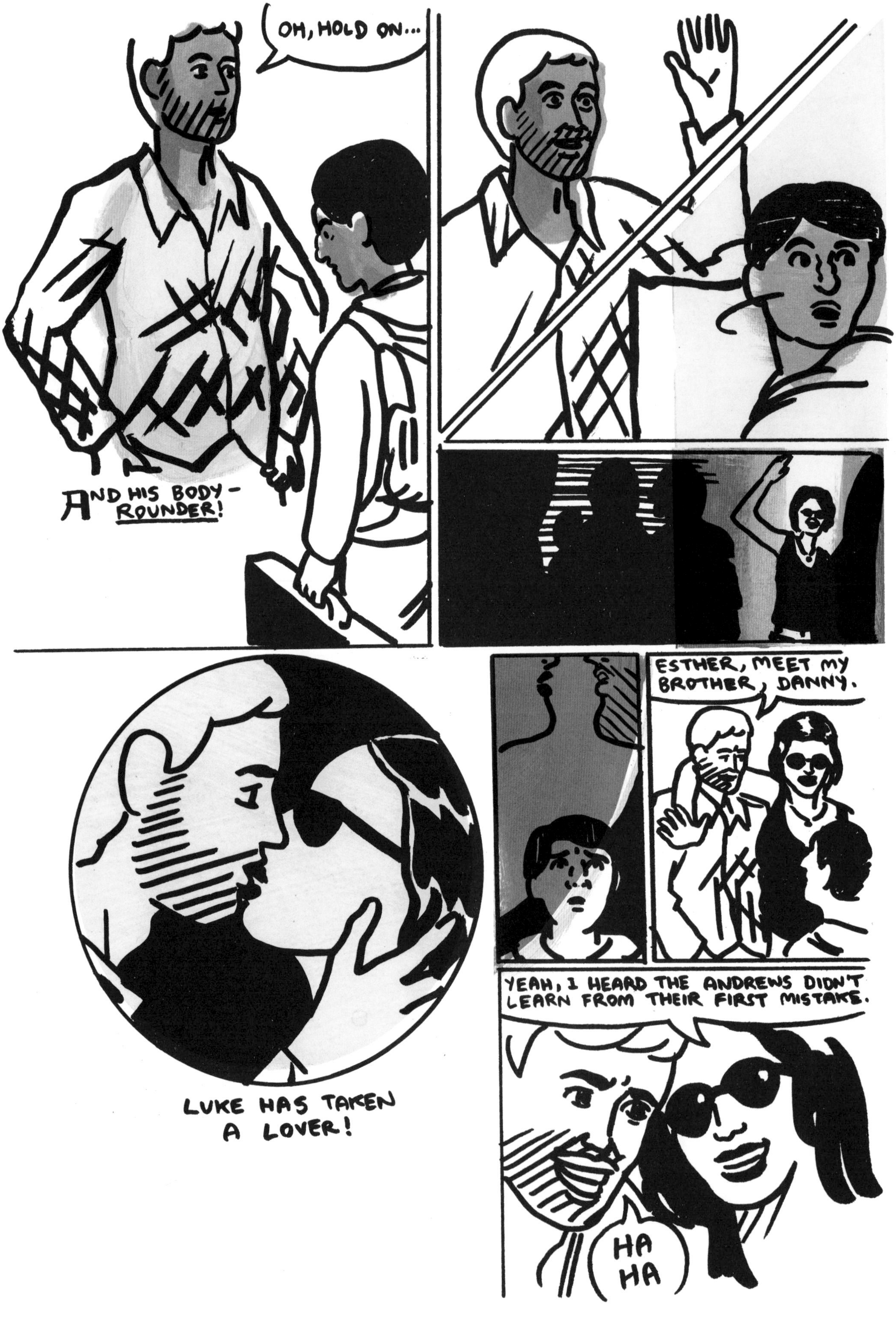
OH, HOLD ON...
AND HIS BODY-ROUNDER!
LUKE HAS TAKEN A LOVER!
ESTHER, MEET MY BROTHER, DANNY.
YEAH, I HEARD THE ANDREWS DIDN'T LEARN FROM THEIR FIRST MISTAKE.
HA HA

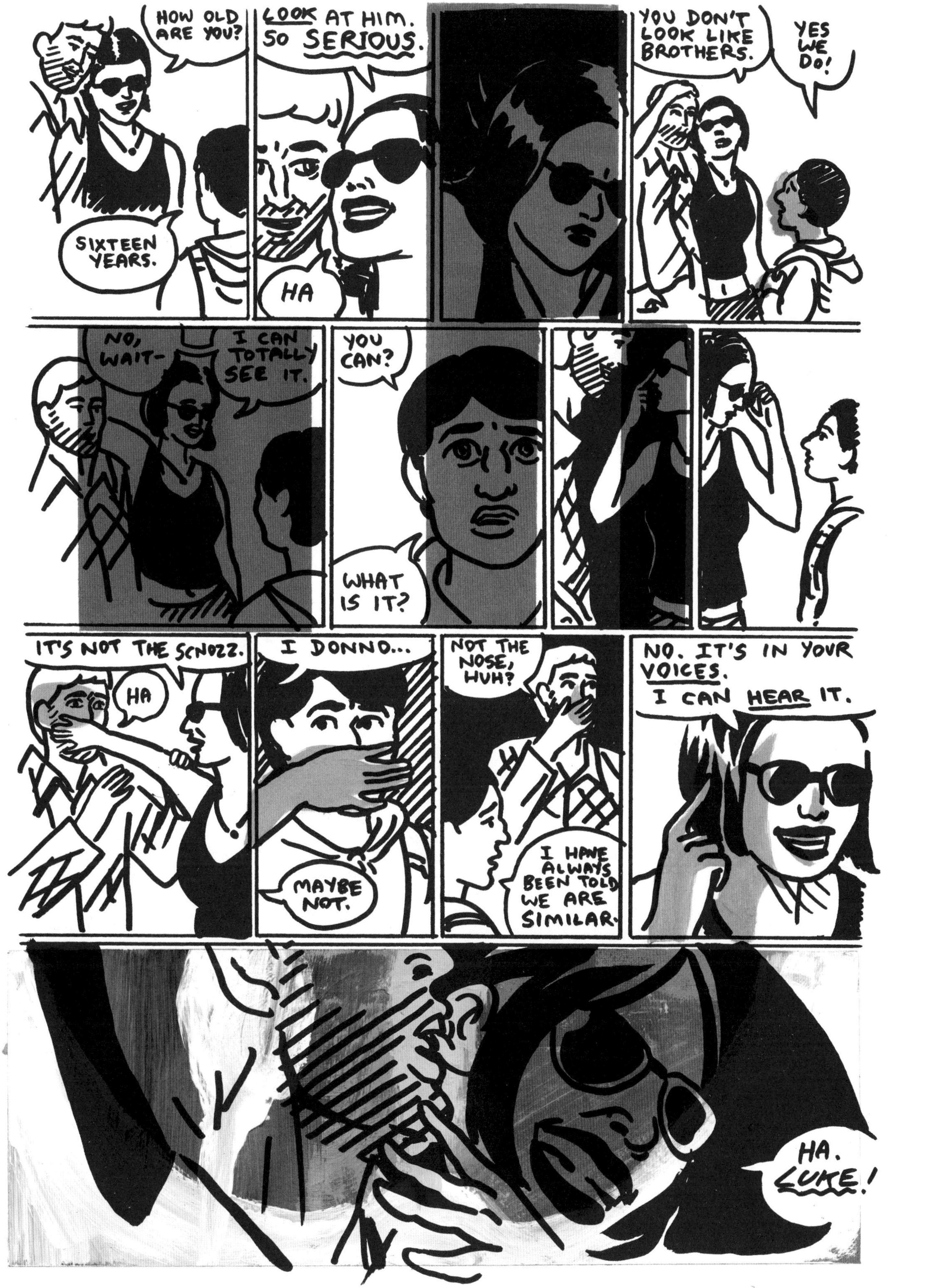
HOW OLD ARE YOU?
SIXTEEN YEARS.
LOOK AT HIM. SO SERIOUS.
HA
YOU DON'T LOOK LIKE BROTHERS.
YES WE DO!
NO, WAIT-
I CAN TOTALLY SEE IT.
YOU CAN?
WHAT IS IT?
IT'S NOT THE SCNOZZ.
HA
I DONNO...
MAYBE NOT.
NOT THE NOSE, HUH?
I HAVE ALWAYS BEEN TOLD WE ARE SIMILAR.
NO. IT'S IN YOUR VOICES.
I CAN HEAR IT.
HA. LUKE!

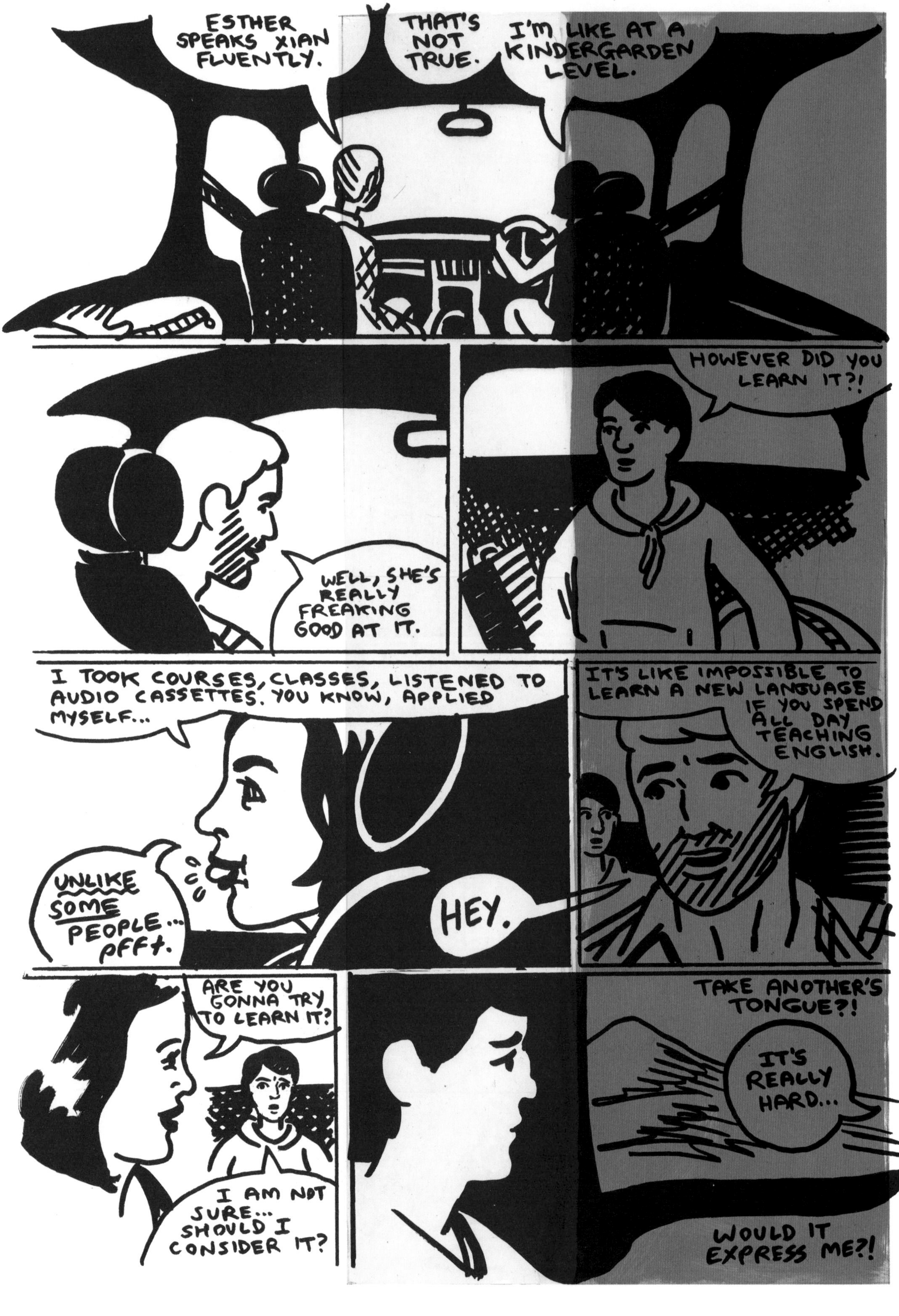
ESTHER SPEAKS XIAN FLUENTLY.
THAT'S NOT TRUE.
I'M LIKE AT A KINDERGARDEN LEVEL.
WELL, SHE'S REALLY FREAKING GOOD AT IT.
HOWEVER DID YOU LEARN IT?!
I TOOK COURSES, CLASSES, LISTENED TO AUDIO CASSETTES. YOU KNOW, APPLIED MYSELF...
UNLIKE SOME PEOPLE... PFFT.
HEY.
IT'S LIKE IMPOSSIBLE TO LEARN A NEW LANGUAGE IF YOU SPEND ALL DAY TEACHING ENGLISH.
ARE YOU GONNA TRY TO LEARN IT?
I AM NOT SURE... SHOULD I CONSIDER IT?
TAKE ANOTHER'S TONGUE?!
IT'S REALLY HARD...
WOULD IT EXPRESS ME?!

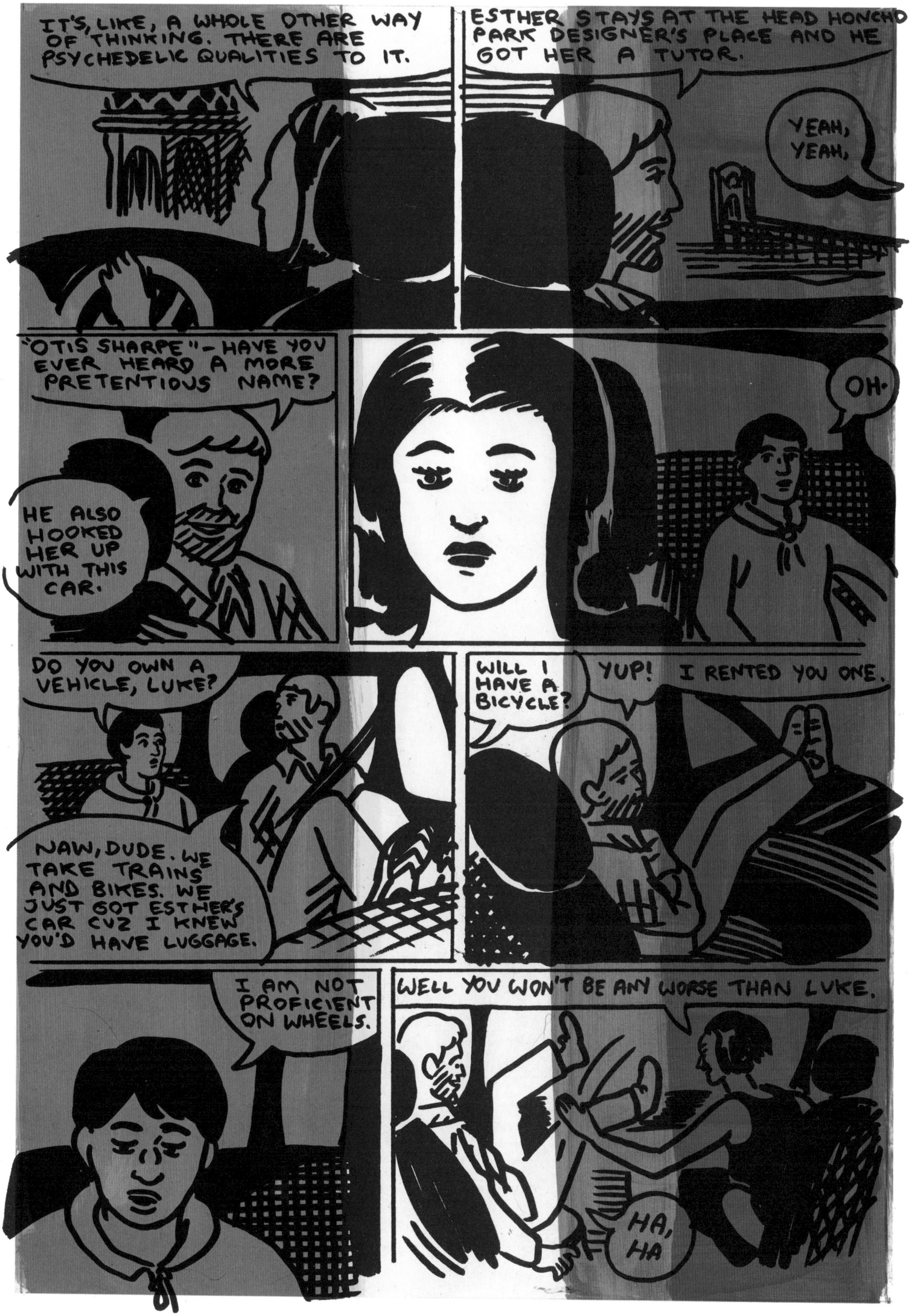
IT'S, LIKE, A WHOLE OTHER WAY OF THINKING. THERE ARE PSYCHEDELIC QUALITIES TO IT.
ESTHER STAYS AT THE HEAD HONCHO PARK DESIGNER'S PLACE AND HE GOT HER A TUTOR.
YEAH, YEAH,
"OTIS SHARPE" - HAVE YOU EVER HEARD A MORE PRETENTIOUS NAME?
HE ALSO HOOKED HER UP WITH THIS CAR.
OH.
DO YOU OWN A VEHICLE, LUKE?
NAW, DUDE. WE TAKE TRAINS AND BIKES. WE JUST GOT ESTHER'S CAR CUZ I KNEW YOU'D HAVE LUGGAGE.
WILL I HAVE A BICYCLE?
YUP! I RENTED YOU ONE.
I AM NOT PROFICIENT ON WHEELS.
WELL YOU WON'T BE ANY WORSE THAN LUKE.
HA, HA

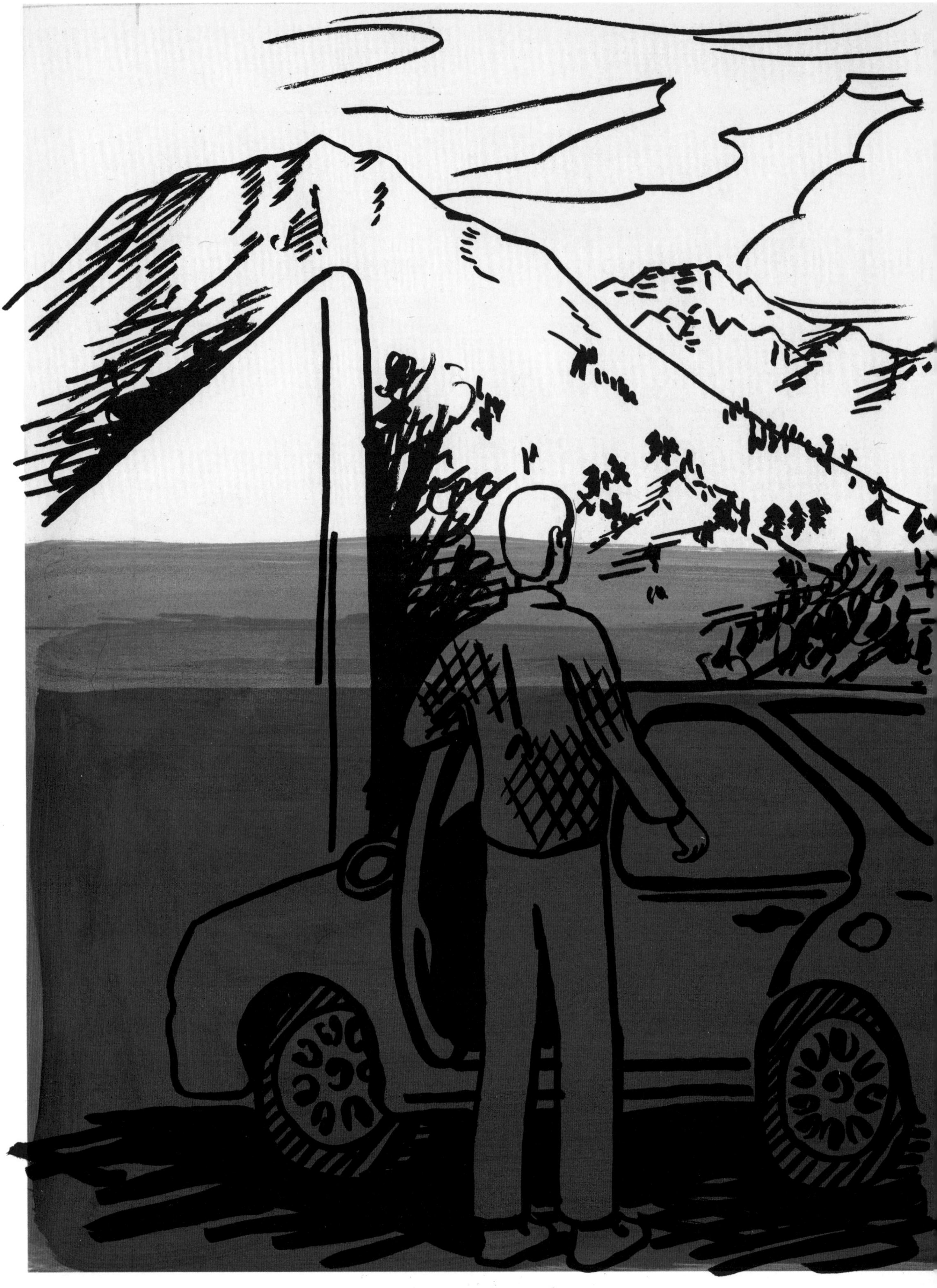

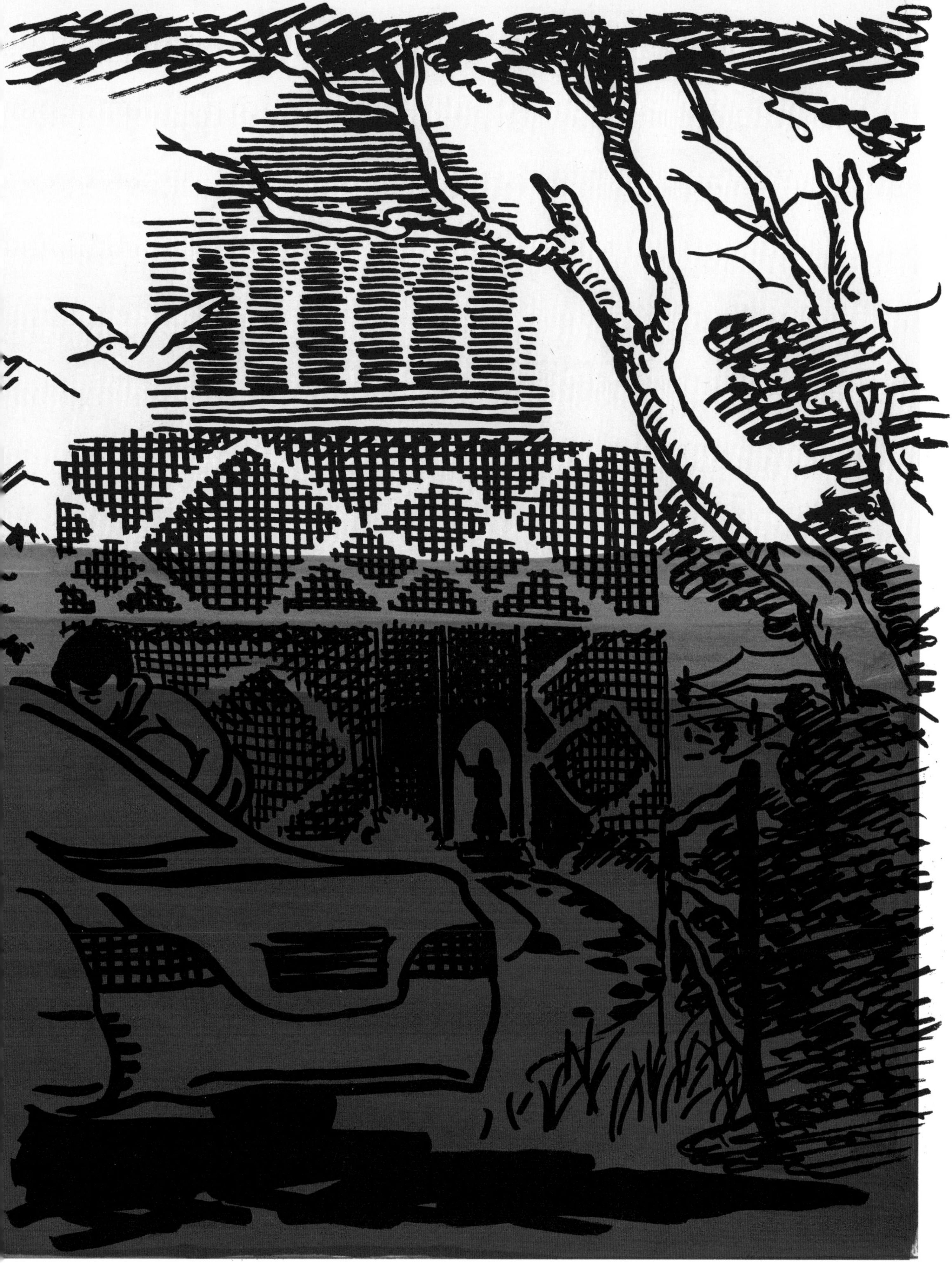

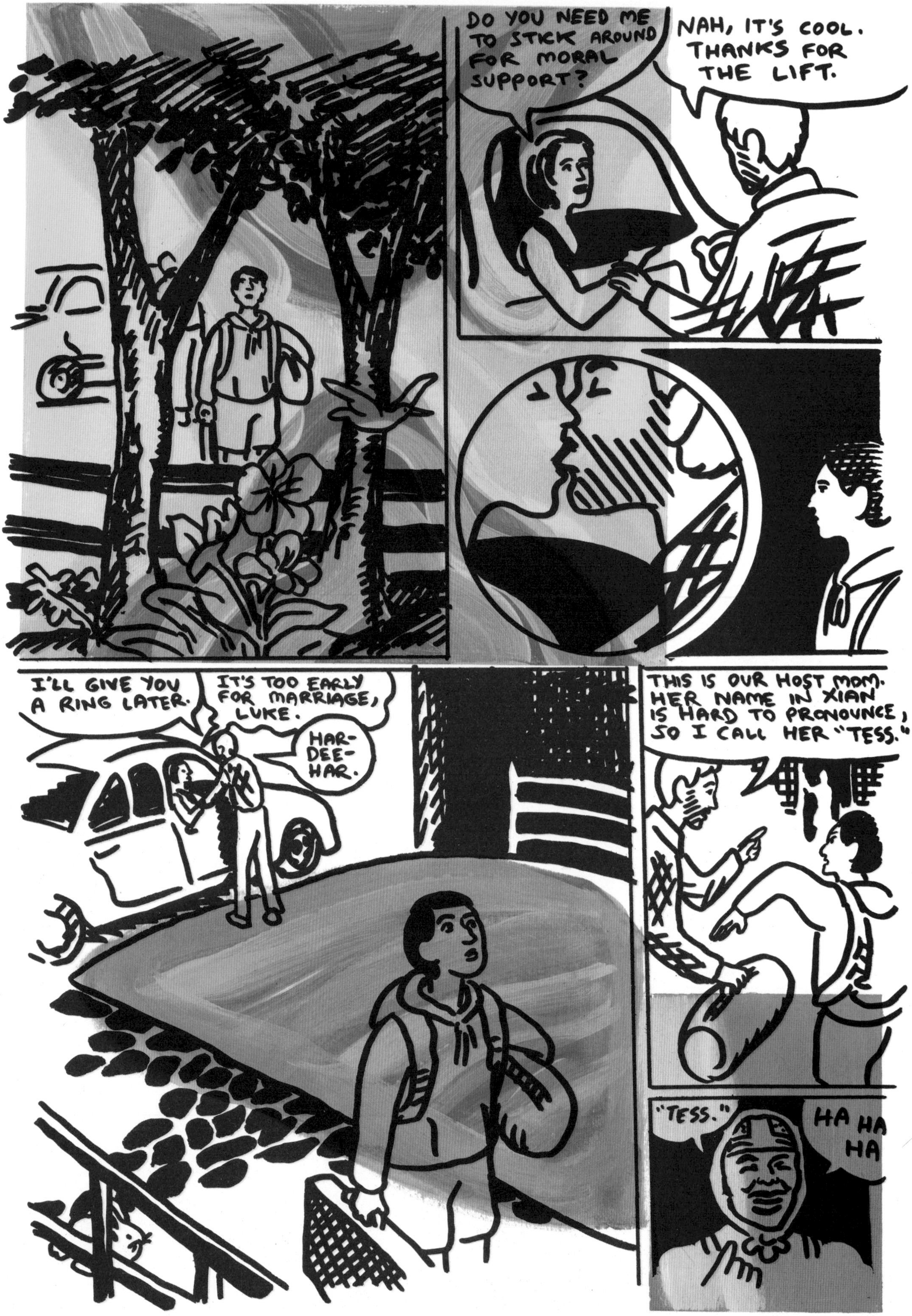
DO YOU NEED ME TO STICK AROUND FOR MORAL SUPPORT?
NAH, IT'S COOL. THANKS FOR THE LIFT.
I'LL GIVE YOU A RING LATER.
IT'S TOO EARLY FOR MARRIAGE, LUKE.
HAR-DEE-HAR.
THIS IS OUR HOST MOM. HER NAME IN XIAN IS HARD TO PRONOUNCE, SO I CALL HER "TESS."
"TESS."
HA HA HA

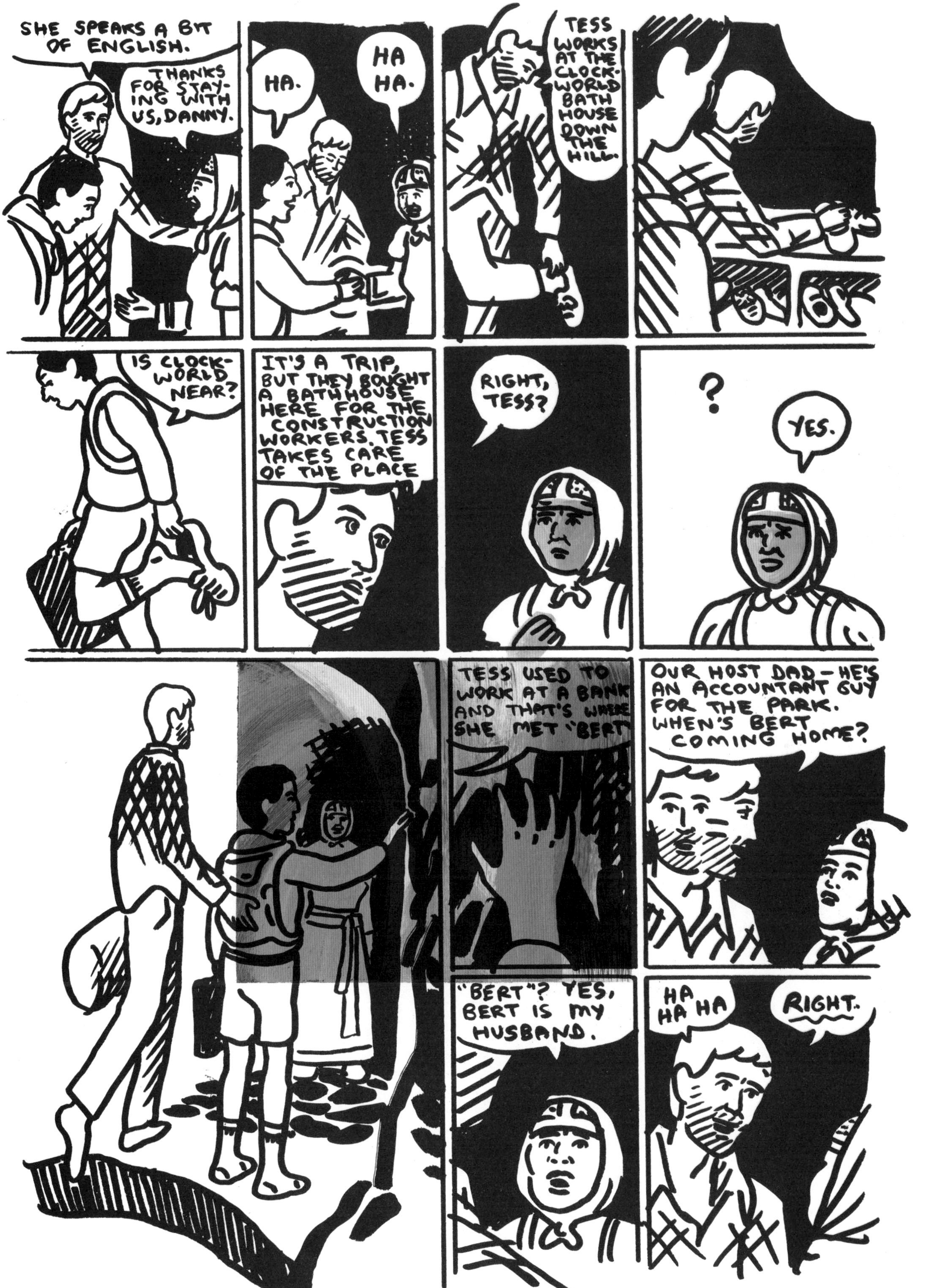
SHE SPEAKS A BIT OF ENGLISH.
THANKS FOR STAYING WITH US, DANNY.
HA.
HA HA.
TESS WORKS AT THE CLOCKWORLD BATH HOUSE DOWN THE HILL.
IS CLOCKWORLD NEAR?
IT'S A TRIP, BUT THEY BOUGHT A BATHHOUSE HERE FOR THE CONSTRUCTION WORKERS. TESS TAKES CARE OF THE PLACE
RIGHT, TESS?
?
YES.
TESS USED TO WORK AT A BANK AND THAT'S WHERE SHE MET "BERT"
OUR HOST DAD—HE'S AN ACCOUNTANT GUY FOR THE PARK. WHEN'S BERT COMING HOME?
"BERT"? YES, BERT IS MY HUSBAND.
HA HA HA
RIGHT.

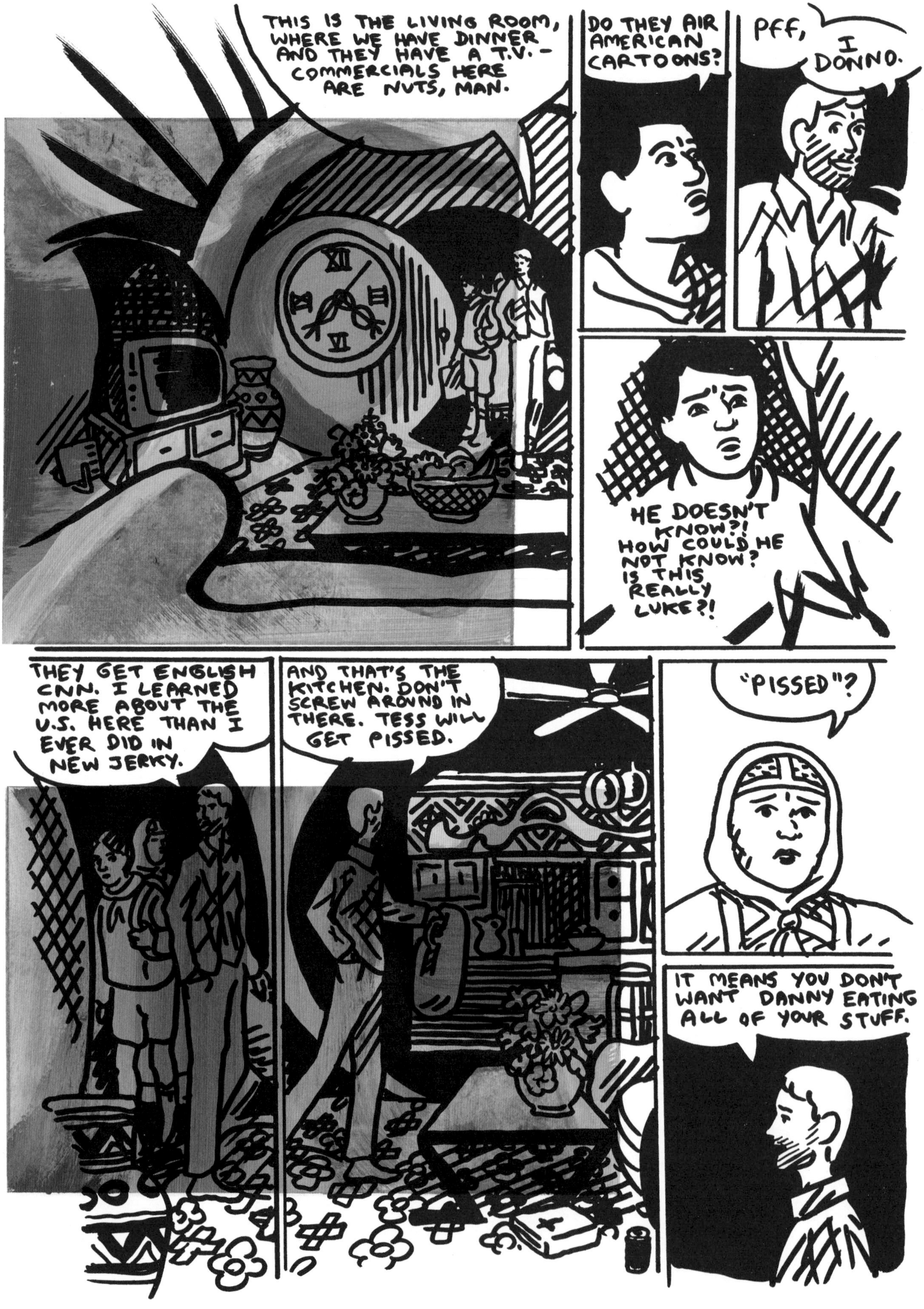
THIS IS THE LIVING ROOM, WHERE WE HAVE DINNER AND THEY HAVE A T.V. - COMMERCIALS HERE ARE NUTS, MAN.
DO THEY AIR AMERICAN CARTOONS?
PFF,
I DONNO.
HE DOESN'T KNOW?! HOW COULD HE NOT KNOW? IS THIS REALLY LUKE?!
THEY GET ENGLISH CNN. I LEARNED MORE ABOUT THE U.S. HERE THAN I EVER DID IN NEW JERKY.
AND THAT'S THE KITCHEN. DON'T SCREW AROUND IN THERE. TESS WILL GET PISSED.
"PISSED"?
IT MEANS YOU DON'T WANT DANNY EATING ALL OF YOUR STUFF.

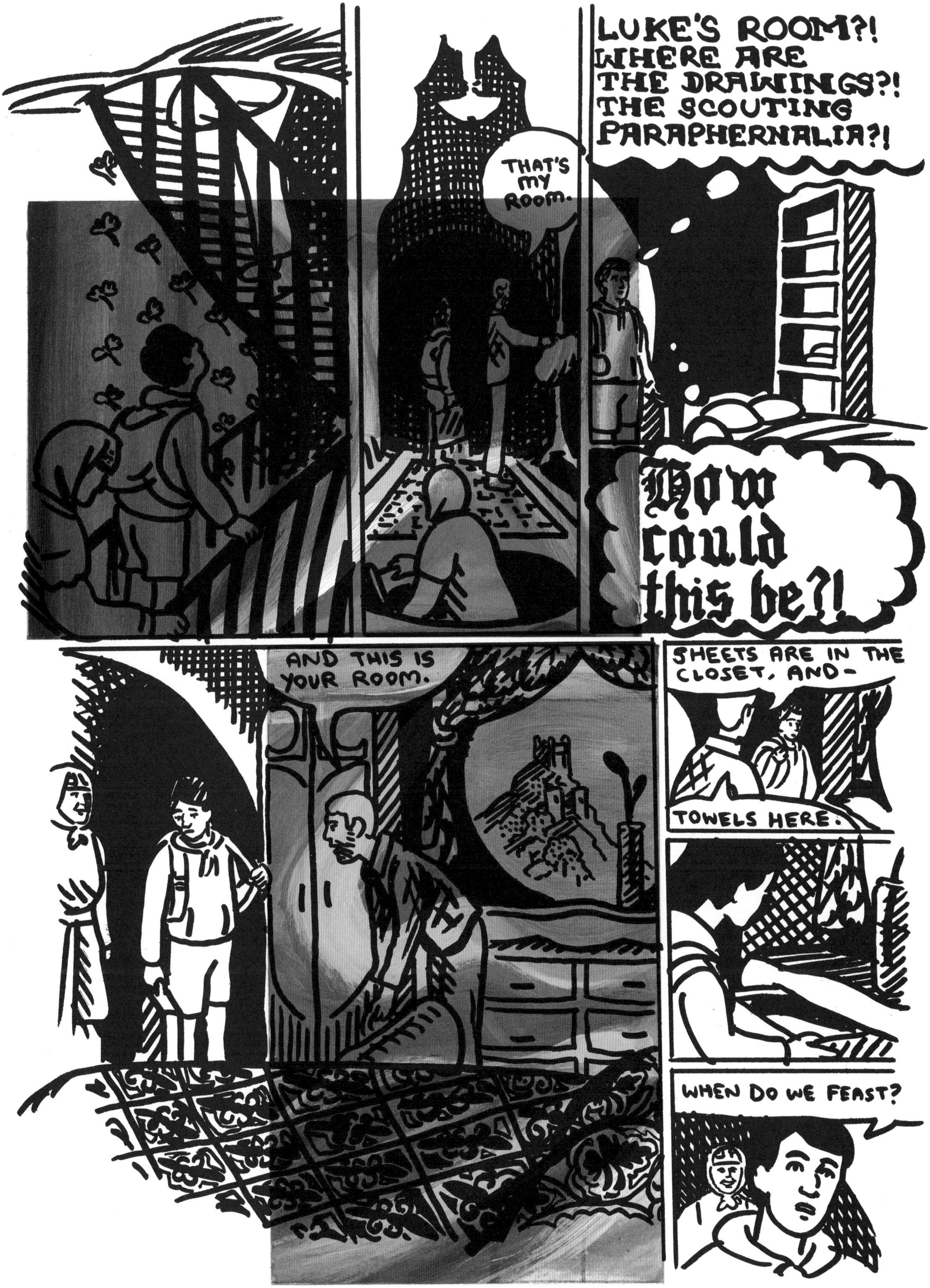
THAT'S MY ROOM.
LUKE'S ROOM?! WHERE ARE THE DRAWINGS?! THE SCOUTING PARAPHERNALIA?!
How could this be?!
AND THIS IS YOUR ROOM.
SHEETS ARE IN THE CLOSET, AND—
TOWELS HERE.
WHEN DO WE FEAST?

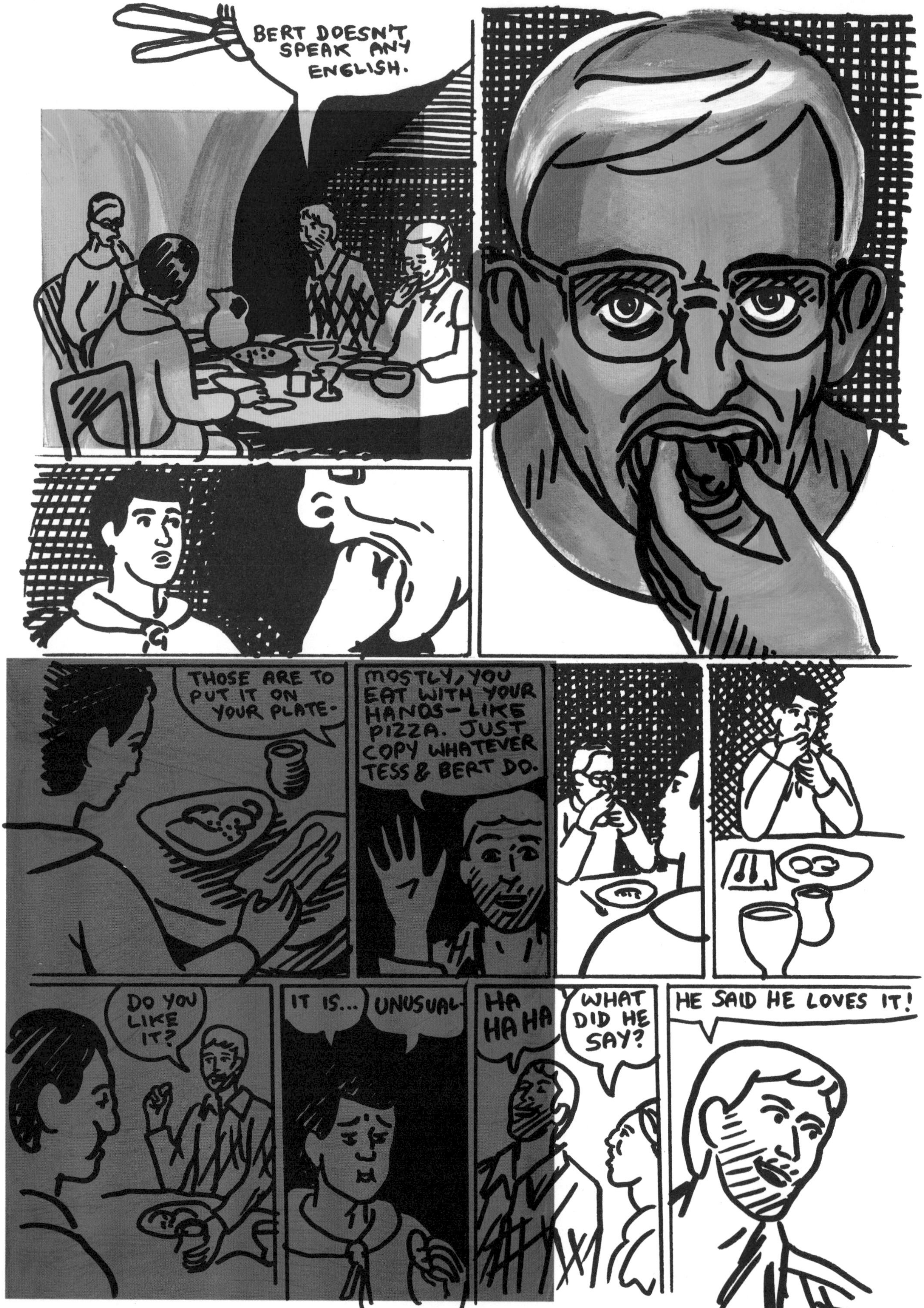
BERT DOESN'T SPEAK ANY ENGLISH.
THOSE ARE TO PUT IT ON YOUR PLATE-
MOSTLY, YOU EAT WITH YOUR HANDS- LIKE PIZZA. JUST COPY WHATEVER TESS & BERT DO.
DO YOU LIKE IT?
IT IS...
UNUSUAL-
HA HA HA
WHAT DID HE SAY?
HE SAID HE LOVES IT!

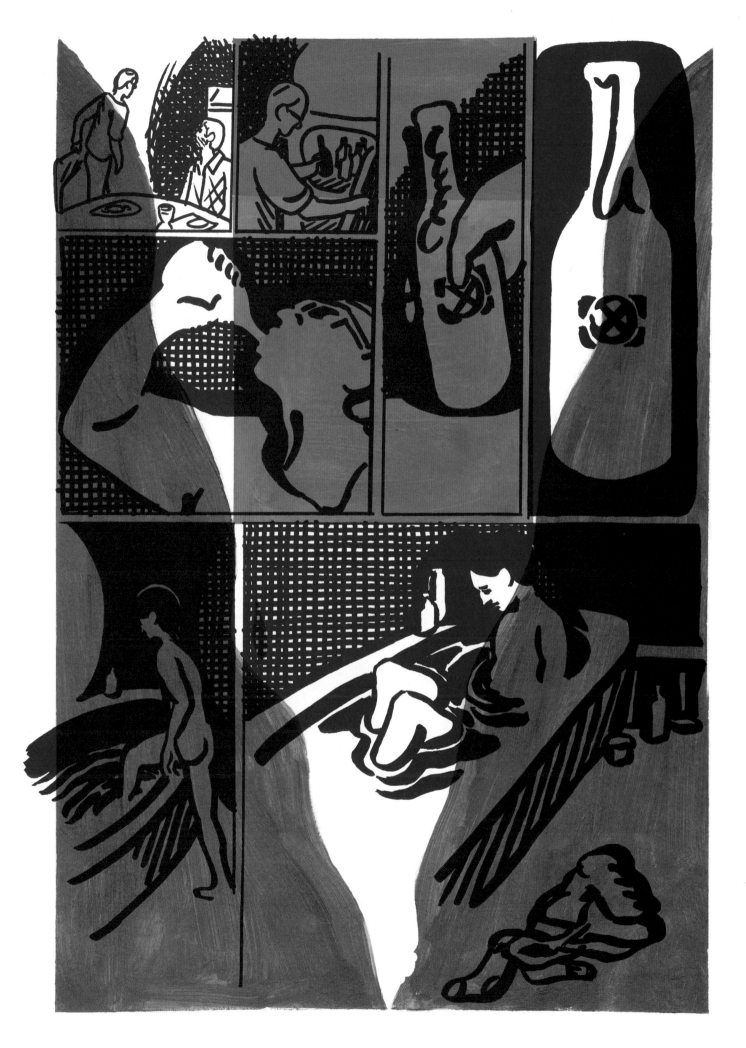

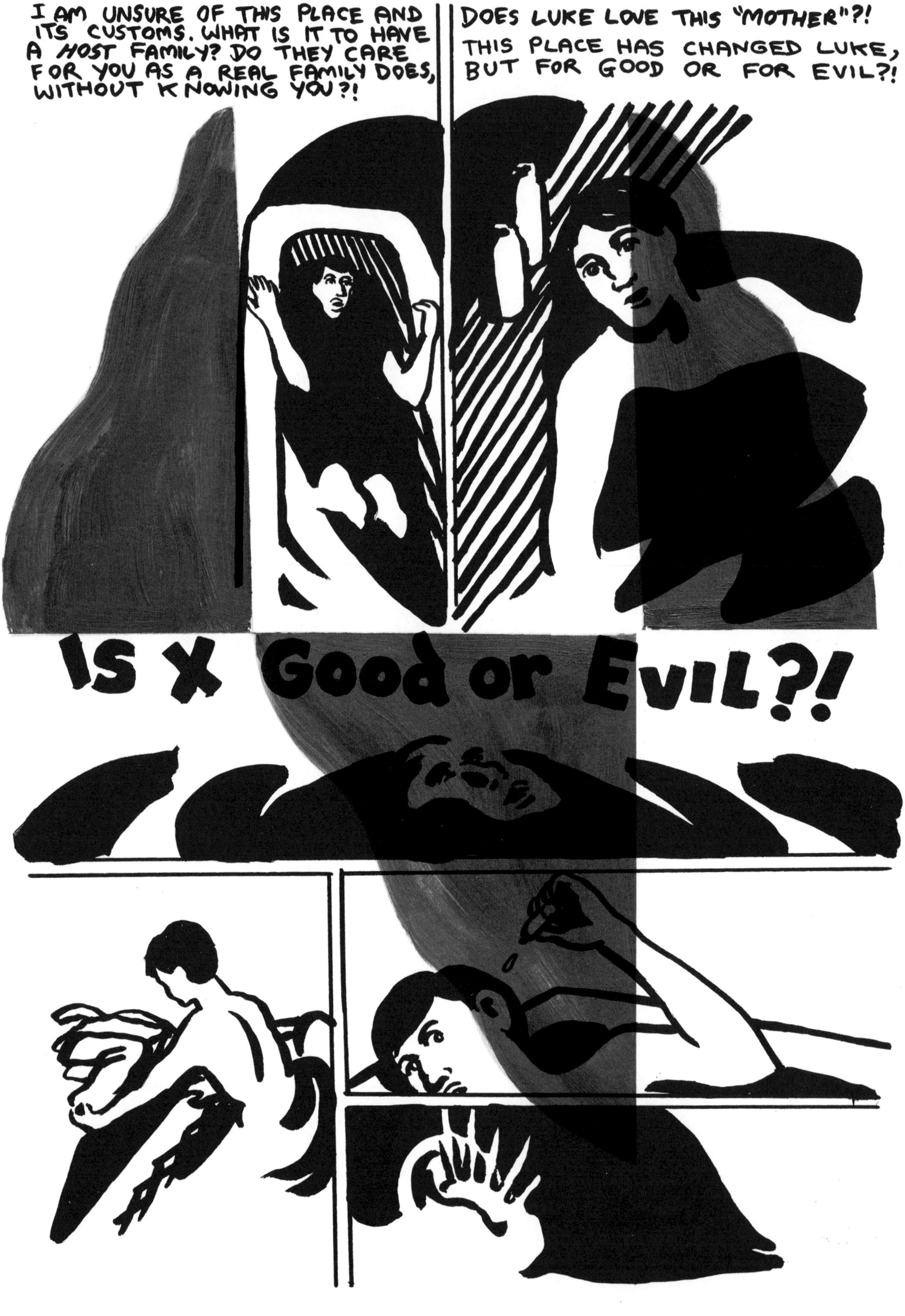
I AM UNSURE OF THIS PLACE AND ITS CUSTOMS. WHAT IS IT TO HAVE A *HOST* FAMILY? DO THEY CARE FOR YOU AS A REAL FAMILY DOES, WITHOUT KNOWING YOU?!
DOES LUKE LOVE THIS "MOTHER"?!
THIS PLACE HAS CHANGED LUKE, BUT FOR GOOD OR FOR EVIL?!
IS X Good or Evil?!

WHAT IS THIS PLACE?

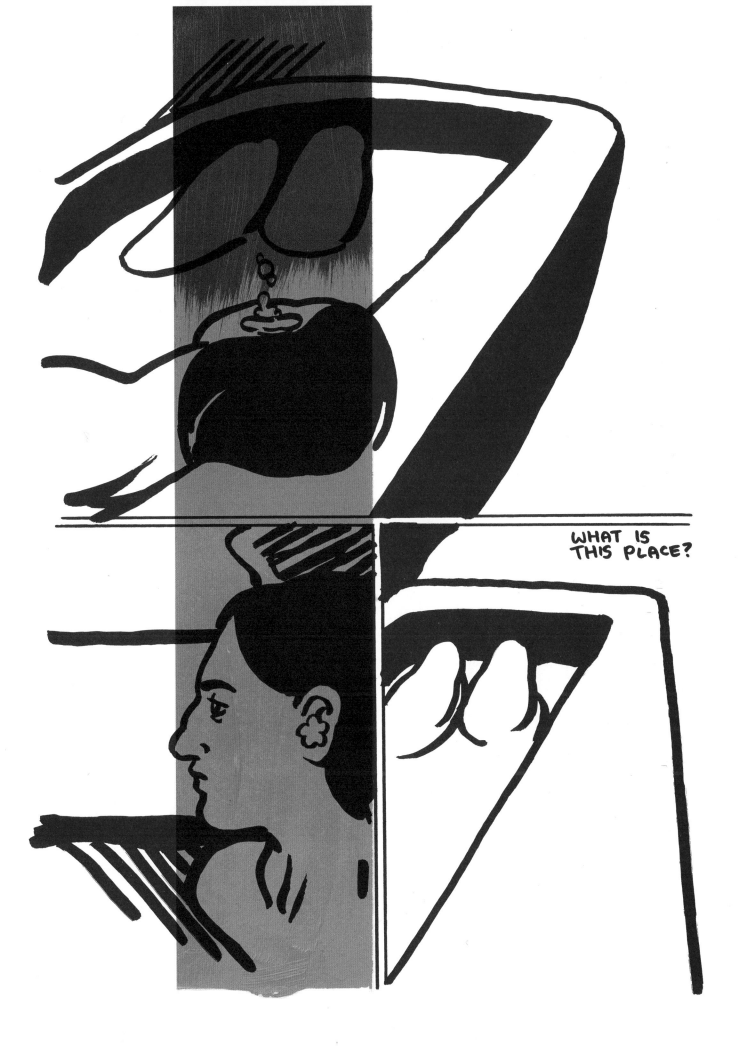

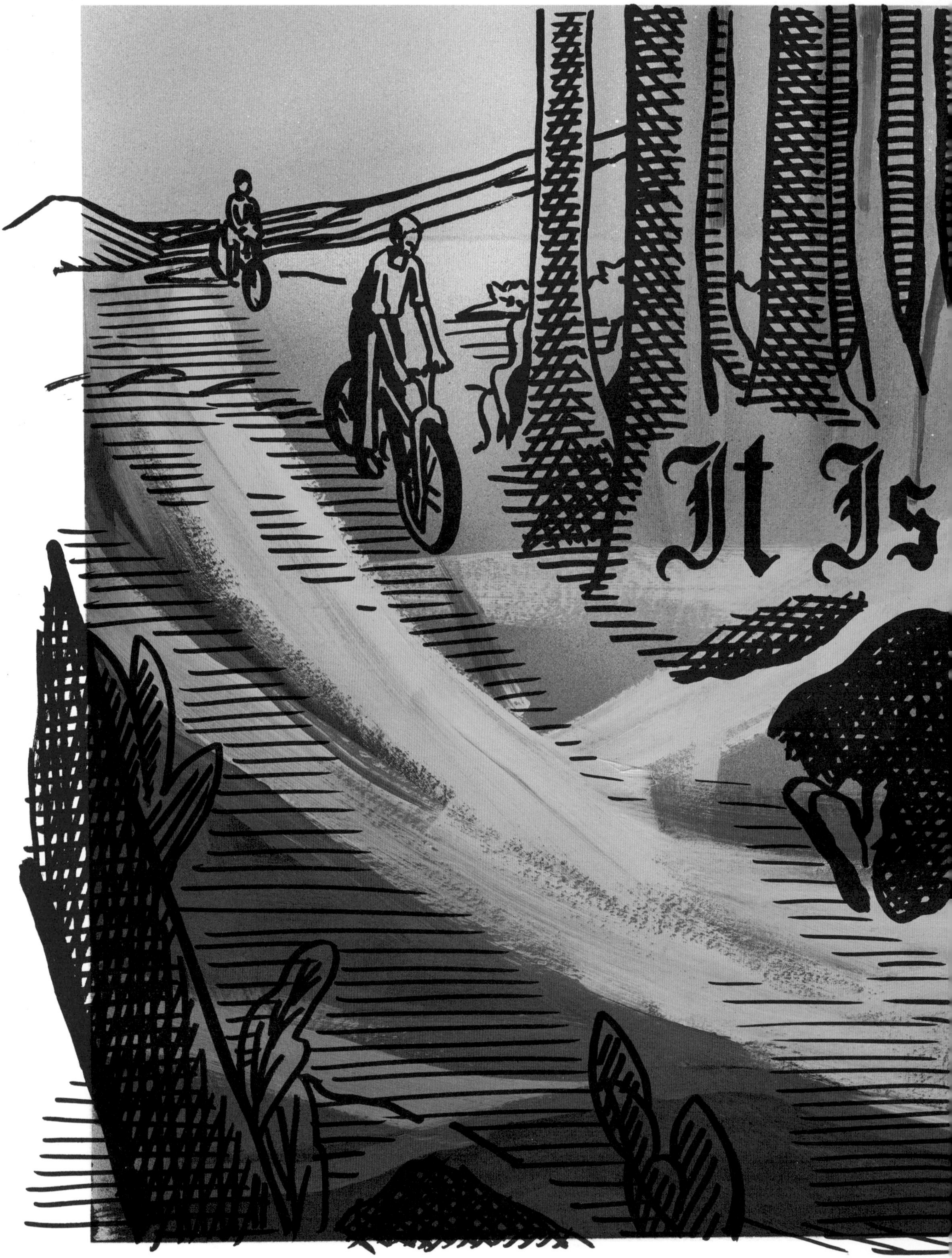
It Is

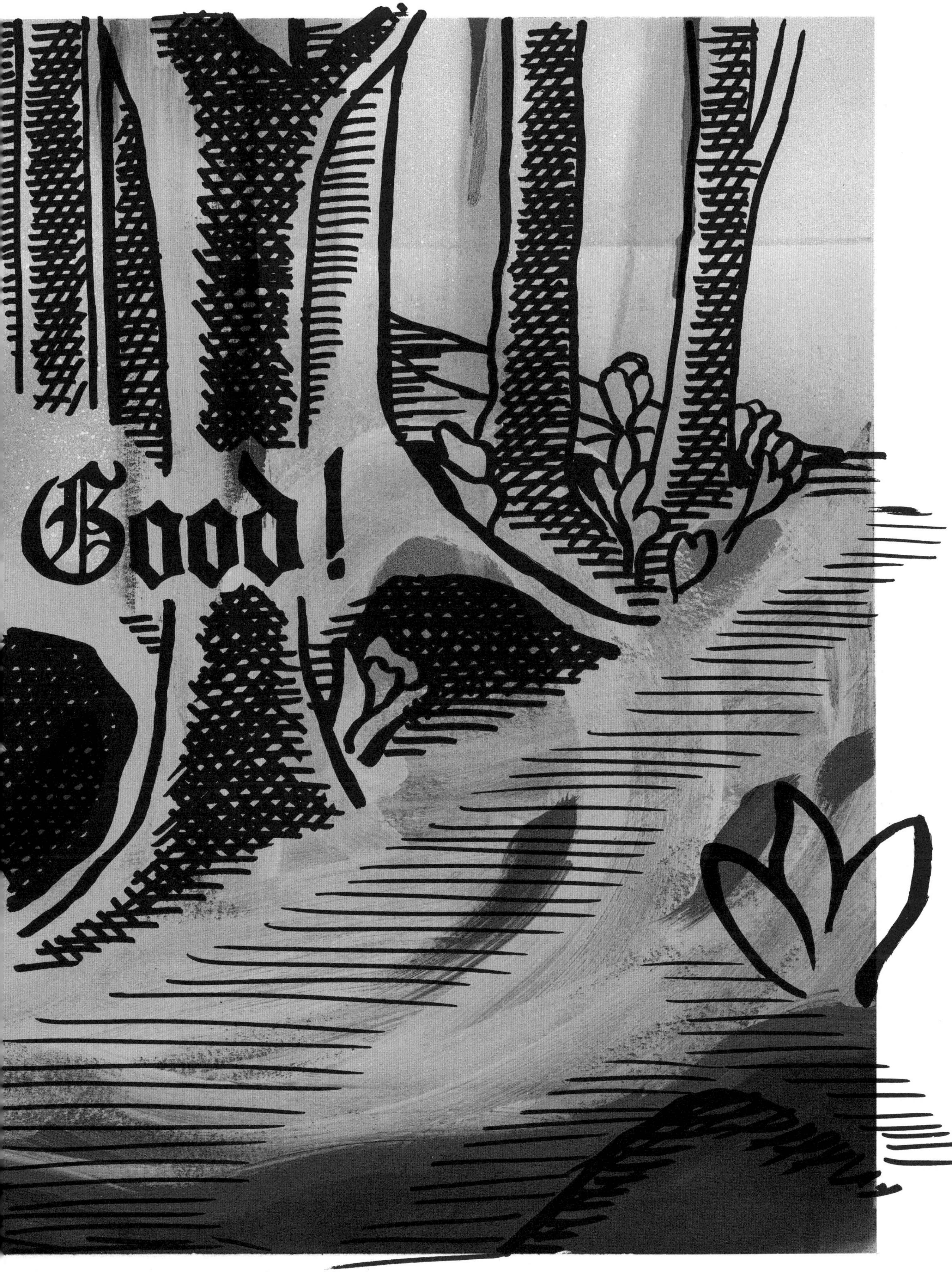
Good!

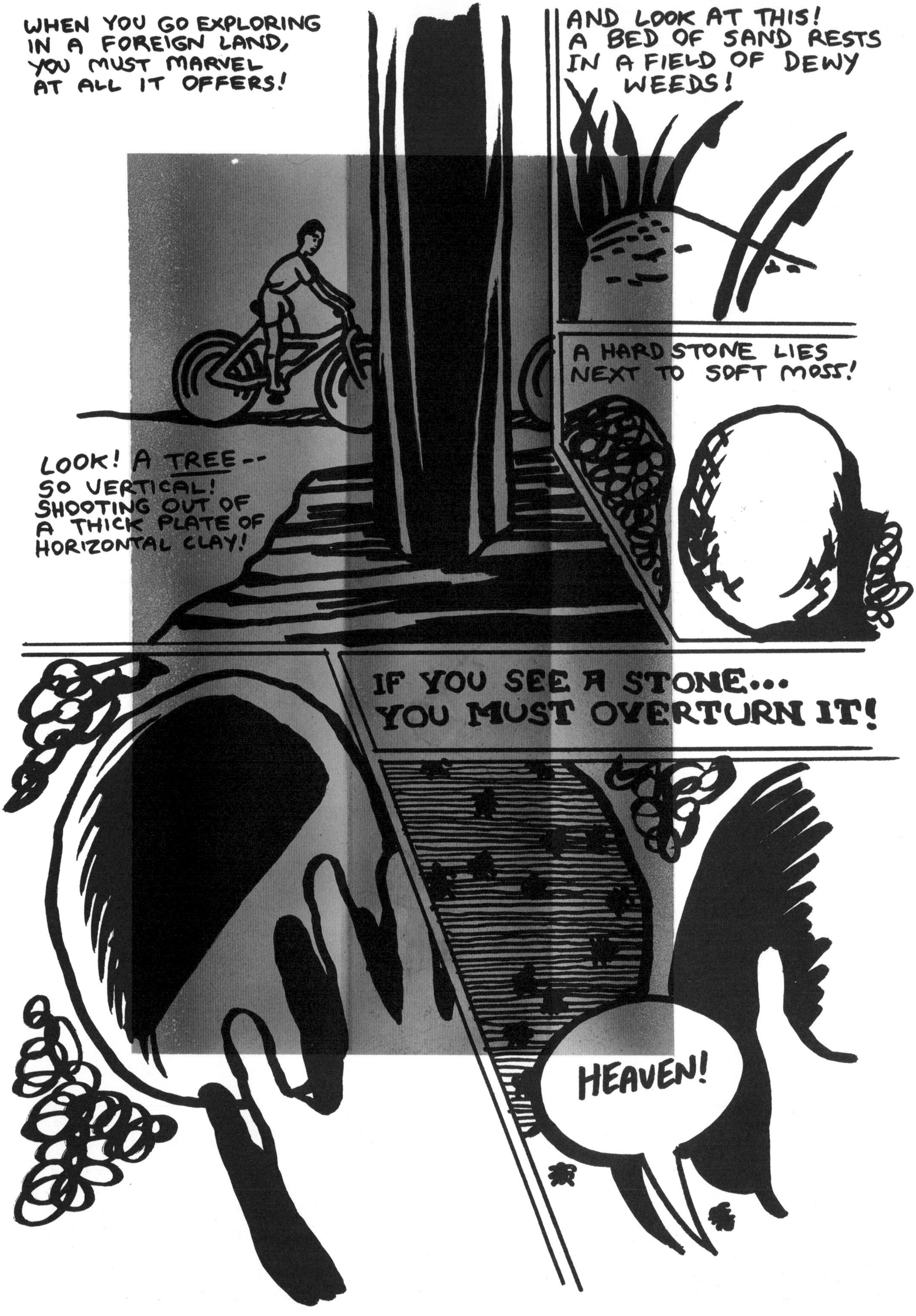
WHEN YOU GO EXPLORING IN A FOREIGN LAND, YOU MUST MARVEL AT ALL IT OFFERS!
AND LOOK AT THIS! A BED OF SAND RESTS IN A FIELD OF DEWY WEEDS!
LOOK! A TREE-- SO VERTICAL! SHOOTING OUT OF A THICK PLATE OF HORIZONTAL CLAY!
A HARD STONE LIES NEXT TO SOFT MOSS!
IF YOU SEE A STONE... YOU MUST OVERTURN IT!
HEAVEN!

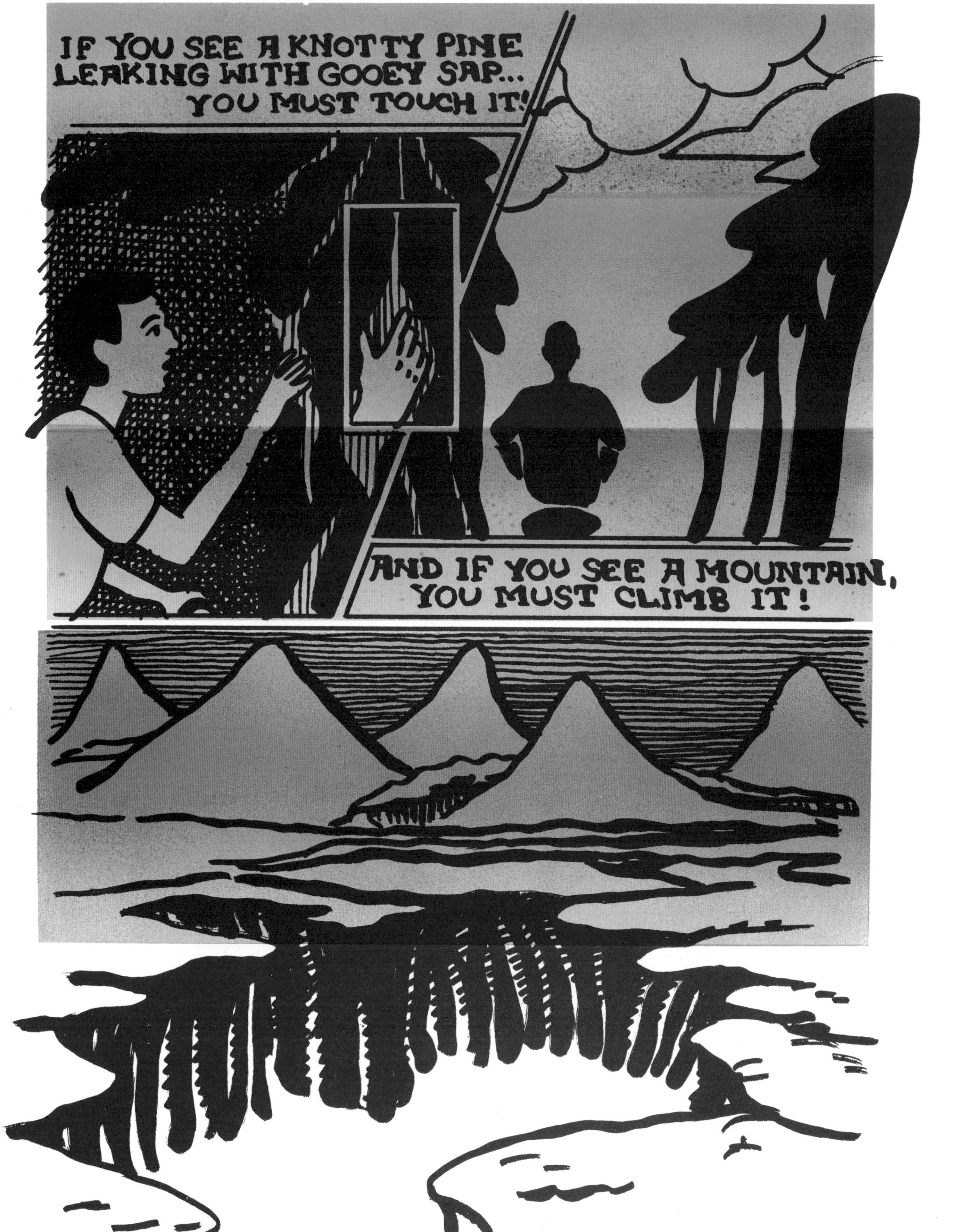
IF YOU SEE A KNOTTY PINE LEAKING WITH GOOEY SAP... YOU MUST TOUCH IT!
AND IF YOU SEE A MOUNTAIN, YOU MUST CLIMB IT!

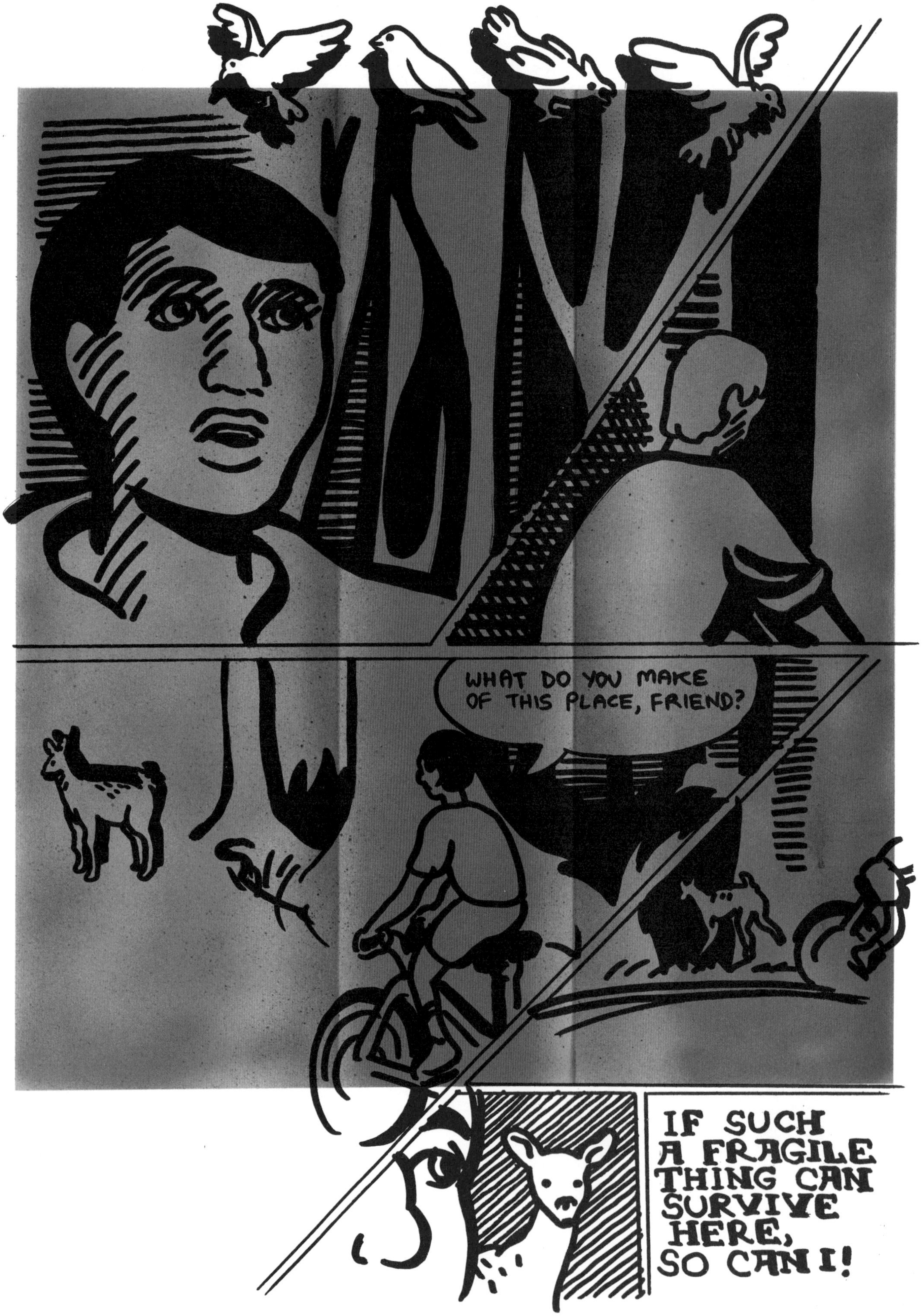
WHAT DO YOU MAKE OF THIS PLACE, FRIEND?
IF SUCH A FRAGILE THING CAN SURVIVE HERE, SO CAN I!

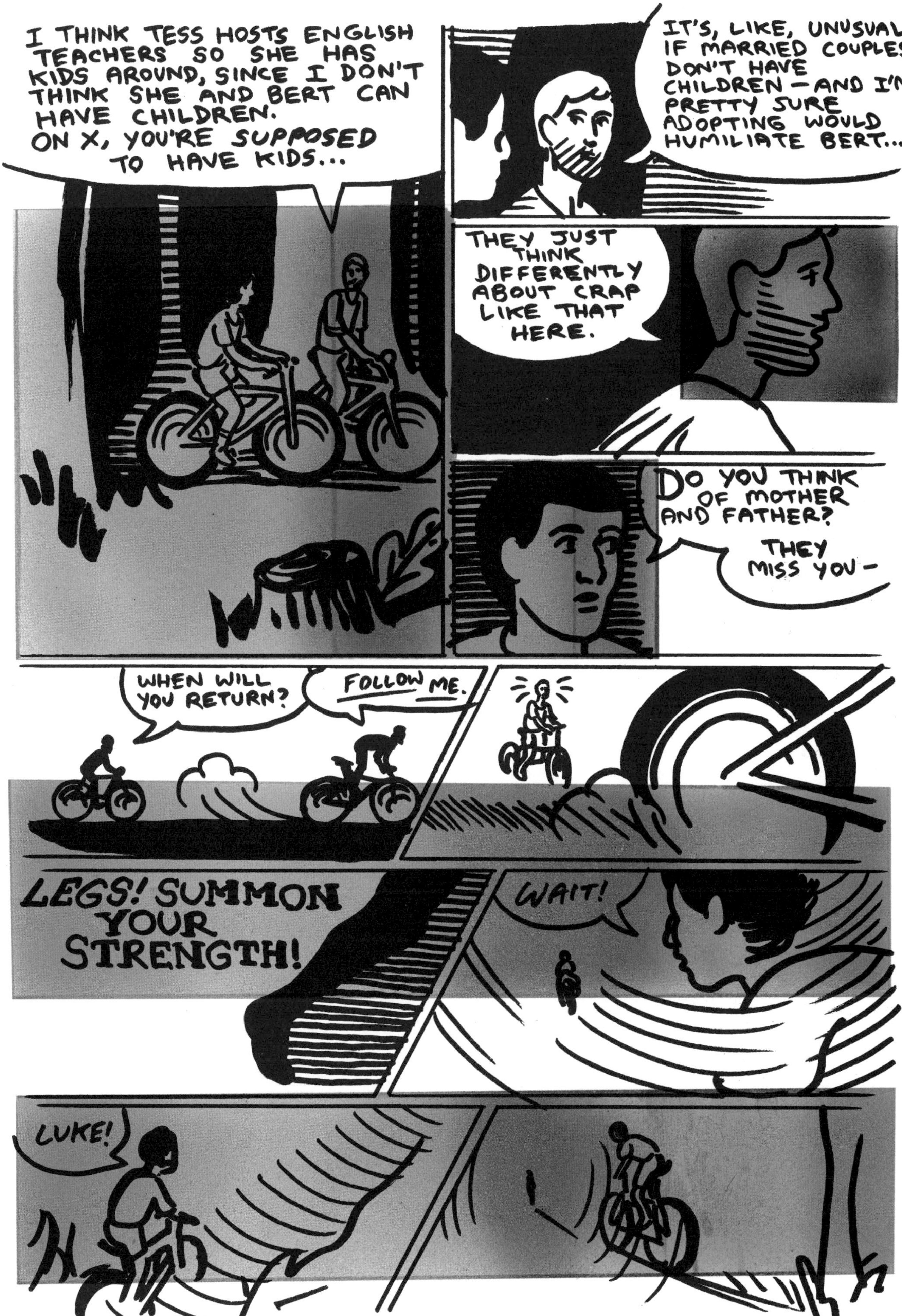

I THINK TESS HOSTS ENGLISH TEACHERS SO SHE HAS KIDS AROUND, SINCE I DON'T THINK SHE AND BERT CAN HAVE CHILDREN.
ON X, YOU'RE SUPPOSED TO HAVE KIDS...
IT'S, LIKE, UNUSUAL IF MARRIED COUPLES DON'T HAVE CHILDREN — AND I'M PRETTY SURE ADOPTING WOULD HUMILIATE BERT...
THEY JUST THINK DIFFERENTLY ABOUT CRAP LIKE THAT HERE.
DO YOU THINK OF MOTHER AND FATHER?
THEY MISS YOU—
WHEN WILL YOU RETURN?
FOLLOW ME.
LEGS! SUMMON YOUR STRENGTH!
WAIT!
LUKE!

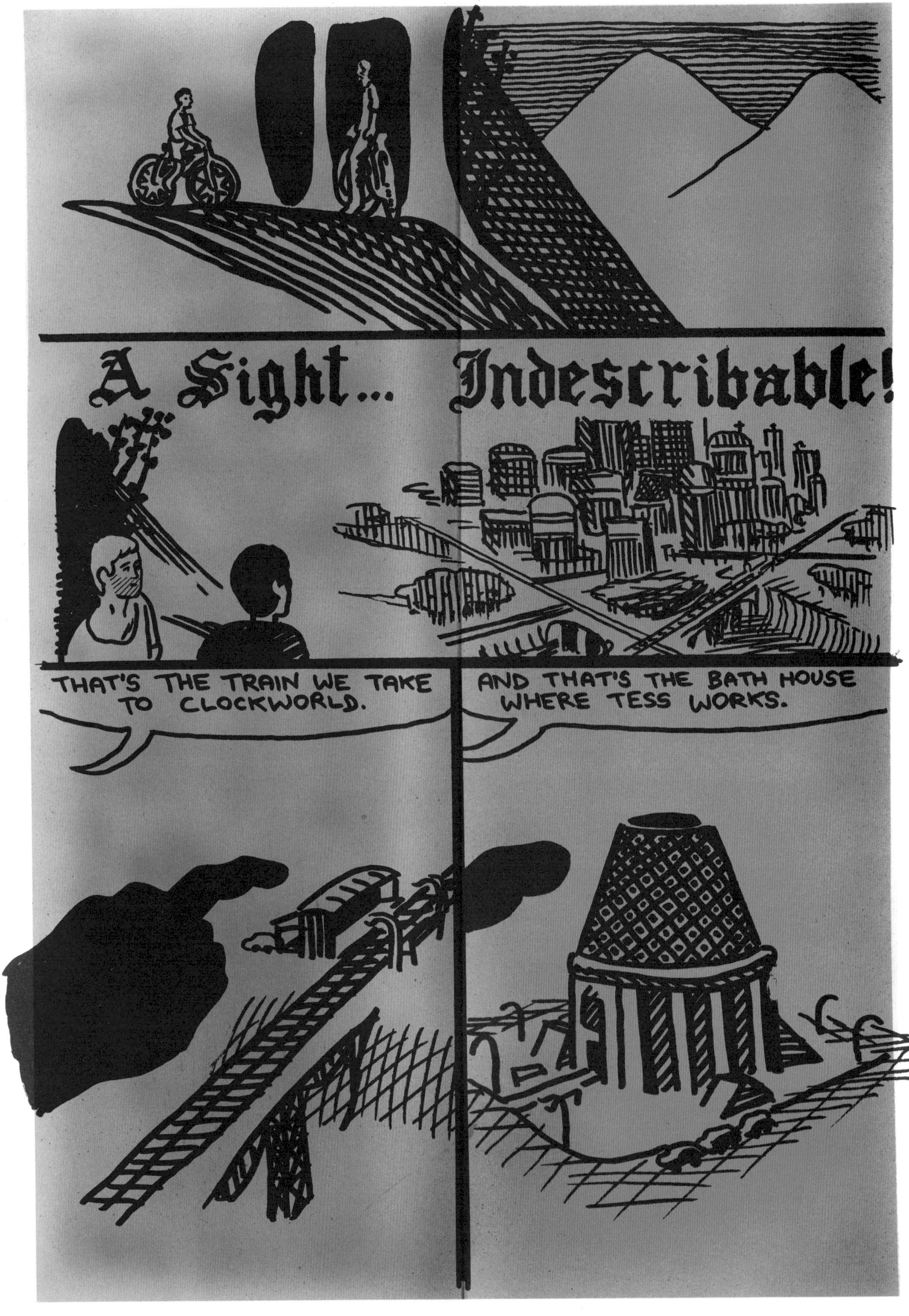
A Sight... Indescribable!
THAT'S THE TRAIN WE TAKE TO CLOCKWORLD.
AND THAT'S THE BATH HOUSE WHERE TESS WORKS.

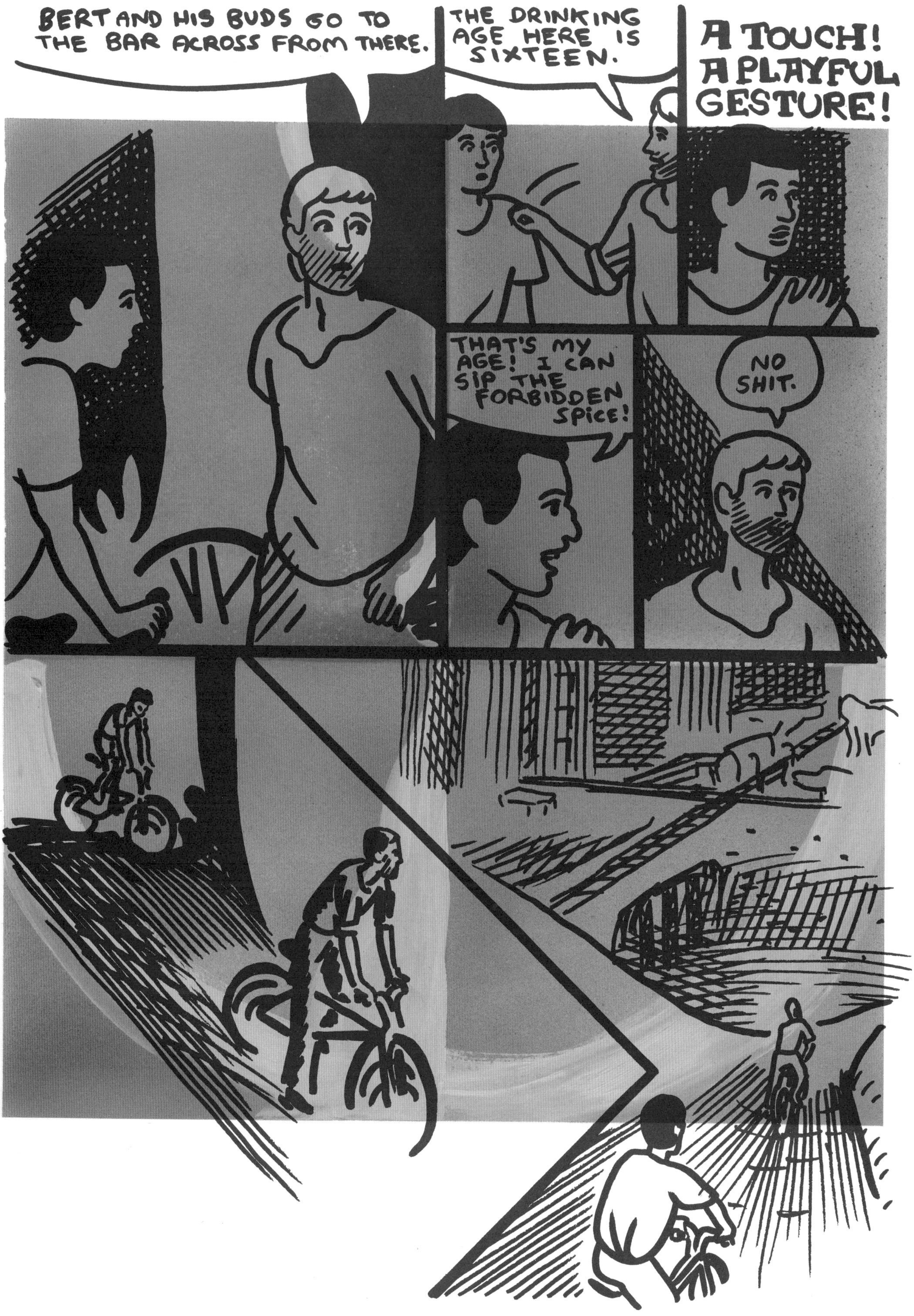
BERT AND HIS BUDS GO TO THE BAR ACROSS FROM THERE.
THE DRINKING AGE HERE IS SIXTEEN.
A TOUCH! A PLAYFUL GESTURE!
THAT'S MY AGE! I CAN SIP THE FORBIDDEN SPICE!
NO SHIT.

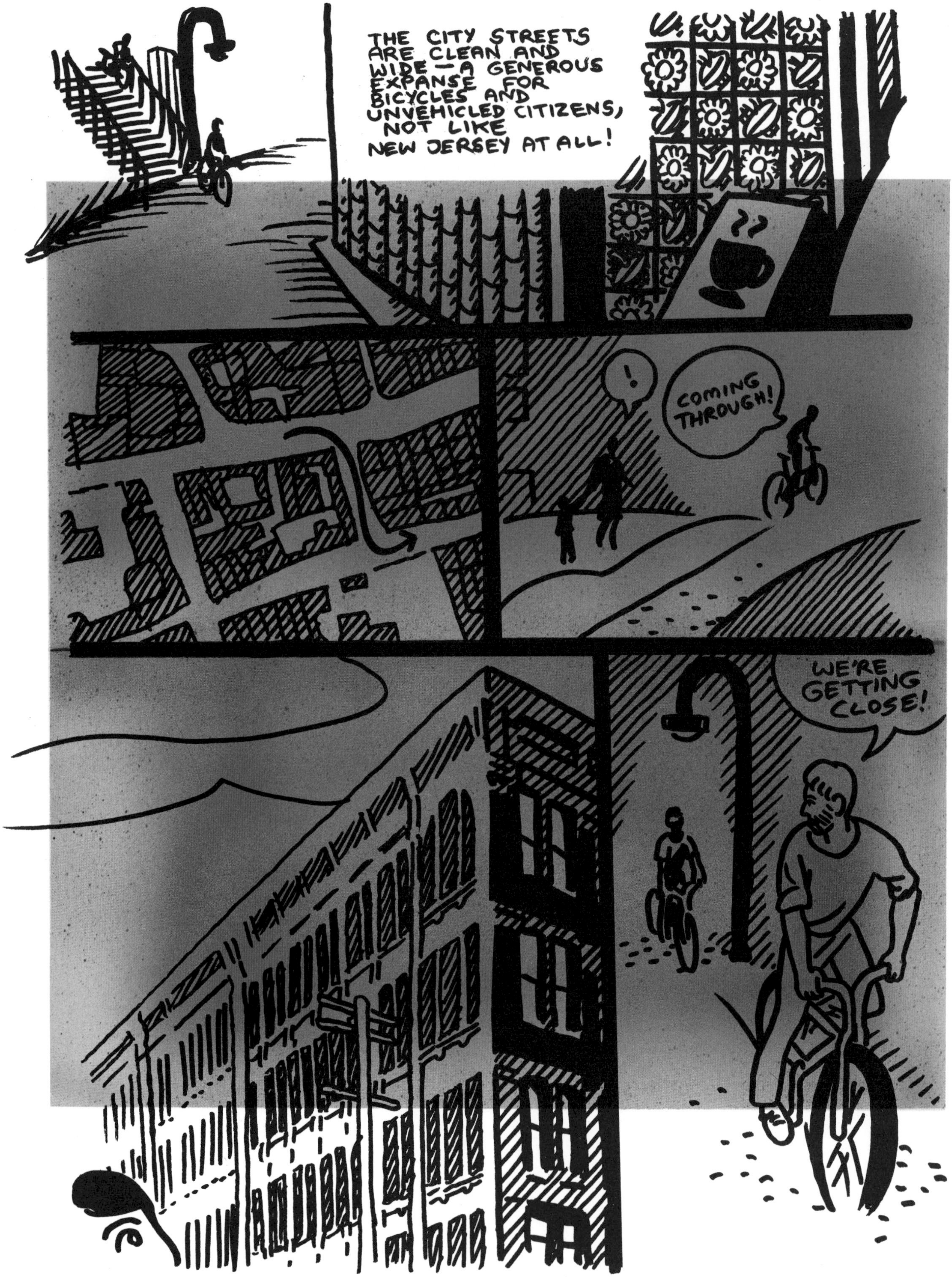
THE CITY STREETS ARE CLEAN AND WIDE—A GENEROUS EXPANSE FOR BICYCLES AND UNVEHICLED CITIZENS, NOT LIKE NEW JERSEY AT ALL!
!
COMING THROUGH!
WE'RE GETTING CLOSE!

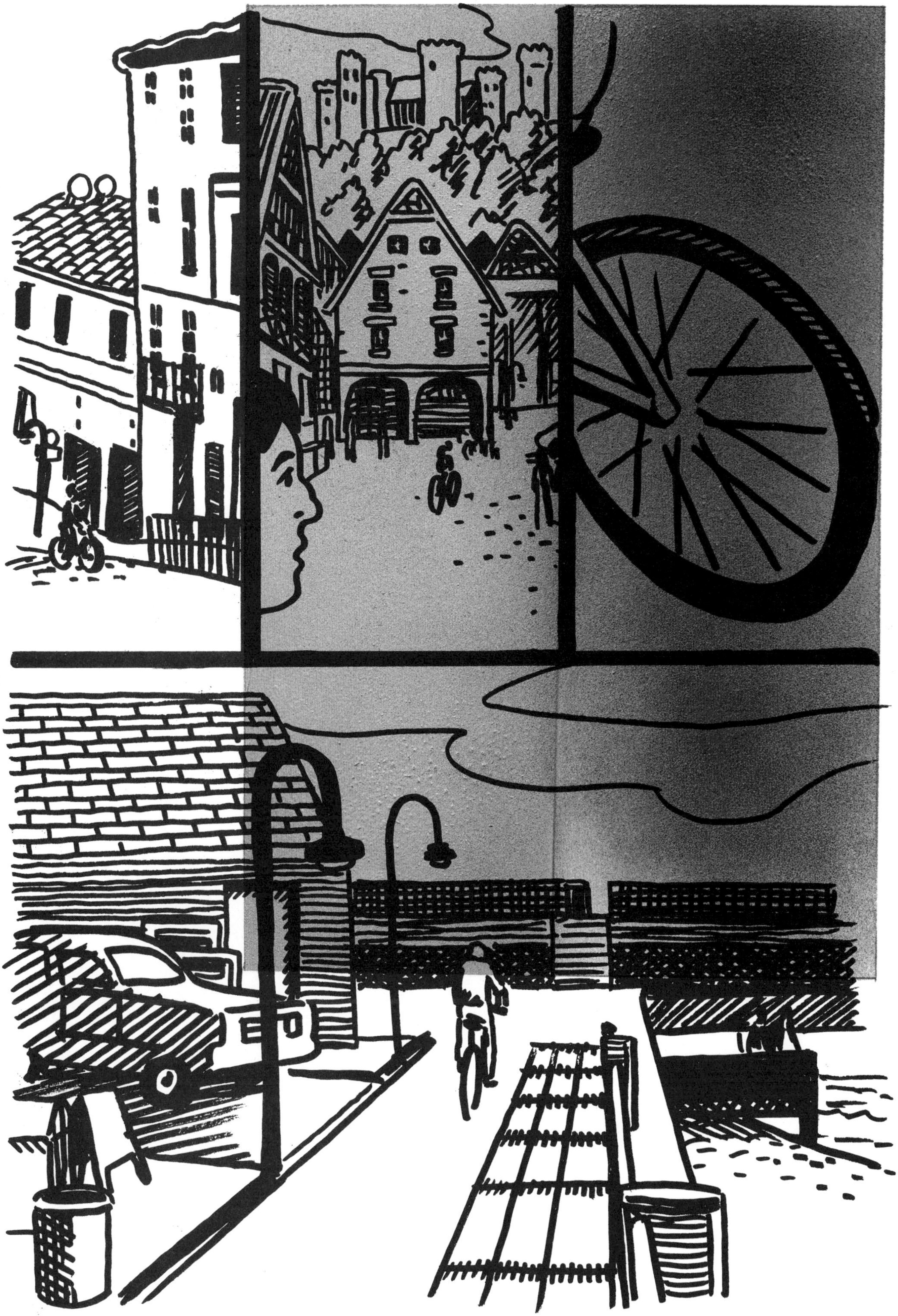

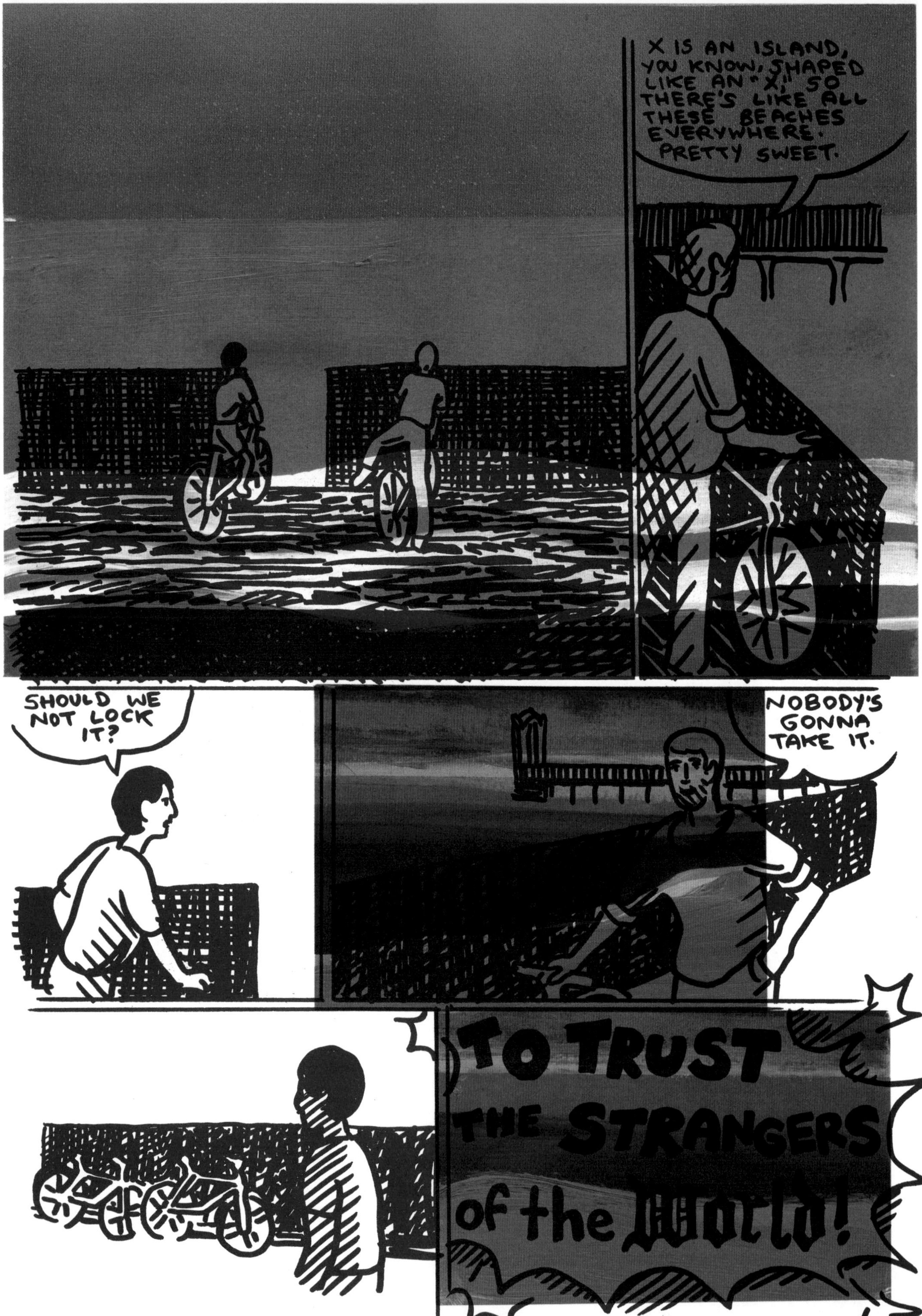
X IS AN ISLAND, YOU KNOW, SHAPED LIKE AN "X," SO THERE'S LIKE ALL THESE BEACHES EVERYWHERE. PRETTY SWEET.
SHOULD WE NOT LOCK IT?
NOBODY'S GONNA TAKE IT.
TO TRUST THE STRANGERS of the World!

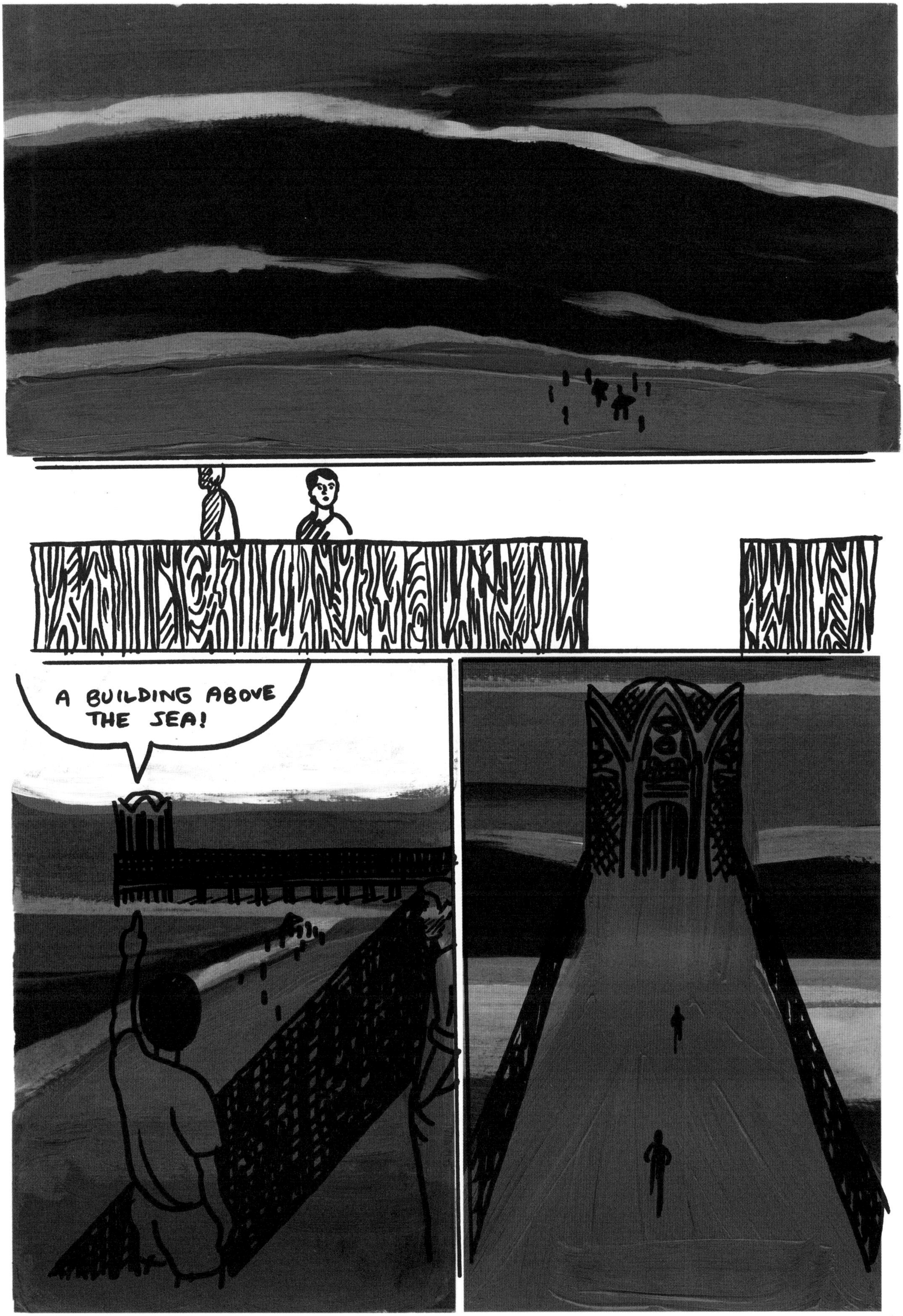
A BUILDING ABOVE THE SEA!

A LIBRARY!

THE BOTTOM FLOOR RESTS BENEATH THE BLUE—

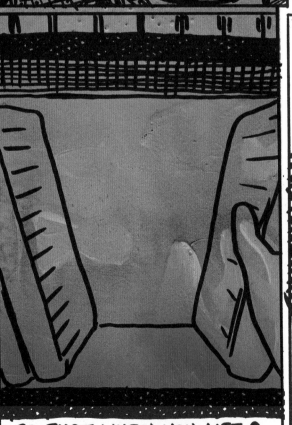

—SO THAT WHEN YOU LIFT A BOOK FROM A SHELF, YOU PEER INTO THE GLISTENING SEA LIFE LIVING BEYOND!

THE DUSK LIGHT PASSES THROUGH THE WATER, ILLUMINATING THE SPACE IN RIPPLING COLOR! HAVE MY EYES EVER SEEN SUCH BEAUTY?! BLISS! BLISS!

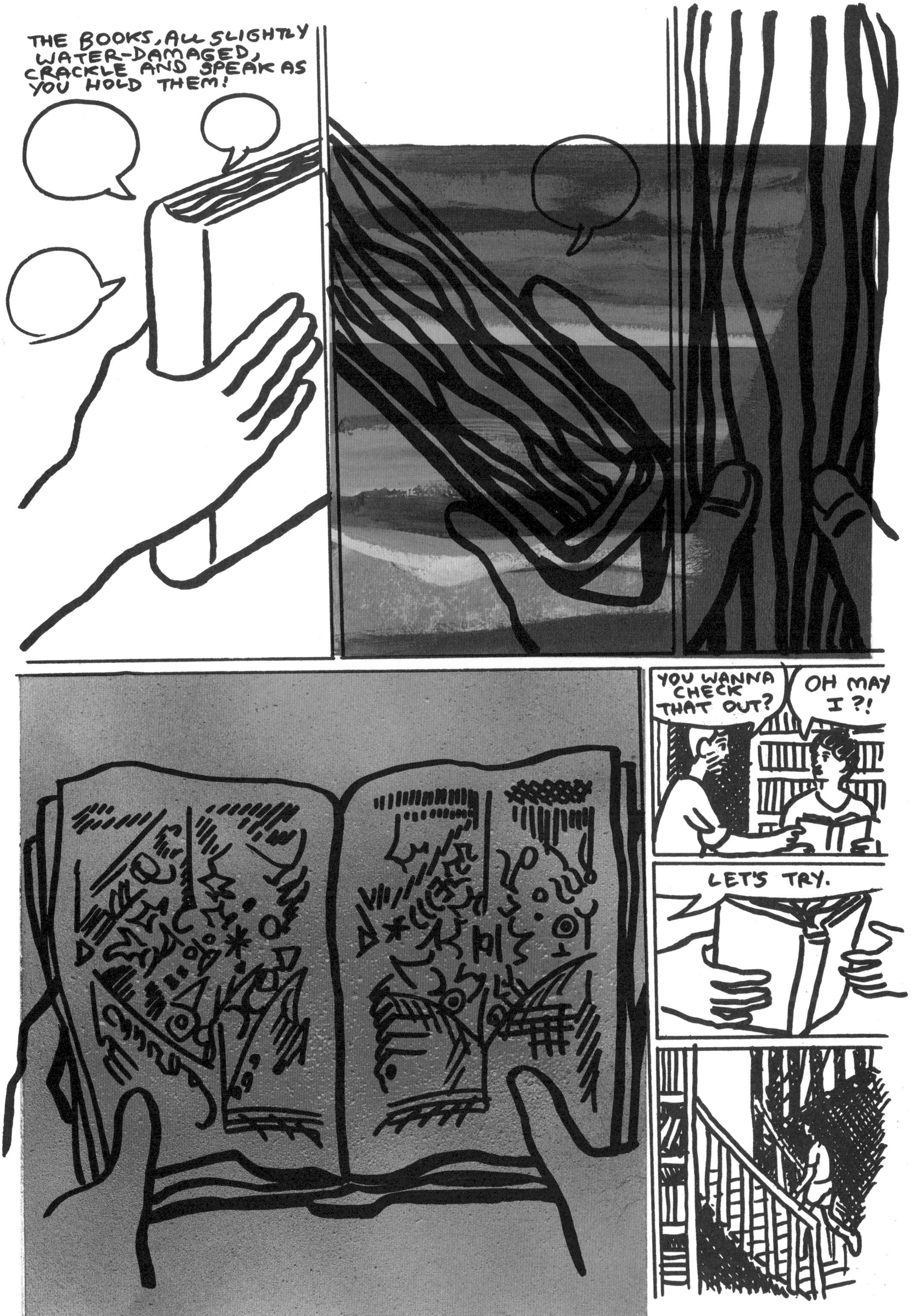

THE BOOKS, ALL SLIGHTLY WATER-DAMAGED, CRACKLE AND SPEAK AS YOU HOLD THEM!
YOU WANNA CHECK THAT OUT?
OH MAY I ?!
LET'S TRY.

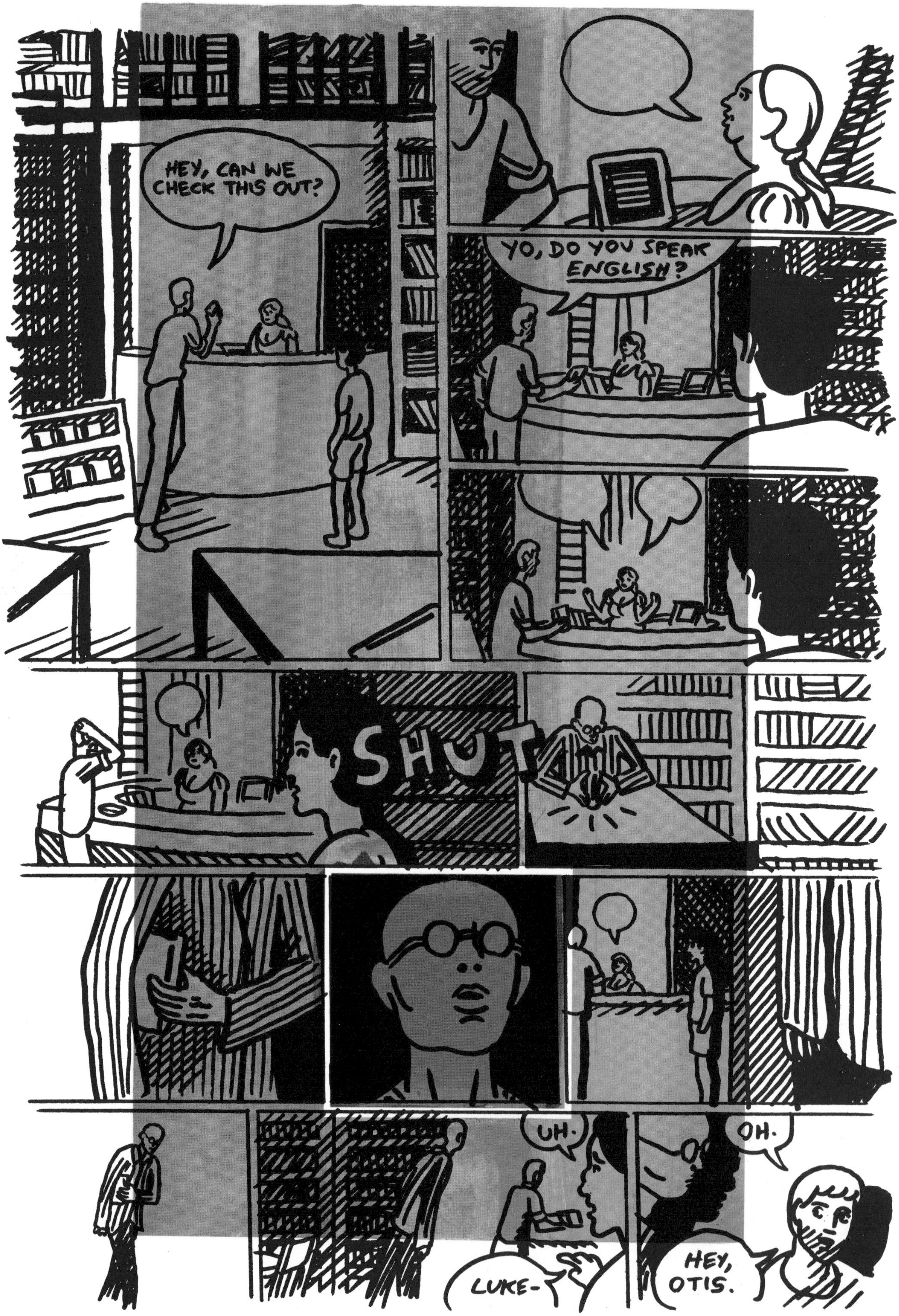
HEY, CAN WE CHECK THIS OUT?
YO, DO YOU SPEAK ENGLISH?
SHUT
UH.
LUKE-
OH.
HEY, OTIS.

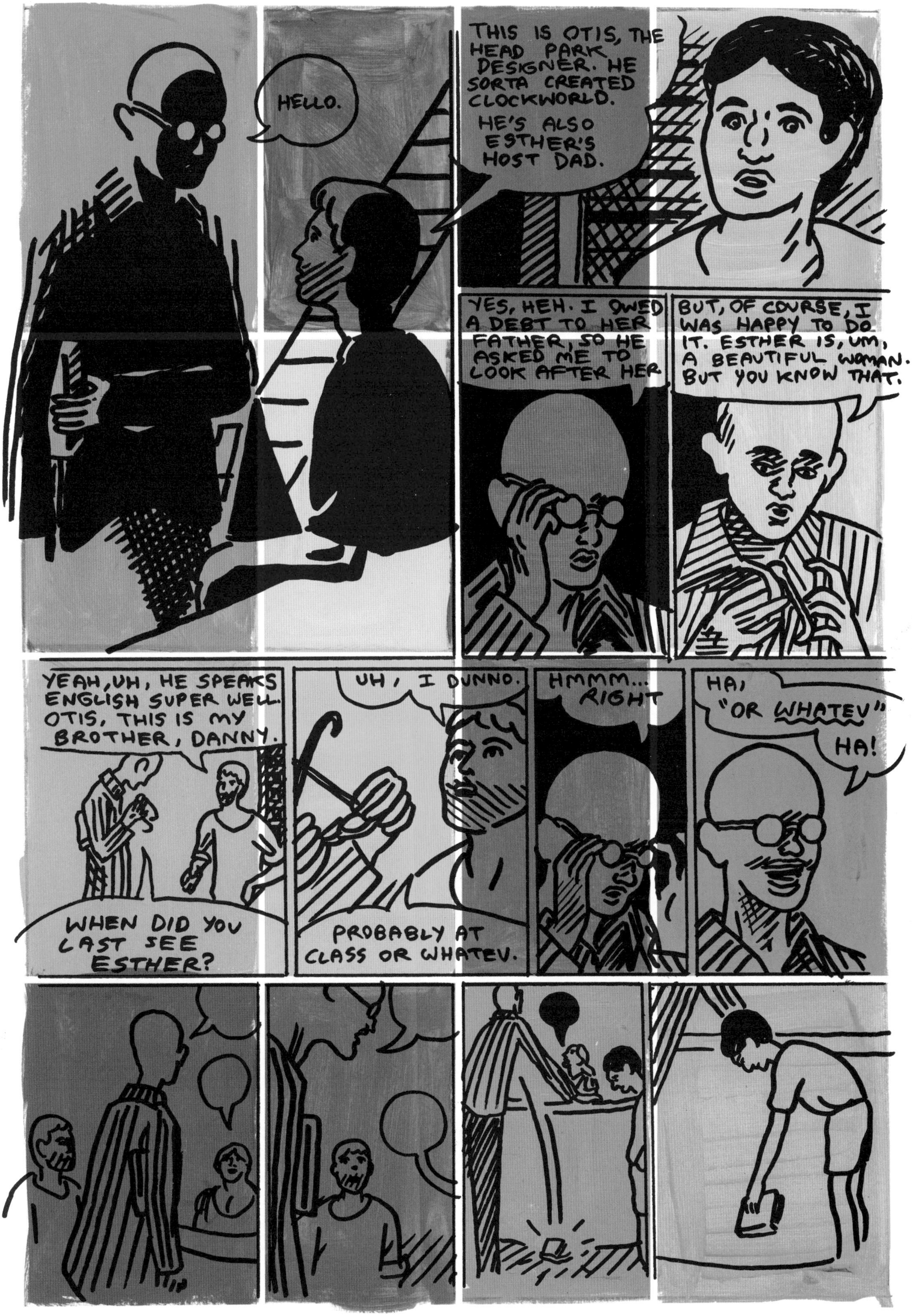
HELLO.
THIS IS OTIS, THE HEAD PARK DESIGNER. HE SORTA CREATED CLOCKWORLD.
HE'S ALSO ESTHER'S HOST DAD.
YES, HEH. I OWED A DEBT TO HER FATHER, SO HE ASKED ME TO LOOK AFTER HER.
BUT, OF COURSE, I WAS HAPPY TO DO IT. ESTHER IS, UM, A BEAUTIFUL WOMAN. BUT YOU KNOW THAT.
YEAH, UH, HE SPEAKS ENGLISH SUPER WELL. OTIS, THIS IS MY BROTHER, DANNY.
WHEN DID YOU LAST SEE ESTHER?
UH, I DUNNO.
PROBABLY AT CLASS OR WHATEV.
HMMM... RIGHT
HA, "OR WHATEV"
HA!

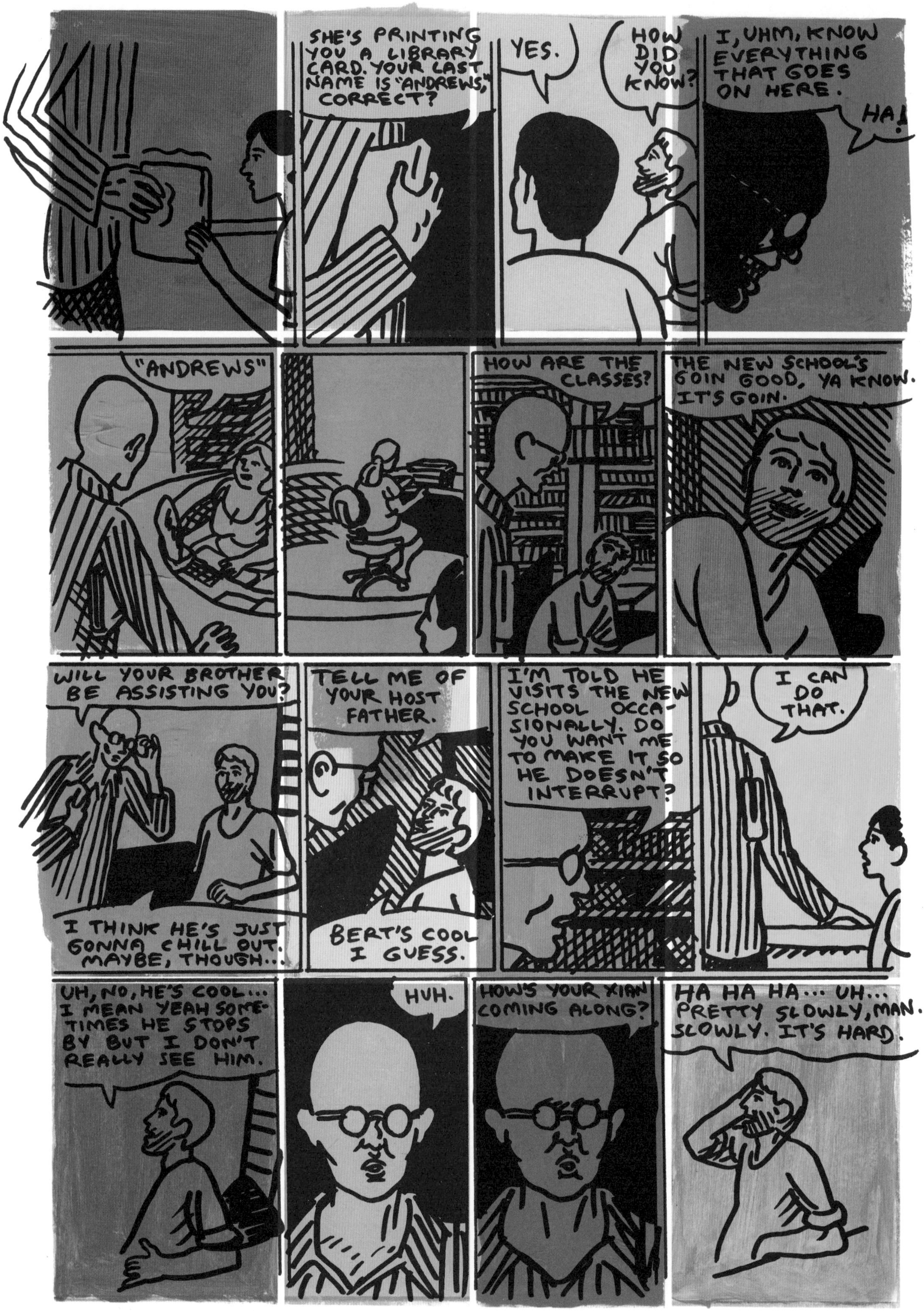
SHE'S PRINTING YOU A LIBRARY CARD. YOUR LAST NAME IS "ANDREWS," CORRECT?
YES.
HOW DID YOU KNOW?
I, UHM, KNOW EVERYTHING THAT GOES ON HERE.
HA!
"ANDREWS"
HOW ARE THE CLASSES?
THE NEW SCHOOL'S GOIN GOOD, YA KNOW. IT'S GOIN.
WILL YOUR BROTHER BE ASSISTING YOU?
I THINK HE'S JUST GONNA CHILL OUT. MAYBE, THOUGH...
TELL ME OF YOUR HOST FATHER.
BERT'S COOL I GUESS.
I'M TOLD HE VISITS THE NEW SCHOOL OCCA-SIONALLY. DO YOU WANT ME TO MAKE IT SO HE DOESN'T INTERRUPT?
I CAN DO THAT.
UH, NO, HE'S COOL... I MEAN YEAH SOME-TIMES HE STOPS BY BUT I DON'T REALLY SEE HIM.
HUH.
HOW'S YOUR XIAN COMING ALONG?
HA HA HA... UH... PRETTY SLOWLY, MAN. SLOWLY. IT'S HARD.

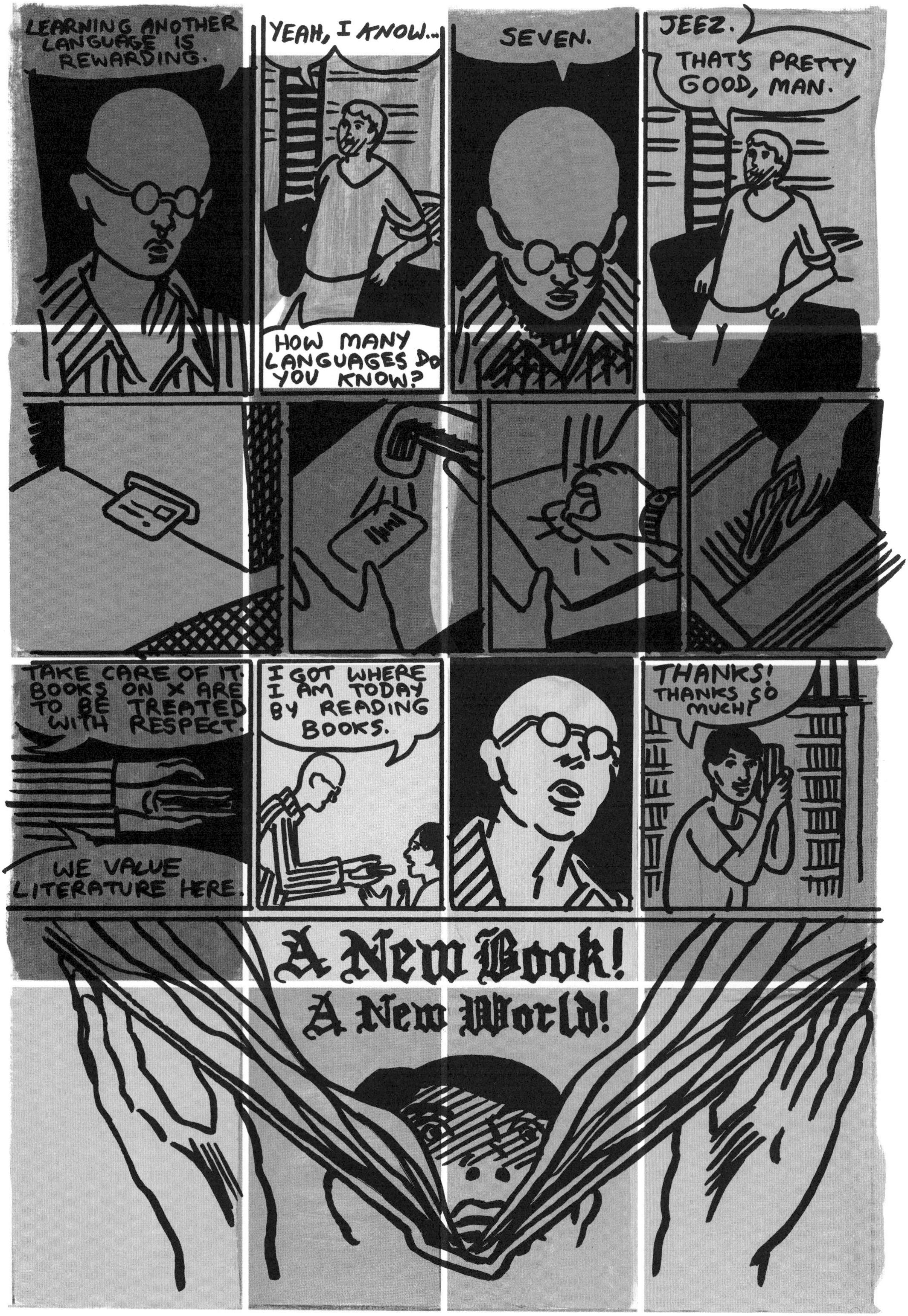
LEARNING ANOTHER LANGUAGE IS REWARDING.
YEAH, I KNOW...
HOW MANY LANGUAGES DO YOU KNOW?
SEVEN.
JEEZ.
THAT'S PRETTY GOOD, MAN.
TAKE CARE OF IT. BOOKS ON X ARE TO BE TREATED WITH RESPECT.
WE VALUE LITERATURE HERE.
I GOT WHERE I AM TODAY BY READING BOOKS.
THANKS! THANKS SO MUCH!
A New Book!
A New World!

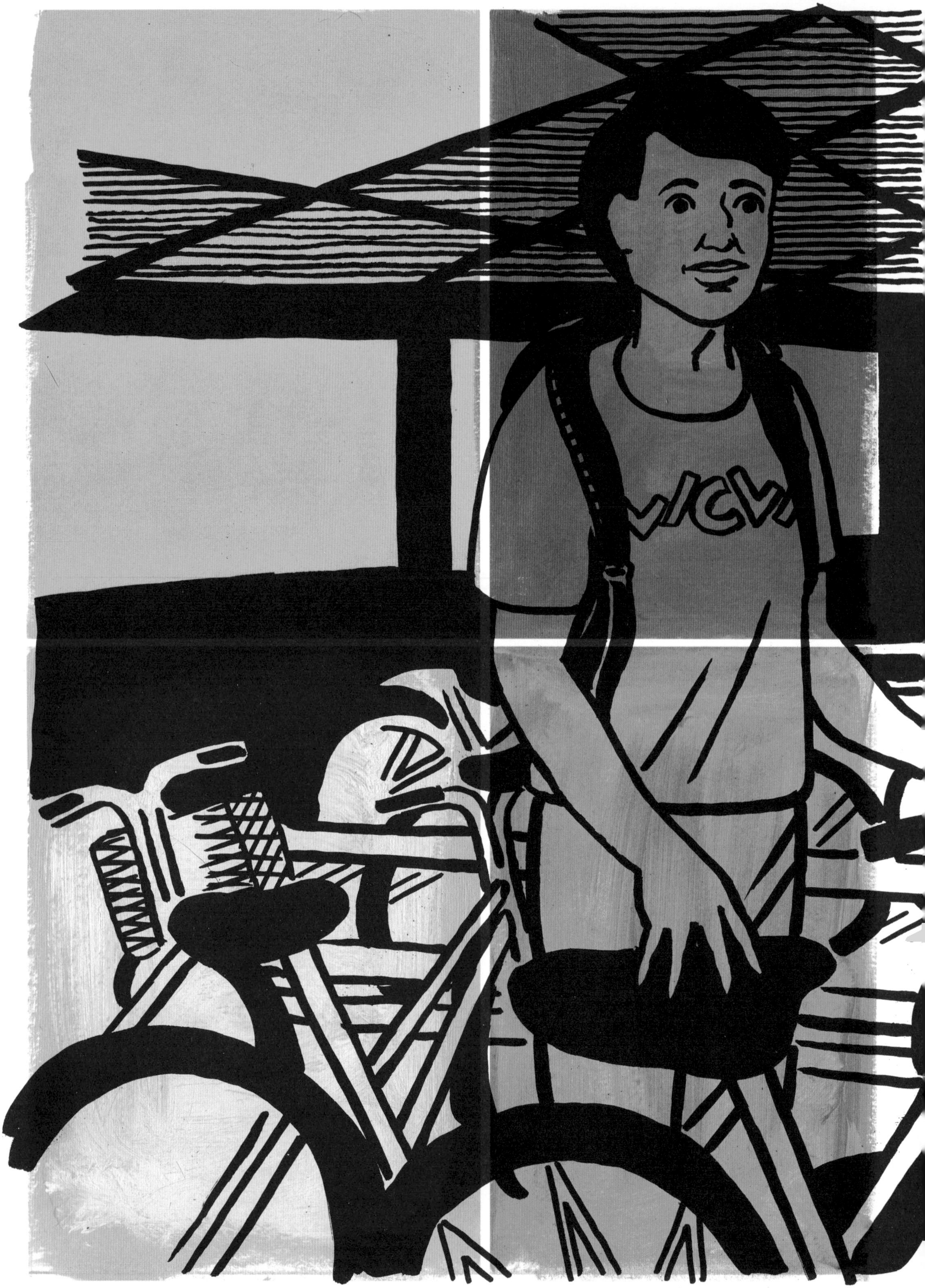

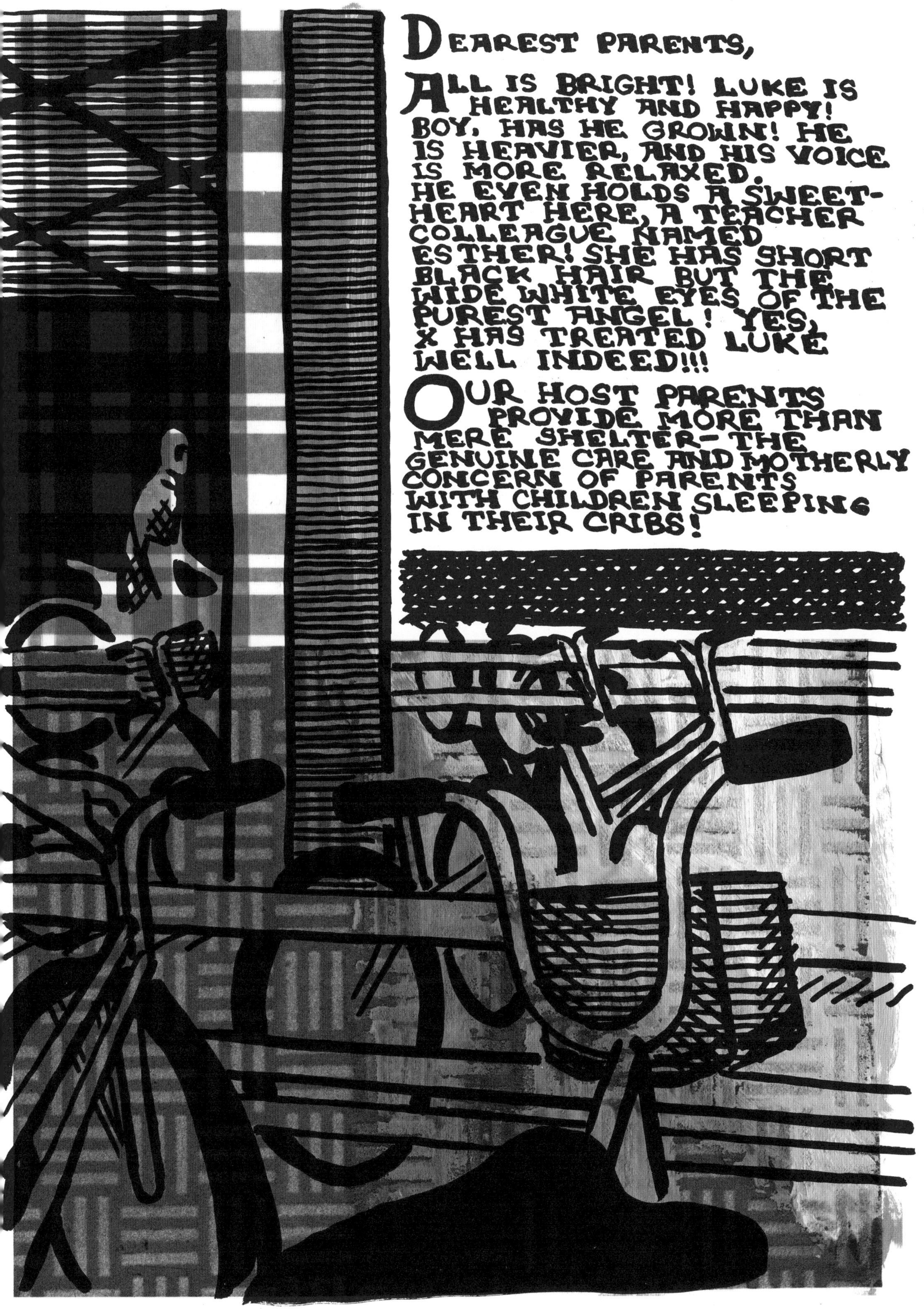
Dearest parents,
All is bright! Luke is healthy and happy! Boy, has he grown! He is heavier, and his voice is more relaxed. He even holds a sweetheart here, a teacher colleague named Esther! She has short black hair but the wide white eyes of the purest angel! Yes, X has treated Luke well indeed!!!
Our host parents provide more than mere shelter— the genuine care and motherly concern of parents with children sleeping in their cribs!

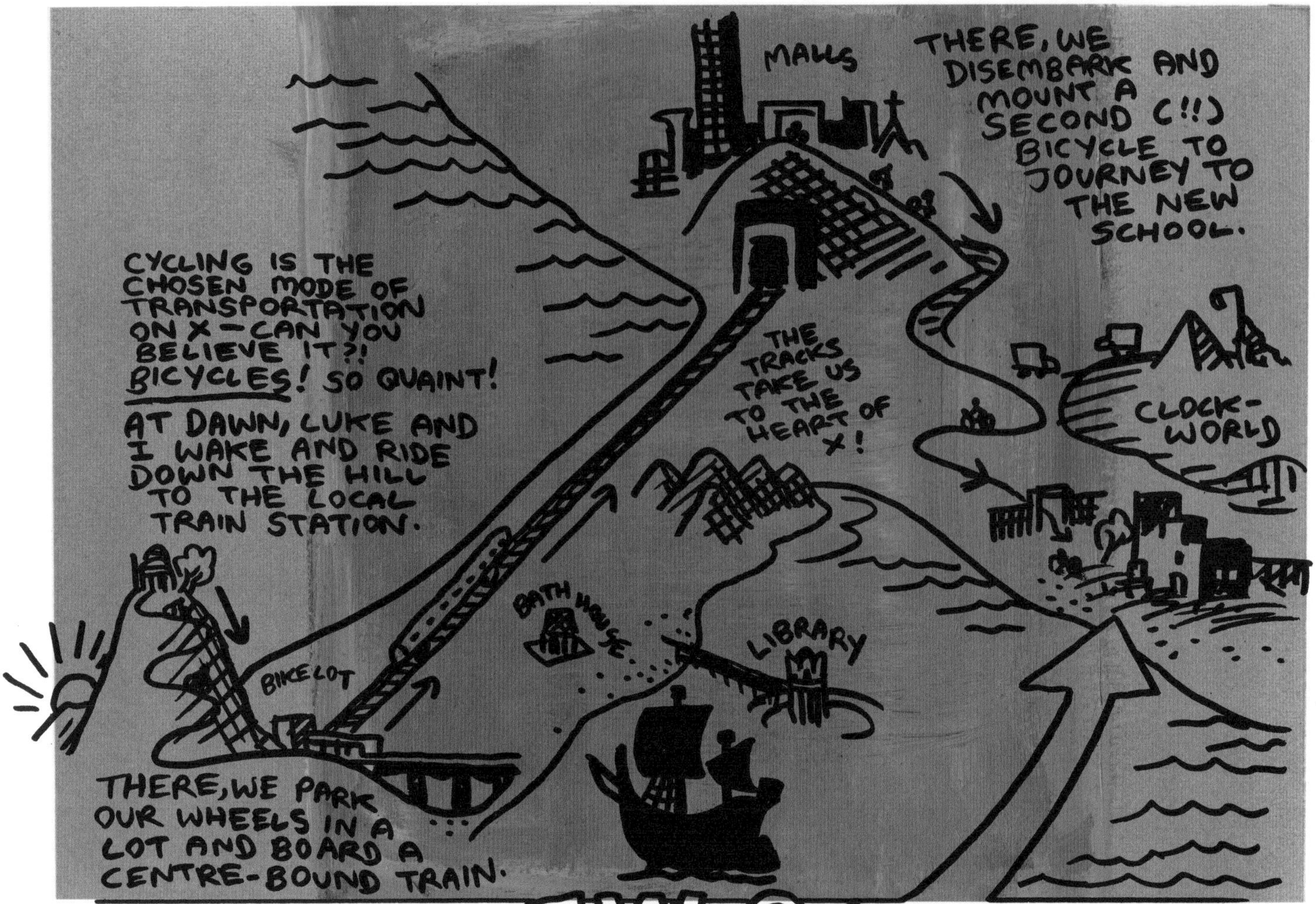

MALLS
THERE, WE DISEMBARK AND MOUNT A SECOND (!!) BICYCLE TO JOURNEY TO THE NEW SCHOOL.
CYCLING IS THE CHOSEN MODE OF TRANSPORTATION ON X—CAN YOU BELIEVE IT?! BICYCLES! SO QUAINT!
AT DAWN, LUKE AND I WAKE AND RIDE DOWN THE HILL TO THE LOCAL TRAIN STATION.
THE TRACKS TAKE US TO THE HEART OF X!
CLOCK-WORLD
BATH HOUSE
LIBRARY
BIKE LOT
THERE, WE PARK OUR WHEELS IN A LOT AND BOARD A CENTRE-BOUND TRAIN.

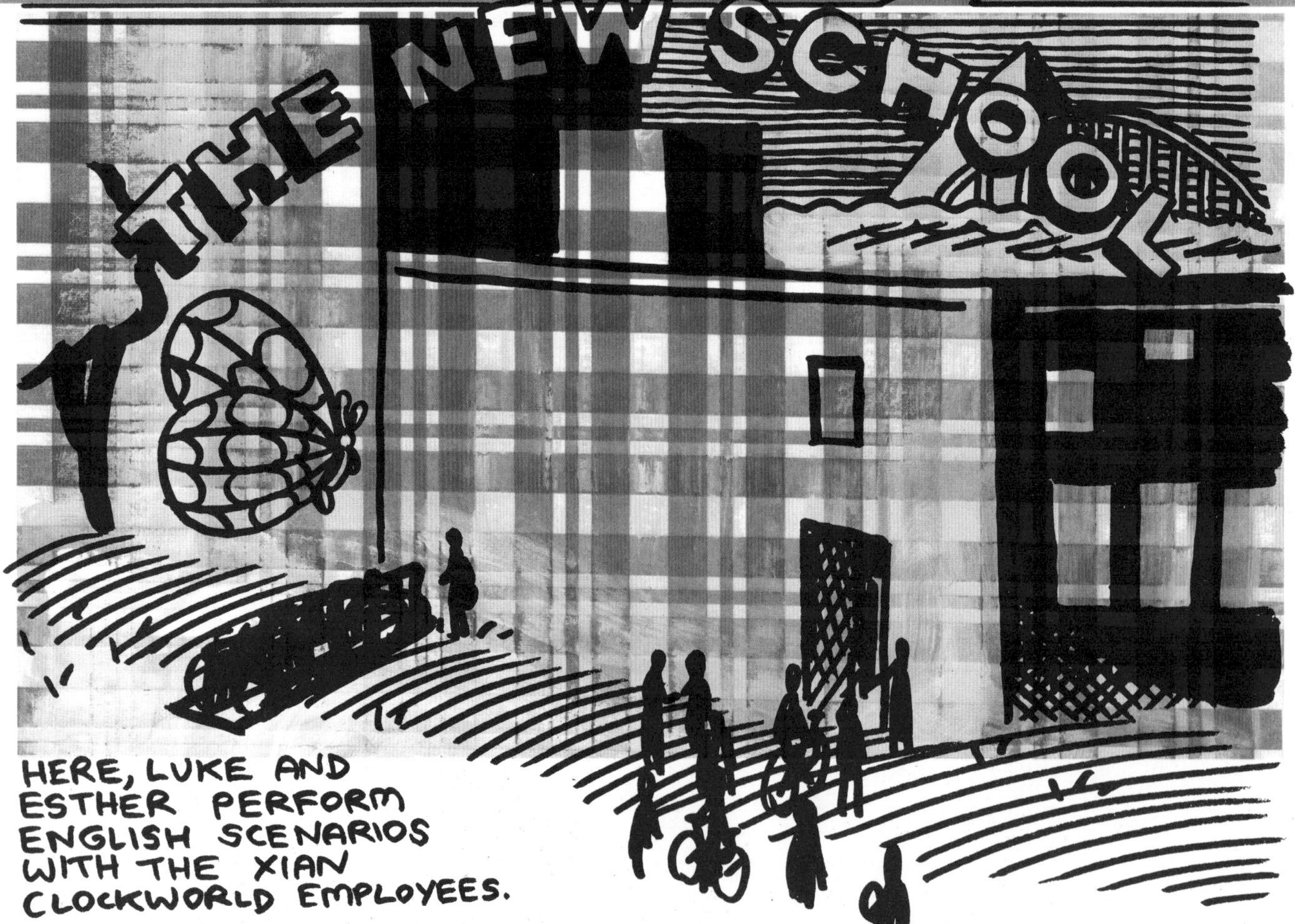

THE NEW SCHOOL
HERE, LUKE AND ESTHER PERFORM ENGLISH SCENARIOS WITH THE XIAN CLOCKWORLD EMPLOYEES.

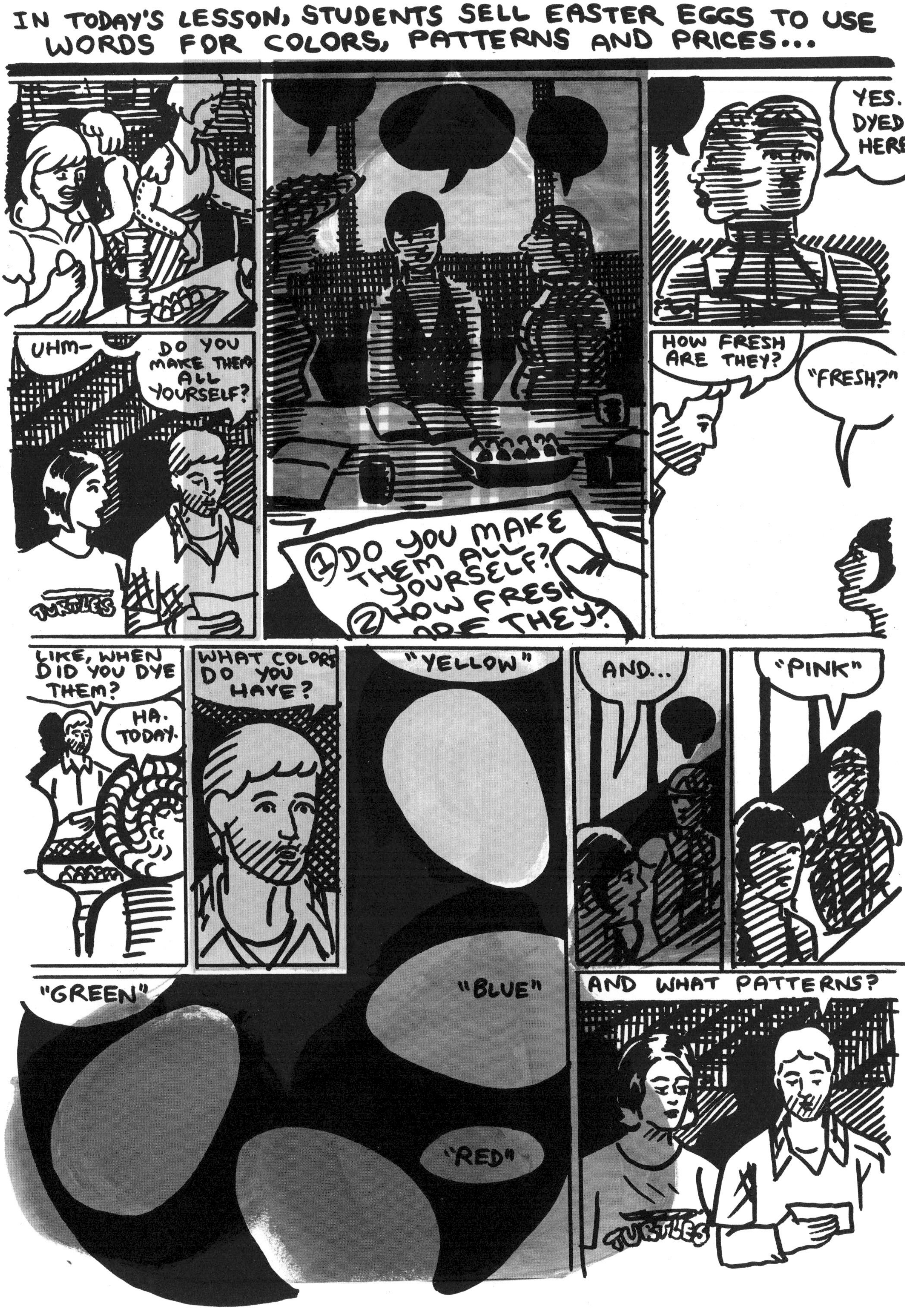
IN TODAY'S LESSON, STUDENTS SELL EASTER EGGS TO USE WORDS FOR COLORS, PATTERNS AND PRICES...
YES. DYED HERE.
UHM—
DO YOU MAKE THEM ALL YOURSELF?
1 DO YOU MAKE THEM ALL YOURSELF? 2 HOW FRESH ARE THEY?
HOW FRESH ARE THEY?
"FRESH?"
LIKE, WHEN DID YOU DYE THEM?
HA. TODAY.
WHAT COLORS DO YOU HAVE?
"YELLOW"
AND...
"PINK"
"GREEN"
"BLUE"
"RED"
AND WHAT PATTERNS?

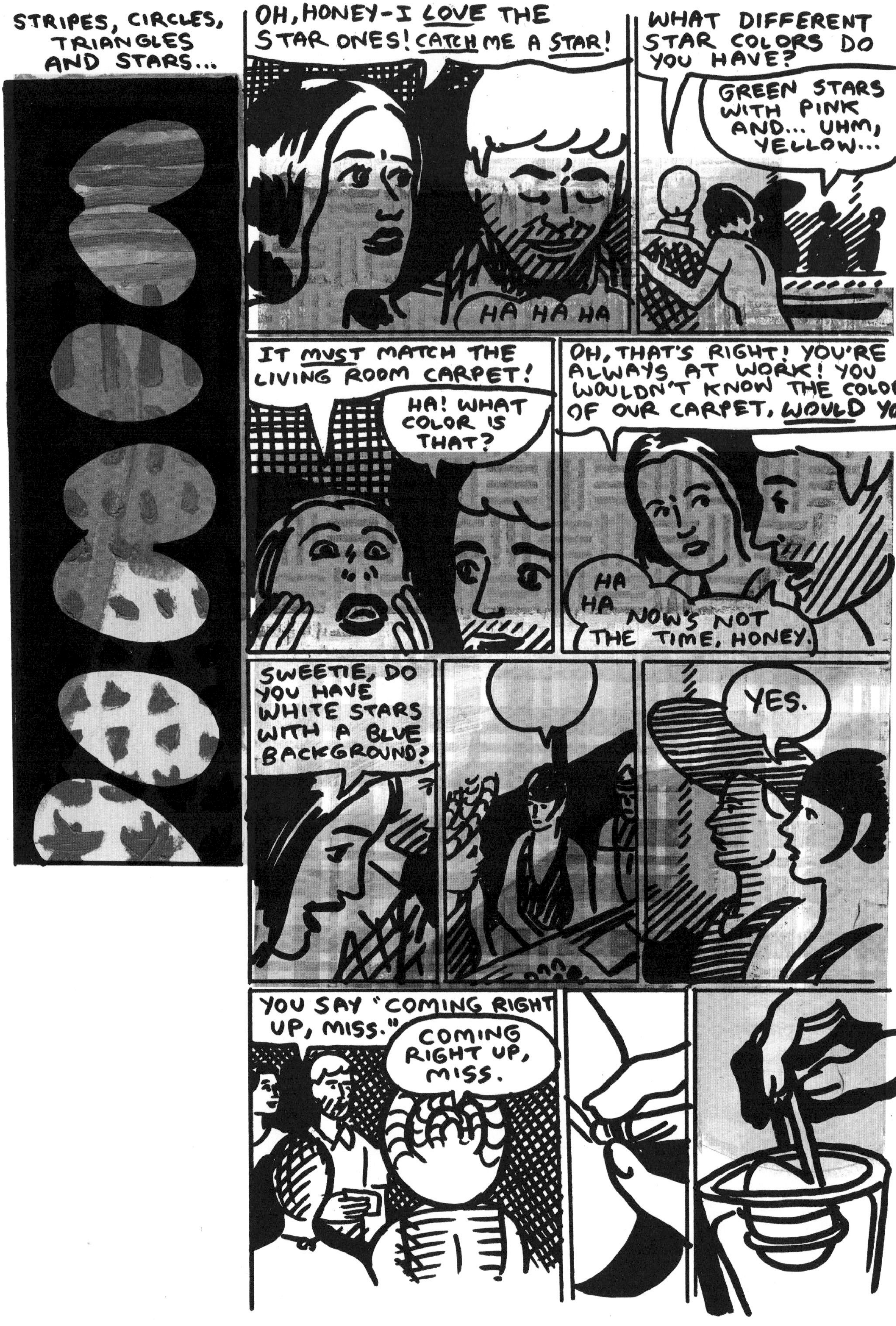
STRIPES, CIRCLES, TRIANGLES AND STARS...
OH, HONEY-I LOVE THE STAR ONES! CATCH ME A STAR!
HA HA HA
WHAT DIFFERENT STAR COLORS DO YOU HAVE?
GREEN STARS WITH PINK AND... UHM, YELLOW...
IT MUST MATCH THE LIVING ROOM CARPET!
HA! WHAT COLOR IS THAT?
OH, THAT'S RIGHT! YOU'RE ALWAYS AT WORK! YOU WOULDN'T KNOW THE COLOR OF OUR CARPET, WOULD YOU?!
HA HA
NOW'S NOT THE TIME, HONEY.
SWEETIE, DO YOU HAVE WHITE STARS WITH A BLUE BACKGROUND?
YES.
YOU SAY "COMING RIGHT UP, MISS."
COMING RIGHT UP, MISS.

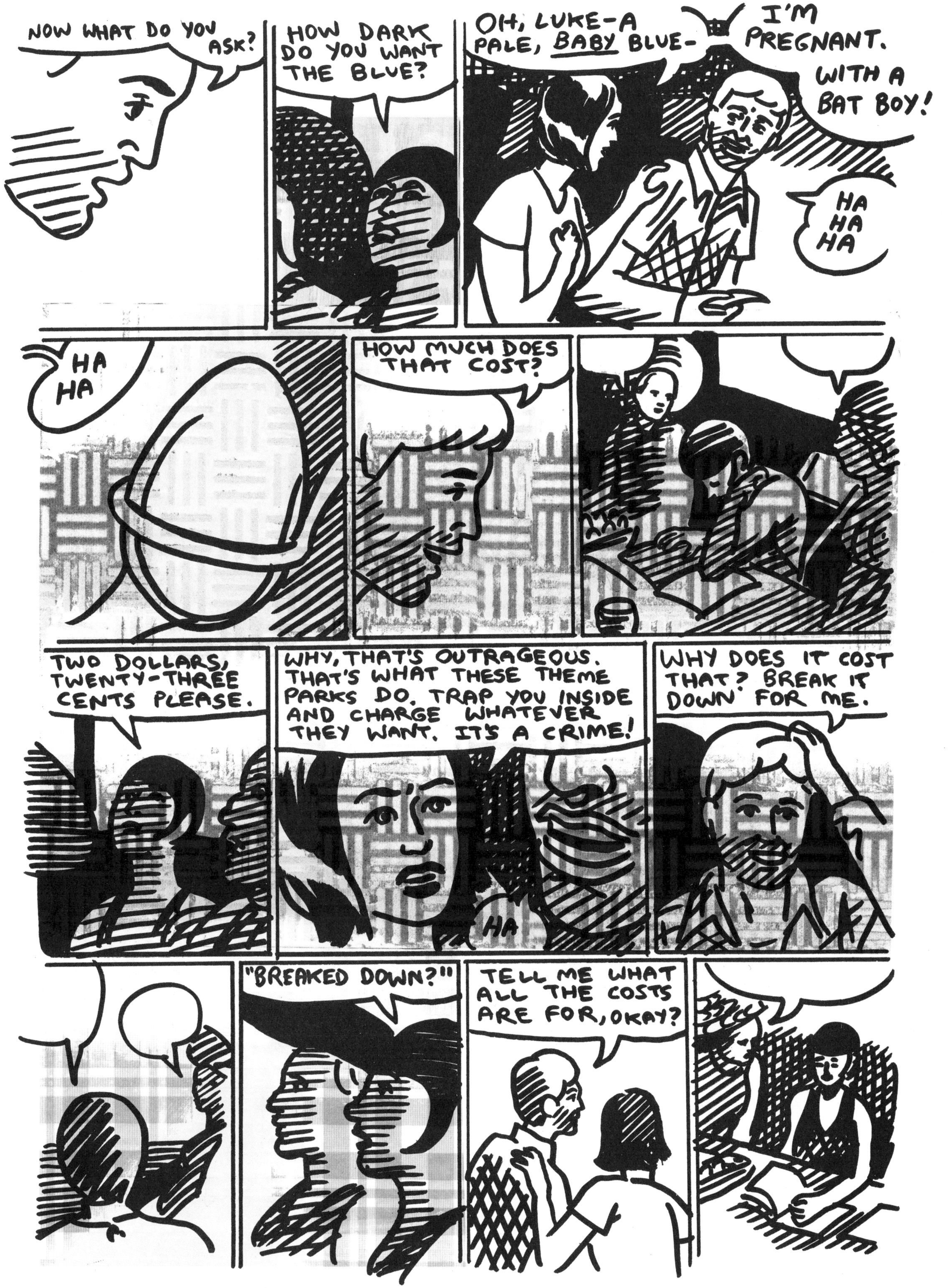
NOW WHAT DO YOU ASK?
HOW DARK DO YOU WANT THE BLUE?
OH, LUKE-A PALE, BABY BLUE-
I'M PREGNANT.
WITH A BAT BOY!
HA HA HA
HA HA
HOW MUCH DOES THAT COST?
TWO DOLLARS, TWENTY-THREE CENTS PLEASE.
WHY, THAT'S OUTRAGEOUS. THAT'S WHAT THESE THEME PARKS DO. TRAP YOU INSIDE AND CHARGE WHATEVER THEY WANT. IT'S A CRIME!
HA
WHY DOES IT COST THAT? BREAK IT DOWN FOR ME.
"BREAKED DOWN?"
TELL ME WHAT ALL THE COSTS ARE FOR, OKAY?

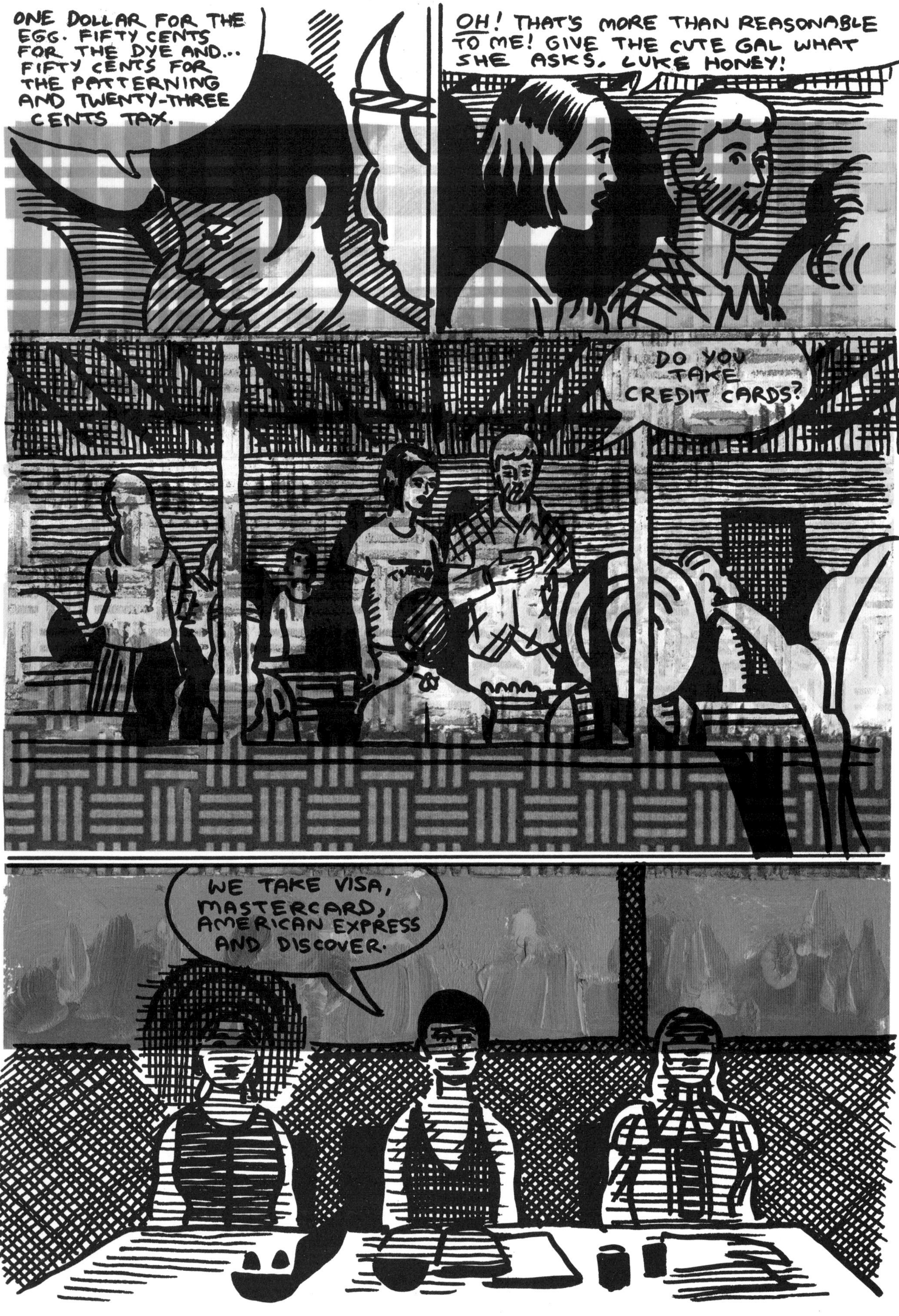
ONE DOLLAR FOR THE EGG. FIFTY CENTS FOR THE DYE AND... FIFTY CENTS FOR THE PATTERNING AND TWENTY-THREE CENTS TAX.
OH! THAT'S MORE THAN REASONABLE TO ME! GIVE THE CUTE GAL WHAT SHE ASKS, LUKE HONEY!
DO YOU TAKE CREDIT CARDS?
WE TAKE VISA, MASTERCARD, AMERICAN EXPRESS AND DISCOVER.

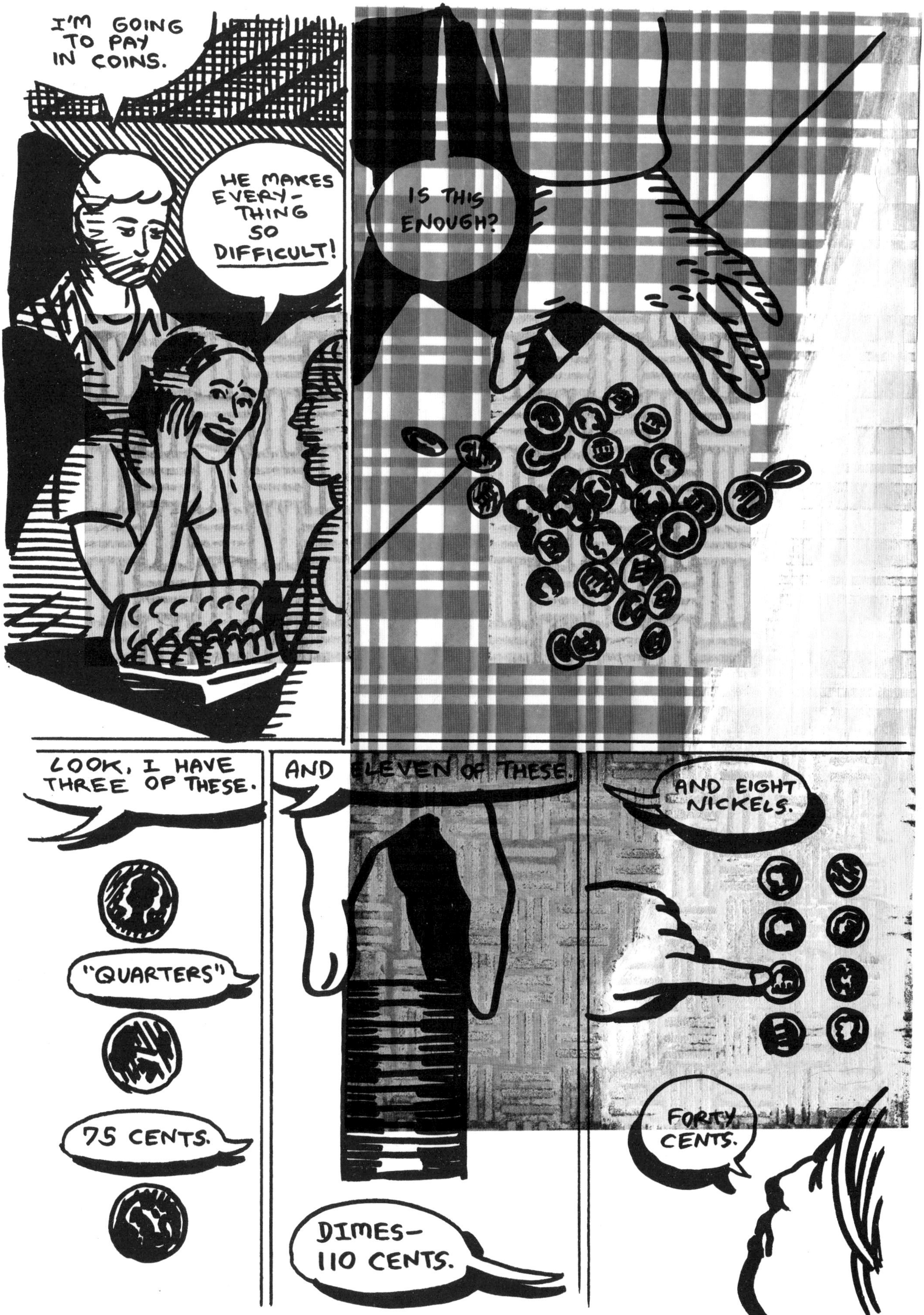
I'M GOING TO PAY IN COINS.
HE MAKES EVERY-THING SO DIFFICULT!
IS THIS ENOUGH?
LOOK, I HAVE THREE OF THESE.
"QUARTERS"
75 CENTS.
AND ELEVEN OF THESE.
DIMES- 110 CENTS.
AND EIGHT NICKELS.
FORTY CENTS.

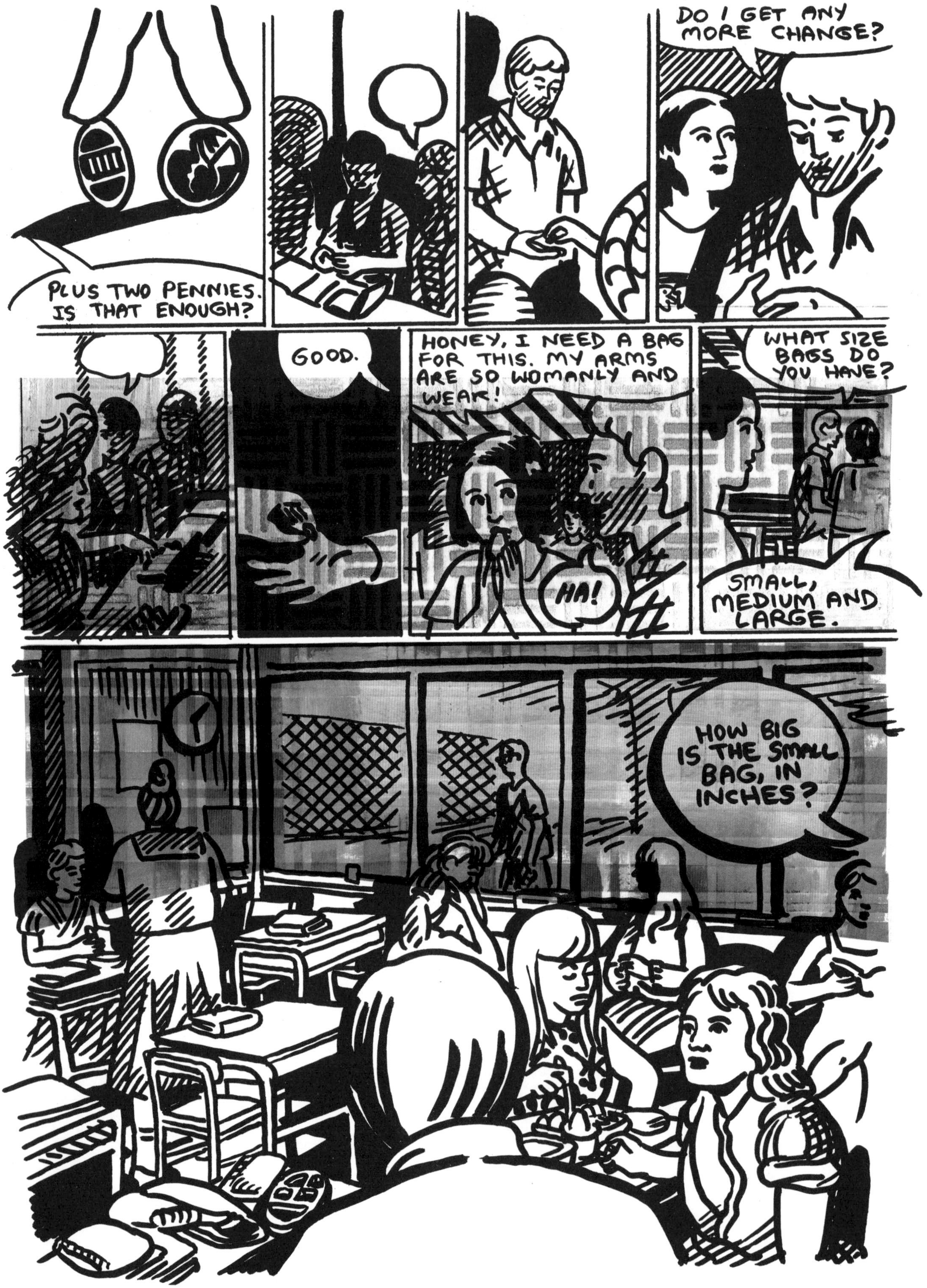
PLUS TWO PENNIES. IS THAT ENOUGH?
DO I GET ANY MORE CHANGE?
GOOD.
HONEY, I NEED A BAG FOR THIS. MY ARMS ARE SO WOMANLY AND WEAK!
HA!
WHAT SIZE BAGS DO YOU HAVE?
SMALL, MEDIUM AND LARGE.
HOW BIG IS THE SMALL BAG, IN INCHES?

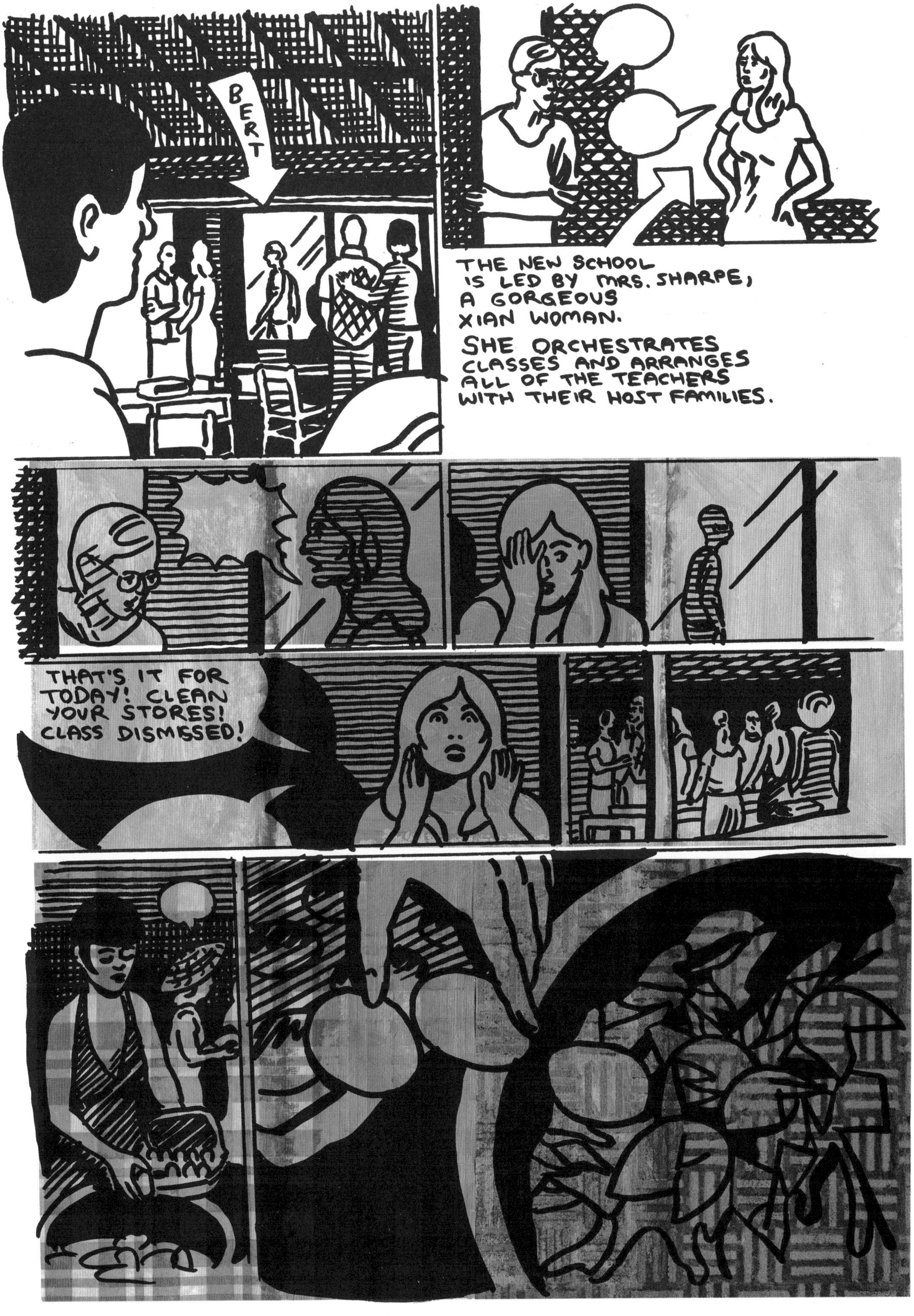
BERT
THE NEW SCHOOL IS LED BY MRS. SHARPE, A GORGEOUS XIAN WOMAN.
SHE ORCHESTRATES CLASSES AND ARRANGES ALL OF THE TEACHERS WITH THEIR HOST FAMILIES.
THAT'S IT FOR TODAY! CLEAN YOUR STORES! CLASS DISMISSED!

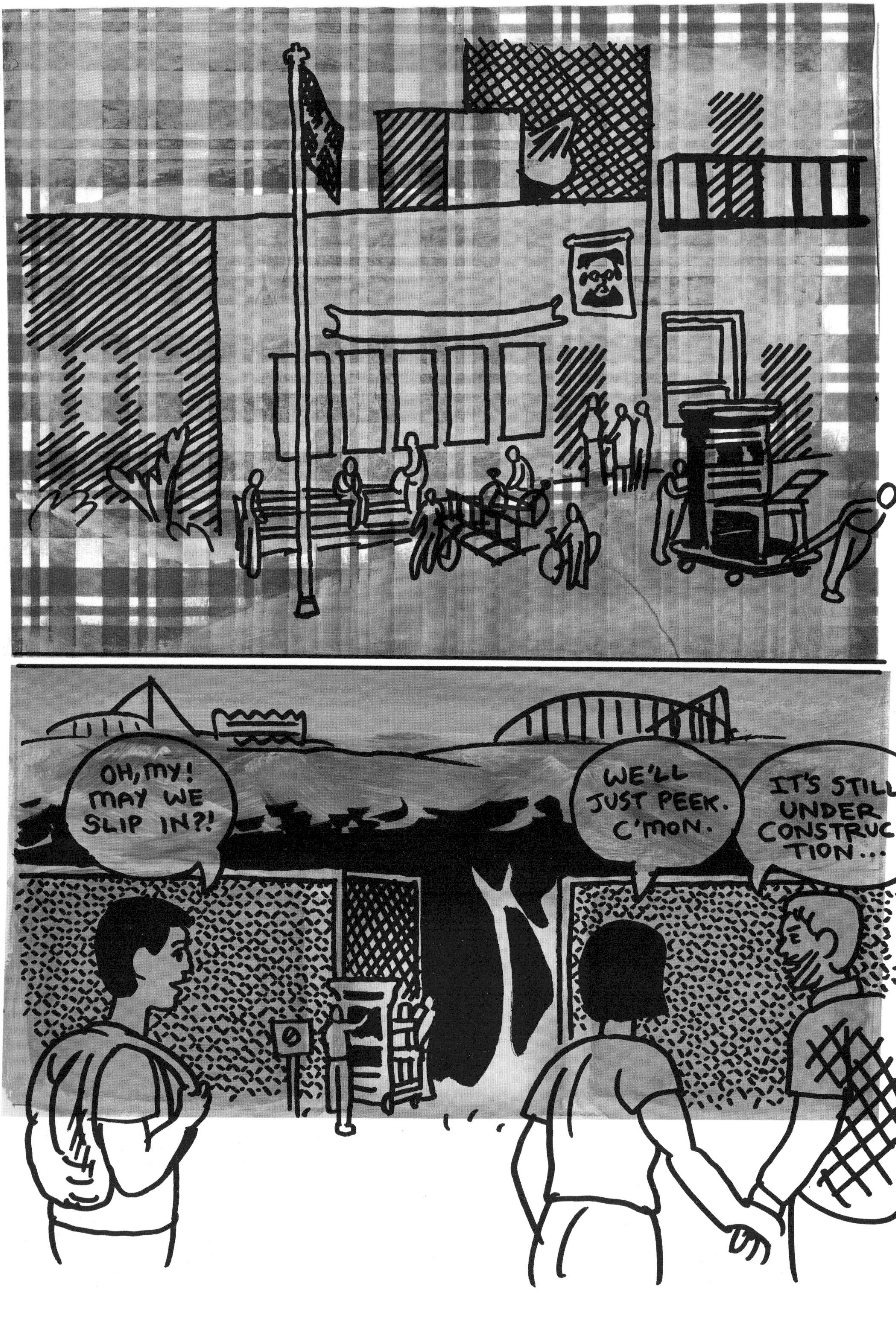
OH, MY! MAY WE SLIP IN?!
WE'LL JUST PEEK. C'MON.
IT'S STILL UNDER CONSTRUCTION...

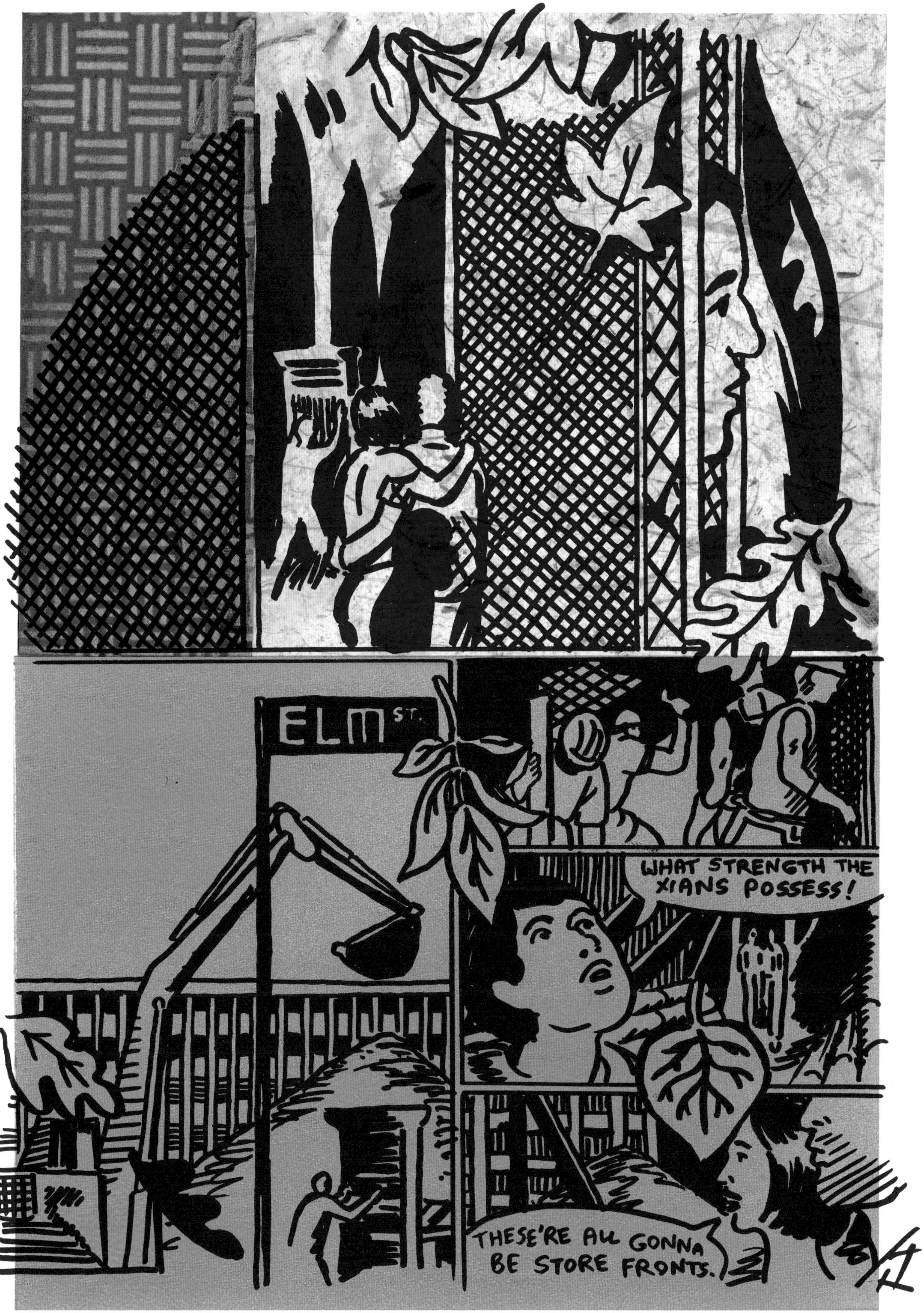
ELM ST.
WHAT STRENGTH THE XIANS POSSESS!
THESE'RE ALL GONNA BE STORE FRONTS.

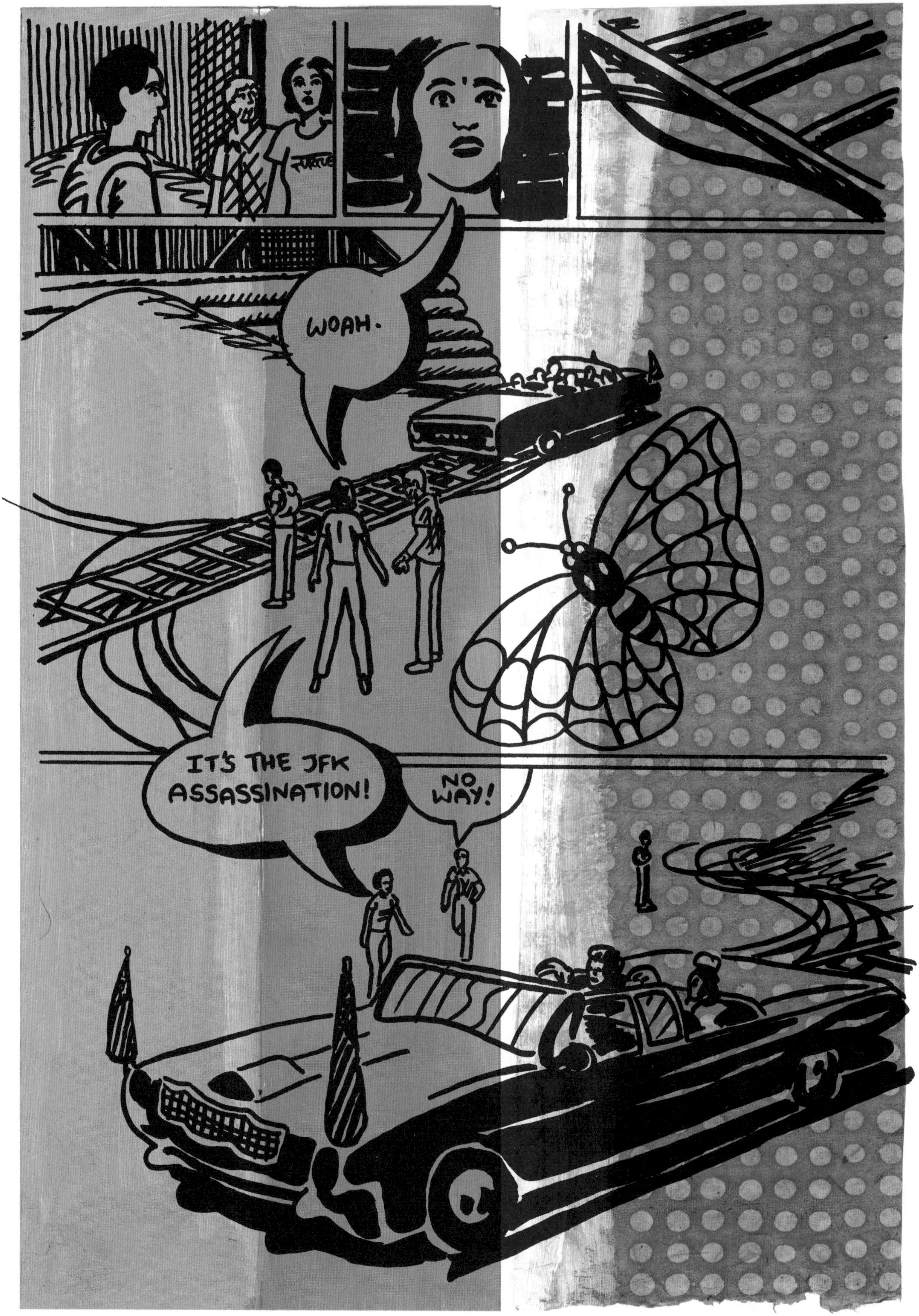
WOAH.
IT'S THE JFK ASSASSINATION!
NO WAY!

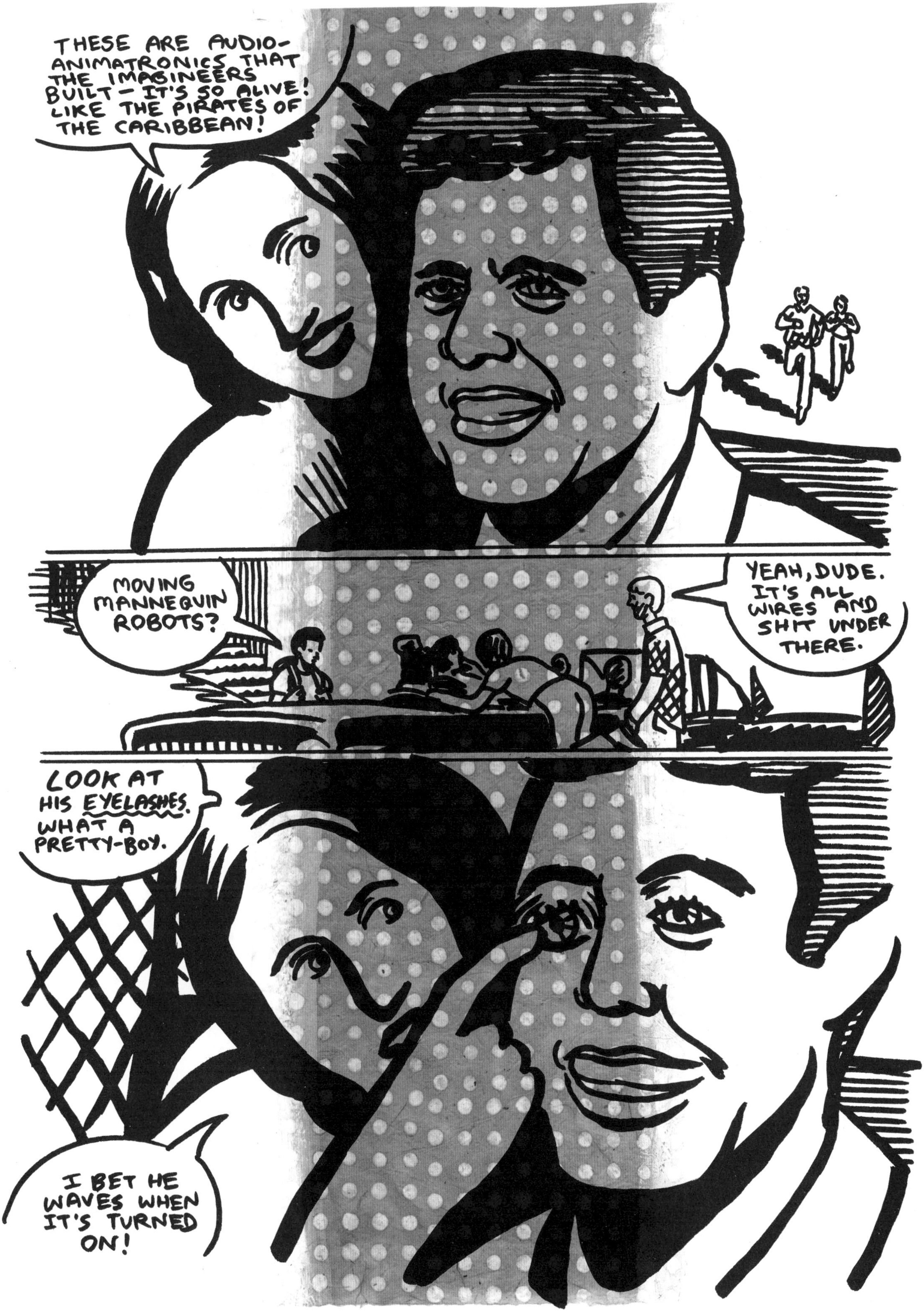
THESE ARE AUDIO-ANIMATRONICS THAT THE IMAGINEERS BUILT—IT'S SO ALIVE! LIKE THE PIRATES OF THE CARIBBEAN!
MOVING MANNEQUIN ROBOTS?
YEAH, DUDE. IT'S ALL WIRES AND SHIT UNDER THERE.
LOOK AT HIS EYELASHES. WHAT A PRETTY-BOY.
I BET HE WAVES WHEN IT'S TURNED ON!

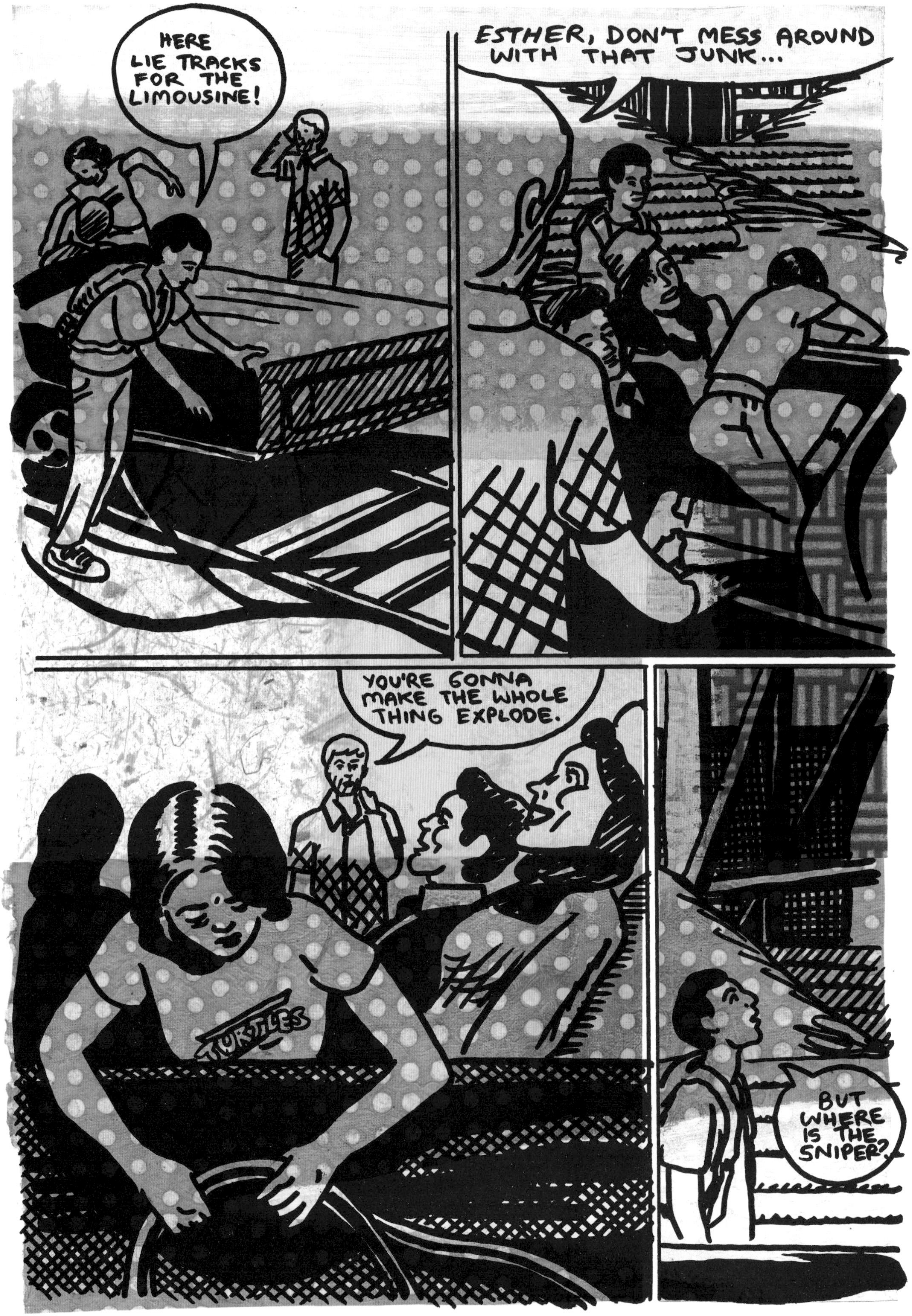
HERE LIE TRACKS FOR THE LIMOUSINE!
ESTHER, DON'T MESS AROUND WITH THAT JUNK...
YOU'RE GONNA MAKE THE WHOLE THING EXPLODE.
TURTLES
BUT WHERE IS THE SNIPER?

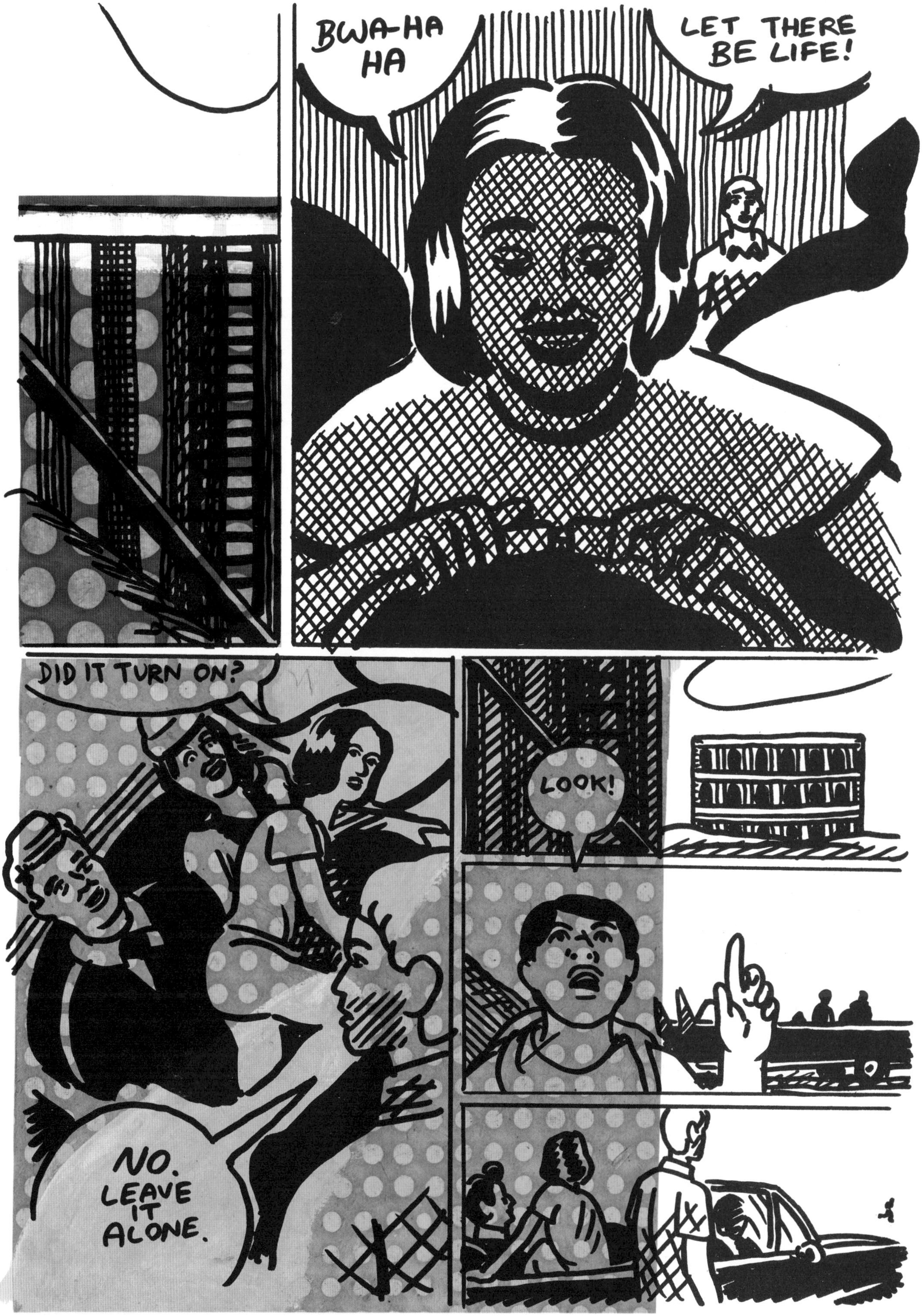
BWA-HA HA
LET THERE BE LIFE!
DID IT TURN ON?
NO. LEAVE IT ALONE.
LOOK!

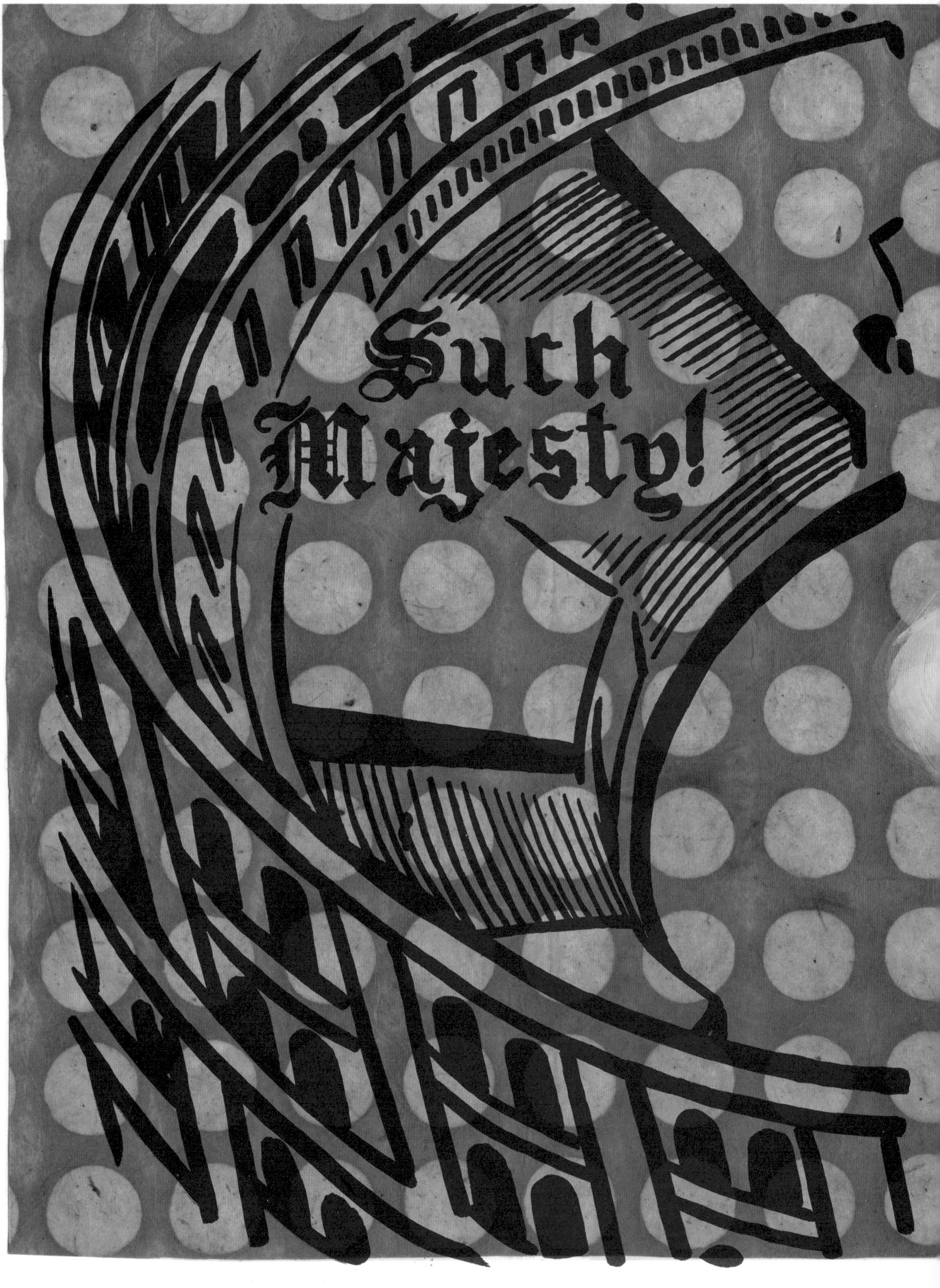
Such
Majesty!

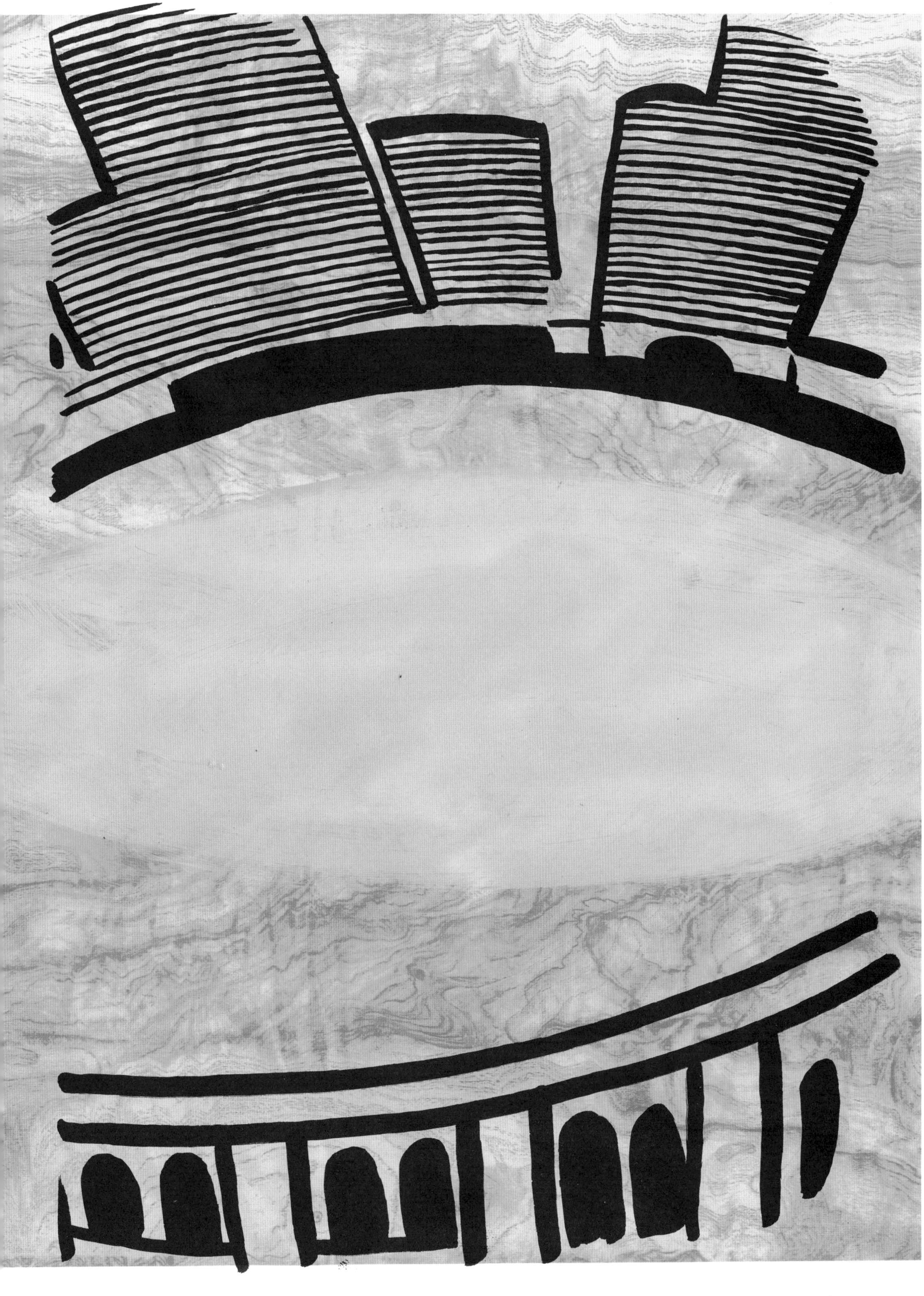

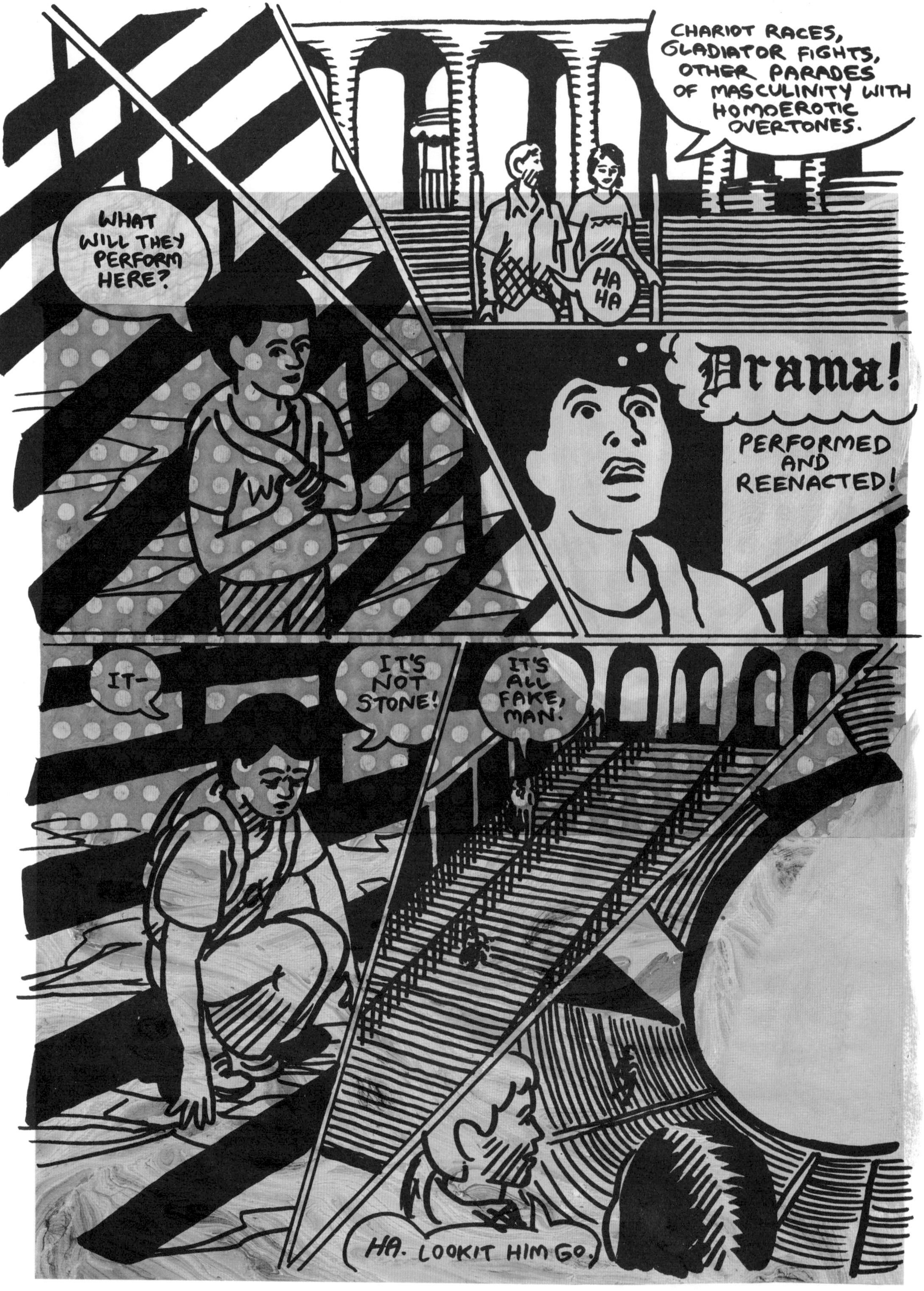
CHARIOT RACES, GLADIATOR FIGHTS, OTHER PARADES OF MASCULINITY WITH HOMOEROTIC OVERTONES.
WHAT WILL THEY PERFORM HERE?
HA HA
Drama!
PERFORMED AND REENACTED!
IT-
IT'S NOT STONE!
IT'S ALL FAKE, MAN.
HA. LOOKIT HIM GO.

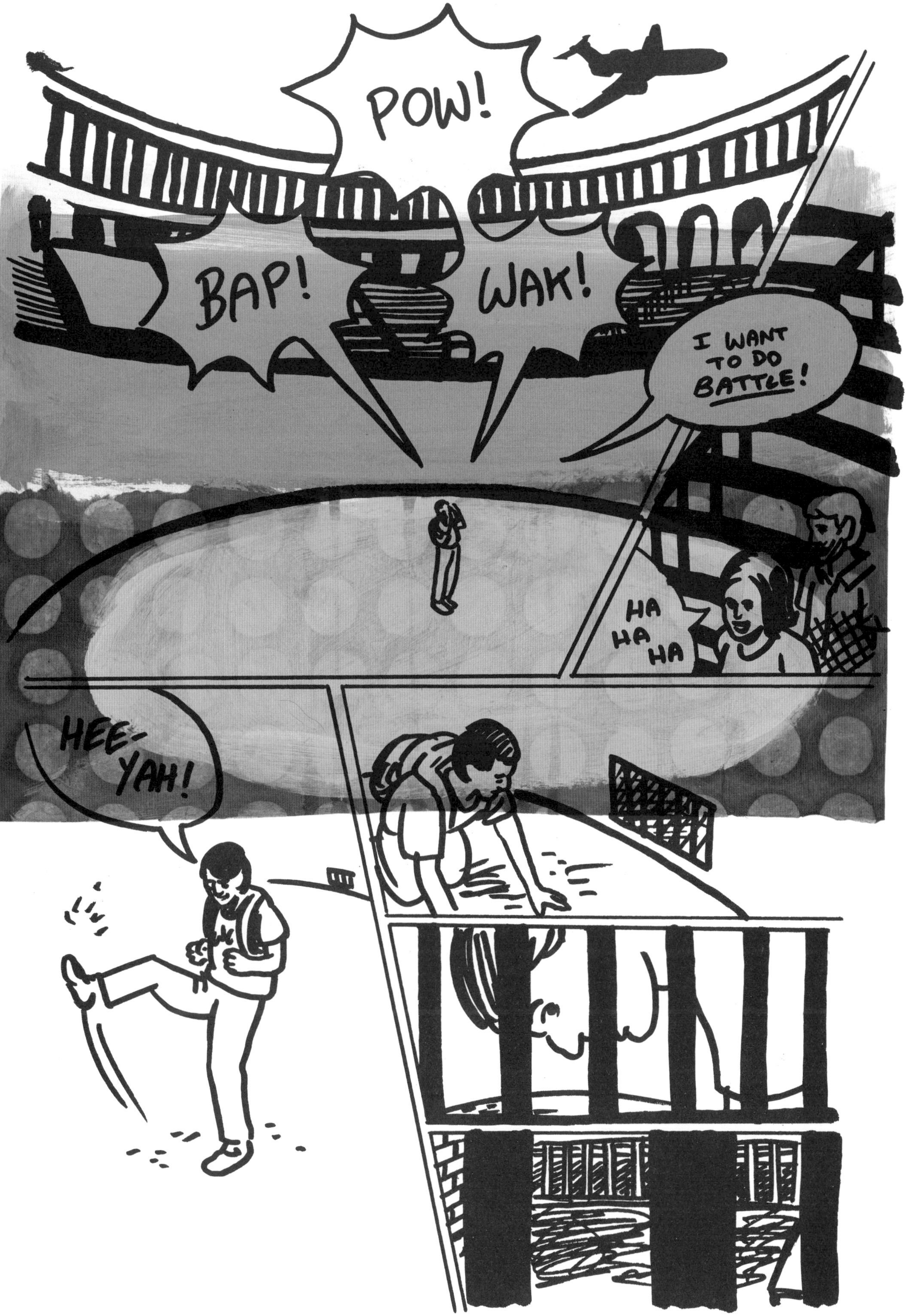
POW!
BAP!
WAK!
I WANT TO DO BATTLE!
HA HA HA
HEE-YAH!

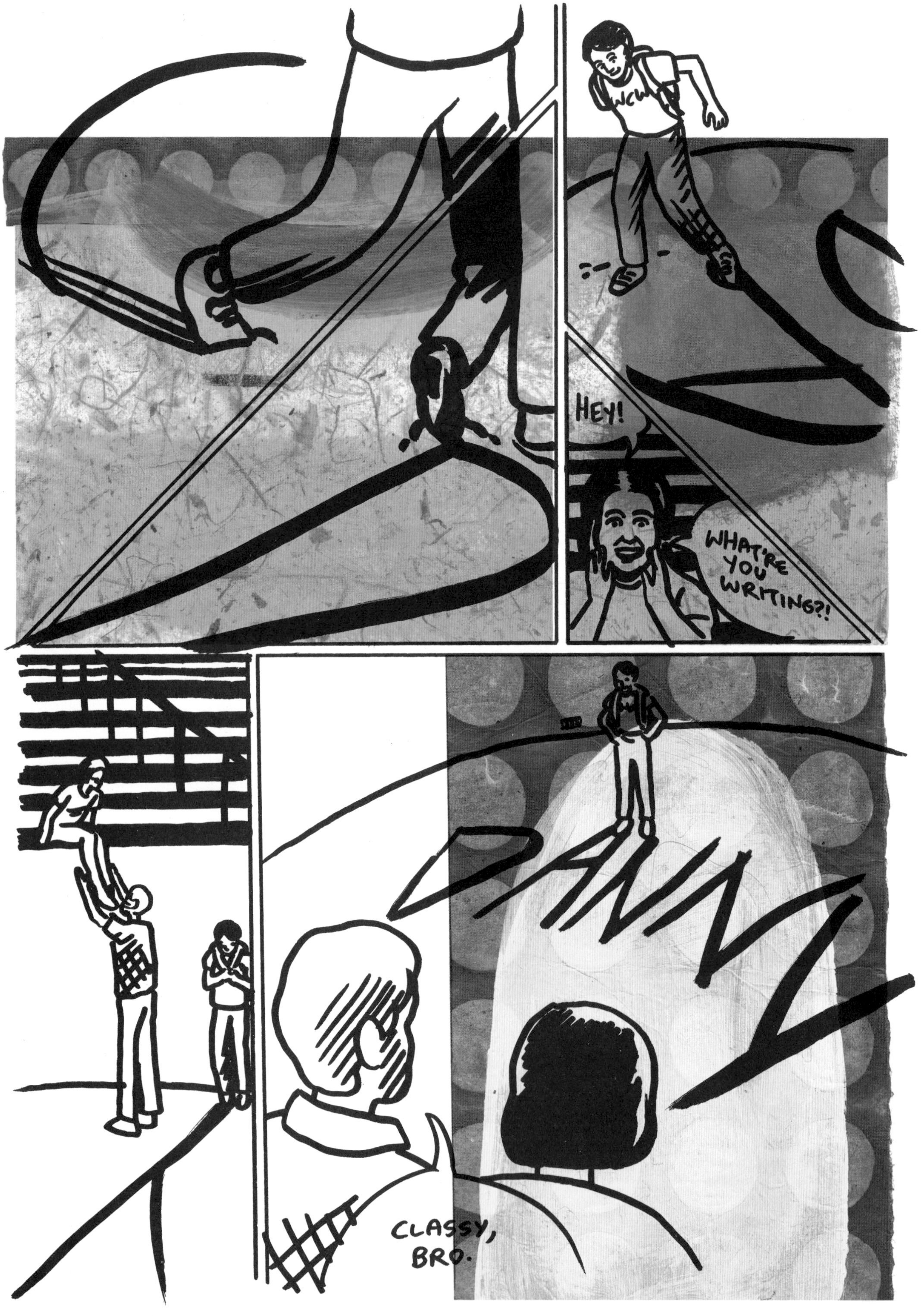
WCW
HEY!
WHAT'RE YOU WRITING?!
DANNY
CLASSY, BRO.

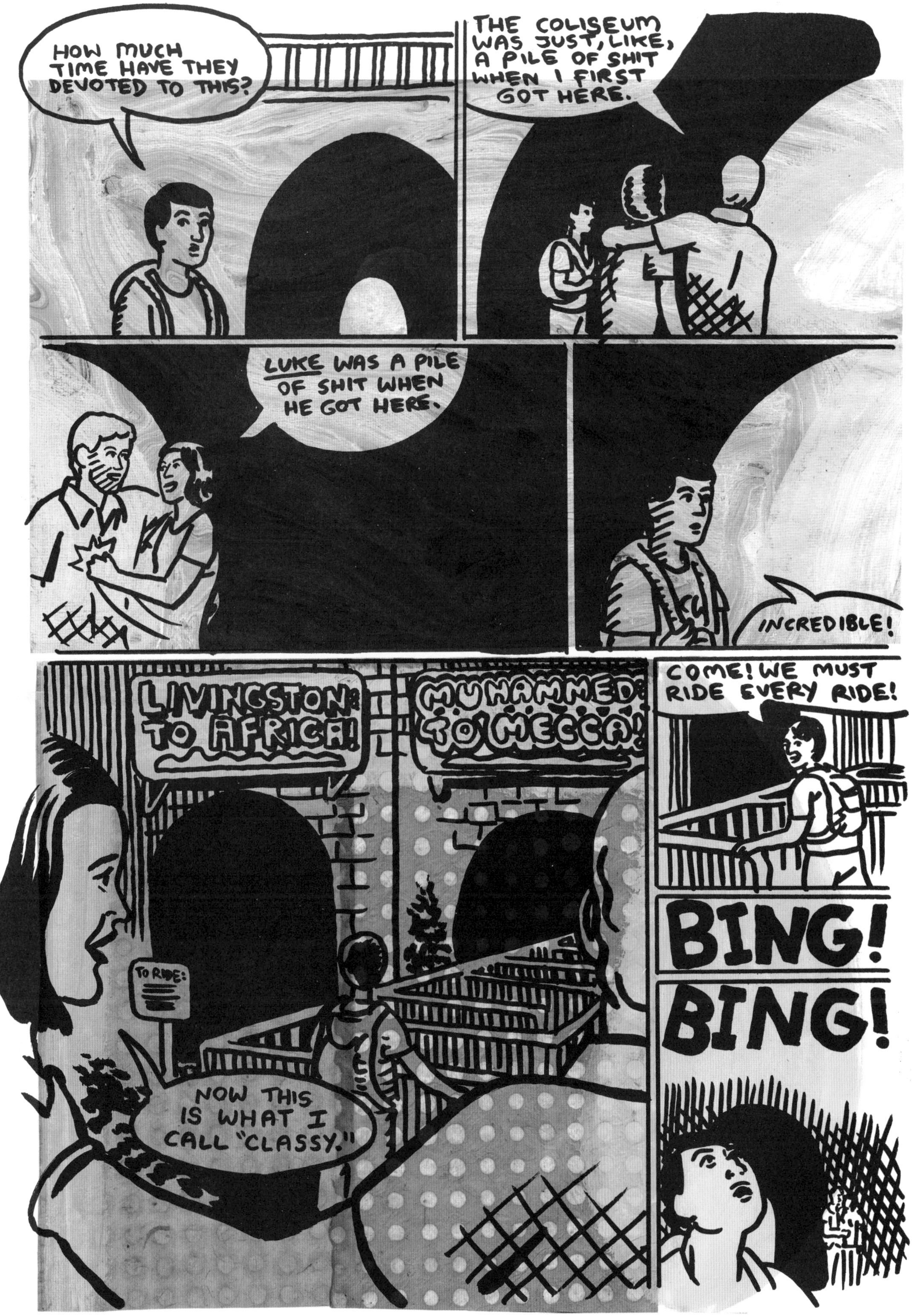
HOW MUCH TIME HAVE THEY DEVOTED TO THIS?
THE COLISEUM WAS JUST, LIKE, A PILE OF SHIT WHEN I FIRST GOT HERE.
LUKE WAS A PILE OF SHIT WHEN HE GOT HERE.
INCREDIBLE!
LIVINGSTON TO AFRICA!
MUHAMMED TO MECCA!
TO RIDE:
NOW THIS IS WHAT I CALL "CLASSY."
COME! WE MUST RIDE EVERY RIDE!
BING!
BING!

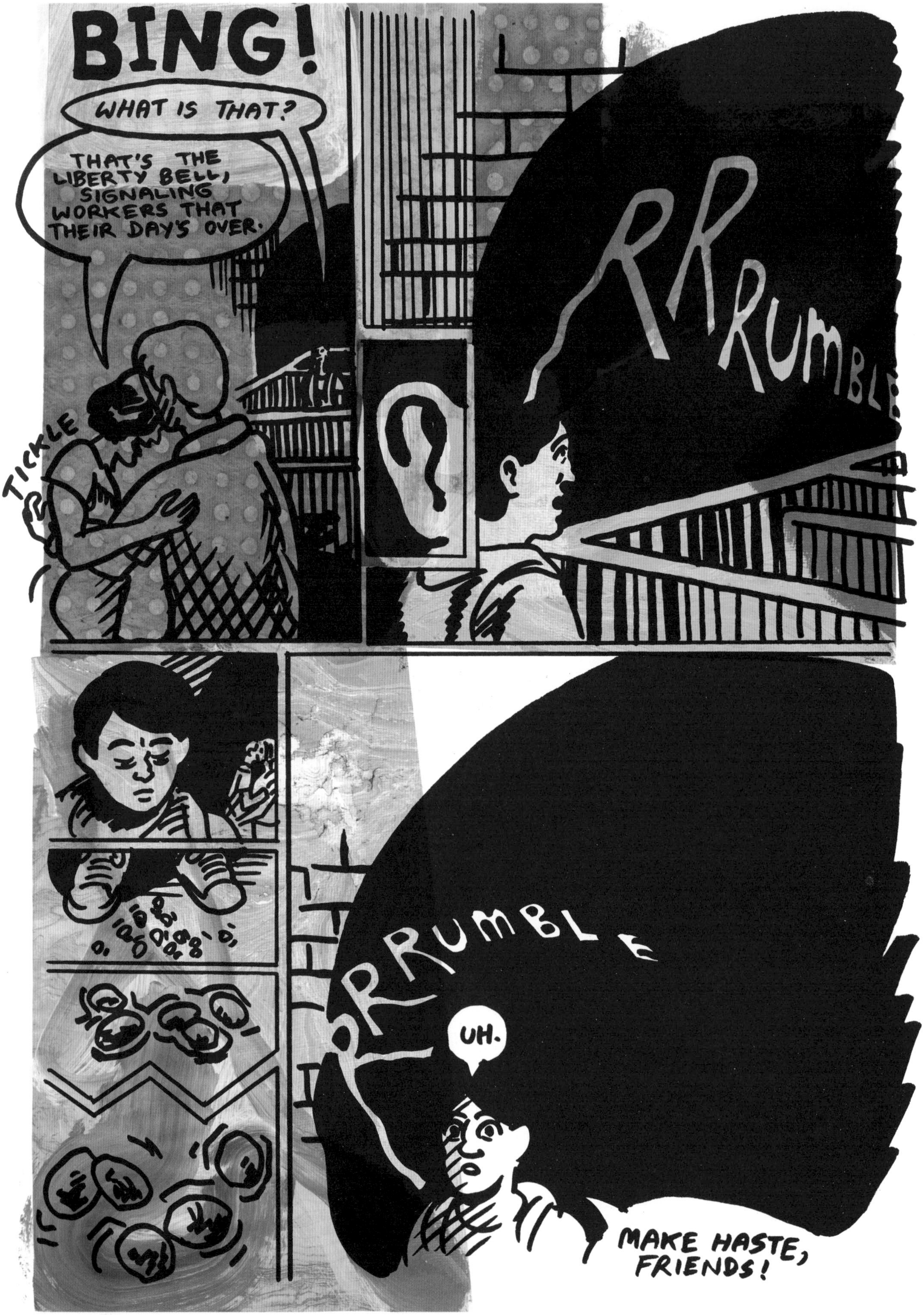
BING!
WHAT IS THAT?
THAT'S THE LIBERTY BELL, SIGNALING WORKERS THAT THEIR DAY'S OVER.
TICKLE
RRRUMBLE
RRUMBLE
UH.
MAKE HASTE, FRIENDS!

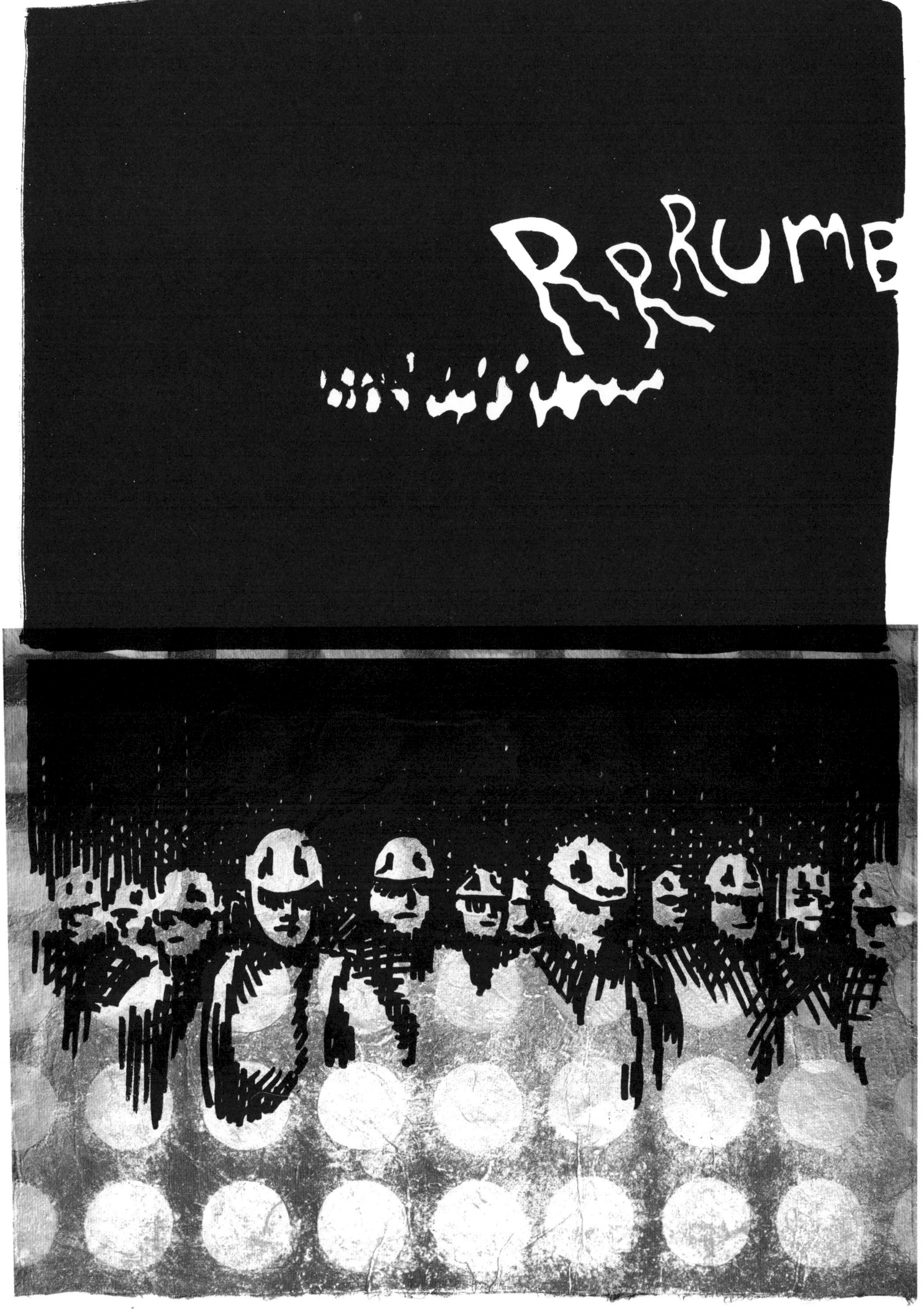
RRRUMB

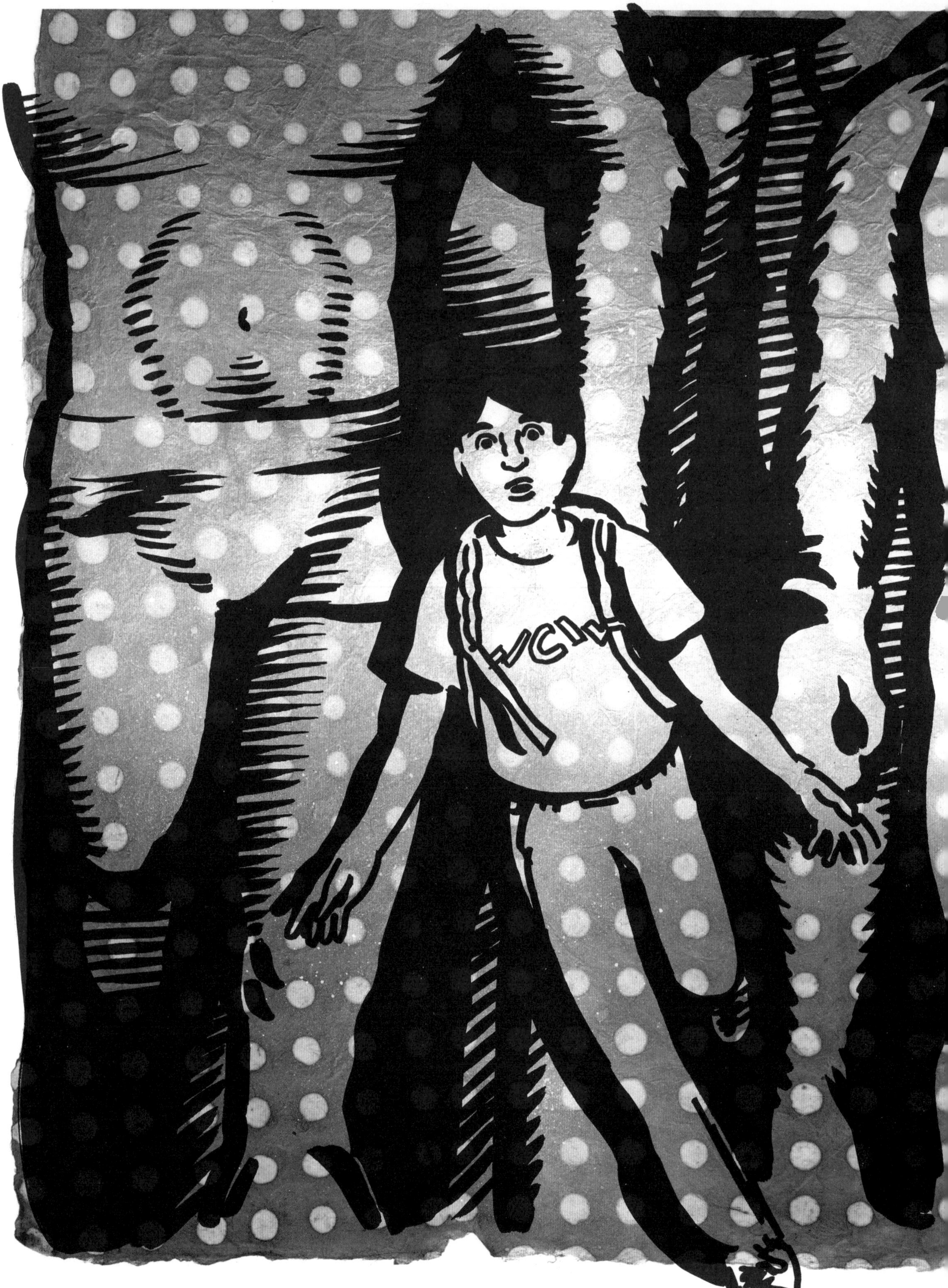

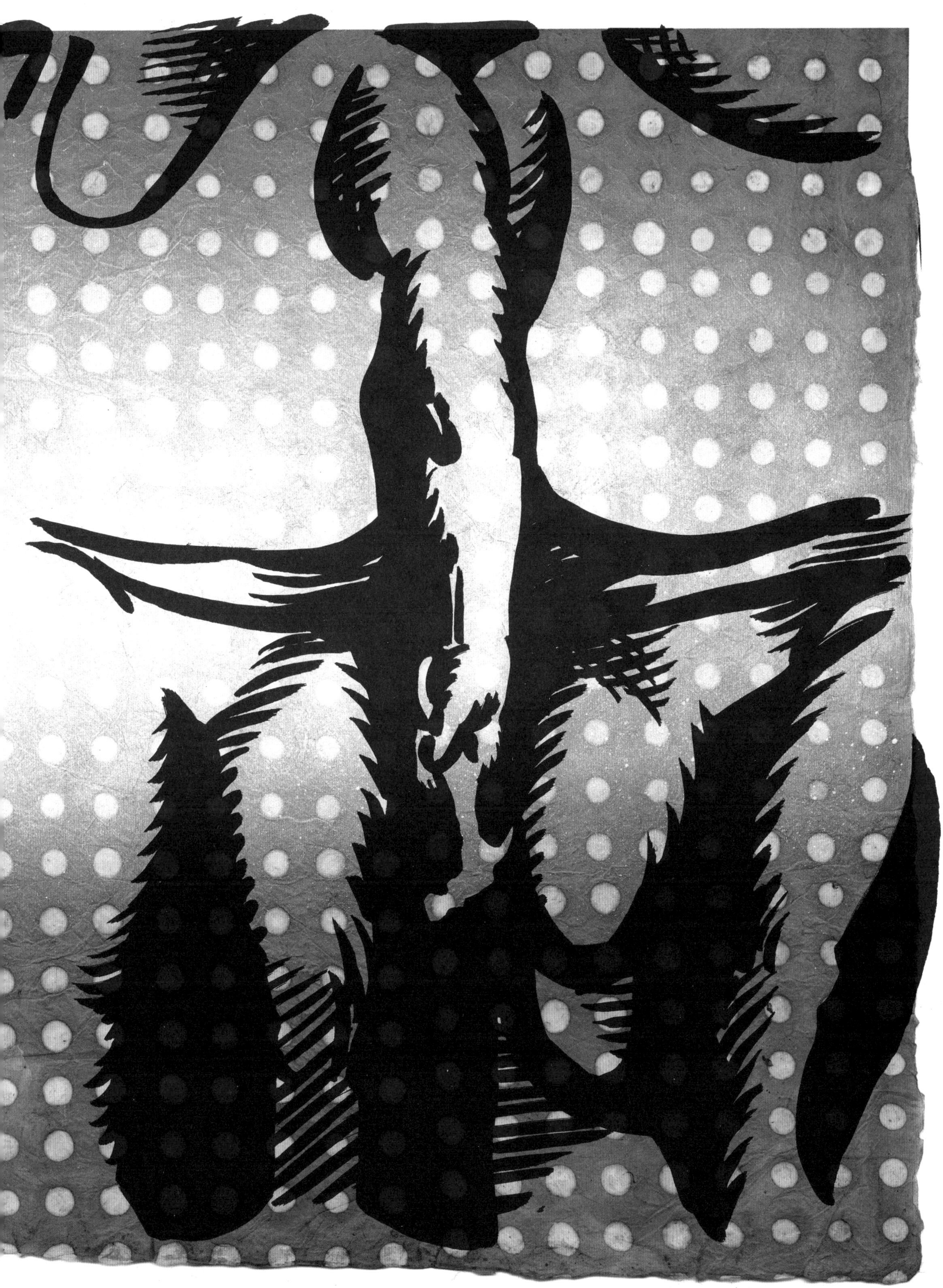

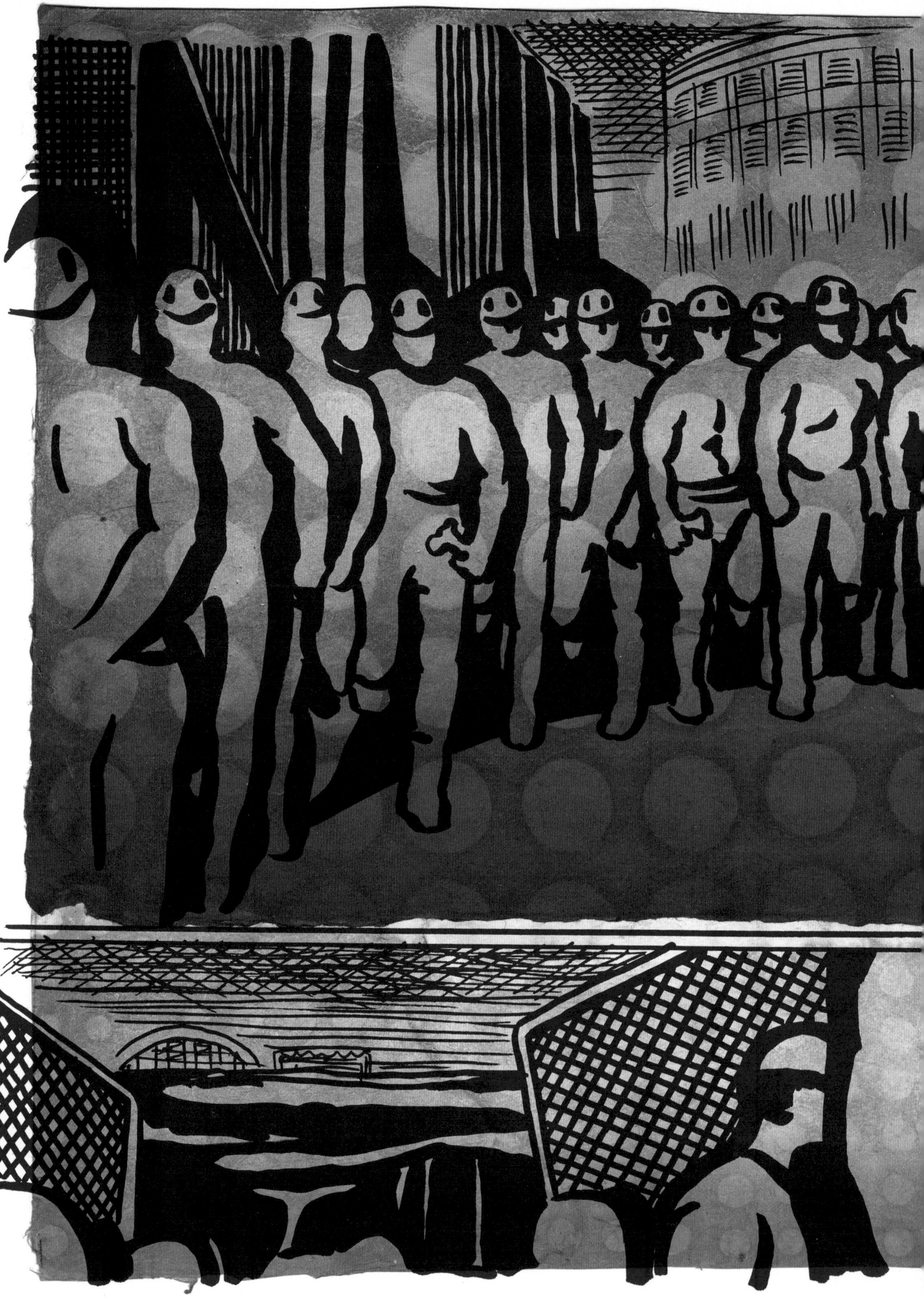

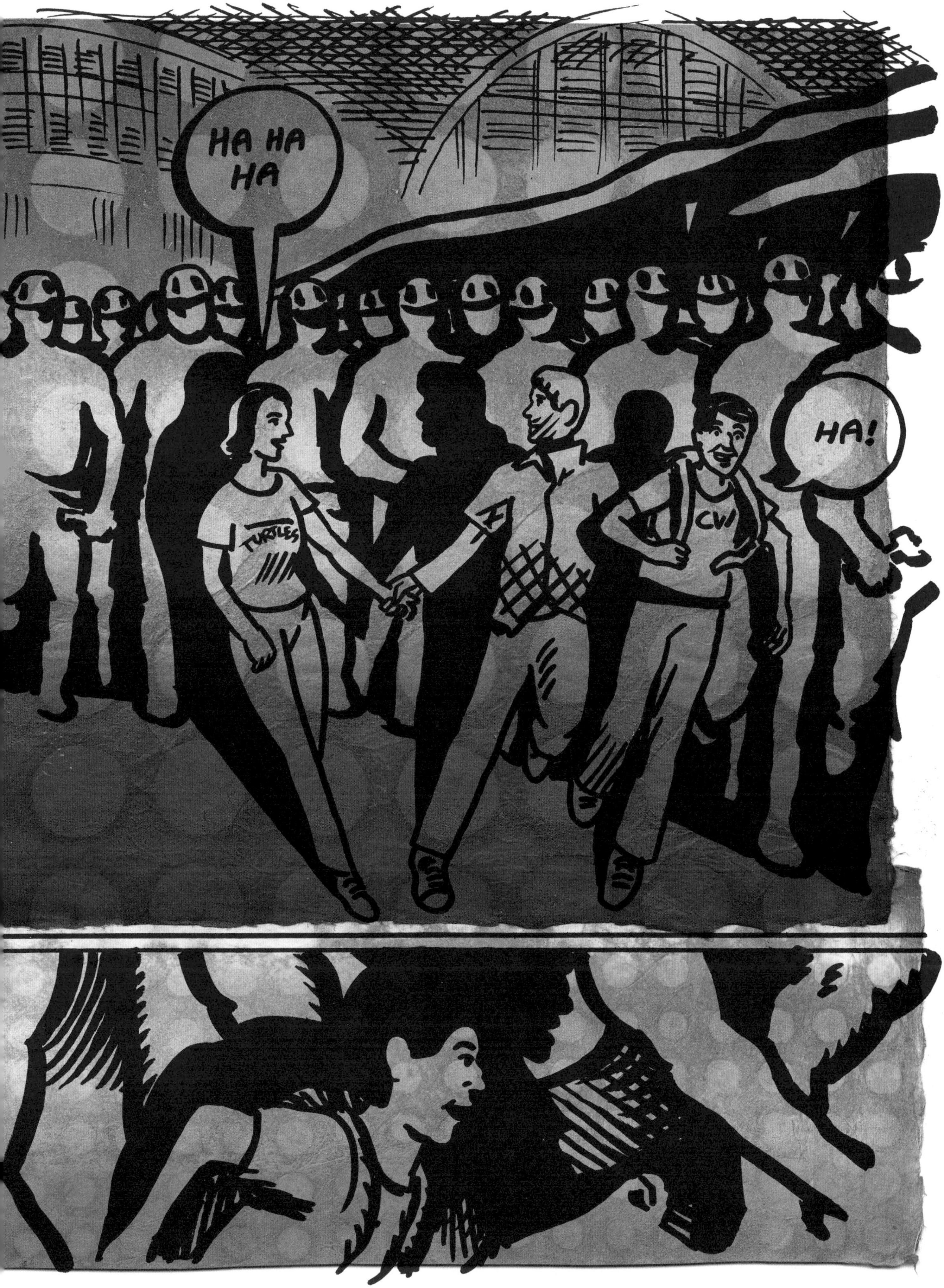
HA HA HA
HA!
TURTLES

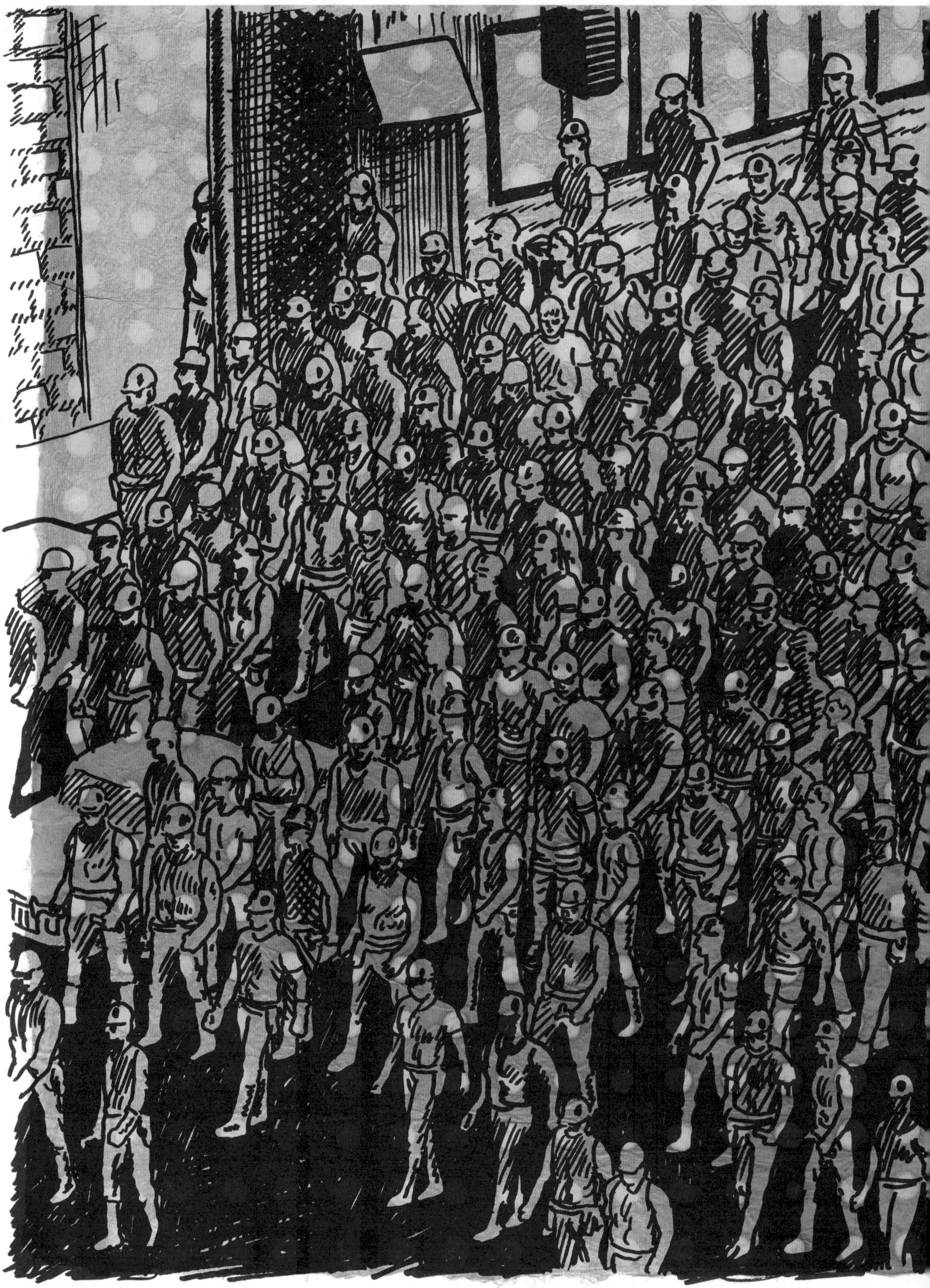

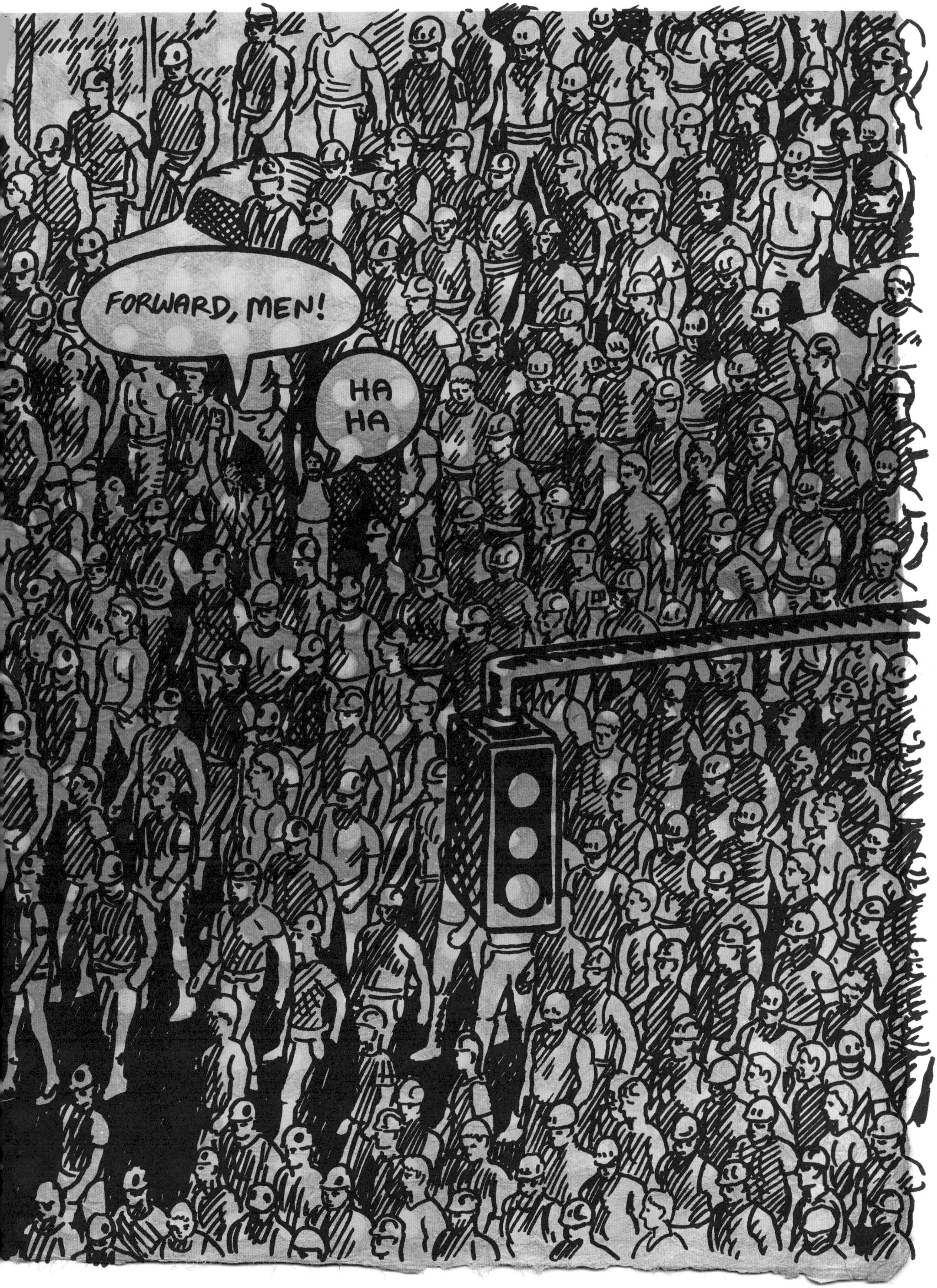
FORWARD, MEN!
HA HA

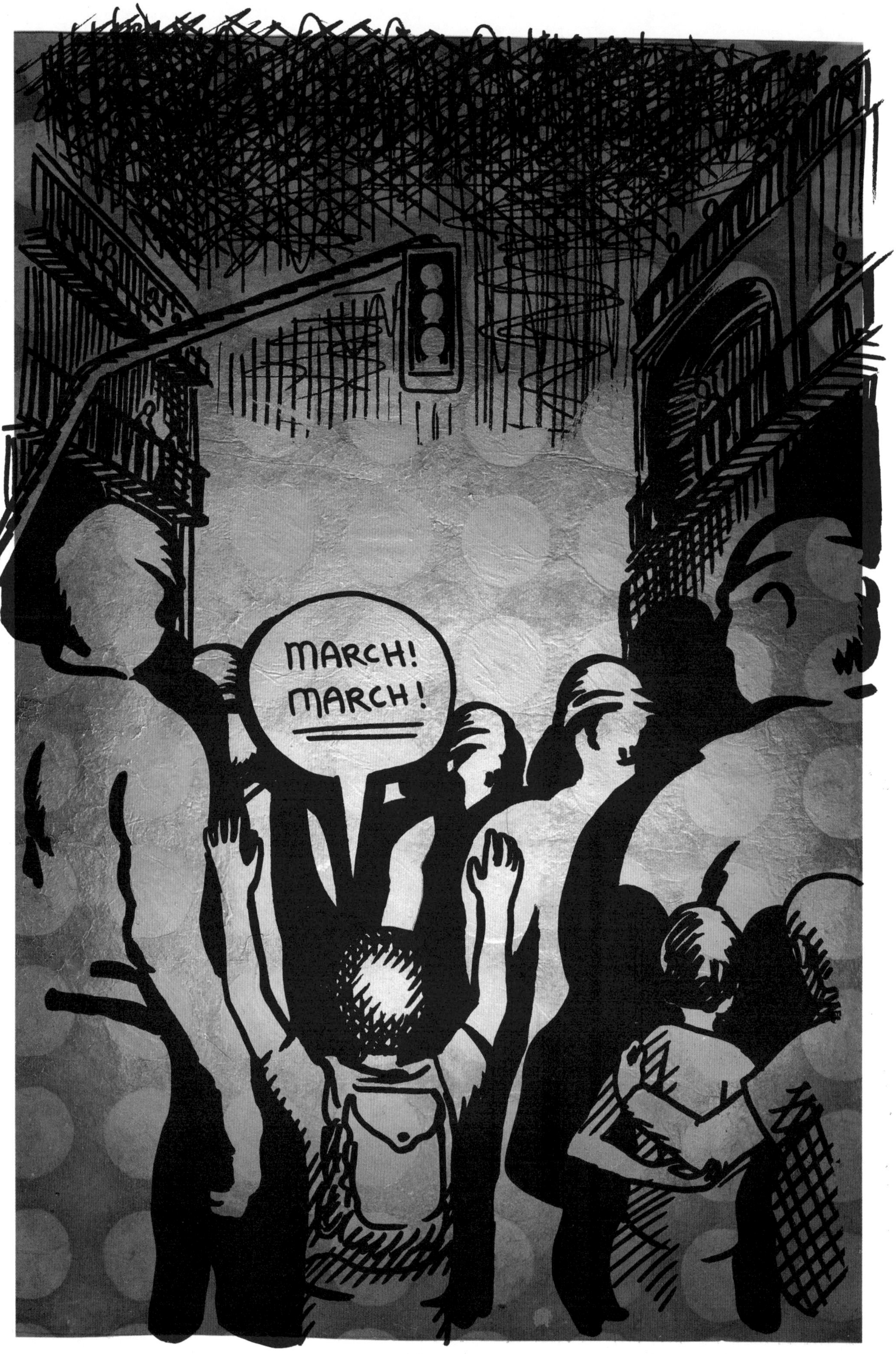
MARCH! MARCH!

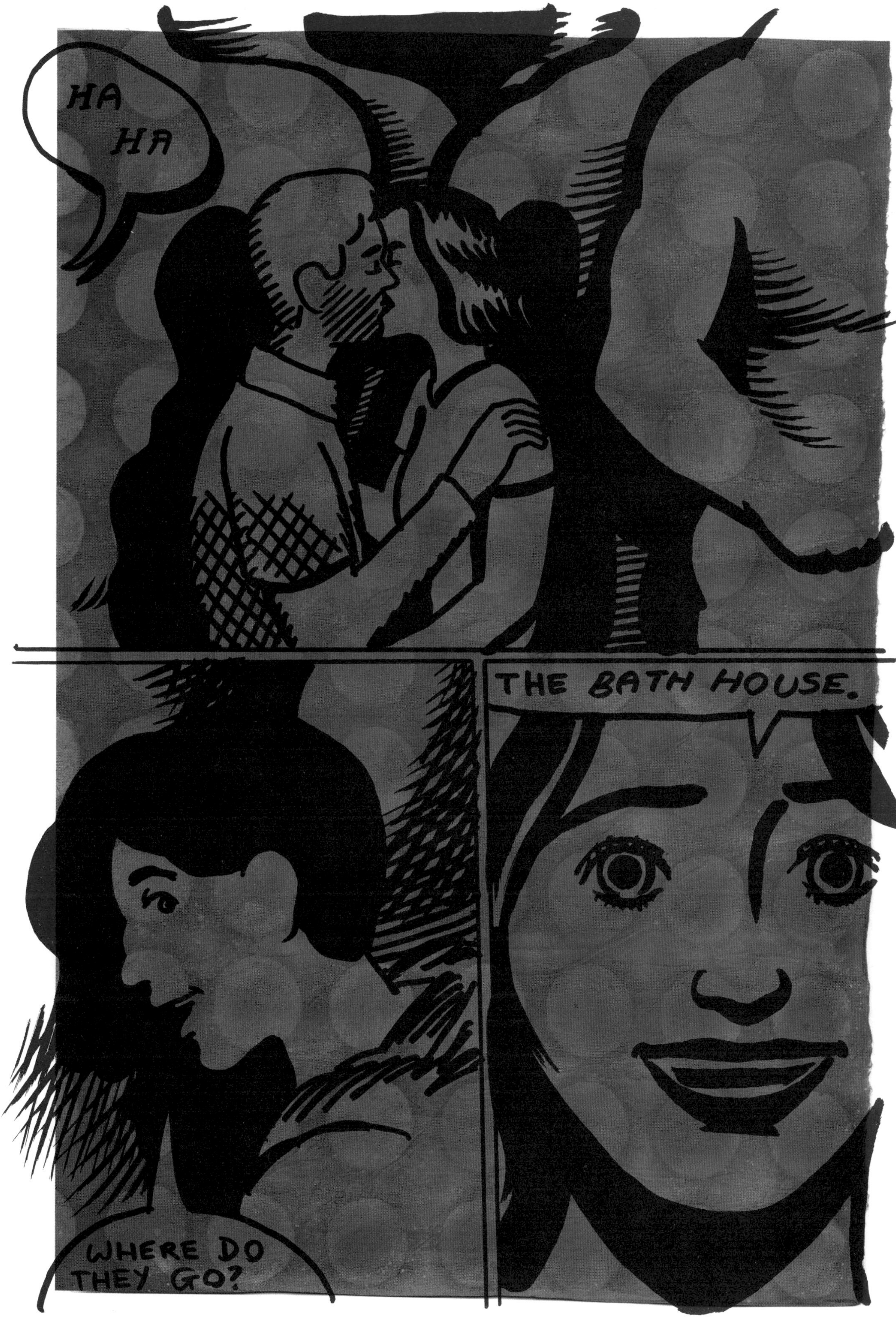
HA HA
WHERE DO THEY GO?
THE BATH HOUSE.

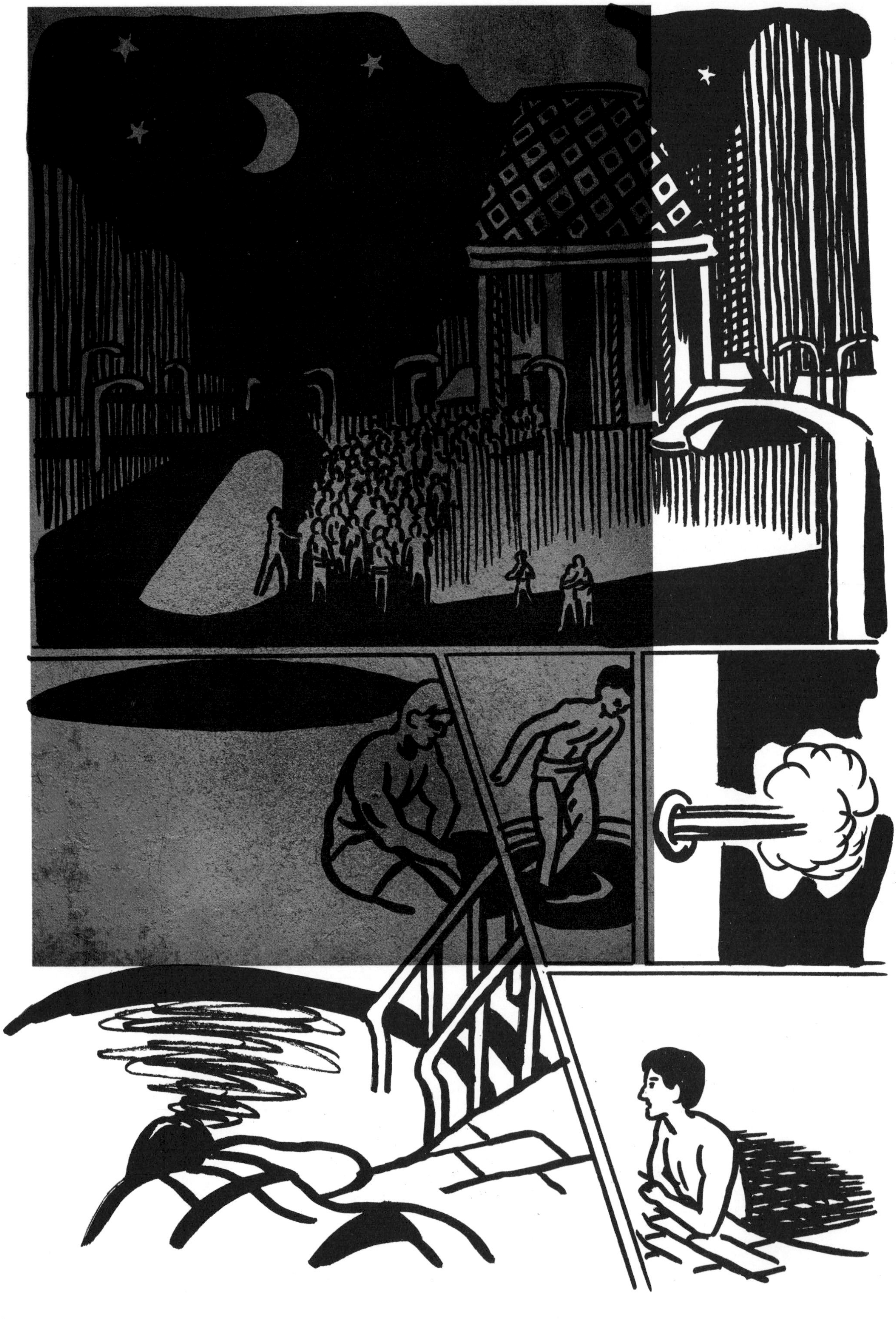

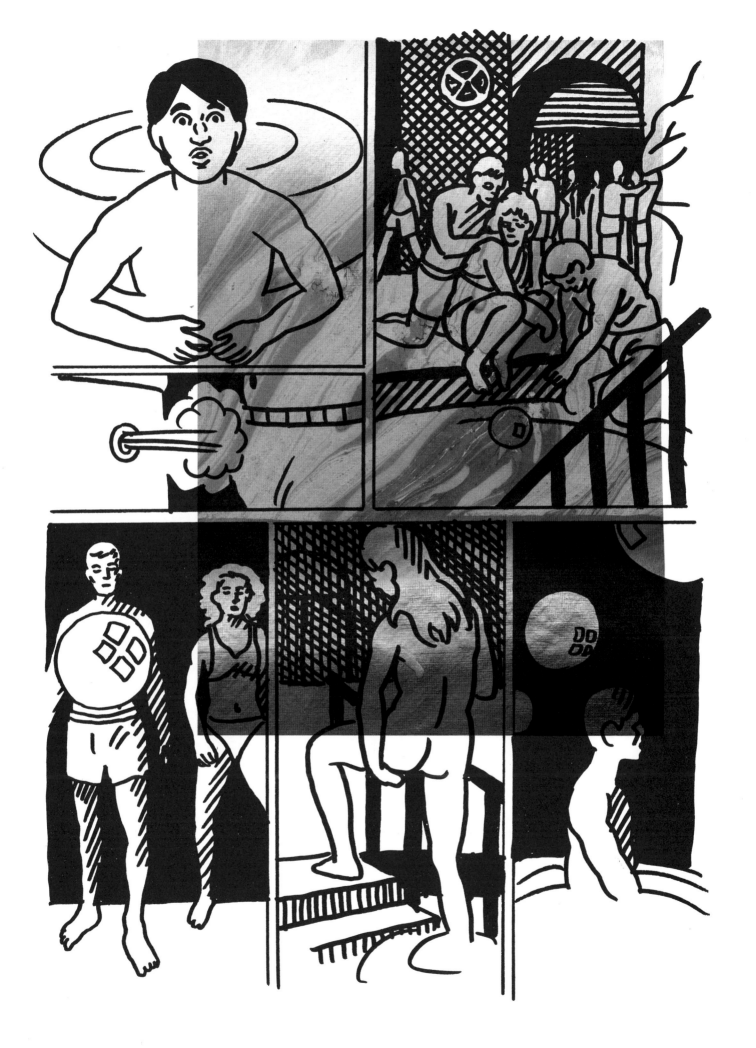

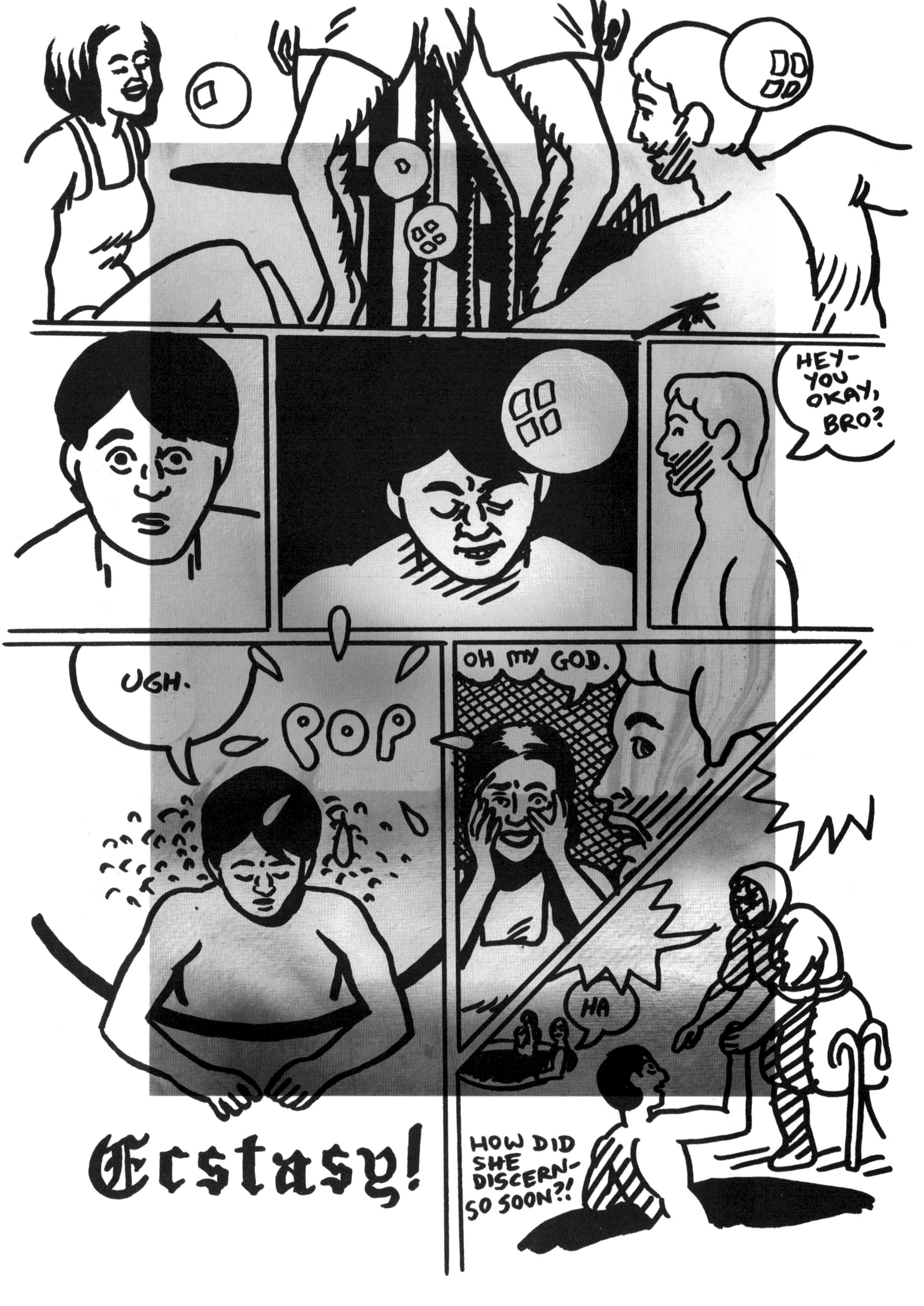
HEY-
YOU
OKAY,
BRO?
UGH.
POP
OH MY GOD.
HA
Ecstasy!
HOW DID
SHE
DISCERN-
SO SOON?!

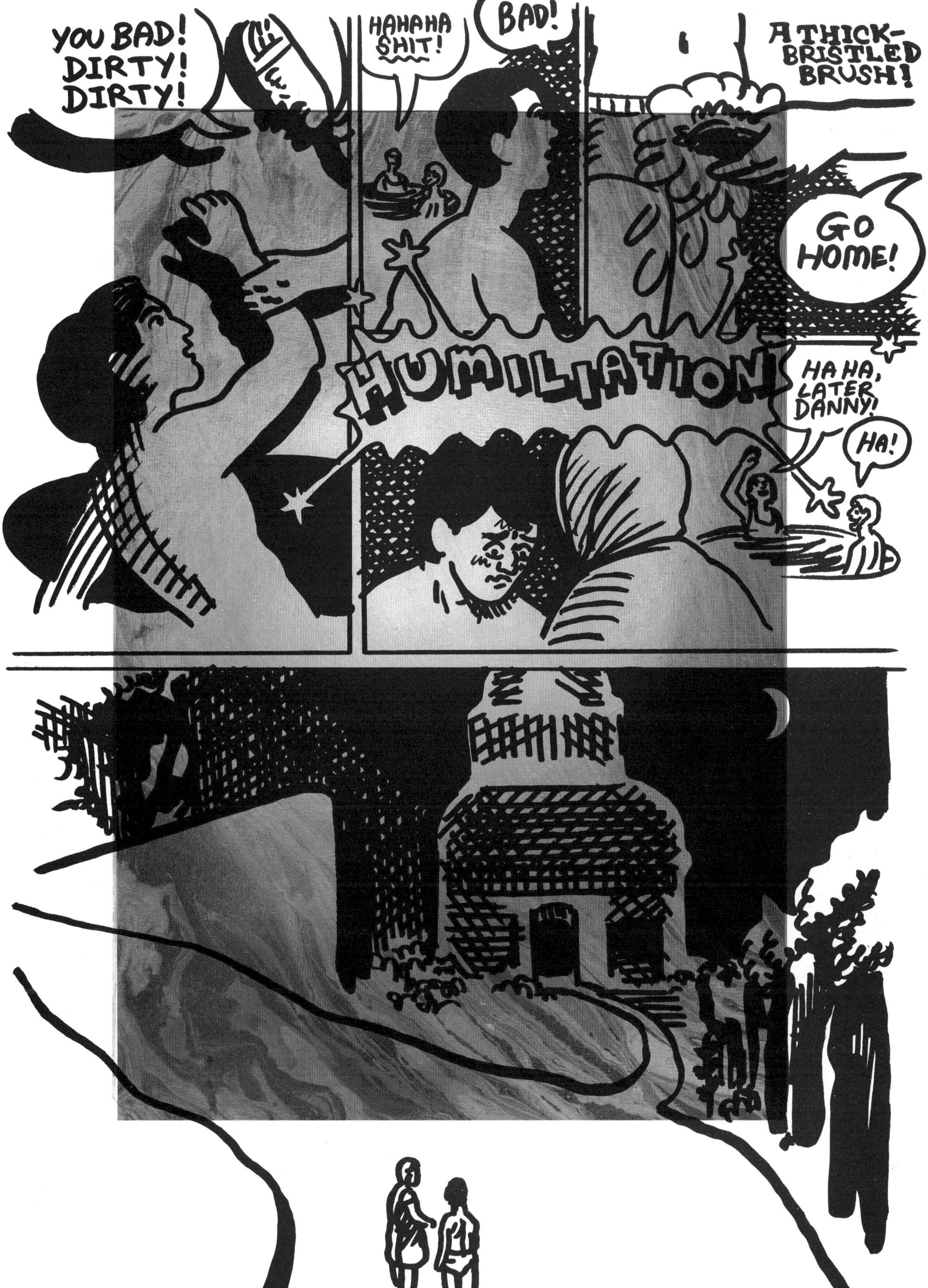
YOU BAD! DIRTY! DIRTY!
HAHAHA SHIT!
BAD!
A THICK-BRISTLED BRUSH!
GO HOME!
HUMILIATION!
HA HA, LATER DANNY!
HA!

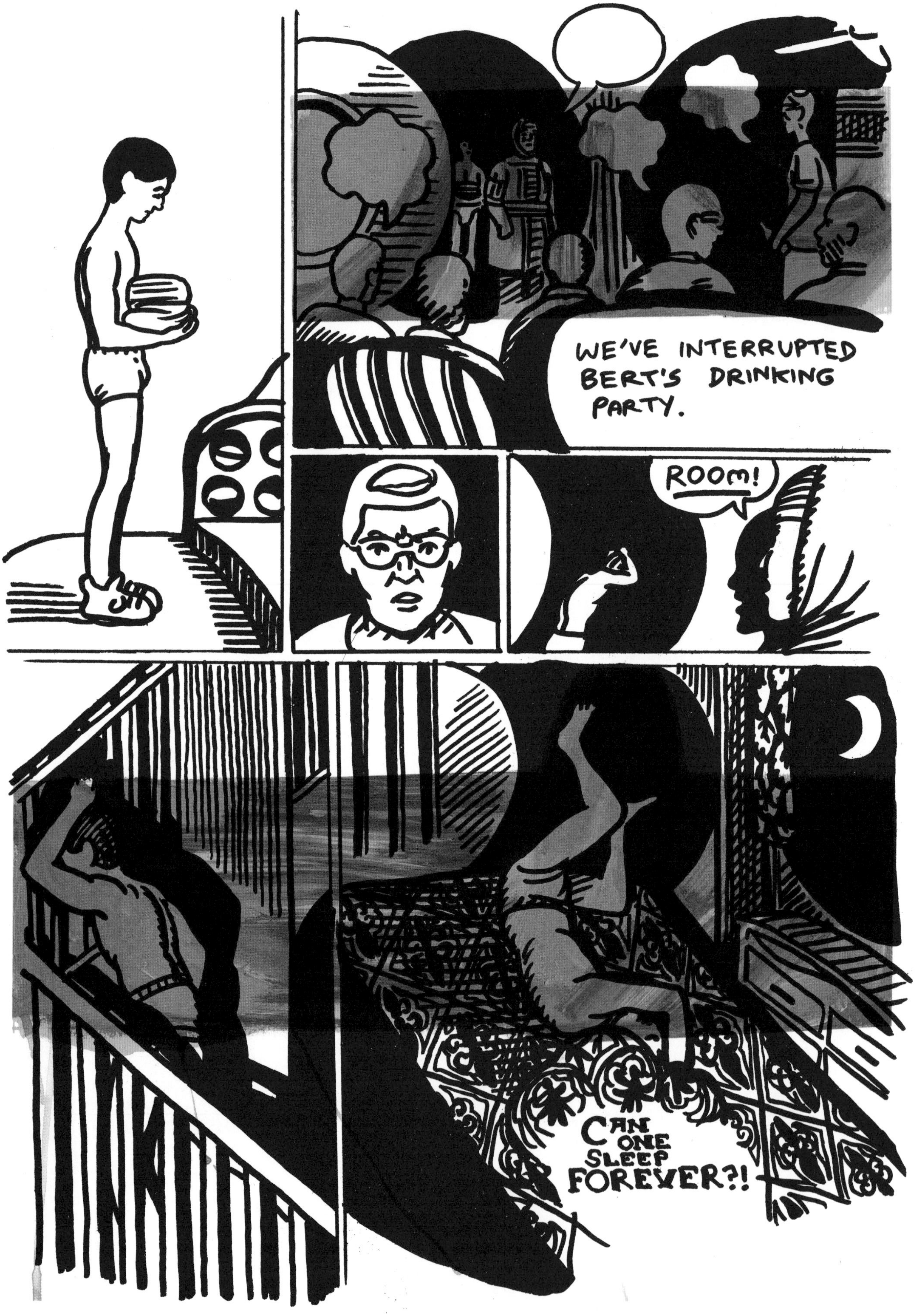
WE'VE INTERRUPTED BERT'S DRINKING PARTY.
ROOM!
CAN ONE SLEEP FOREVER?!

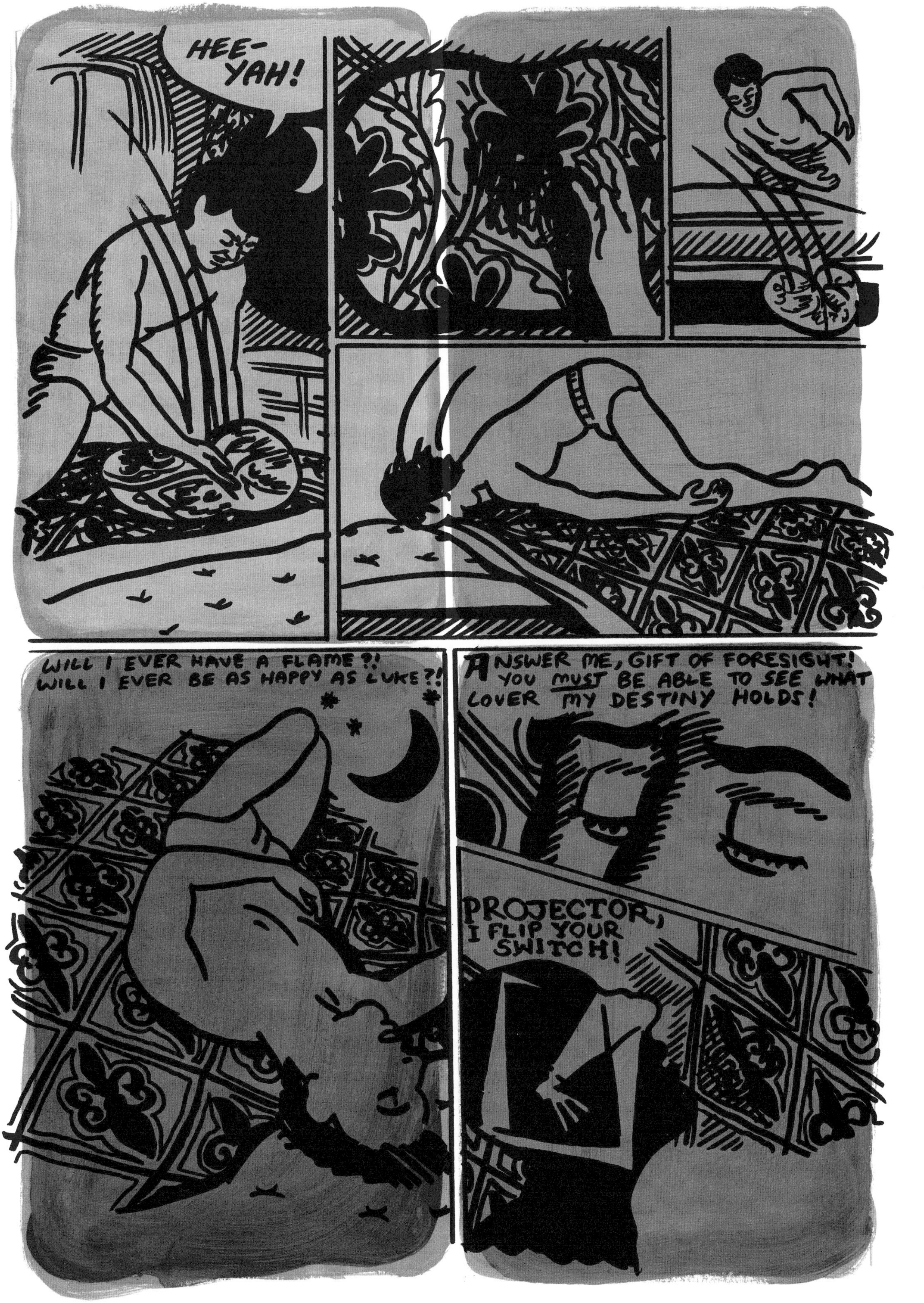
HEE-YAH!
WILL I EVER HAVE A FLAME?! WILL I EVER BE AS HAPPY AS LUKE?!
ANSWER ME, GIFT OF FORESIGHT! YOU MUST BE ABLE TO SEE WHAT LOVER MY DESTINY HOLDS!
PROJECTOR, I FLIP YOUR SWITCH!

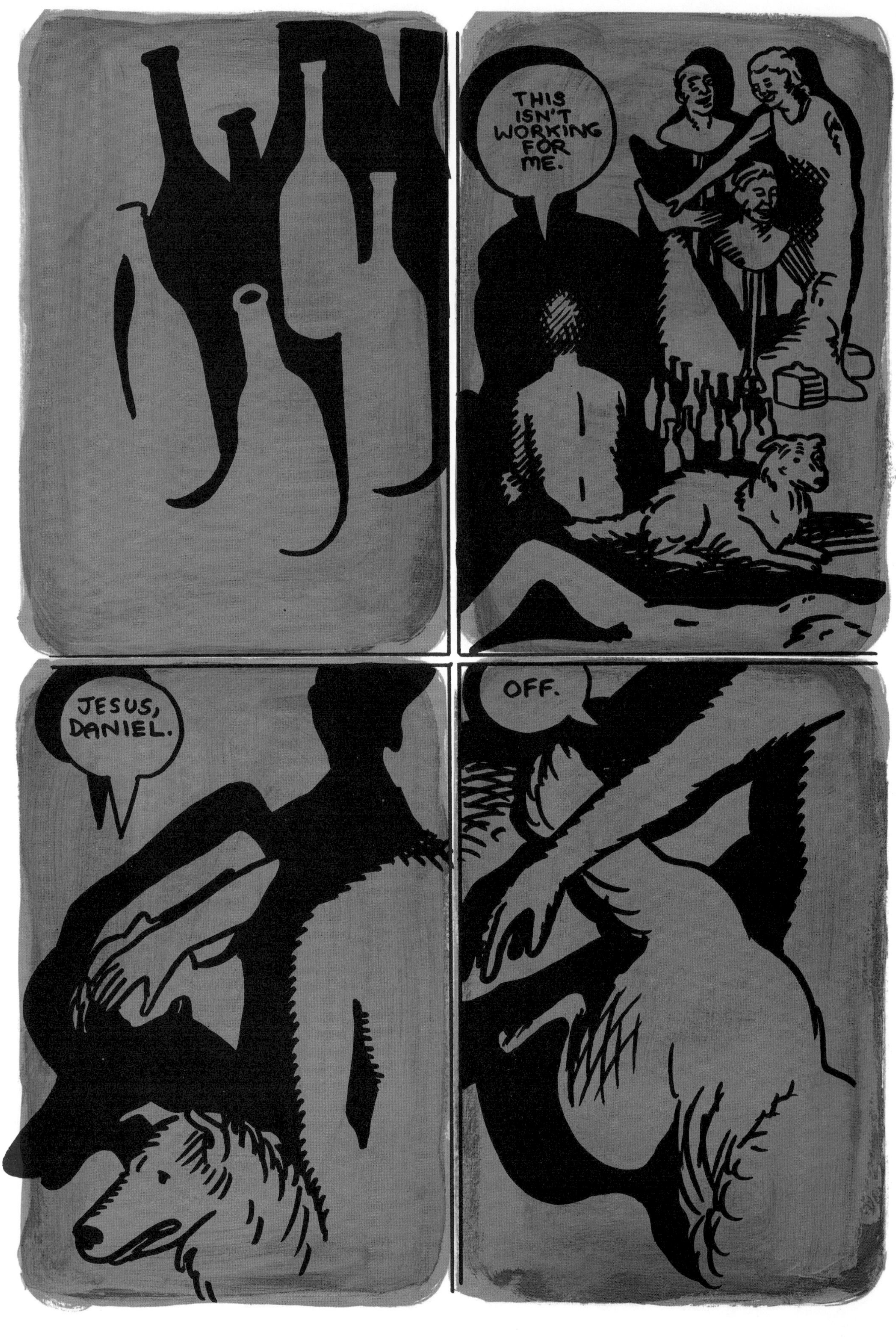
THIS ISN'T WORKING FOR ME.
JESUS, DANIEL.
OFF.

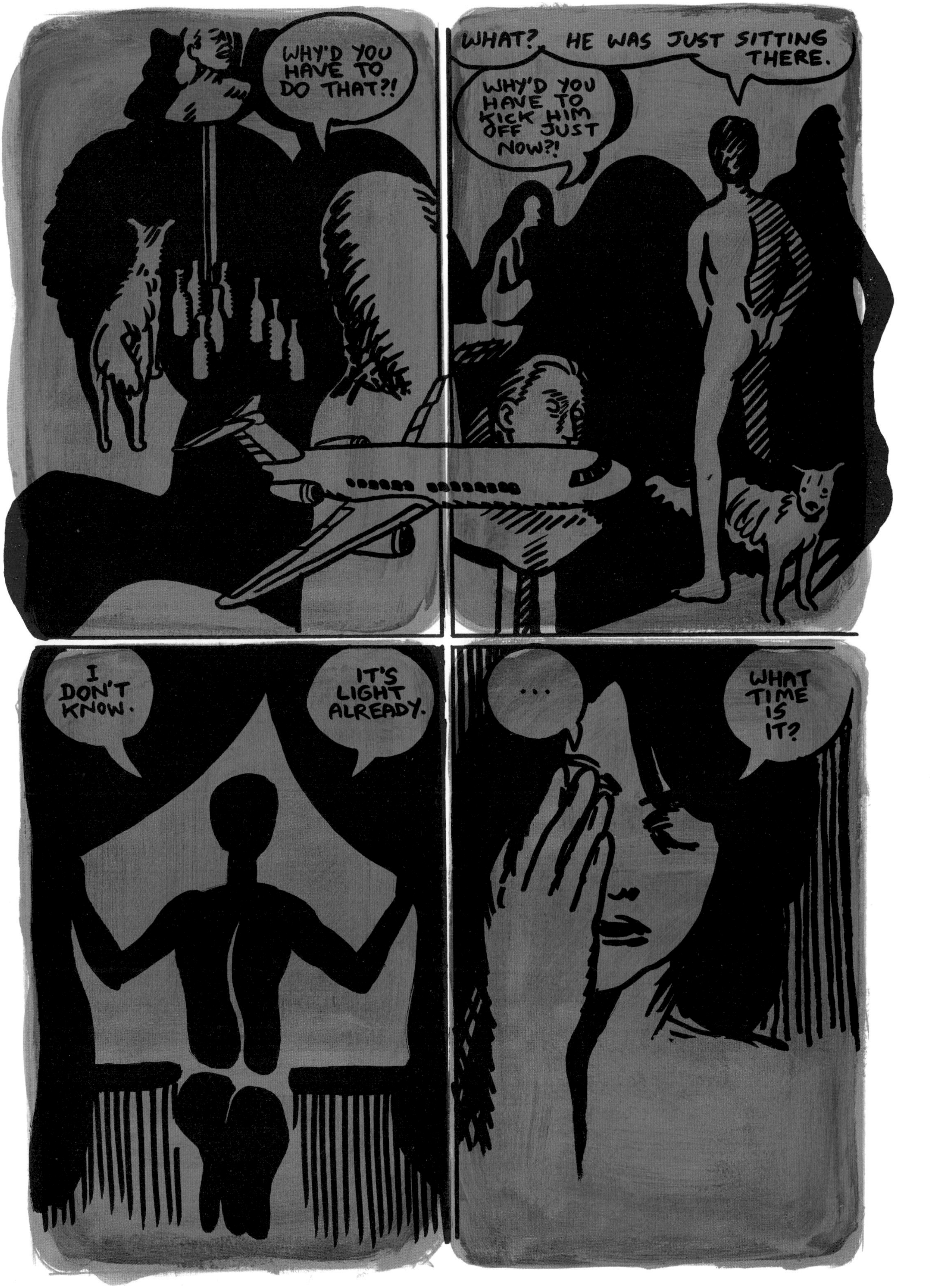
WHY'D YOU HAVE TO DO THAT?!
WHAT? HE WAS JUST SITTING THERE.
WHY'D YOU HAVE TO KICK HIM OFF JUST NOW?!
I DON'T KNOW.
IT'S LIGHT ALREADY.
...
WHAT TIME IS IT?

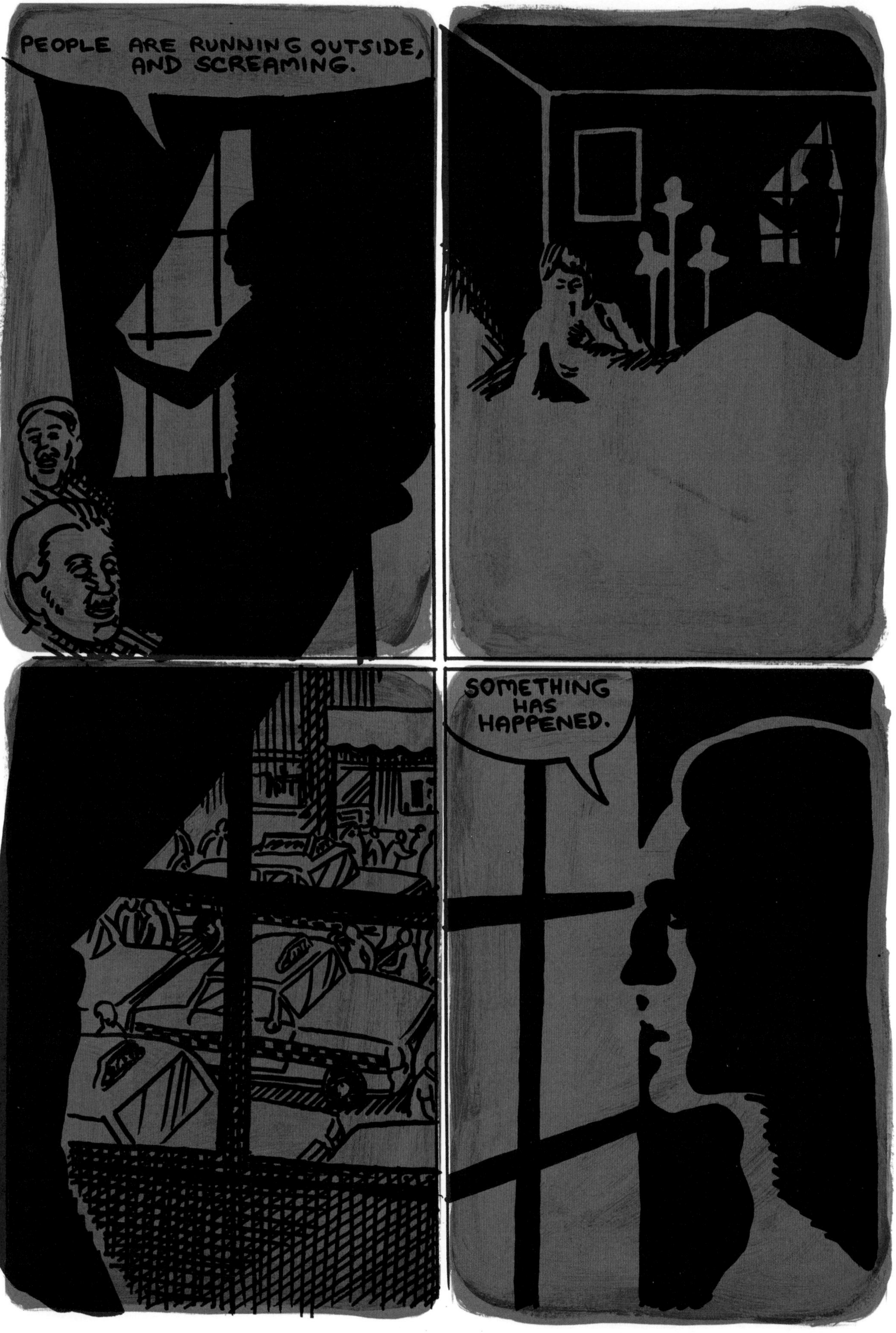
PEOPLE ARE RUNNING OUTSIDE, AND SCREAMING.
SOMETHING HAS HAPPENED.

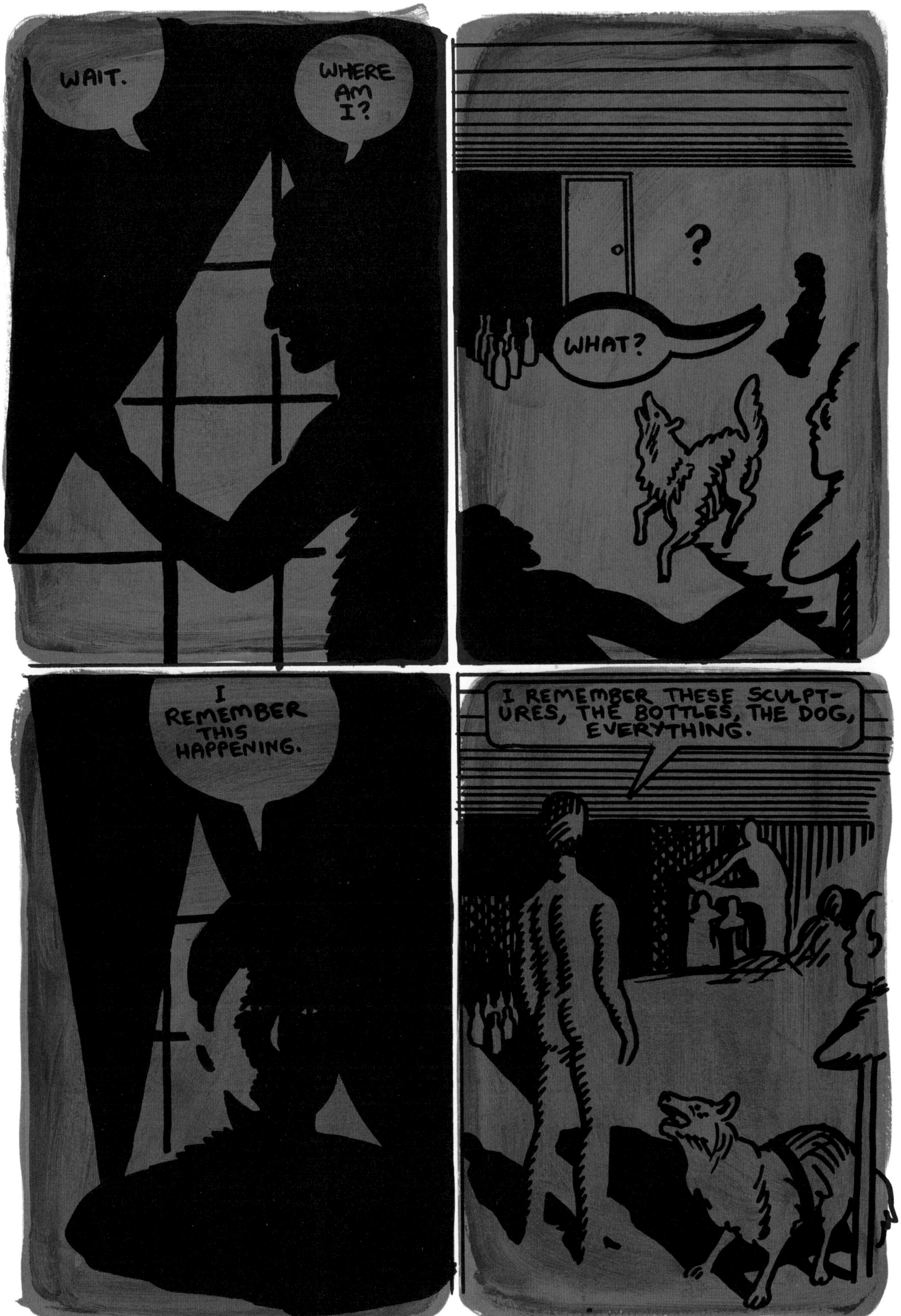
WAIT.
WHERE AM I?
?
WHAT?
I REMEMBER THIS HAPPENING.
I REMEMBER THESE SCULPTURES, THE BOTTLES, THE DOG, EVERYTHING.

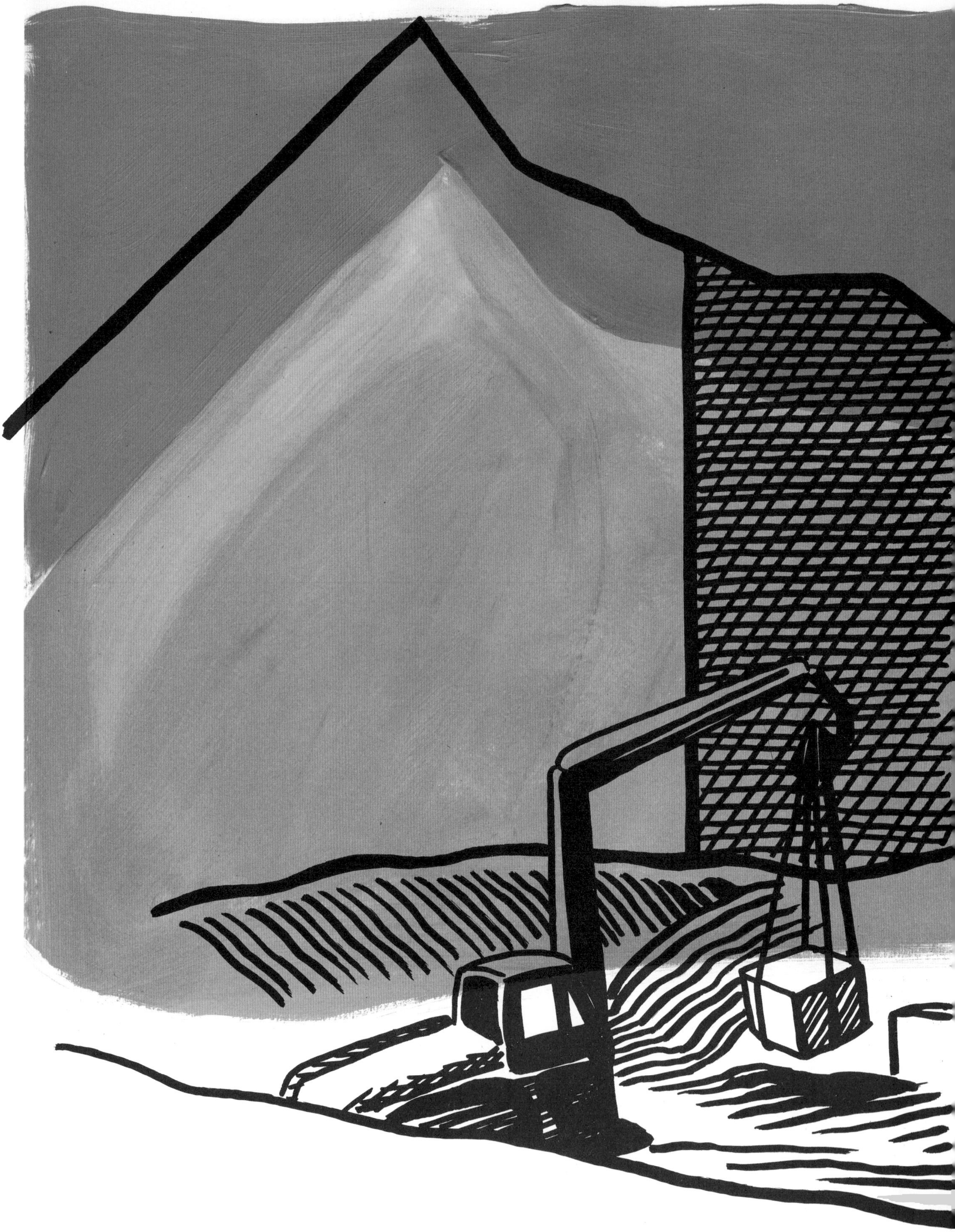

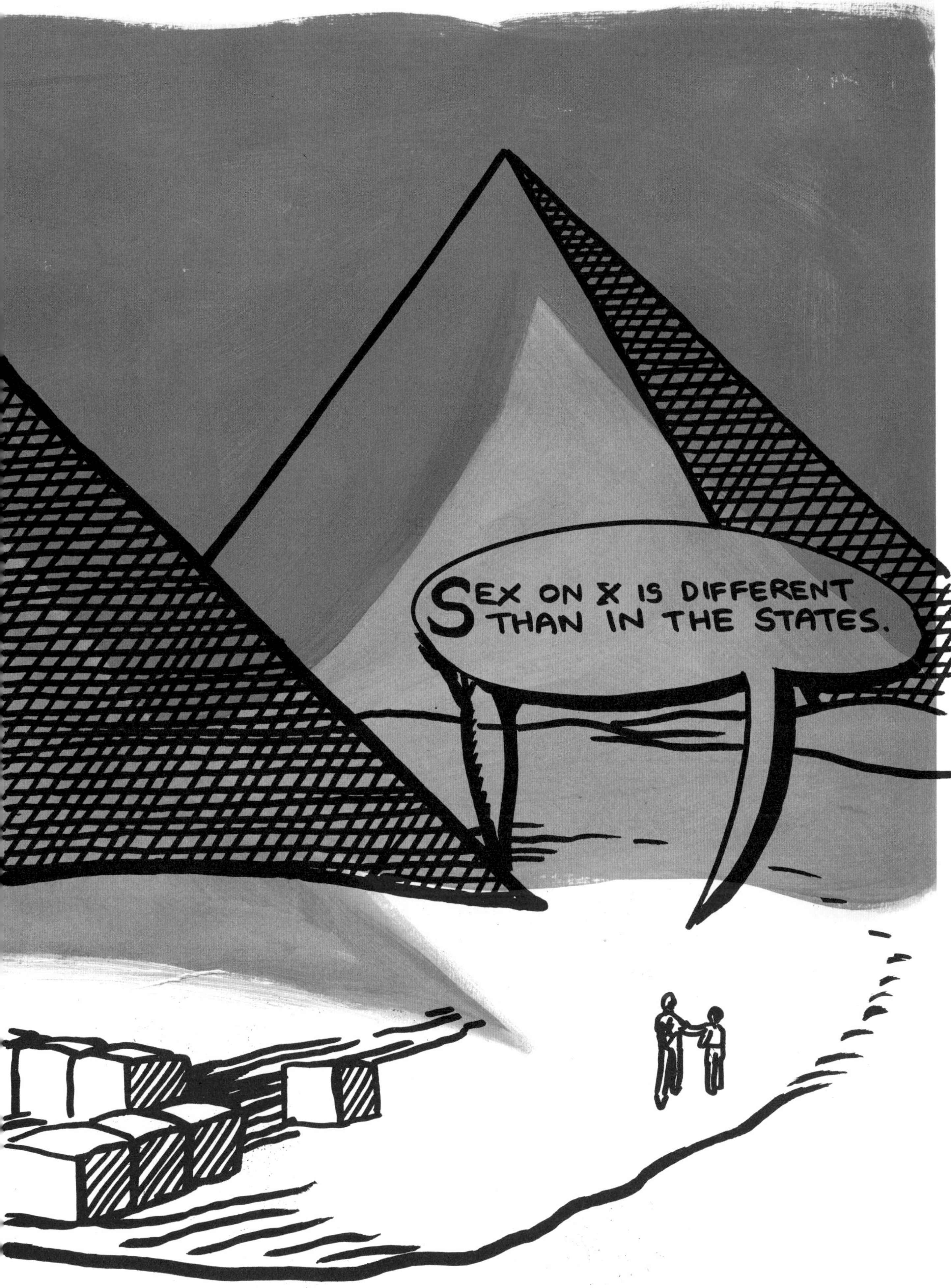
SEX ON X IS DIFFERENT THAN IN THE STATES.

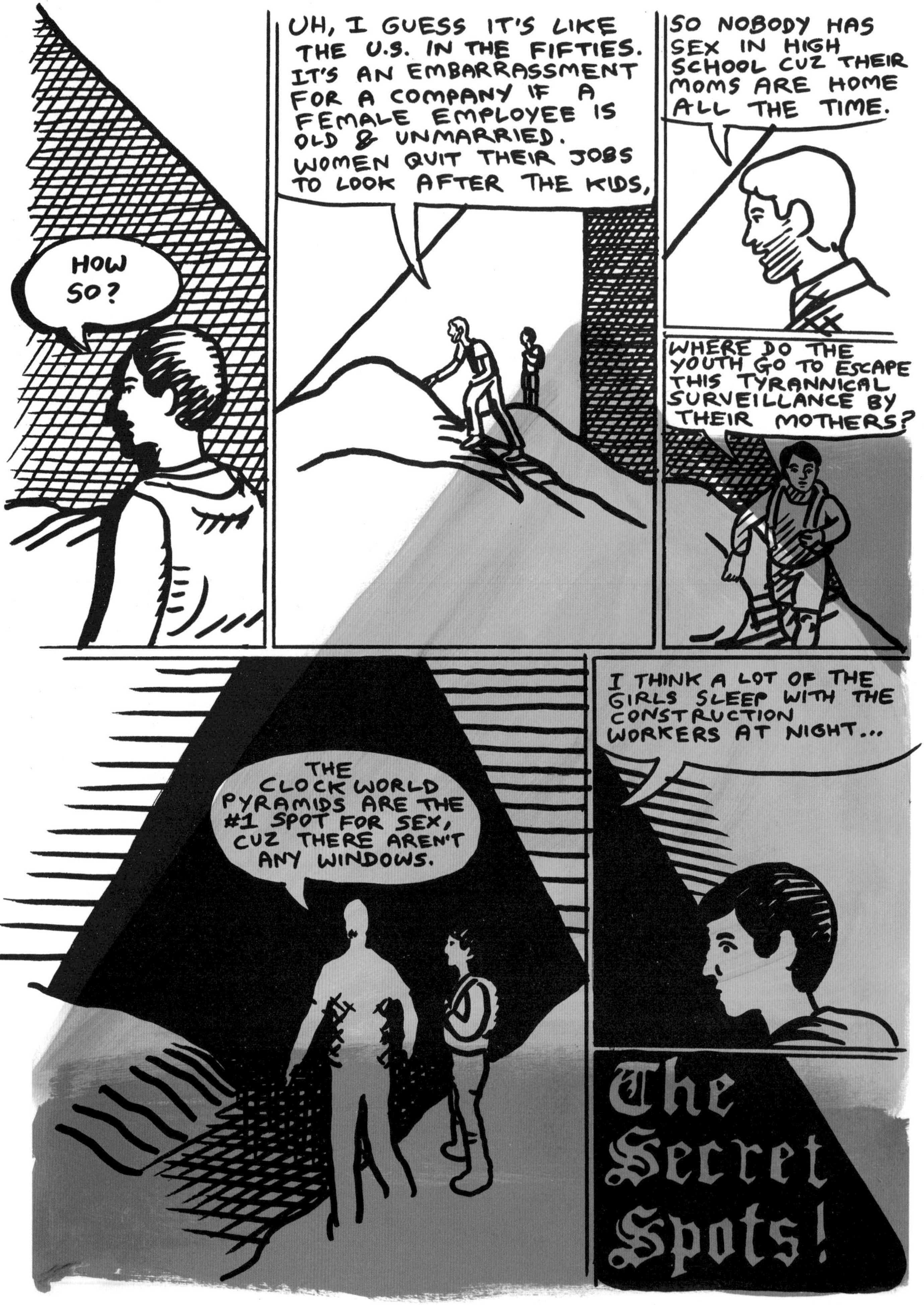
HOW SO?
UH, I GUESS IT'S LIKE THE U.S. IN THE FIFTIES. IT'S AN EMBARRASSMENT FOR A COMPANY IF A FEMALE EMPLOYEE IS OLD & UNMARRIED. WOMEN QUIT THEIR JOBS TO LOOK AFTER THE KIDS,
SO NOBODY HAS SEX IN HIGH SCHOOL CUZ THEIR MOMS ARE HOME ALL THE TIME.
WHERE DO THE YOUTH GO TO ESCAPE THIS TYRANNICAL SURVEILLANCE BY THEIR MOTHERS?
THE CLOCKWORLD PYRAMIDS ARE THE #1 SPOT FOR SEX, CUZ THERE AREN'T ANY WINDOWS.
I THINK A LOT OF THE GIRLS SLEEP WITH THE CONSTRUCTION WORKERS AT NIGHT...
The Secret Spots!

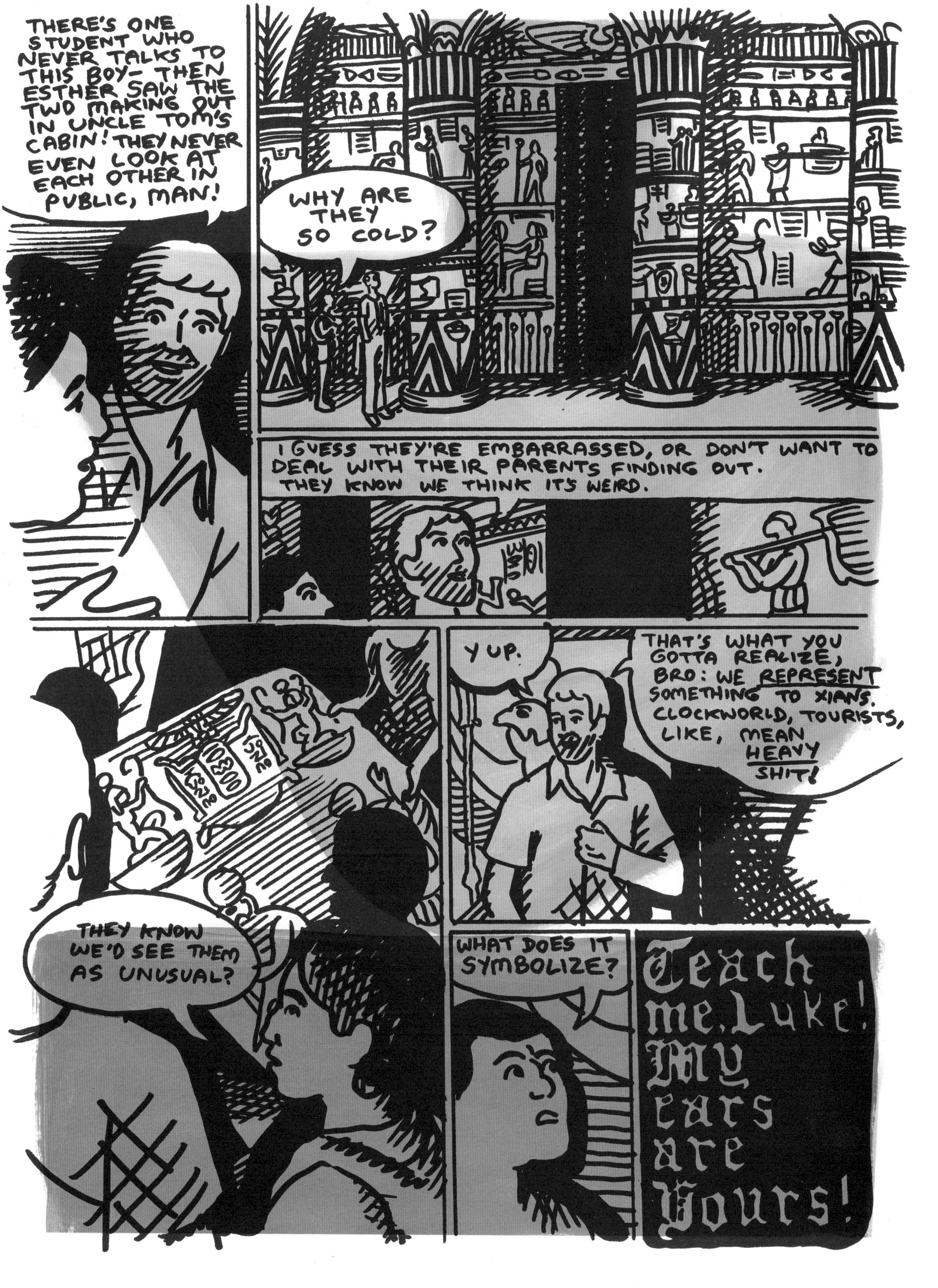
THERE'S ONE STUDENT WHO NEVER TALKS TO THIS BOY- THEN ESTHER SAW THE TWO MAKING OUT IN UNCLE TOM'S CABIN! THEY NEVER EVEN LOOK AT EACH OTHER IN PUBLIC, MAN!
WHY ARE THEY SO COLD?
I GUESS THEY'RE EMBARRASSED, OR DON'T WANT TO DEAL WITH THEIR PARENTS FINDING OUT. THEY KNOW WE THINK IT'S WEIRD.
YUP.
THAT'S WHAT YOU GOTTA REALIZE, BRO: WE REPRESENT SOMETHING TO XIANS. CLOCKWORLD, TOURISTS, LIKE, MEAN HEAVY SHIT!
THEY KNOW WE'D SEE THEM AS UNUSUAL?
WHAT DOES IT SYMBOLIZE?
Teach me, Luke! My ears are yours!

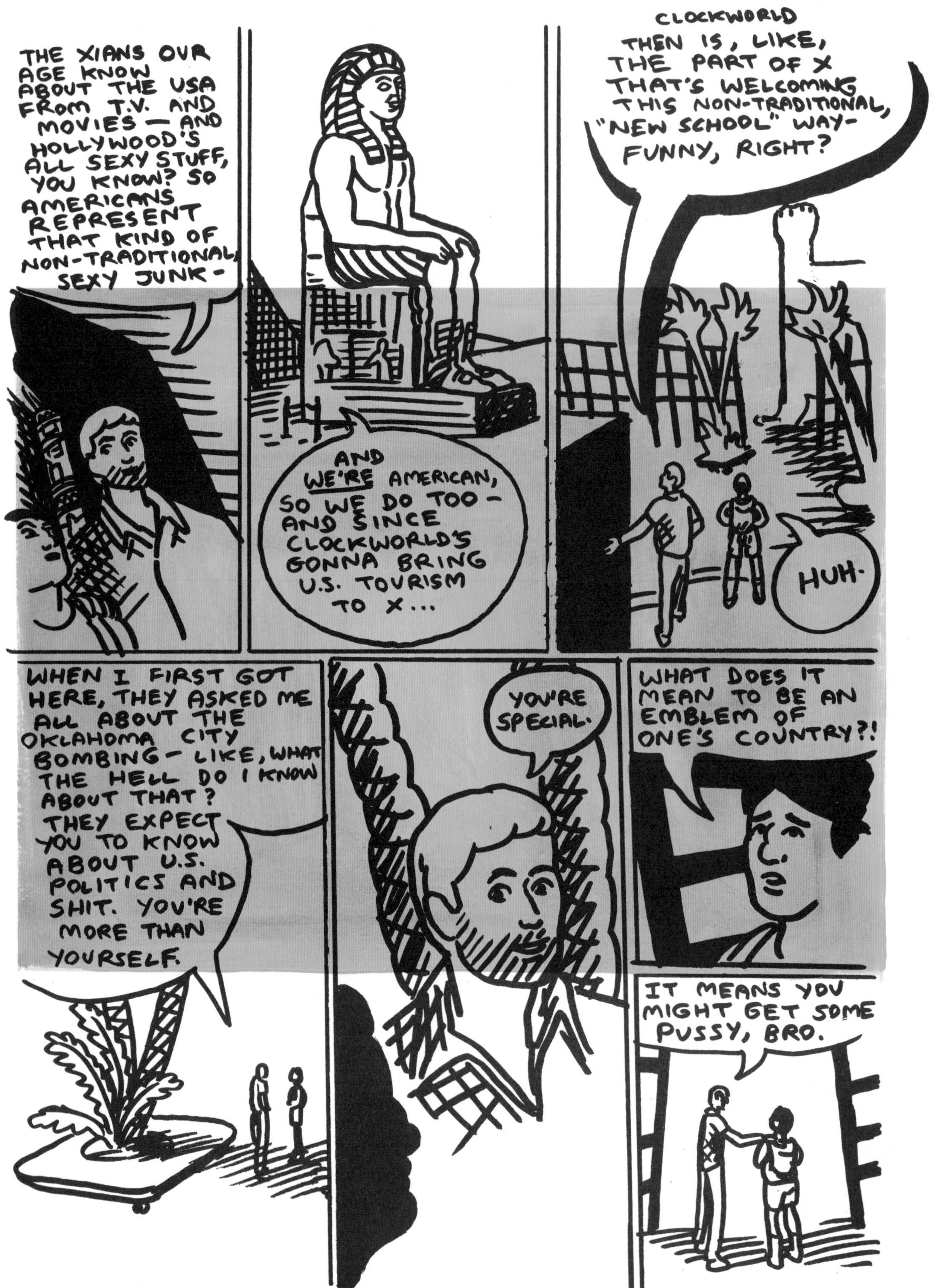
THE XIANS OUR AGE KNOW ABOUT THE USA FROM T.V. AND MOVIES — AND HOLLYWOOD'S ALL SEXY STUFF, YOU KNOW? SO AMERICANS REPRESENT THAT KIND OF NON-TRADITIONAL, SEXY JUNK-
AND WE'RE AMERICAN, SO WE DO TOO- AND SINCE CLOCKWORLD'S GONNA BRING U.S. TOURISM TO X...
CLOCKWORLD THEN IS, LIKE, THE PART OF X THAT'S WELCOMING THIS NON-TRADITIONAL, "NEW SCHOOL" WAY- FUNNY, RIGHT?
HUH.
WHEN I FIRST GOT HERE, THEY ASKED ME ALL ABOUT THE OKLAHOMA CITY BOMBING- LIKE, WHAT THE HELL DO I KNOW ABOUT THAT? THEY EXPECT YOU TO KNOW ABOUT U.S. POLITICS AND SHIT. YOU'RE MORE THAN YOURSELF.
YOU'RE SPECIAL.
WHAT DOES IT MEAN TO BE AN EMBLEM OF ONE'S COUNTRY?!
IT MEANS YOU MIGHT GET SOME PUSSY, BRO.

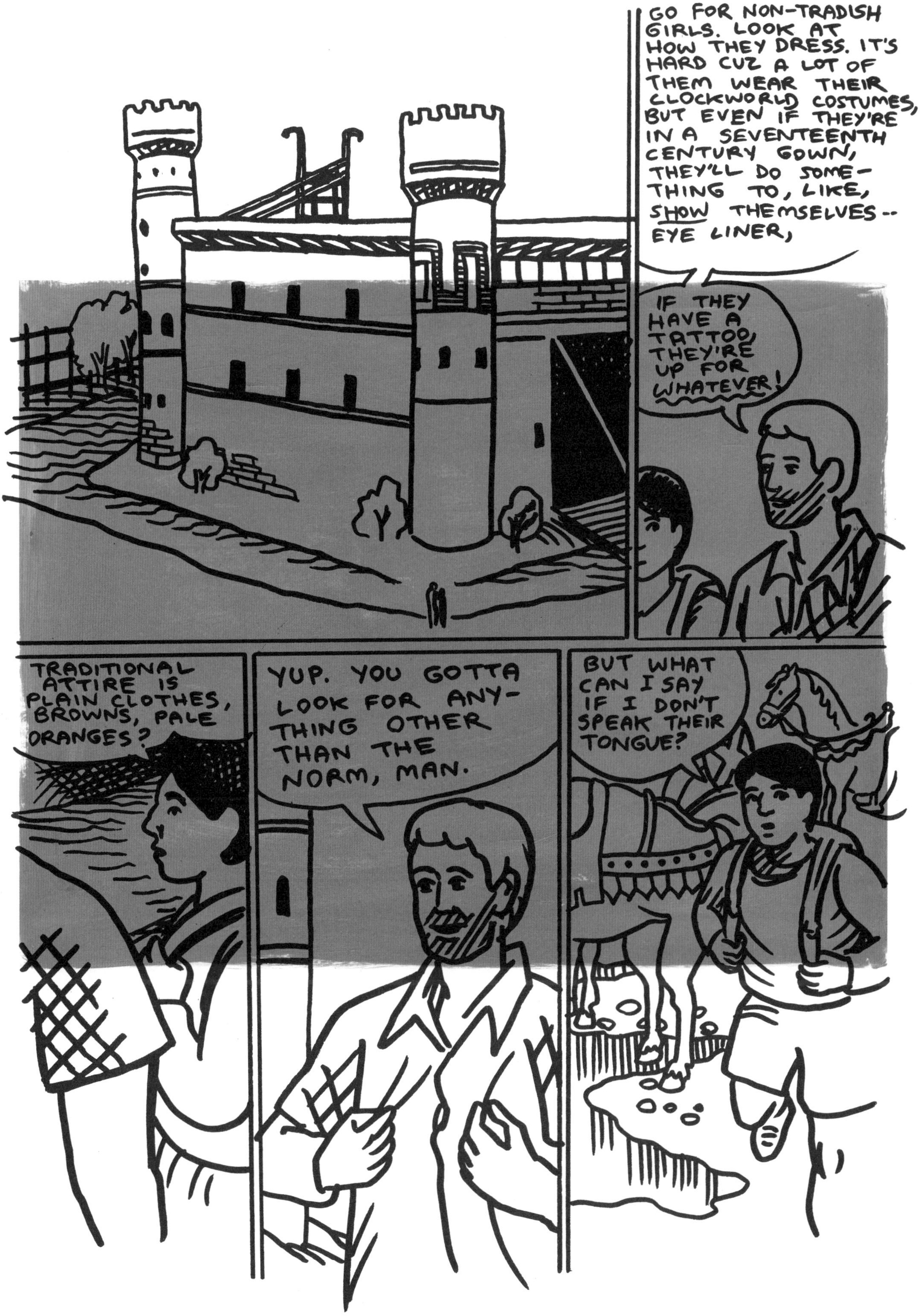
GO FOR NON-TRADISH GIRLS. LOOK AT HOW THEY DRESS. IT'S HARD CUZ A LOT OF THEM WEAR THEIR CLOCKWORLD COSTUMES, BUT EVEN IF THEY'RE IN A SEVENTEENTH CENTURY GOWN, THEY'LL DO SOME-THING TO, LIKE, SHOW THEMSELVES-- EYE LINER,
IF THEY HAVE A TATTOO, THEY'RE UP FOR WHATEVER!
TRADITIONAL ATTIRE IS PLAIN CLOTHES, BROWNS, PALE ORANGES?
YUP. YOU GOTTA LOOK FOR ANY-THING OTHER THAN THE NORM, MAN.
BUT WHAT CAN I SAY IF I DON'T SPEAK THEIR TONGUE?

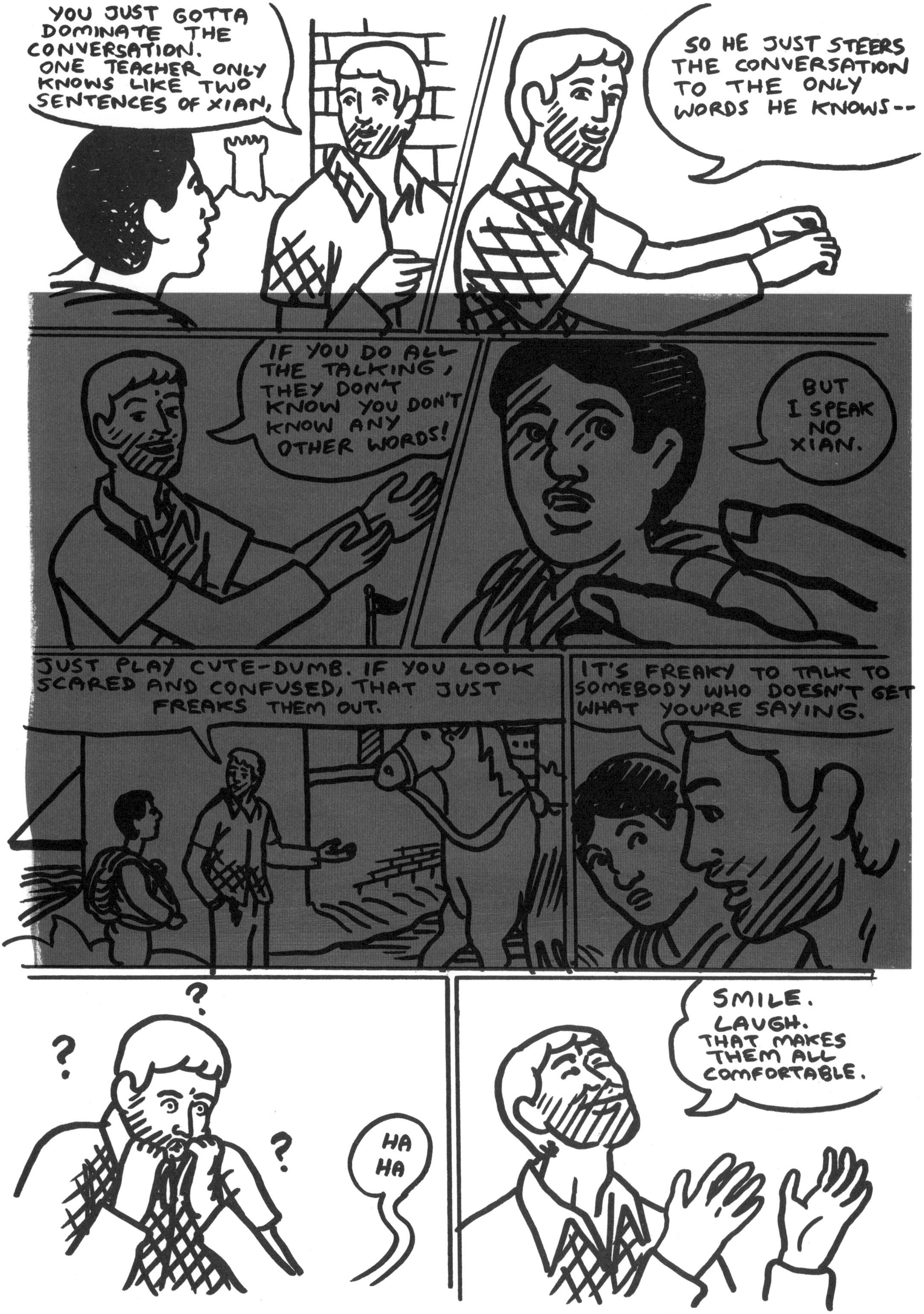
YOU JUST GOTTA DOMINATE THE CONVERSATION. ONE TEACHER ONLY KNOWS LIKE TWO SENTENCES OF XIAN,
SO HE JUST STEERS THE CONVERSATION TO THE ONLY WORDS HE KNOWS--
IF YOU DO ALL THE TALKING, THEY DON'T KNOW YOU DON'T KNOW ANY OTHER WORDS!
BUT I SPEAK NO XIAN.
JUST PLAY CUTE-DUMB. IF YOU LOOK SCARED AND CONFUSED, THAT JUST FREAKS THEM OUT.
IT'S FREAKY TO TALK TO SOMEBODY WHO DOESN'T GET WHAT YOU'RE SAYING.
?
?
?
HA HA
SMILE. LAUGH. THAT MAKES THEM ALL COMFORTABLE.

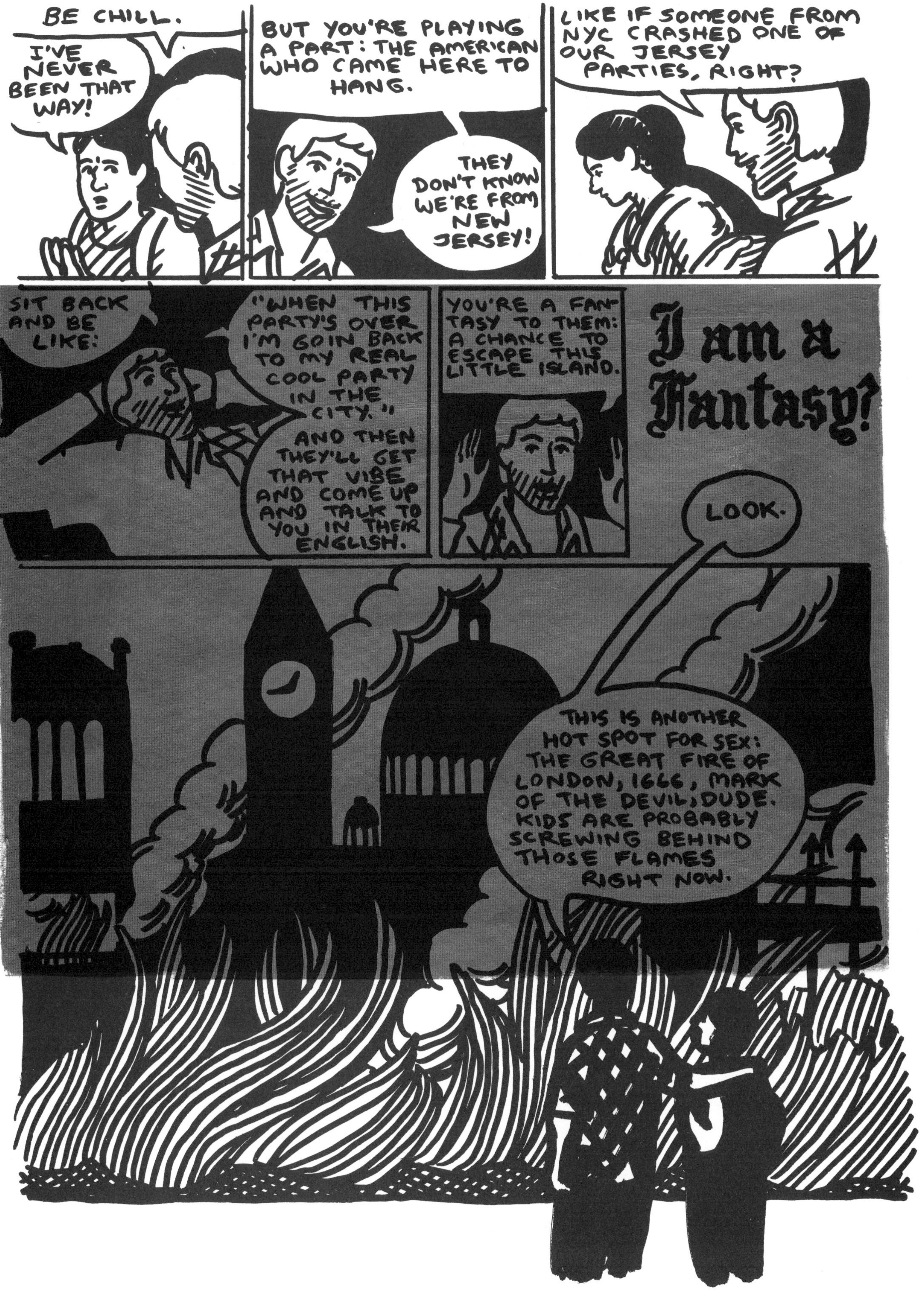
BE CHILL.
I'VE NEVER BEEN THAT WAY!
BUT YOU'RE PLAYING A PART: THE AMERICAN WHO CAME HERE TO HANG.
THEY DON'T KNOW WE'RE FROM NEW JERSEY!
LIKE IF SOMEONE FROM NYC CRASHED ONE OF OUR JERSEY PARTIES, RIGHT?
SIT BACK AND BE LIKE:
"WHEN THIS PARTY'S OVER I'M GOIN BACK TO MY REAL COOL PARTY IN THE CITY."
AND THEN THEY'LL GET THAT VIBE AND COME UP AND TALK TO YOU IN THEIR ENGLISH.
YOU'RE A FANTASY TO THEM: A CHANCE TO ESCAPE THIS LITTLE ISLAND.
I am a Fantasy?
LOOK.
THIS IS ANOTHER HOT SPOT FOR SEX: THE GREAT FIRE OF LONDON, 1666, MARK OF THE DEVIL, DUDE. KIDS ARE PROBABLY SCREWING BEHIND THOSE FLAMES RIGHT NOW.

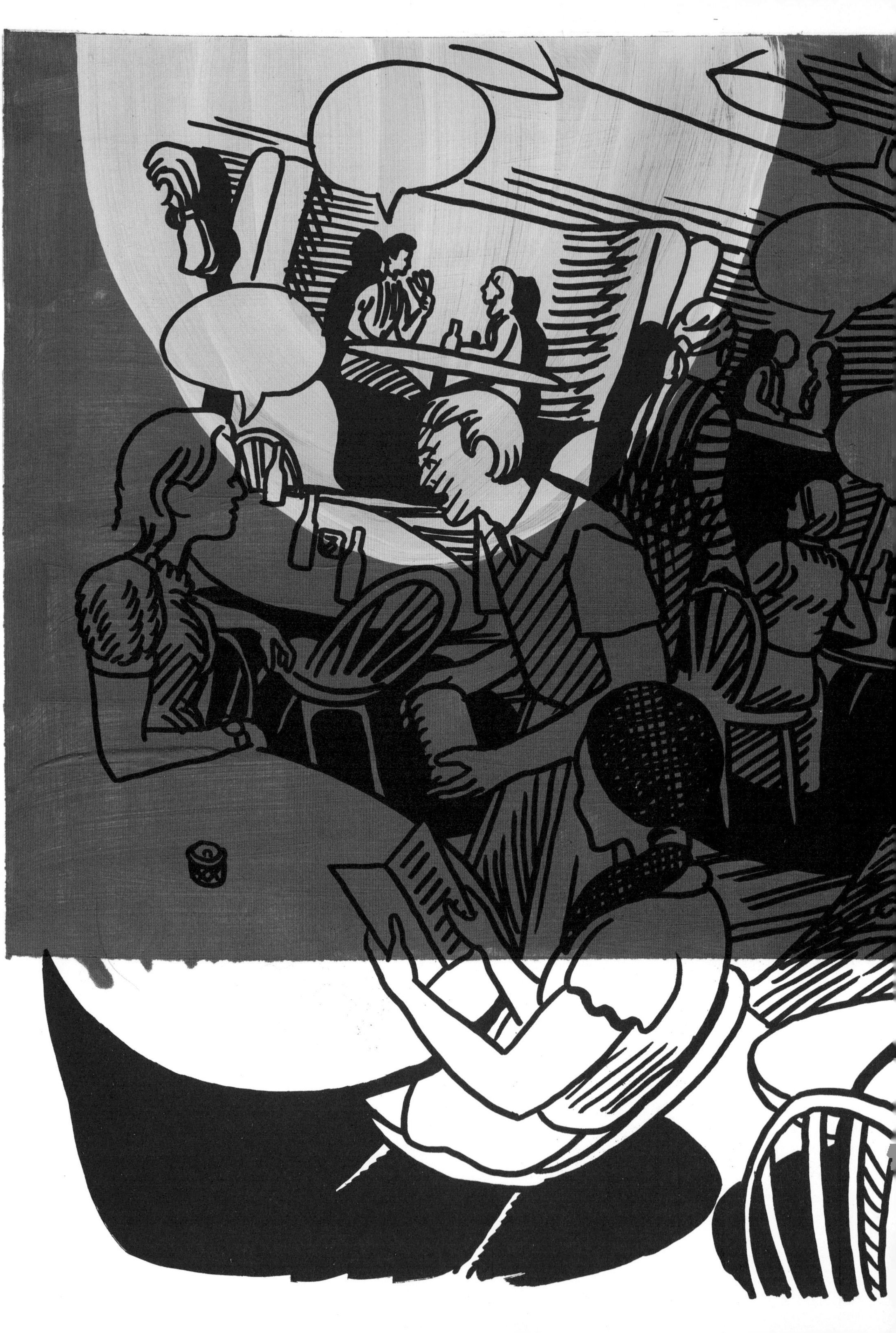

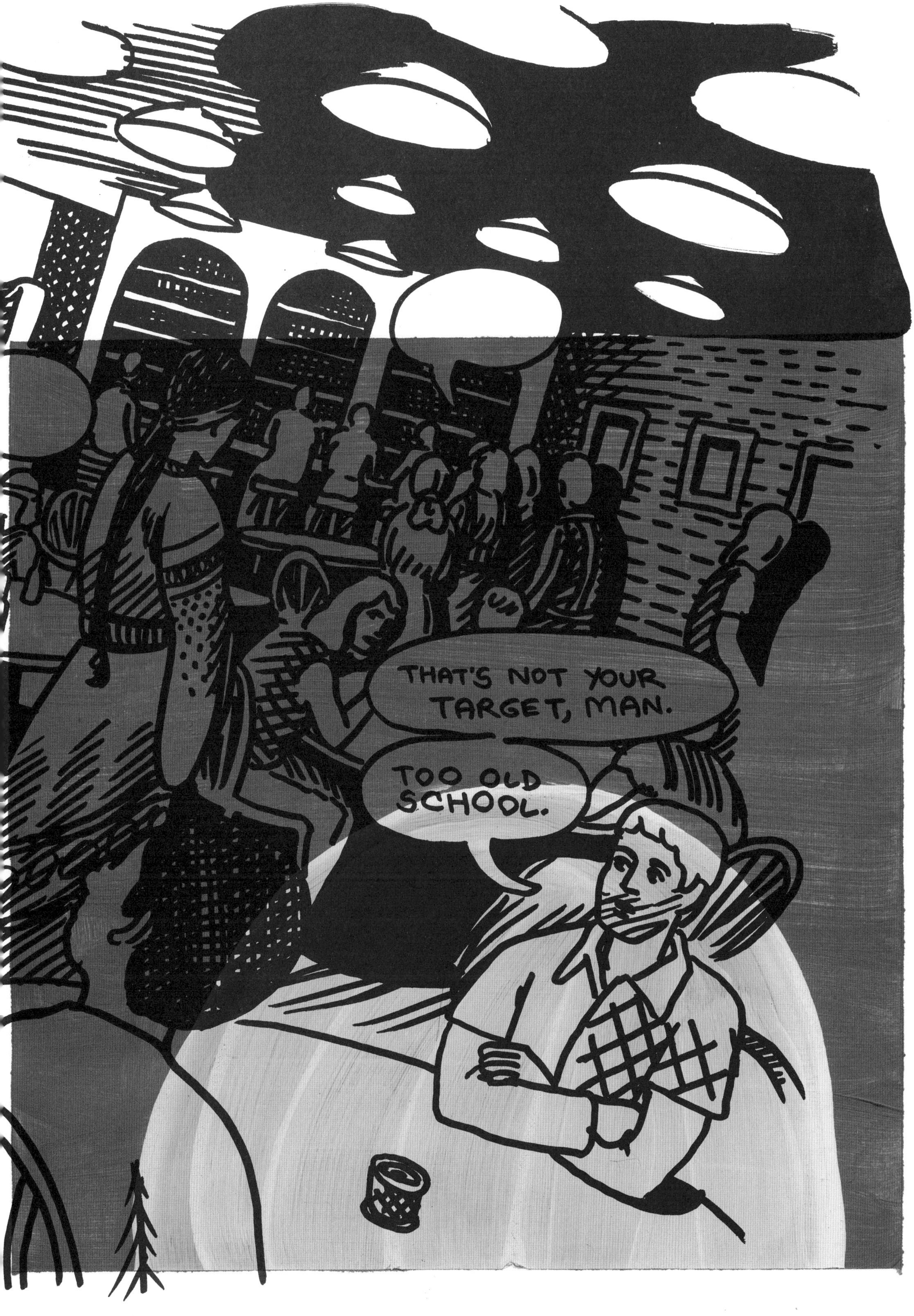
THAT'S NOT YOUR TARGET, MAN.
TOO OLD SCHOOL.

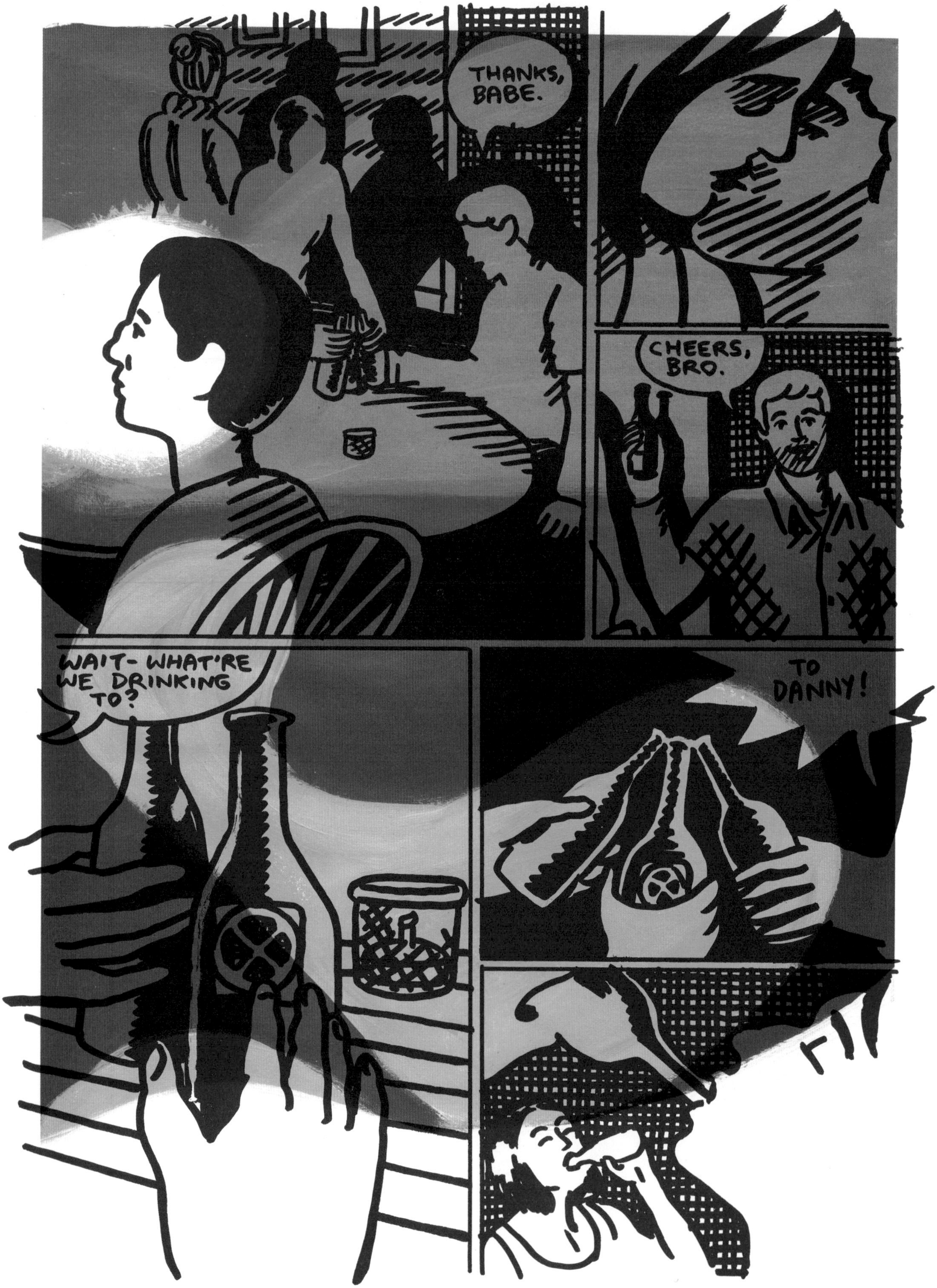
THANKS, BABE.
CHEERS, BRO.
WAIT- WHAT'RE WE DRINKING TO?
TO DANNY!

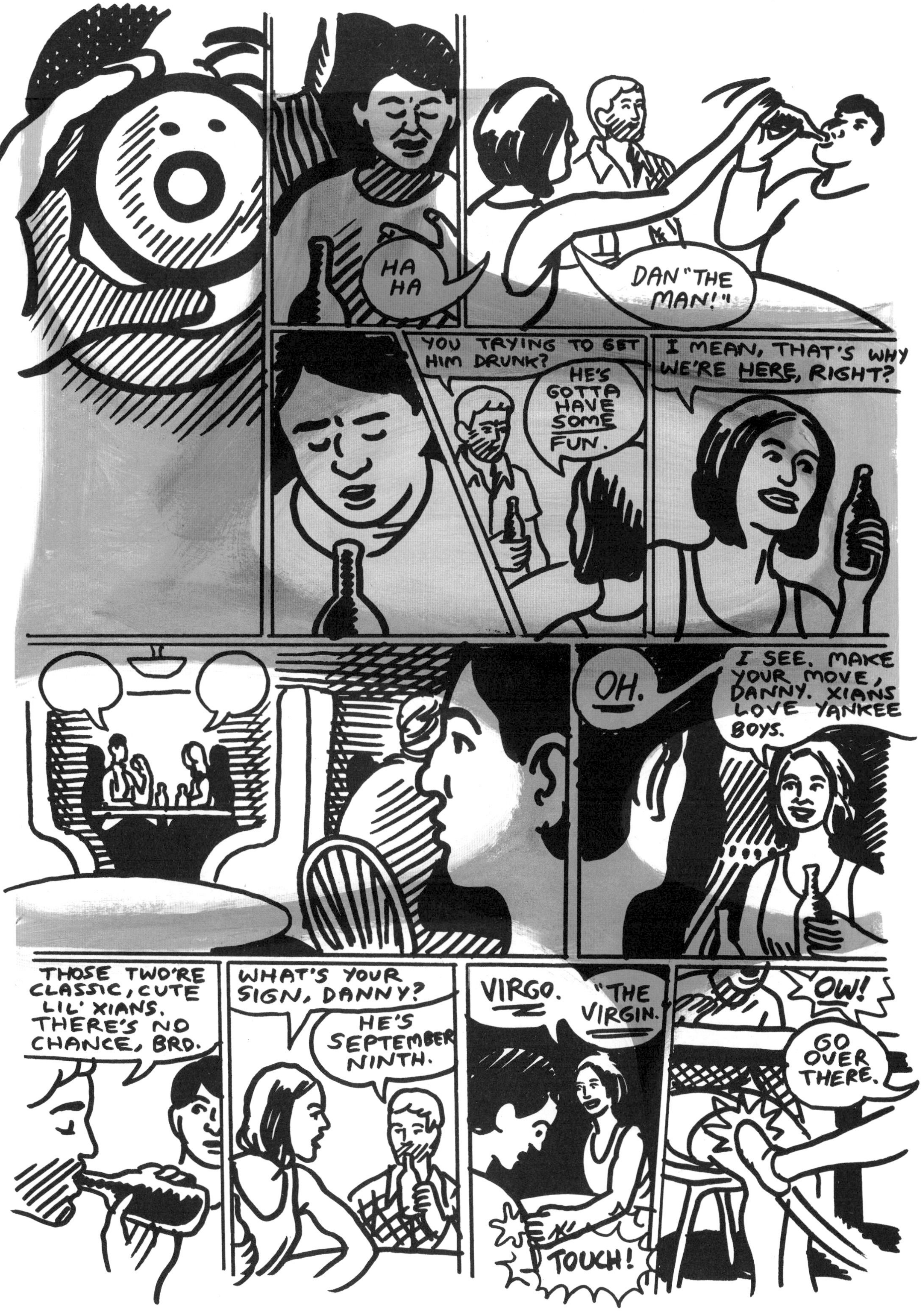

HA HA
DAN "THE MAN!"
YOU TRYING TO GET HIM DRUNK?
HE'S GOTTA HAVE SOME FUN.
I MEAN, THAT'S WHY WE'RE HERE, RIGHT?
OH.
I SEE. MAKE YOUR MOVE, DANNY. XIANS LOVE YANKEE BOYS.
THOSE TWO'RE CLASSIC, CUTE LIL' XIANS. THERE'S NO CHANCE, BRO.
WHAT'S YOUR SIGN, DANNY?
HE'S SEPTEMBER NINTH.
VIRGO.
"THE VIRGIN."
TOUCH!
OW!
GO OVER THERE.

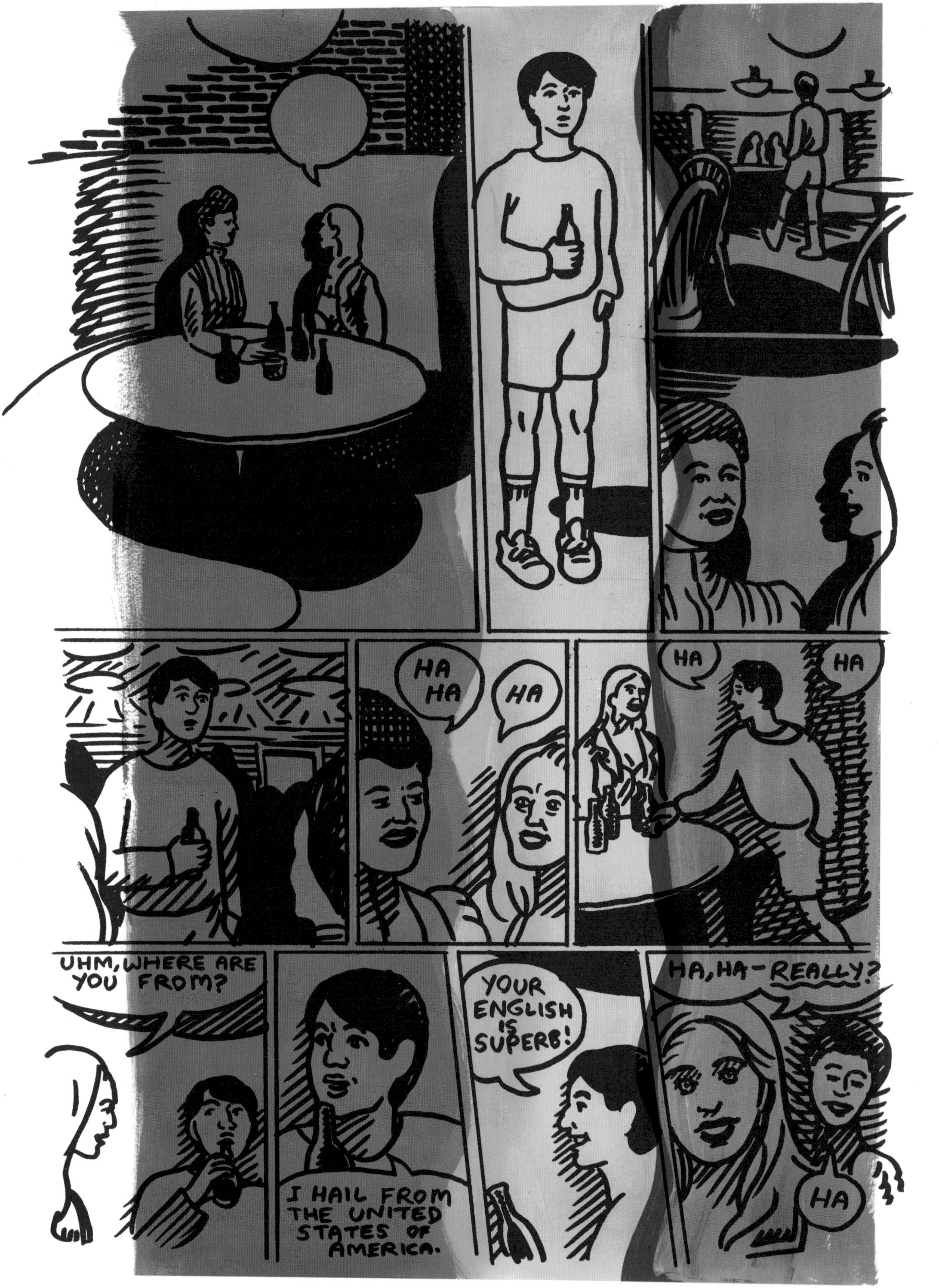
HA HA
HA
HA
HA
UHM, WHERE ARE YOU FROM?
I HAIL FROM THE UNITED STATES OF AMERICA.
YOUR ENGLISH IS SUPERB!
HA, HA-REALLY?
HA

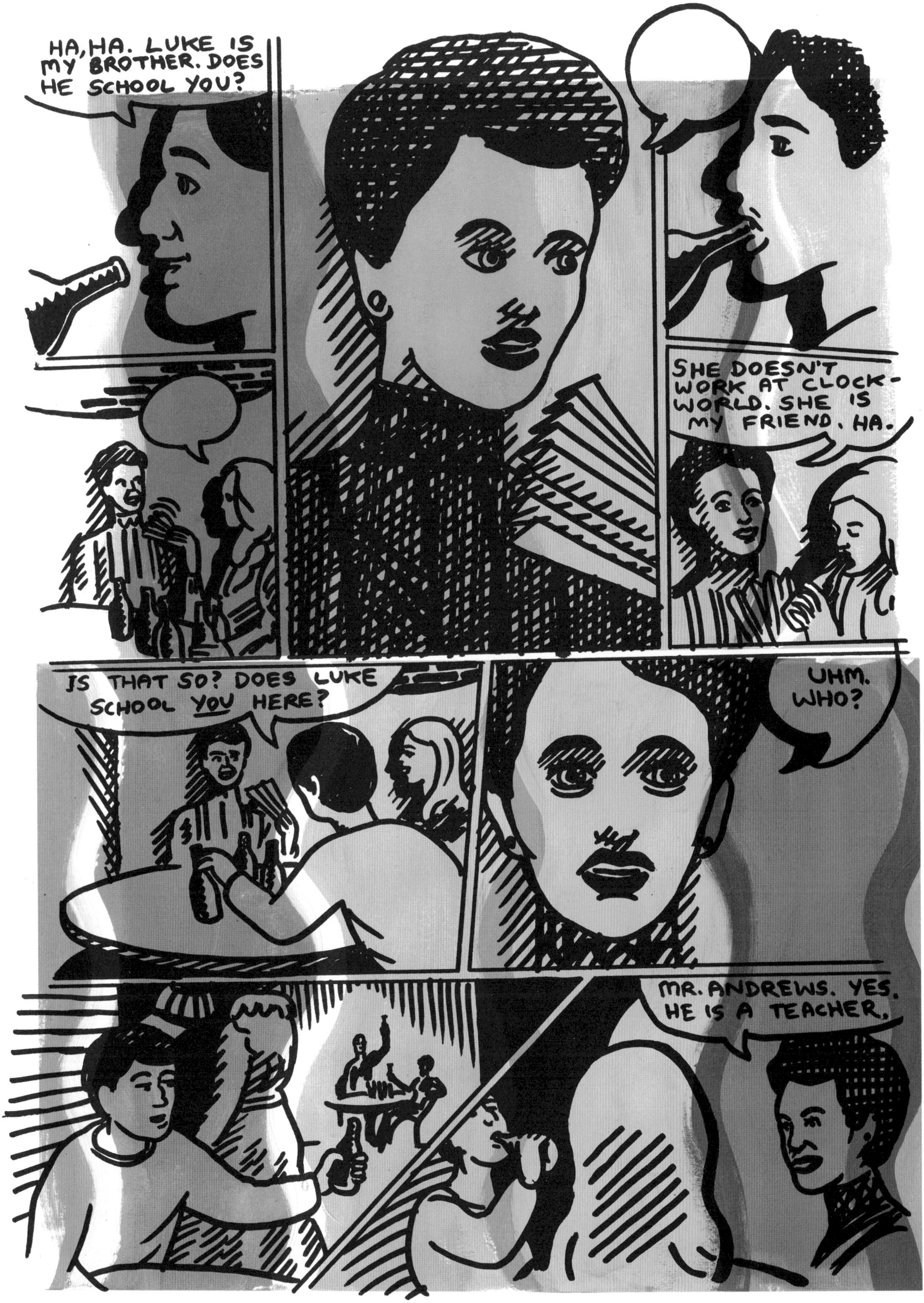
HA, HA. LUKE IS MY BROTHER. DOES HE SCHOOL YOU?
SHE DOESN'T WORK AT CLOCK-WORLD. SHE IS MY FRIEND. HA.
IS THAT SO? DOES LUKE SCHOOL YOU HERE?
UHM. WHO?
MR. ANDREWS. YES. HE IS A TEACHER.

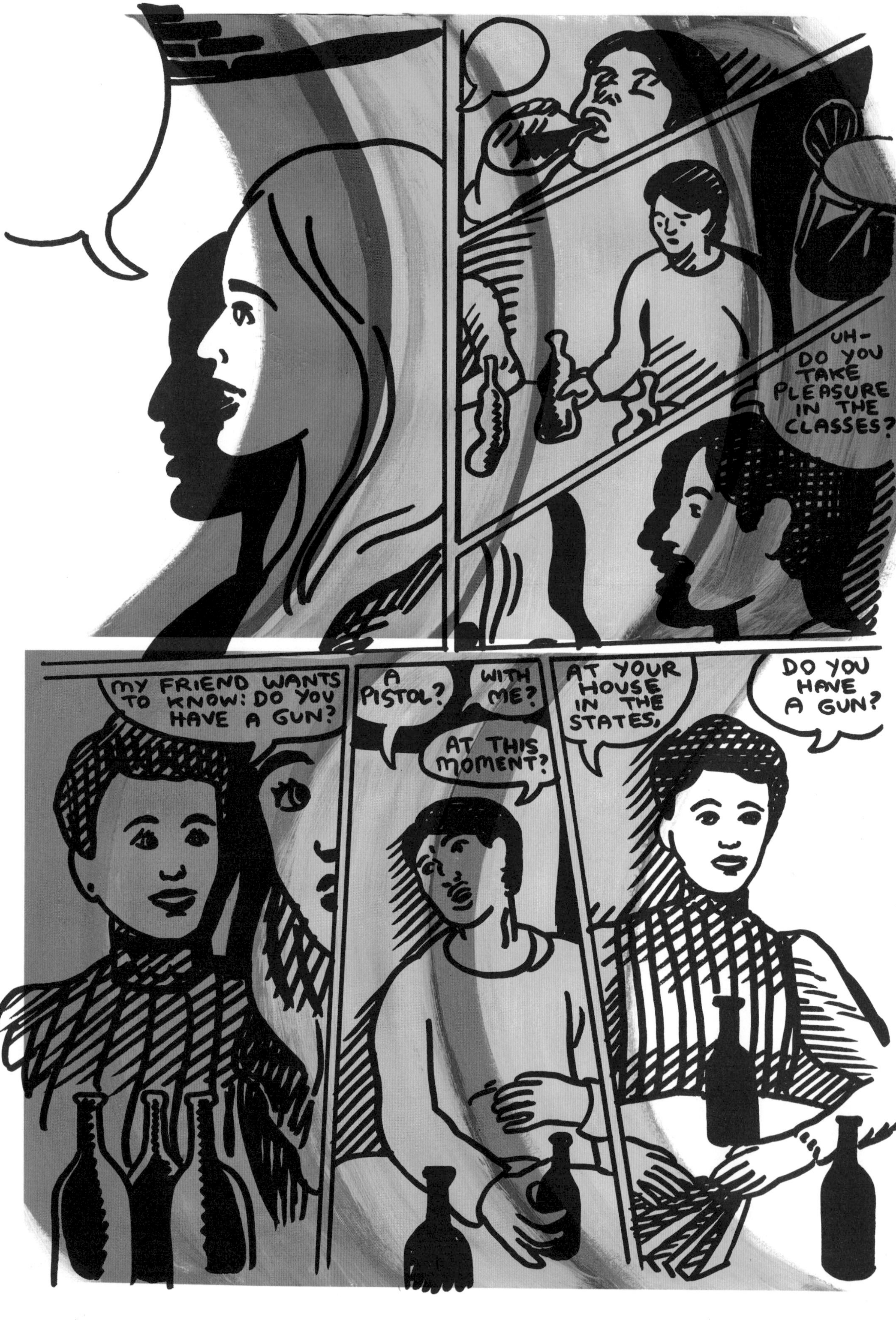
UH-
DO YOU TAKE PLEASURE IN THE CLASSES?
MY FRIEND WANTS TO KNOW: DO YOU HAVE A GUN?
A PISTOL?
WITH ME?
AT THIS MOMENT?
AT YOUR HOUSE IN THE STATES,
DO YOU HAVE A GUN?

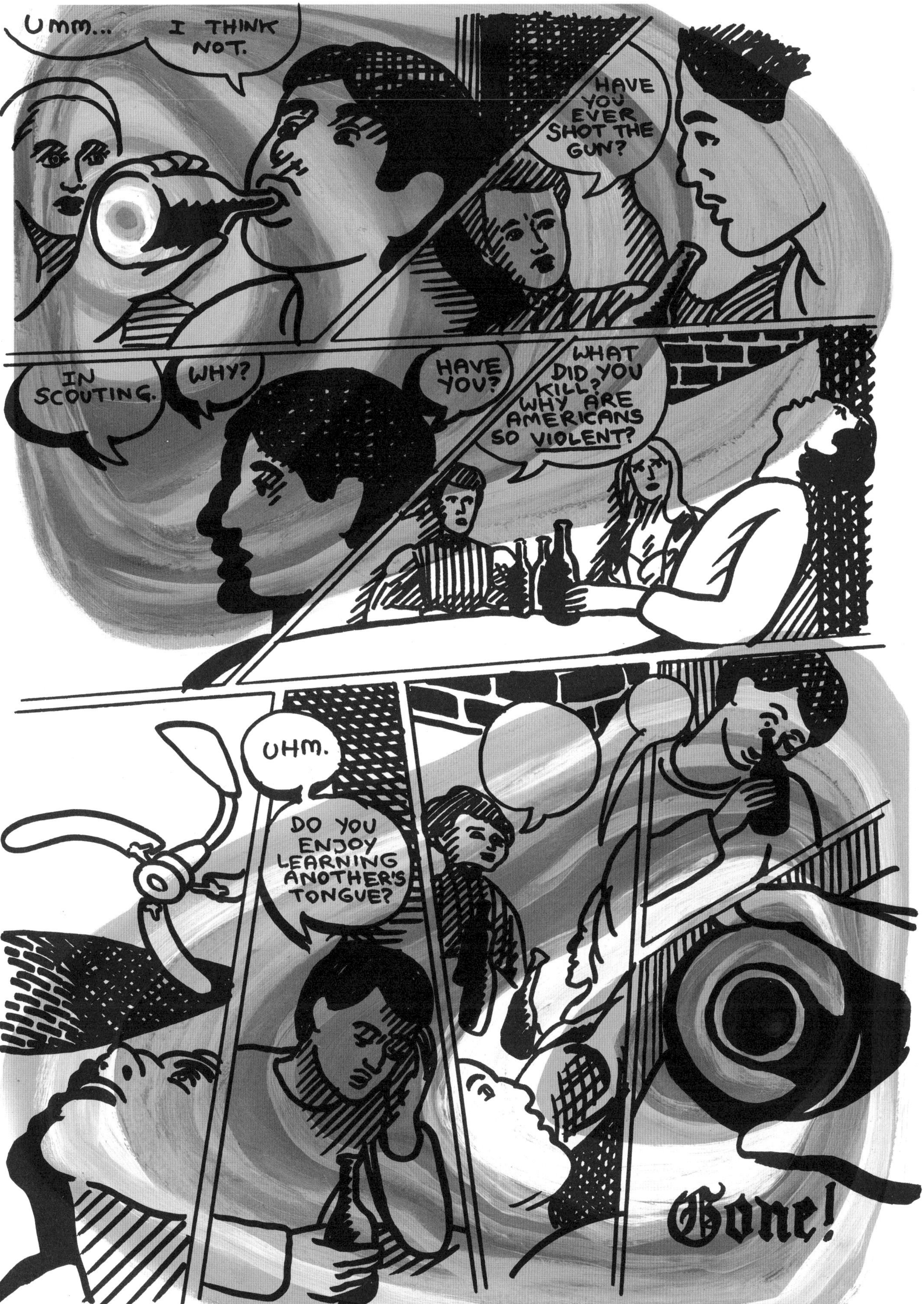
UMM...
I THINK NOT.
HAVE YOU EVER SHOT THE GUN?
IN SCOUTING.
WHY?
HAVE YOU?
WHAT DID YOU KILL? WHY ARE AMERICANS SO VIOLENT?
UHM.
DO YOU ENJOY LEARNING ANOTHER'S TONGUE?
Gone!

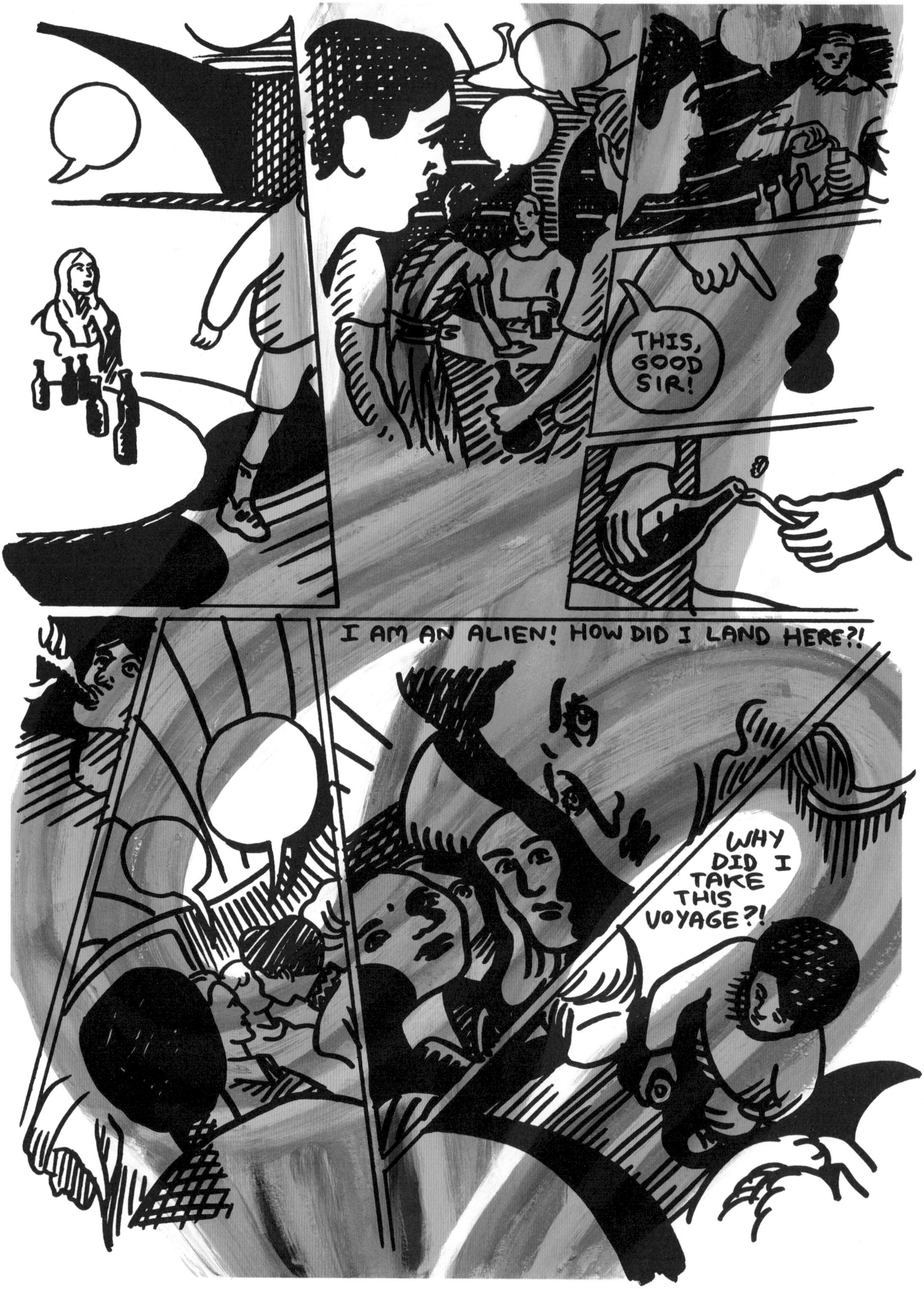
THIS, GOOD SIR!
I AM AN ALIEN! HOW DID I LAND HERE?!
WHY DID I TAKE THIS VOYAGE?!

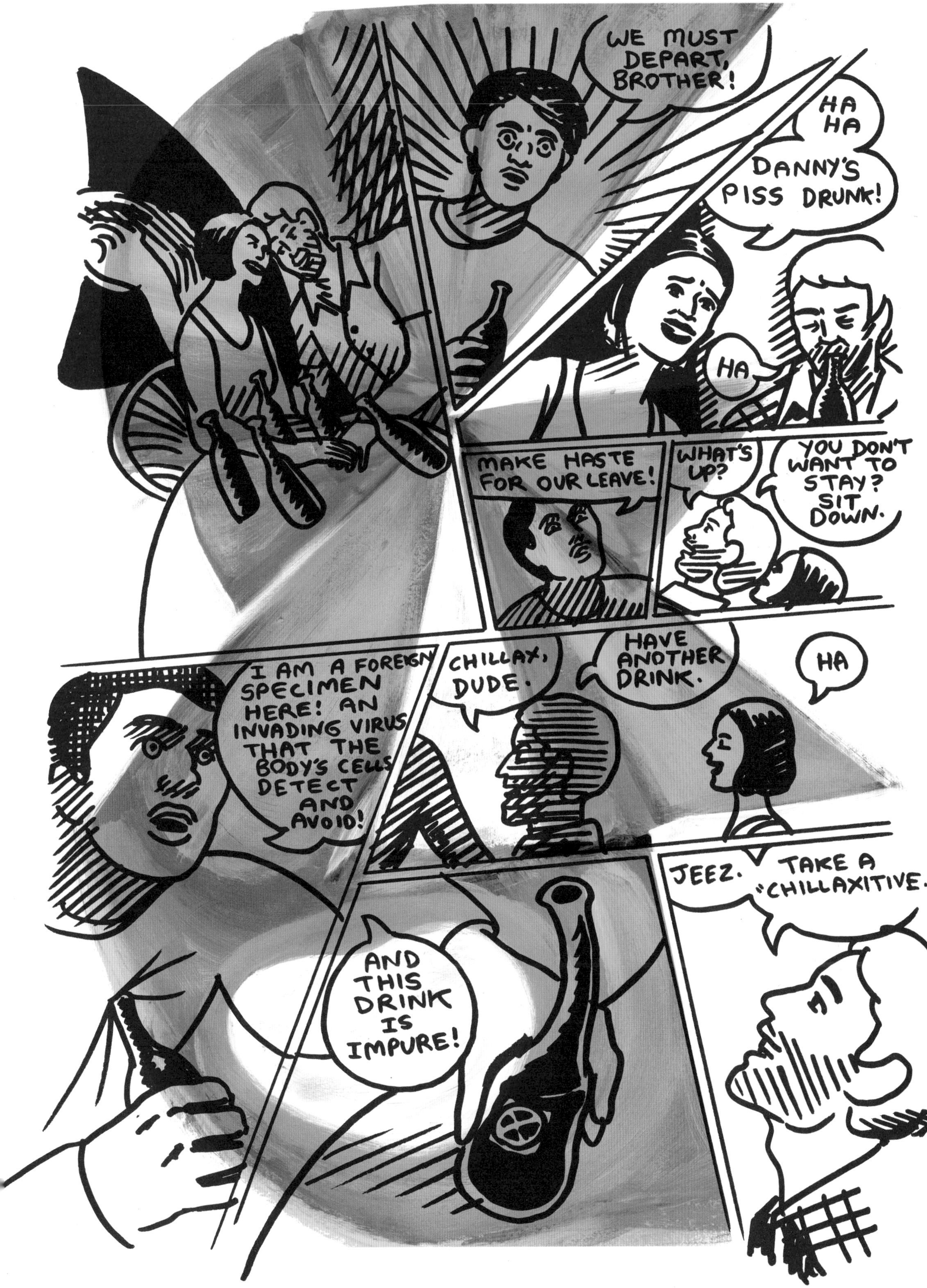
WE MUST DEPART, BROTHER!
HA HA
DANNY'S PISS DRUNK!
HA
MAKE HASTE FOR OUR LEAVE!
WHAT'S UP?
YOU DON'T WANT TO STAY? SIT DOWN.
I AM A FOREIGN SPECIMEN HERE! AN INVADING VIRUS THAT THE BODY'S CELLS DETECT AND AVOID!
CHILLAX, DUDE.
HAVE ANOTHER DRINK.
HA
AND THIS DRINK IS IMPURE!
JEEZ.
TAKE A "CHILLAXITIVE."

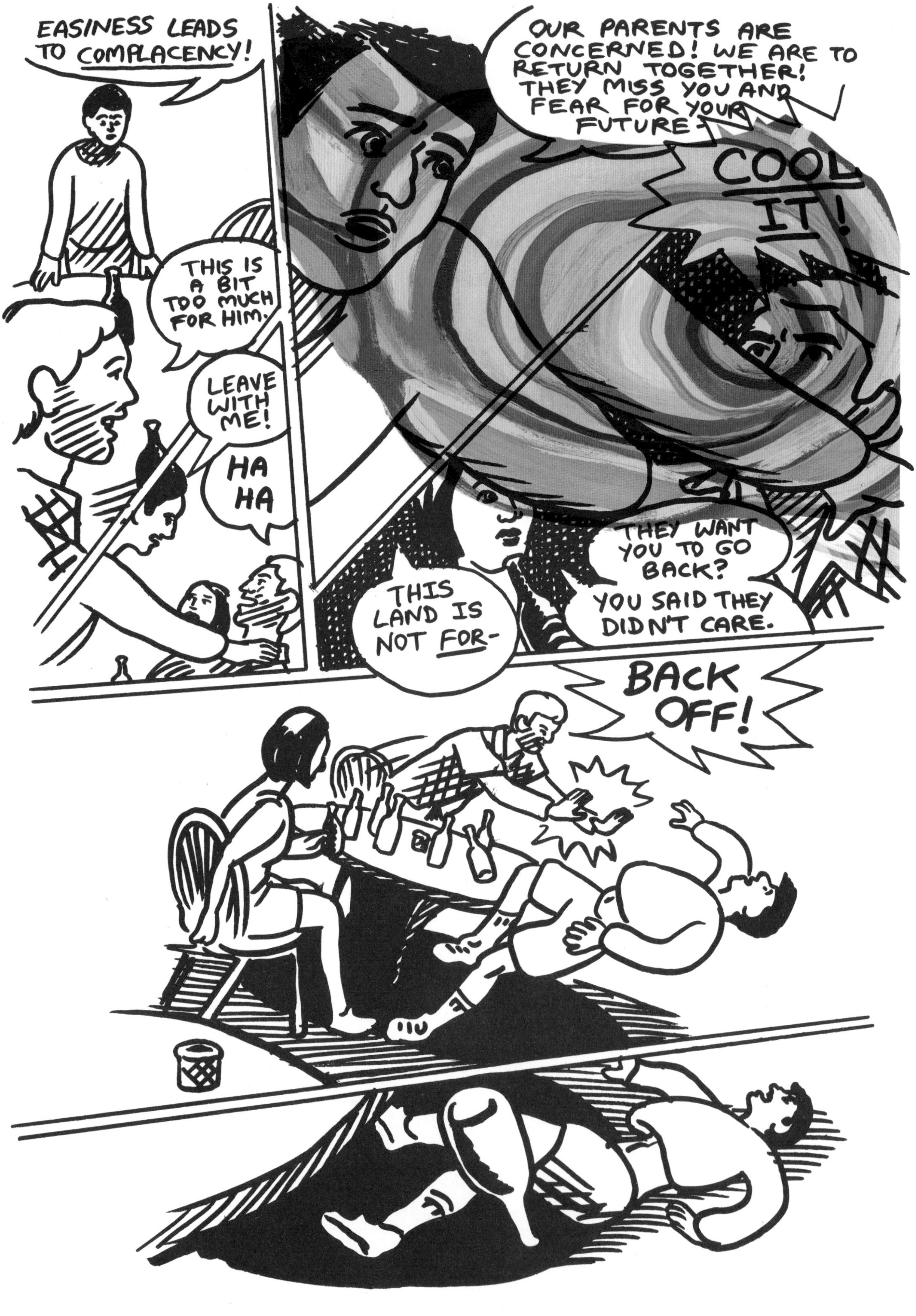
EASINESS LEADS TO COMPLACENCY!
THIS IS A BIT TOO MUCH FOR HIM.
LEAVE WITH ME!
HA HA
OUR PARENTS ARE CONCERNED! WE ARE TO RETURN TOGETHER! THEY MISS YOU AND FEAR FOR YOUR FUTURE-
COOL IT!
THEY WANT YOU TO GO BACK?
YOU SAID THEY DIDN'T CARE.
THIS LAND IS NOT FOR-
BACK OFF!

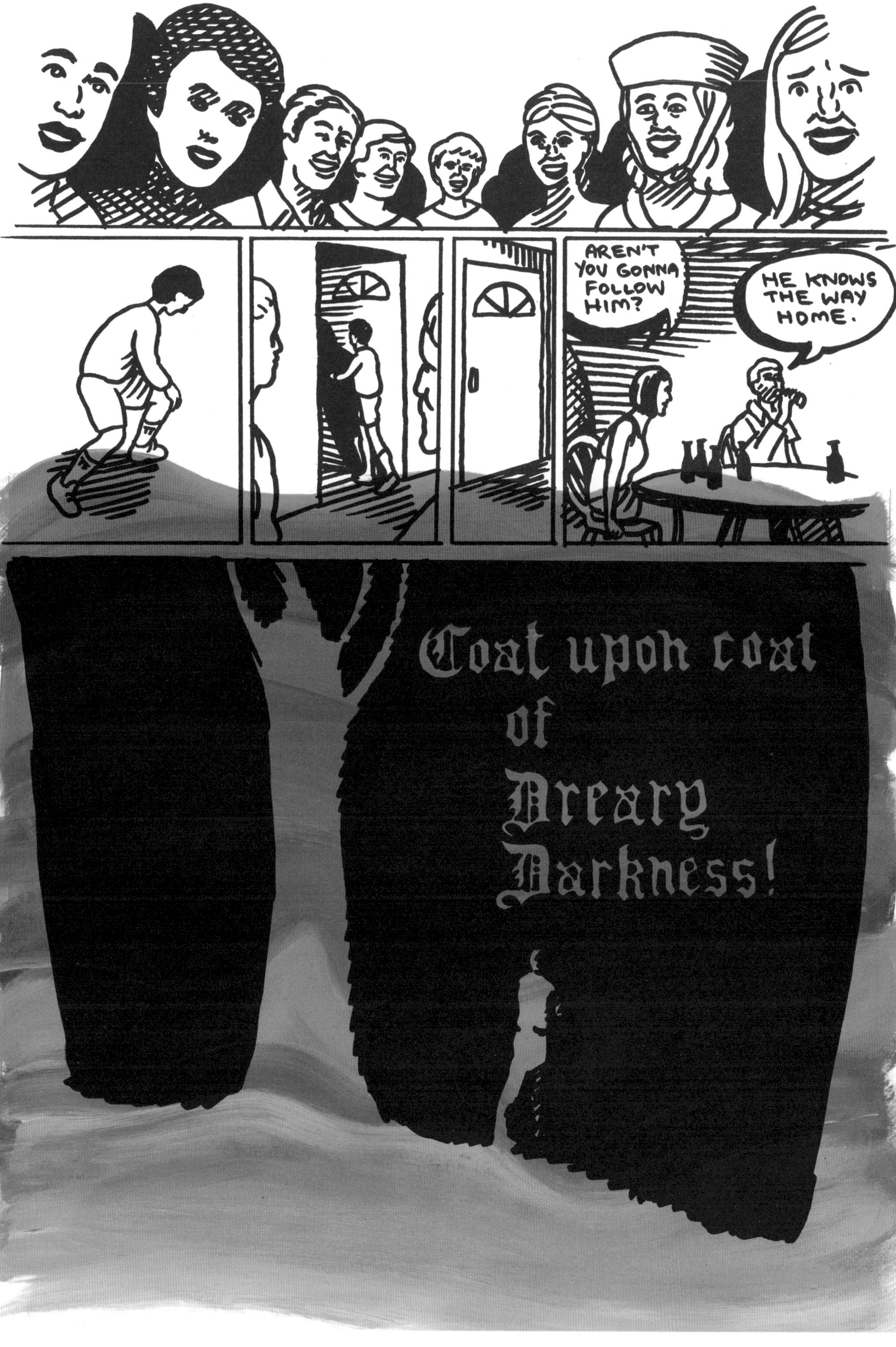
AREN'T YOU GONNA FOLLOW HIM?
HE KNOWS THE WAY HOME.
Coat upon coat of Dreary Darkness!

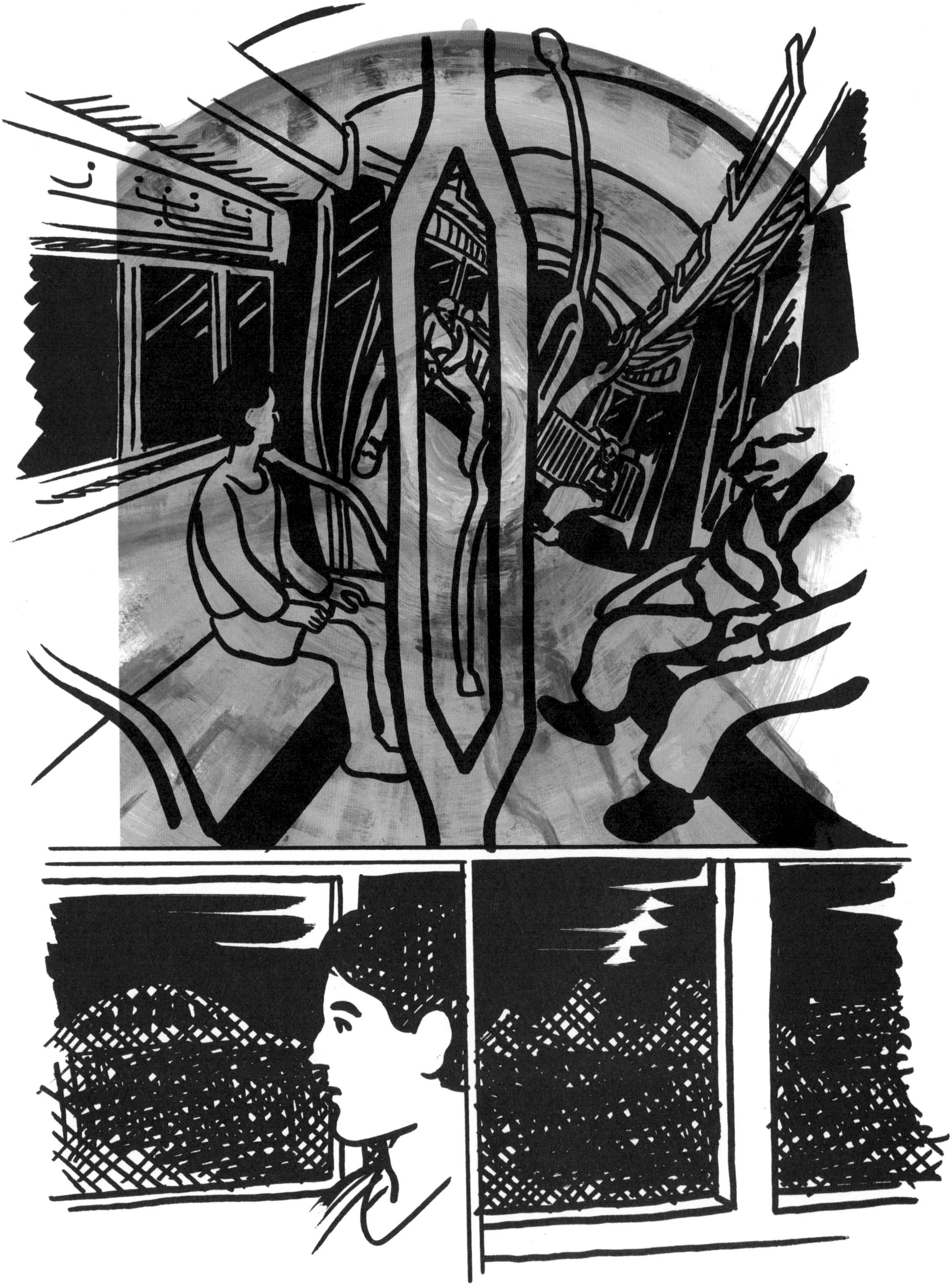

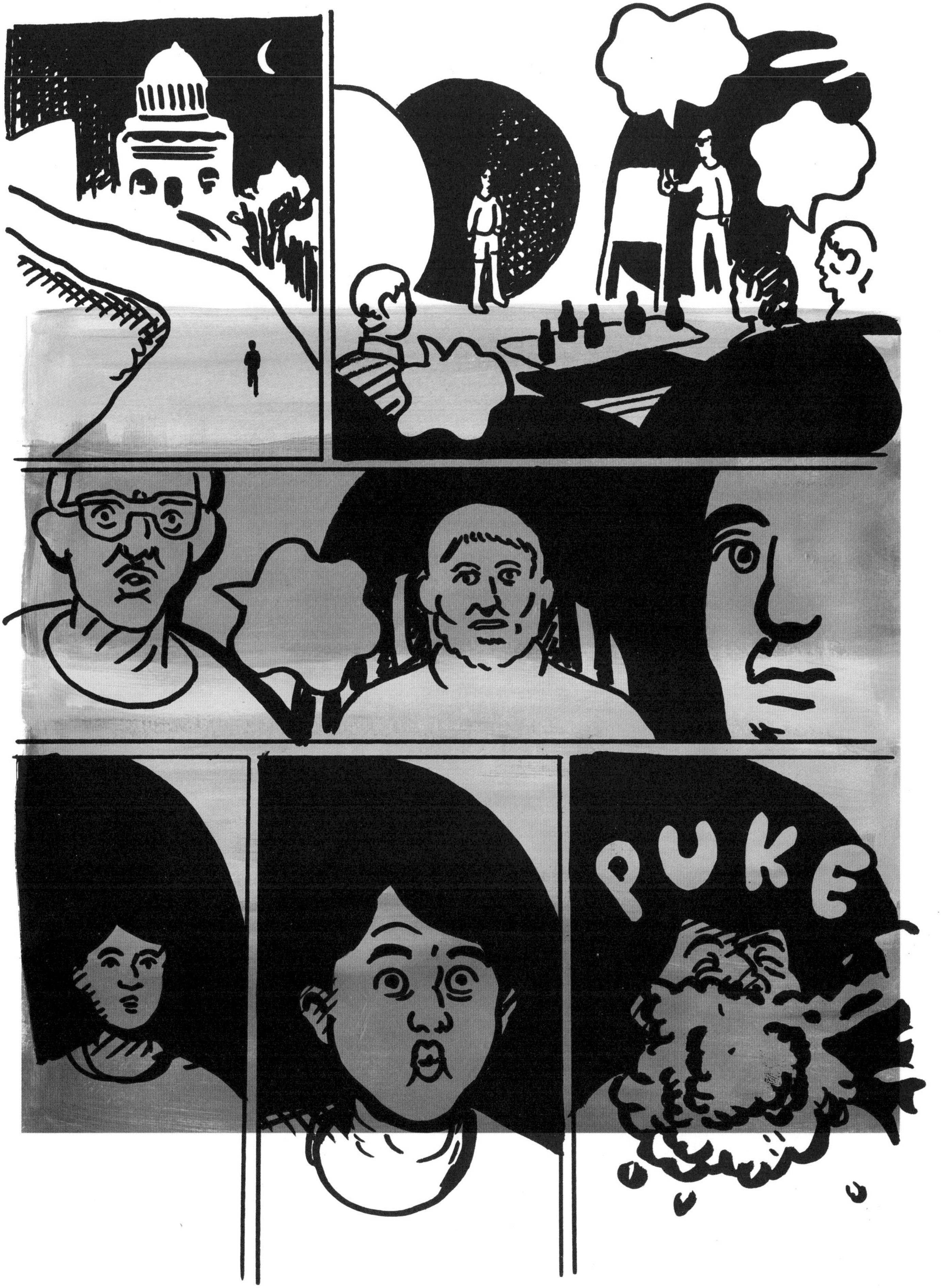
PUKE

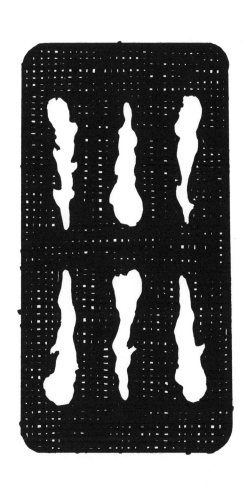

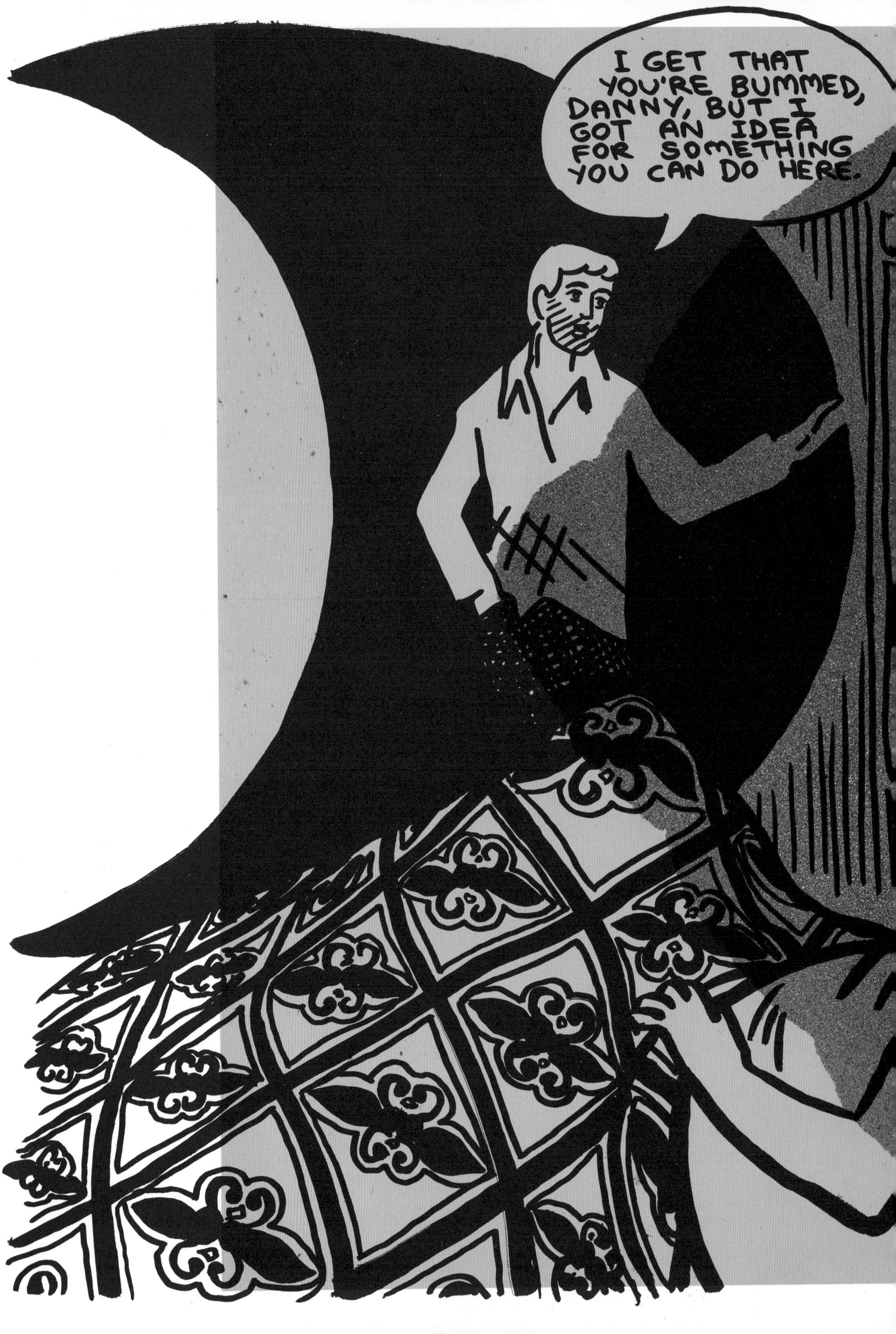
I GET THAT YOU'RE BUMMED, DANNY, BUT I GOT AN IDEA FOR SOMETHING YOU CAN DO HERE.

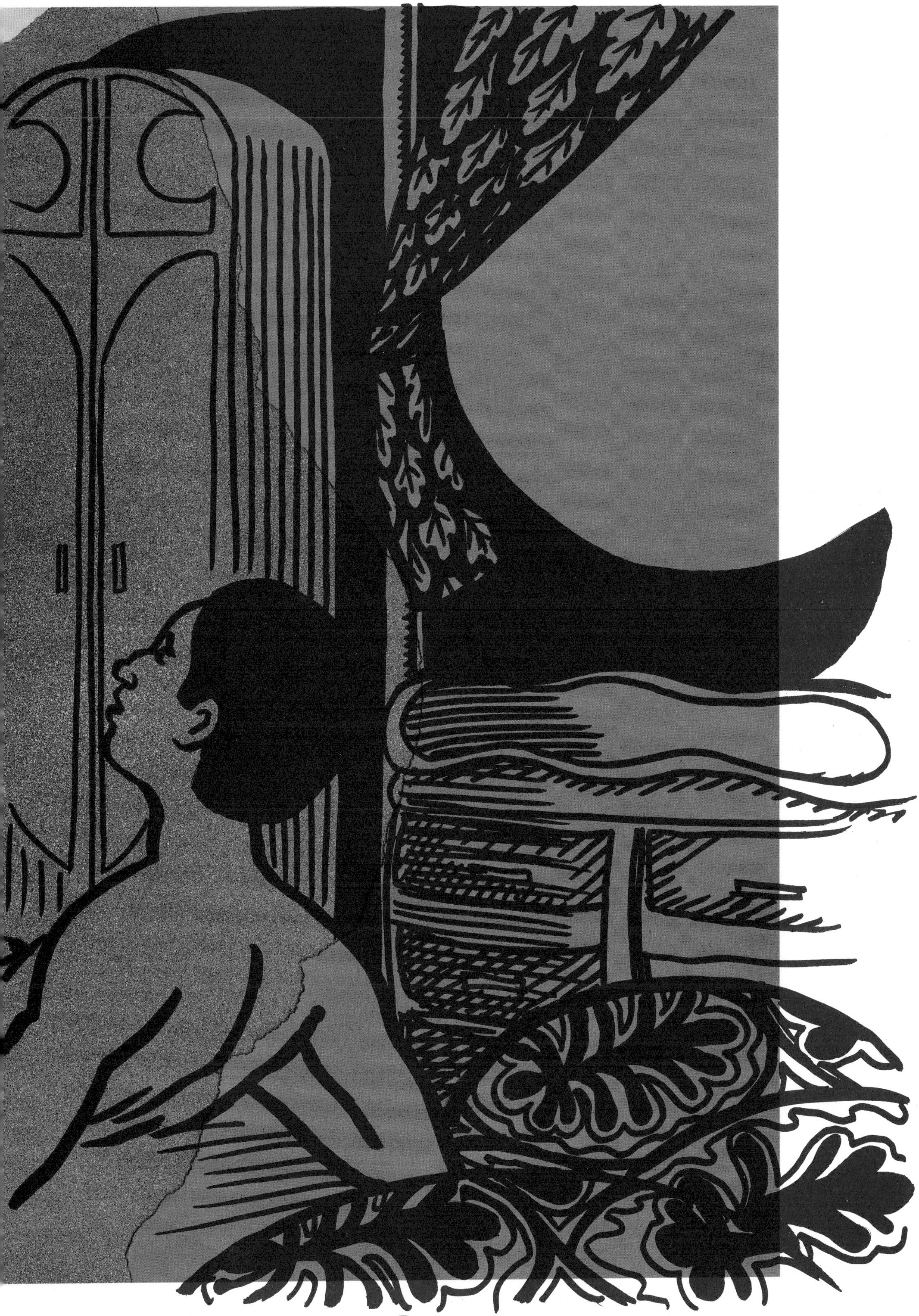

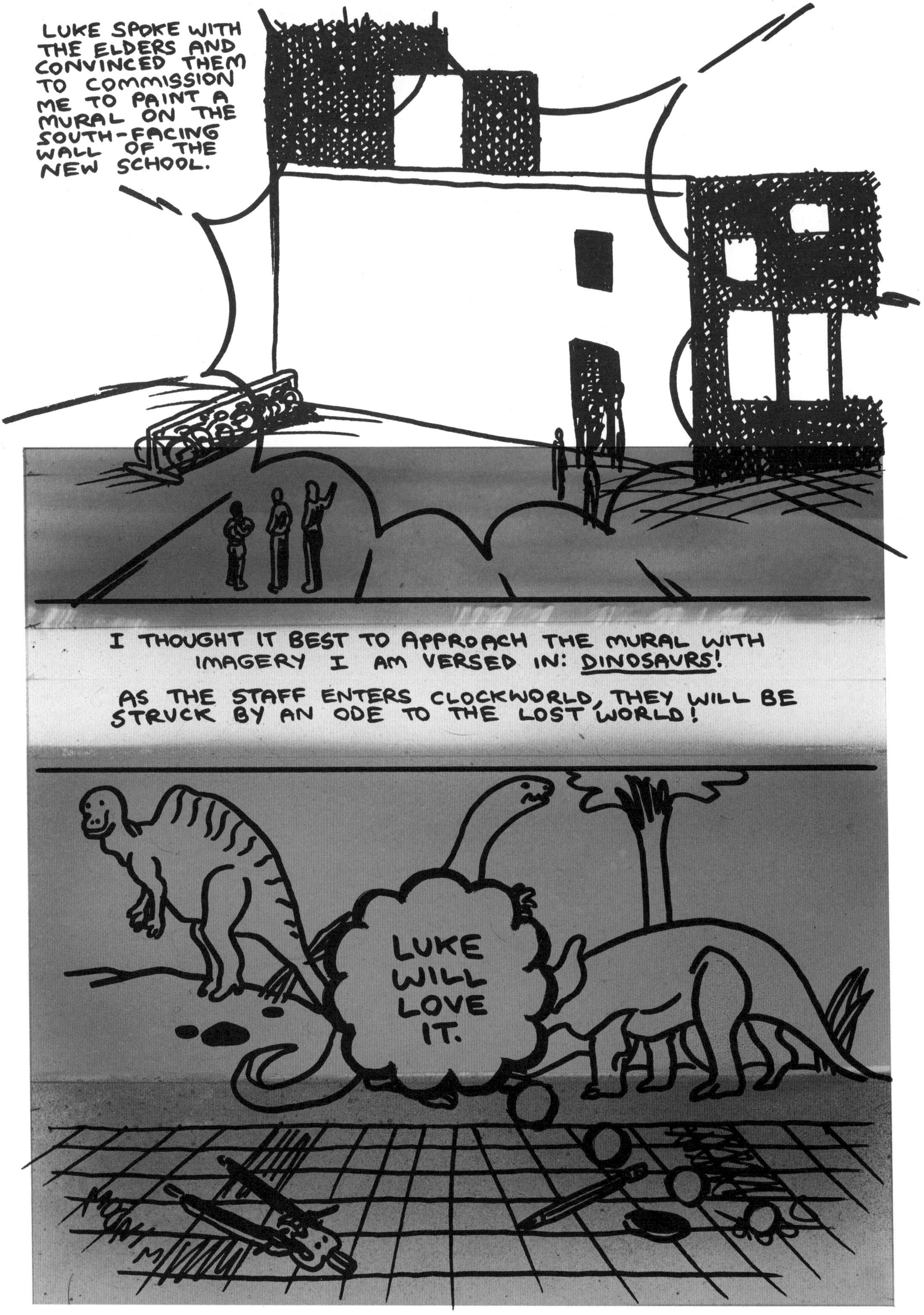
LUKE SPOKE WITH THE ELDERS AND CONVINCED THEM TO COMMISSION ME TO PAINT A MURAL ON THE SOUTH-FACING WALL OF THE NEW SCHOOL.
I THOUGHT IT BEST TO APPROACH THE MURAL WITH IMAGERY I AM VERSED IN: DINOSAURS!
AS THE STAFF ENTERS CLOCKWORLD, THEY WILL BE STRUCK BY AN ODE TO THE LOST WORLD!
LUKE WILL LOVE IT.

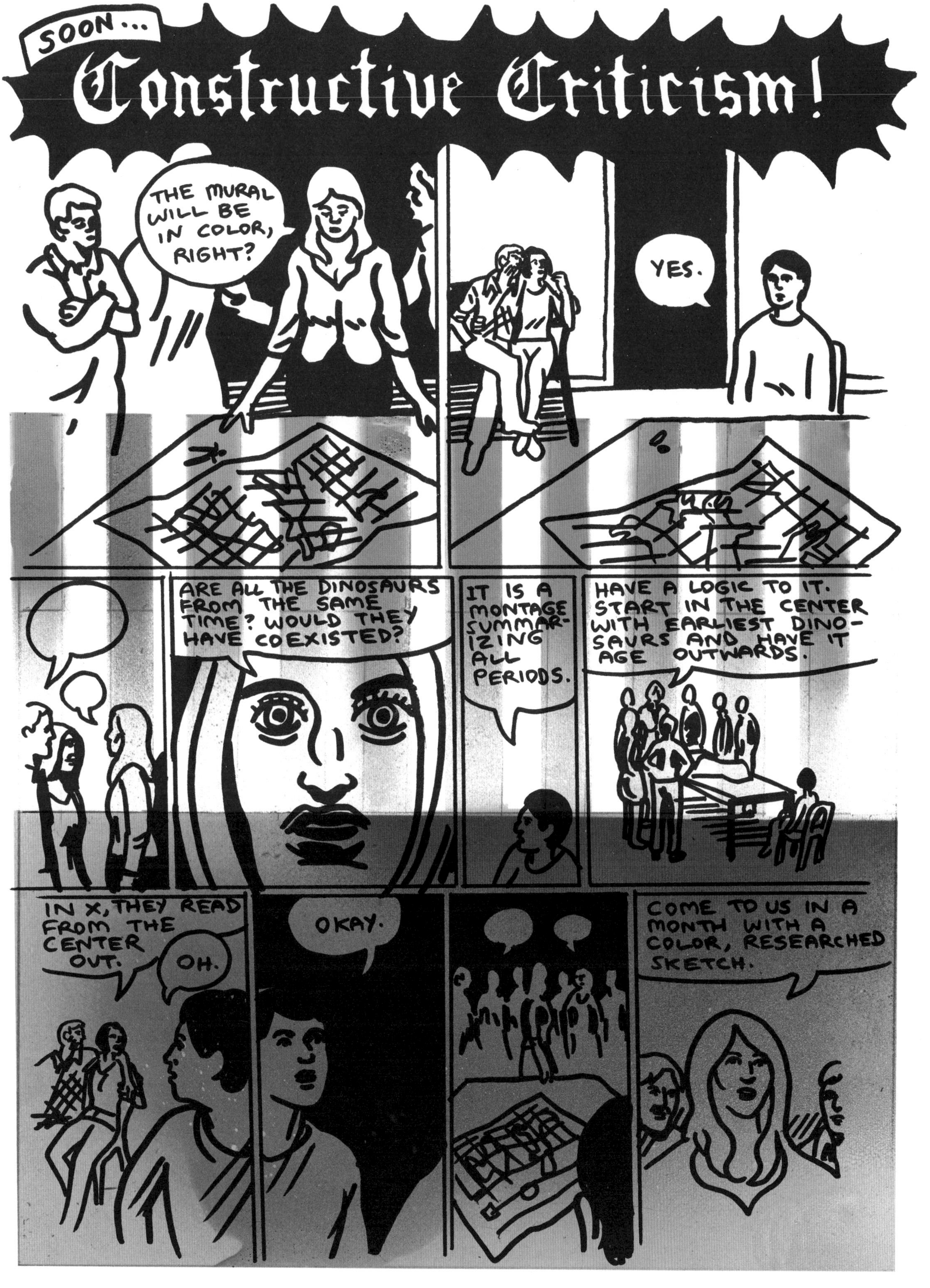
SOON...
Constructive Criticism!
THE MURAL WILL BE IN COLOR, RIGHT?
YES.
ARE ALL THE DINOSAURS FROM THE SAME TIME? WOULD THEY HAVE COEXISTED?
IT IS A MONTAGE SUMMARIZING ALL PERIODS.
HAVE A LOGIC TO IT. START IN THE CENTER WITH EARLIEST DINOSAURS AND HAVE IT AGE OUTWARDS.
IN X, THEY READ FROM THE CENTER OUT.
OH.
OKAY.
COME TO US IN A MONTH WITH A COLOR, RESEARCHED SKETCH.

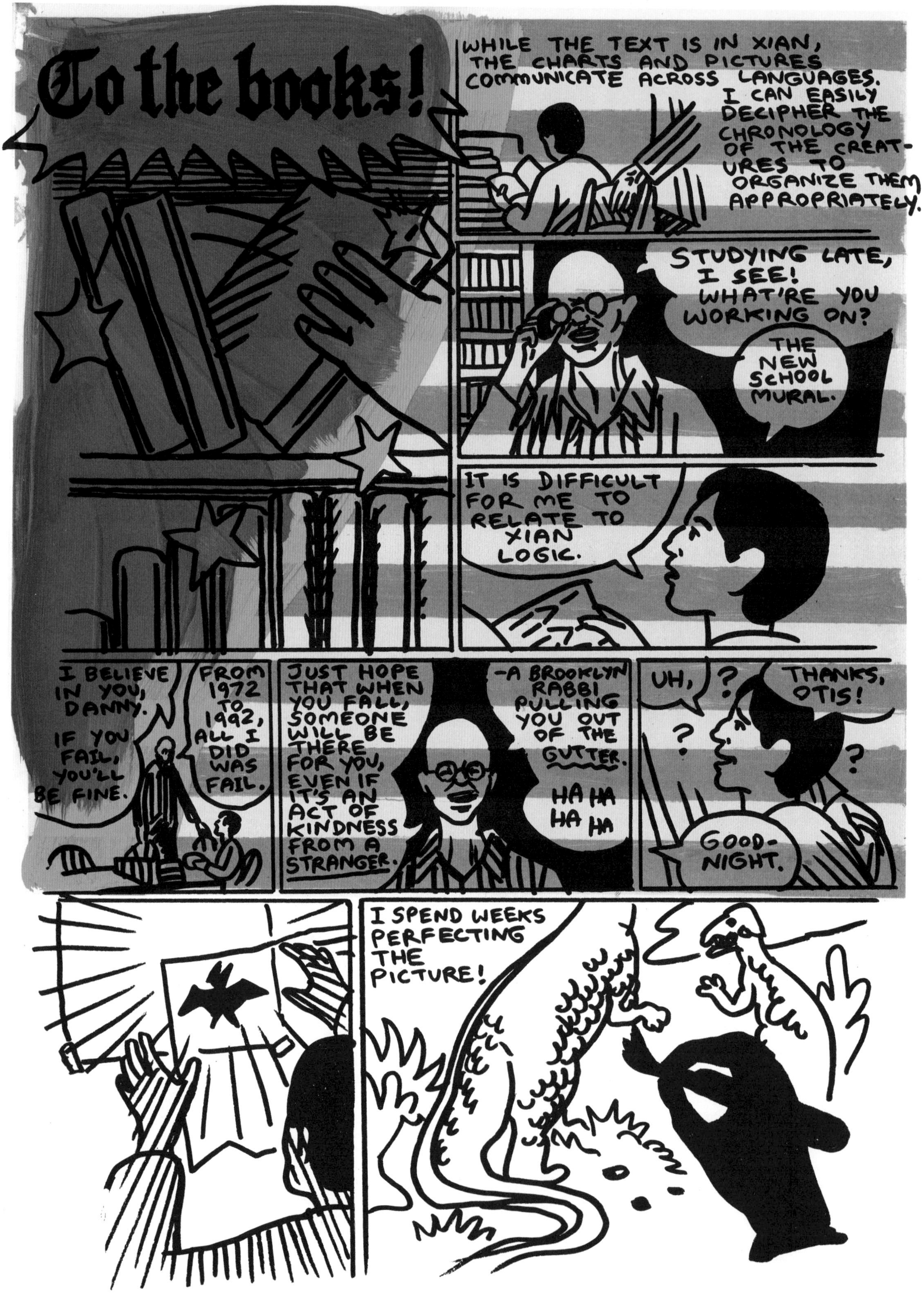
To the books!
WHILE THE TEXT IS IN XIAN, THE CHARTS AND PICTURES COMMUNICATE ACROSS LANGUAGES.
I CAN EASILY DECIPHER THE CHRONOLOGY OF THE CREATURES TO ORGANIZE THEM APPROPRIATELY.
STUDYING LATE, I SEE! WHAT'RE YOU WORKING ON?
THE NEW SCHOOL MURAL.
IT IS DIFFICULT FOR ME TO RELATE TO XIAN LOGIC.
I BELIEVE IN YOU, DANNY.
IF YOU FAIL, YOU'LL BE FINE.
FROM 1972 TO 1992, ALL I DID WAS FAIL.
JUST HOPE THAT WHEN YOU FALL, SOMEONE WILL BE THERE FOR YOU, EVEN IF IT'S AN ACT OF KINDNESS FROM A STRANGER.
-A BROOKLYN RABBI PULLING YOU OUT OF THE GUTTER.
HA HA HA HA
UH,
? ? ?
THANKS, OTIS!
GOOD-NIGHT.
I SPEND WEEKS PERFECTING THE PICTURE!

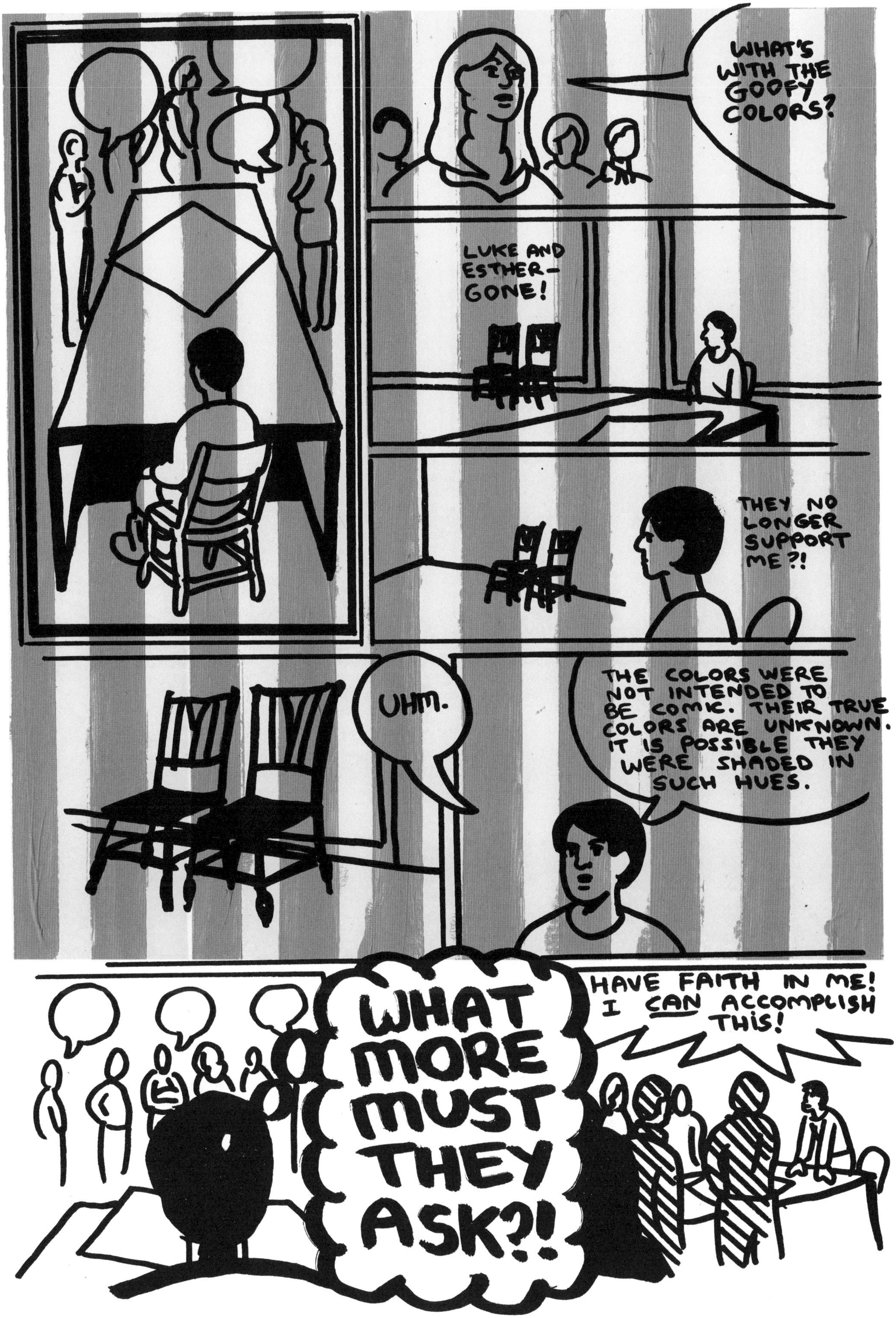
WHAT'S WITH THE GOOFY COLORS?
LUKE AND ESTHER— GONE!
THEY NO LONGER SUPPORT ME?!
UHM.
THE COLORS WERE NOT INTENDED TO BE COMIC. THEIR TRUE COLORS ARE UNKNOWN. IT IS POSSIBLE THEY WERE SHADED IN SUCH HUES.
WHAT MORE MUST THEY ASK?!
HAVE FAITH IN ME! I CAN ACCOMPLISH THIS!

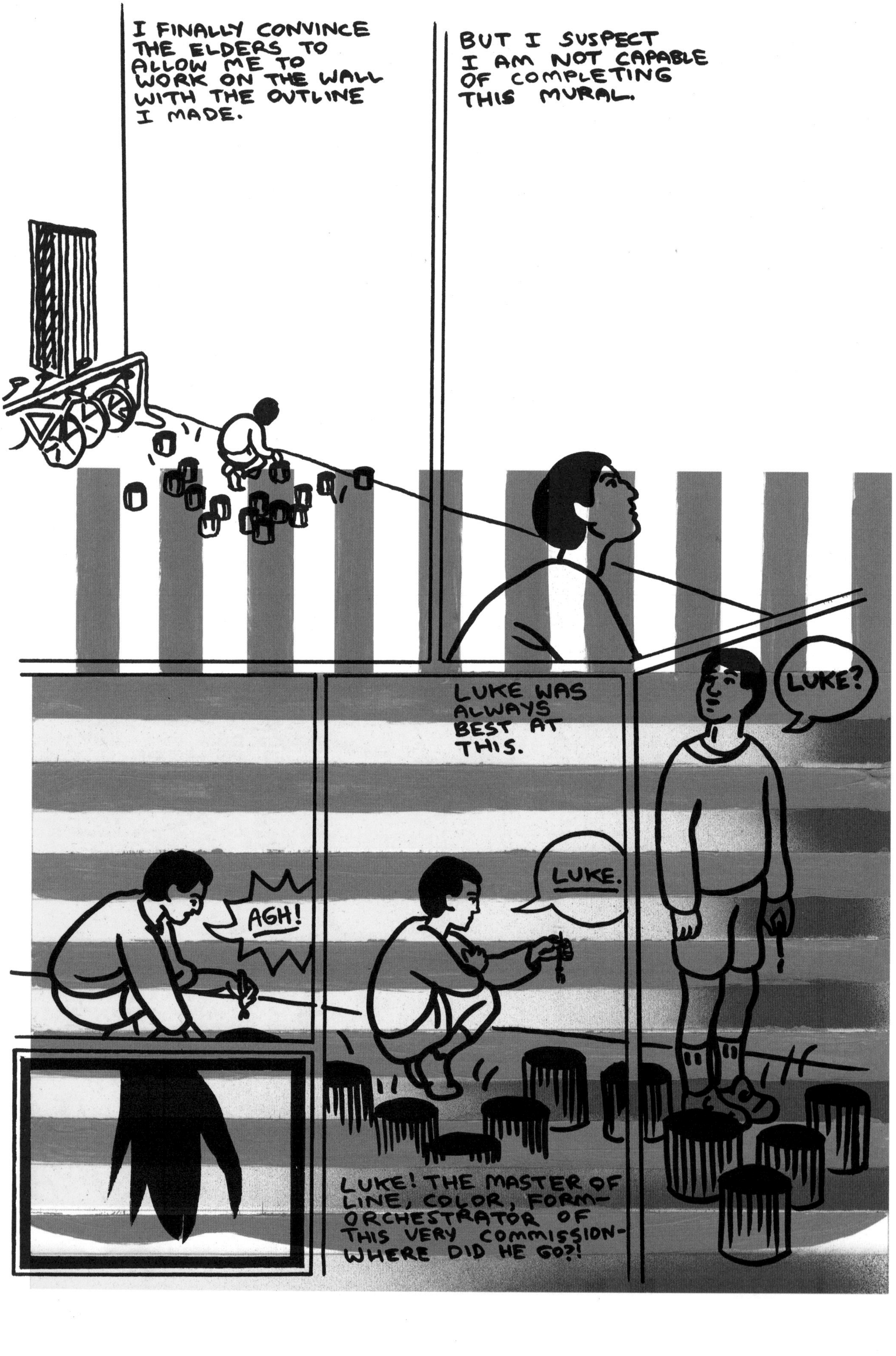

I FINALLY CONVINCE THE ELDERS TO ALLOW ME TO WORK ON THE WALL WITH THE OUTLINE I MADE.
BUT I SUSPECT I AM NOT CAPABLE OF COMPLETING THIS MURAL.
LUKE WAS ALWAYS BEST AT THIS.
LUKE?
AGH!
LUKE.
LUKE! THE MASTER OF LINE, COLOR, FORM-ORCHESTRATOR OF THIS VERY COMMISSION-WHERE DID HE GO?!

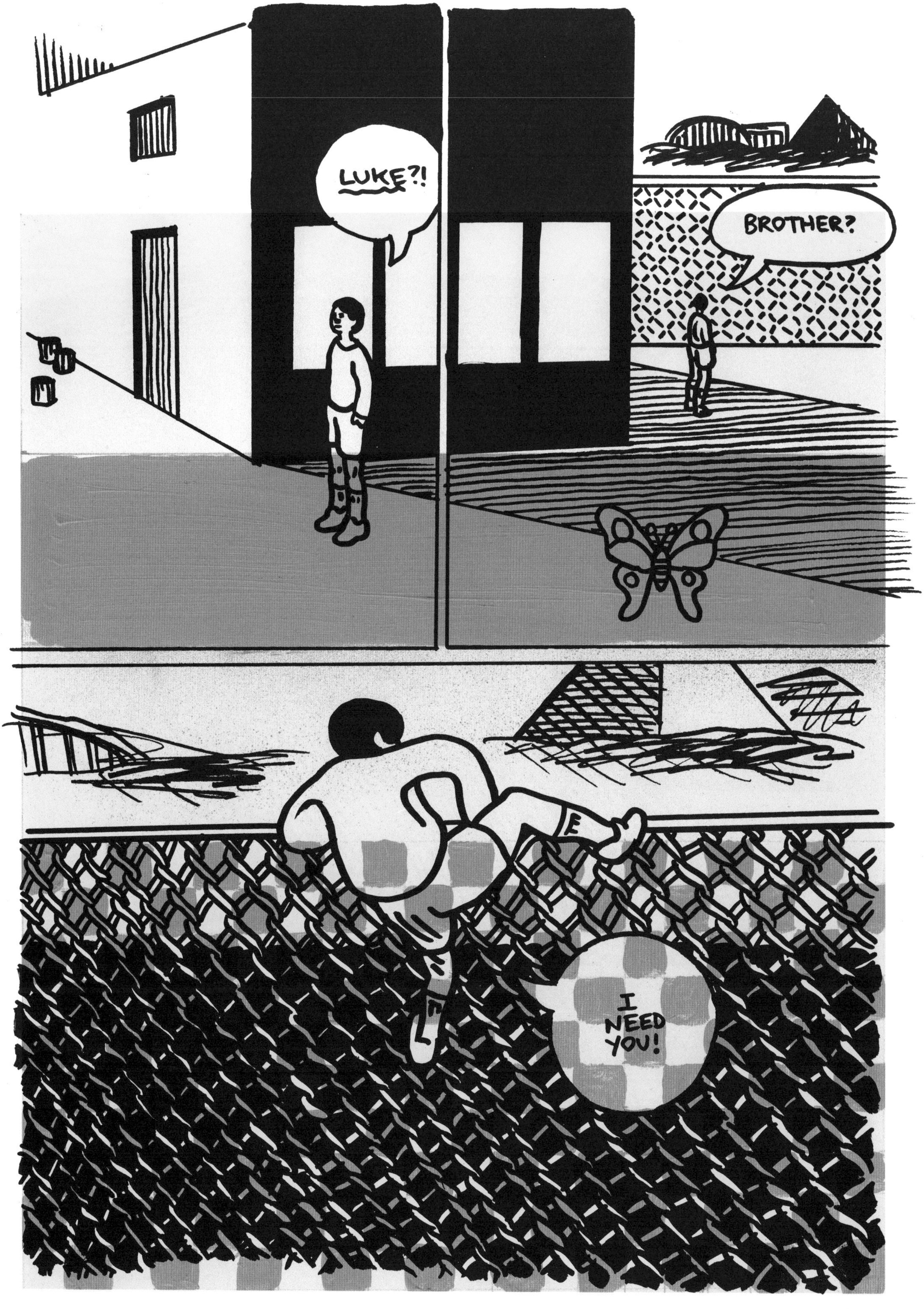
LUKE?!
BROTHER?
I NEED YOU!

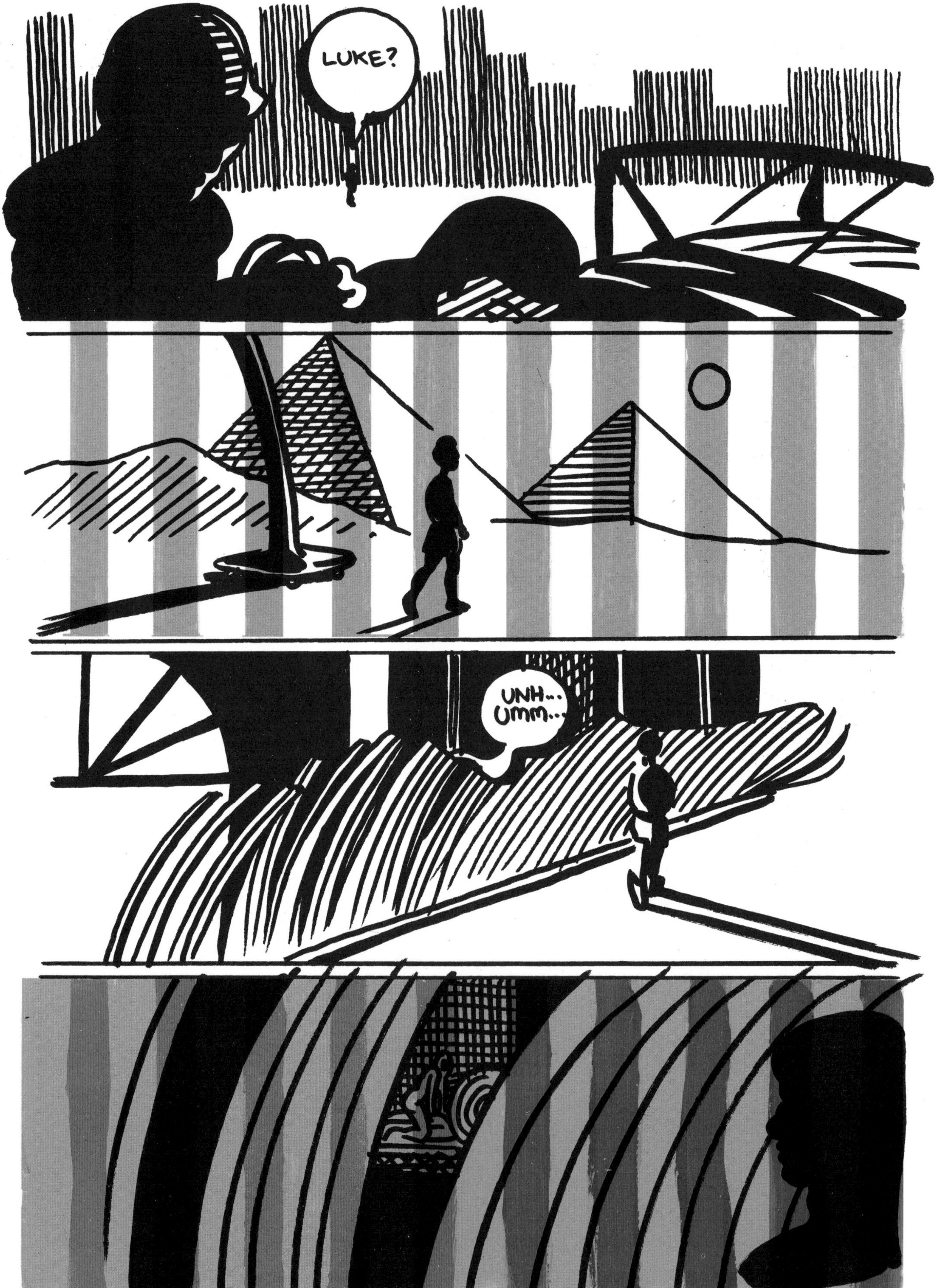
LUKE?
UNH.. UMM..

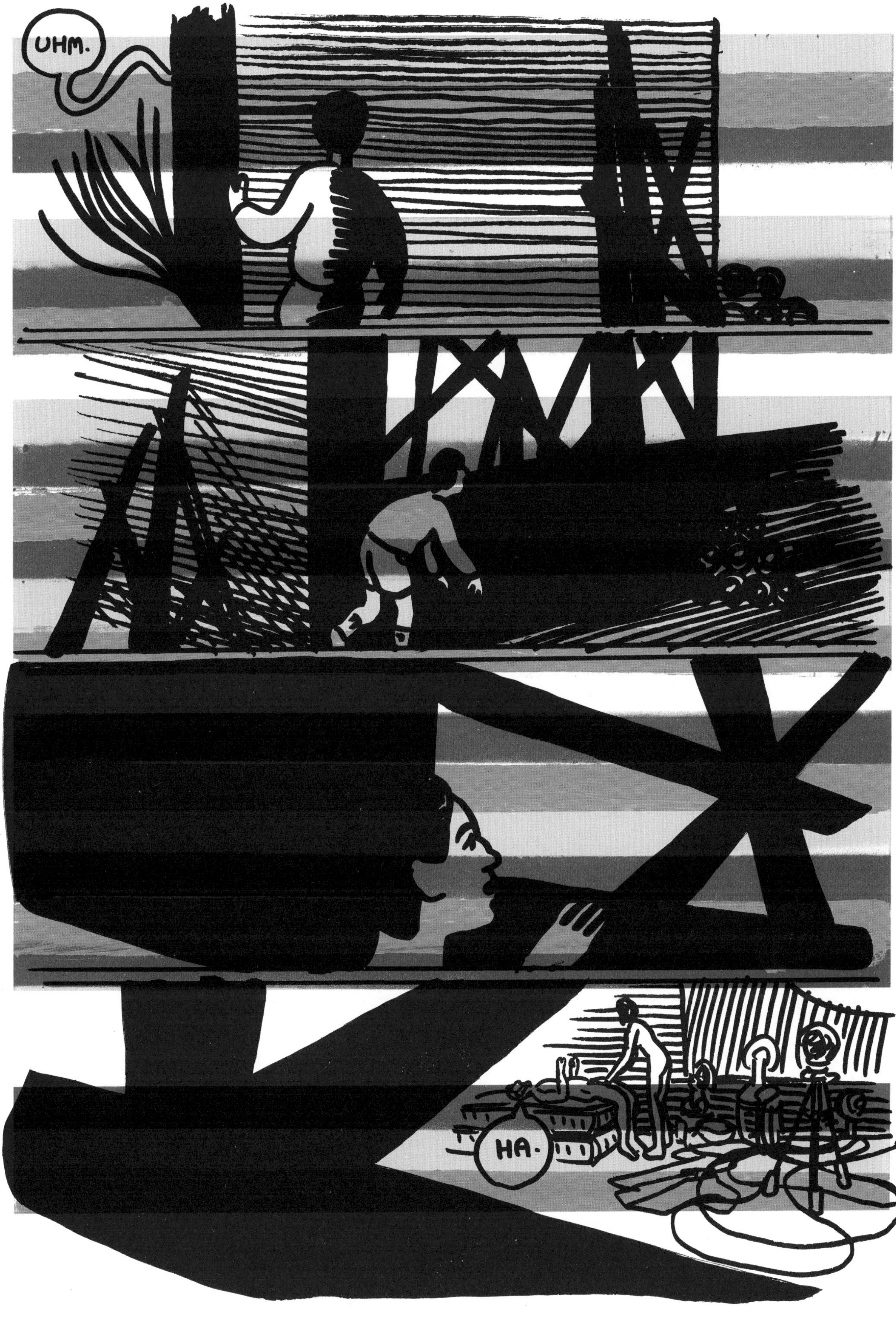
UHM.
HA.

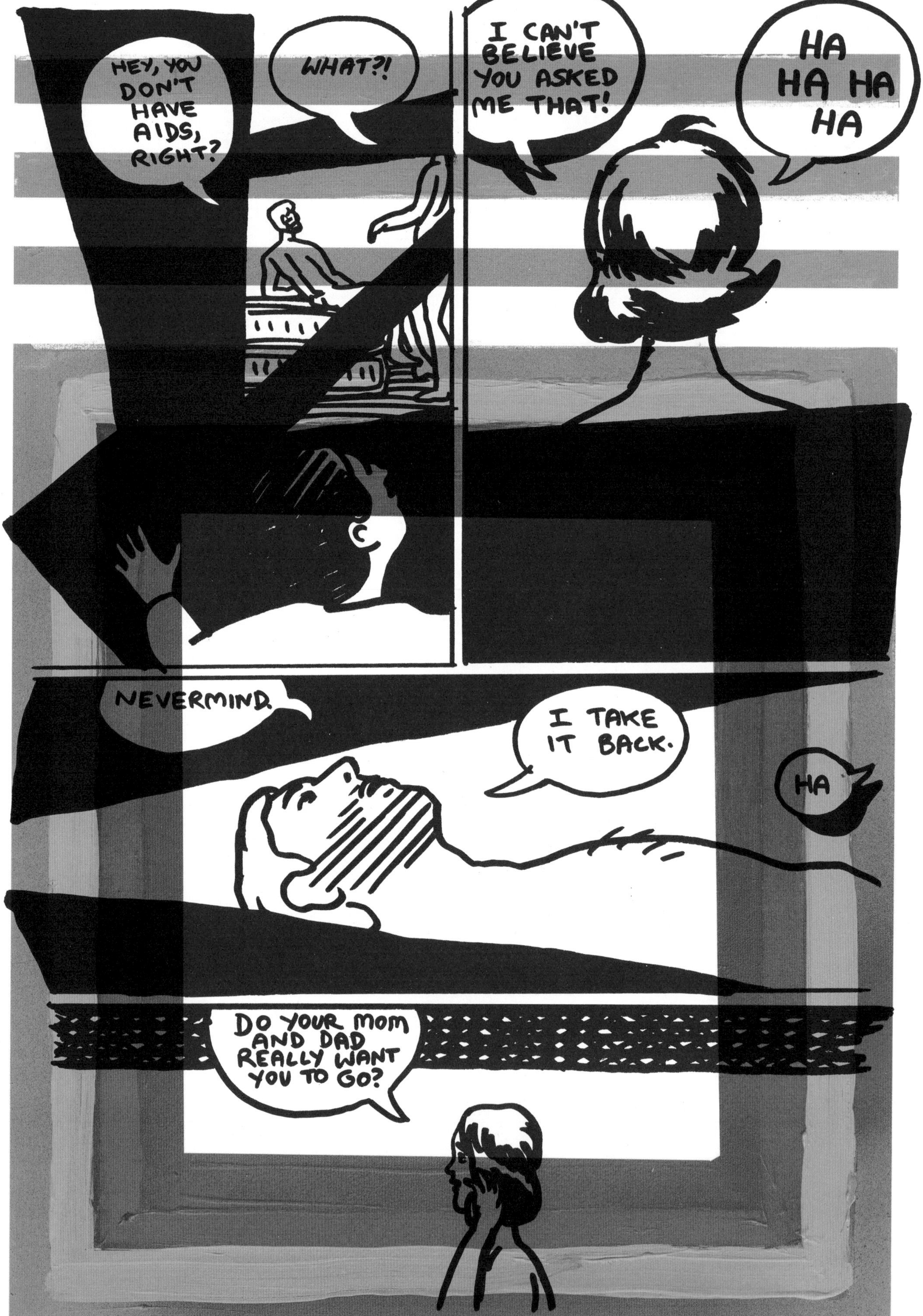
HEY, YOU DON'T HAVE AIDS, RIGHT?
WHAT?!
I CAN'T BELIEVE YOU ASKED ME THAT!
HA HA HA HA
NEVERMIND.
I TAKE IT BACK.
HA
DO YOUR MOM AND DAD REALLY WANT YOU TO GO?

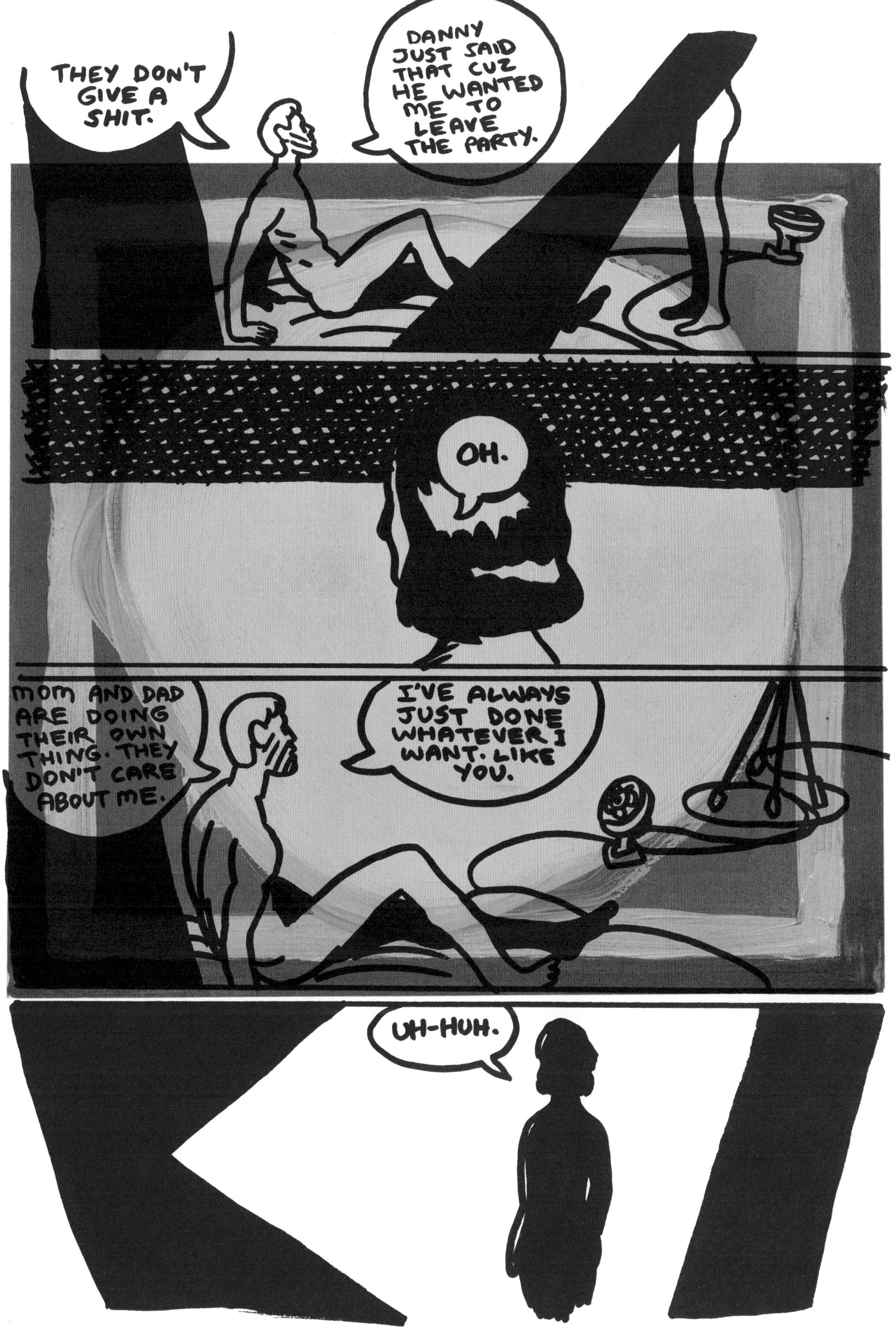
THEY DON'T GIVE A SHIT.
DANNY JUST SAID THAT CUZ HE WANTED ME TO LEAVE THE PARTY.
OH.
MOM AND DAD ARE DOING THEIR OWN THING. THEY DON'T CARE ABOUT ME.
I'VE ALWAYS JUST DONE WHATEVER I WANT. LIKE YOU.
UH-HUH.

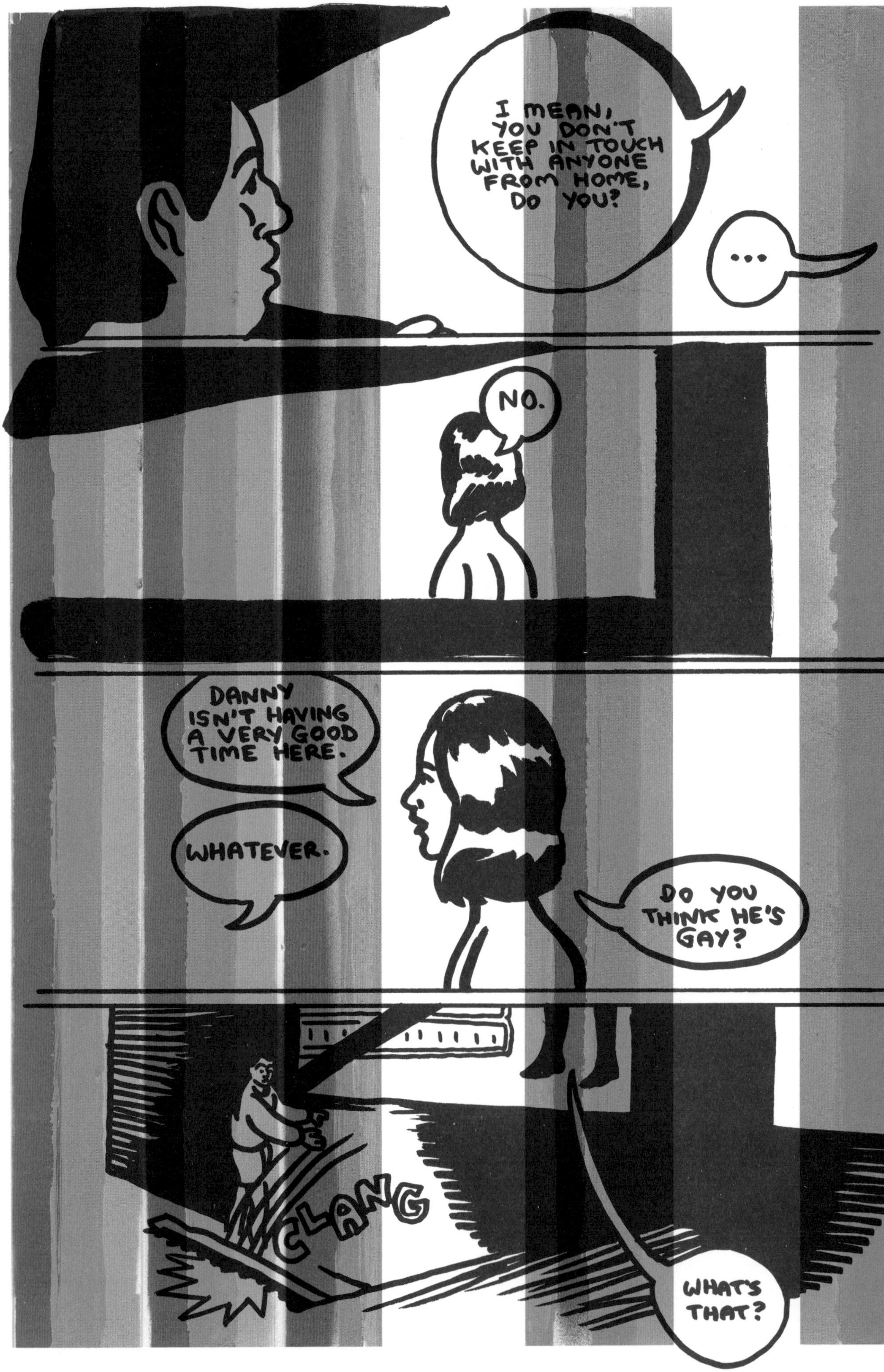
I MEAN, YOU DON'T KEEP IN TOUCH WITH ANYONE FROM HOME, DO YOU?
...
NO.
DANNY ISN'T HAVING A VERY GOOD TIME HERE.
WHATEVER.
DO YOU THINK HE'S GAY?
CLANG
WHAT'S THAT?

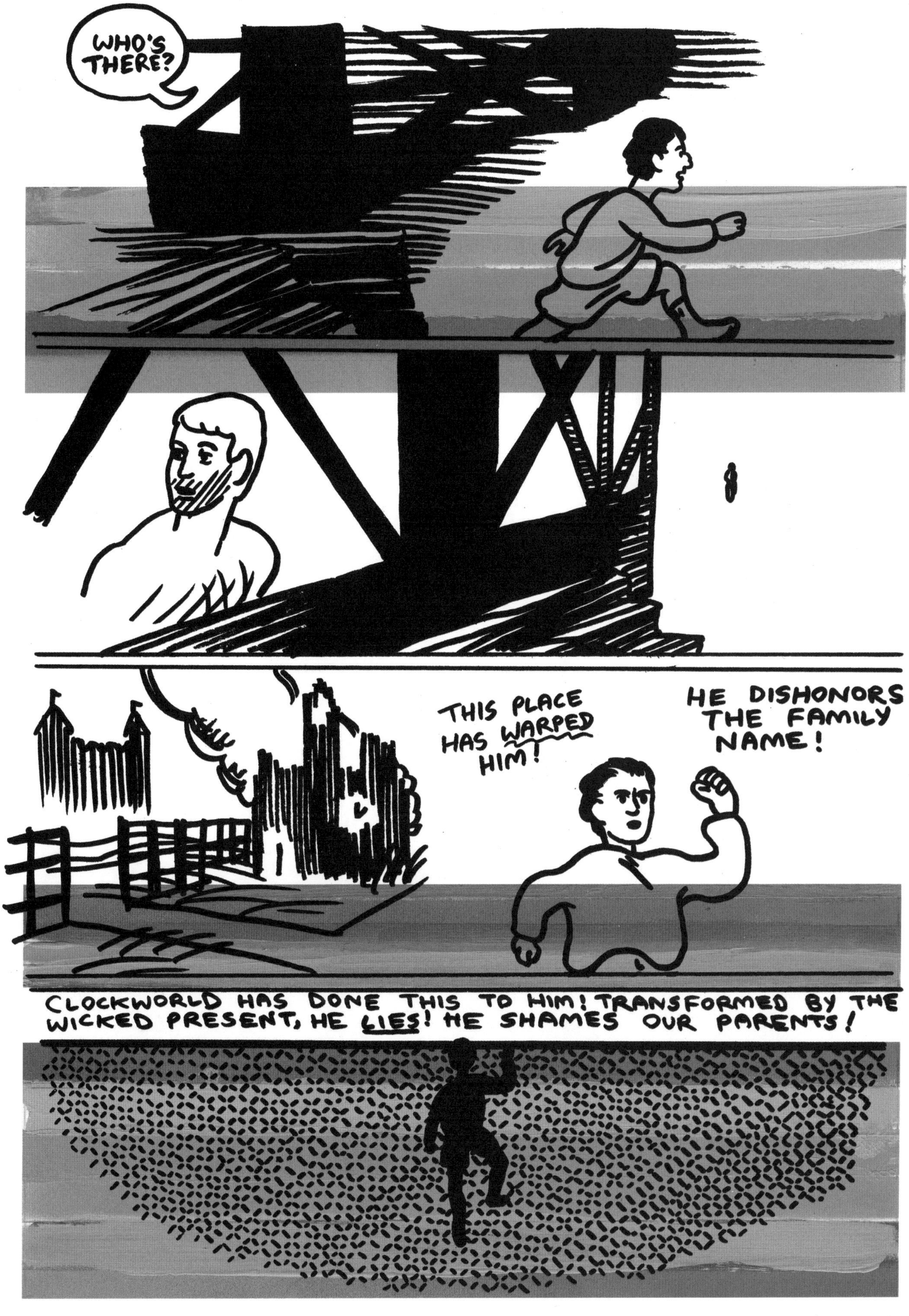
WHO'S THERE?
THIS PLACE HAS WARPED HIM!
HE DISHONORS THE FAMILY NAME!
CLOCKWORLD HAS DONE THIS TO HIM! TRANSFORMED BY THE WICKED PRESENT, HE LIES! HE SHAMES OUR PARENTS!

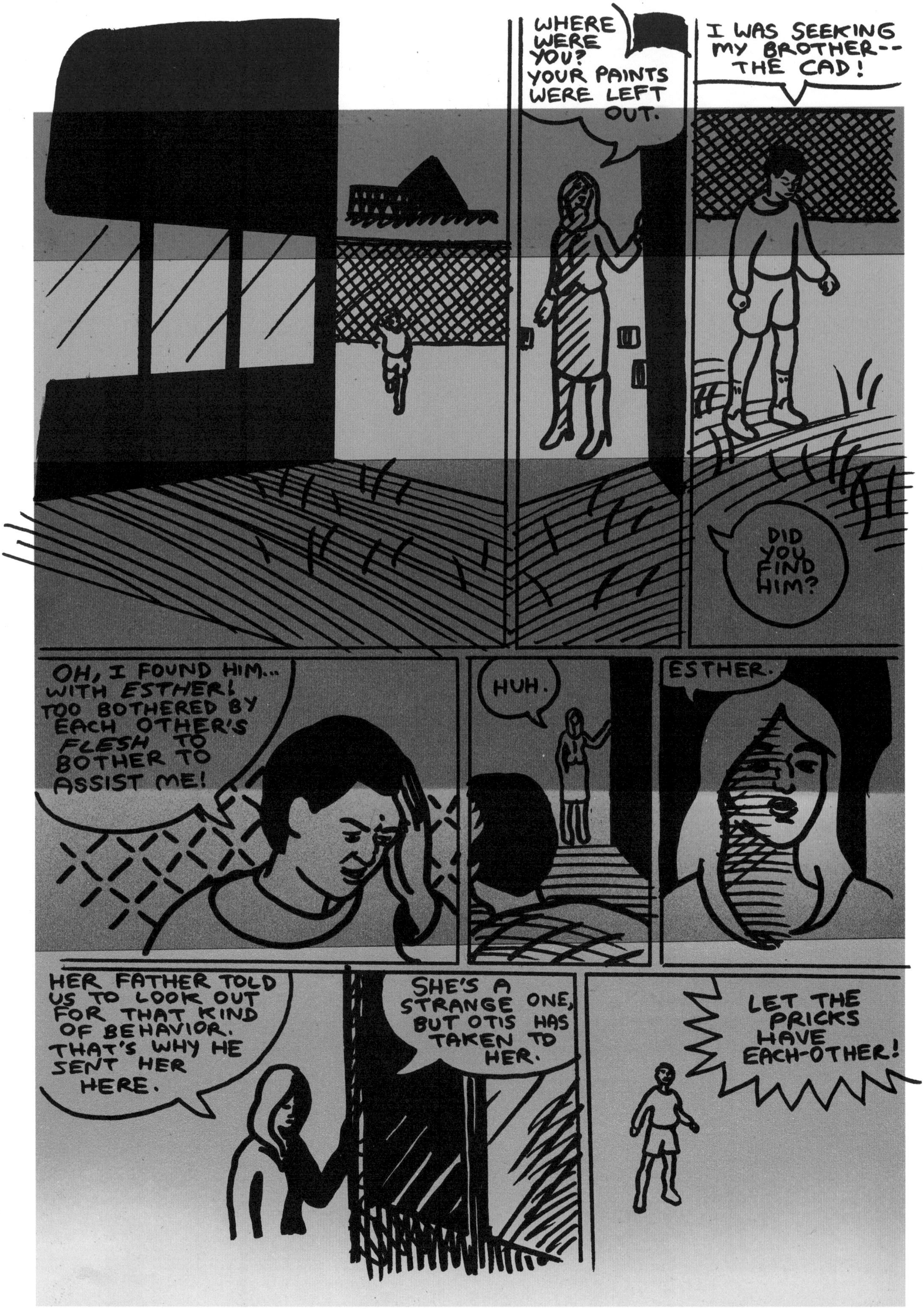
WHERE WERE YOU? YOUR PAINTS WERE LEFT OUT.
I WAS SEEKING MY BROTHER-- THE CAD!
DID YOU FIND HIM?
OH, I FOUND HIM... WITH *ESTHER*! TOO BOTHERED BY EACH OTHER'S *FLESH* TO BOTHER TO ASSIST ME!
HUH.
ESTHER.
HER FATHER TOLD US TO LOOK OUT FOR THAT KIND OF BEHAVIOR. THAT'S WHY HE SENT HER HERE.
SHE'S A STRANGE ONE, BUT OTIS HAS TAKEN TO HER.
LET THE PRICKS HAVE EACH-OTHER!

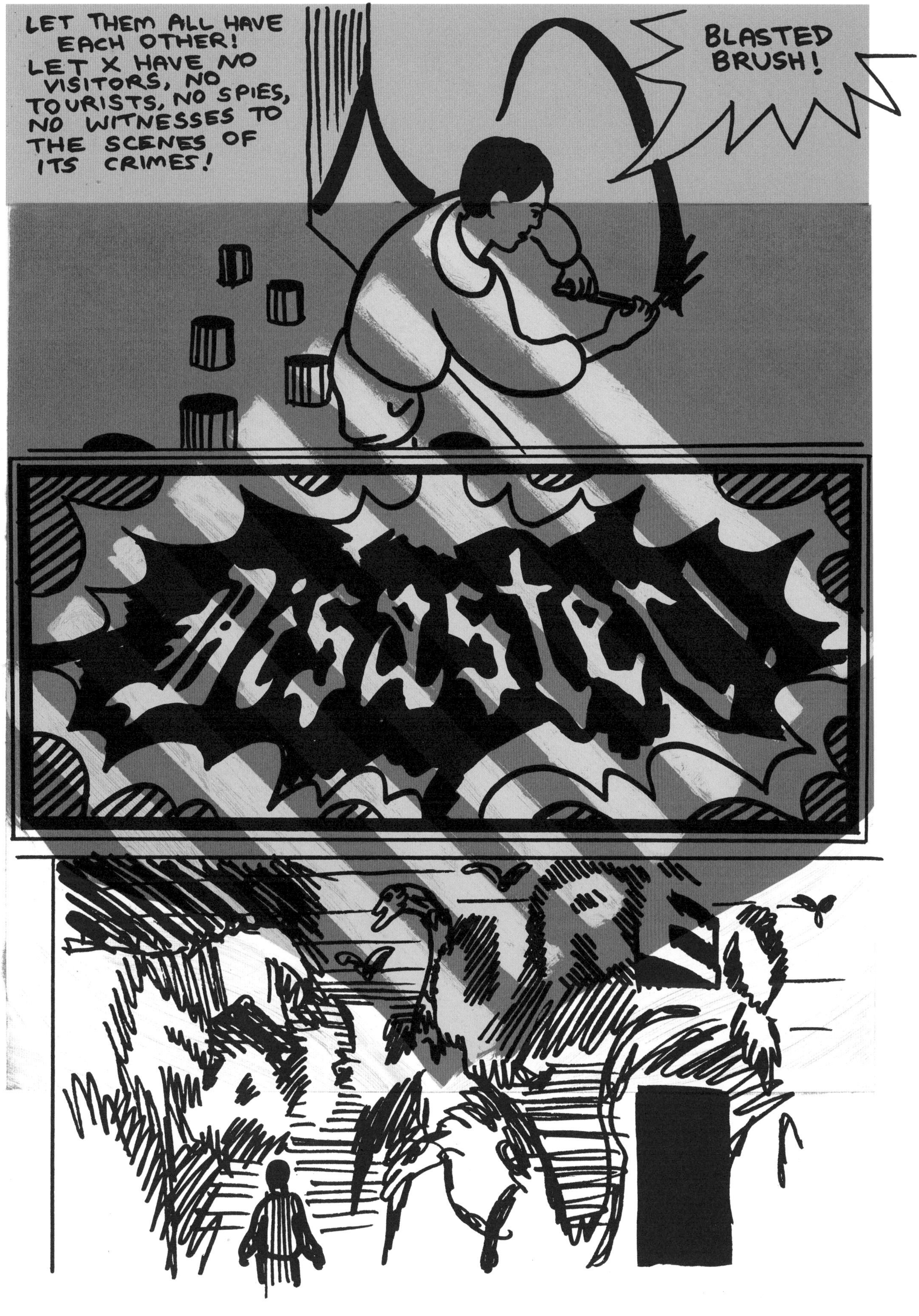
LET THEM ALL HAVE EACH OTHER! LET X HAVE NO VISITORS, NO TOURISTS, NO SPIES, NO WITNESSES TO THE SCENES OF ITS CRIMES!
BLASTED BRUSH!
disaster

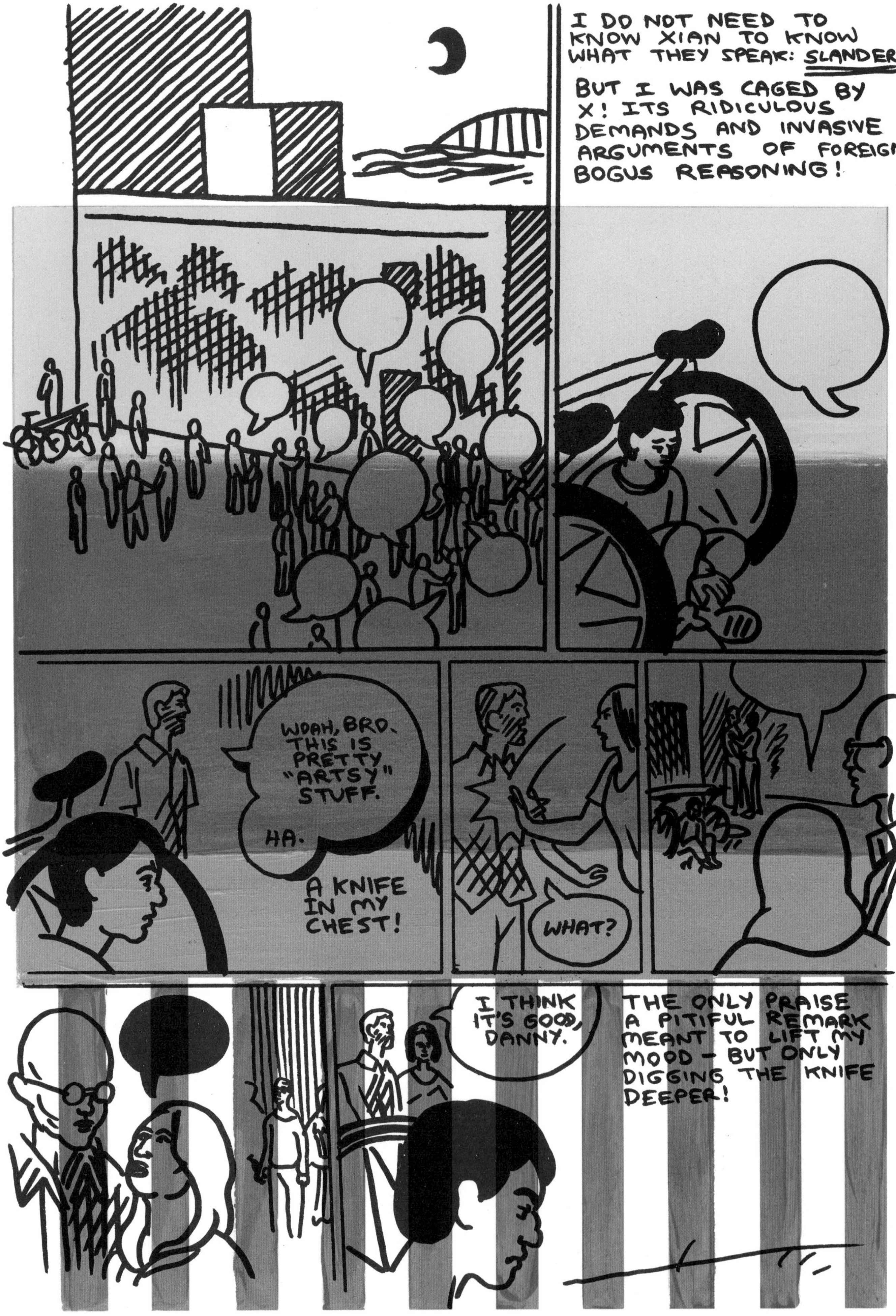
I DO NOT NEED TO KNOW XIAN TO KNOW WHAT THEY SPEAK: SLANDER!
BUT I WAS CAGED BY X! ITS RIDICULOUS DEMANDS AND INVASIVE ARGUMENTS OF FOREIGN, BOGUS REASONING!
WOAH, BRO. THIS IS PRETTY "ARTSY" STUFF.
HA.
A KNIFE IN MY CHEST!
WHAT?
I THINK IT'S GOOD, DANNY.
THE ONLY PRAISE A PITIFUL REMARK MEANT TO LIFT MY MOOD – BUT ONLY DIGGING THE KNIFE DEEPER!

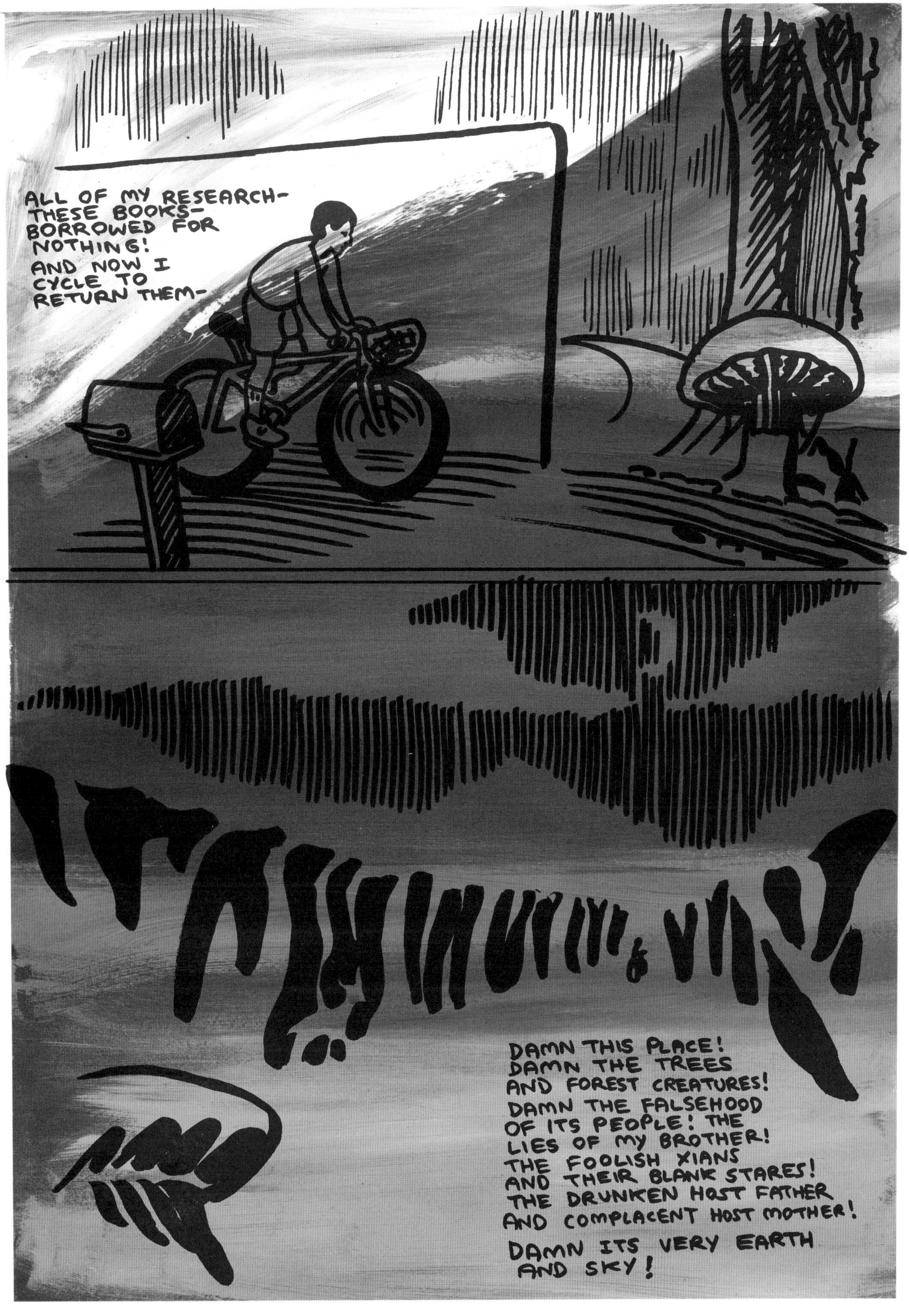
ALL OF MY RESEARCH- THESE BOOKS- BORROWED FOR NOTHING! AND NOW I CYCLE TO RETURN THEM-
DAMN THIS PLACE! DAMN THE TREES AND FOREST CREATURES! DAMN THE FALSEHOOD OF ITS PEOPLE! THE LIES OF MY BROTHER! THE FOOLISH XIANS AND THEIR BLANK STARES! THE DRUNKEN HOST FATHER AND COMPLACENT HOST MOTHER!
DAMN ITS VERY EARTH AND SKY!

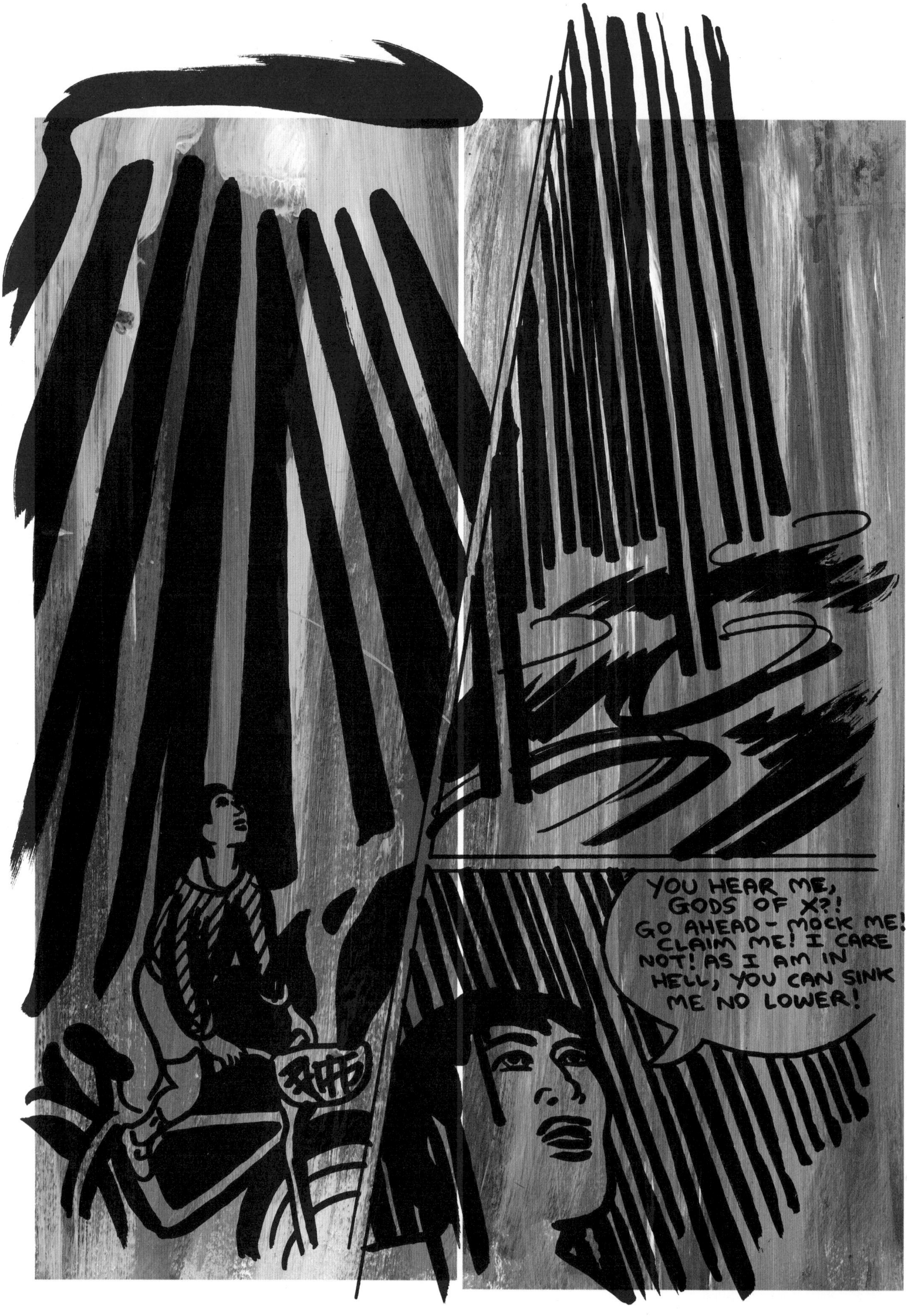
YOU HEAR ME, GODS OF X?! GO AHEAD - MOCK ME! CLAIM ME! I CARE NOT! AS I AM IN HELL, YOU CAN SINK ME NO LOWER!

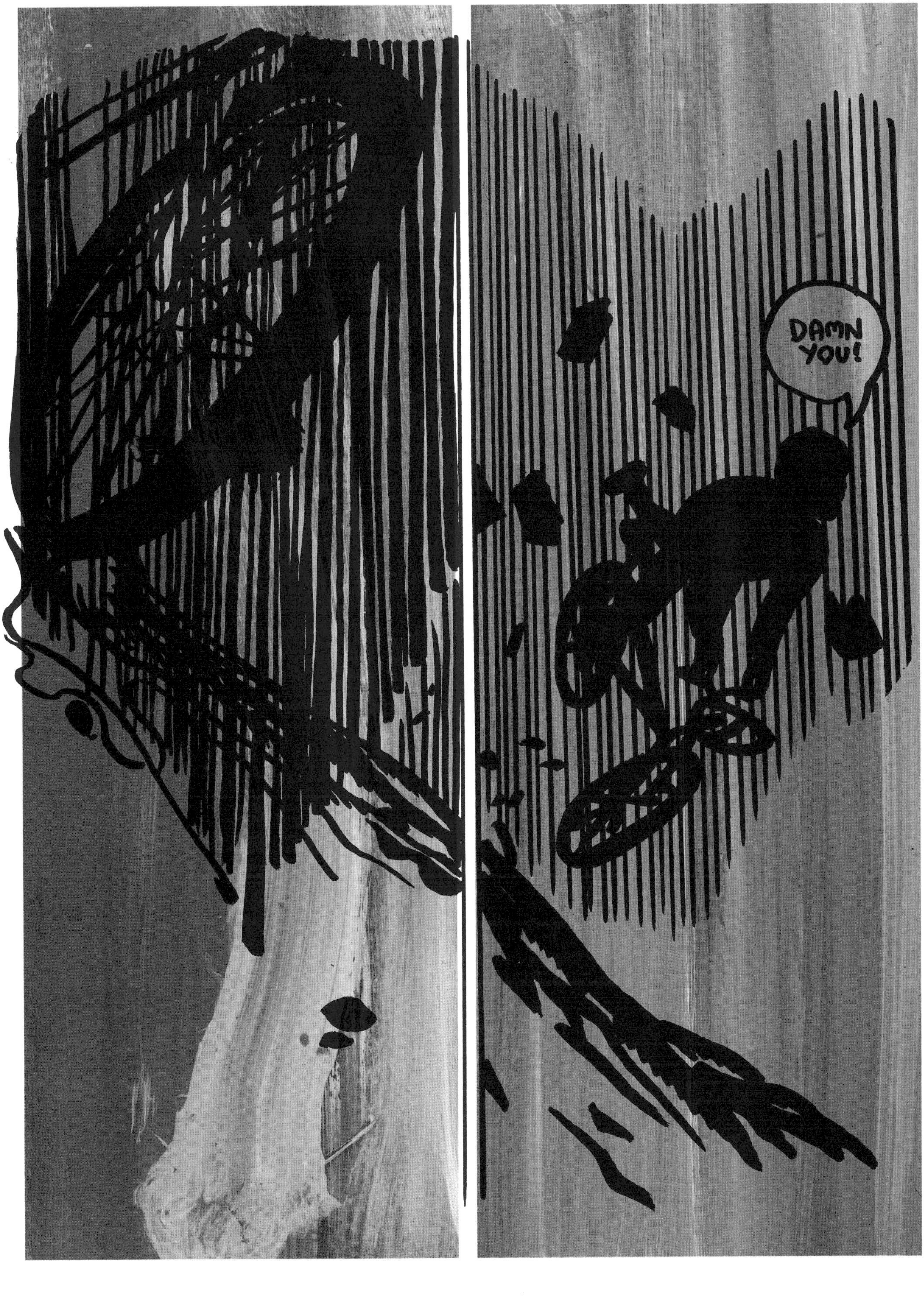
DAMN YOU!

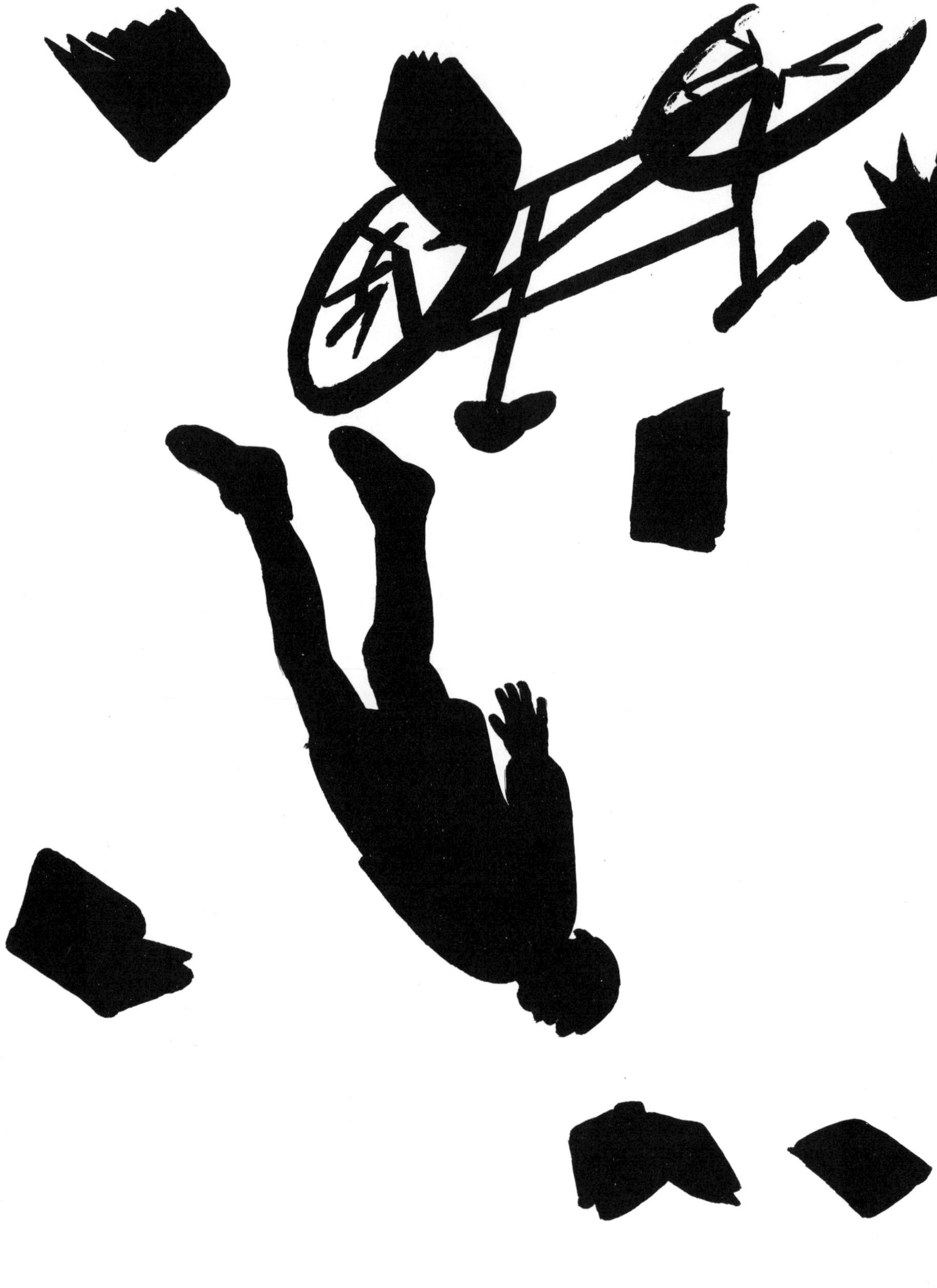

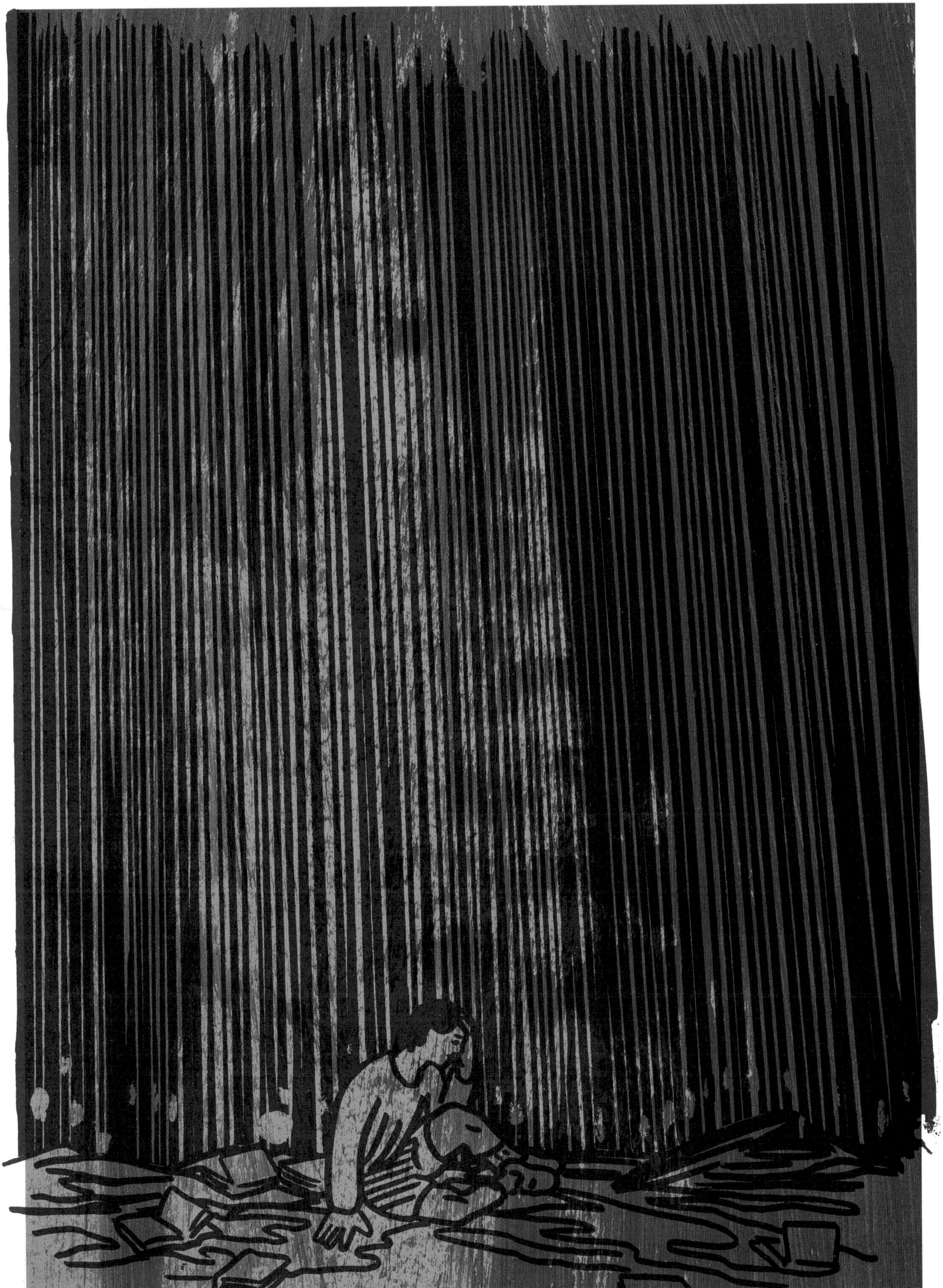

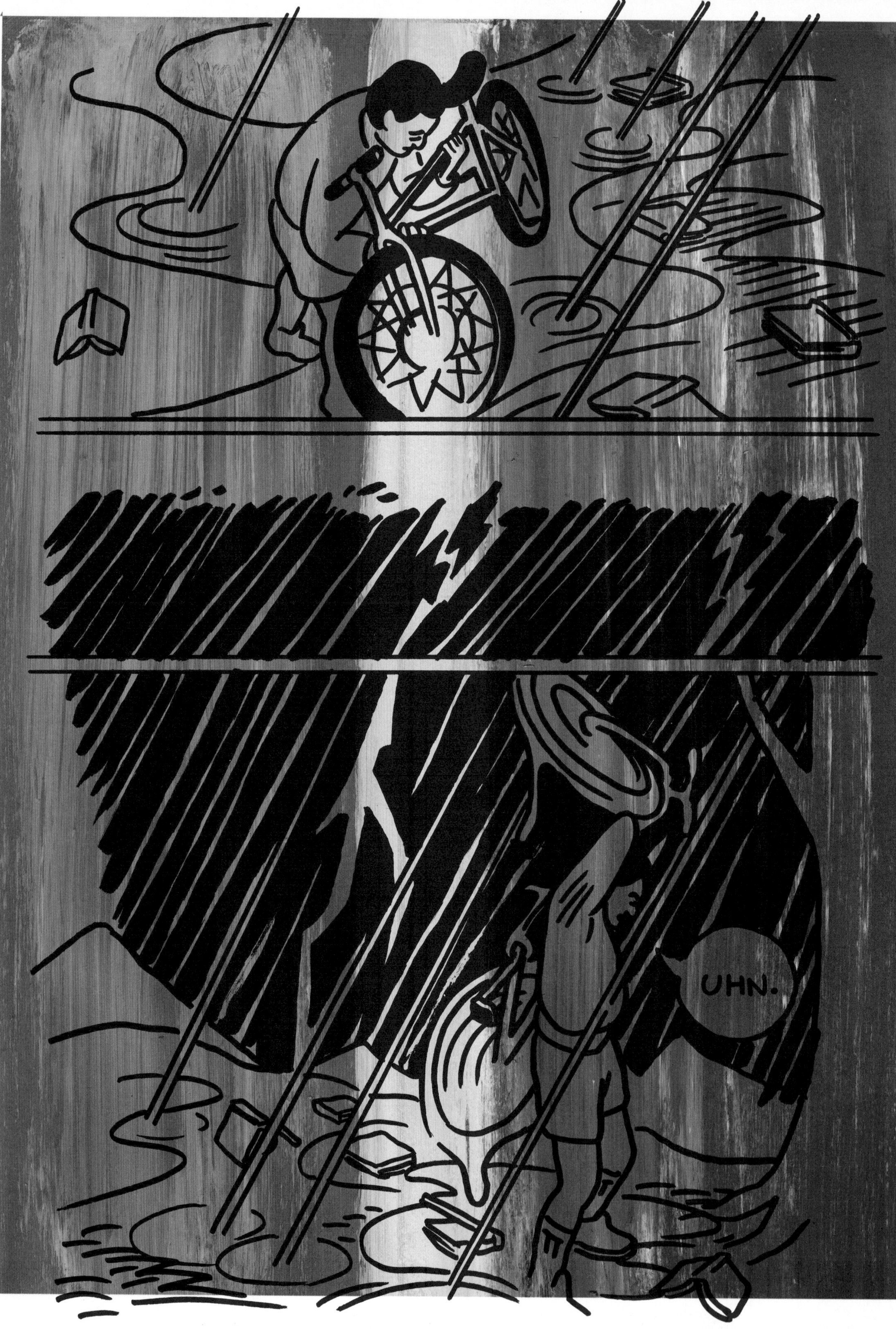
UHN.

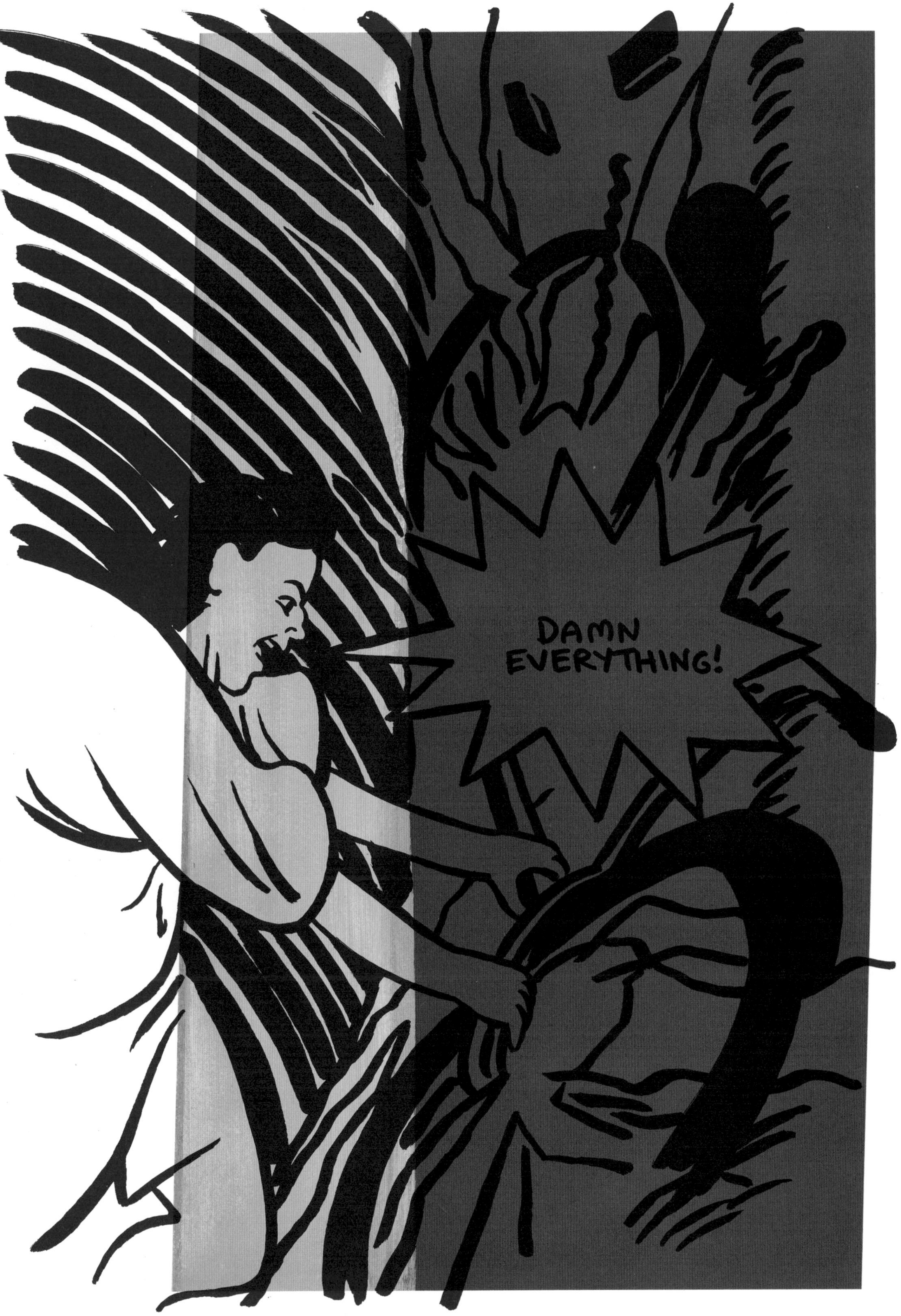
DAMN EVERYTHING!

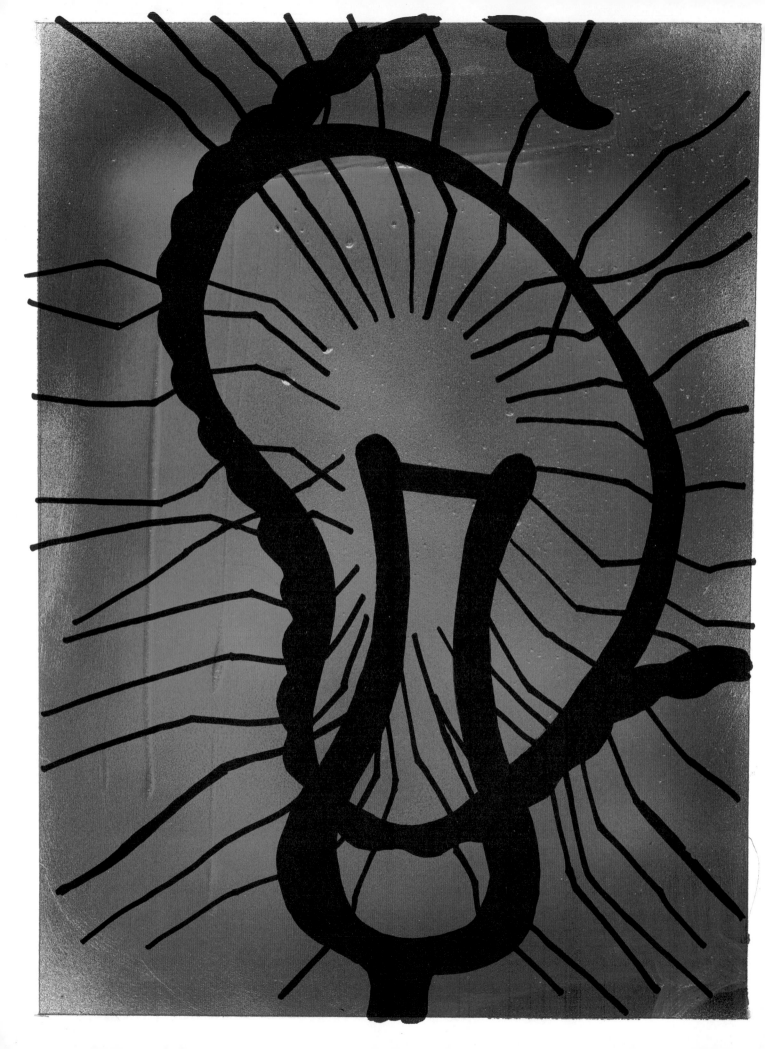

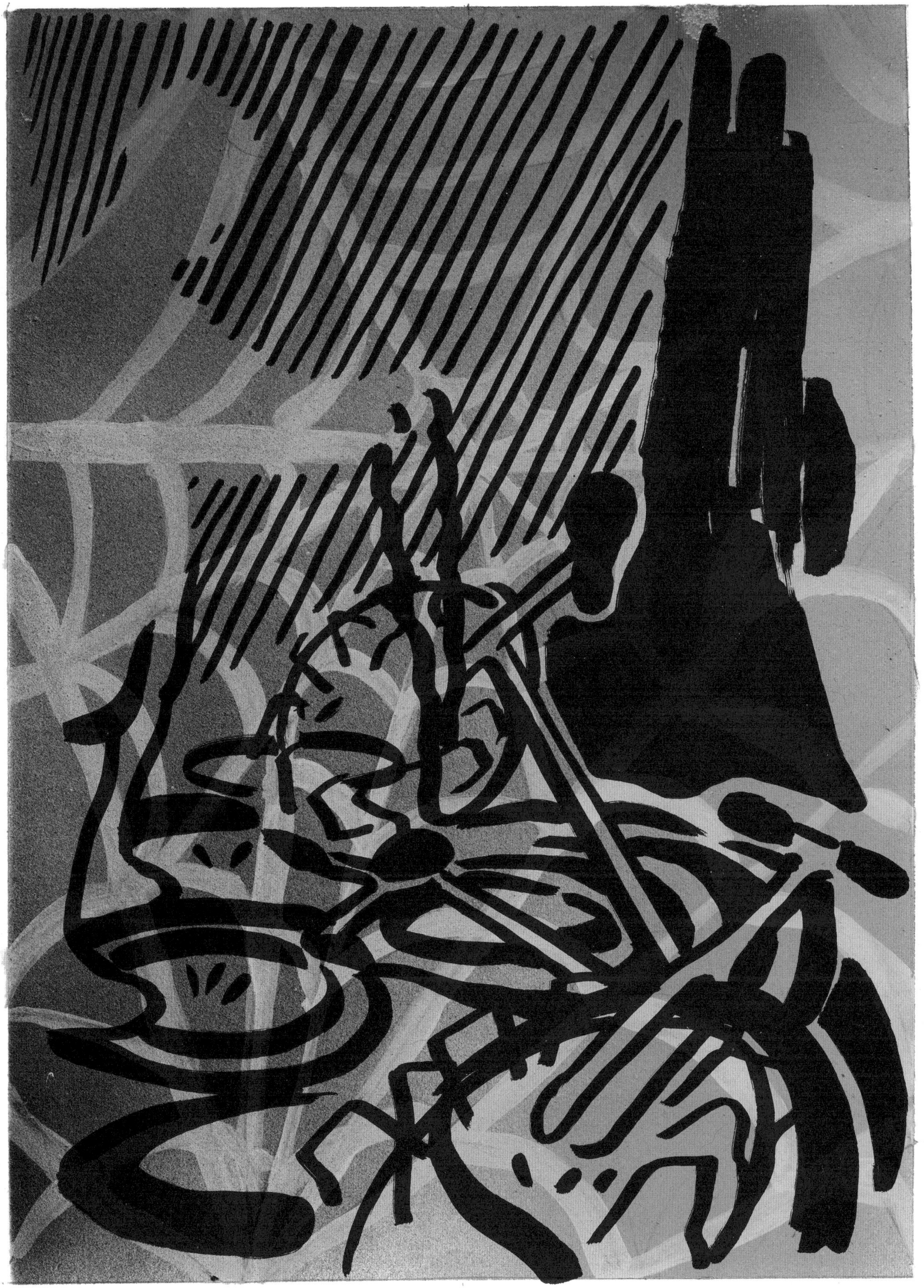

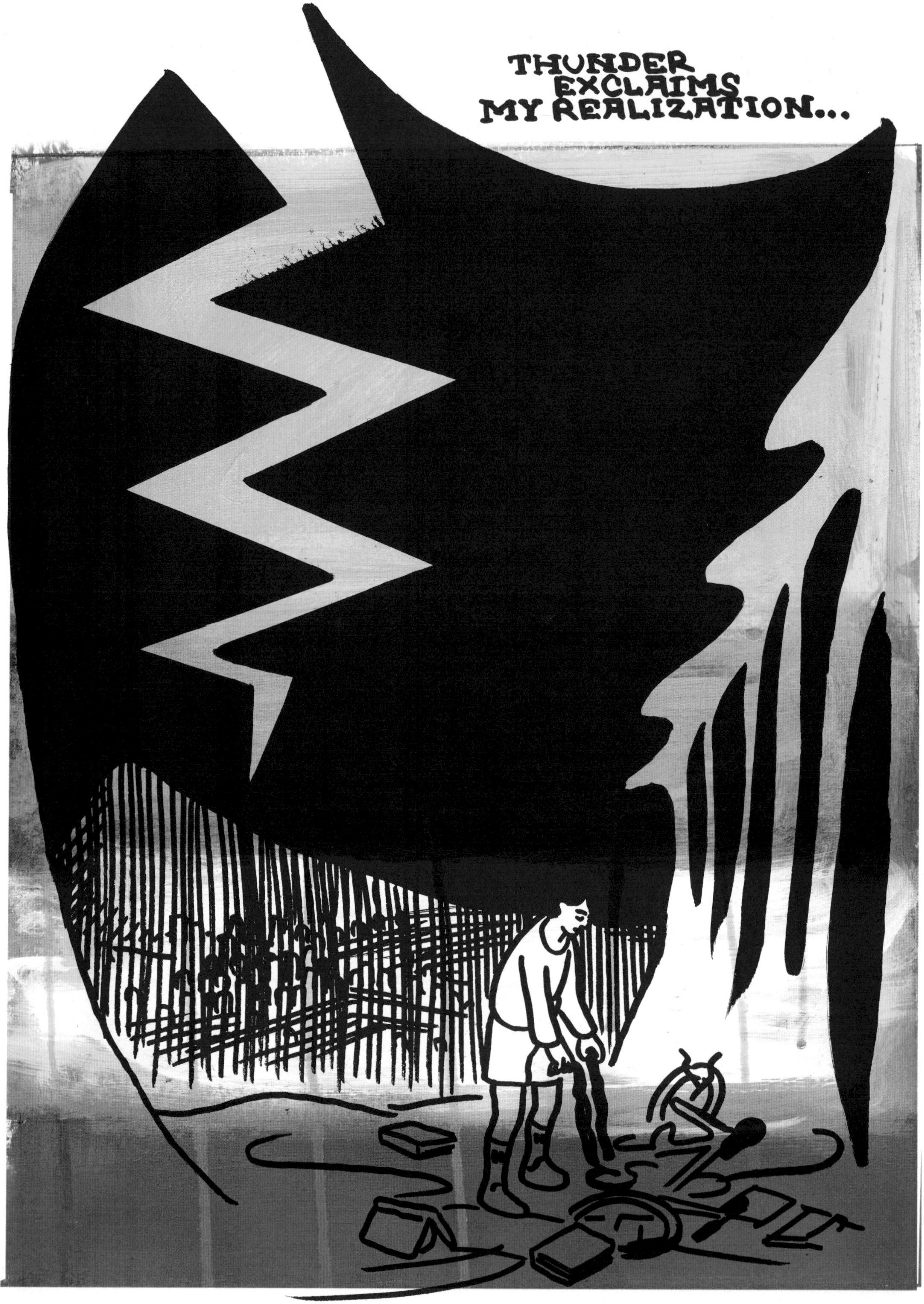
THUNDER EXCLAIMS MY REALIZATION...

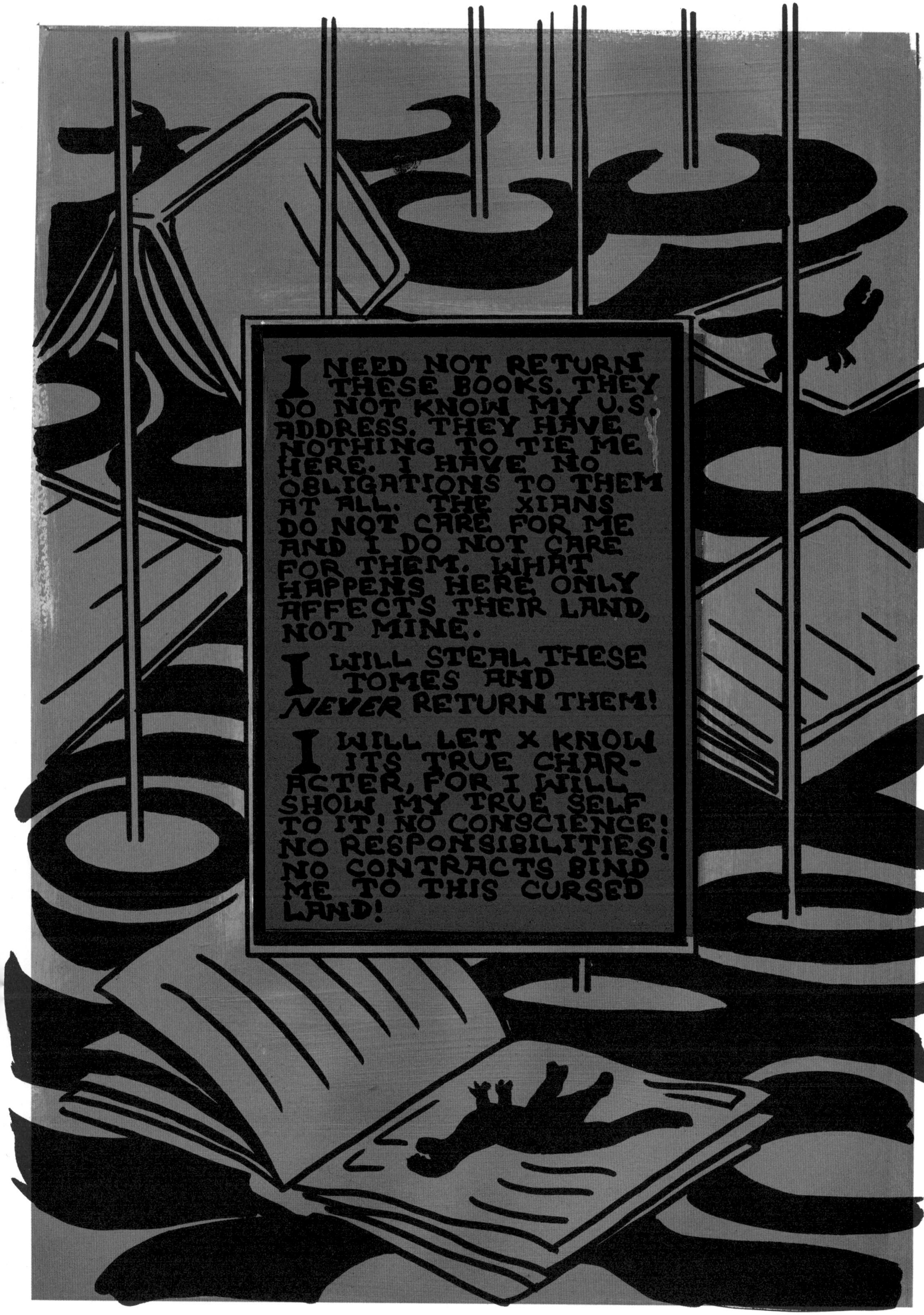
I NEED NOT RETURN THESE BOOKS. THEY DO NOT KNOW MY U.S. ADDRESS. THEY HAVE NOTHING TO TIE ME HERE. I HAVE NO OBLIGATIONS TO THEM AT ALL. THE XIANS DO NOT CARE FOR ME AND I DO NOT CARE FOR THEM. WHAT HAPPENS HERE ONLY AFFECTS THEIR LAND, NOT MINE.
I WILL STEAL THESE TOMES AND NEVER RETURN THEM!
I WILL LET X KNOW ITS TRUE CHARACTER, FOR I WILL SHOW MY TRUE SELF TO IT! NO CONSCIENCE! NO RESPONSIBILITIES! NO CONTRACTS BIND ME TO THIS CURSED LAND!

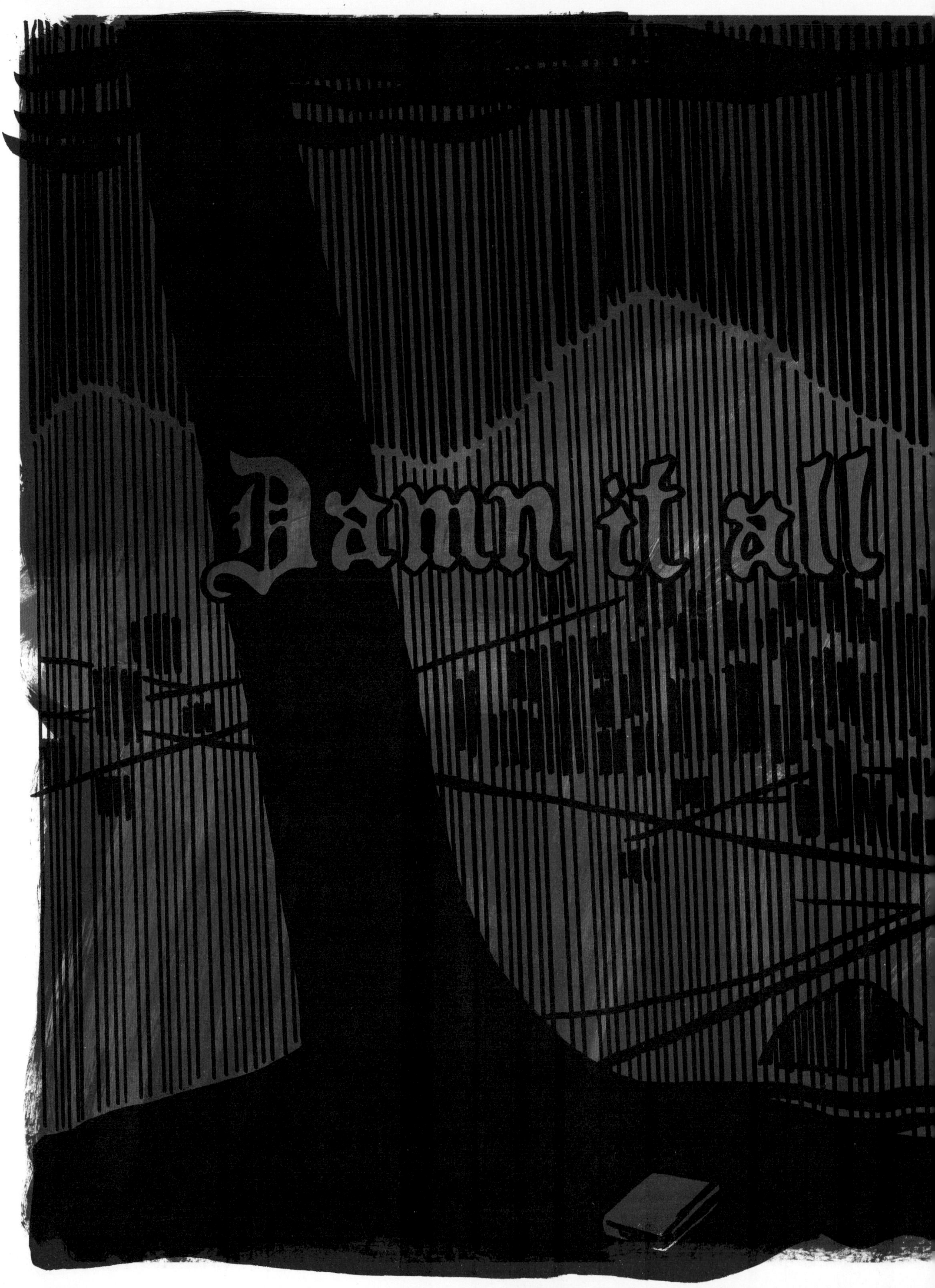
Damn it all

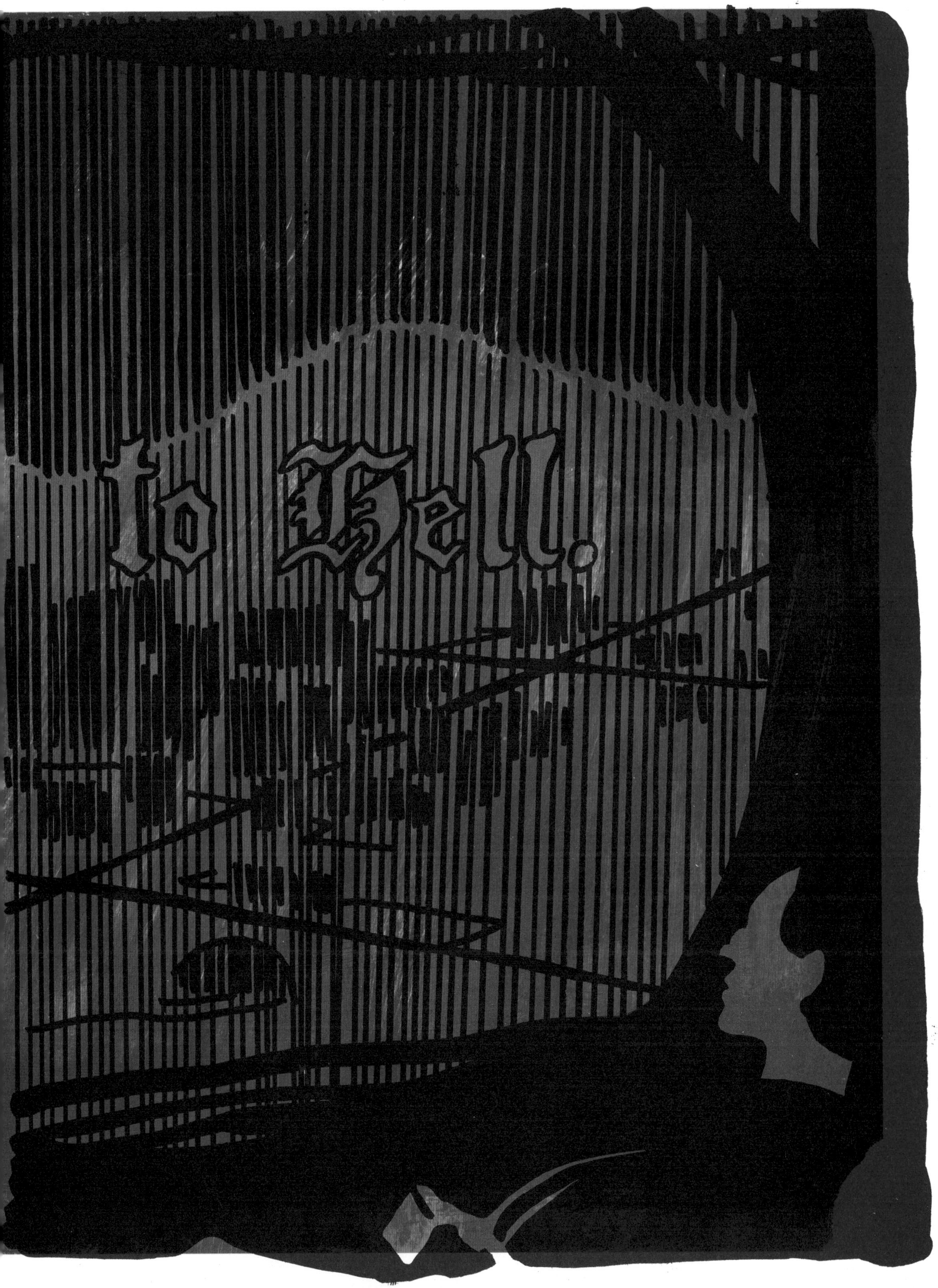
to Hell.

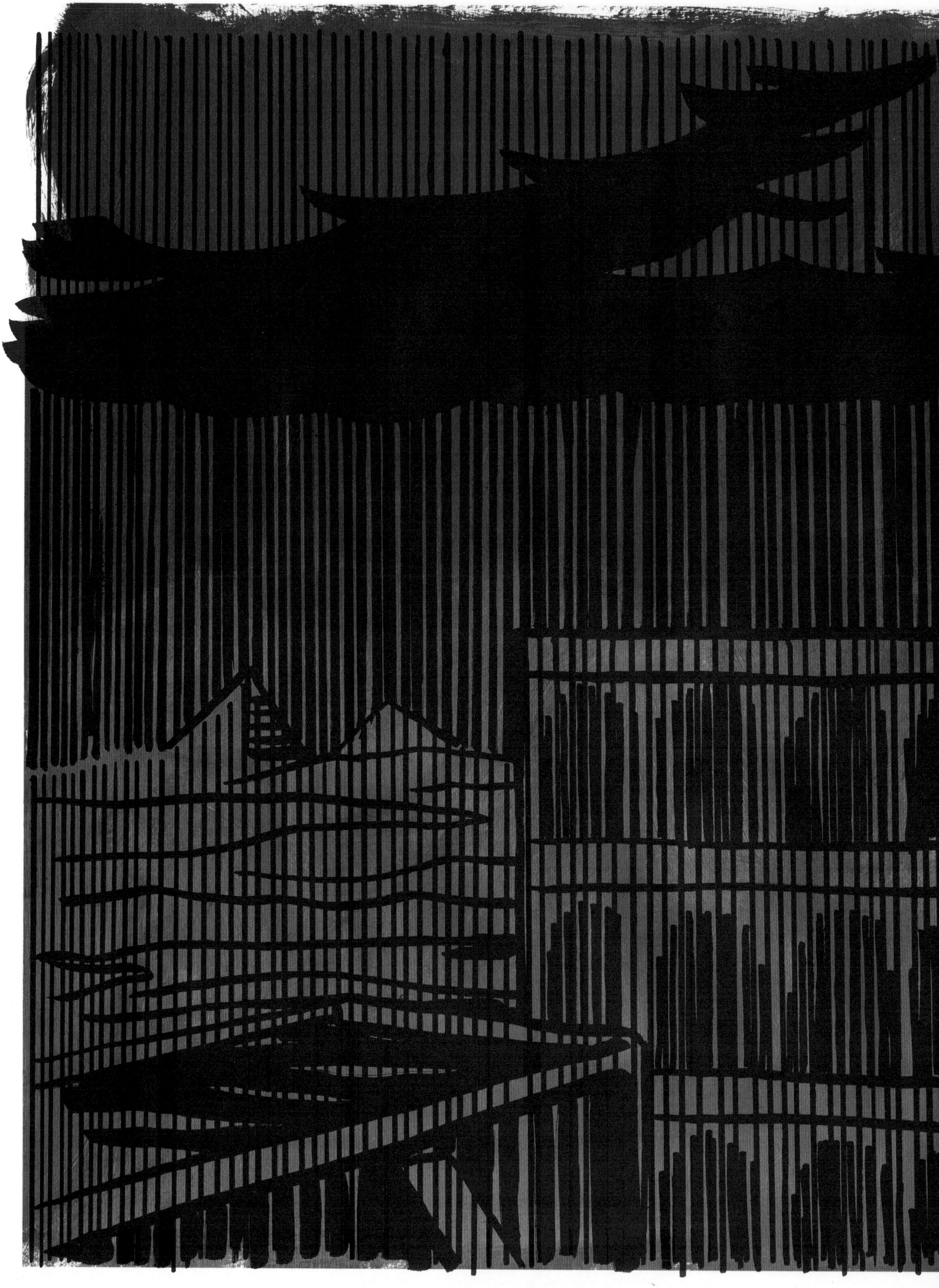

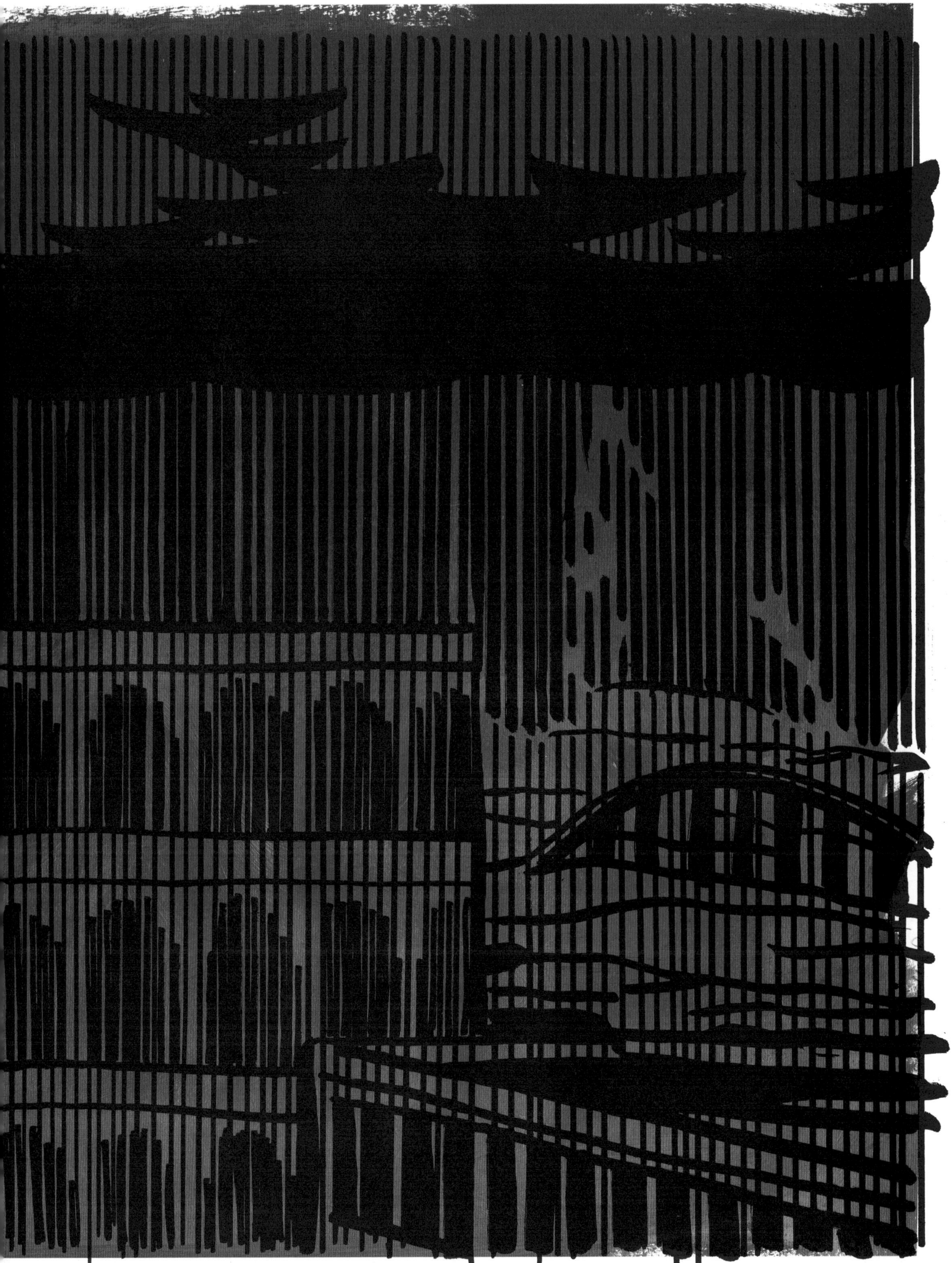

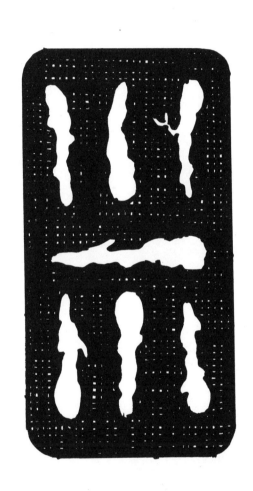

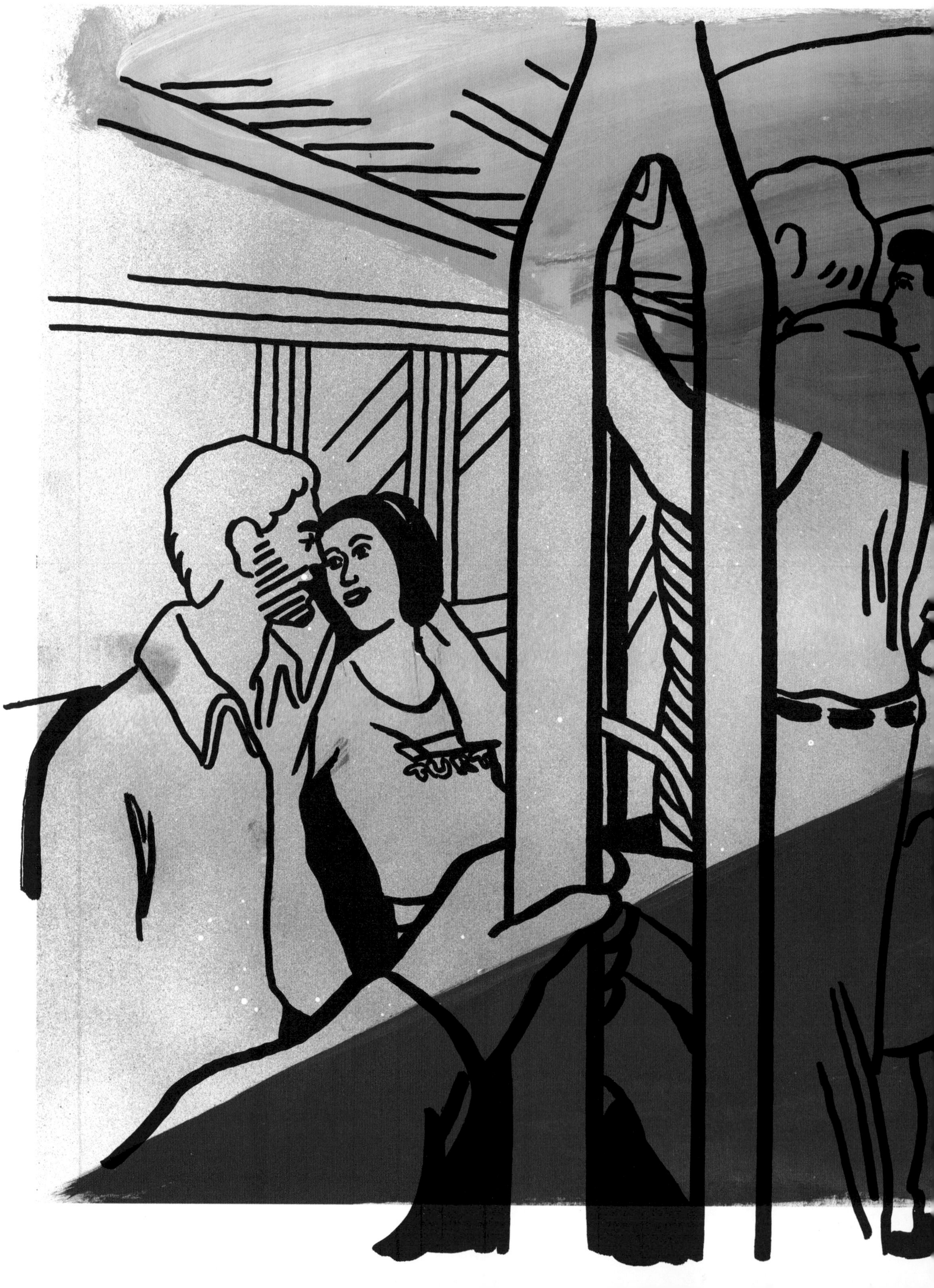

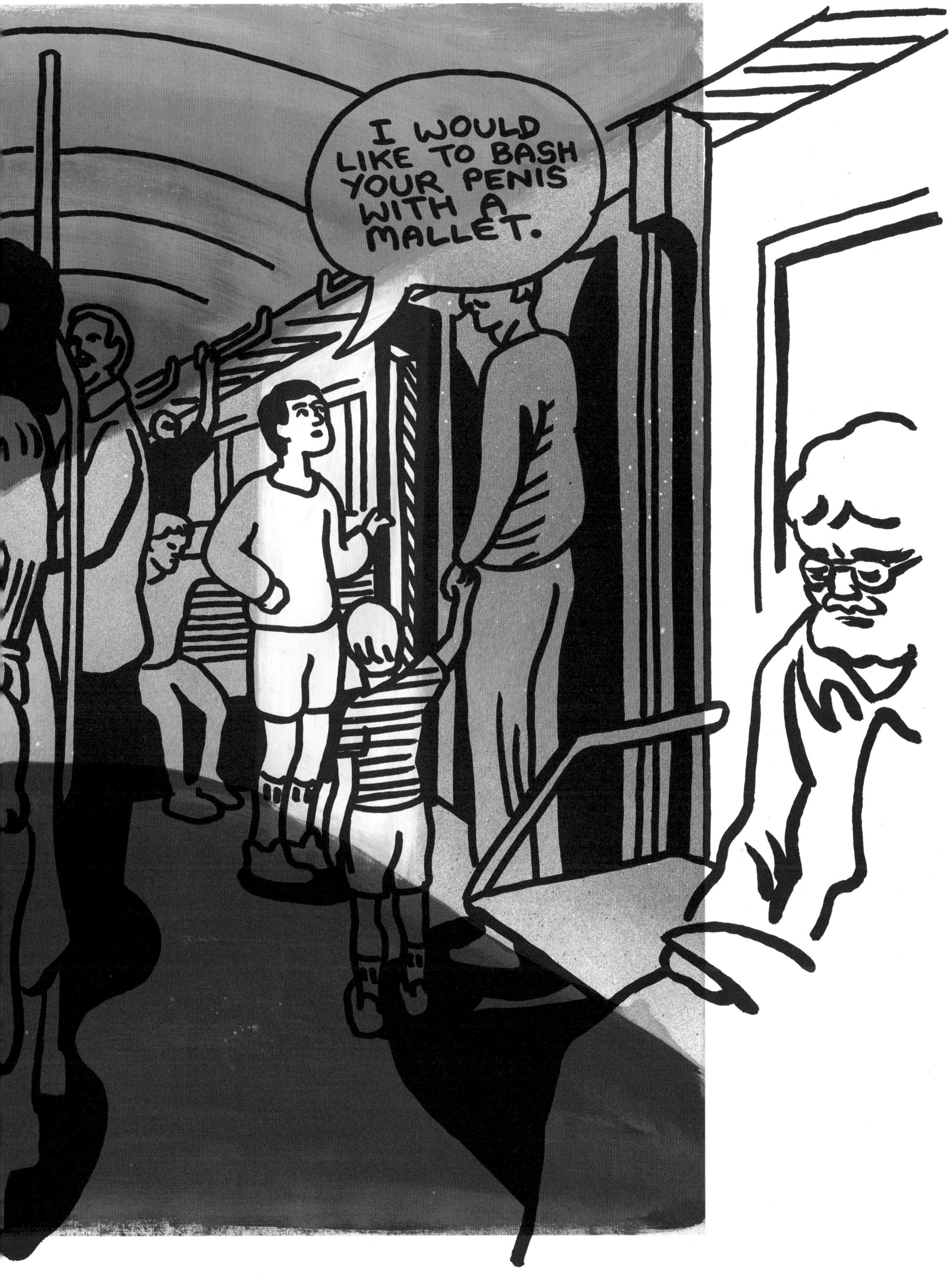
I WOULD LIKE TO BASH YOUR PENIS WITH A MALLET.

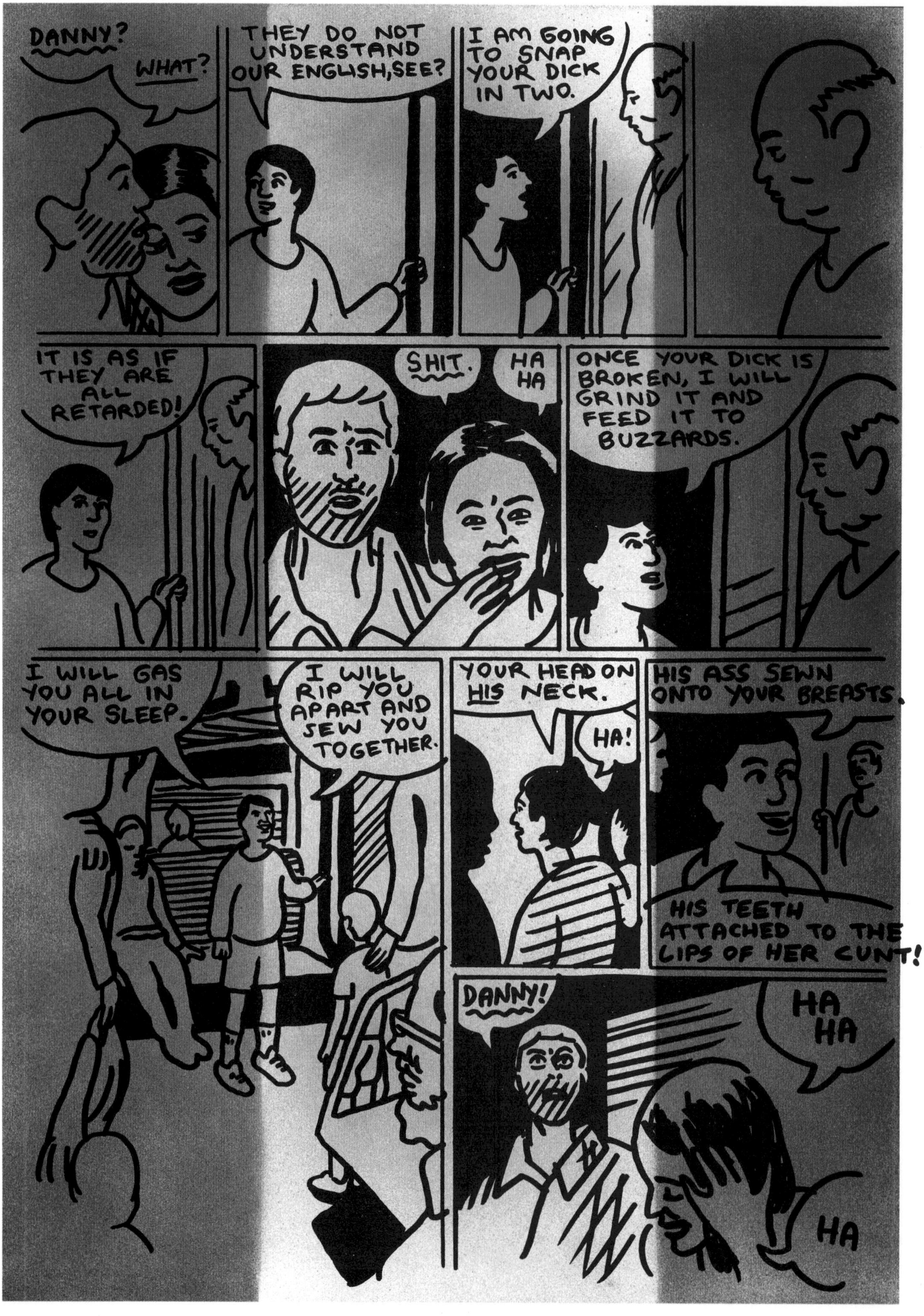
DANNY?
WHAT?
THEY DO NOT UNDERSTAND OUR ENGLISH, SEE?
I AM GOING TO SNAP YOUR DICK IN TWO.
IT IS AS IF THEY ARE ALL RETARDED!
SHIT.
HA HA
ONCE YOUR DICK IS BROKEN, I WILL GRIND IT AND FEED IT TO BUZZARDS.
I WILL GAS YOU ALL IN YOUR SLEEP.
I WILL RIP YOU APART AND SEW YOU TOGETHER.
YOUR HEAD ON HIS NECK.
HA!
HIS ASS SEWN ONTO YOUR BREASTS.
HIS TEETH ATTACHED TO THE LIPS OF HER CUNT!
DANNY!
HA HA
HA

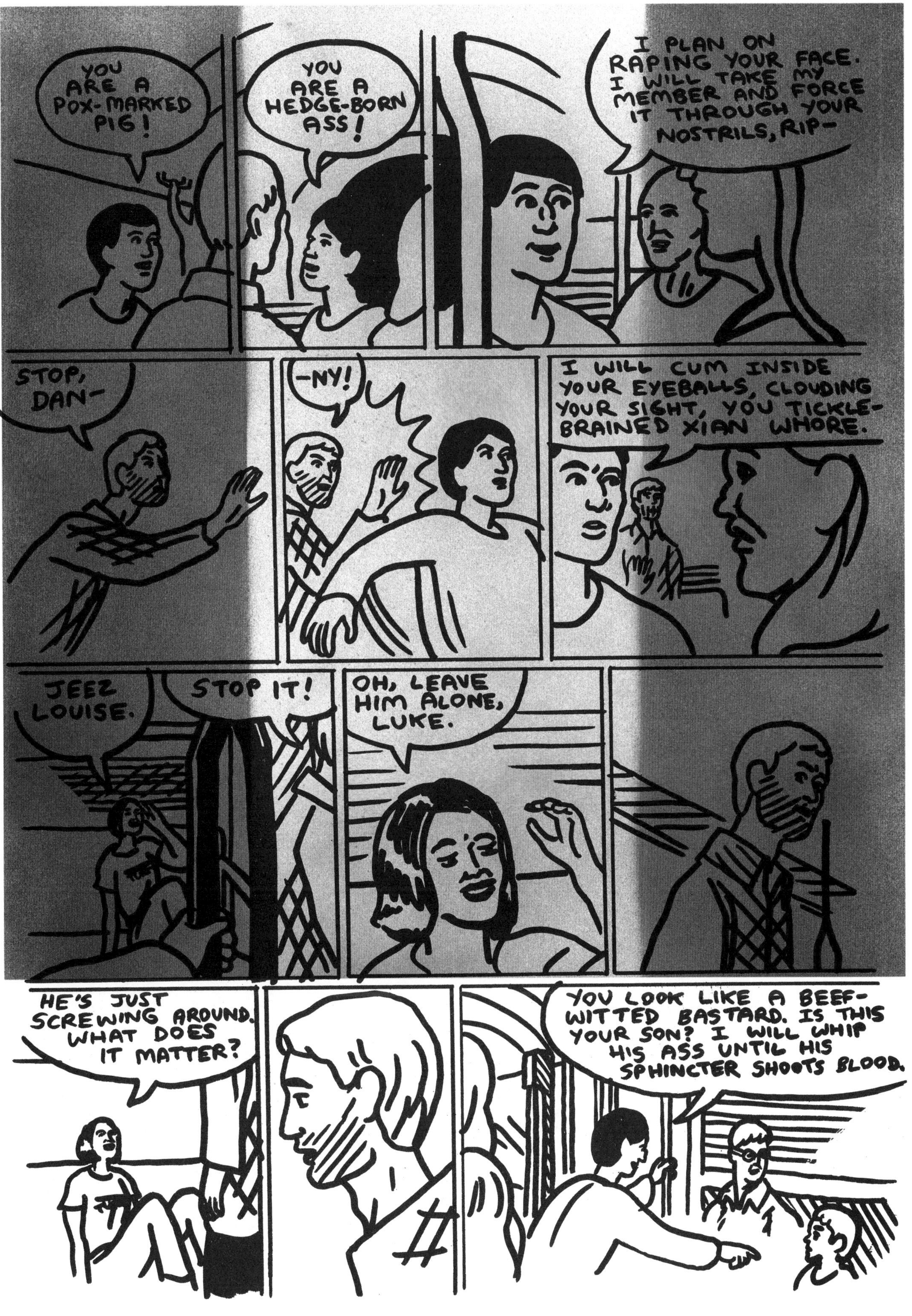
YOU ARE A POX-MARKED PIG!
YOU ARE A HEDGE-BORN ASS!
I PLAN ON RAPING YOUR FACE. I WILL TAKE MY MEMBER AND FORCE IT THROUGH YOUR NOSTRILS, RIP-
STOP, DAN-
-NY!
I WILL CUM INSIDE YOUR EYEBALLS, CLOUDING YOUR SIGHT, YOU TICKLE-BRAINED XIAN WHORE.
JEEZ LOUISE.
STOP IT!
OH, LEAVE HIM ALONE, LUKE.
HE'S JUST SCREWING AROUND. WHAT DOES IT MATTER?
YOU LOOK LIKE A BEEF-WITTED BASTARD. IS THIS YOUR SON? I WILL WHIP HIS ASS UNTIL HIS SPHINCTER SHOOTS BLOOD.

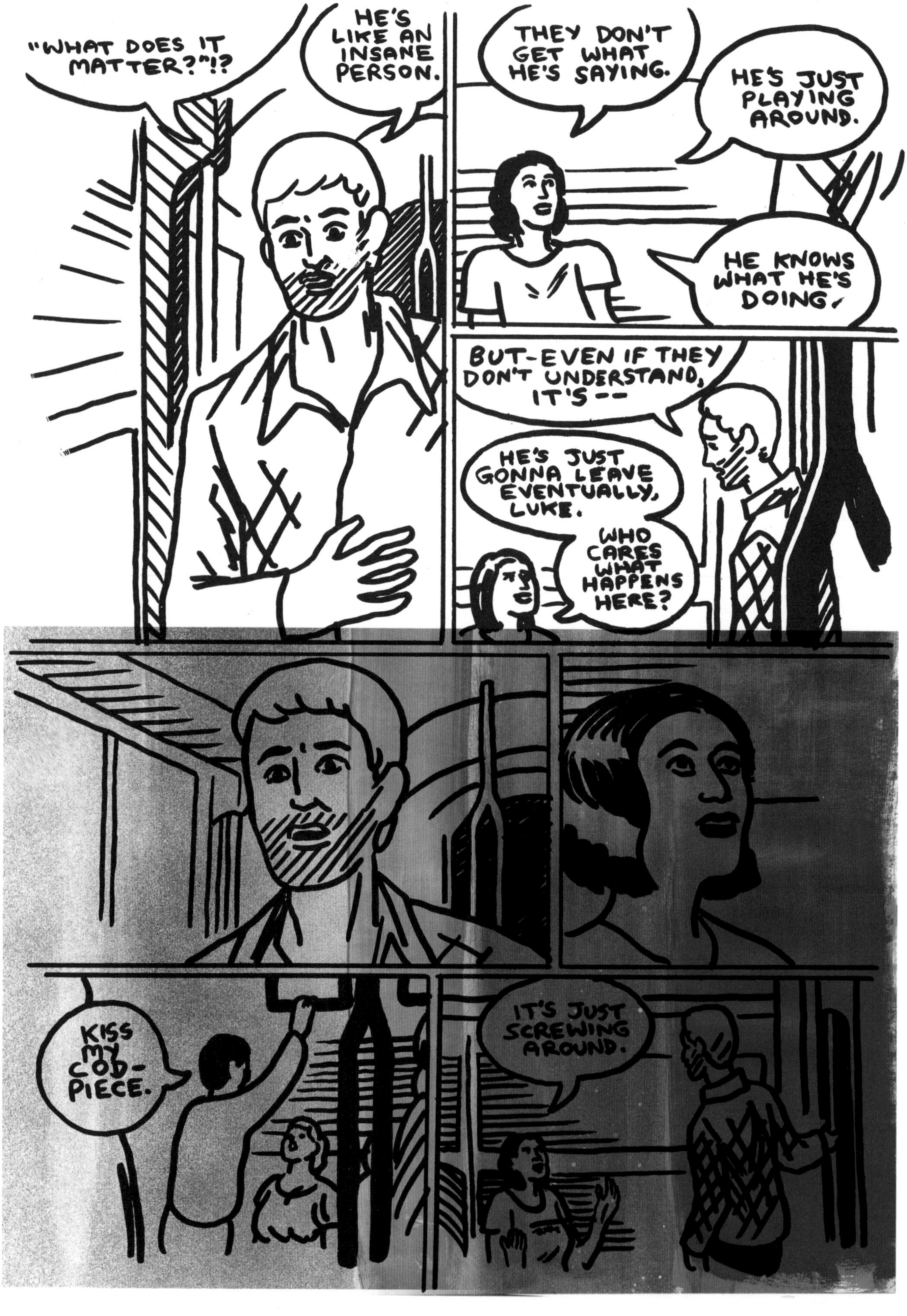
"WHAT DOES IT MATTER?"!?
HE'S LIKE AN INSANE PERSON.
THEY DON'T GET WHAT HE'S SAYING.
HE'S JUST PLAYING AROUND.
HE KNOWS WHAT HE'S DOING.
BUT-EVEN IF THEY DON'T UNDERSTAND, IT'S --
HE'S JUST GONNA LEAVE EVENTUALLY, LUKE.
WHO CARES WHAT HAPPENS HERE?
KISS MY COD-PIECE.
IT'S JUST SCREWING AROUND.

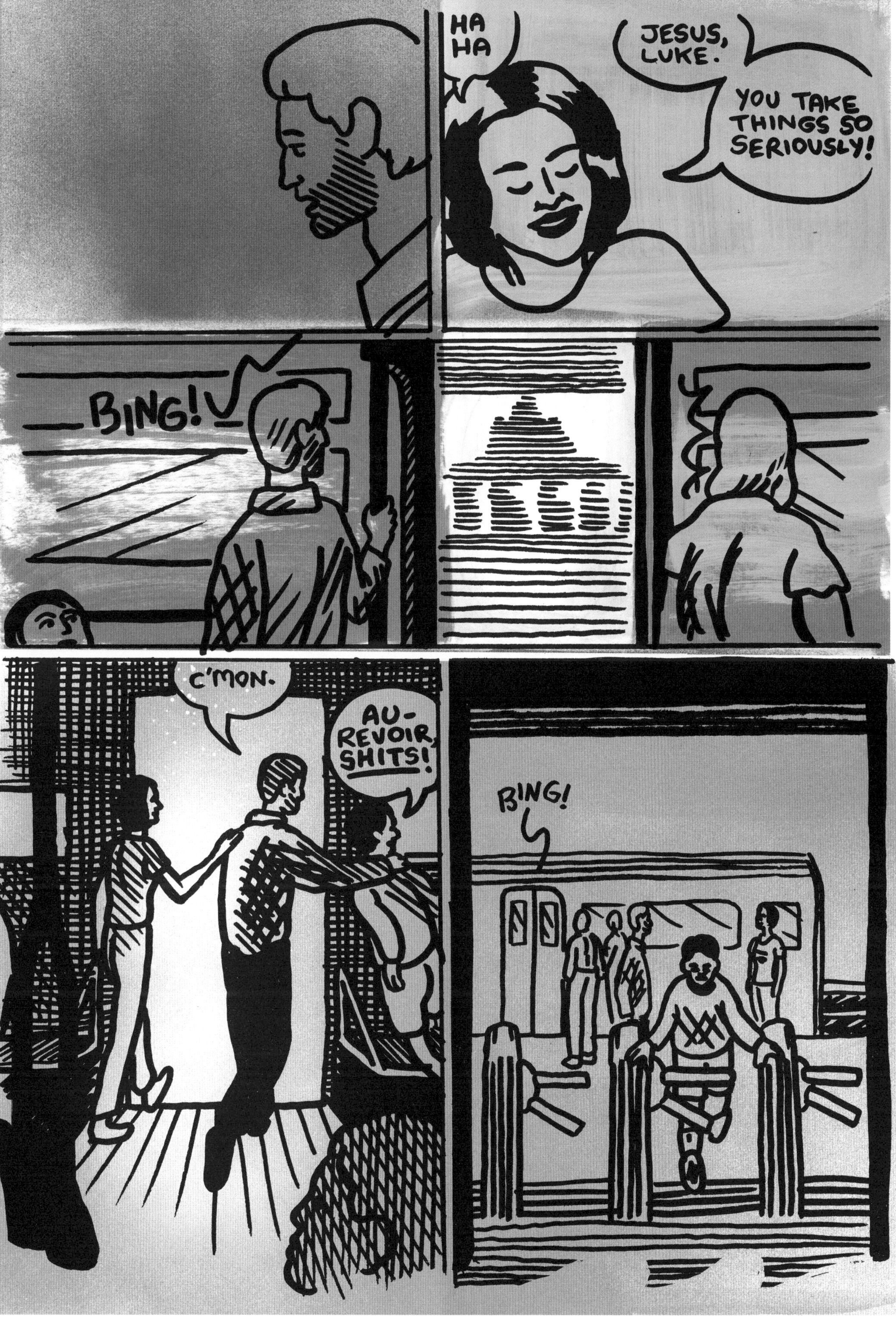
HA HA
JESUS, LUKE.
YOU TAKE THINGS SO SERIOUSLY!
BING!
C'MON.
AU-REVOIR, SHITS!
BING!

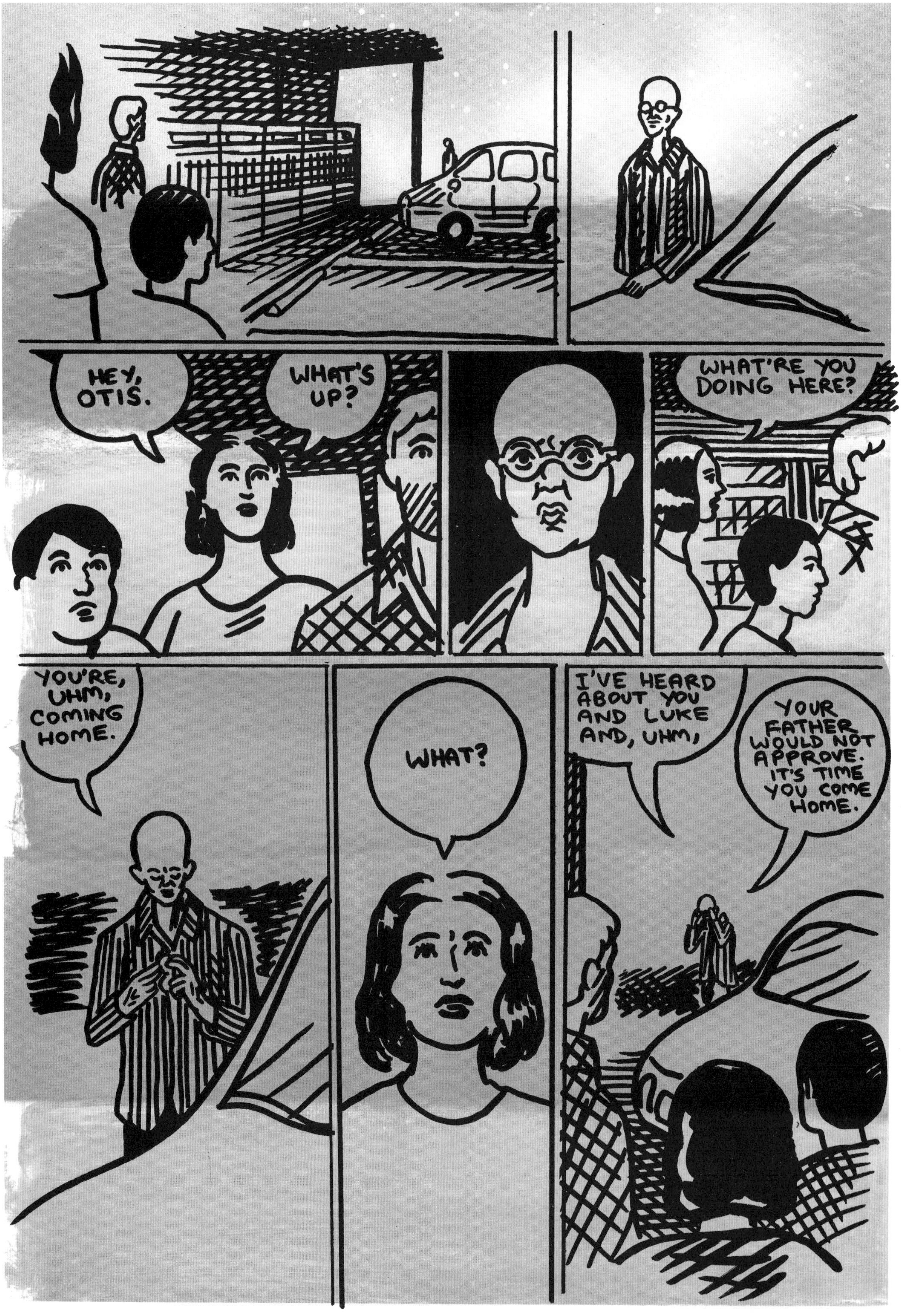
HEY, OTIS.
WHAT'S UP?
WHAT'RE YOU DOING HERE?
YOU'RE, UHM, COMING HOME.
WHAT?
I'VE HEARD ABOUT YOU AND LUKE AND, UHM,
YOUR FATHER WOULD NOT APPROVE. IT'S TIME YOU COME HOME.

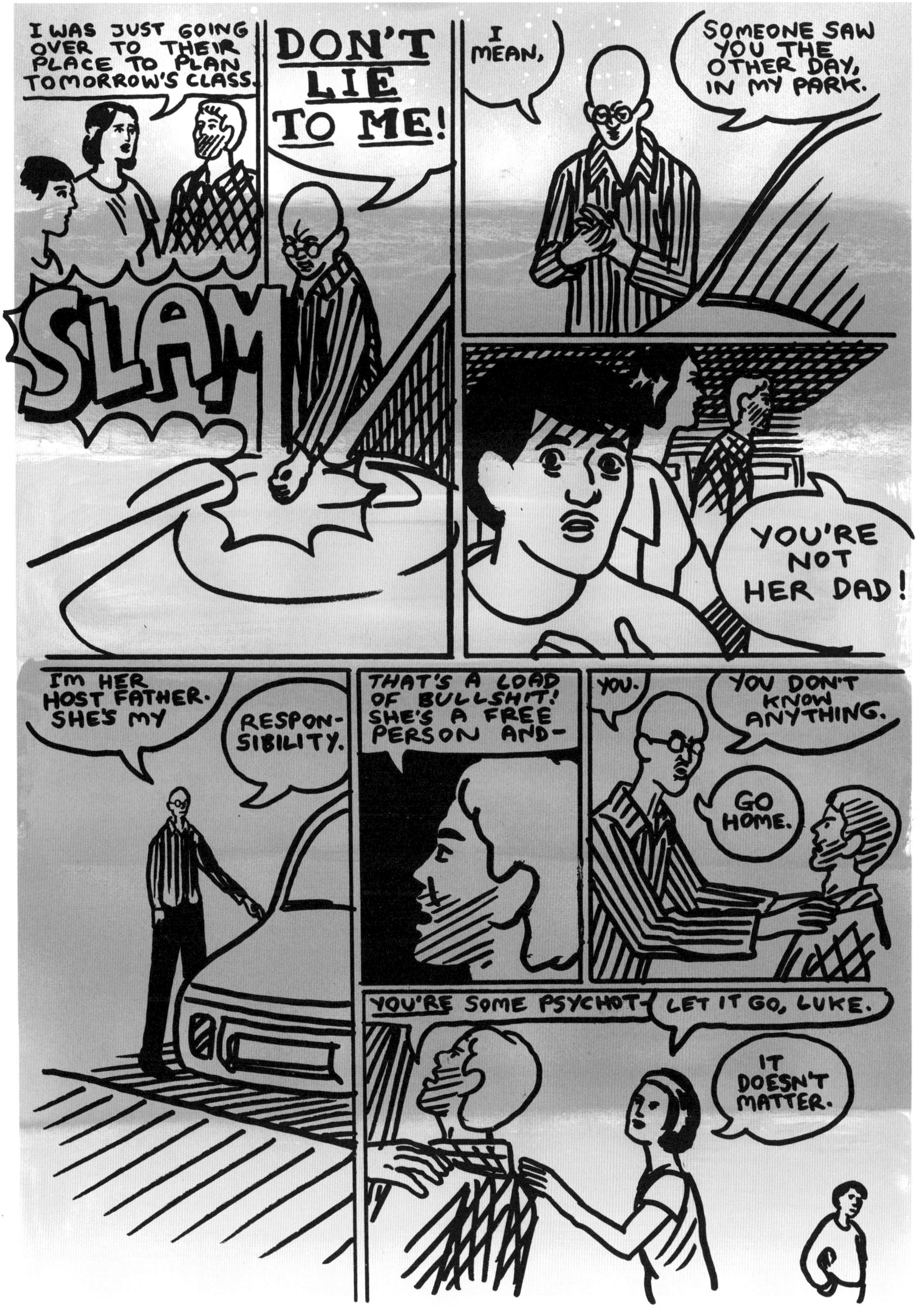
I WAS JUST GOING OVER TO THEIR PLACE TO PLAN TOMORROW'S CLASS.
DON'T LIE TO ME!
SLAM
I MEAN,
SOMEONE SAW YOU THE OTHER DAY, IN MY PARK.
YOU'RE NOT HER DAD!
I'M HER HOST FATHER. SHE'S MY
RESPON-SIBILITY.
THAT'S A LOAD OF BULLSHIT! SHE'S A FREE PERSON AND-
YOU.
YOU DON'T KNOW ANYTHING.
GO HOME.
YOU'RE SOME PSYCHOT-
LET IT GO, LUKE.
IT DOESN'T MATTER.

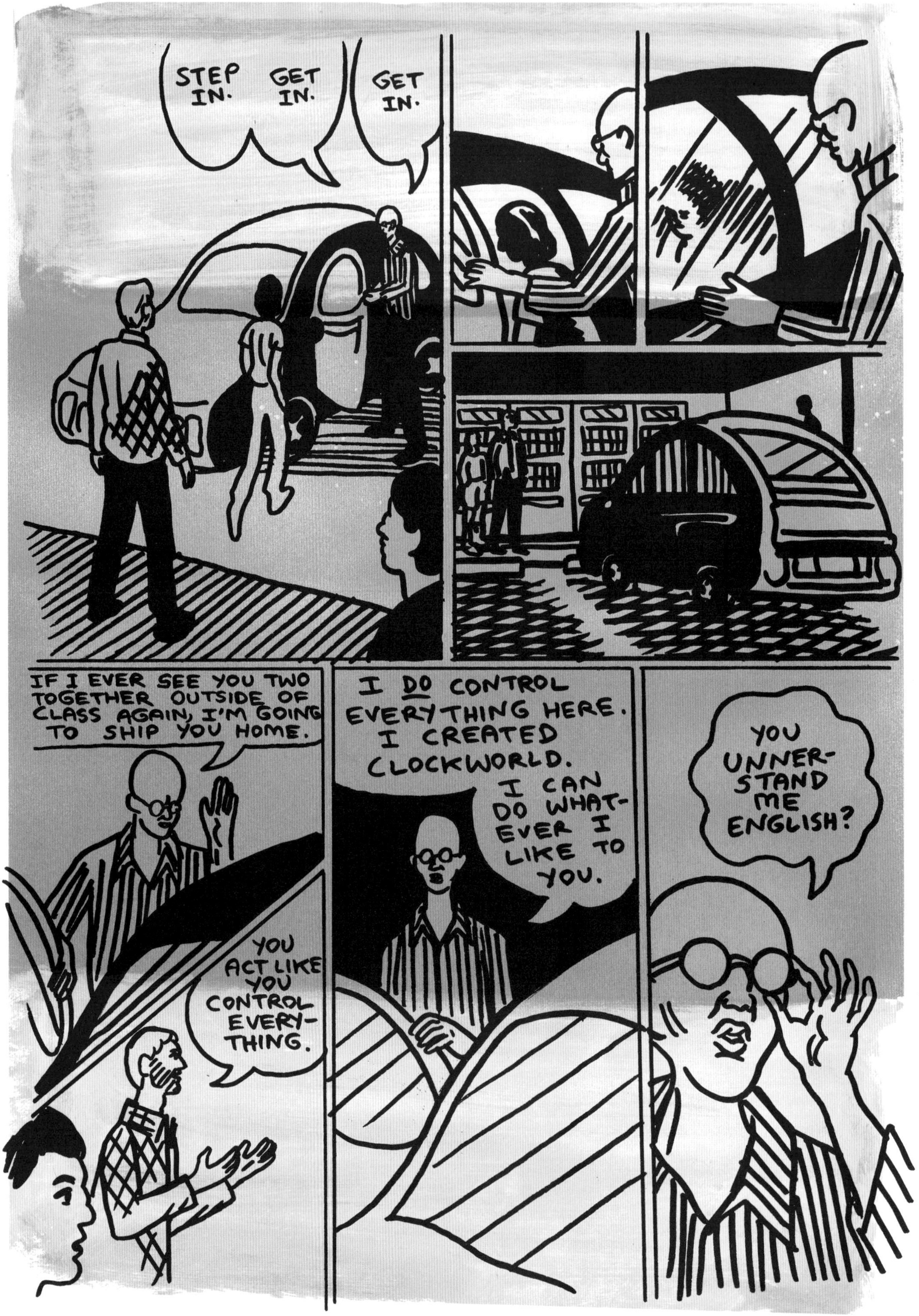
STEP IN. GET IN.
GET IN.
IF I EVER SEE YOU TWO TOGETHER OUTSIDE OF CLASS AGAIN, I'M GOING TO SHIP YOU HOME.
YOU ACT LIKE YOU CONTROL EVERY-THING.
I DO CONTROL EVERYTHING HERE. I CREATED CLOCKWORLD.
I CAN DO WHAT-EVER I LIKE TO YOU.
YOU UNNER-STAND ME ENGLISH?

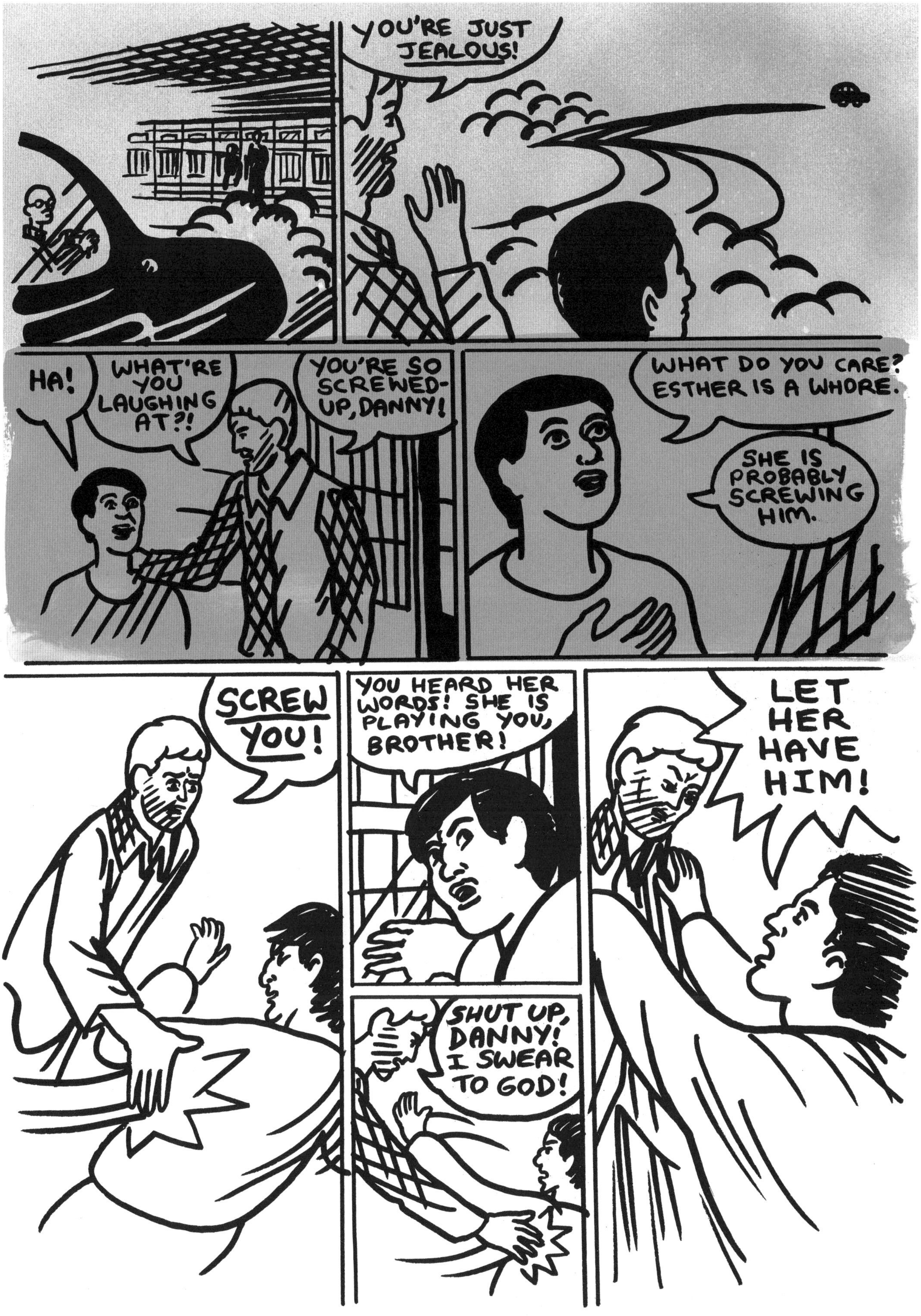
YOU'RE JUST JEALOUS!
HA!
WHAT'RE YOU LAUGHING AT?!
YOU'RE SO SCREWED-UP, DANNY!
WHAT DO YOU CARE? ESTHER IS A WHORE.
SHE IS PROBABLY SCREWING HIM.
SCREW YOU!
YOU HEARD HER WORDS! SHE IS PLAYING YOU, BROTHER!
SHUT UP, DANNY! I SWEAR TO GOD!
LET HER HAVE HIM!

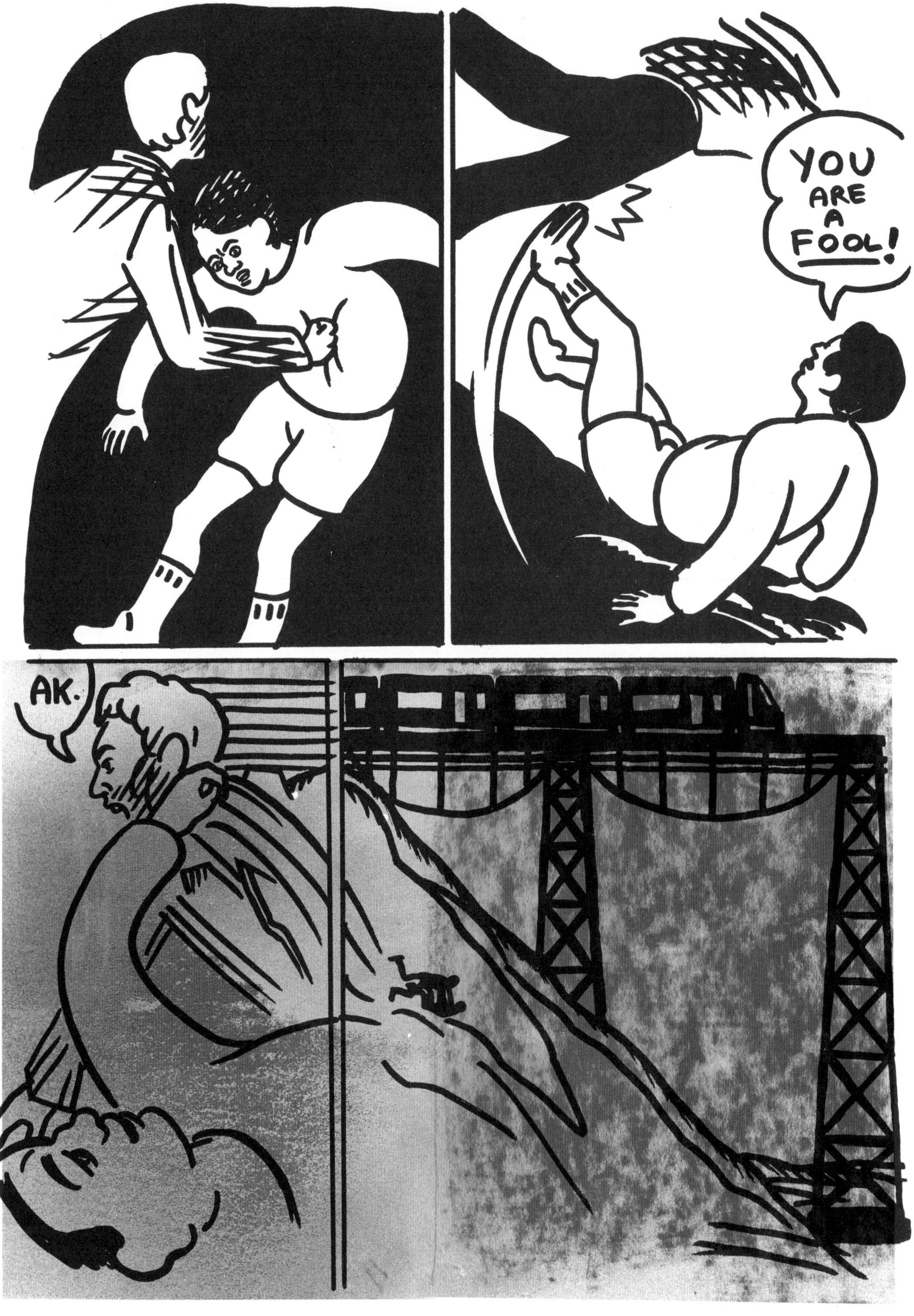
YOU ARE A FOOL!
AK.

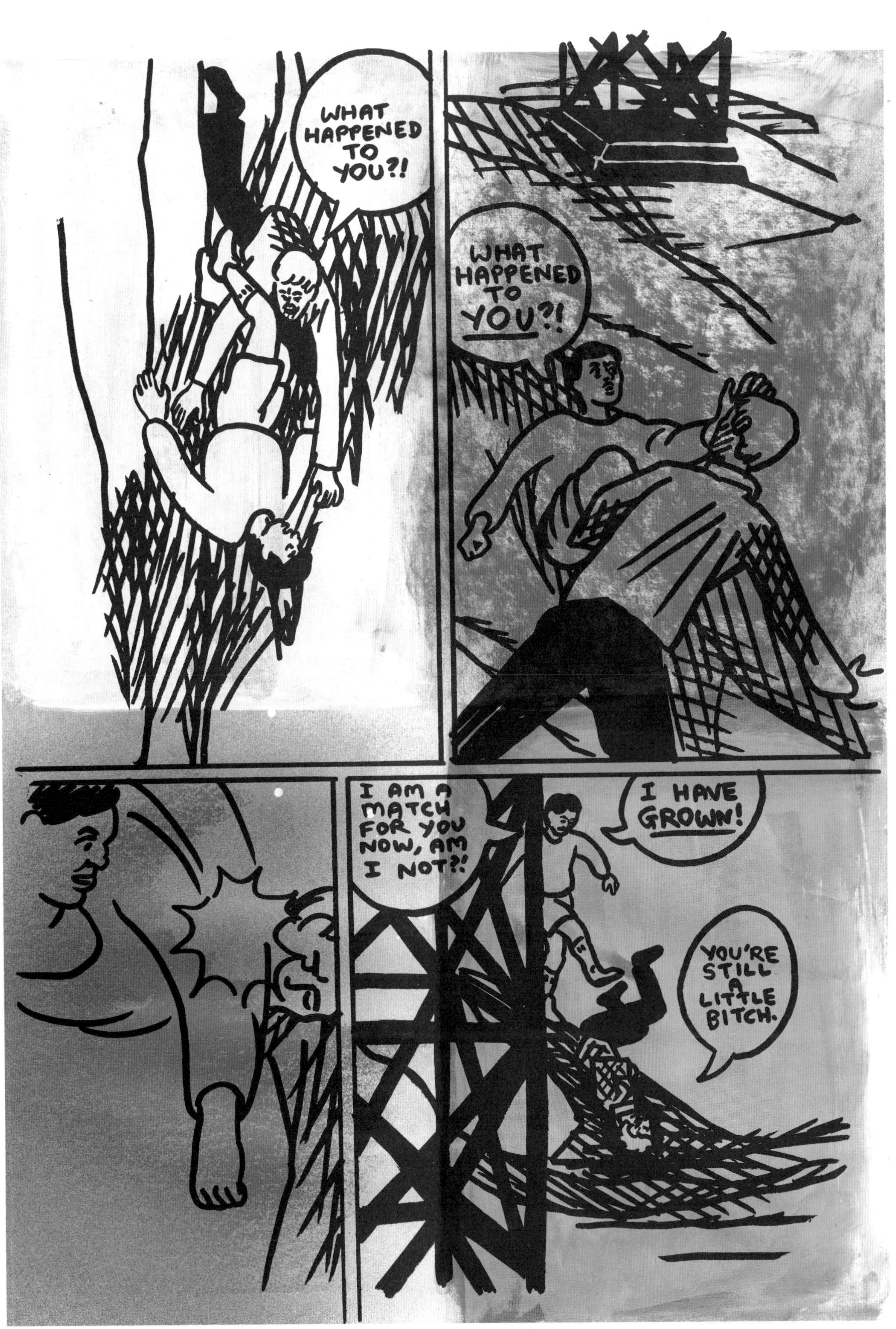
WHAT HAPPENED TO YOU?!
WHAT HAPPENED TO YOU?!
I AM A MATCH FOR YOU NOW, AM I NOT?!
I HAVE GROWN!
YOU'RE STILL A LITTLE BITCH.

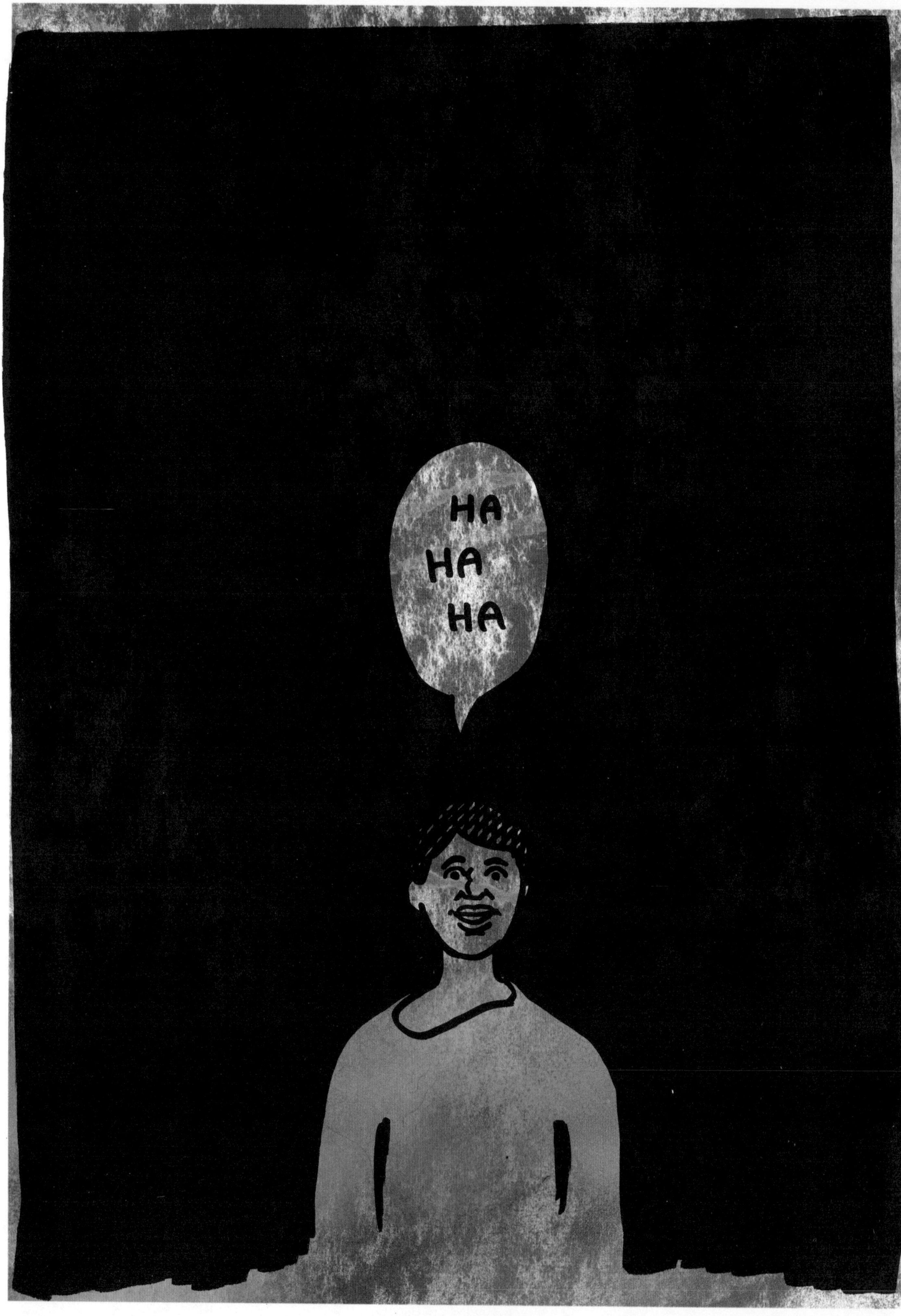
HA
HA
HA

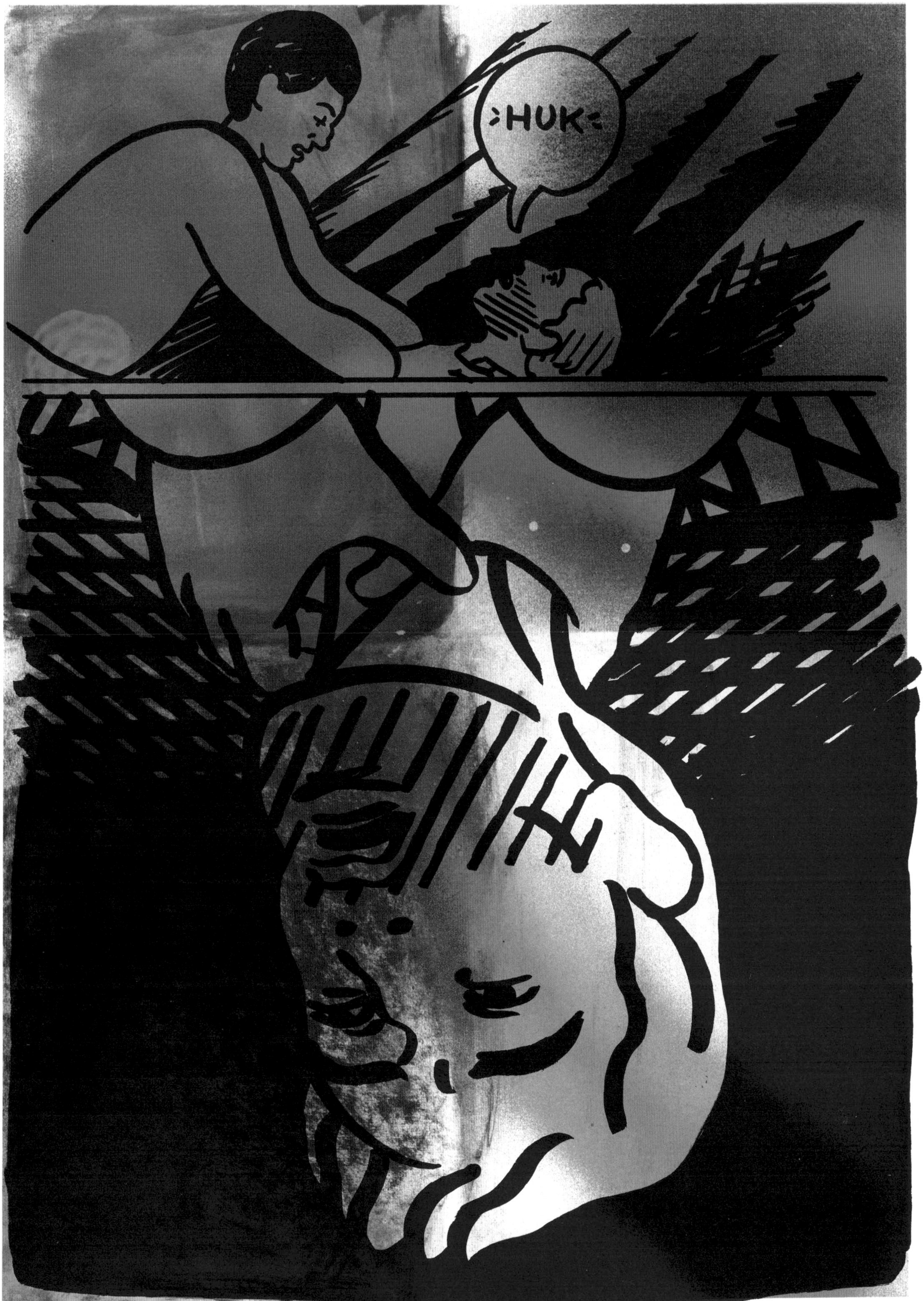
HUK

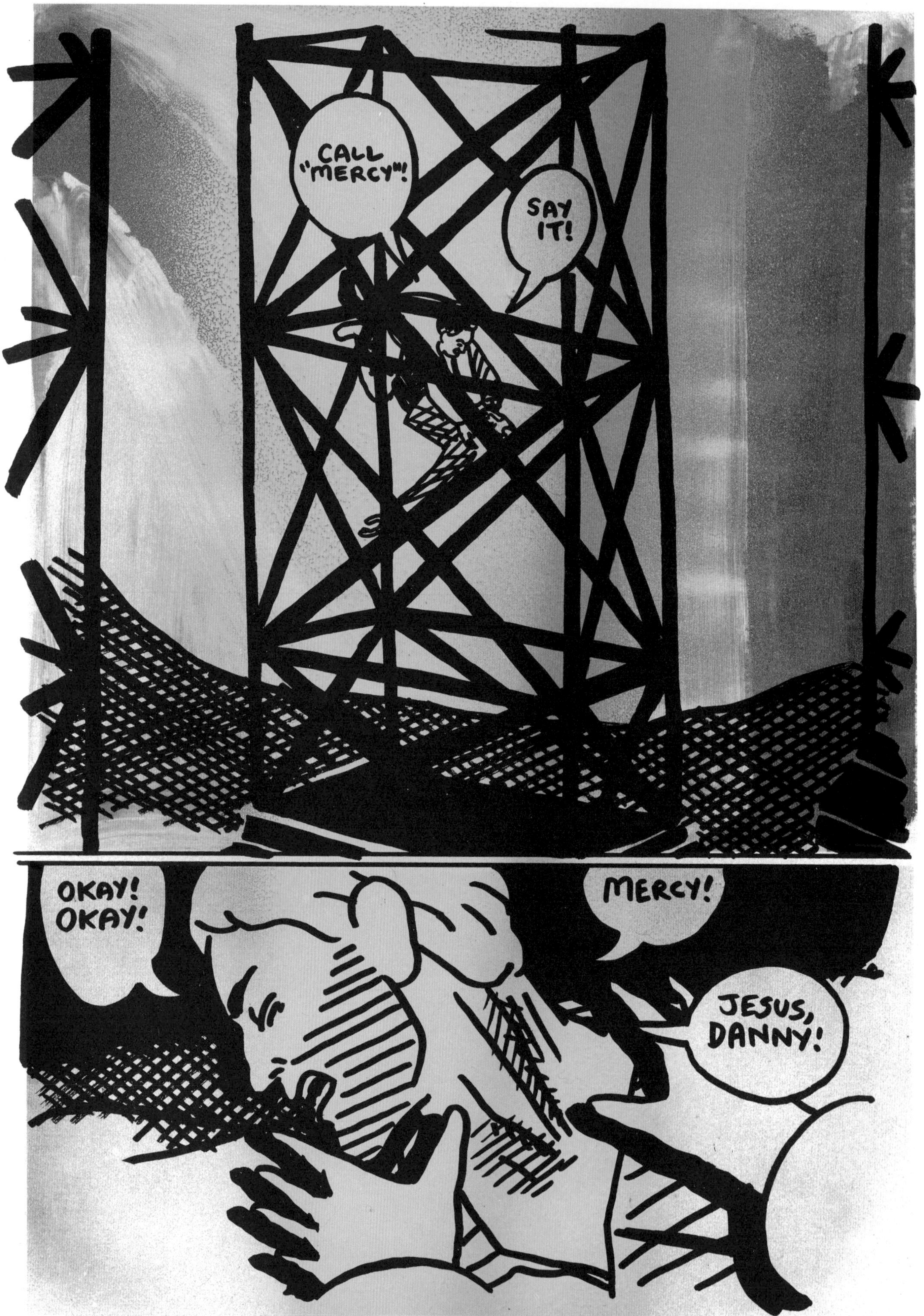
CALL "MERCY"!
SAY IT!
OKAY! OKAY!
MERCY!
JESUS, DANNY!

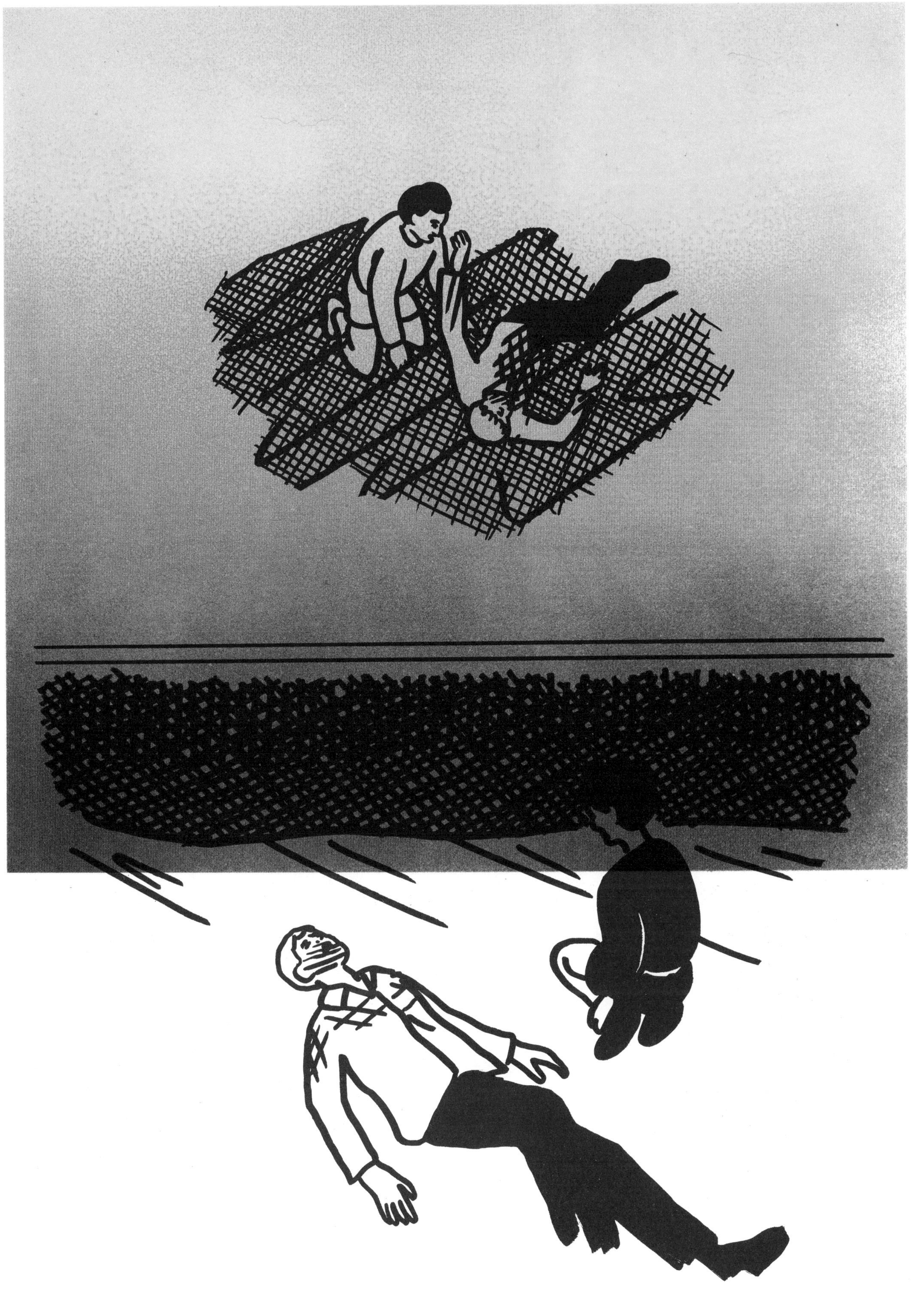

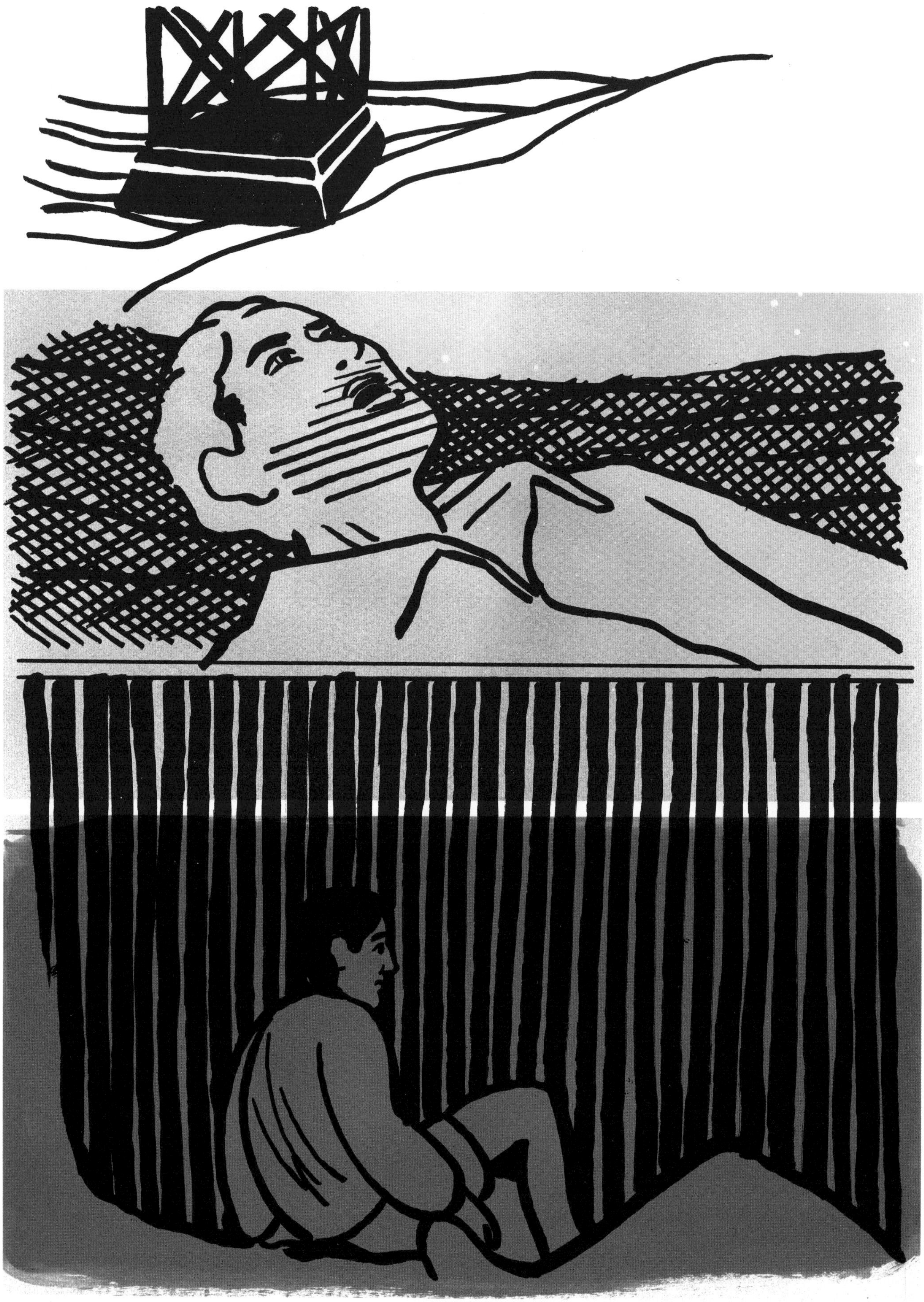

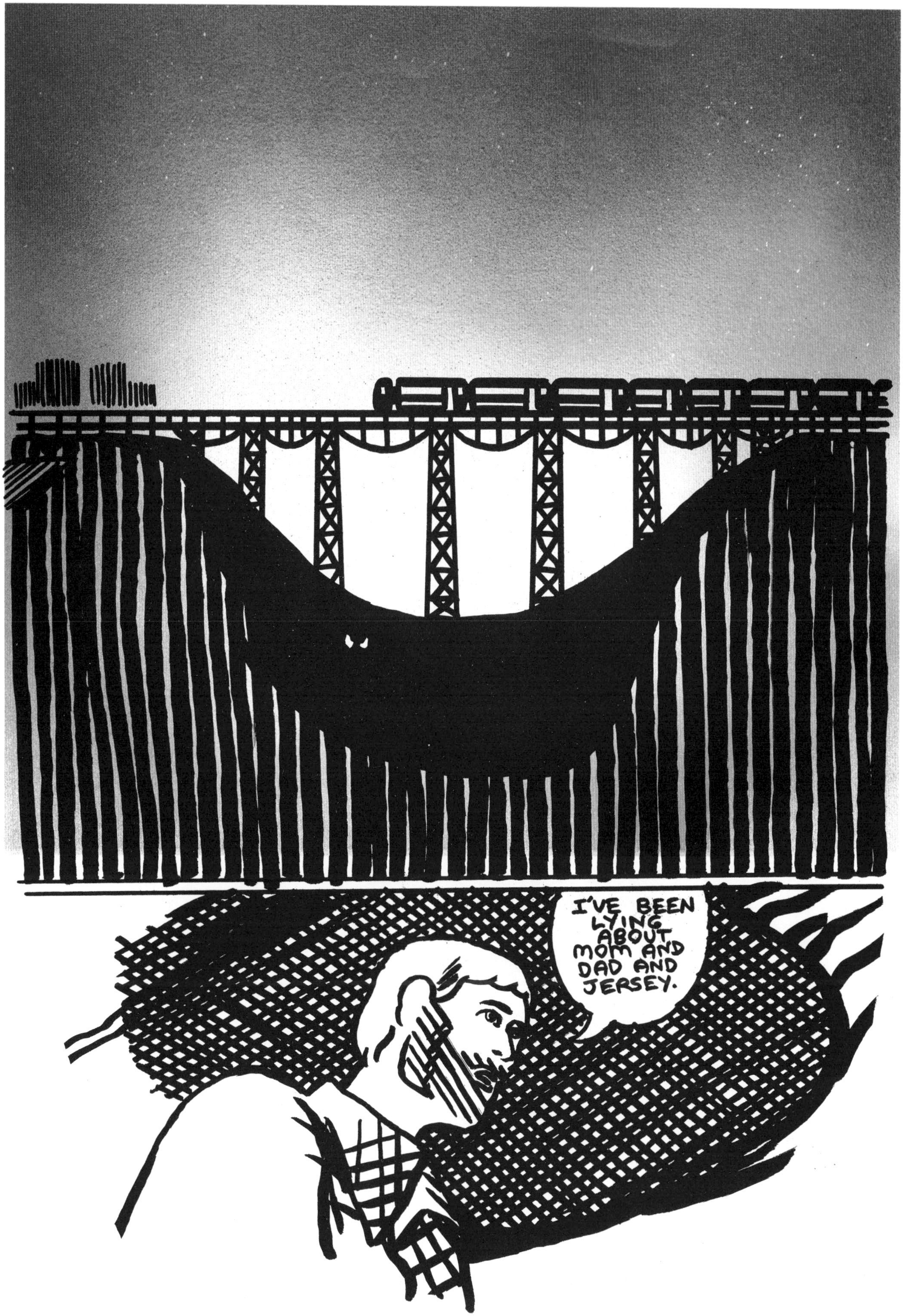
I'VE BEEN LYING ABOUT MOM AND DAD AND JERSEY.

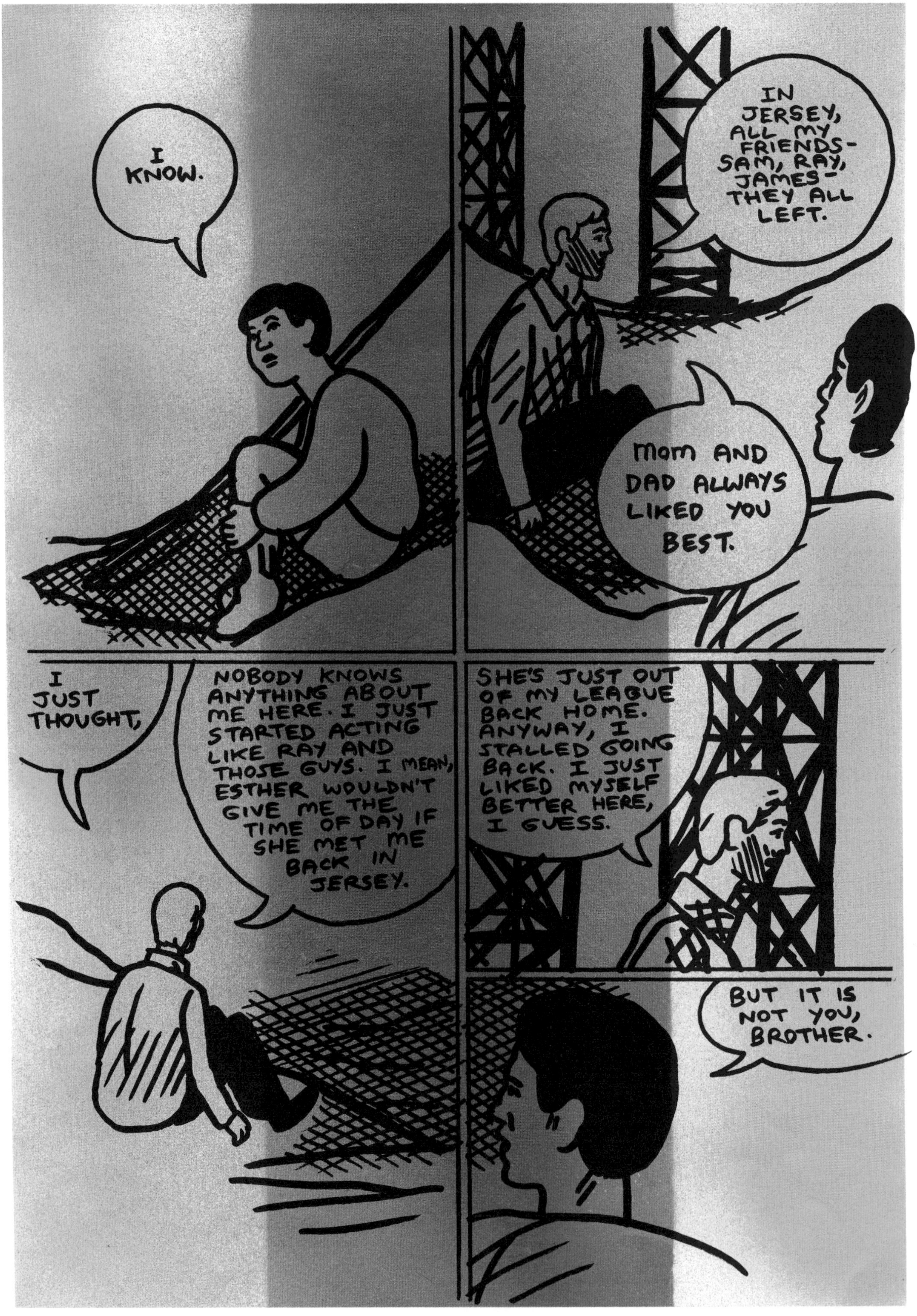
I KNOW.
IN JERSEY, ALL MY FRIENDS- SAM, RAY, JAMES- THEY ALL LEFT.
MOM AND DAD ALWAYS LIKED YOU BEST.
I JUST THOUGHT,
NOBODY KNOWS ANYTHING ABOUT ME HERE. I JUST STARTED ACTING LIKE RAY AND THOSE GUYS. I MEAN, ESTHER WOULDN'T GIVE ME THE TIME OF DAY IF SHE MET ME BACK IN JERSEY.
SHE'S JUST OUT OF MY LEAGUE BACK HOME. ANYWAY, I STALLED GOING BACK. I JUST LIKED MYSELF BETTER HERE, I GUESS.
BUT IT IS NOT YOU, BROTHER.

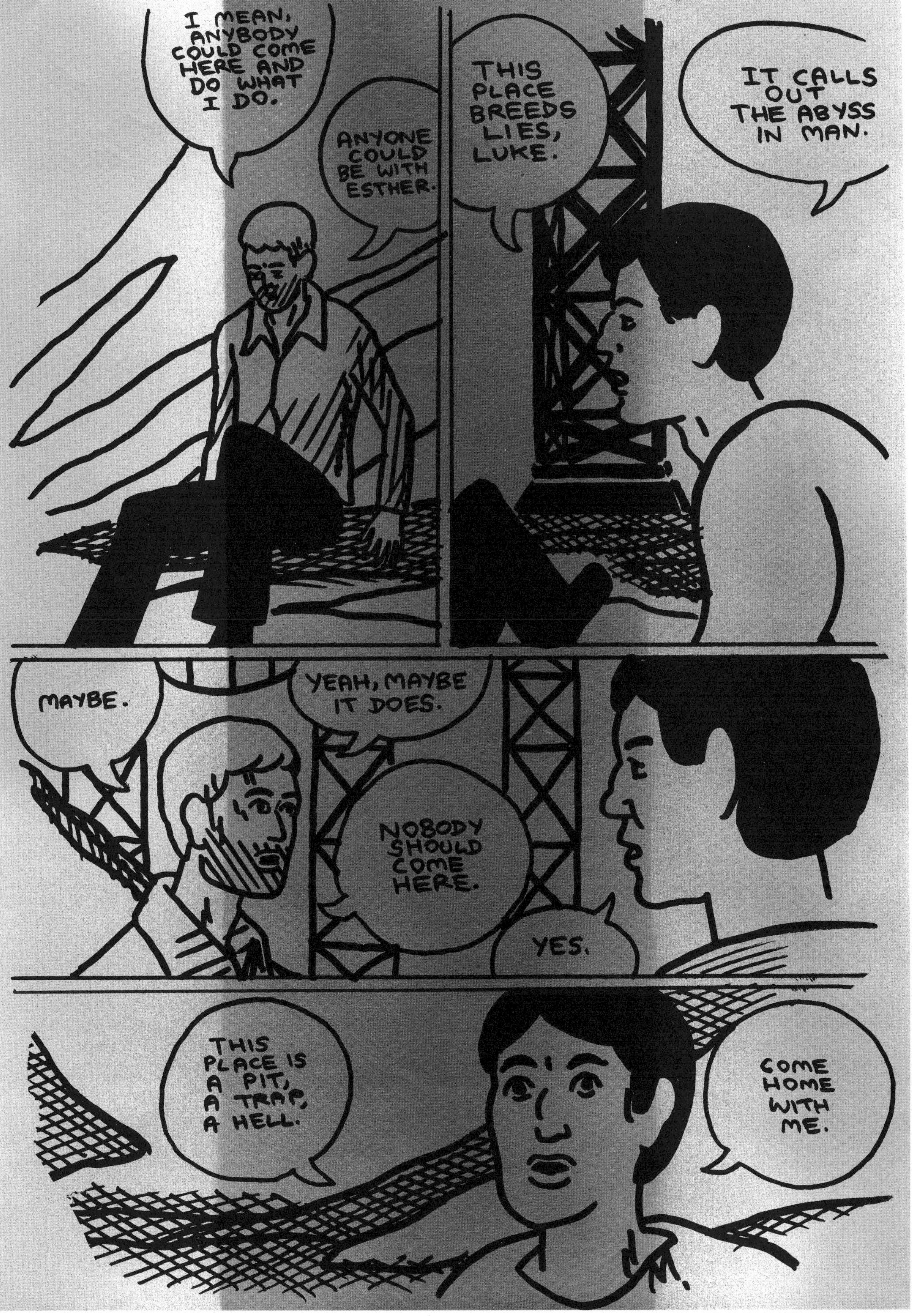
I MEAN, ANYBODY COULD COME HERE AND DO WHAT I DO.
ANYONE COULD BE WITH ESTHER.
THIS PLACE BREEDS LIES, LUKE.
IT CALLS OUT THE ABYSS IN MAN.
MAYBE.
YEAH, MAYBE IT DOES.
NOBODY SHOULD COME HERE.
YES.
THIS PLACE IS A PIT, A TRAP, A HELL.
COME HOME WITH ME.

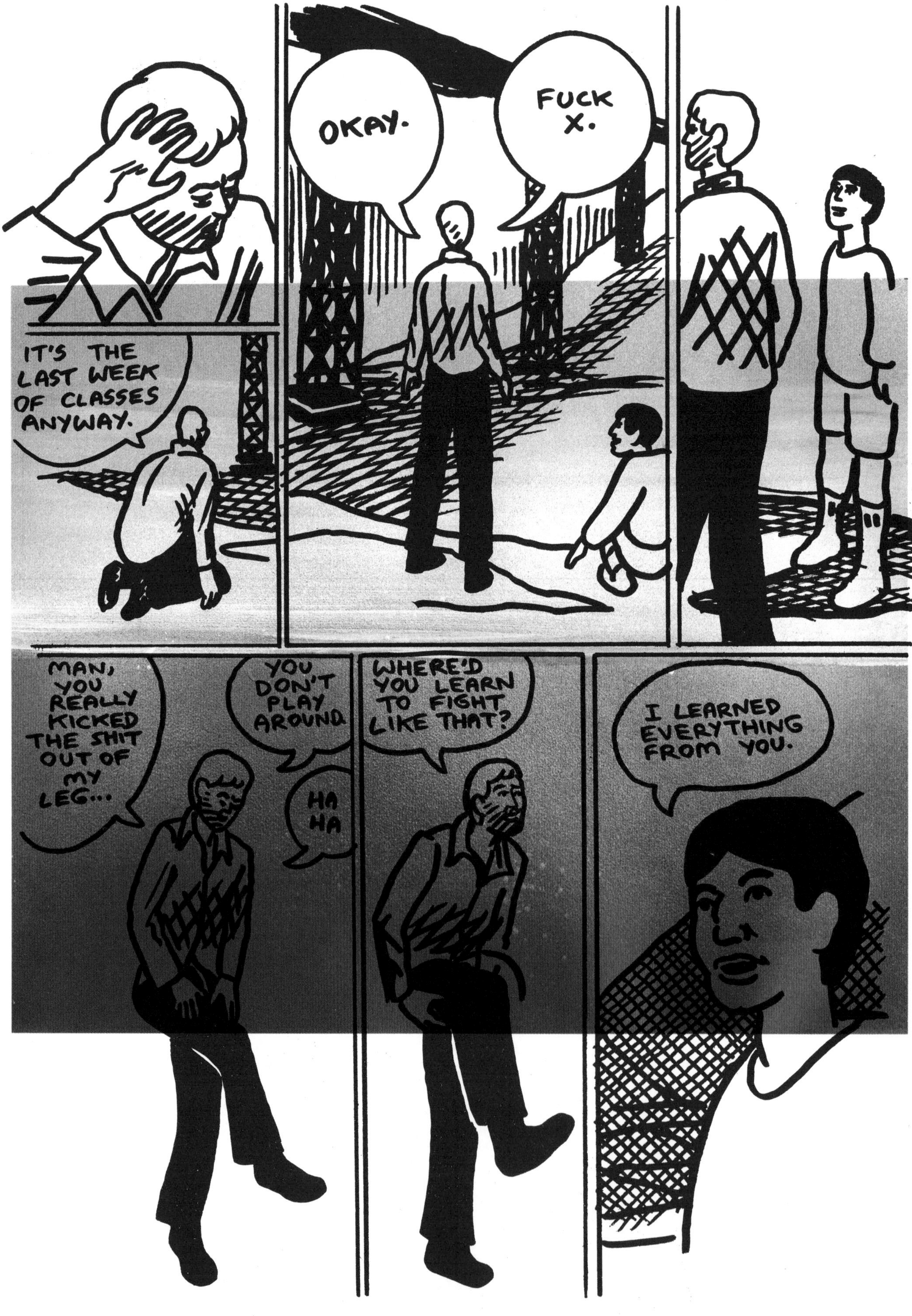
IT'S THE LAST WEEK OF CLASSES ANYWAY.
OKAY.
FUCK X.
MAN, YOU REALLY KICKED THE SHIT OUT OF MY LEG...
YOU DON'T PLAY AROUND.
HA HA
WHERE'D YOU LEARN TO FIGHT LIKE THAT?
I LEARNED EVERYTHING FROM YOU.

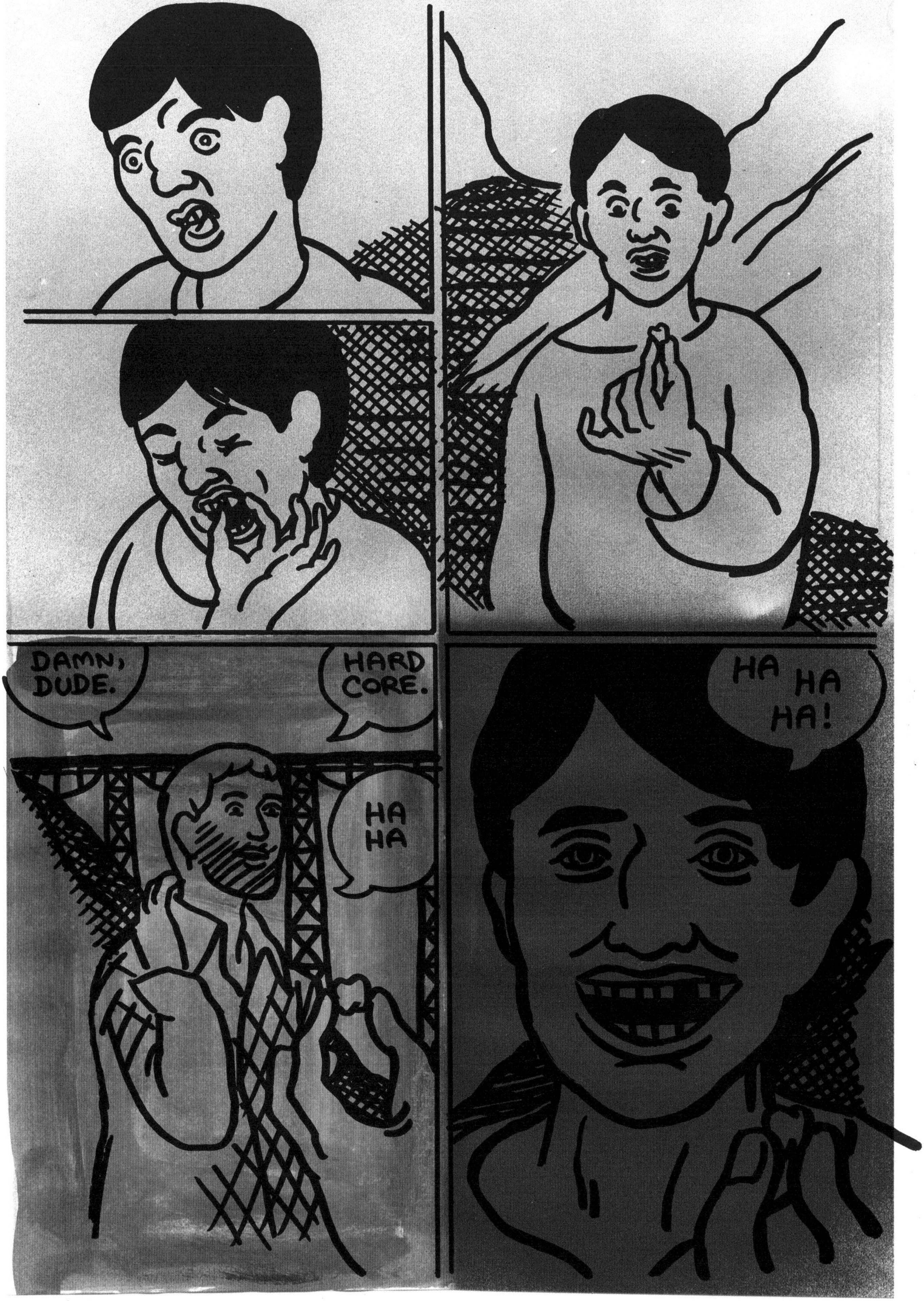
DAMN, DUDE.
HARD CORE.
HA HA
HA HA HA!

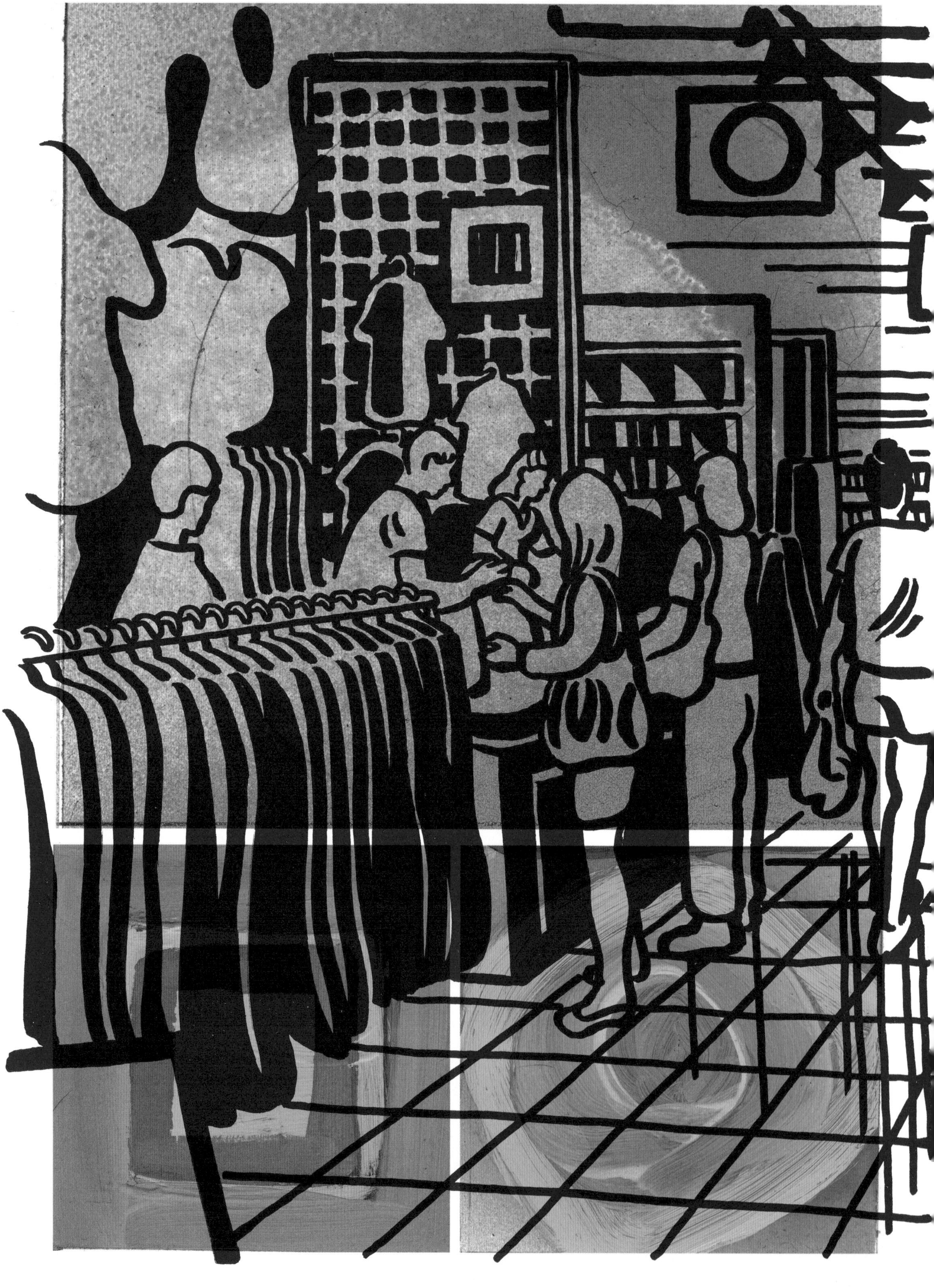

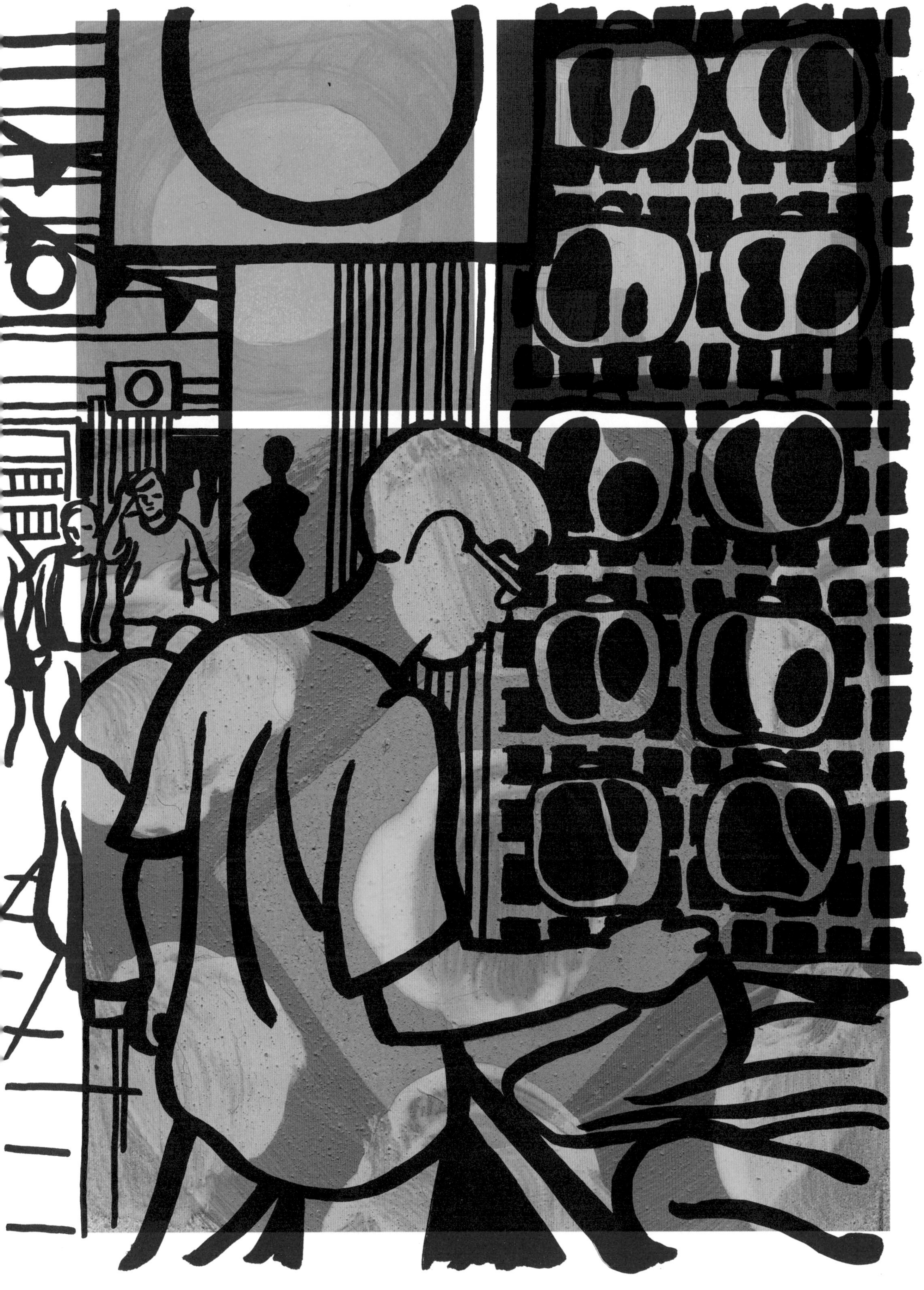

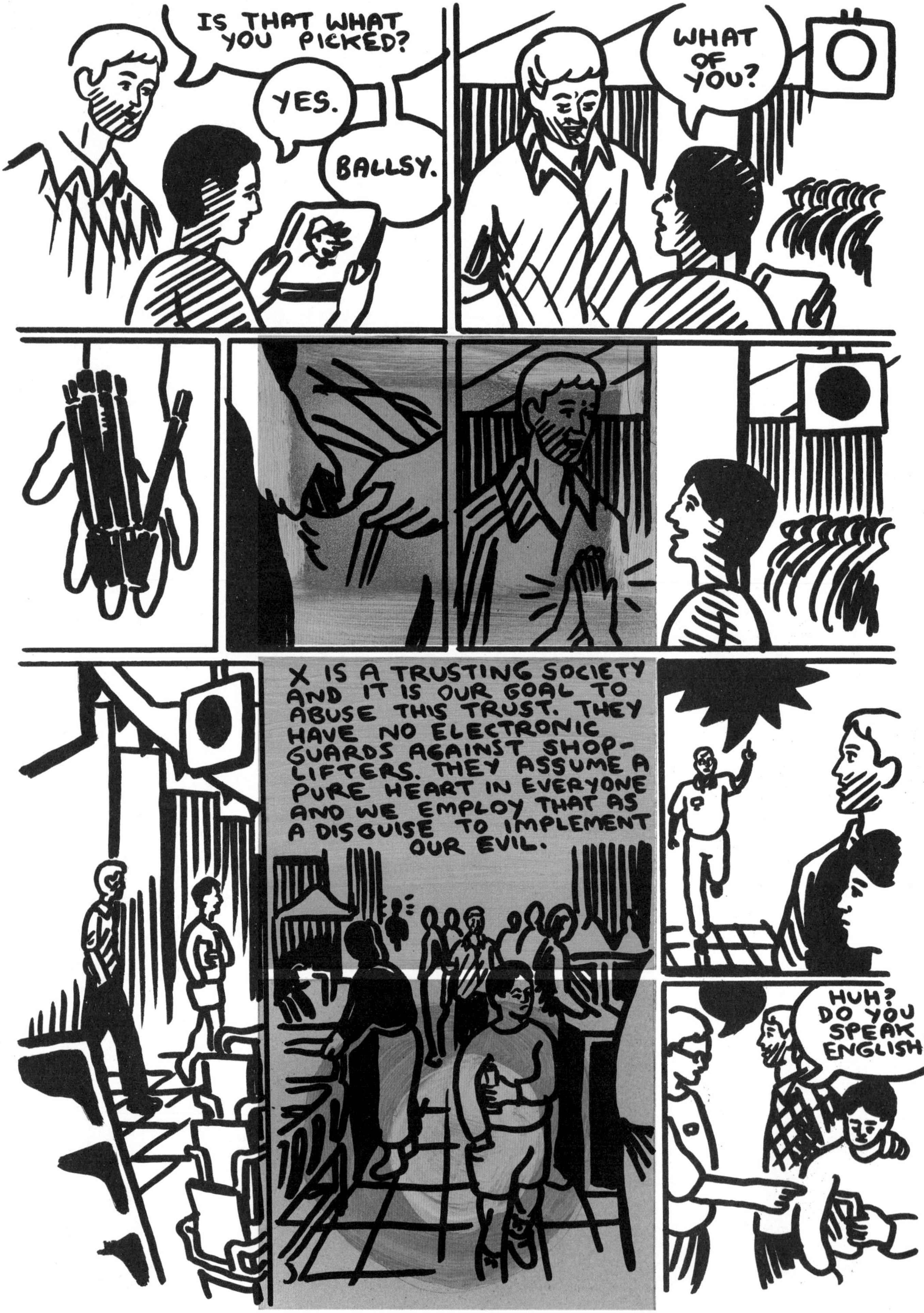
IS THAT WHAT YOU PICKED?
YES.
BALLSY.
WHAT OF YOU?
X IS A TRUSTING SOCIETY AND IT IS OUR GOAL TO ABUSE THIS TRUST. THEY HAVE NO ELECTRONIC GUARDS AGAINST SHOP-LIFTERS. THEY ASSUME A PURE HEART IN EVERYONE AND WE EMPLOY THAT AS A DISGUISE TO IMPLEMENT OUR EVIL.
HUH? DO YOU SPEAK ENGLISH?

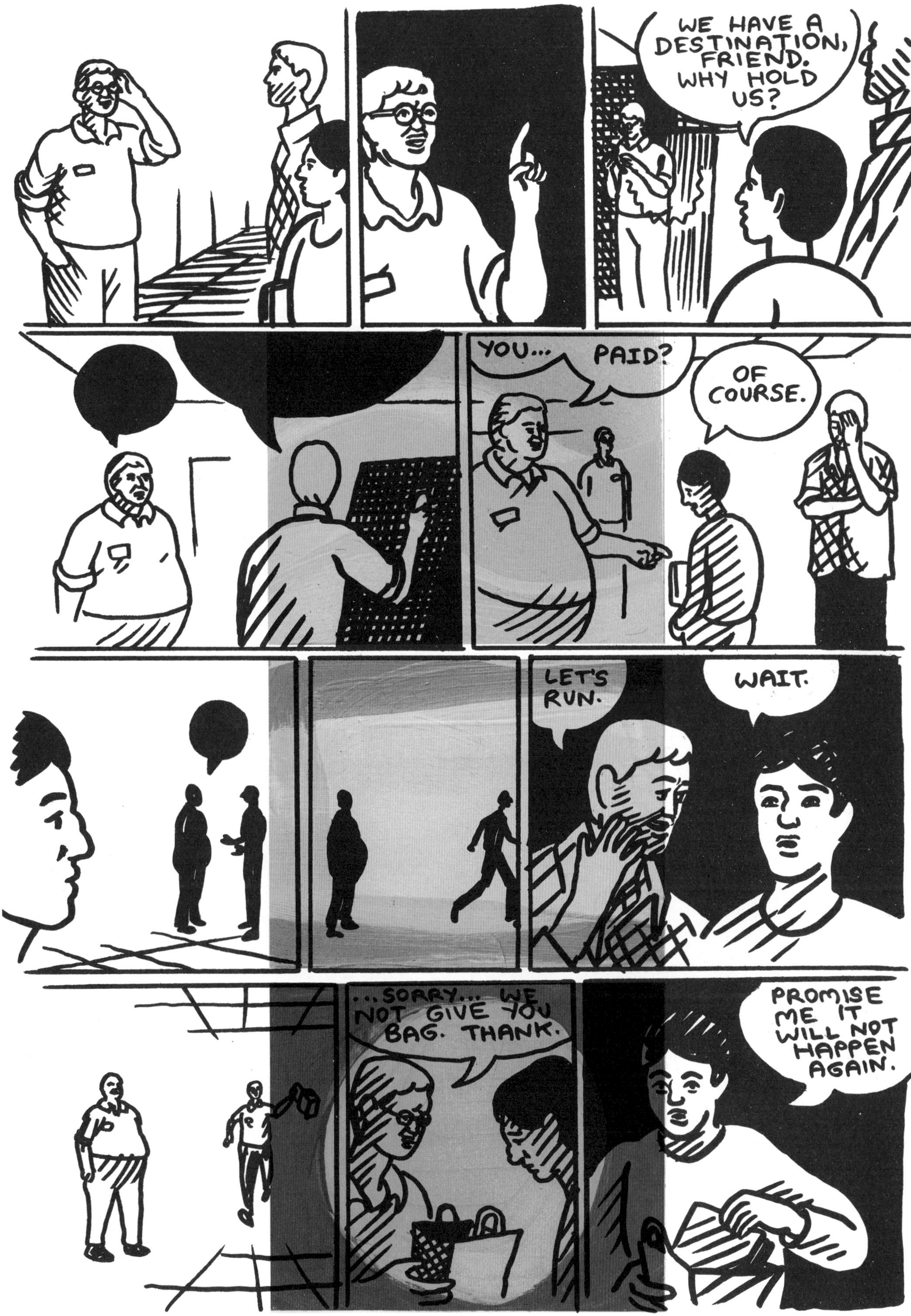
WE HAVE A DESTINATION, FRIEND. WHY HOLD US?
YOU... PAID?
OF COURSE.
LET'S RUN.
WAIT.
...SORRY... WE NOT GIVE YOU BAG. THANK.
PROMISE ME IT WILL NOT HAPPEN AGAIN.

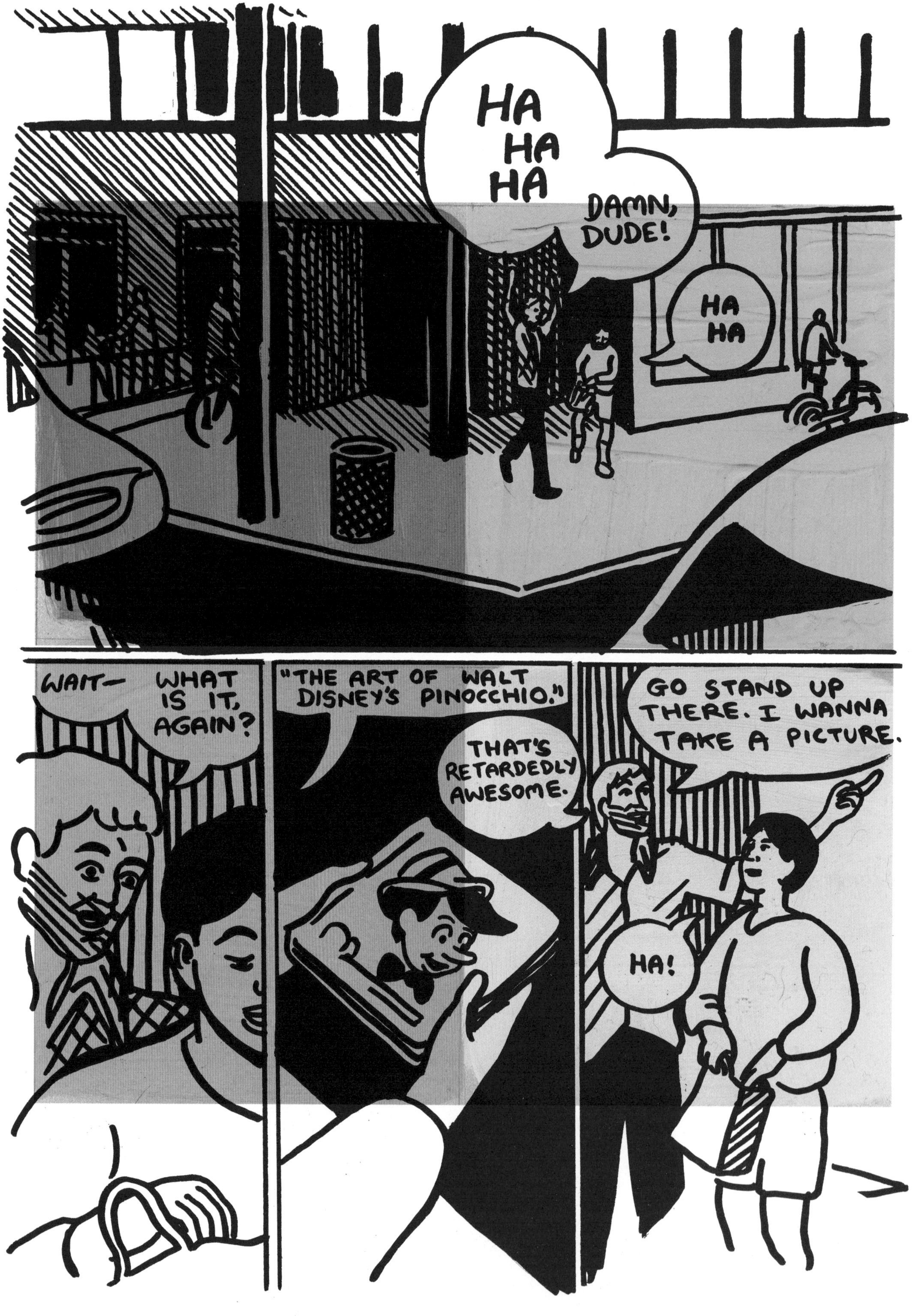

HA HA HA
DAMN, DUDE!
HA HA
WAIT— WHAT IS IT, AGAIN?
"THE ART OF WALT DISNEY'S PINOCCHIO."
THAT'S RETARDEDLY AWESOME.
GO STAND UP THERE. I WANNA TAKE A PICTURE.
HA!

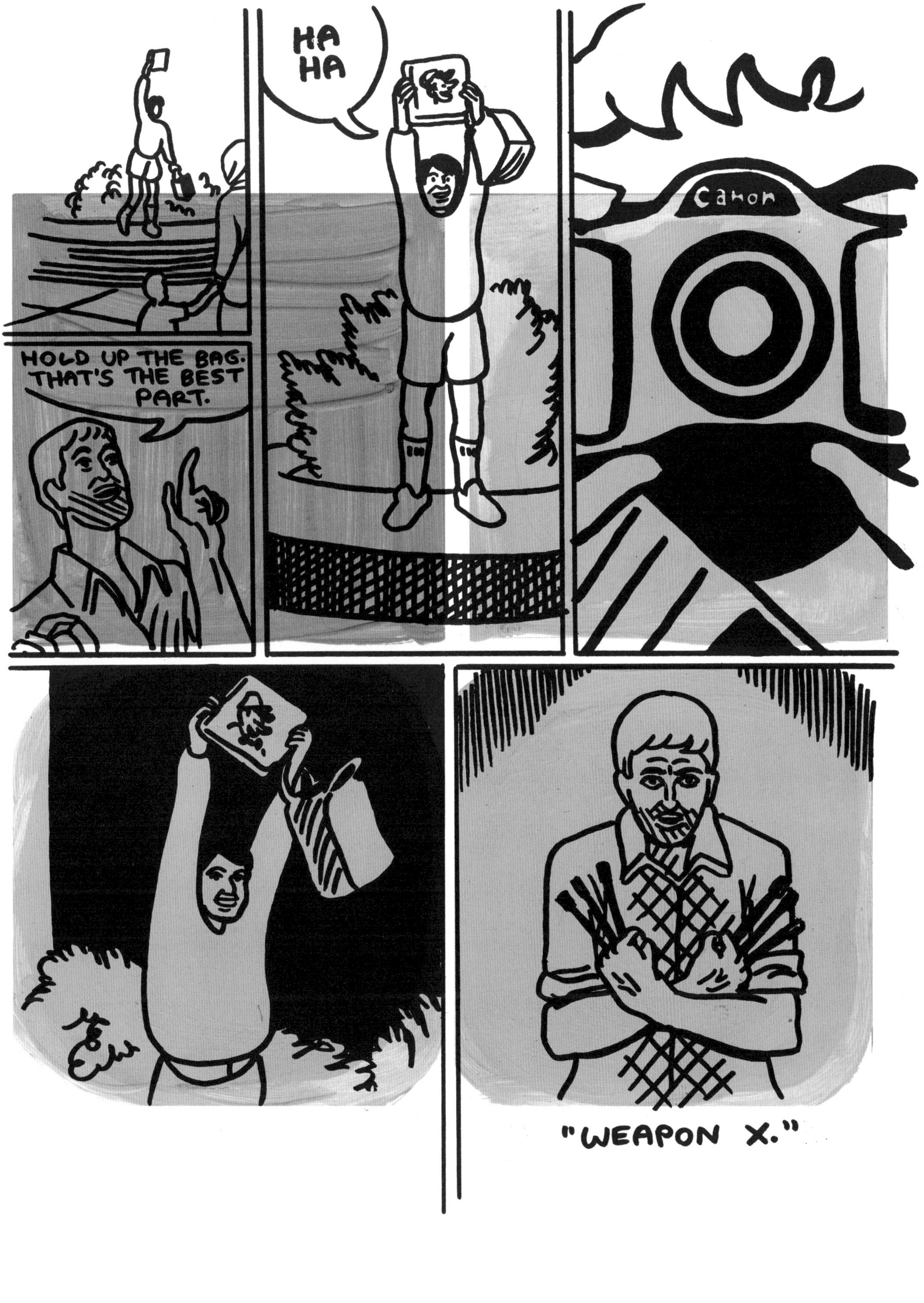
HOLD UP THE BAG. THAT'S THE BEST PART.
HA HA
Canon
"WEAPON X."

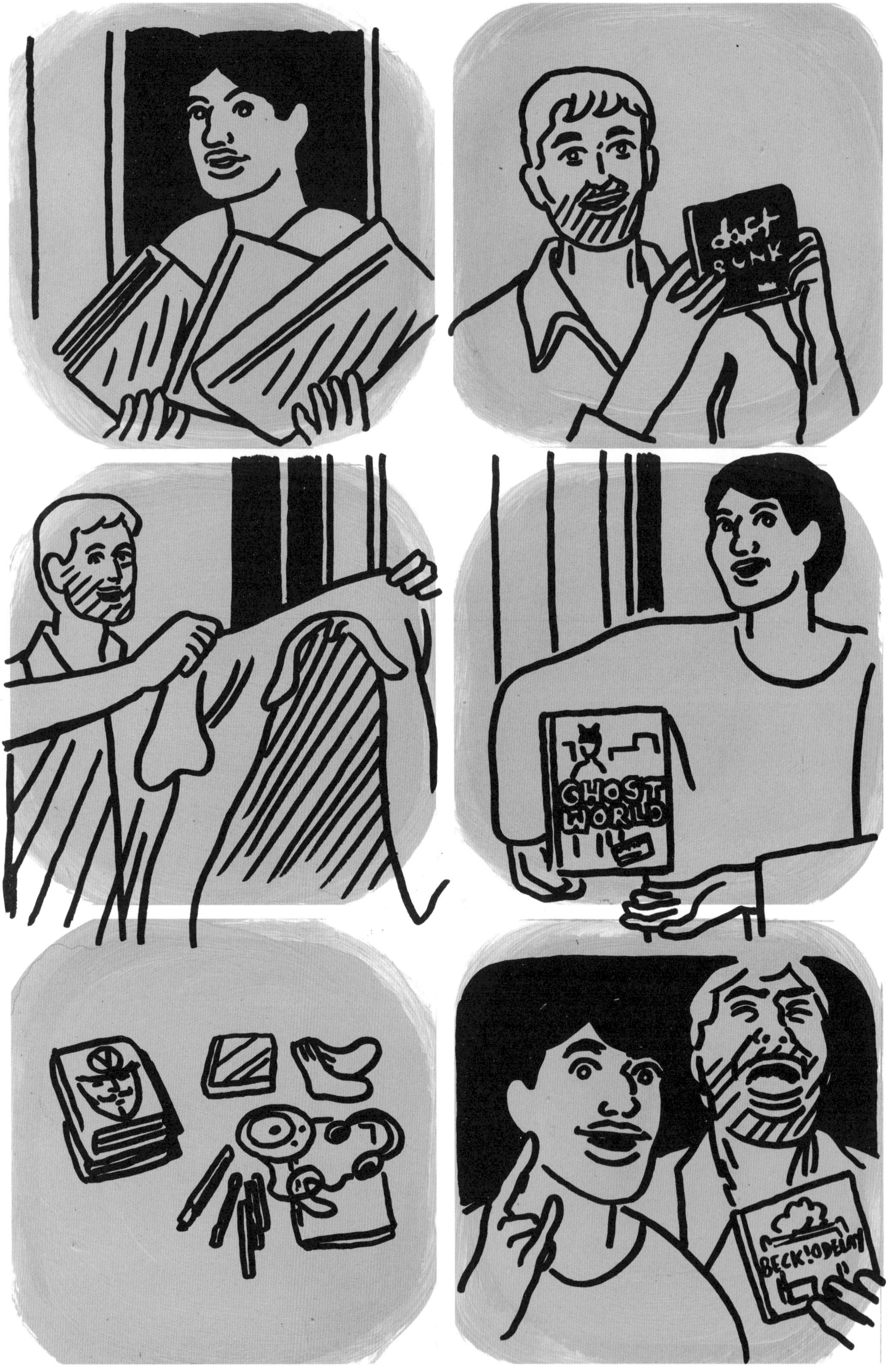
GHOST WORLD
BECK!ODELAY

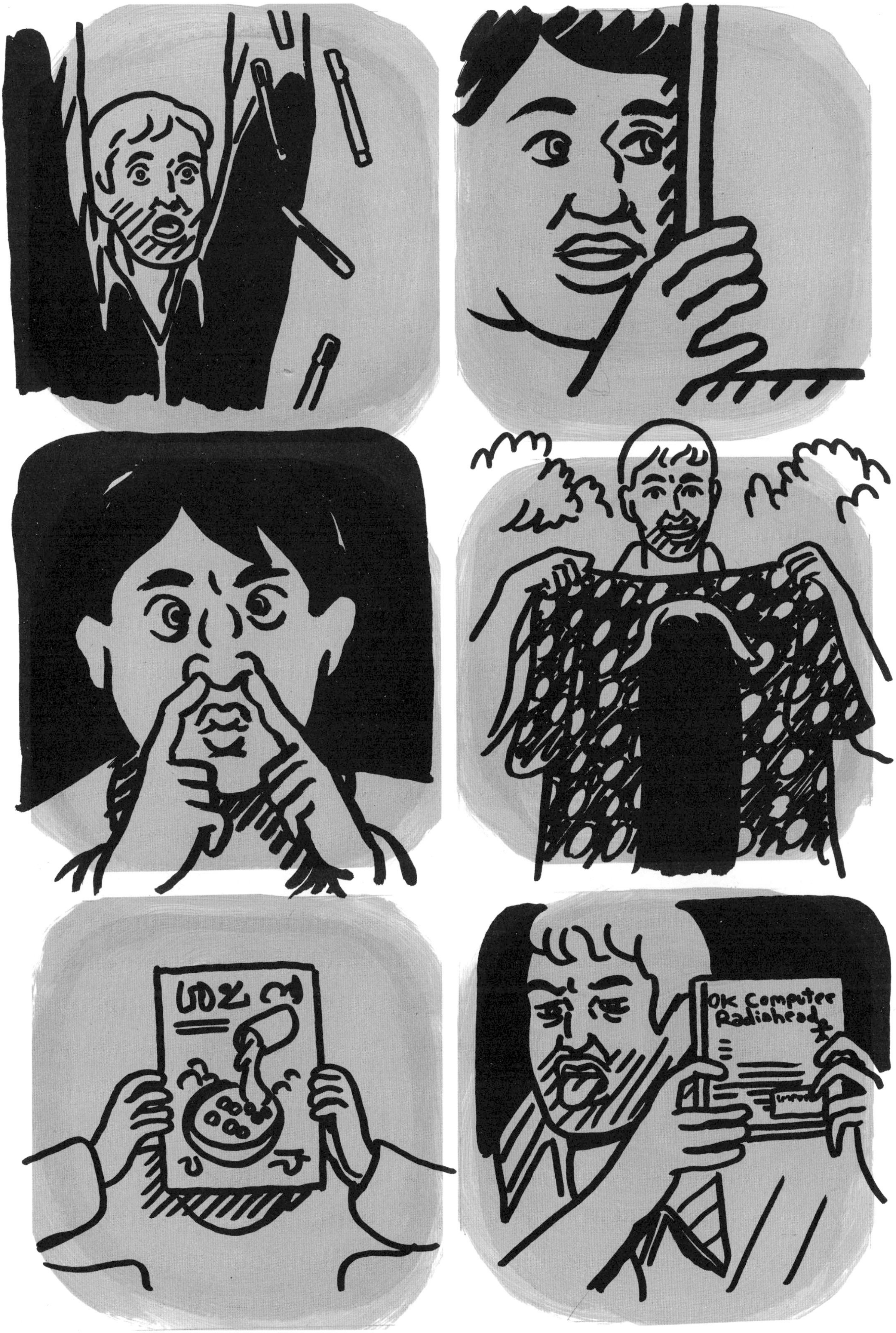
OK Computer
Radiohead

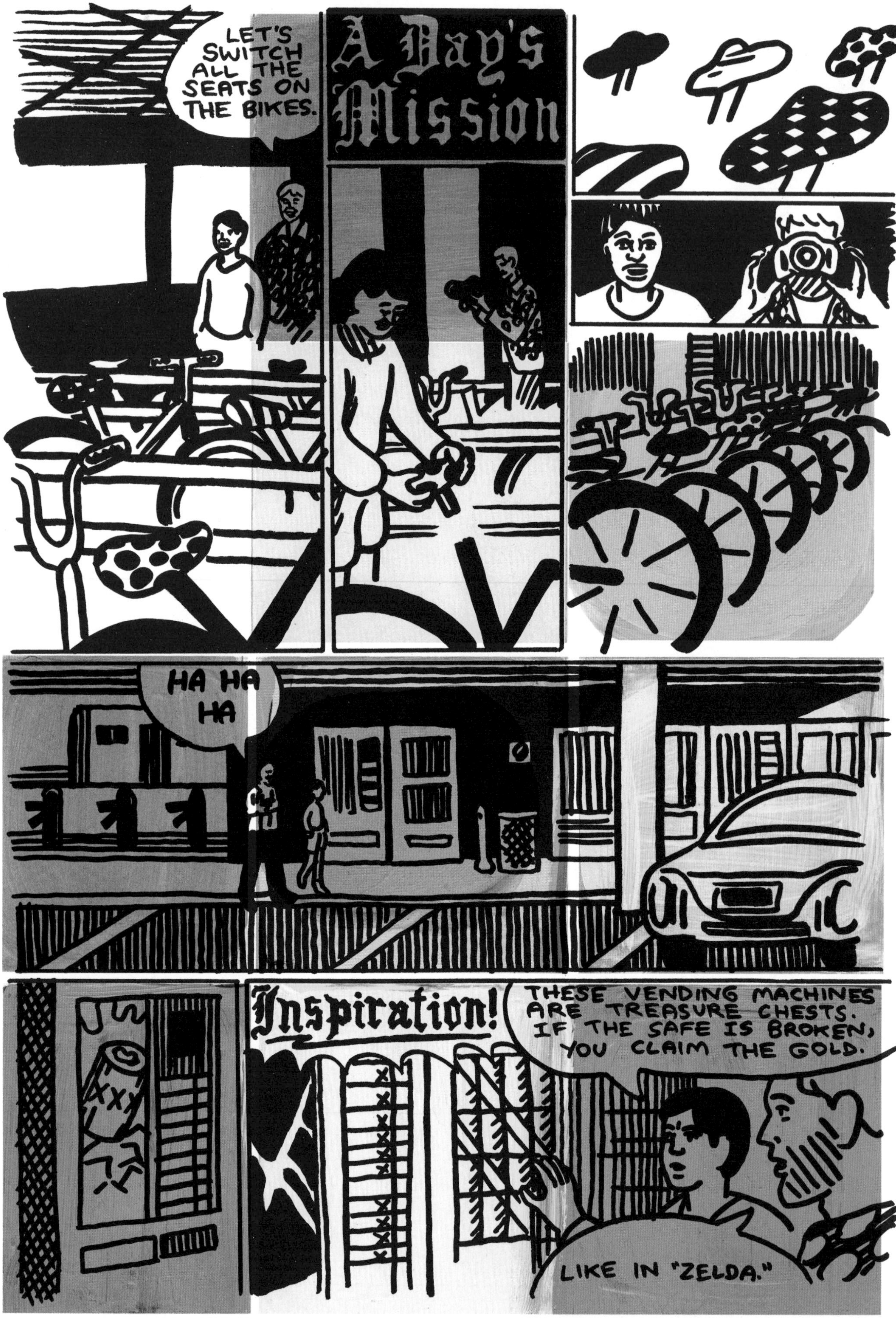
LET'S SWITCH ALL THE SEATS ON THE BIKES.
A Day's Mission
HA HA HA
Inspiration!
THESE VENDING MACHINES ARE TREASURE CHESTS. IF THE SAFE IS BROKEN, YOU CLAIM THE GOLD.
LIKE IN "ZELDA."

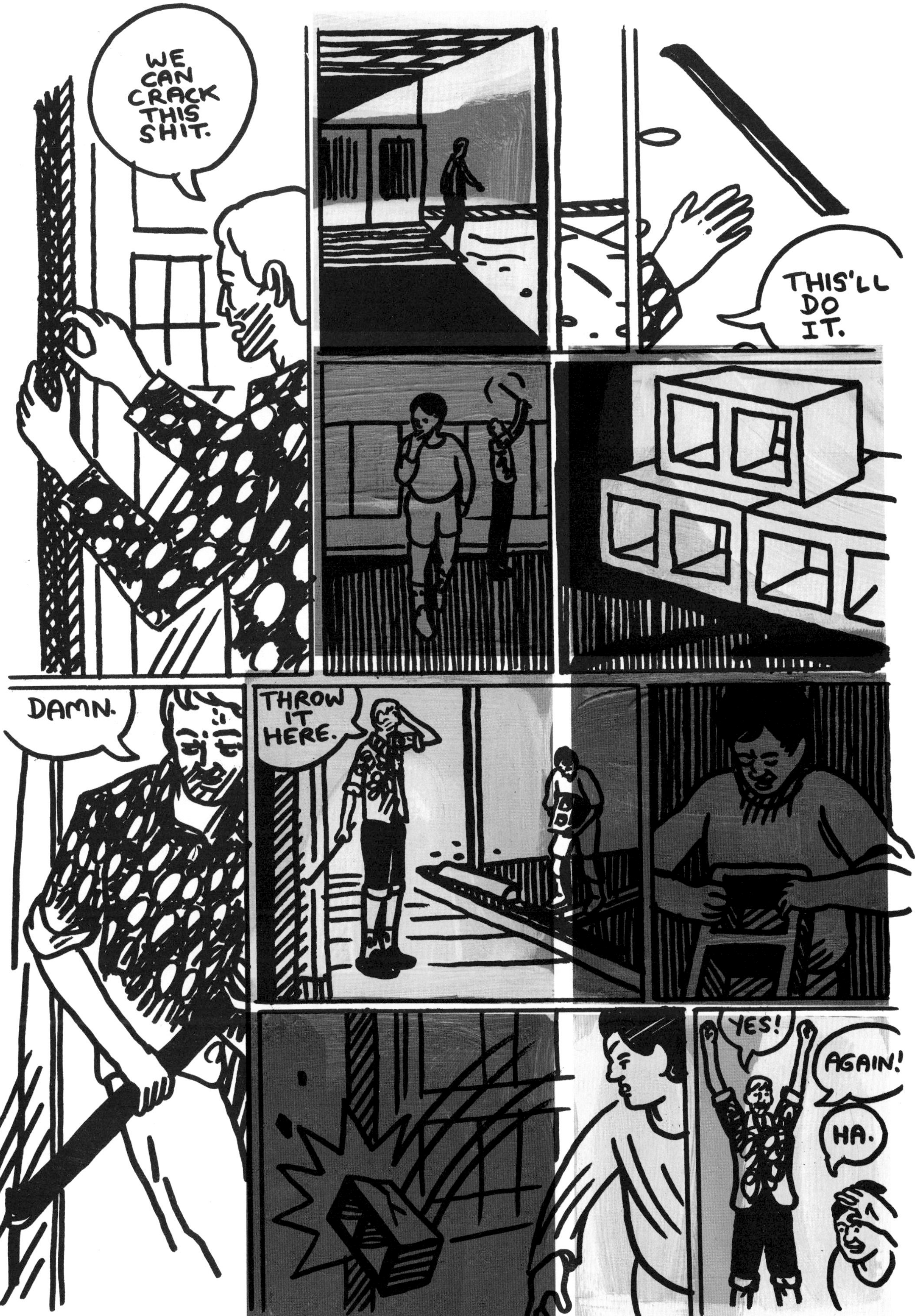
WE CAN CRACK THIS SHIT.
THIS'LL DO IT.
DAMN.
THROW IT HERE.
YES!
AGAIN!
HA.

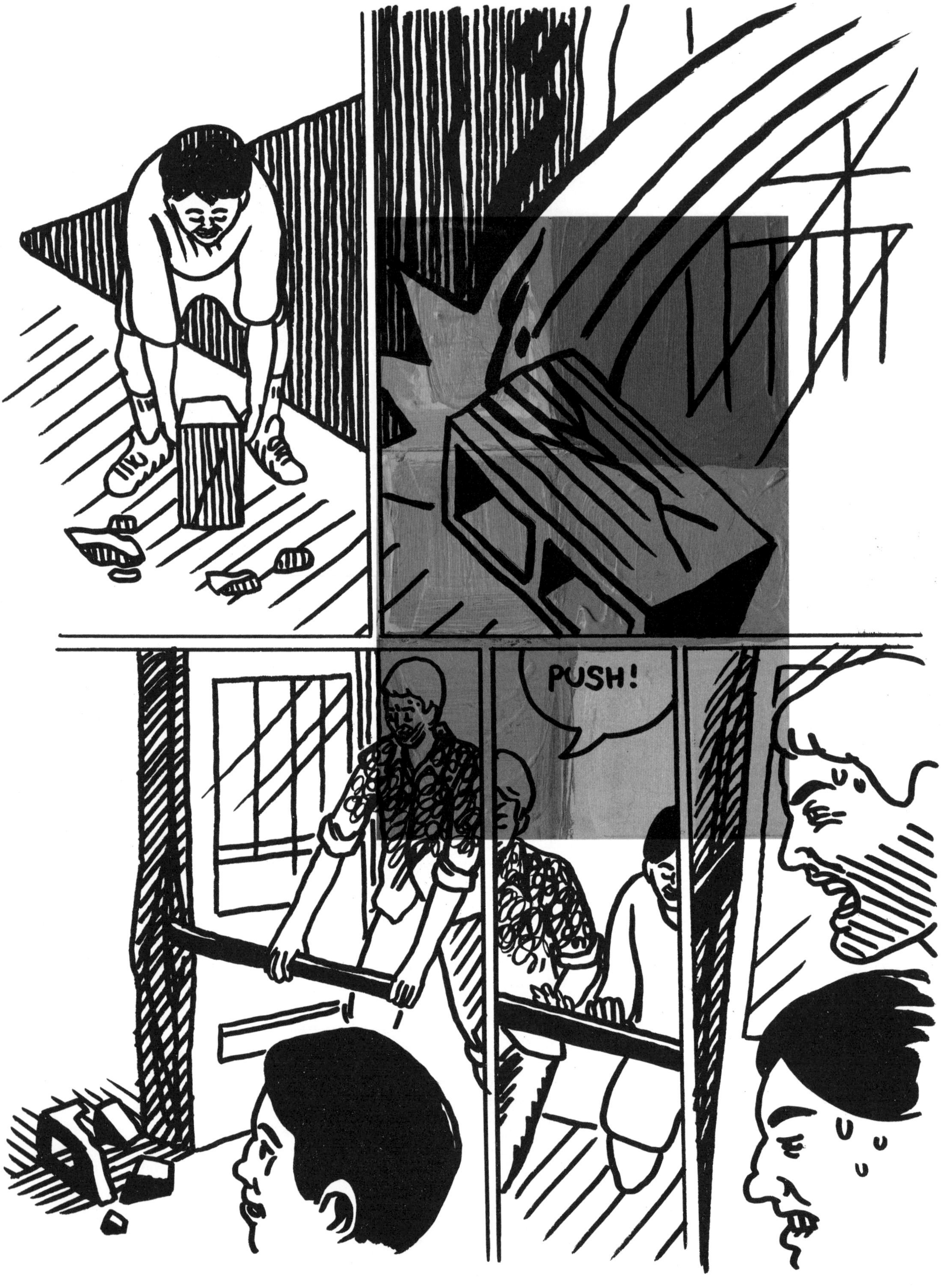
PUSH!

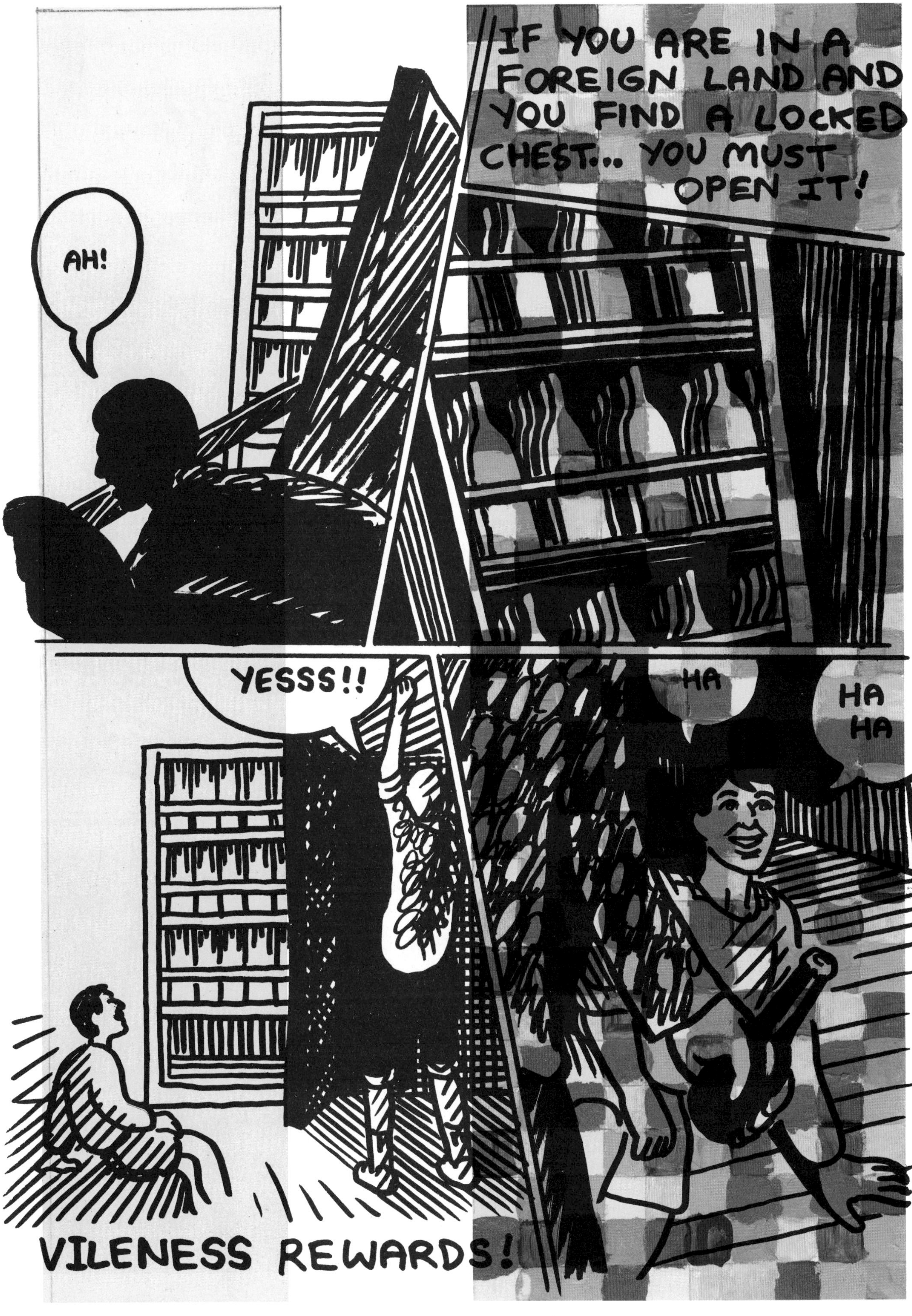
IF YOU ARE IN A FOREIGN LAND AND YOU FIND A LOCKED CHEST... YOU MUST OPEN IT!
AH!
YESSS!!
HA
HA HA
VILENESS REWARDS!

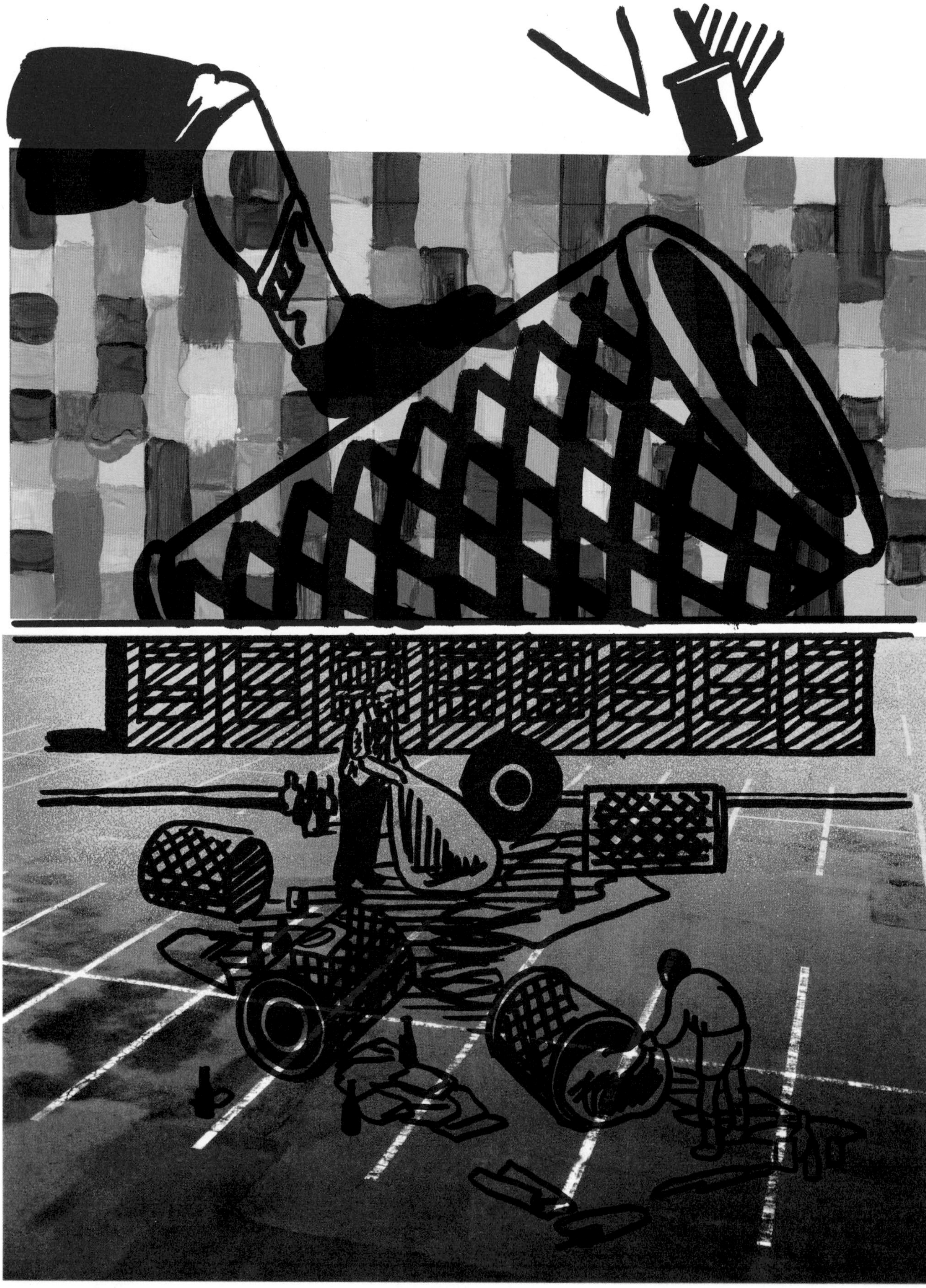

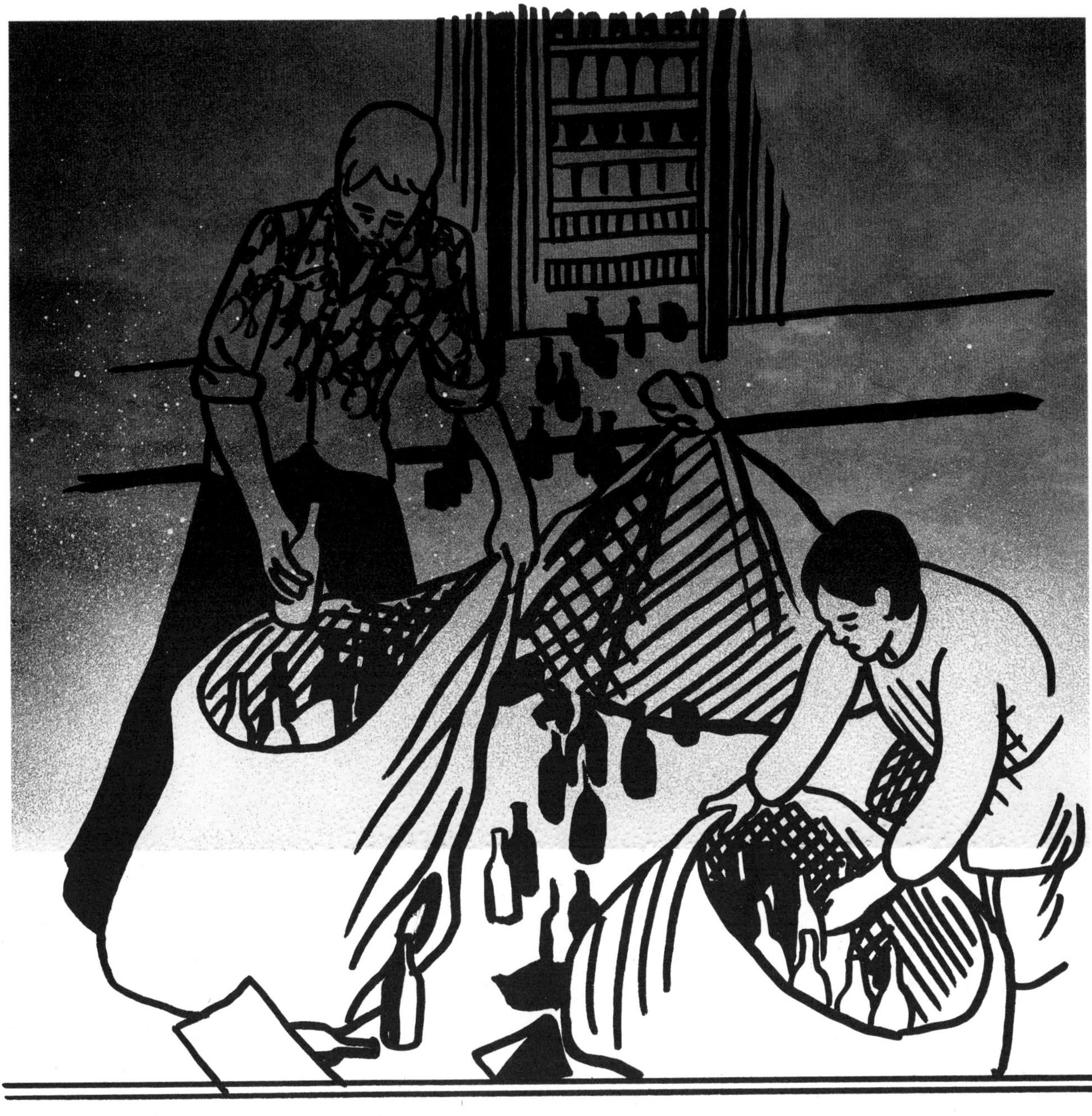

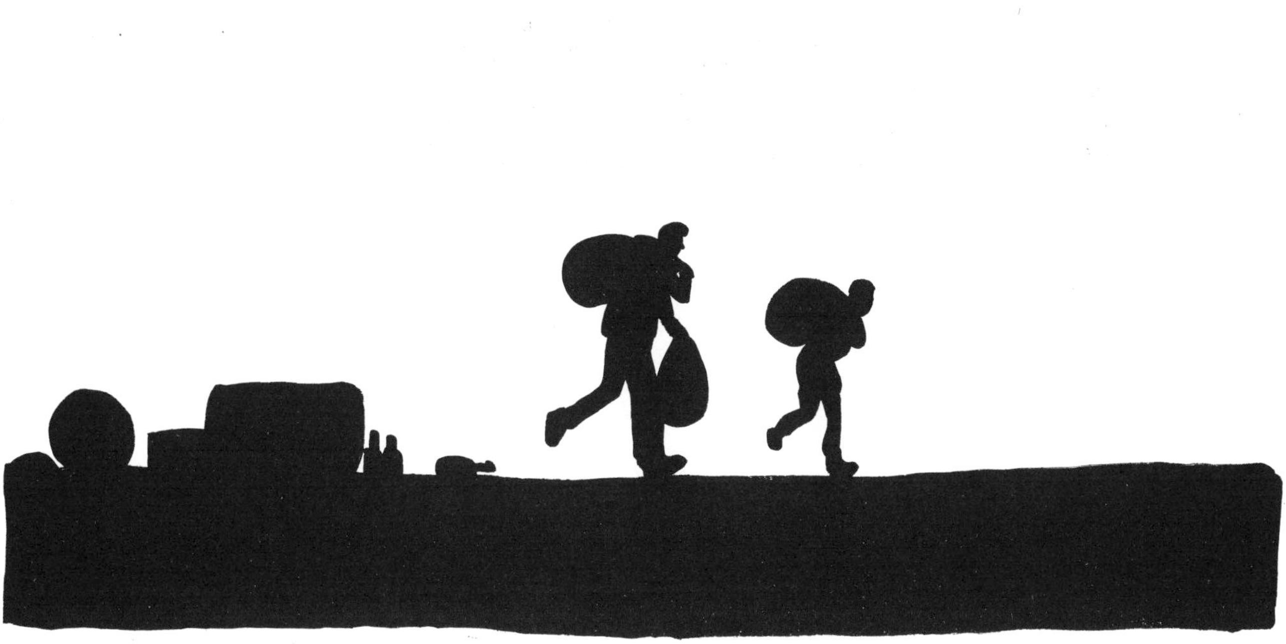

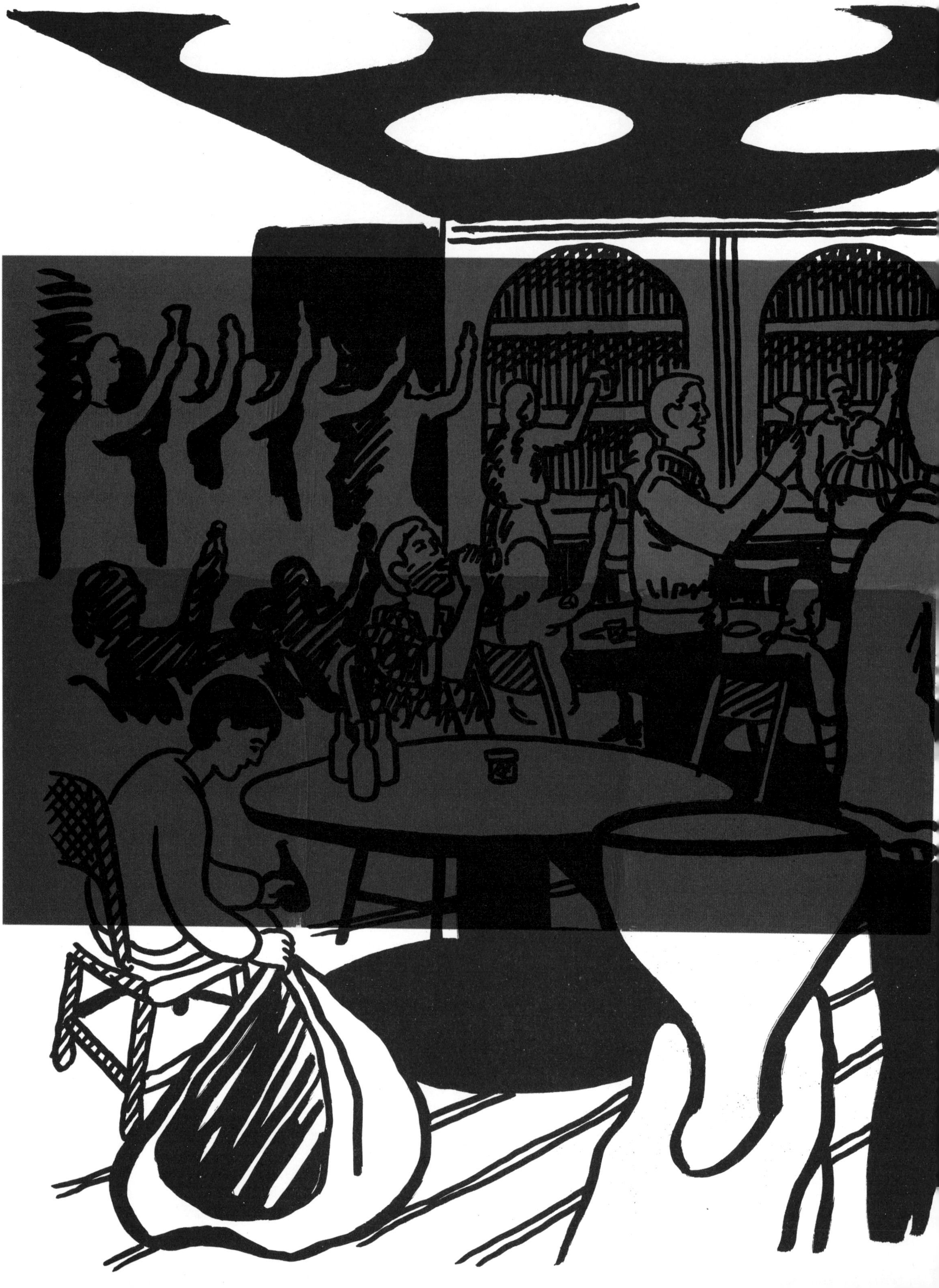

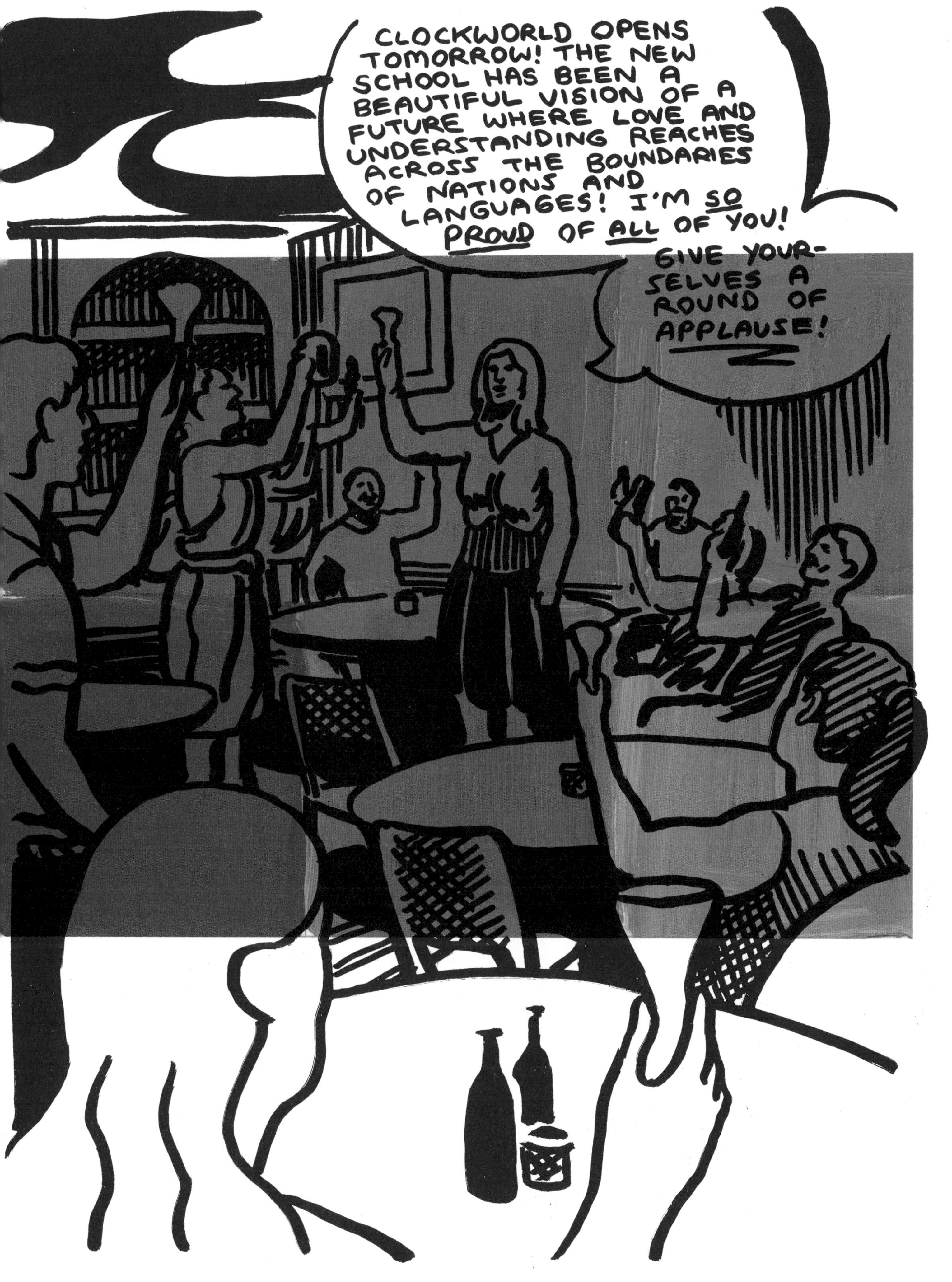
CLOCKWORLD OPENS TOMORROW! THE NEW SCHOOL HAS BEEN A BEAUTIFUL VISION OF A FUTURE WHERE LOVE AND UNDERSTANDING REACHES ACROSS THE BOUNDARIES OF NATIONS AND LANGUAGES! I'M SO PROUD OF ALL OF YOU!
GIVE YOURSELVES A ROUND OF APPLAUSE!

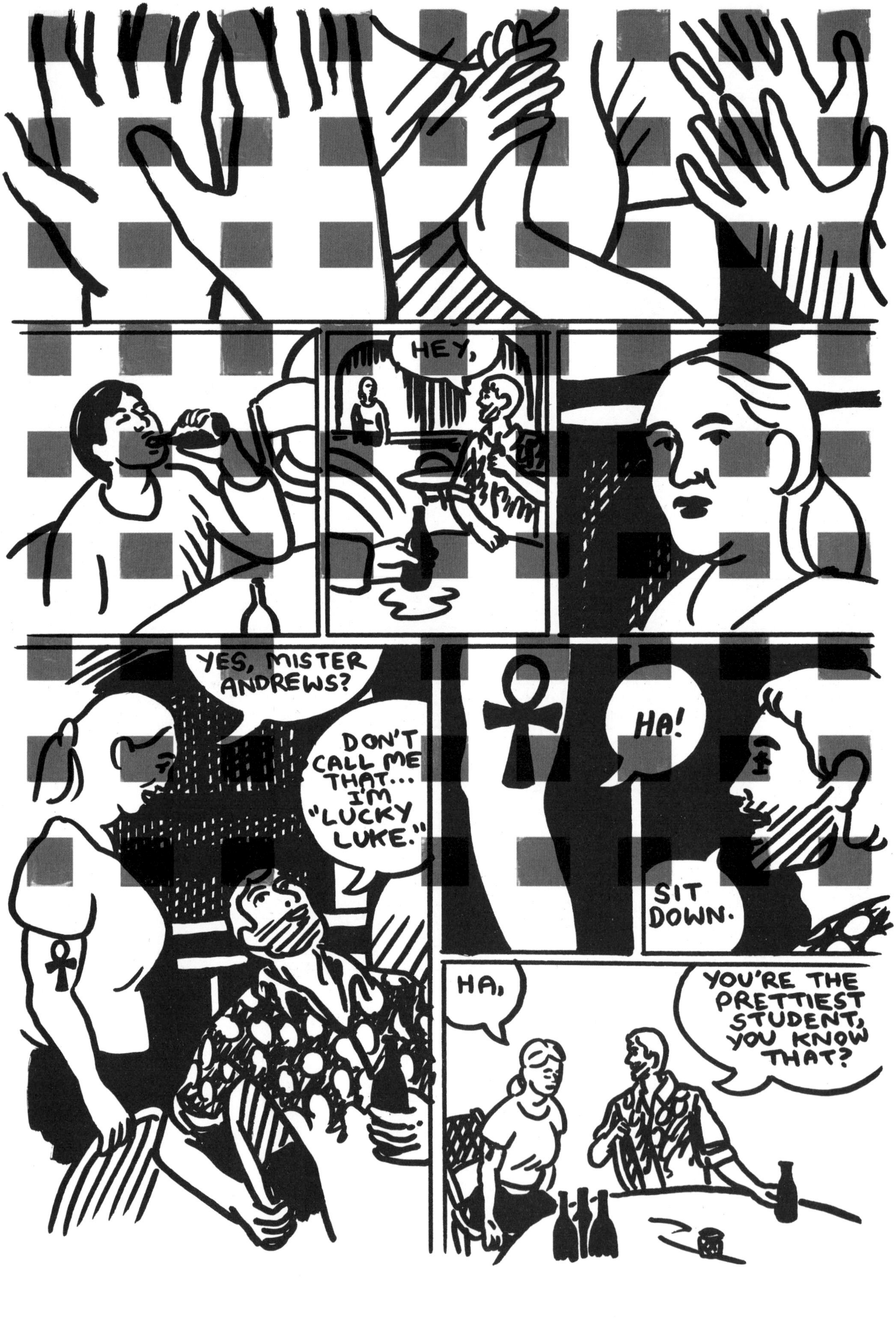
HEY,
YES, MISTER ANDREWS?
DON'T CALL ME THAT... I'M "LUCKY LUKE."
HA!
SIT DOWN.
HA,
YOU'RE THE PRETTIEST STUDENT, YOU KNOW THAT?

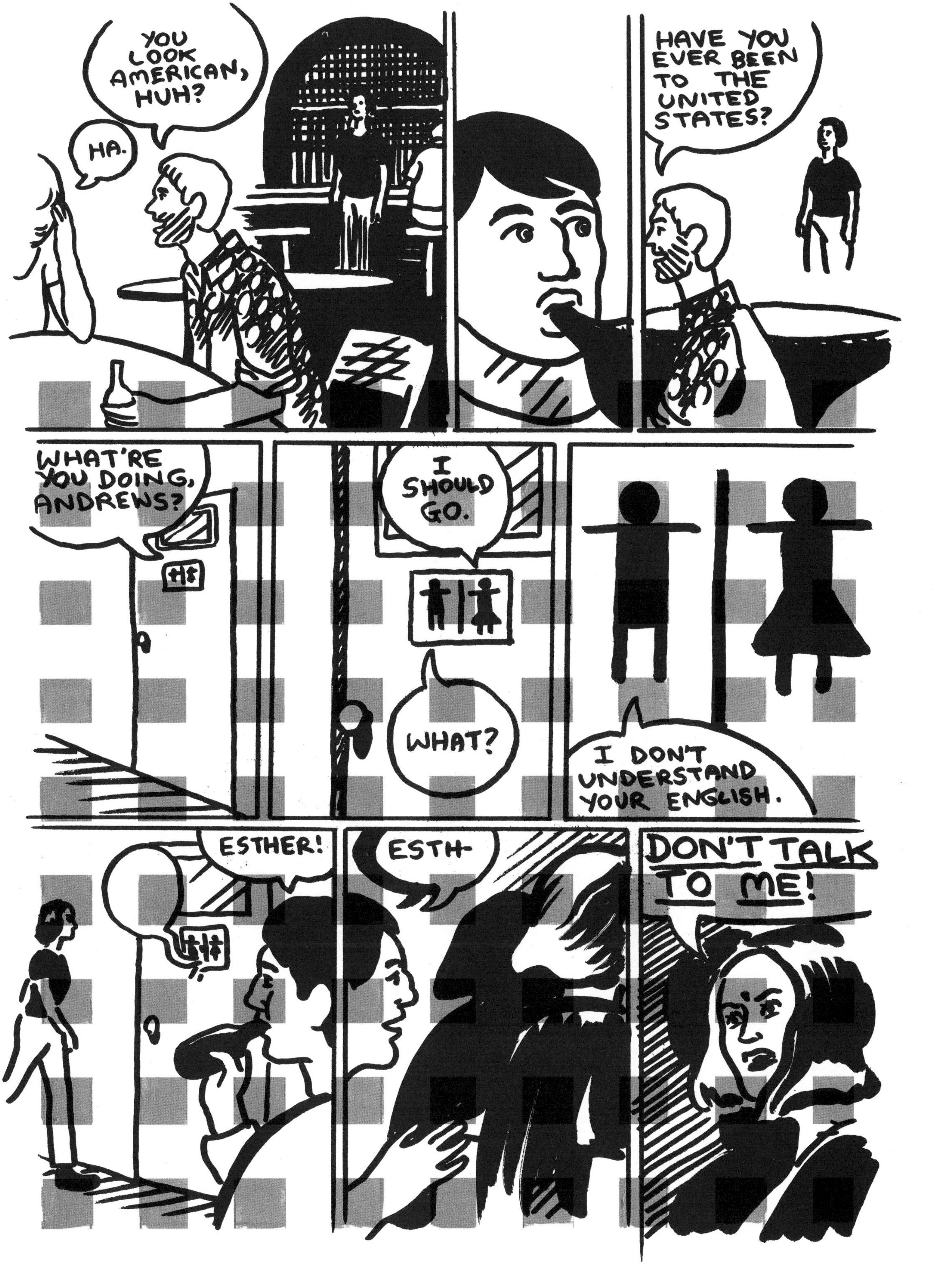
YOU LOOK AMERICAN, HUH?
HA.
HAVE YOU EVER BEEN TO THE UNITED STATES?
WHAT'RE YOU DOING, ANDREWS?
I SHOULD GO.
WHAT?
I DON'T UNDERSTAND YOUR ENGLISH.
ESTHER!
ESTH-
DON'T TALK TO ME!

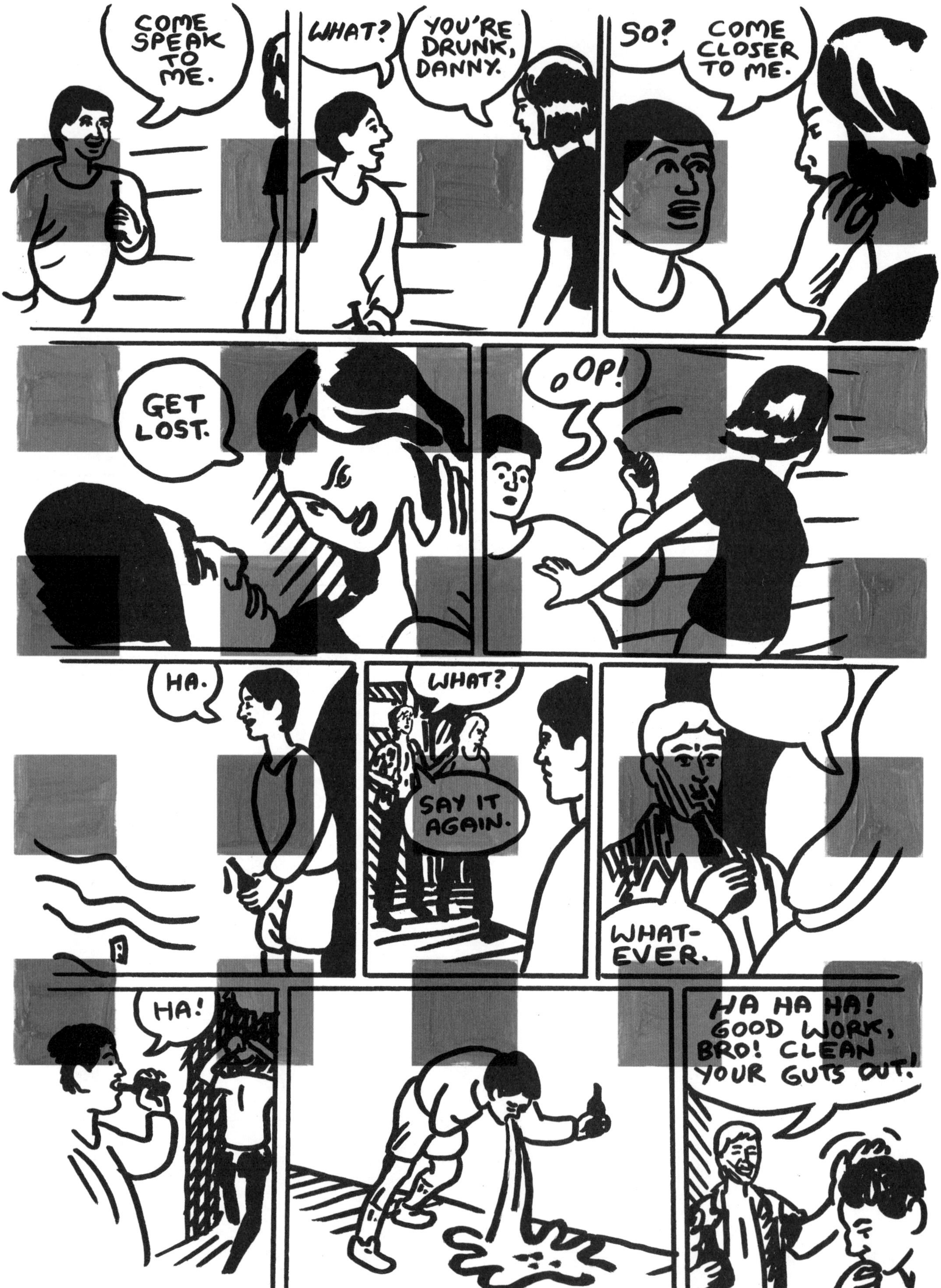
COME SPEAK TO ME.
WHAT?
YOU'RE DRUNK, DANNY.
SO?
COME CLOSER TO ME.
GET LOST.
OOP!
HA.
WHAT?
SAY IT AGAIN.
WHAT-EVER.
HA!
HA HA HA! GOOD WORK, BRO! CLEAN YOUR GUTS OUT!

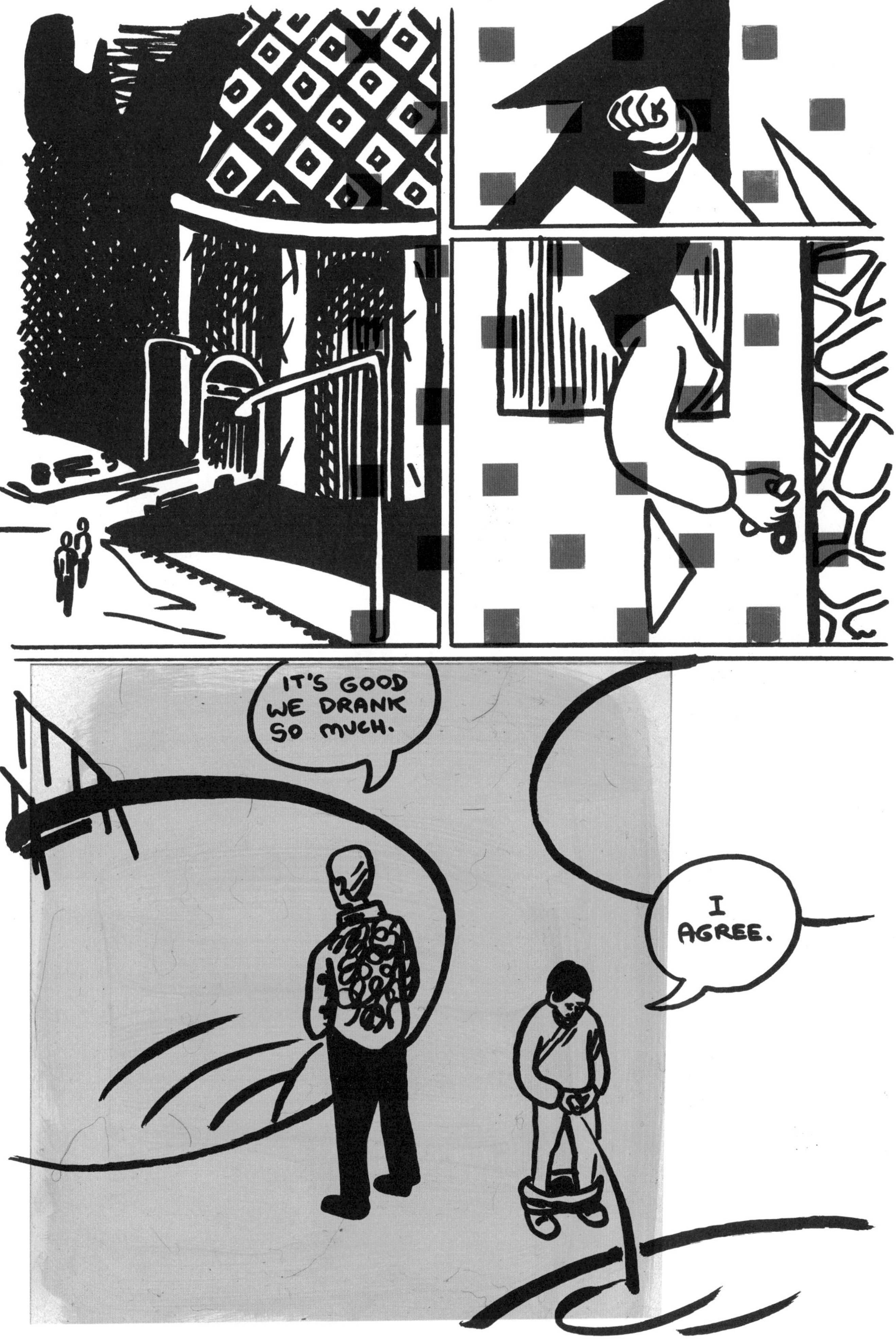
IT'S GOOD WE DRANK SO MUCH.
I AGREE.

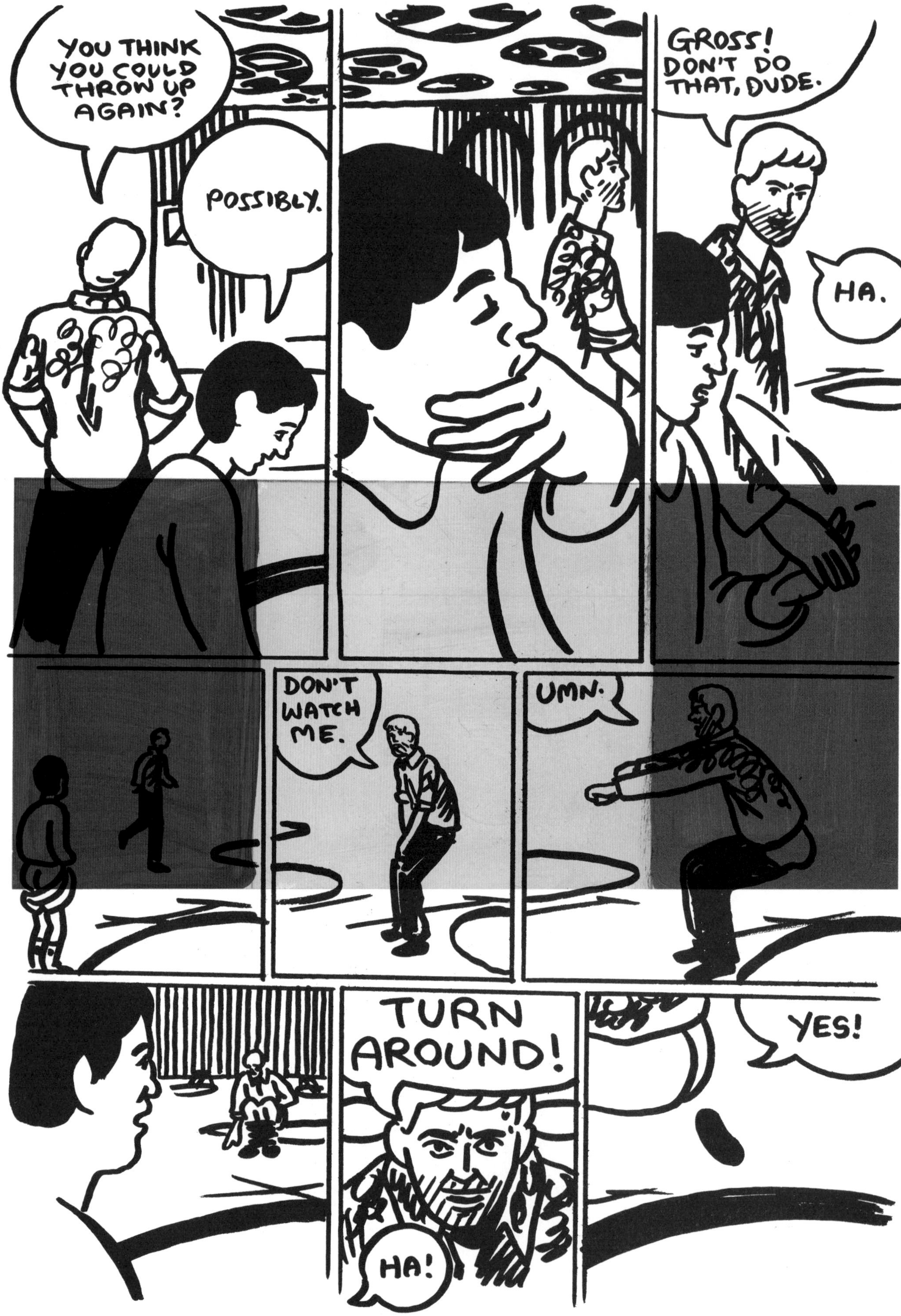
YOU THINK YOU COULD THROW UP AGAIN?
POSSIBLY.
GROSS! DON'T DO THAT, DUDE.
HA.
DON'T WATCH ME.
UMN.
TURN AROUND!
HA!
YES!

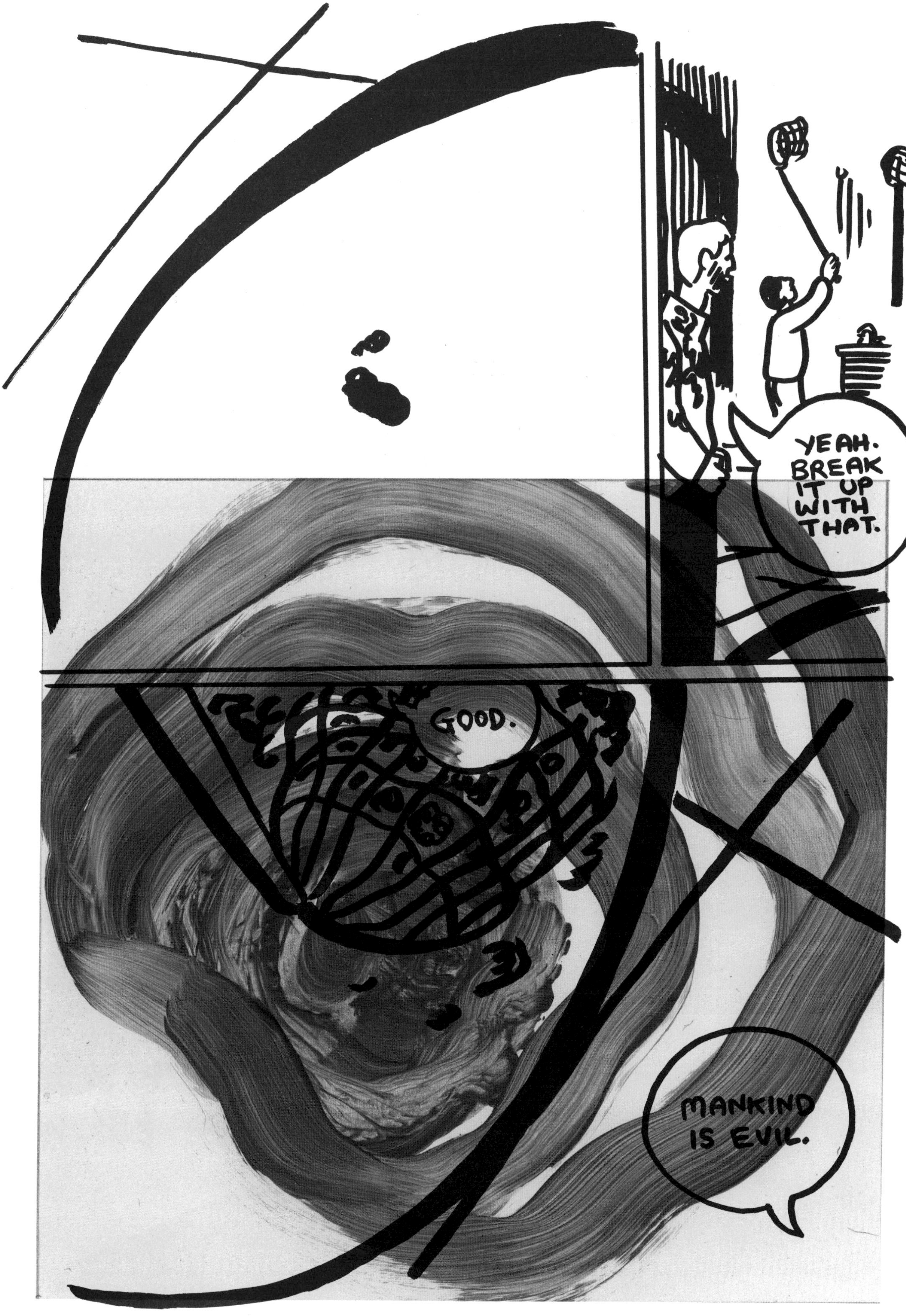
YEAH. BREAK IT UP WITH THAT.
GOOD.
MANKIND IS EVIL.

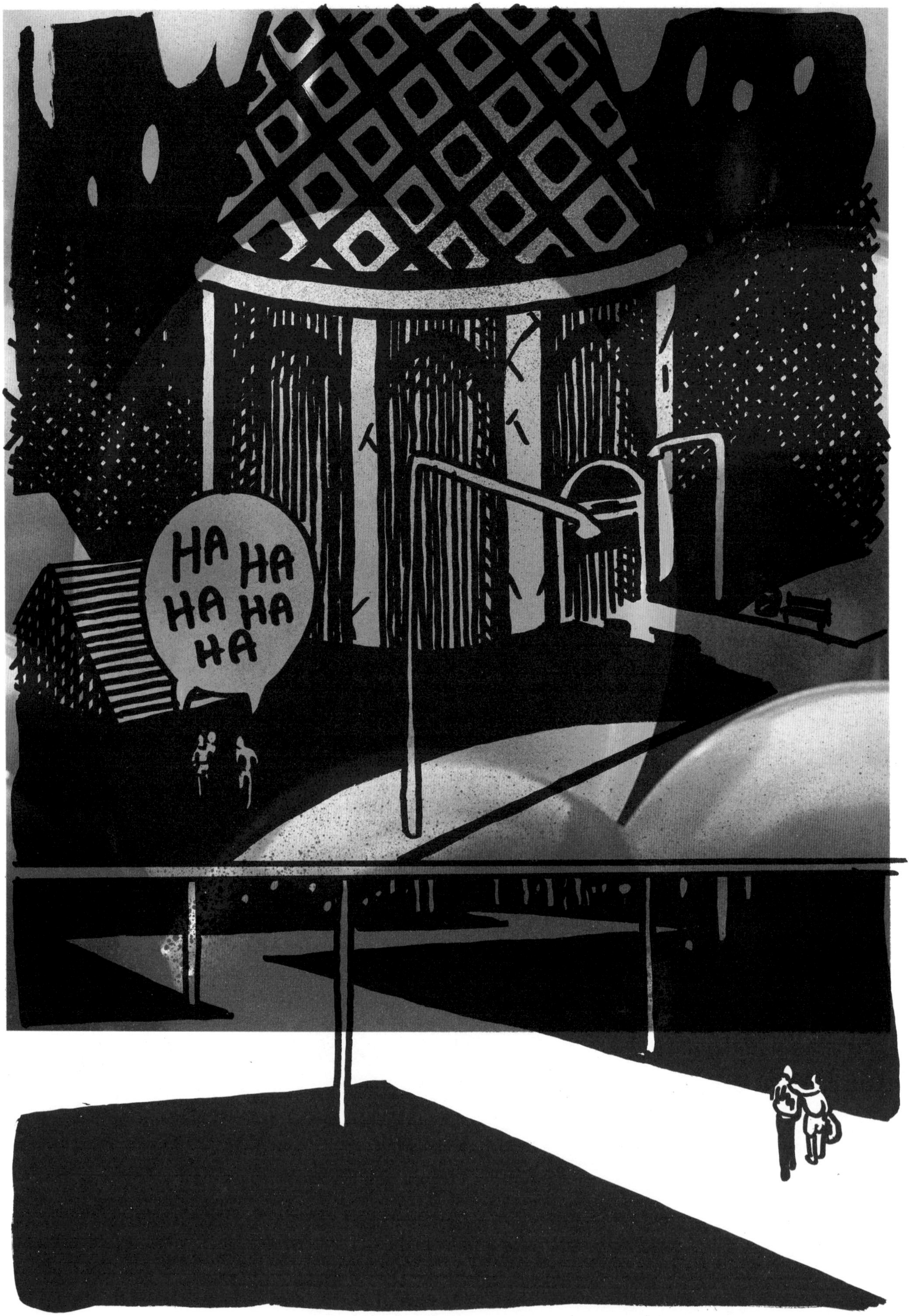
HA HA HA HA HA

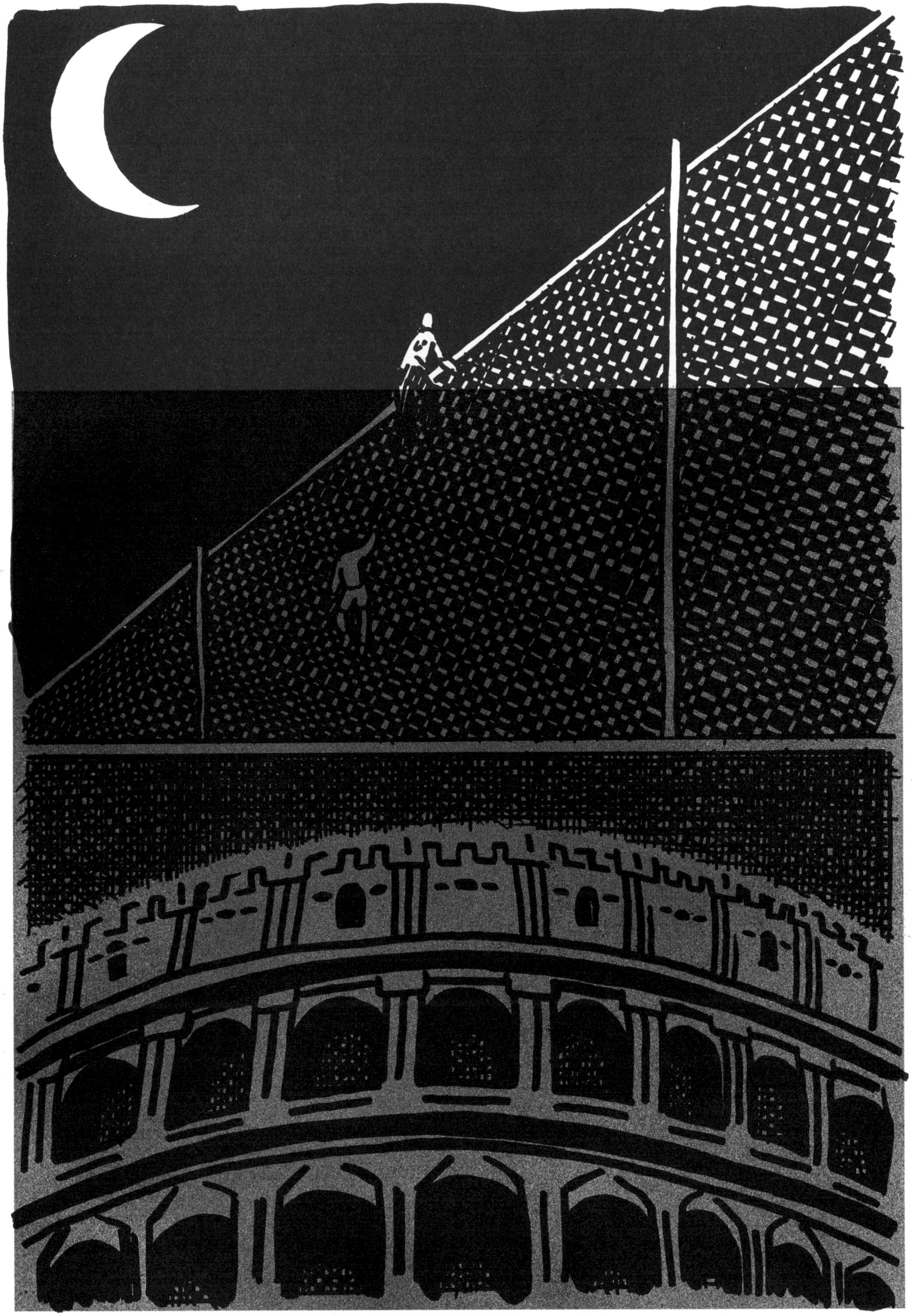

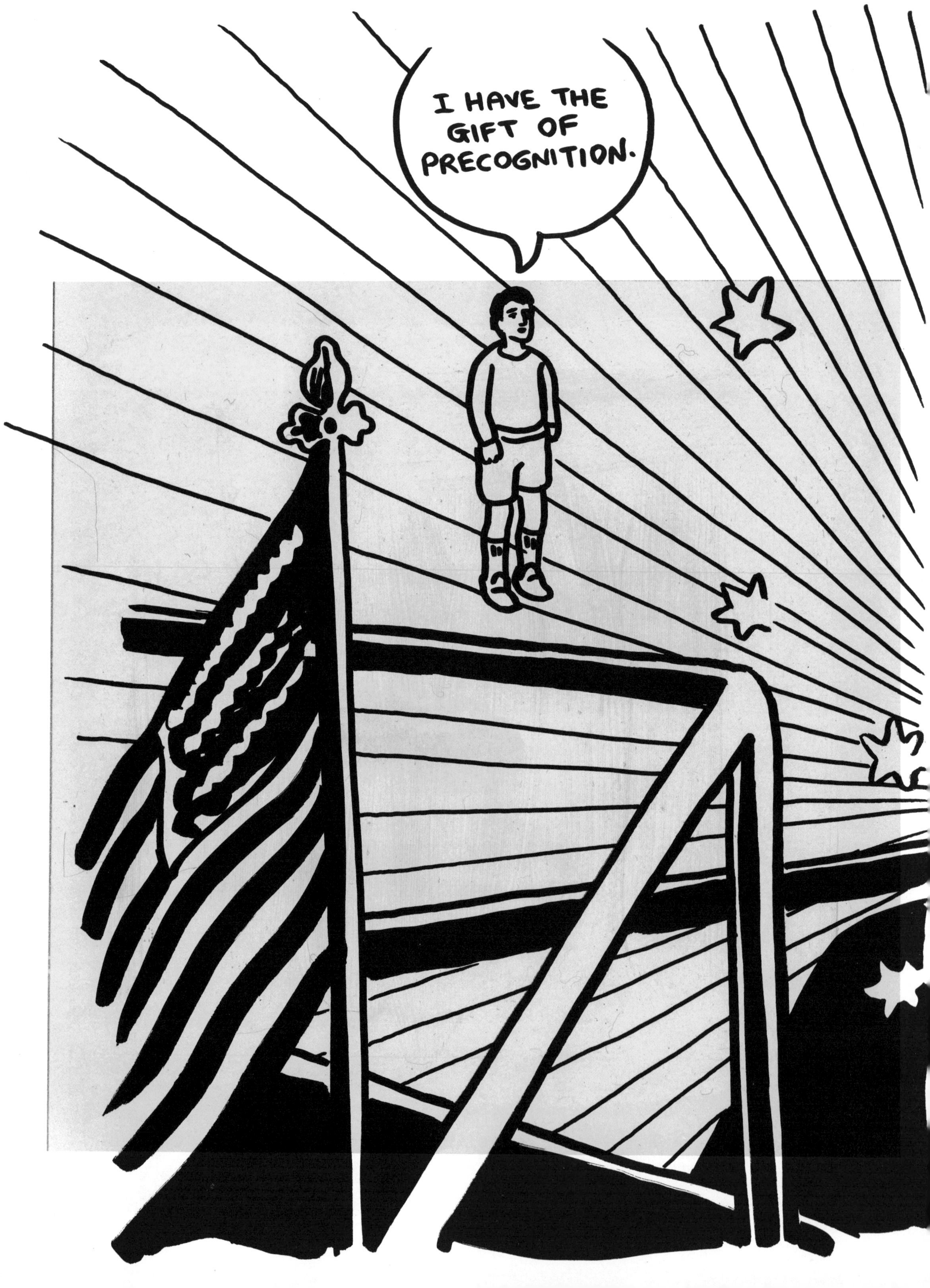
I HAVE THE GIFT OF PRECOGNITION.

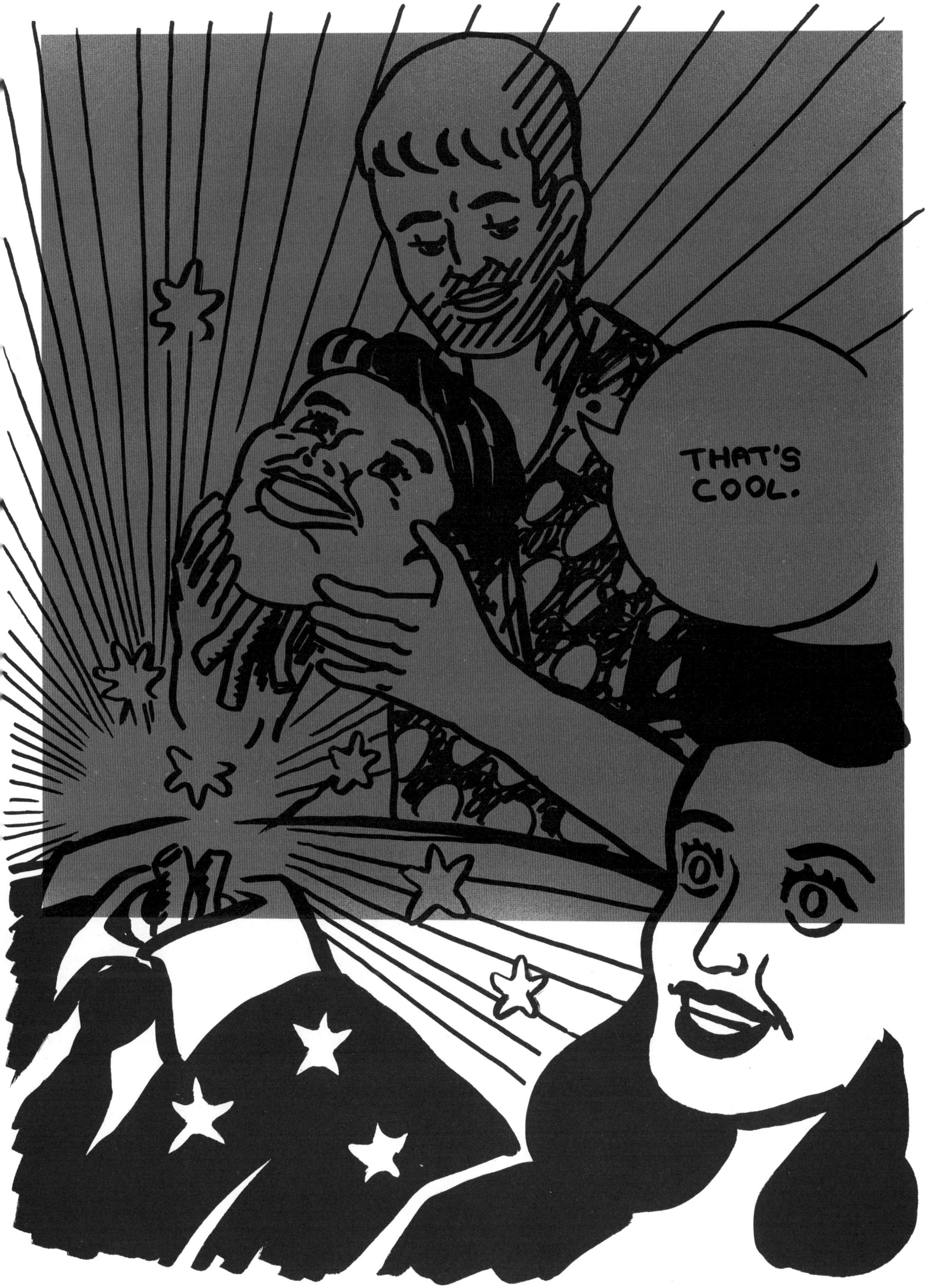
THAT'S COOL.

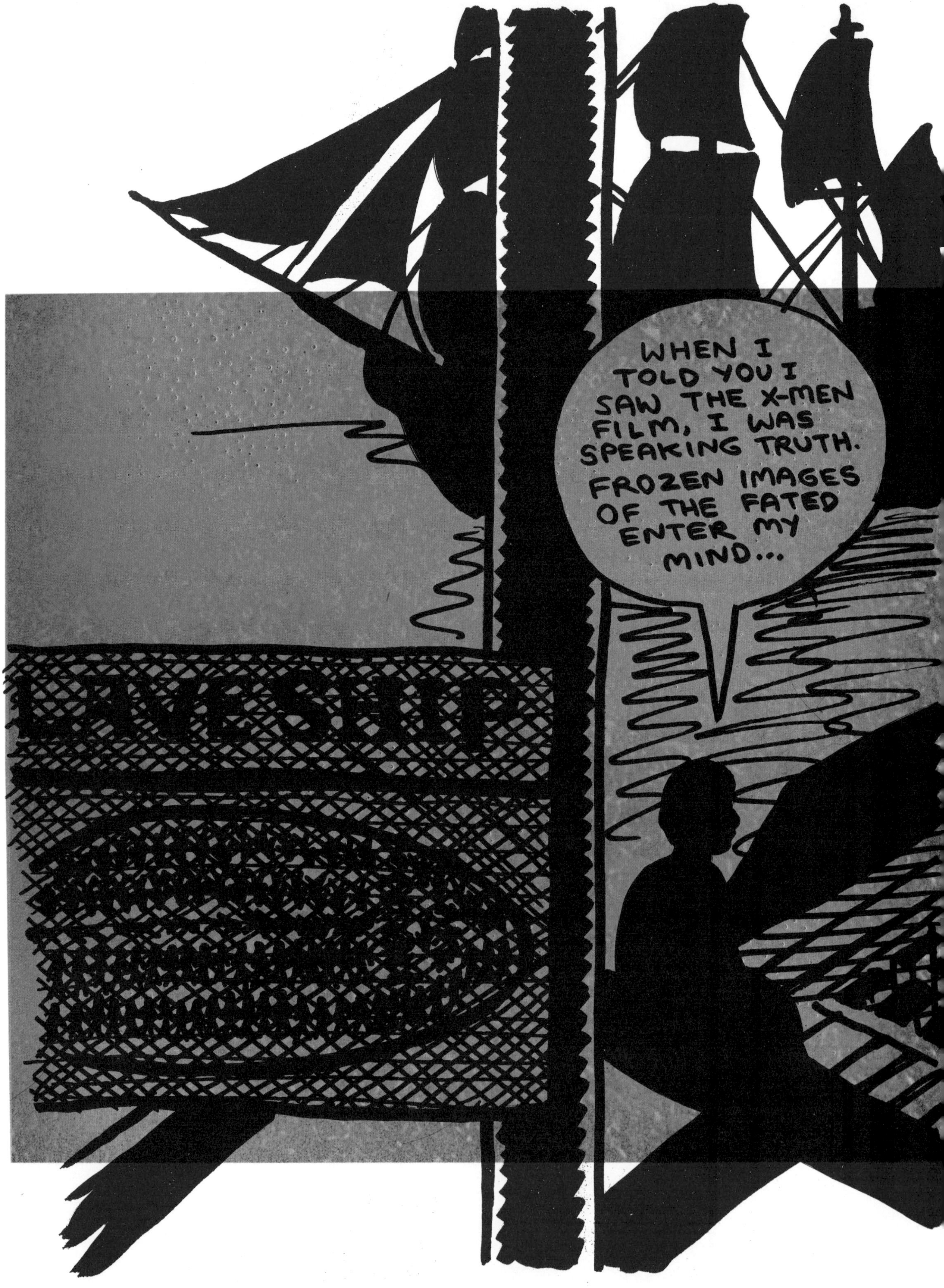
WHEN I TOLD YOU I SAW THE X-MEN FILM, I WAS SPEAKING TRUTH. FROZEN IMAGES OF THE FATED ENTER MY MIND...

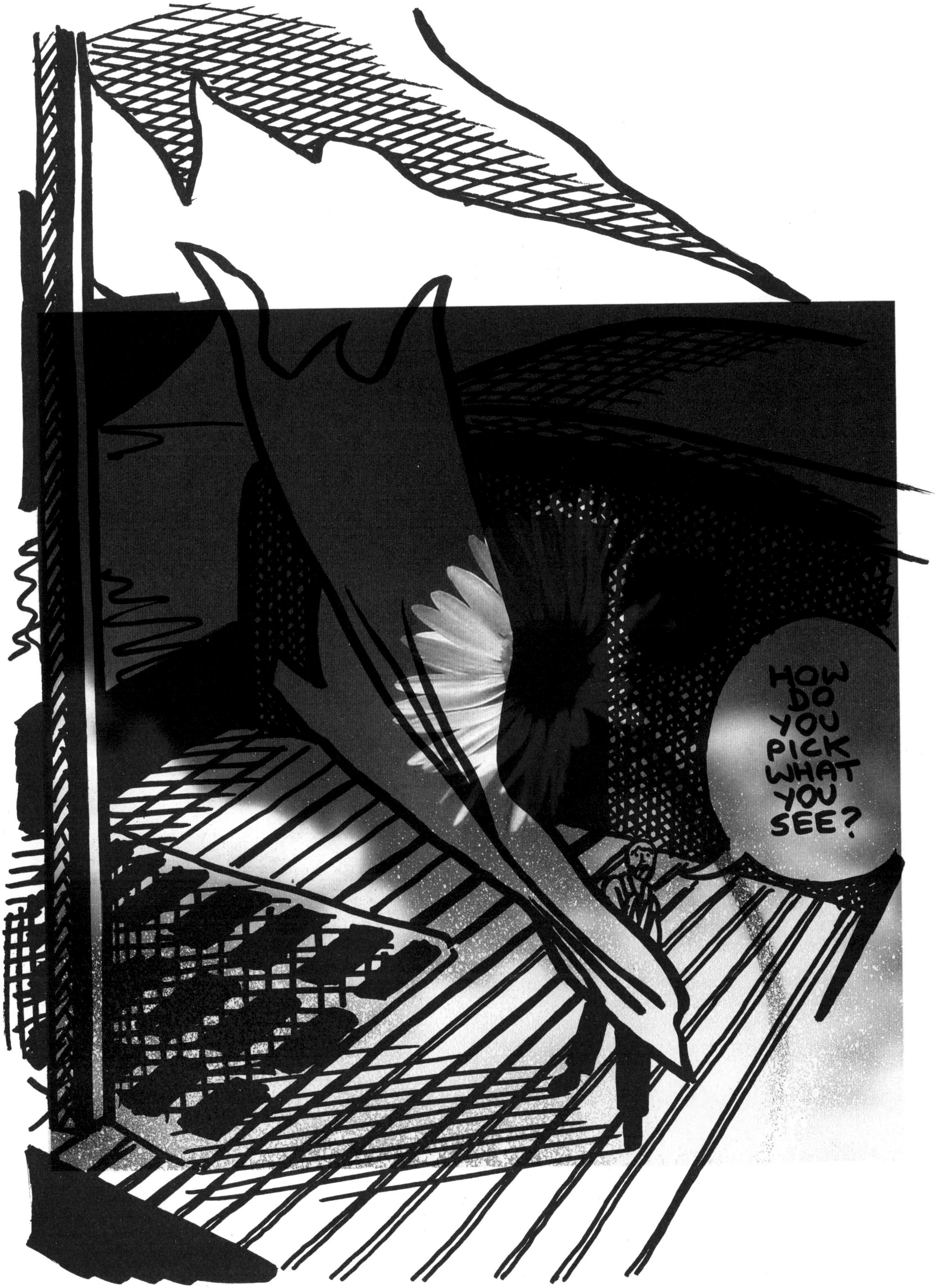
HOW DO YOU PICK WHAT YOU SEE?

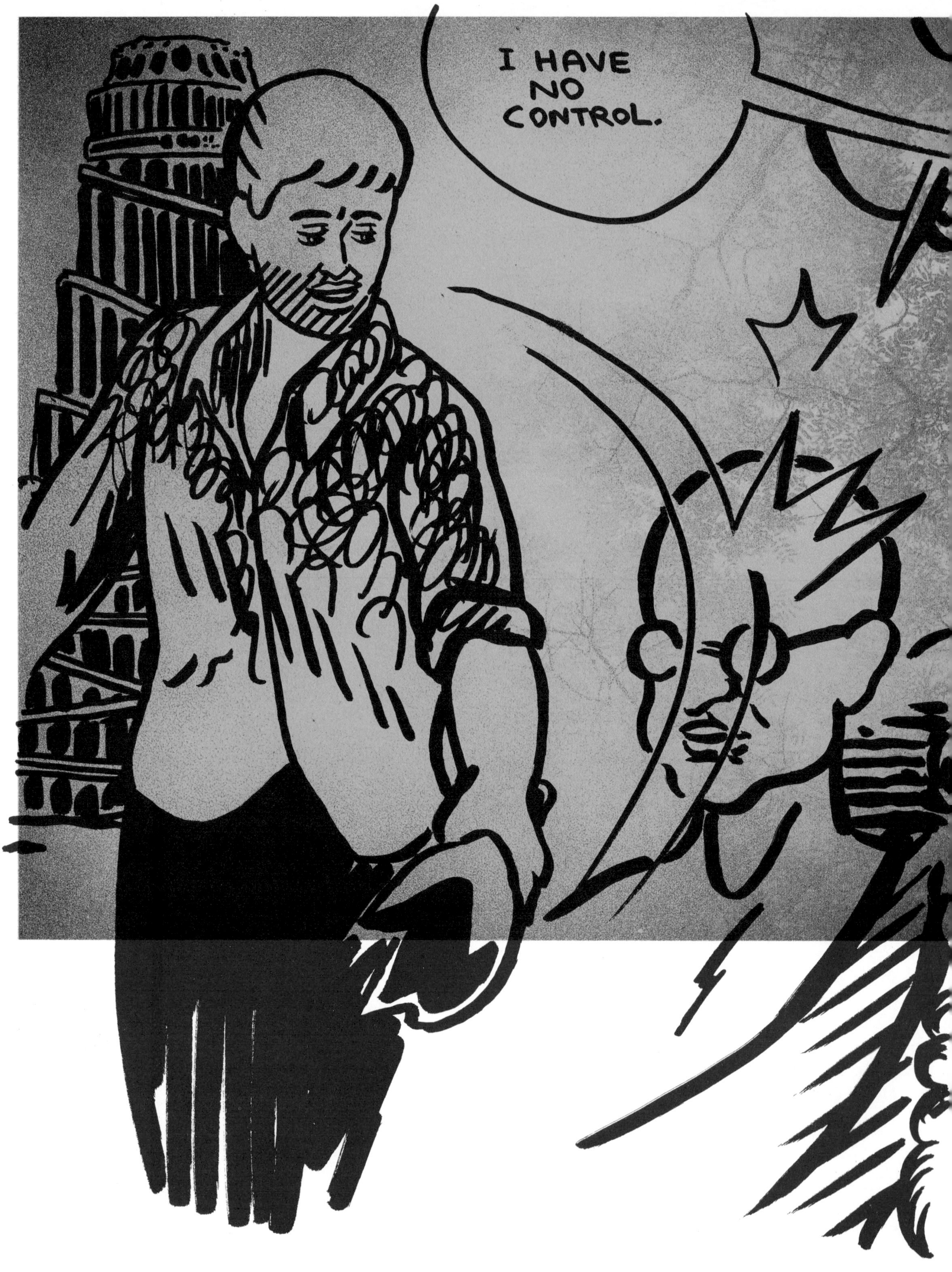
I HAVE NO CONTROL.

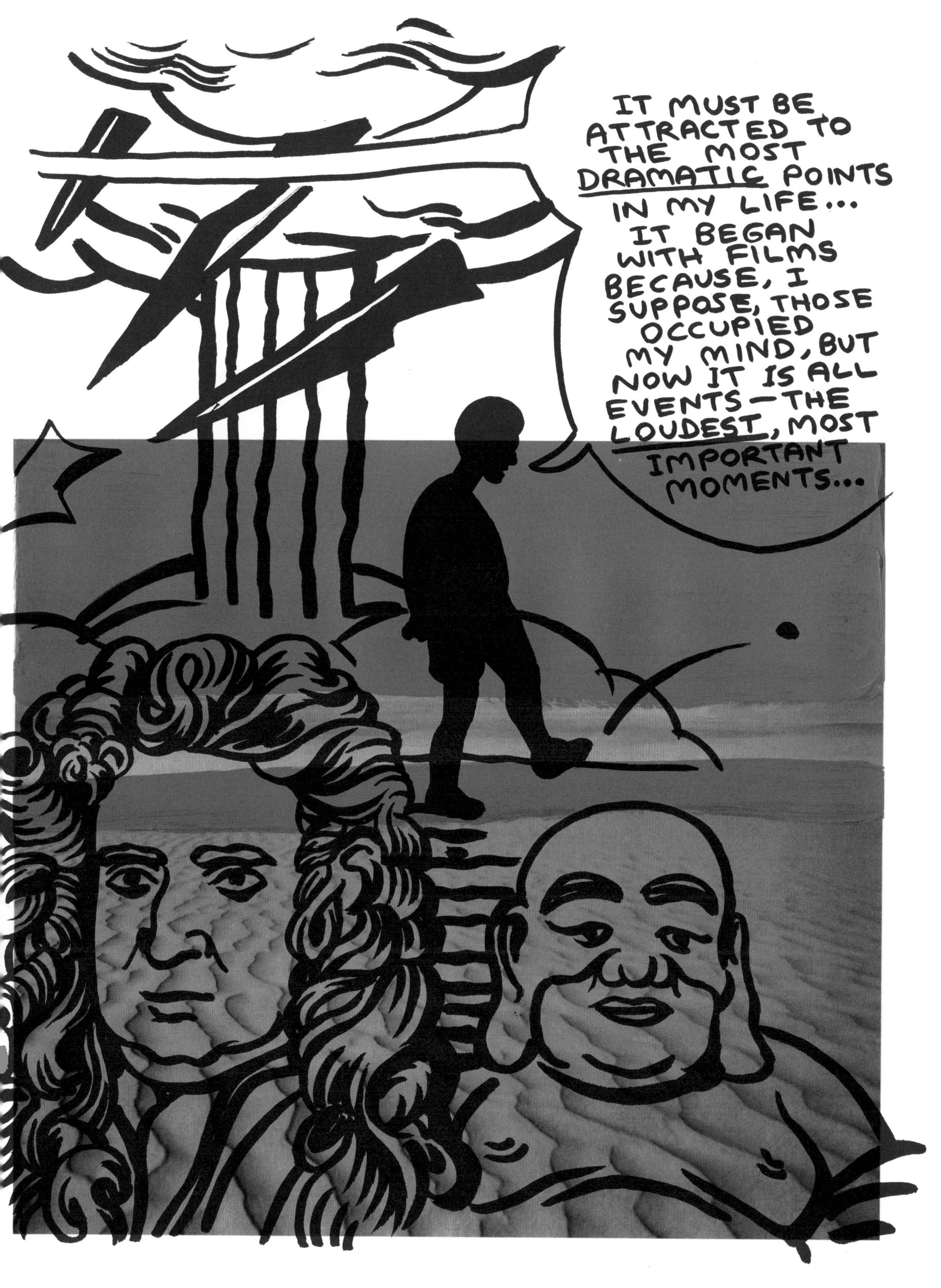
IT MUST BE ATTRACTED TO THE MOST DRAMATIC POINTS IN MY LIFE... IT BEGAN WITH FILMS BECAUSE, I SUPPOSE, THOSE OCCUPIED MY MIND, BUT NOW IT IS ALL EVENTS—THE LOUDEST, MOST IMPORTANT MOMENTS...

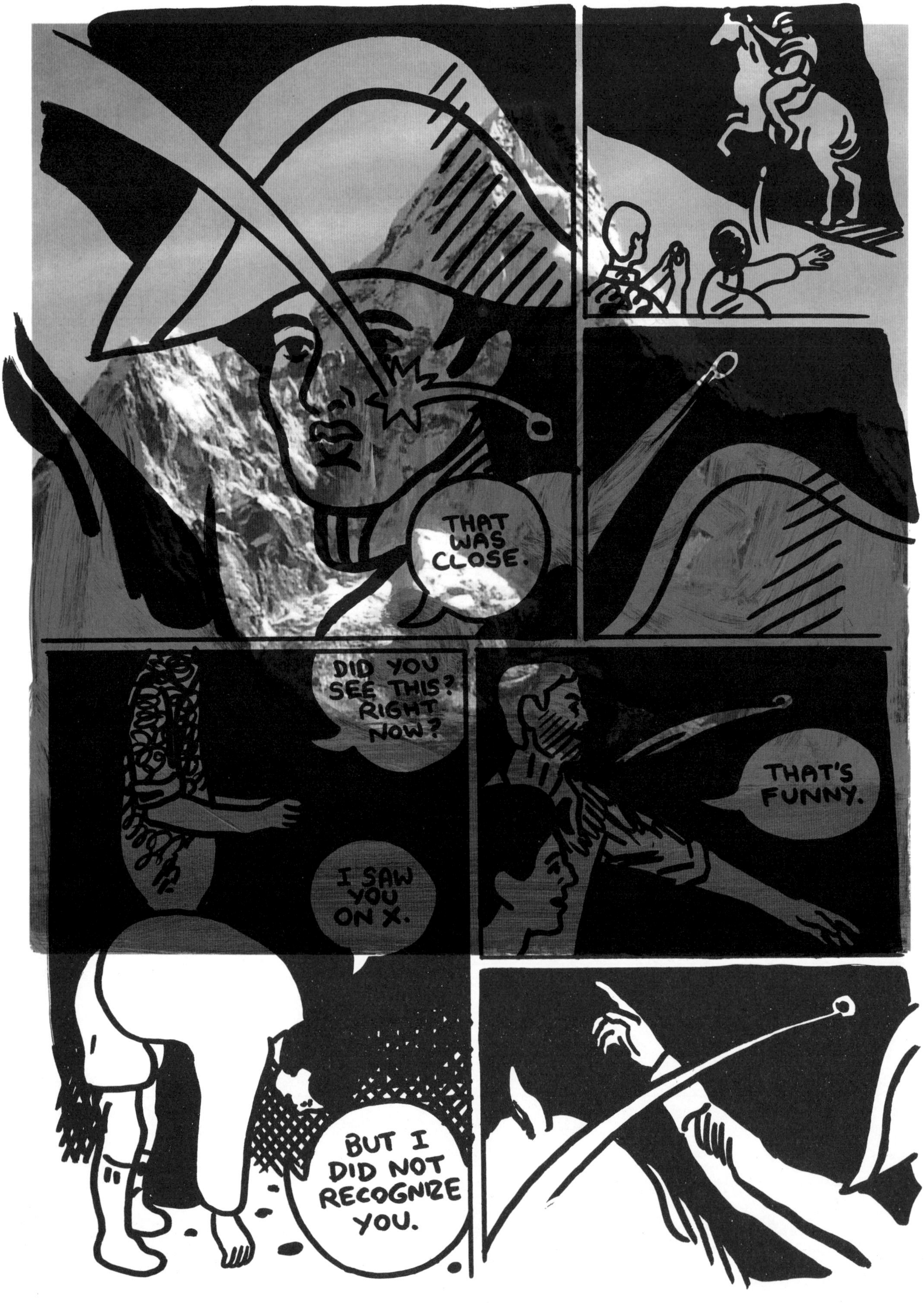
THAT WAS CLOSE.
DID YOU SEE THIS? RIGHT NOW?
THAT'S FUNNY.
I SAW YOU ON X.
BUT I DID NOT RECOGNIZE YOU.

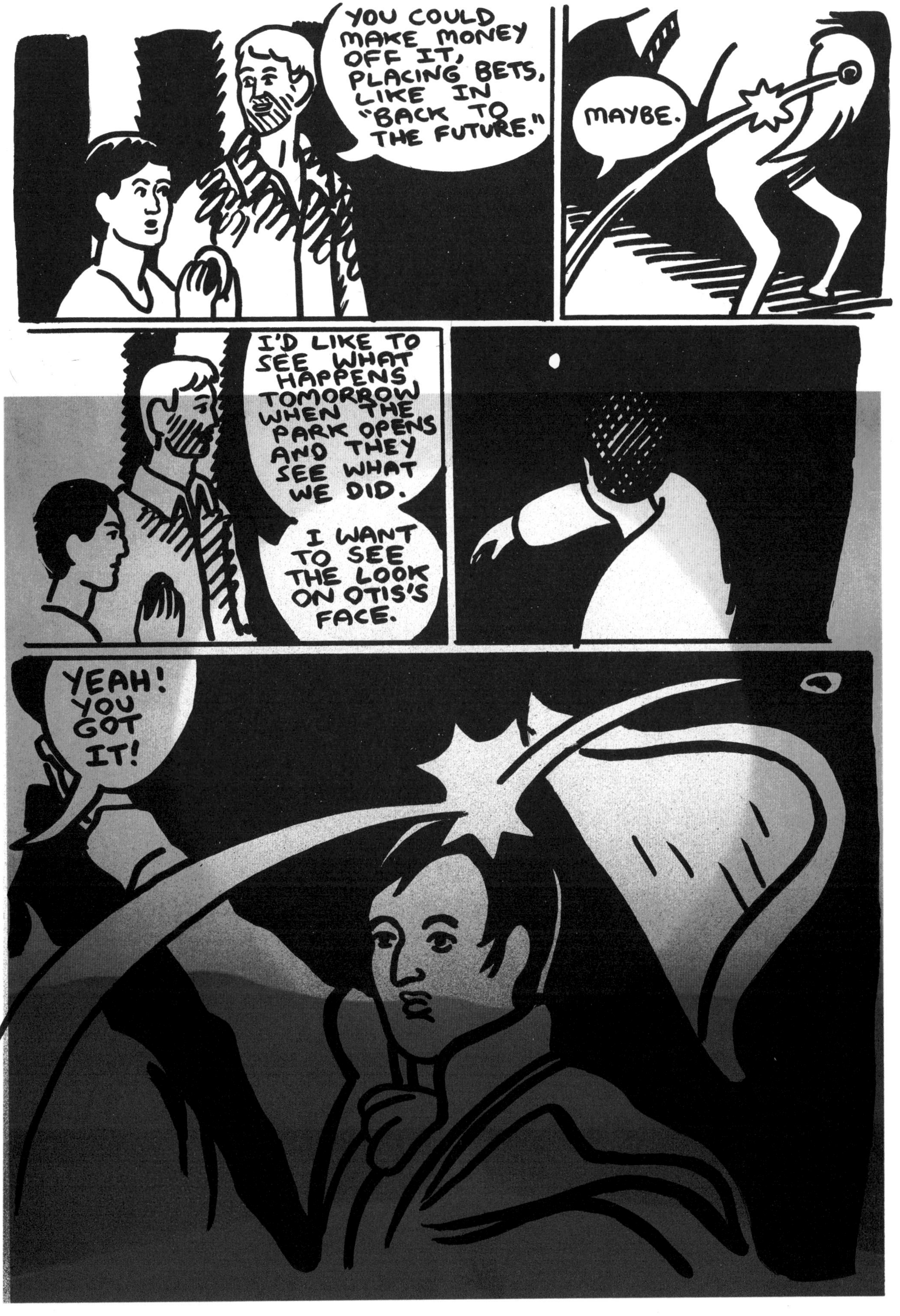
YOU COULD MAKE MONEY OFF IT, PLACING BETS, LIKE IN "BACK TO THE FUTURE."
MAYBE.
I'D LIKE TO SEE WHAT HAPPENS TOMORROW WHEN THE PARK OPENS AND THEY SEE WHAT WE DID.
I WANT TO SEE THE LOOK ON OTIS'S FACE.
YEAH! YOU GOT IT!

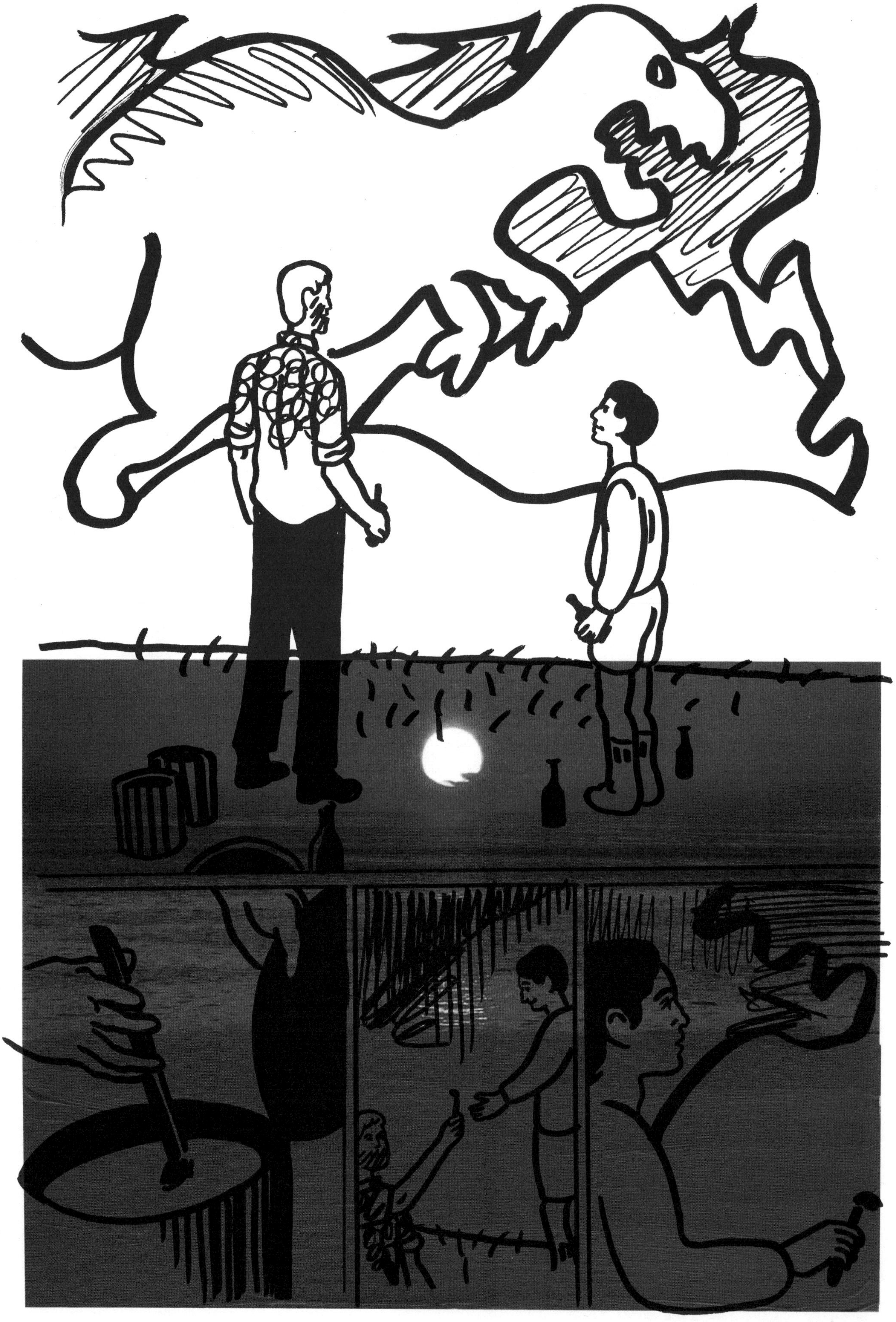

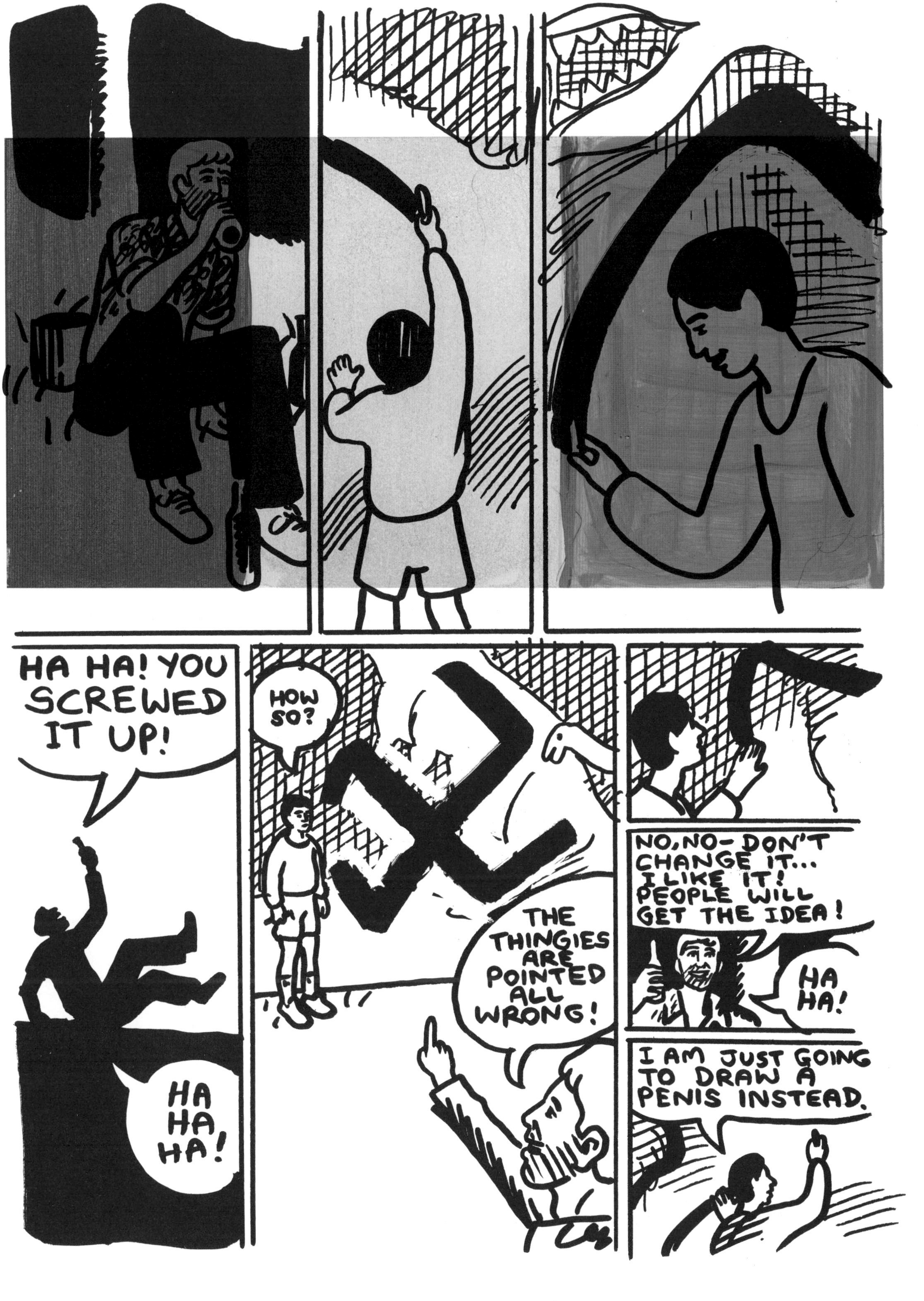
HA HA! YOU SCREWED IT UP!
HA HA HA!
HOW SO?
THE THINGIES ARE POINTED ALL WRONG!
NO, NO- DON'T CHANGE IT... I LIKE IT! PEOPLE WILL GET THE IDEA!
HA HA!
I AM JUST GOING TO DRAW A PENIS INSTEAD.

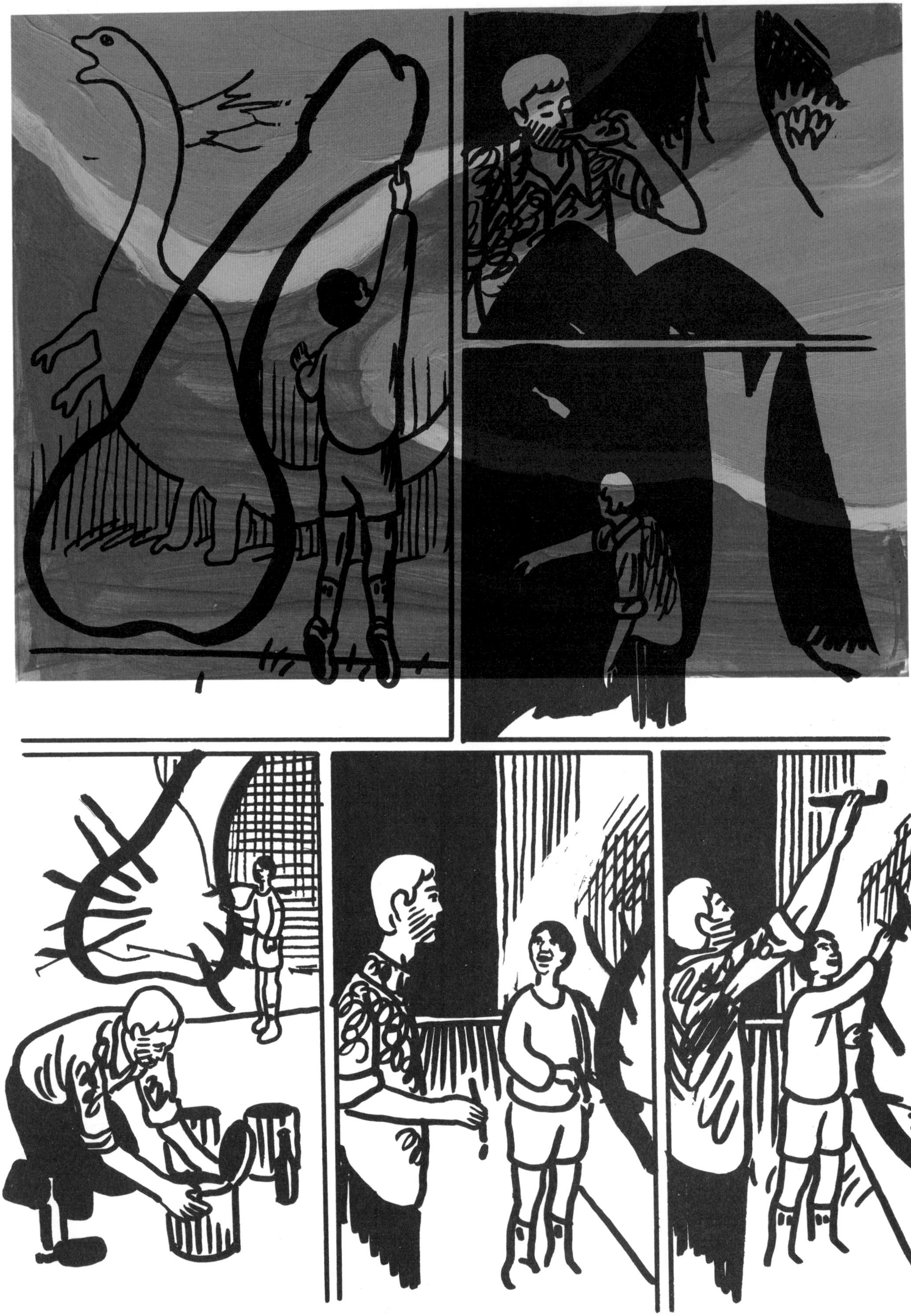

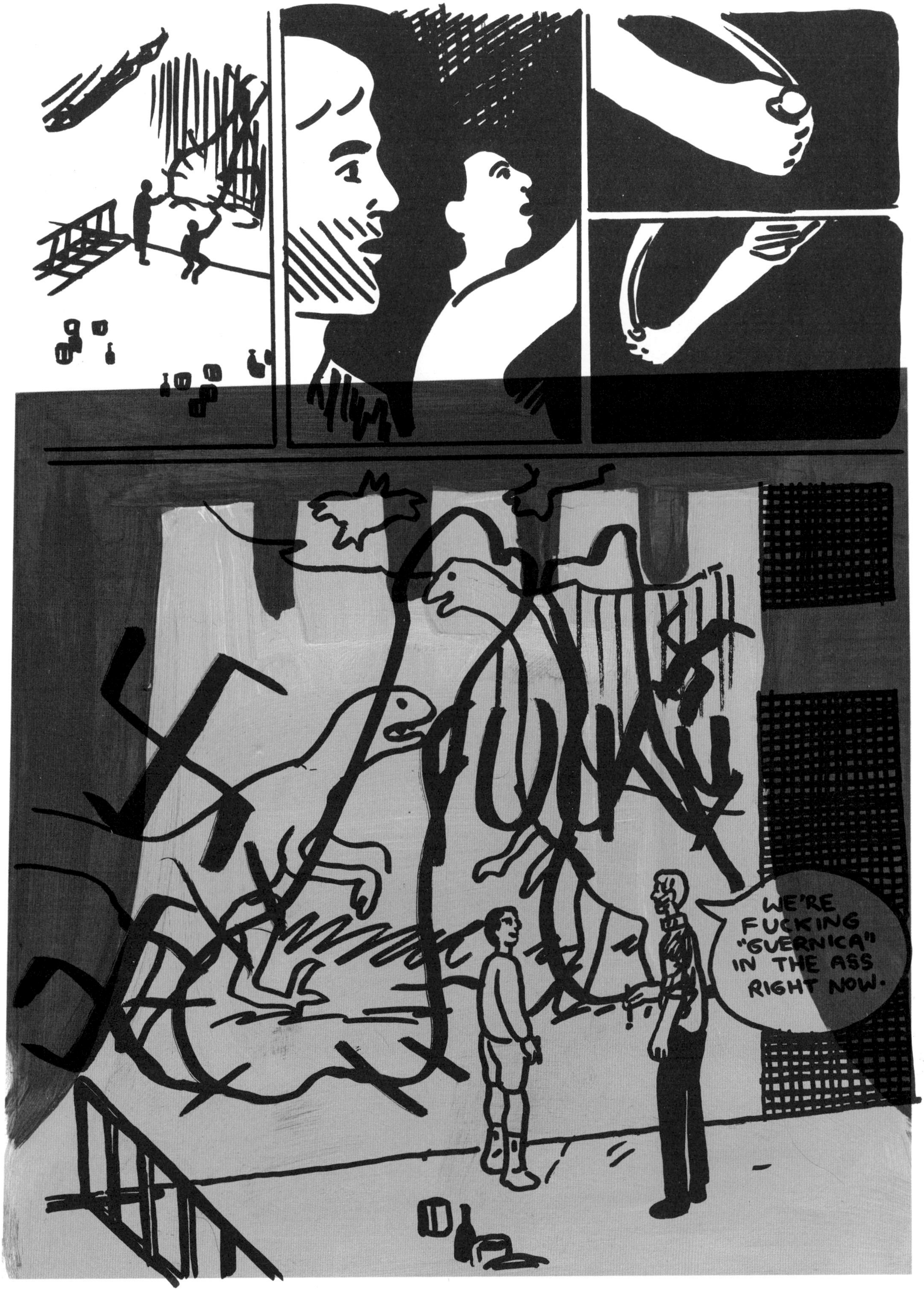
WE'RE FUCKING "GUERNICA" IN THE ASS RIGHT NOW.

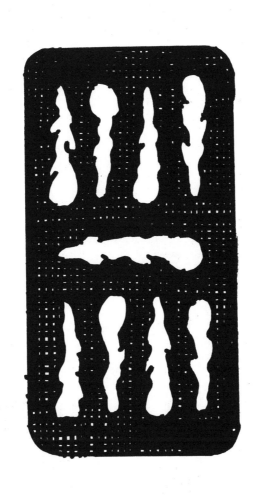

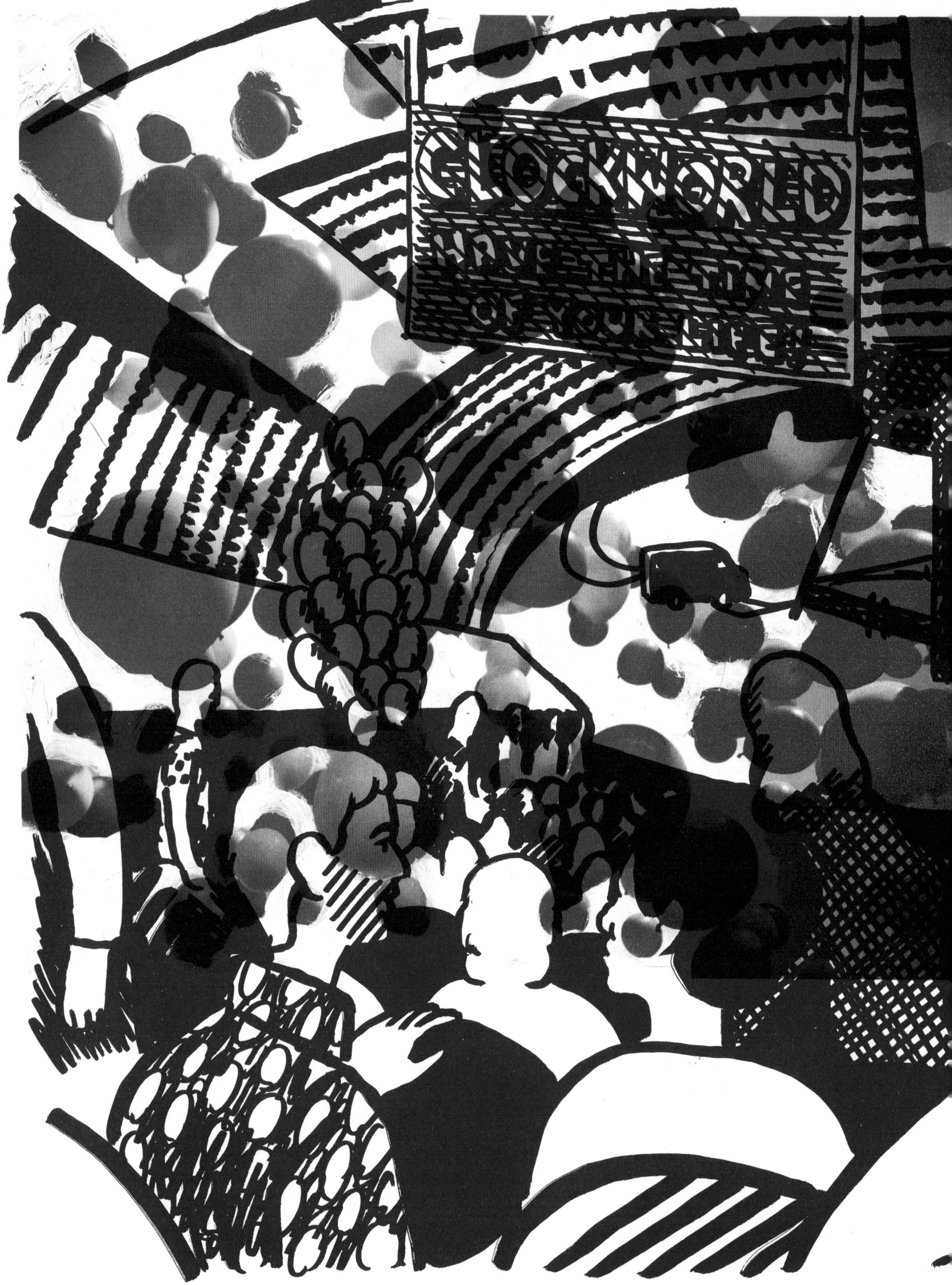
CLOCKWORLD
HAVE THE TIME
OF YOUR

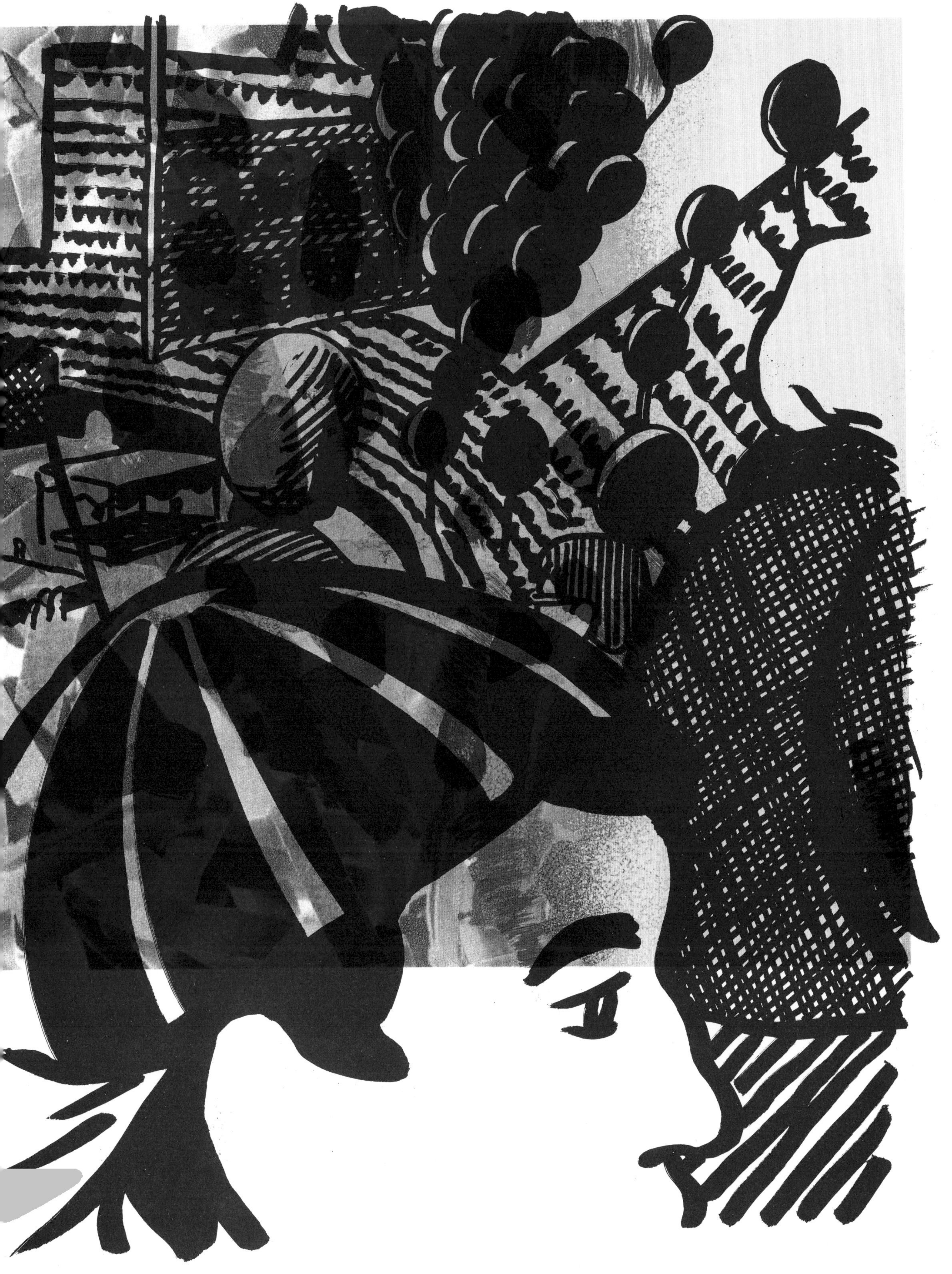

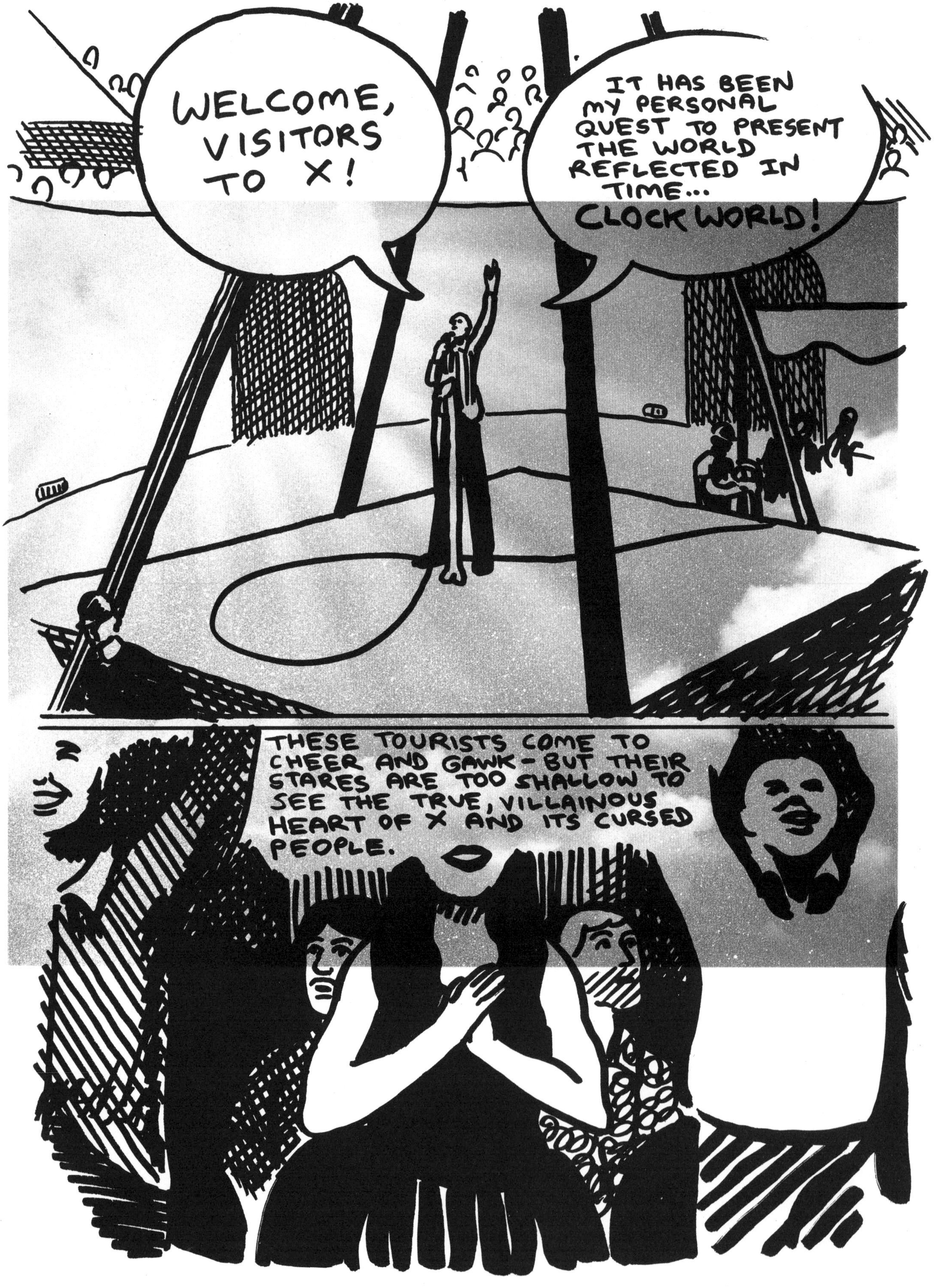
WELCOME, VISITORS TO X!
IT HAS BEEN MY PERSONAL QUEST TO PRESENT THE WORLD REFLECTED IN TIME... CLOCKWORLD!
THESE TOURISTS COME TO CHEER AND GAWK - BUT THEIR STARES ARE TOO SHALLOW TO SEE THE TRUE, VILLAINOUS HEART OF X AND ITS CURSED PEOPLE.

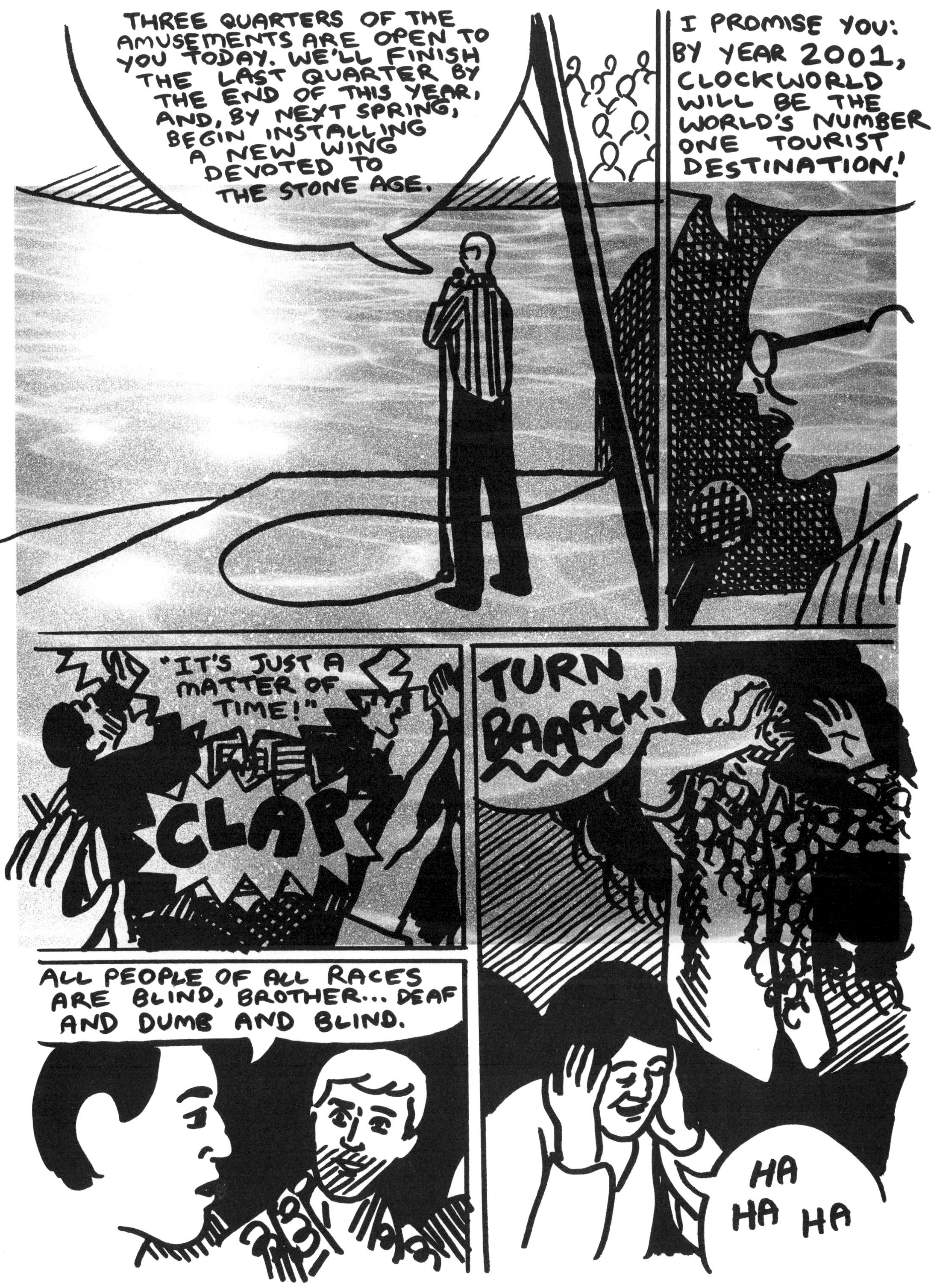
THREE QUARTERS OF THE AMUSEMENTS ARE OPEN TO YOU TODAY. WE'LL FINISH THE LAST QUARTER BY THE END OF THIS YEAR, AND, BY NEXT SPRING, BEGIN INSTALLING A NEW WING DEVOTED TO THE STONE AGE.
I PROMISE YOU: BY YEAR 2001, CLOCKWORLD WILL BE THE WORLD'S NUMBER ONE TOURIST DESTINATION!
"IT'S JUST A MATTER OF TIME!"
CLAP
TURN BAAACK!
ALL PEOPLE OF ALL RACES ARE BLIND, BROTHER... DEAF AND DUMB AND BLIND.
HA HA HA

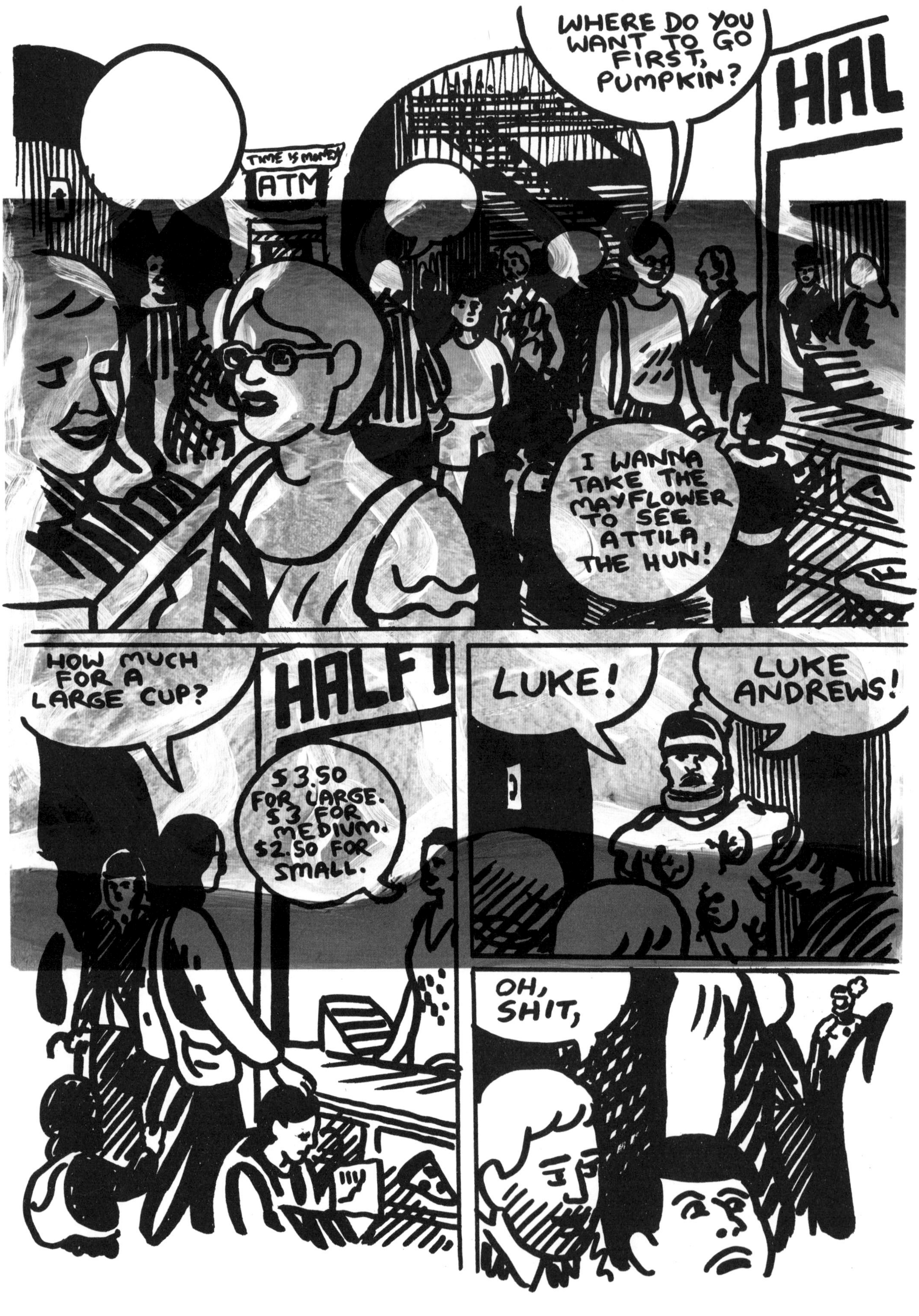
TIME IS MONEY
ATM
WHERE DO YOU WANT TO GO FIRST, PUMPKIN?
HAL
I WANNA TAKE THE MAYFLOWER TO SEE ATTILA THE HUN!
HOW MUCH FOR A LARGE CUP?
HALF!
$3.50 FOR LARGE. $3 FOR MEDIUM. $2.50 FOR SMALL.
LUKE!
LUKE ANDREWS!
OH, SHIT,

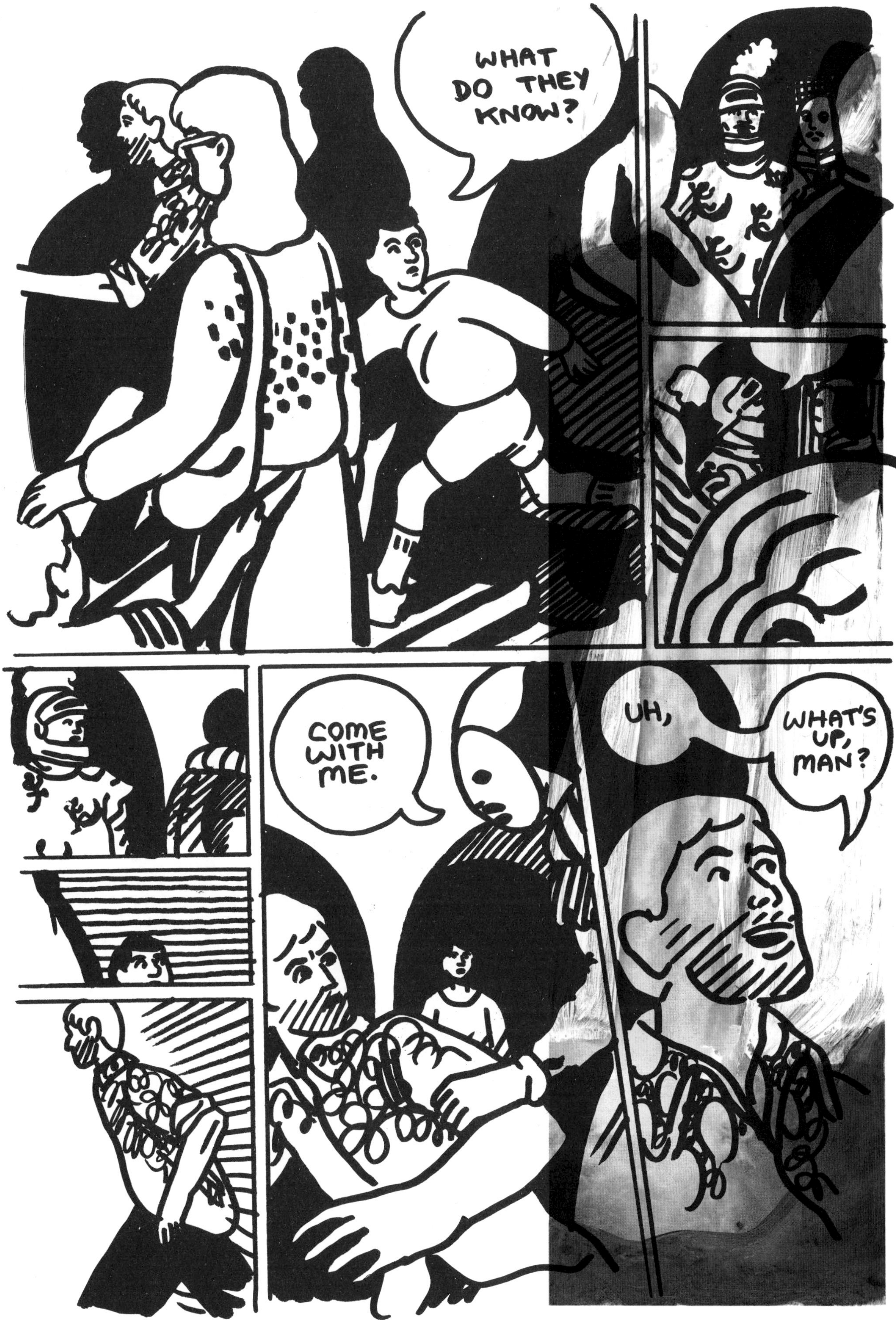
WHAT DO THEY KNOW?
COME WITH ME.
UH,
WHAT'S UP, MAN?

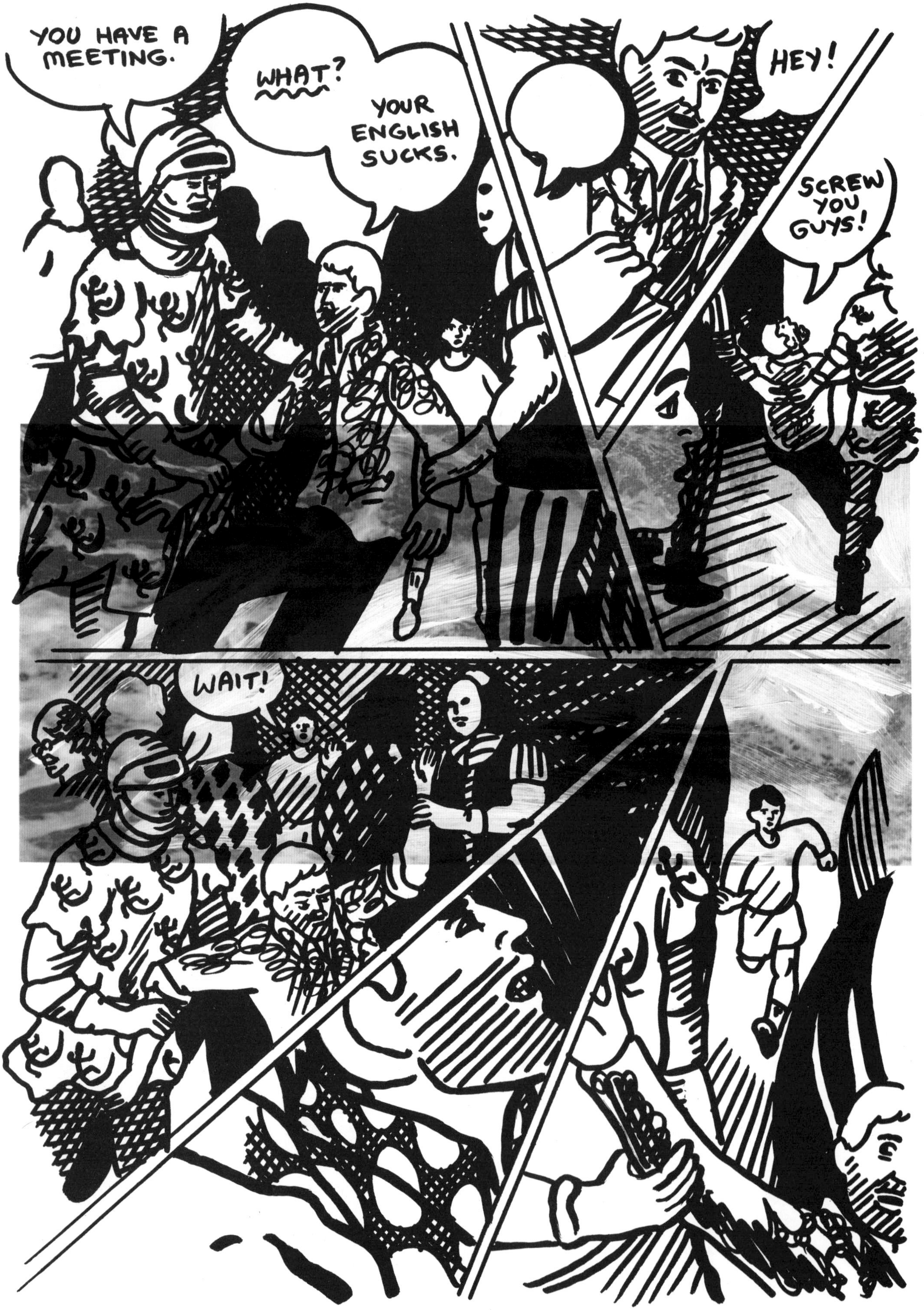
YOU HAVE A MEETING.
WHAT?
YOUR ENGLISH SUCKS.
HEY!
SCREW YOU GUYS!
WAIT!

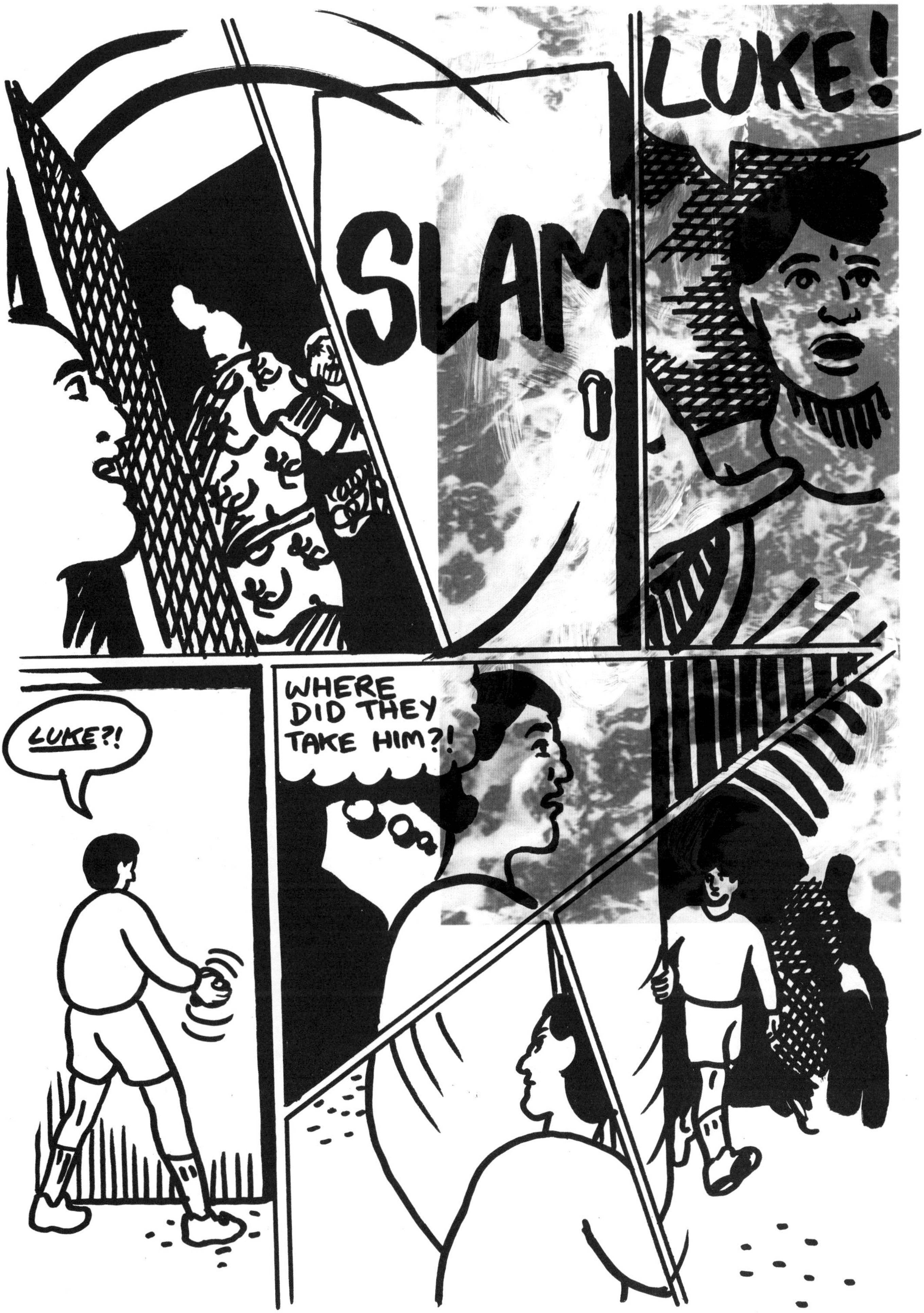
SLAM
LUKE!
LUKE?!
WHERE DID THEY TAKE HIM?!

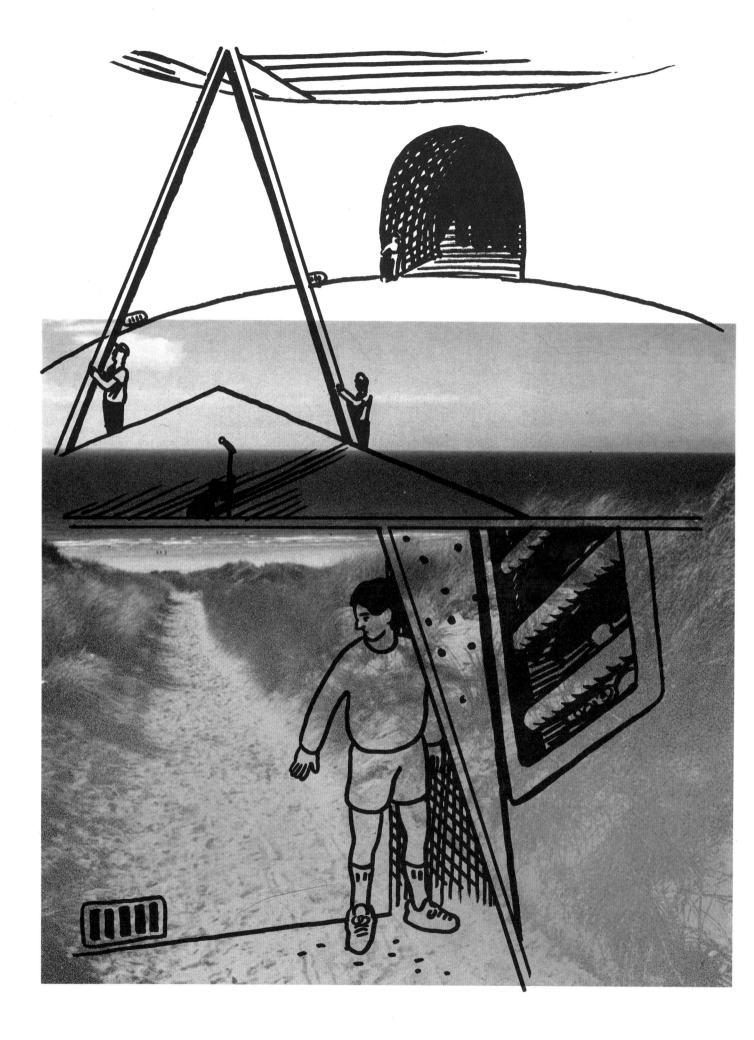

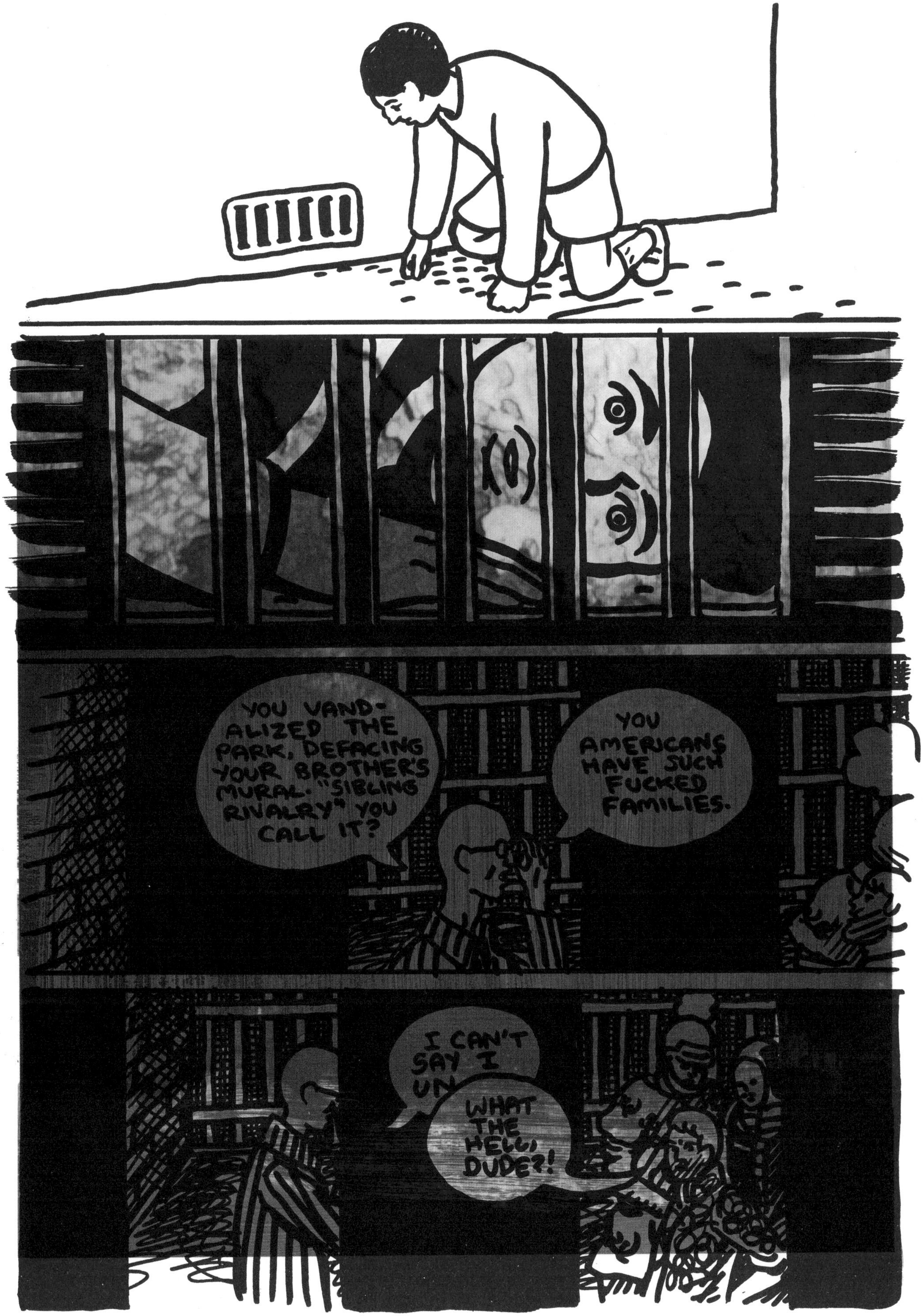
YOU VANDALIZED THE PARK, DEFACING YOUR BROTHER'S MURAL. "SIBLING RIVALRY" YOU CALL IT?
YOU AMERICANS HAVE SUCH FUCKED FAMILIES.
I CAN'T SAY I UN
WHAT THE HELL, DUDE?!

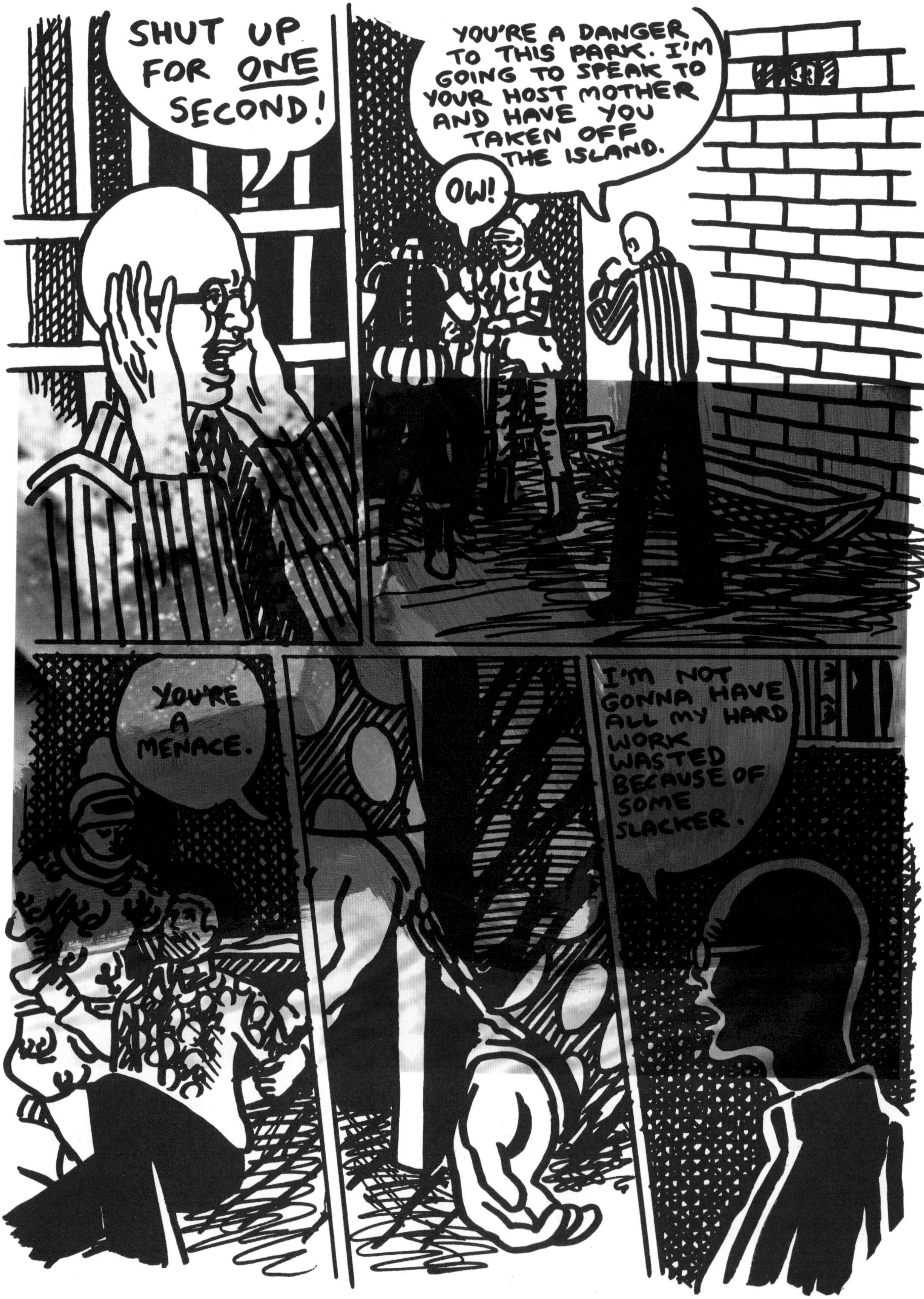
SHUT UP FOR ONE SECOND!
YOU'RE A DANGER TO THIS PARK. I'M GOING TO SPEAK TO YOUR HOST MOTHER AND HAVE YOU TAKEN OFF THE ISLAND.
OW!
YOU'RE A MENACE.
I'M NOT GONNA HAVE ALL MY HARD WORK WASTED BECAUSE OF SOME SLACKER.

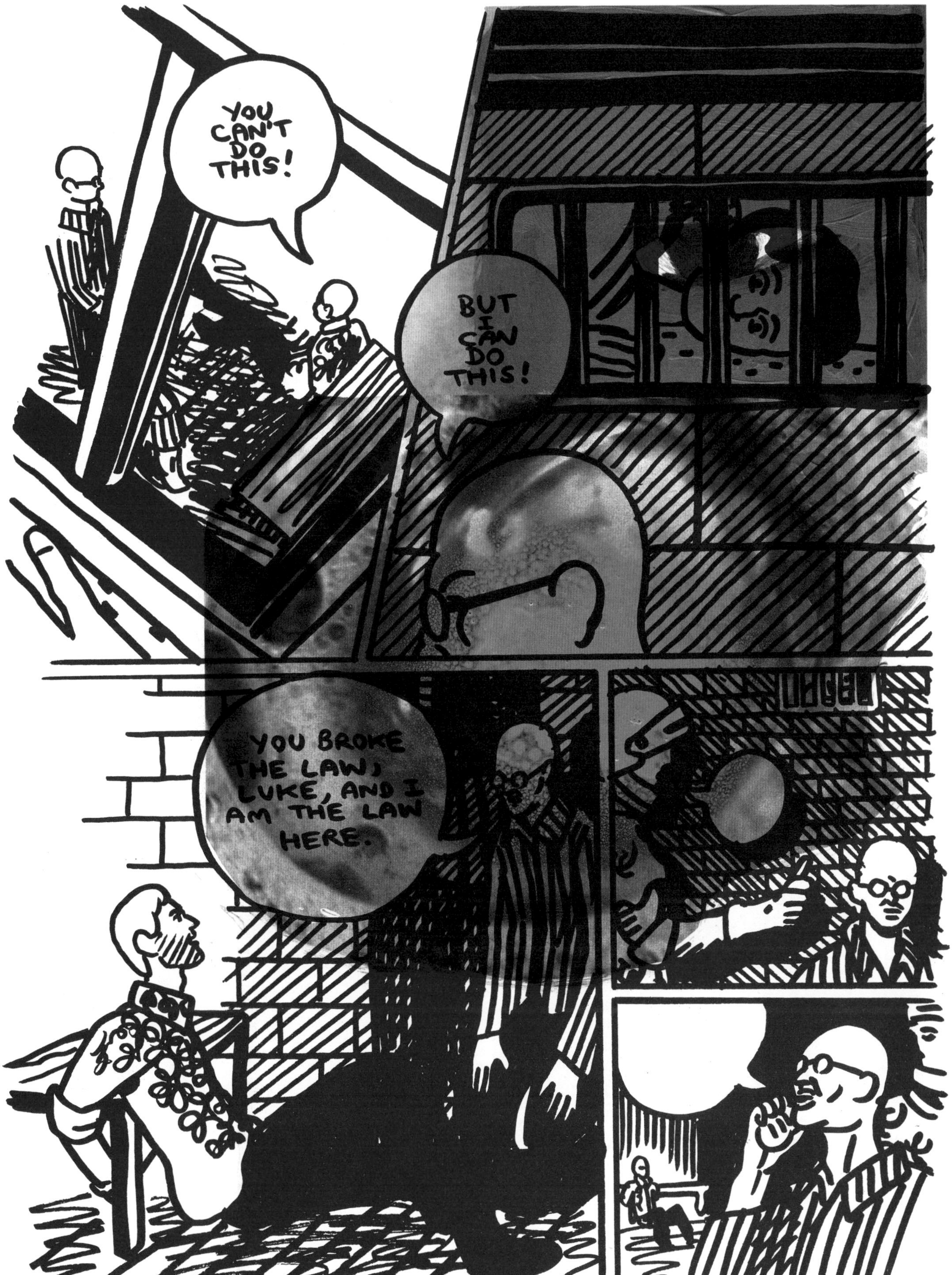
YOU CAN'T DO THIS!
BUT I CAN DO THIS!
YOU BROKE THE LAW, LUKE, AND I AM THE LAW HERE.

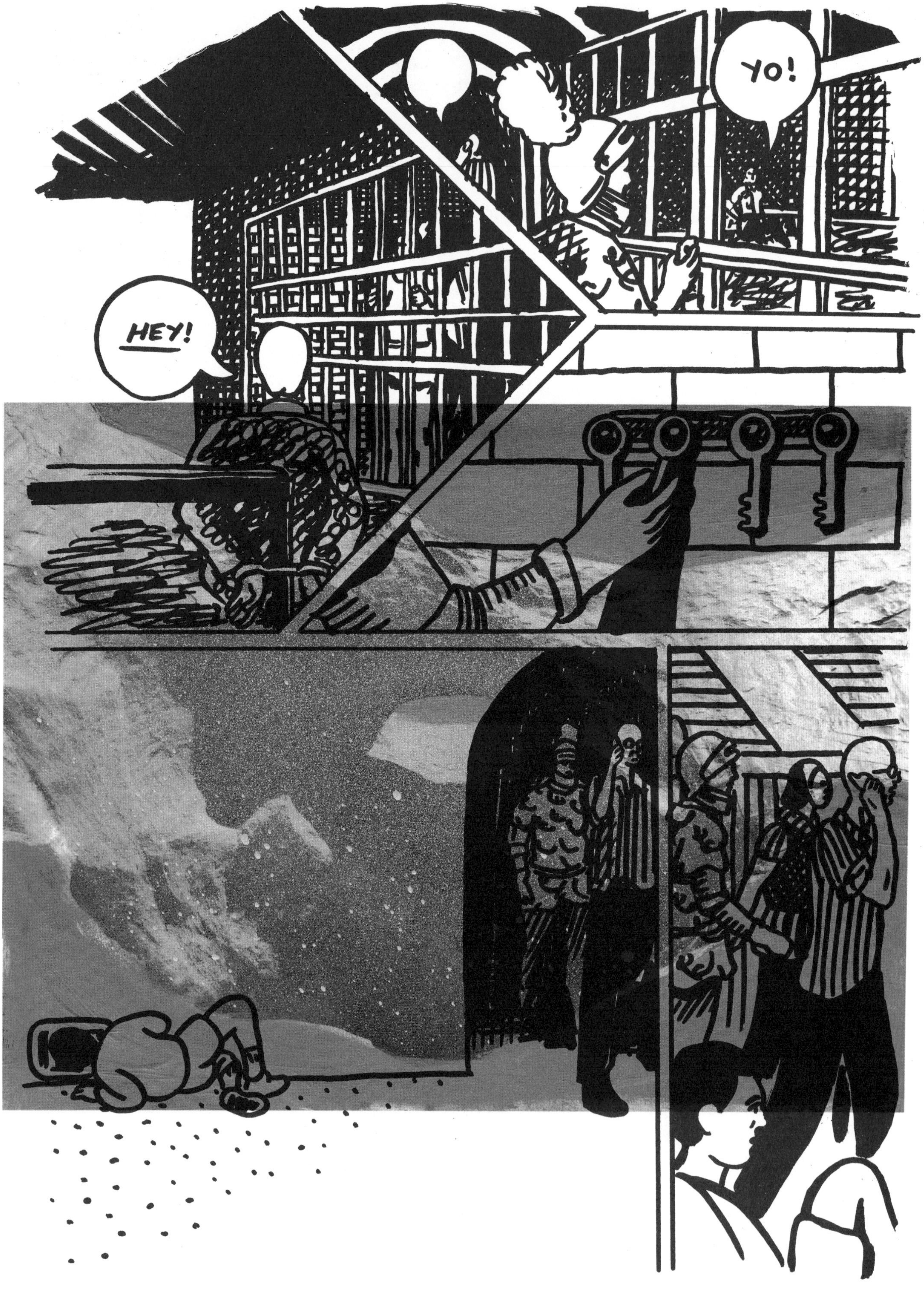
YO!
HEY!

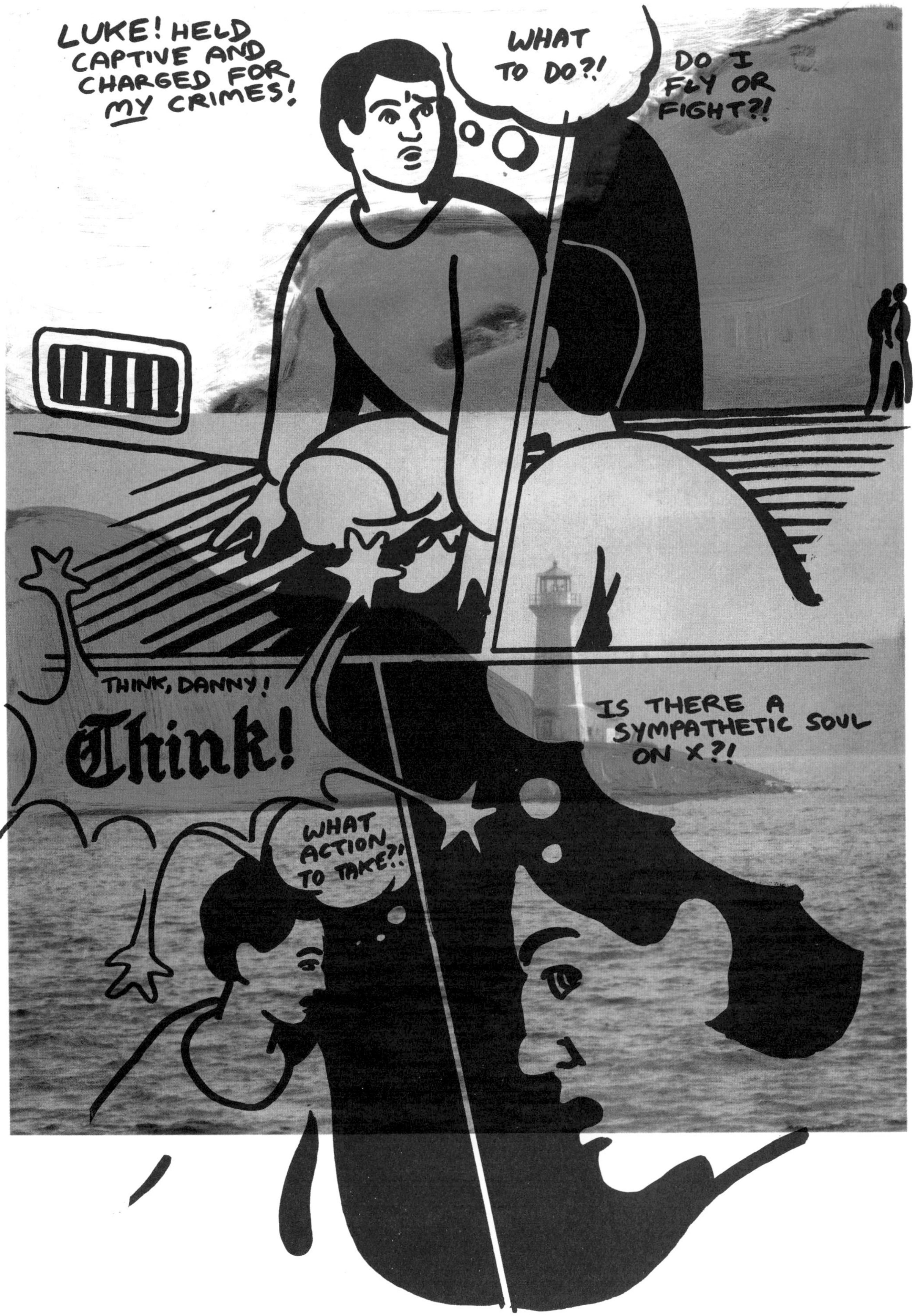

LUKE! HELD CAPTIVE AND CHARGED FOR MY CRIMES!
WHAT TO DO?!
DO I FLY OR FIGHT?!
THINK, DANNY!
Think!
IS THERE A SYMPATHETIC SOUL ON X?!
WHAT ACTION TO TAKE?!

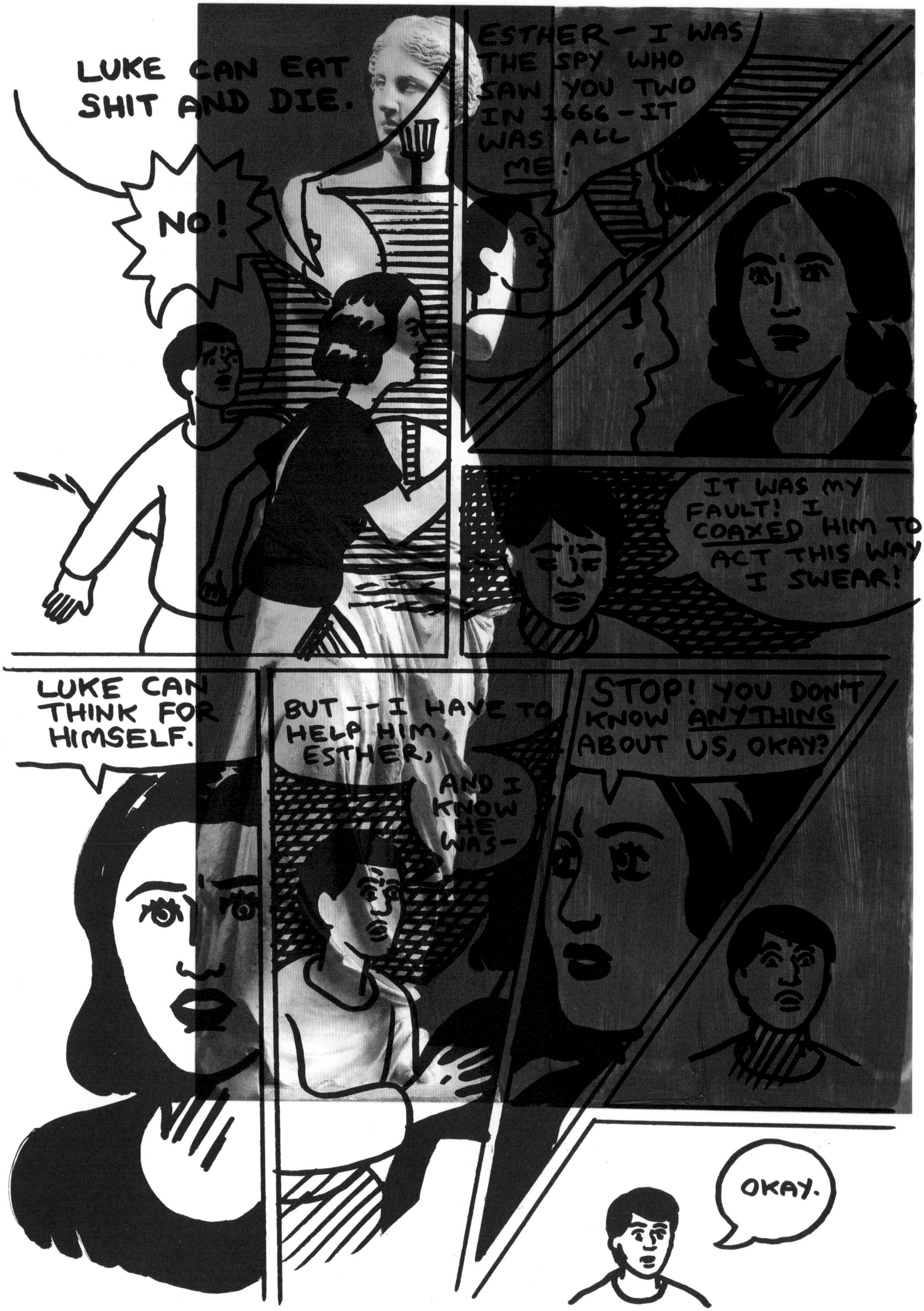
LUKE CAN EAT SHIT AND DIE.
NO!
ESTHER - I WAS THE SPY WHO SAW YOU TWO IN 1666 - IT WAS ALL ME!
IT WAS MY FAULT! I COAXED HIM TO ACT THIS WAY! I SWEAR!
LUKE CAN THINK FOR HIMSELF.
BUT -- I HAVE TO HELP HIM, ESTHER,
AND I KNOW HE WAS-
STOP! YOU DON'T KNOW ANYTHING ABOUT US, OKAY?
OKAY.

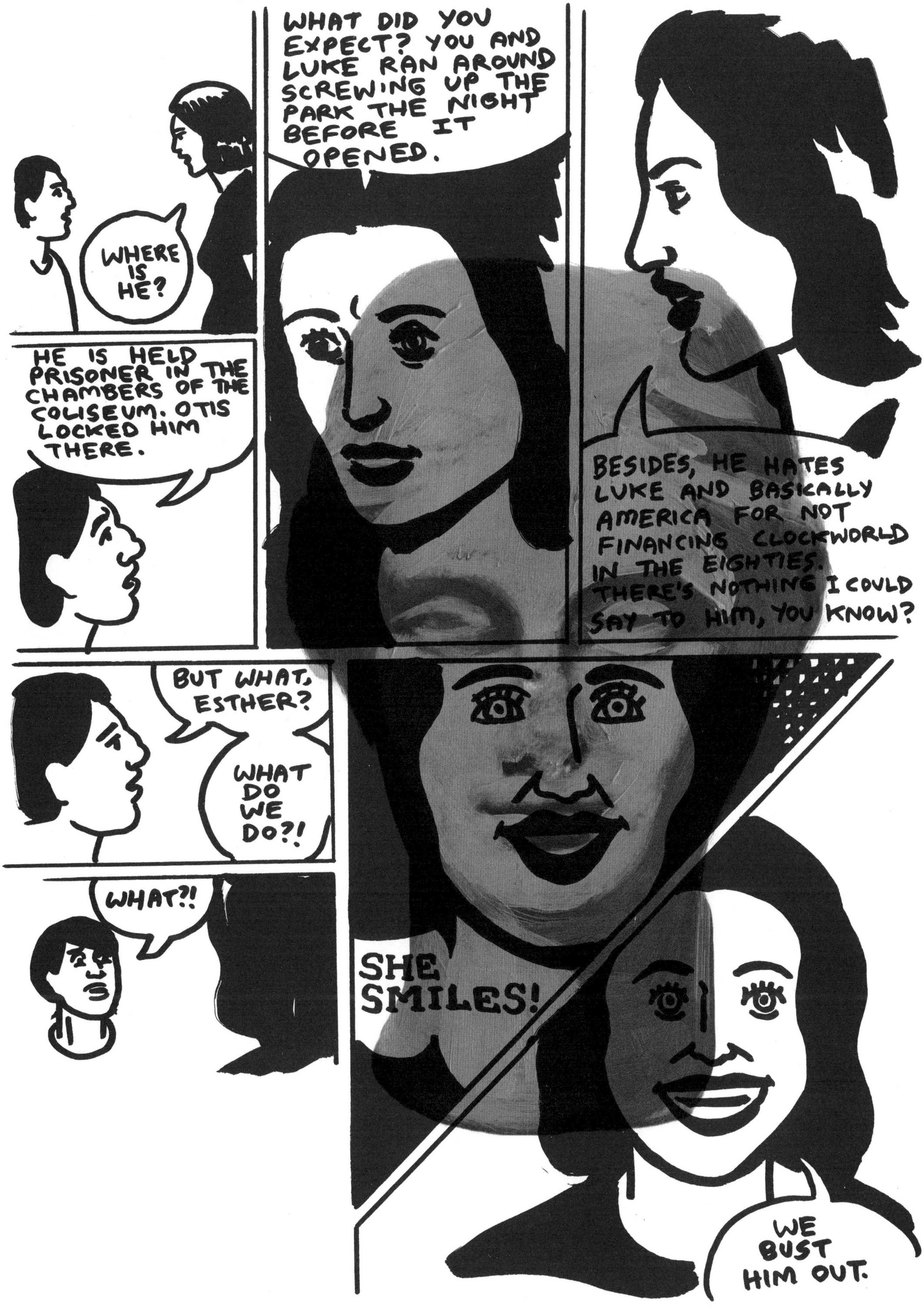

WHERE IS HE?
WHAT DID YOU EXPECT? YOU AND LUKE RAN AROUND SCREWING UP THE PARK THE NIGHT BEFORE IT OPENED.
HE IS HELD PRISONER IN THE CHAMBERS OF THE COLISEUM. OTIS LOCKED HIM THERE.
BESIDES, HE HATES LUKE AND BASICALLY AMERICA FOR NOT FINANCING CLOCKWORLD IN THE EIGHTIES. THERE'S NOTHING I COULD SAY TO HIM, YOU KNOW?
BUT WHAT, ESTHER?
WHAT DO WE DO?!
WHAT?!
SHE SMILES!
WE BUST HIM OUT.

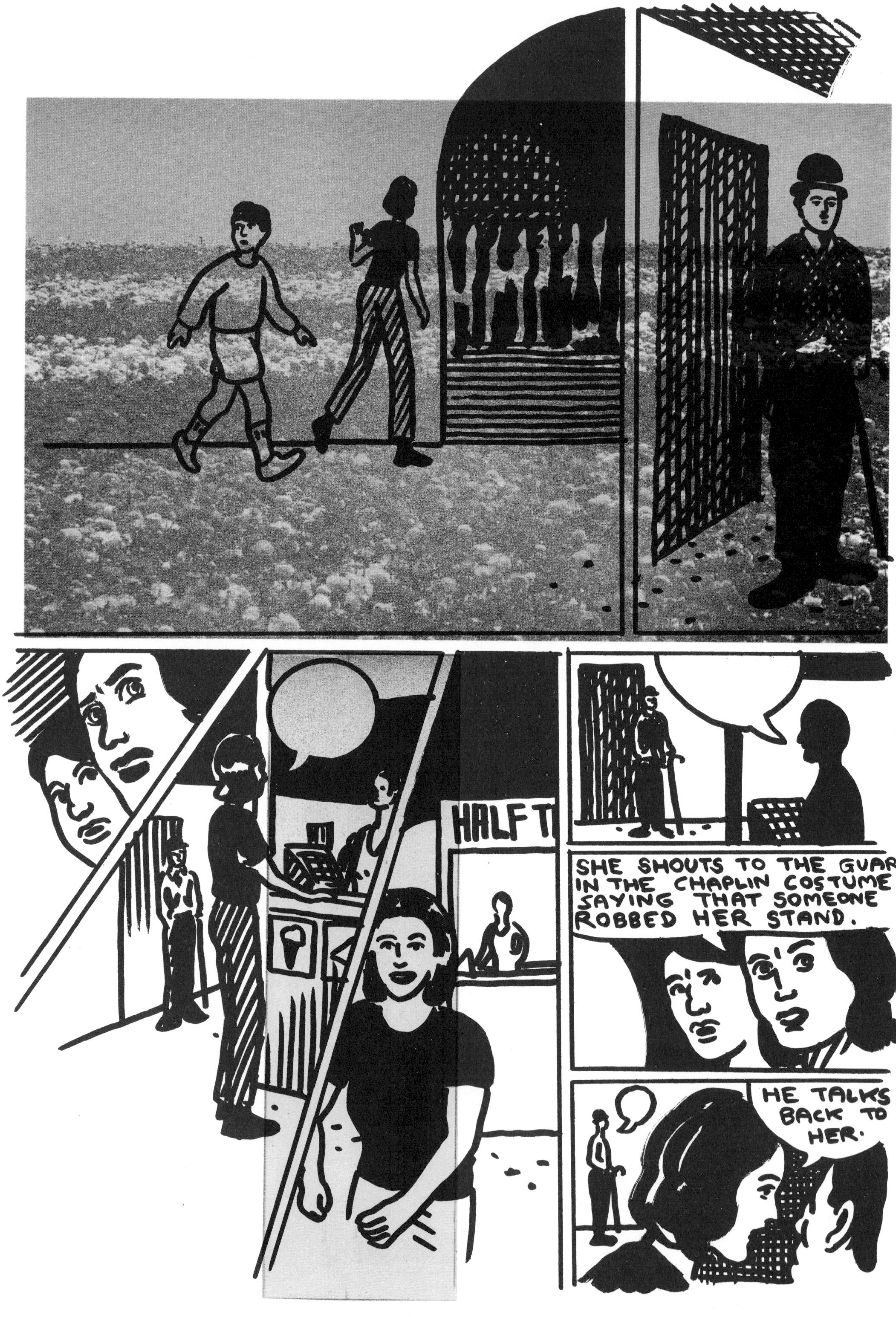
HALF T
SHE SHOUTS TO THE GUARD IN THE CHAPLIN COSTUME, SAYING THAT SOMEONE ROBBED HER STAND.
HE TALKS BACK TO HER.

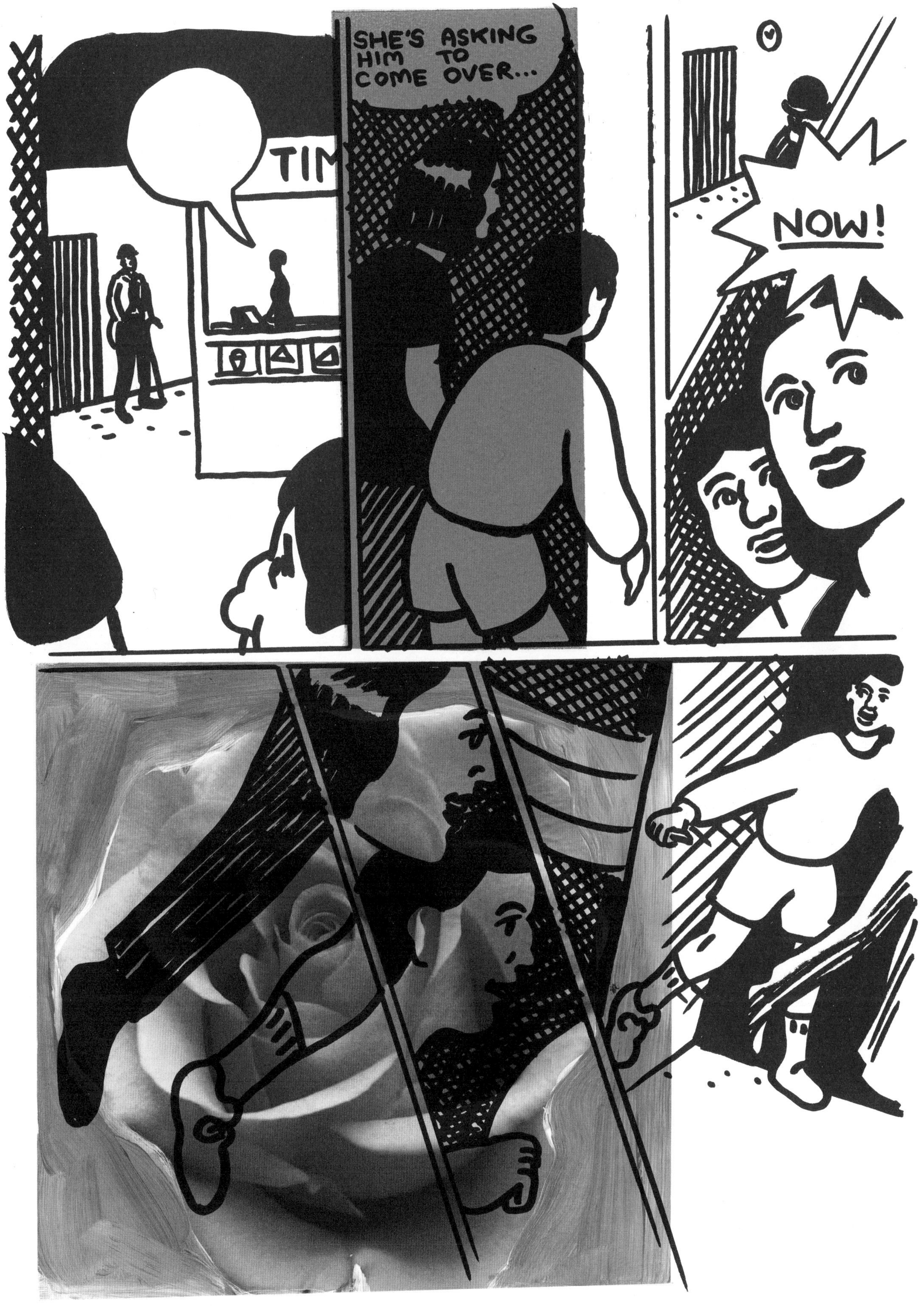

TIM
SHE'S ASKING HIM TO COME OVER...
NOW!

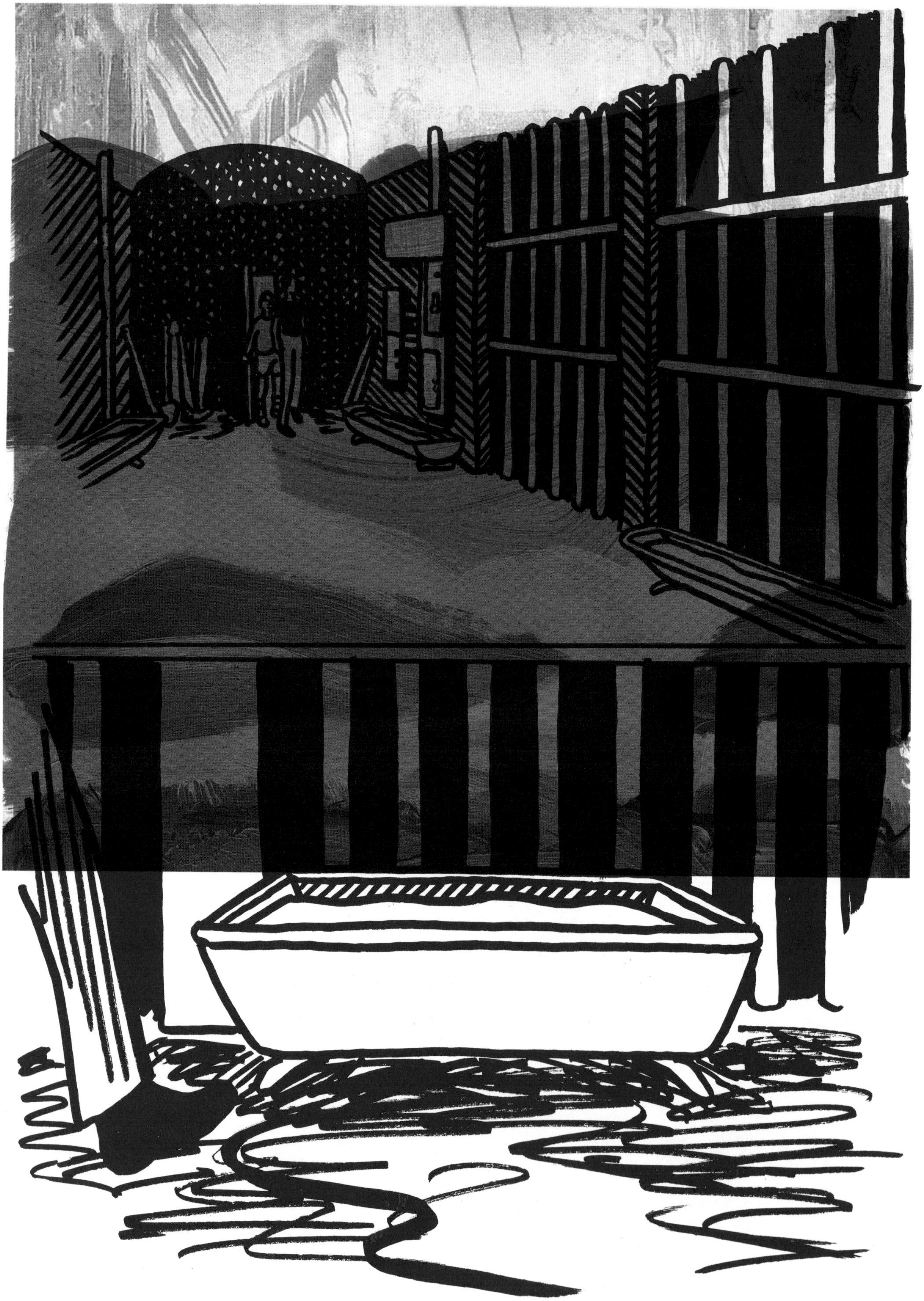

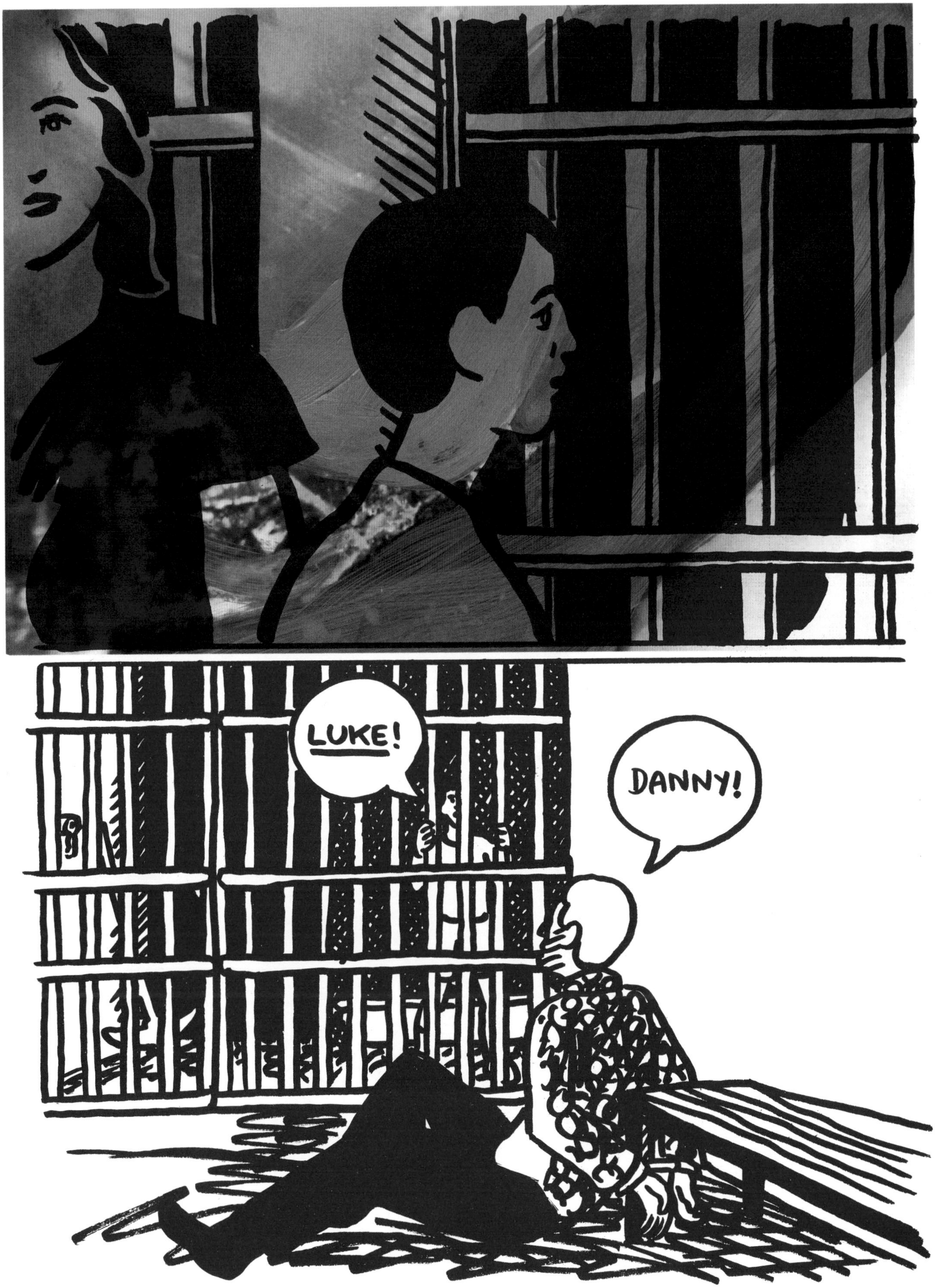
LUKE!
DANNY!

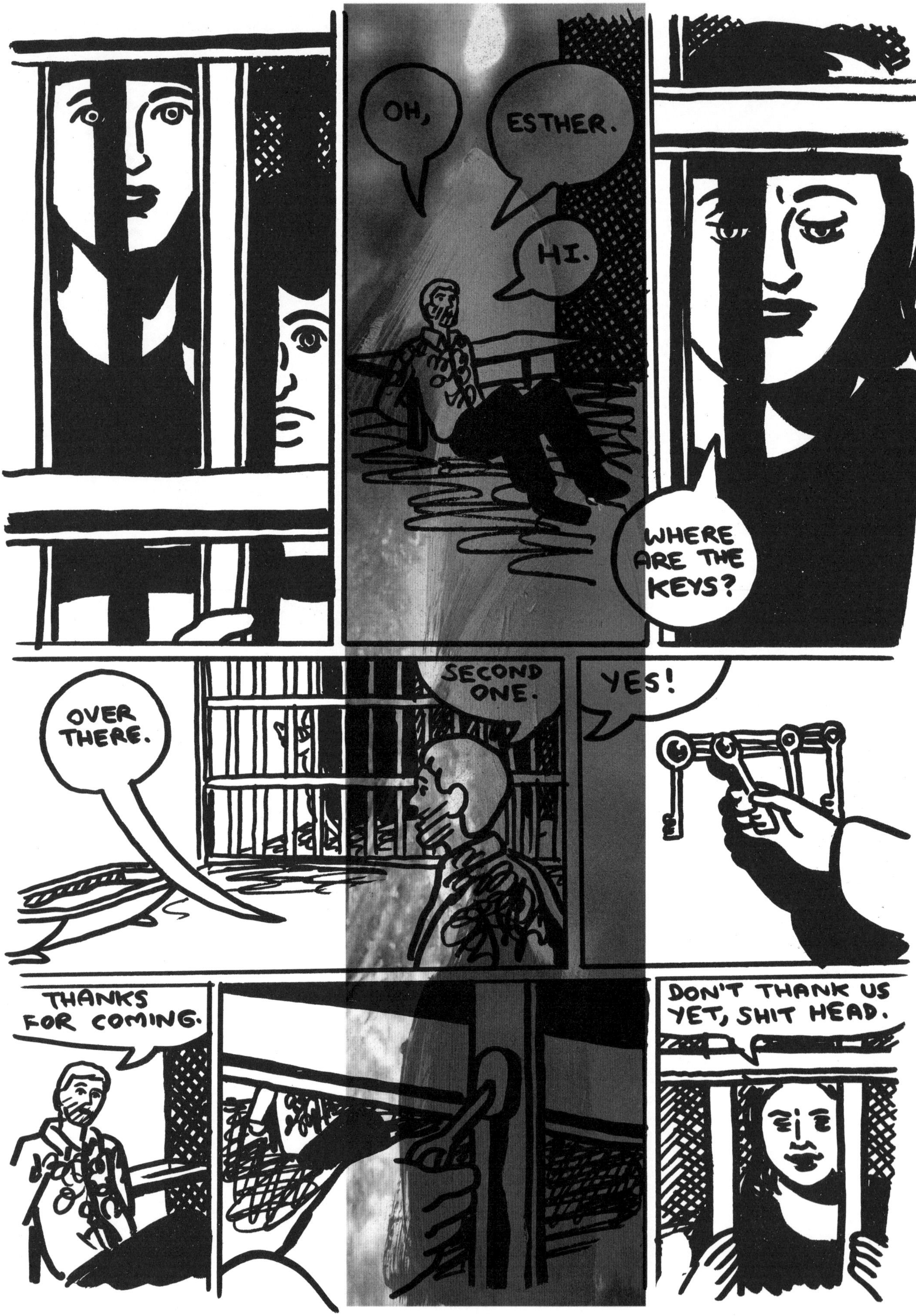
OH,
ESTHER.
HI.
WHERE ARE THE KEYS?
OVER THERE.
SECOND ONE.
YES!
THANKS FOR COMING.
DON'T THANK US YET, SHIT HEAD.

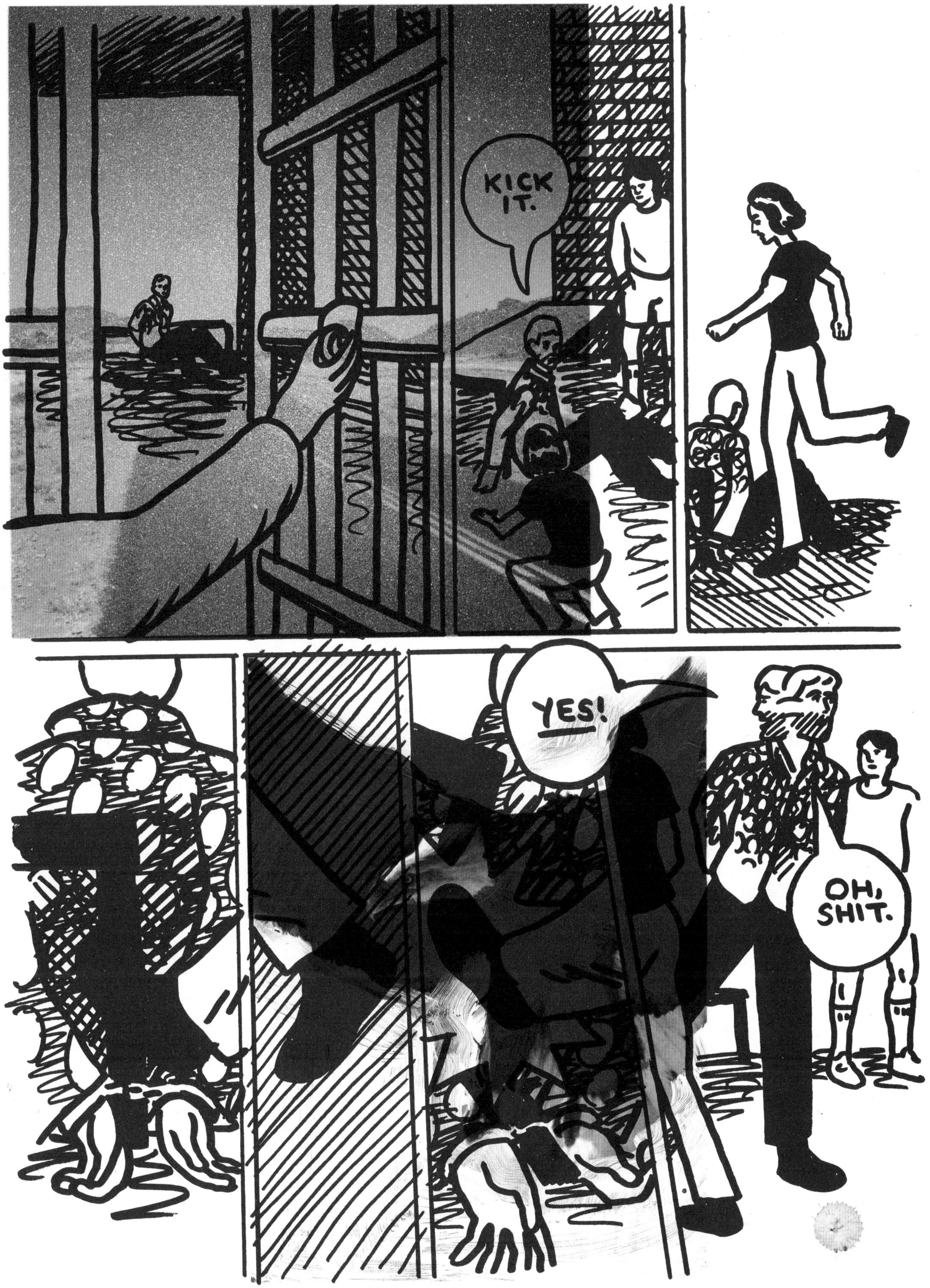
KICK IT.
YES!
OH, SHIT.

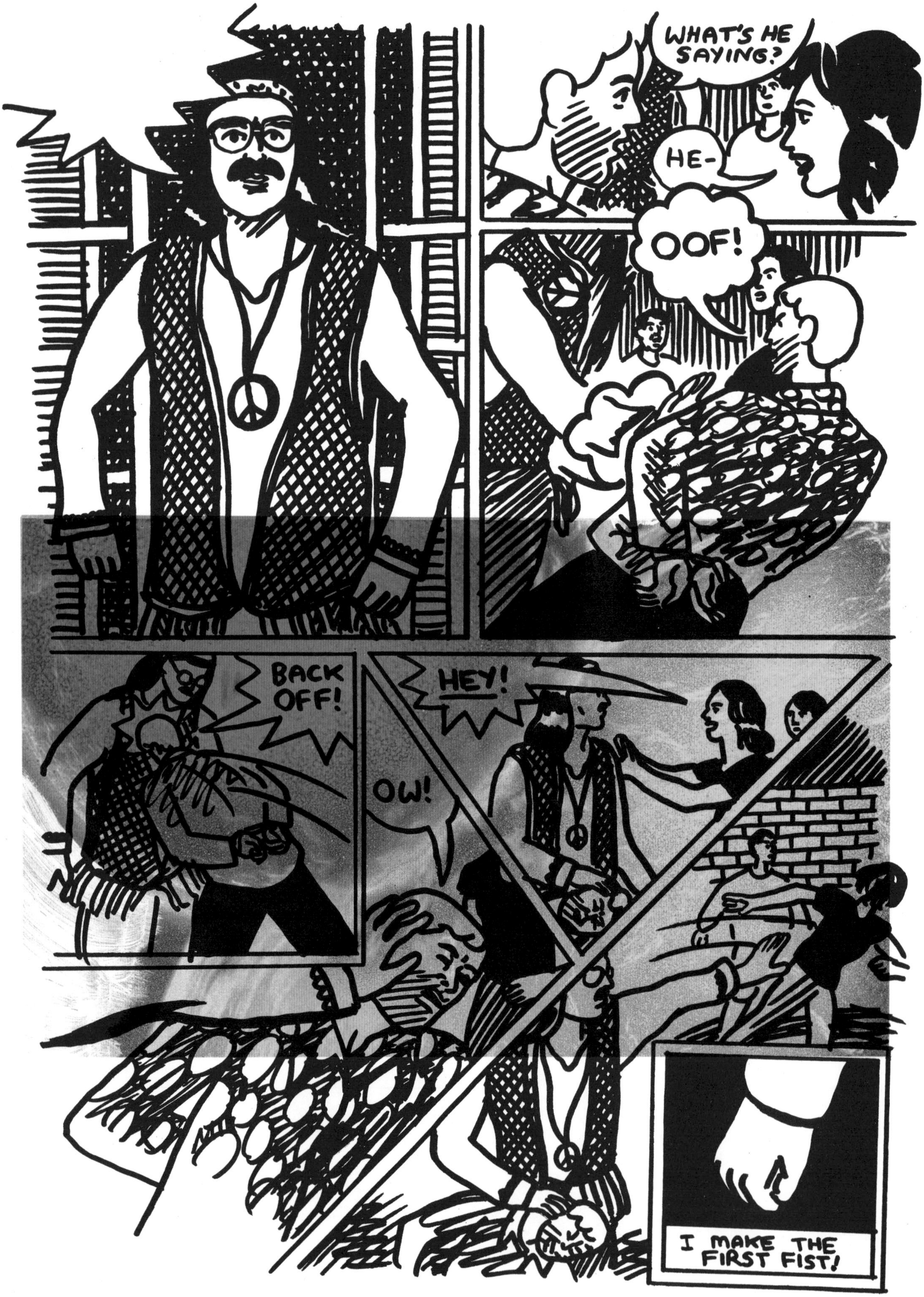

WHAT'S HE SAYING?
HE-
OOF!
BACK OFF!
HEY!
OW!
I MAKE THE FIRST FIST!

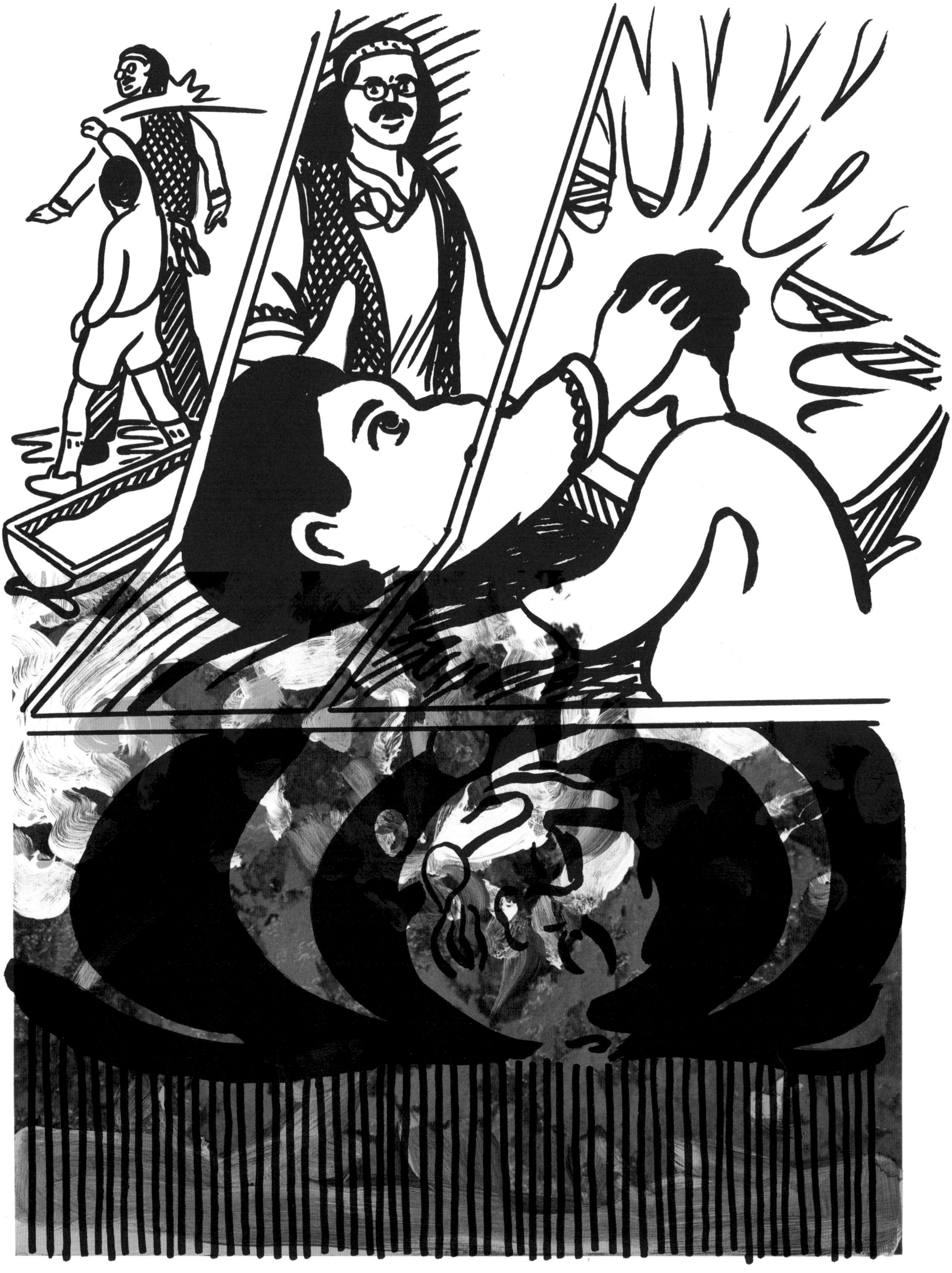

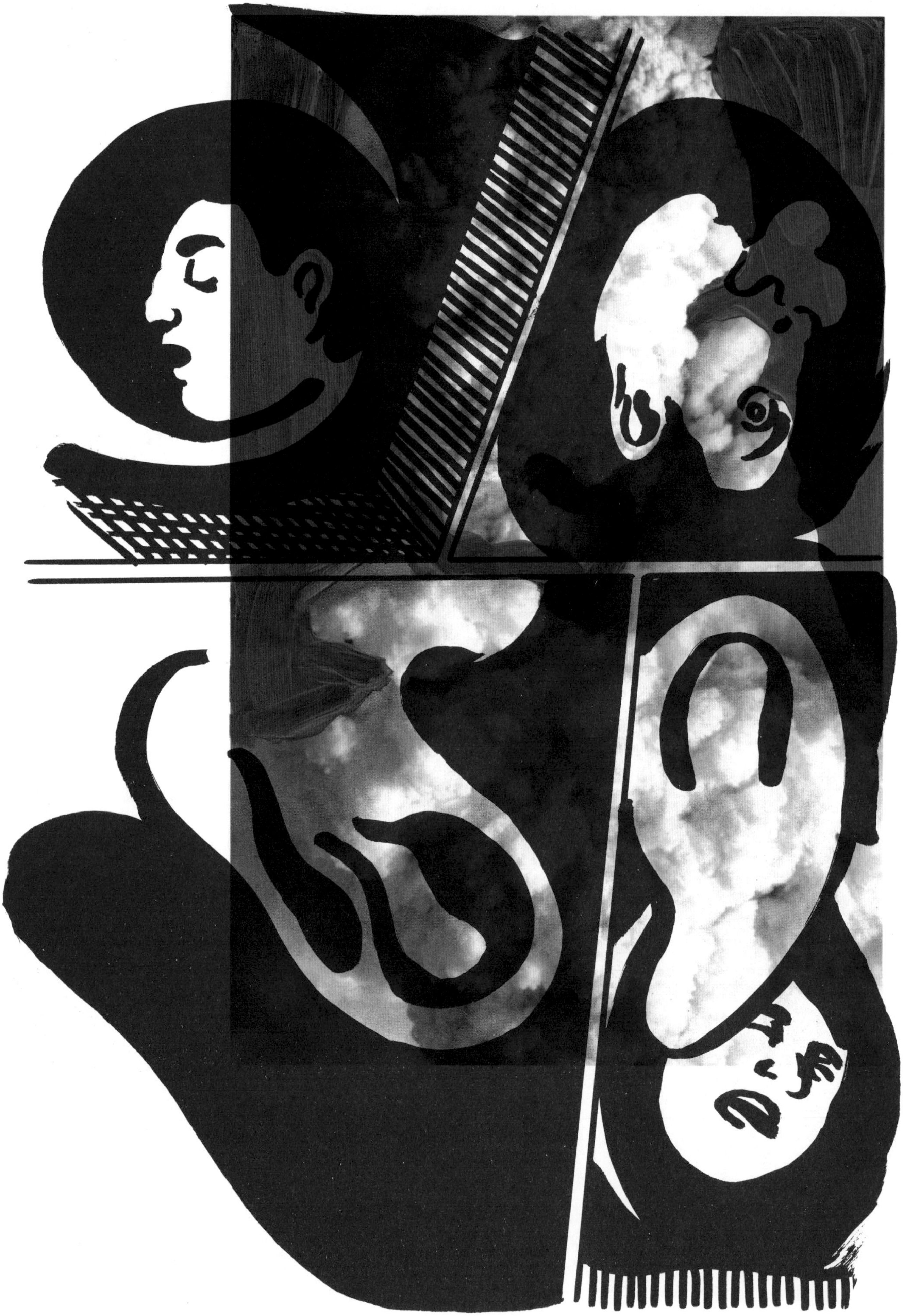

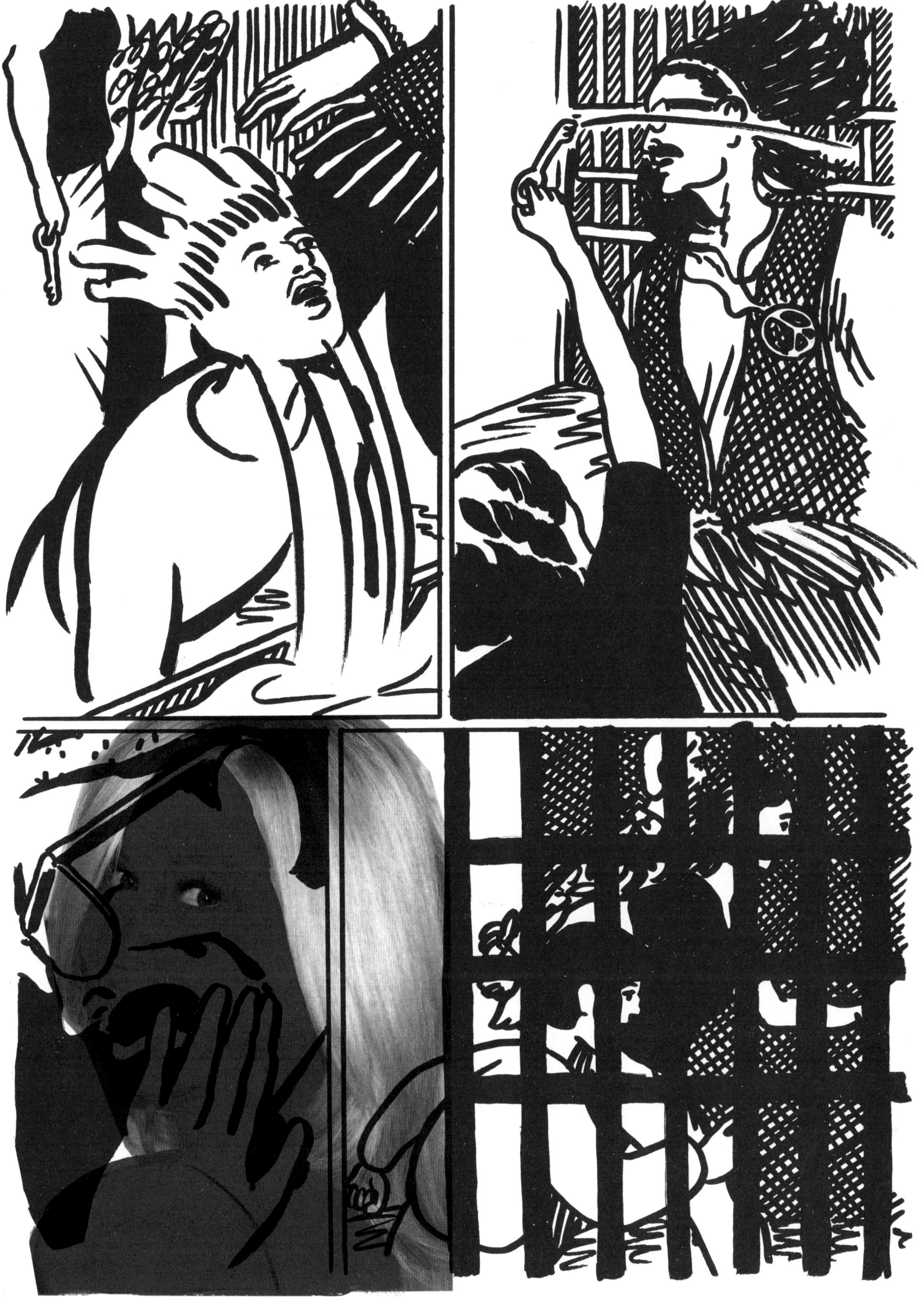

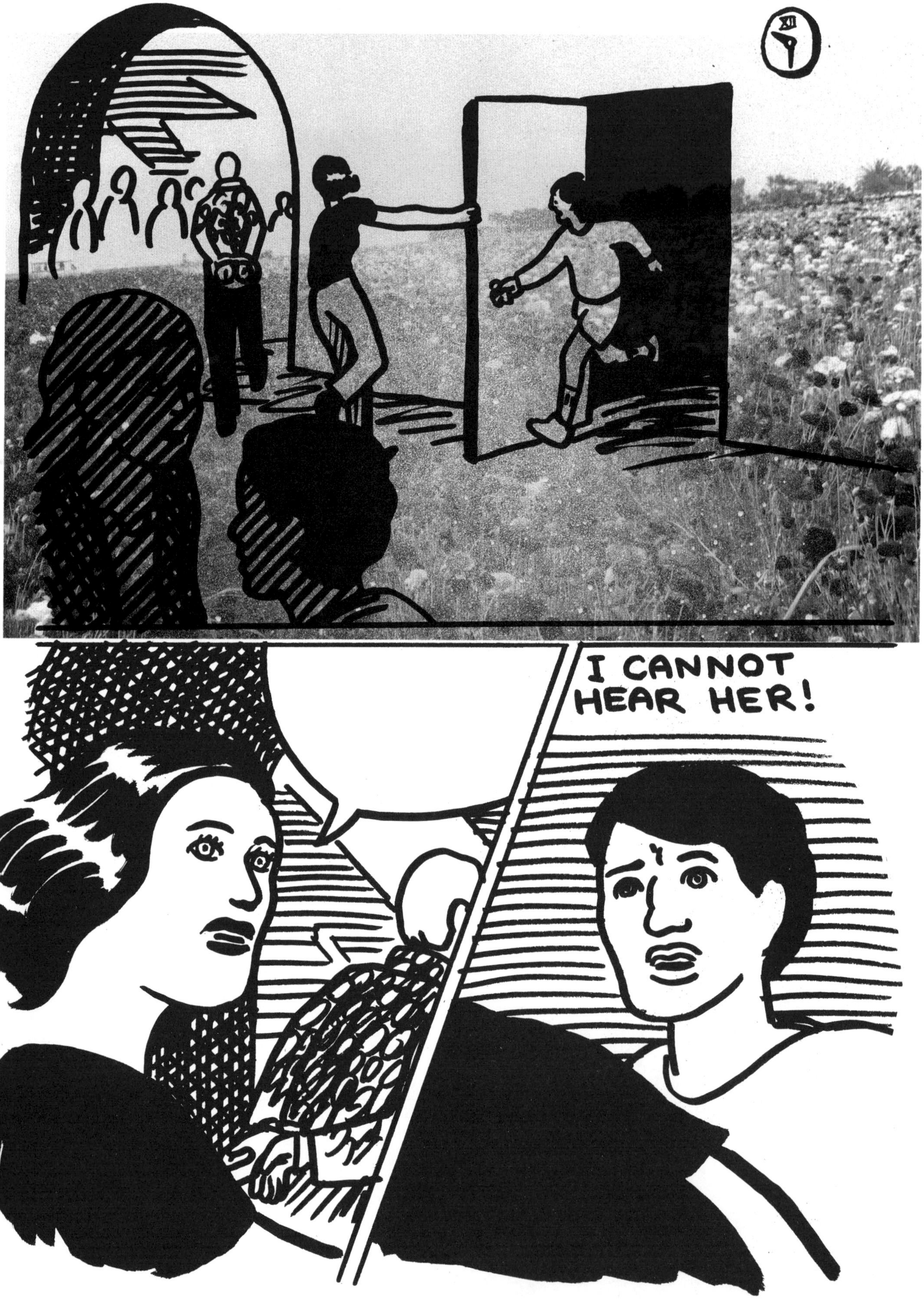
I CANNOT HEAR HER!

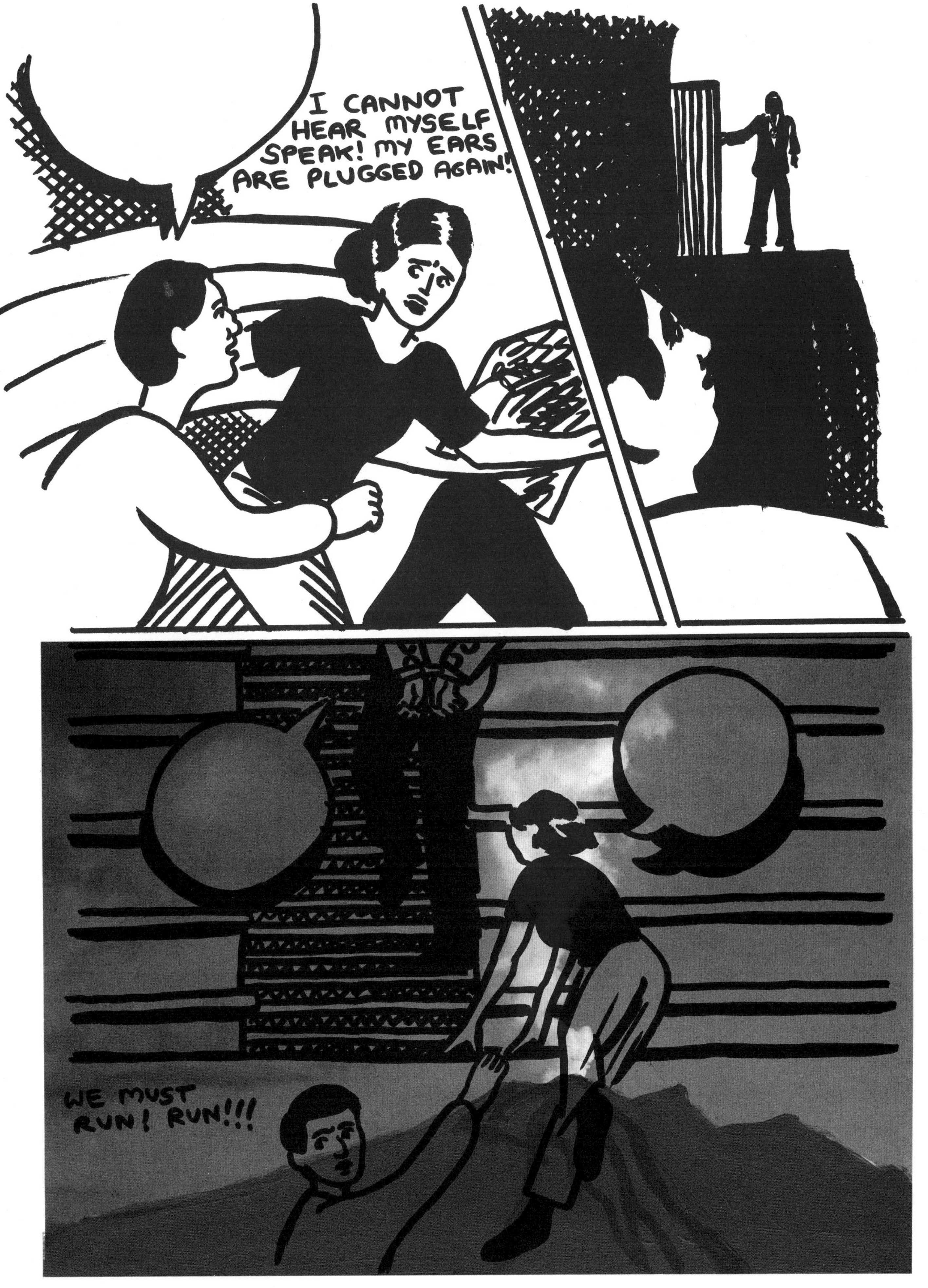
I CANNOT HEAR MYSELF SPEAK! MY EARS ARE PLUGGED AGAIN!
WE MUST RUN! RUN!!!

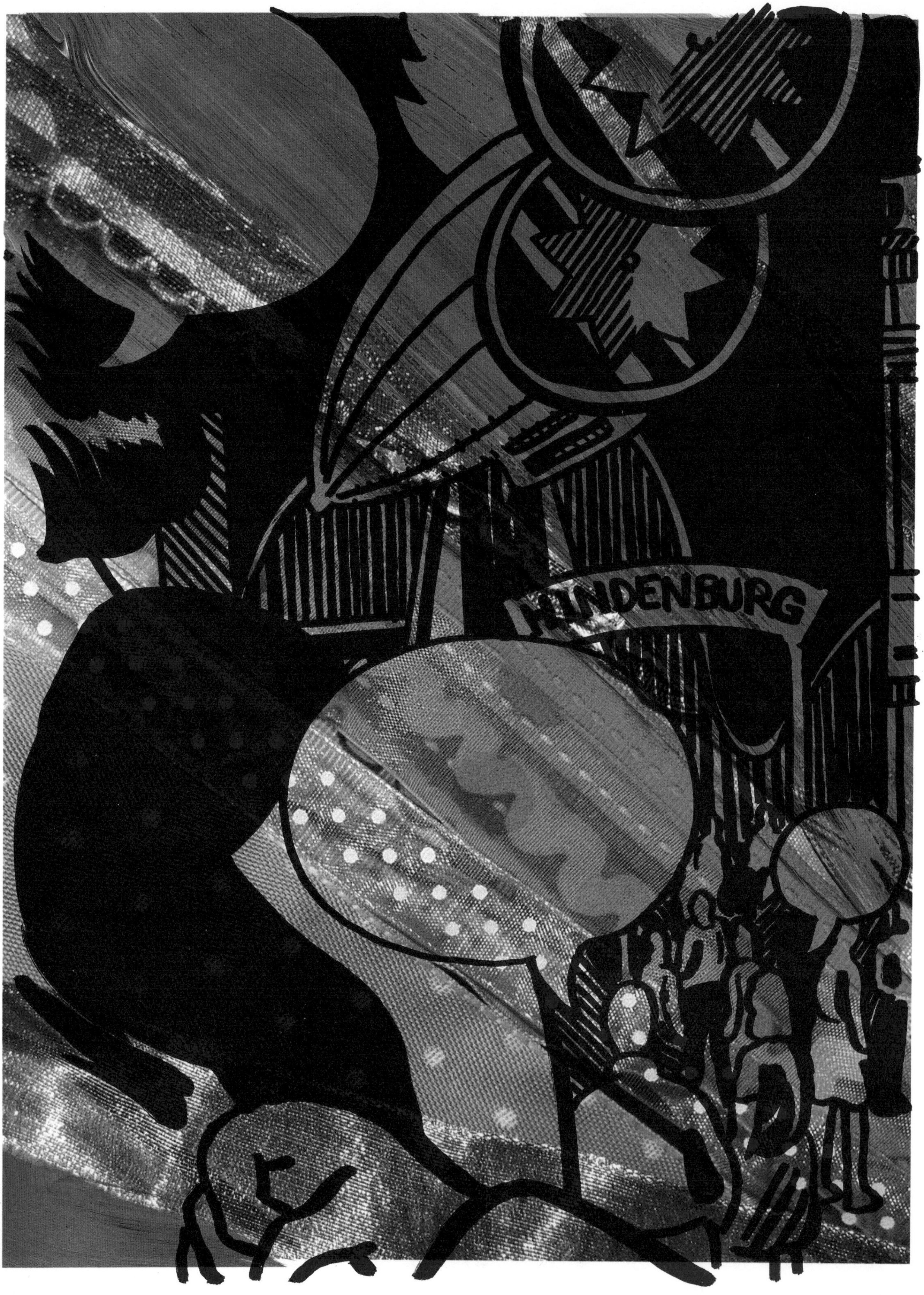
HINDENBURG

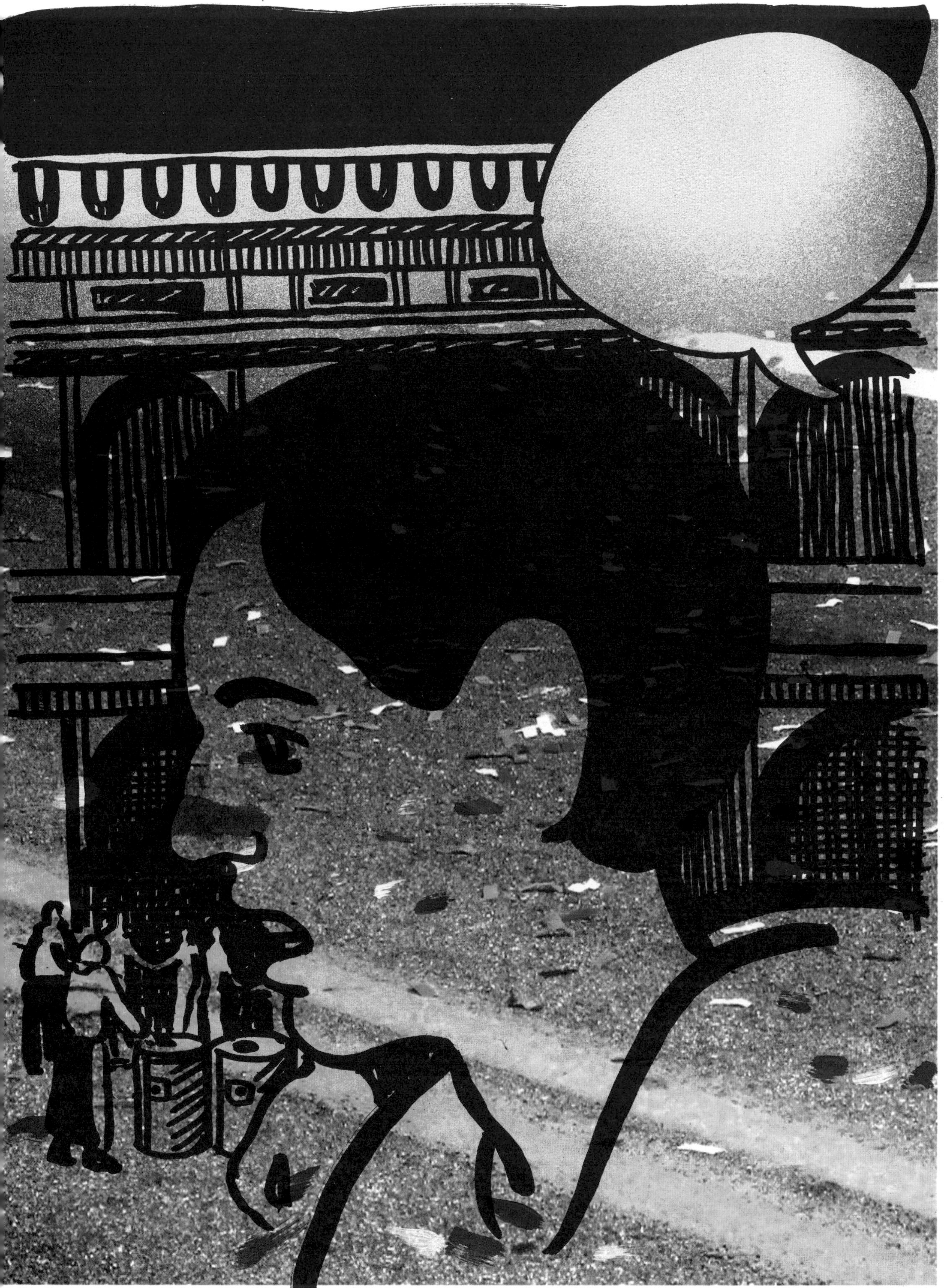

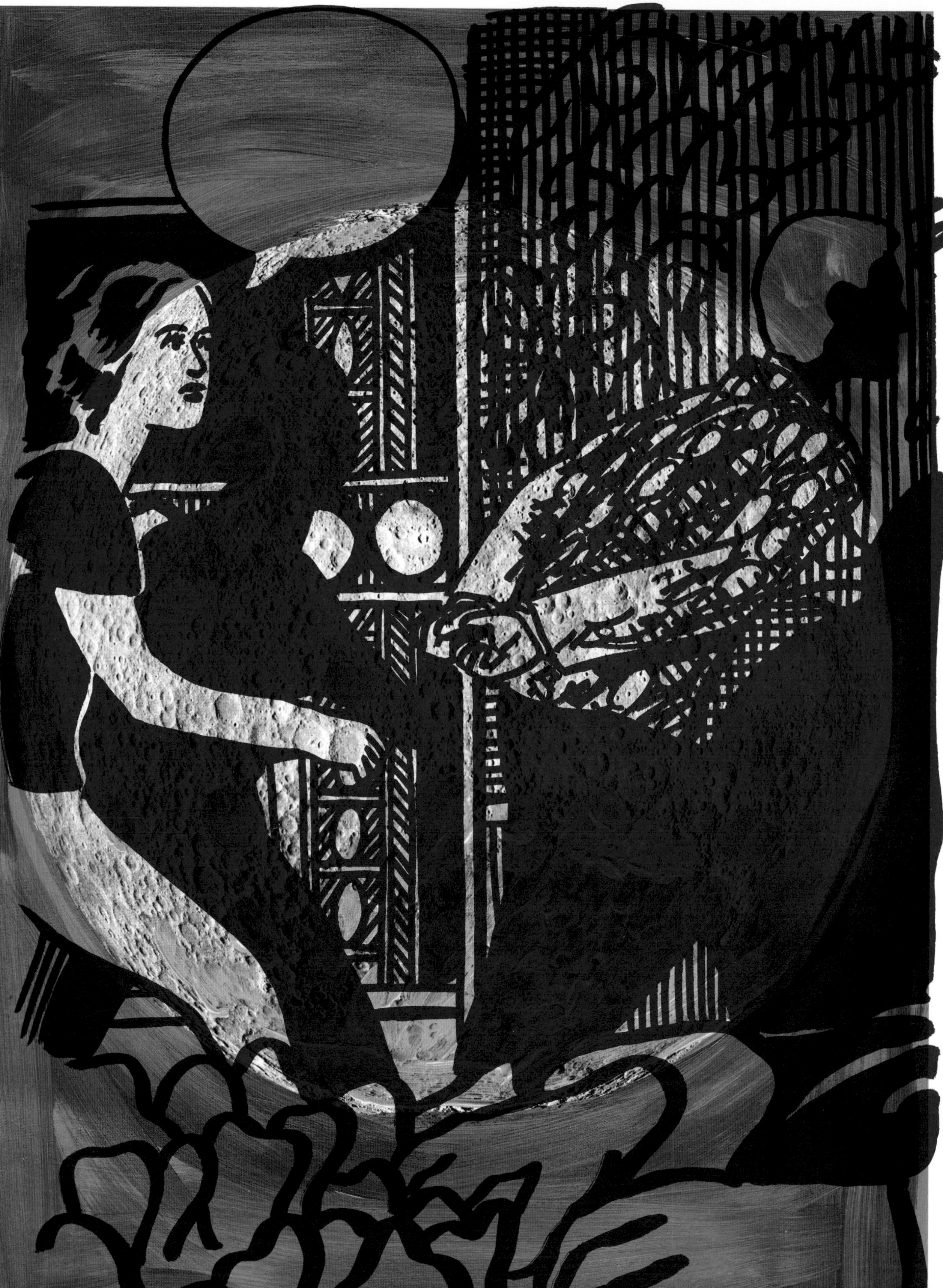

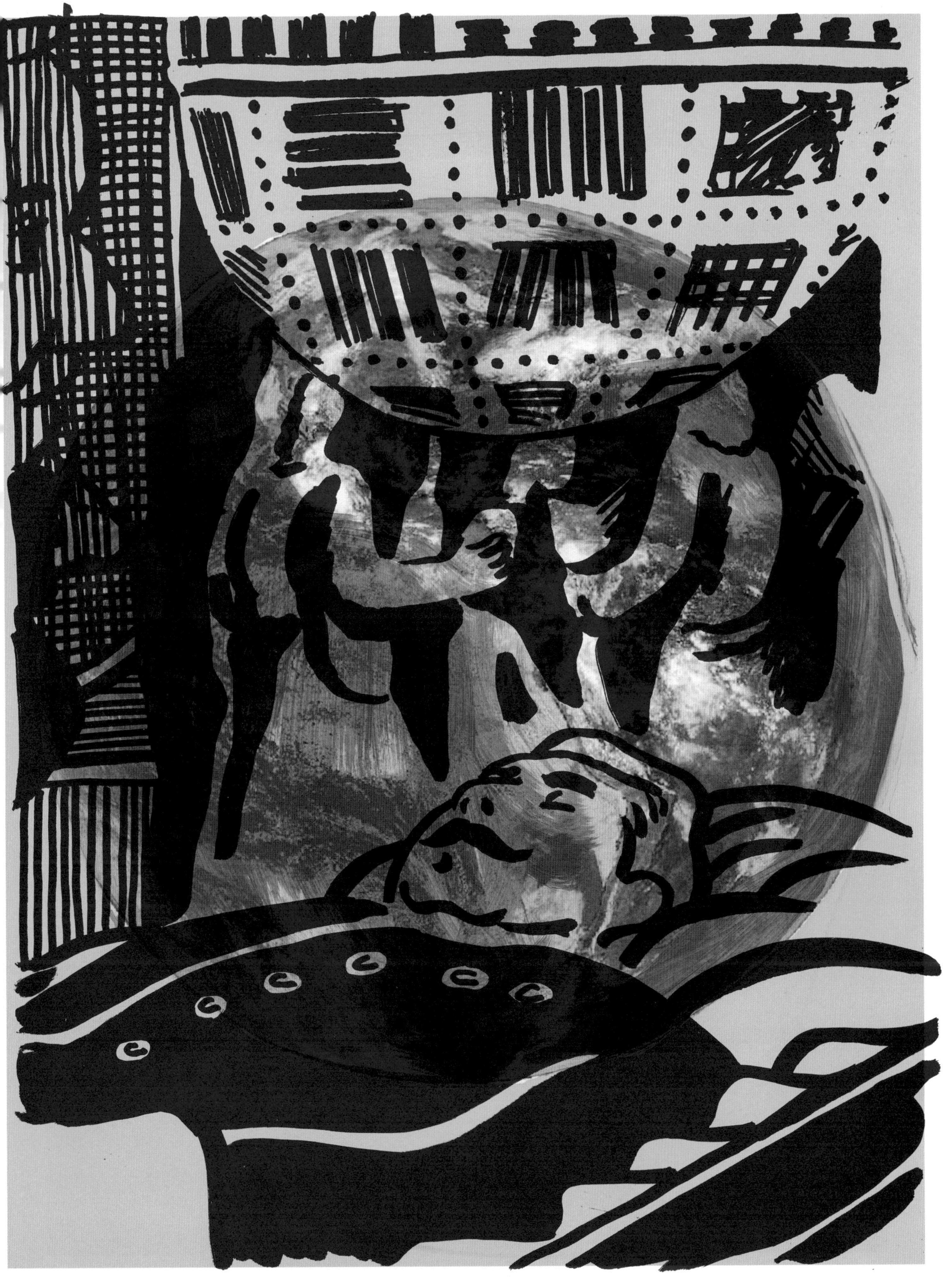

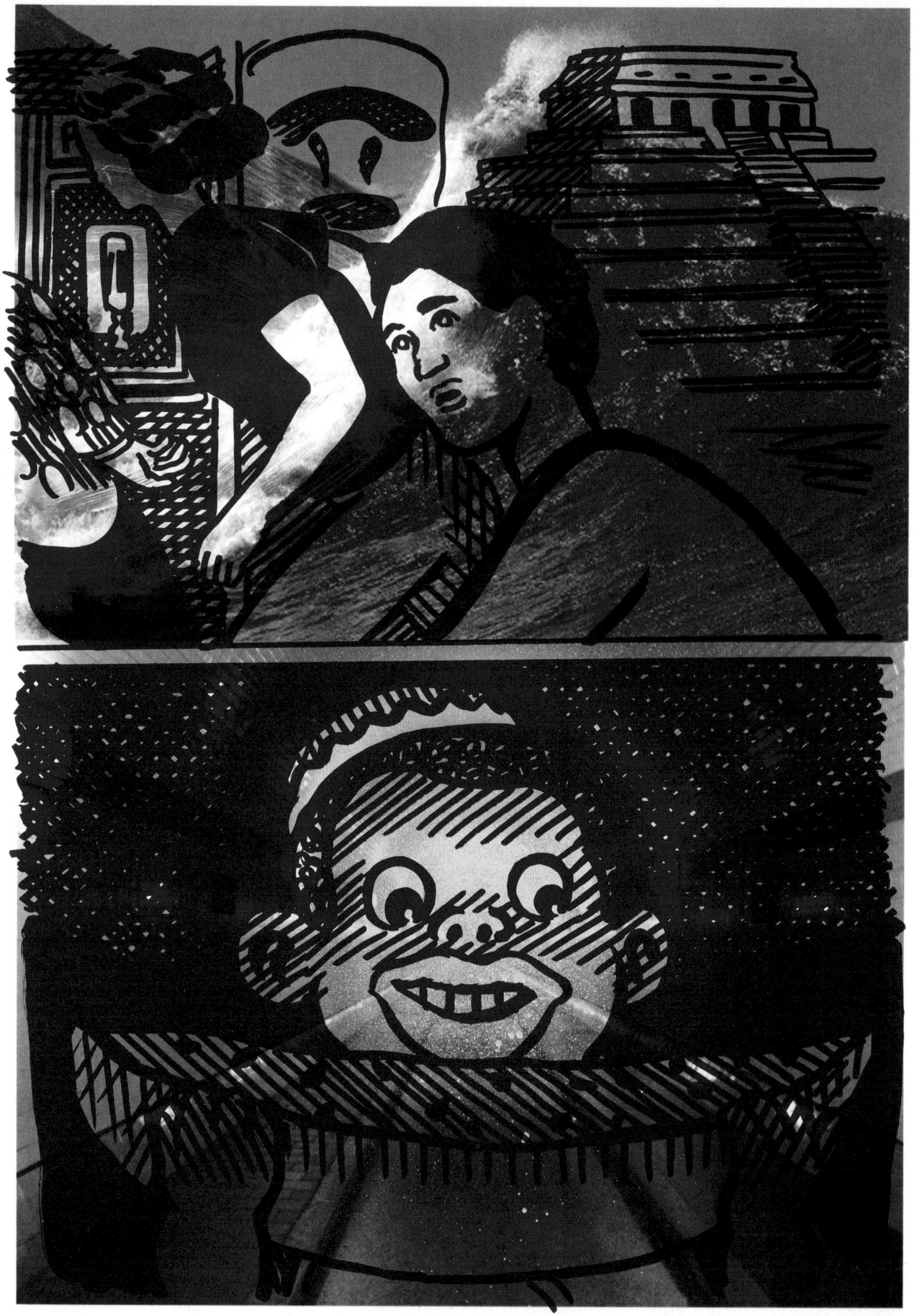

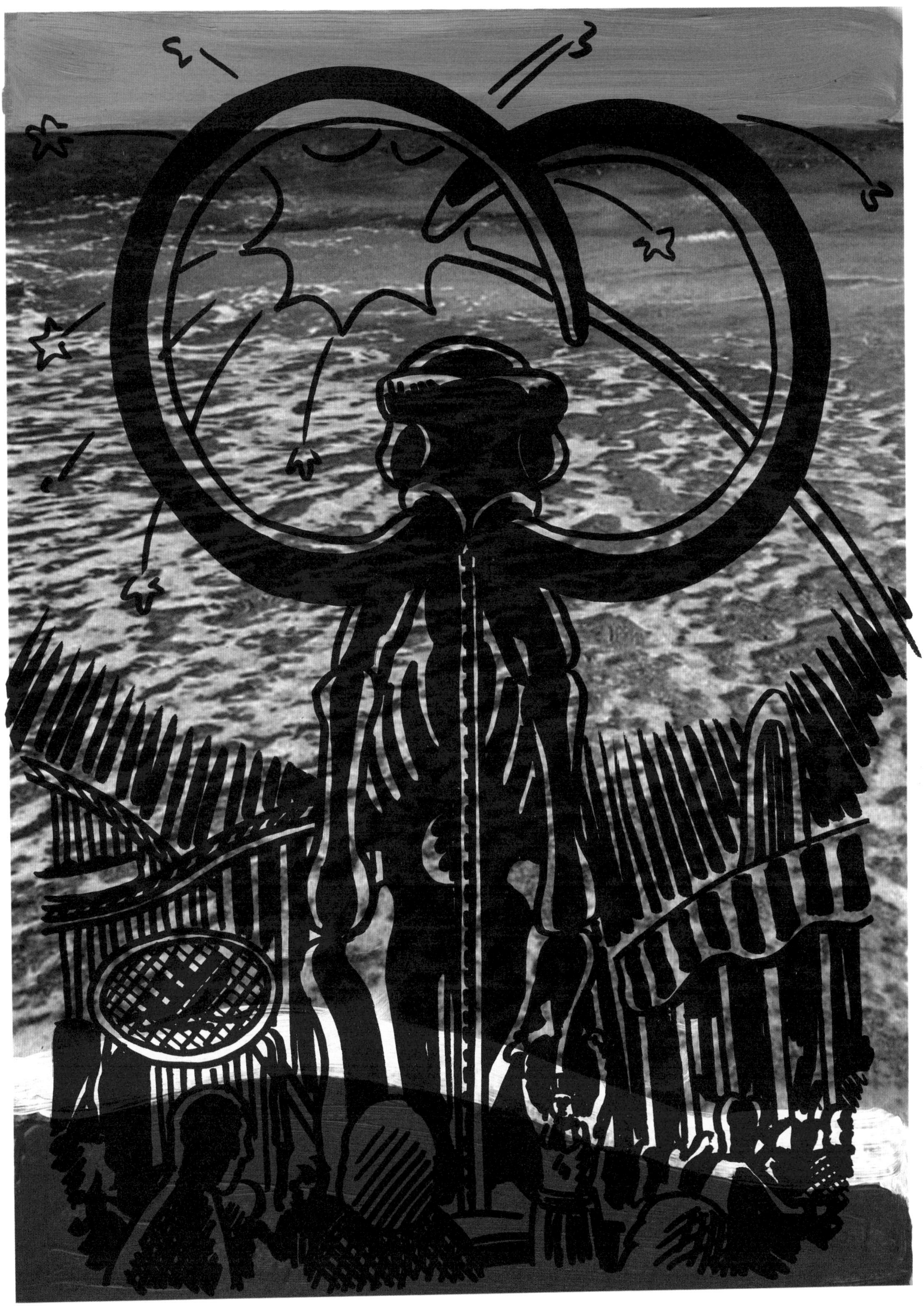

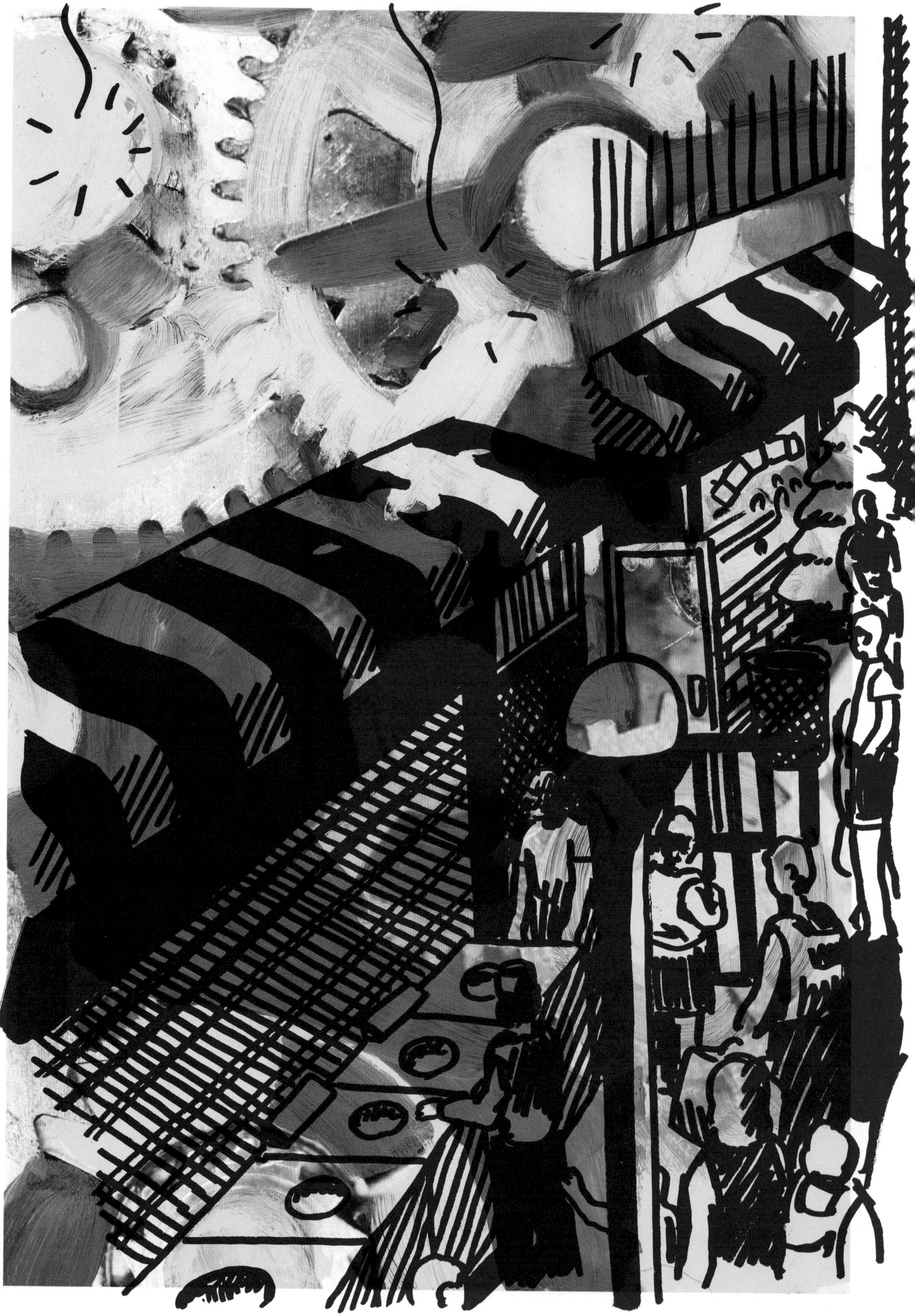

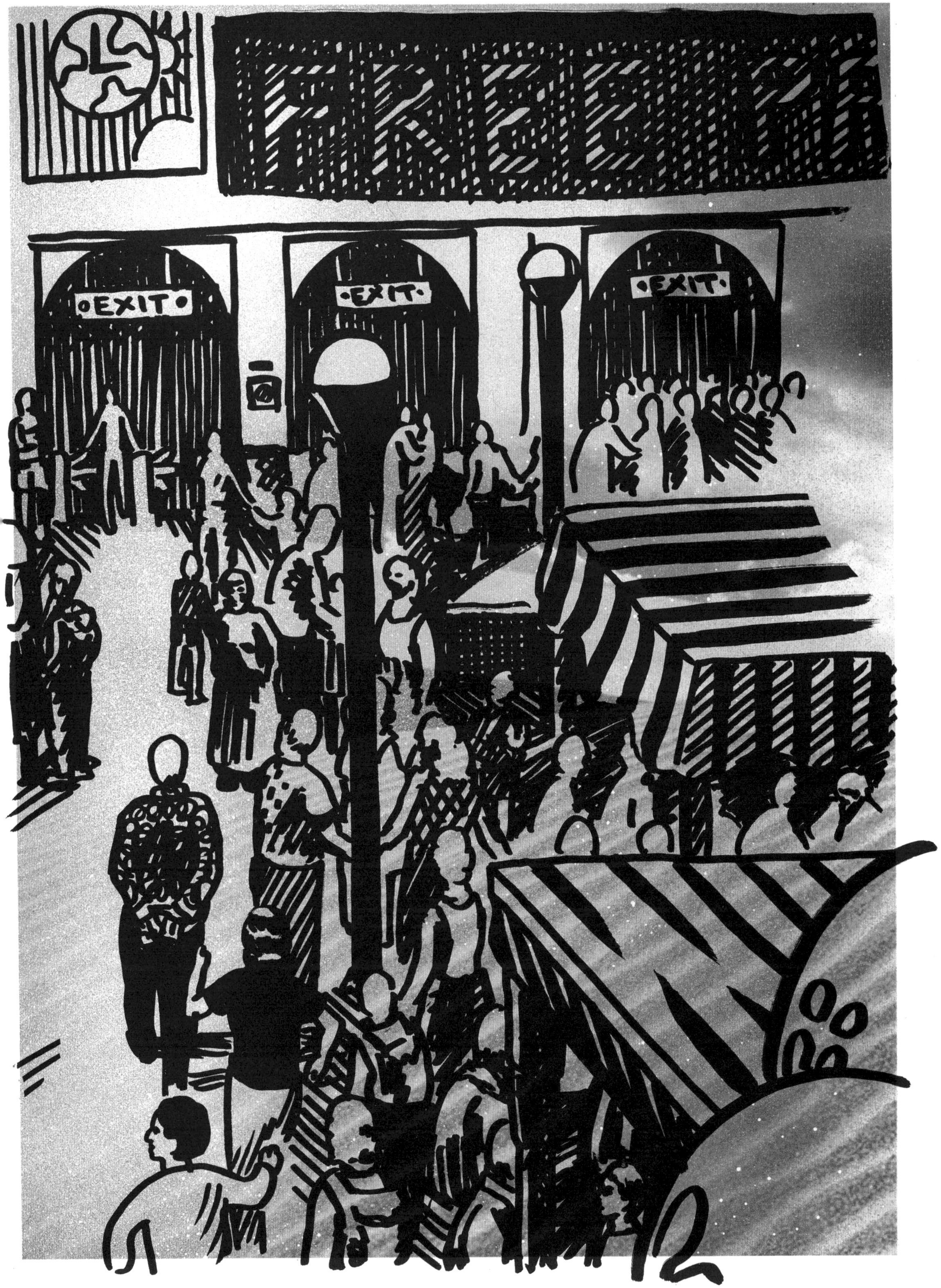
EXIT
EXIT
EXIT

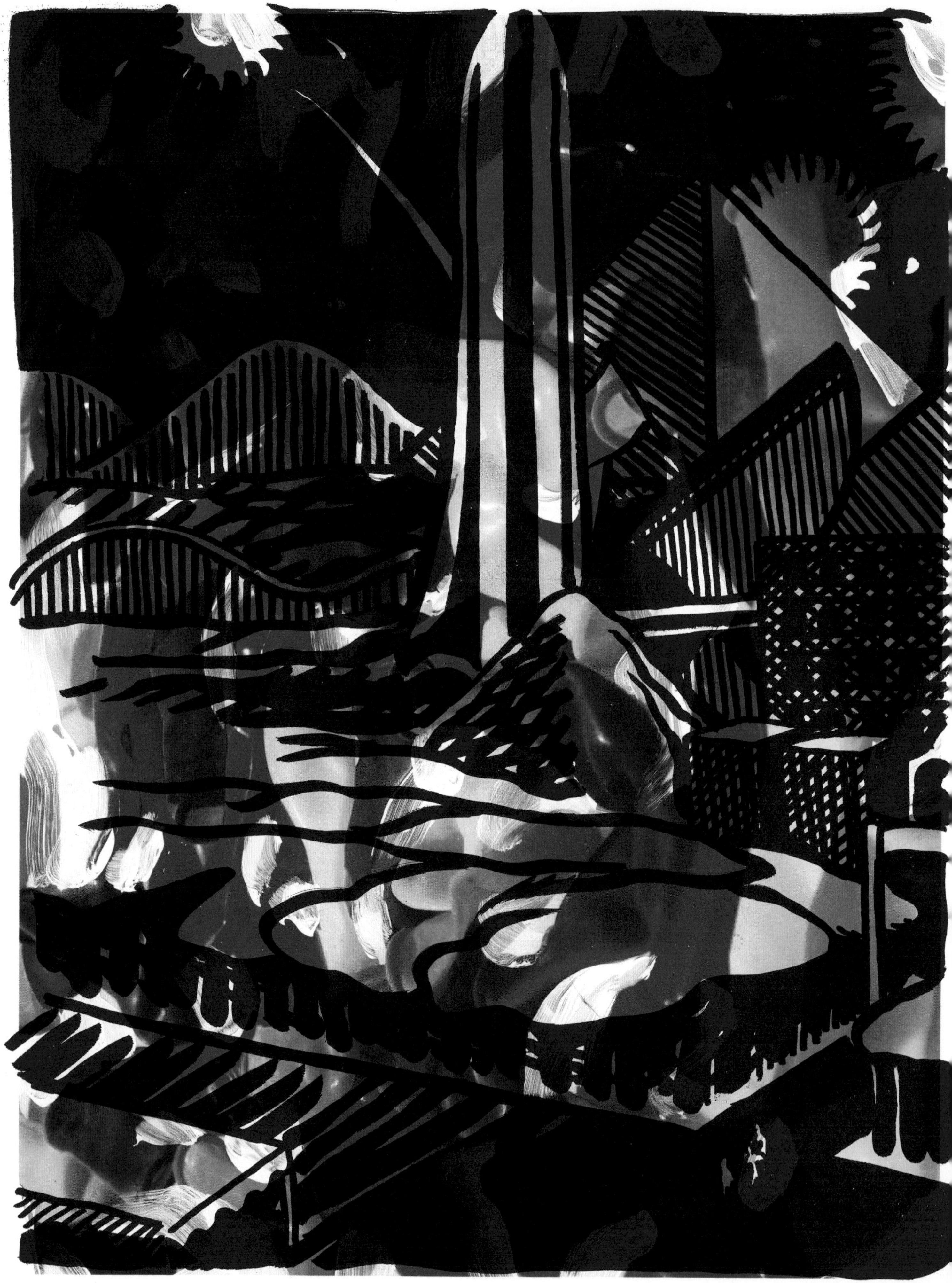

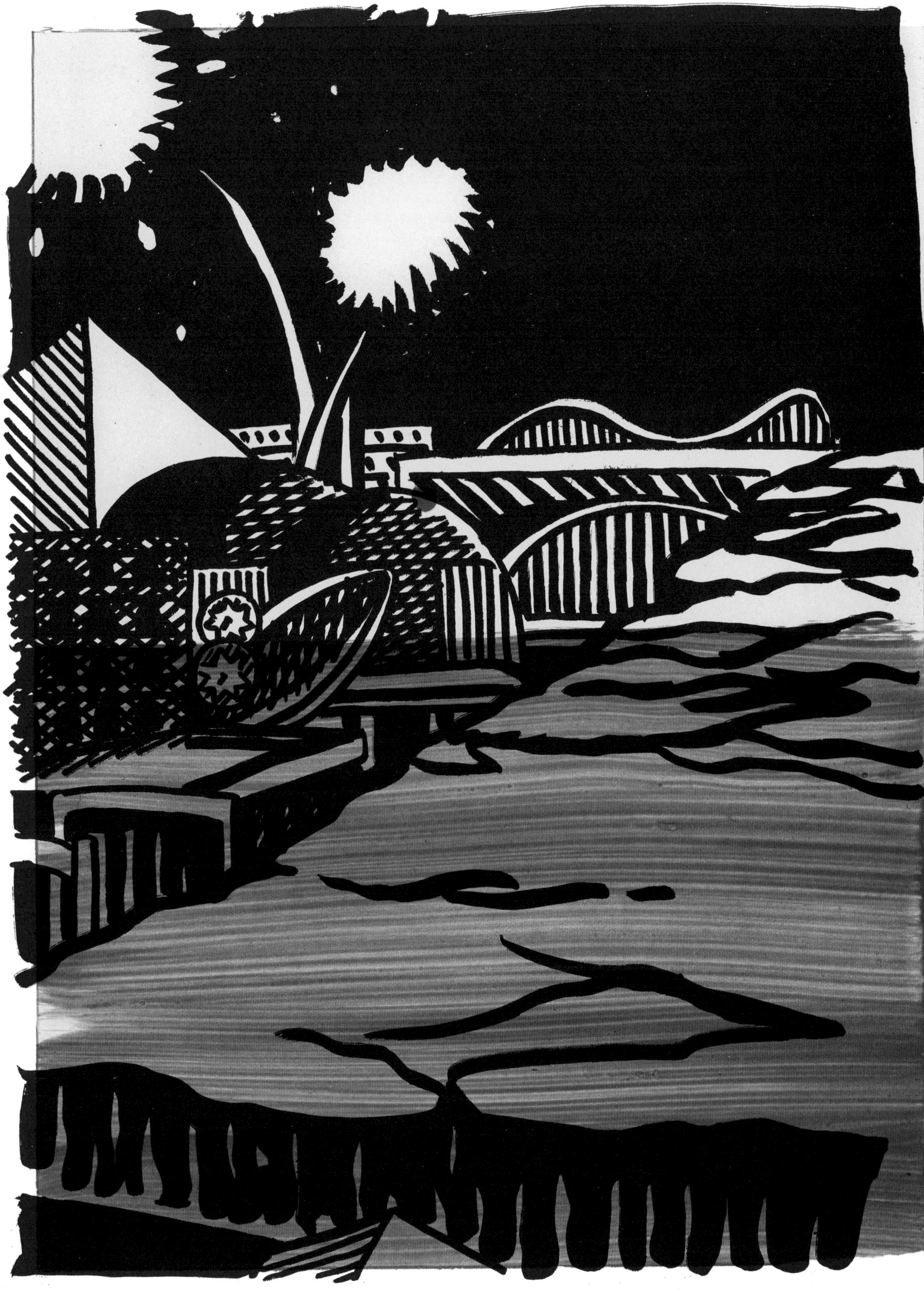

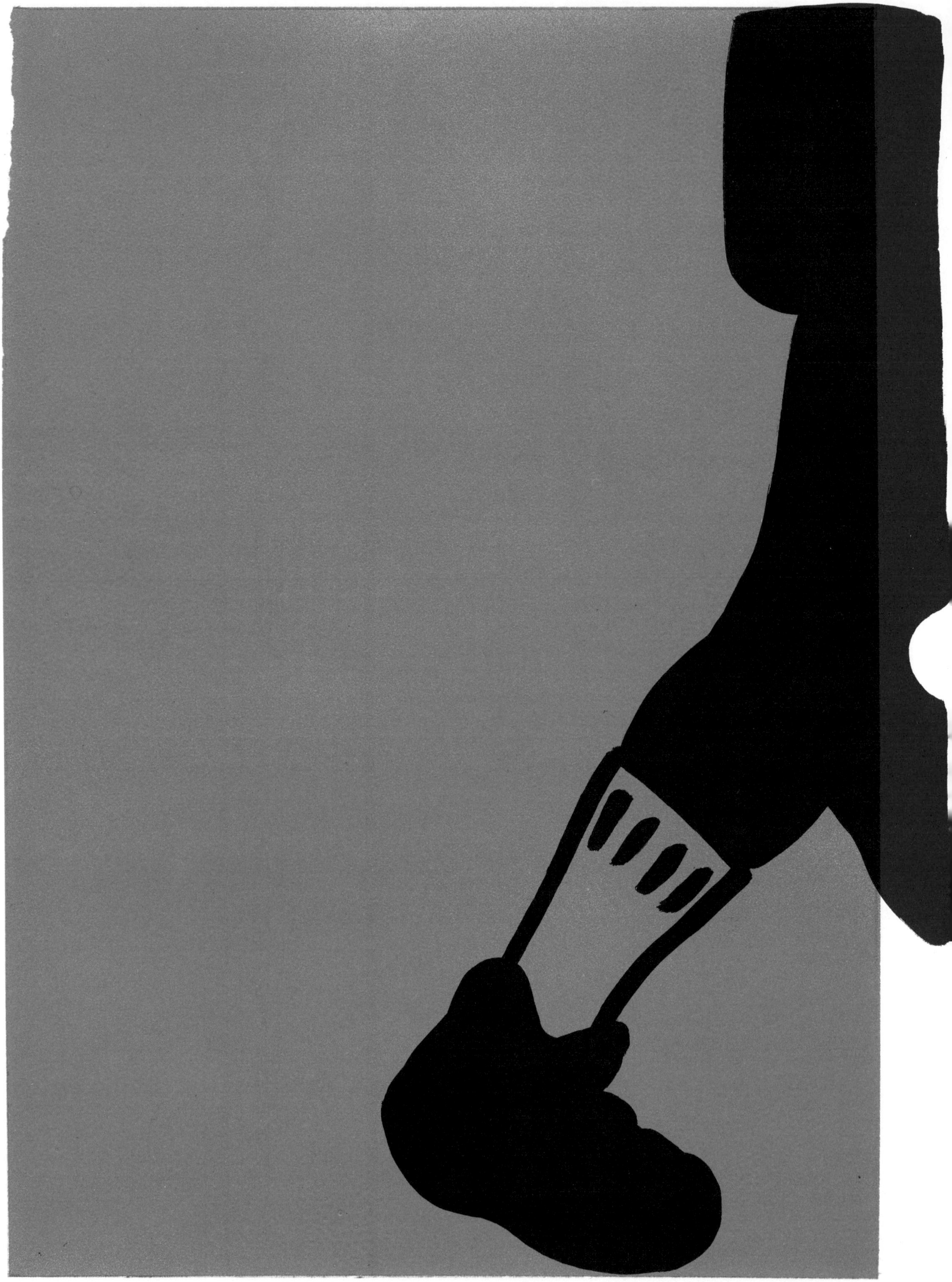

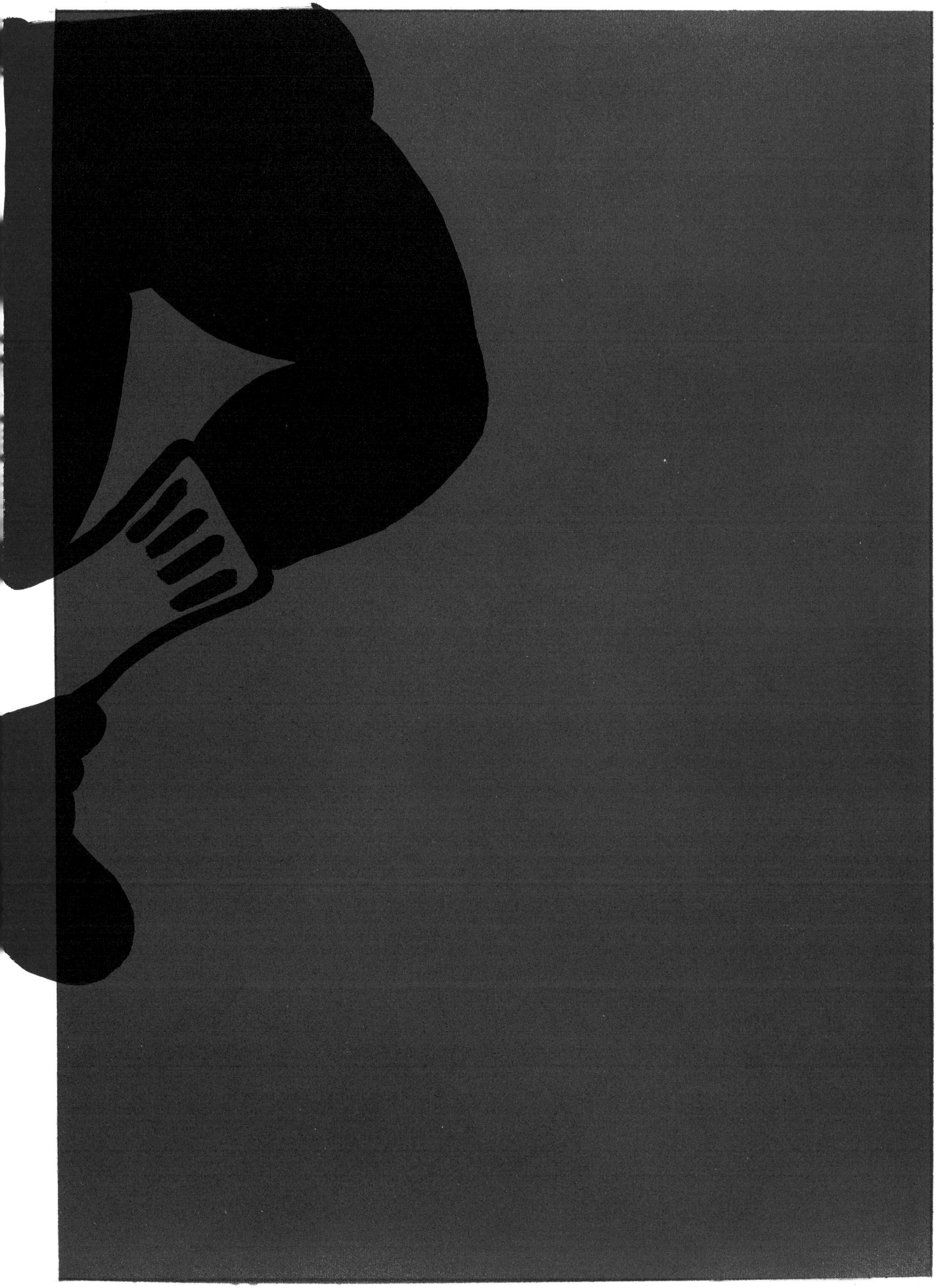

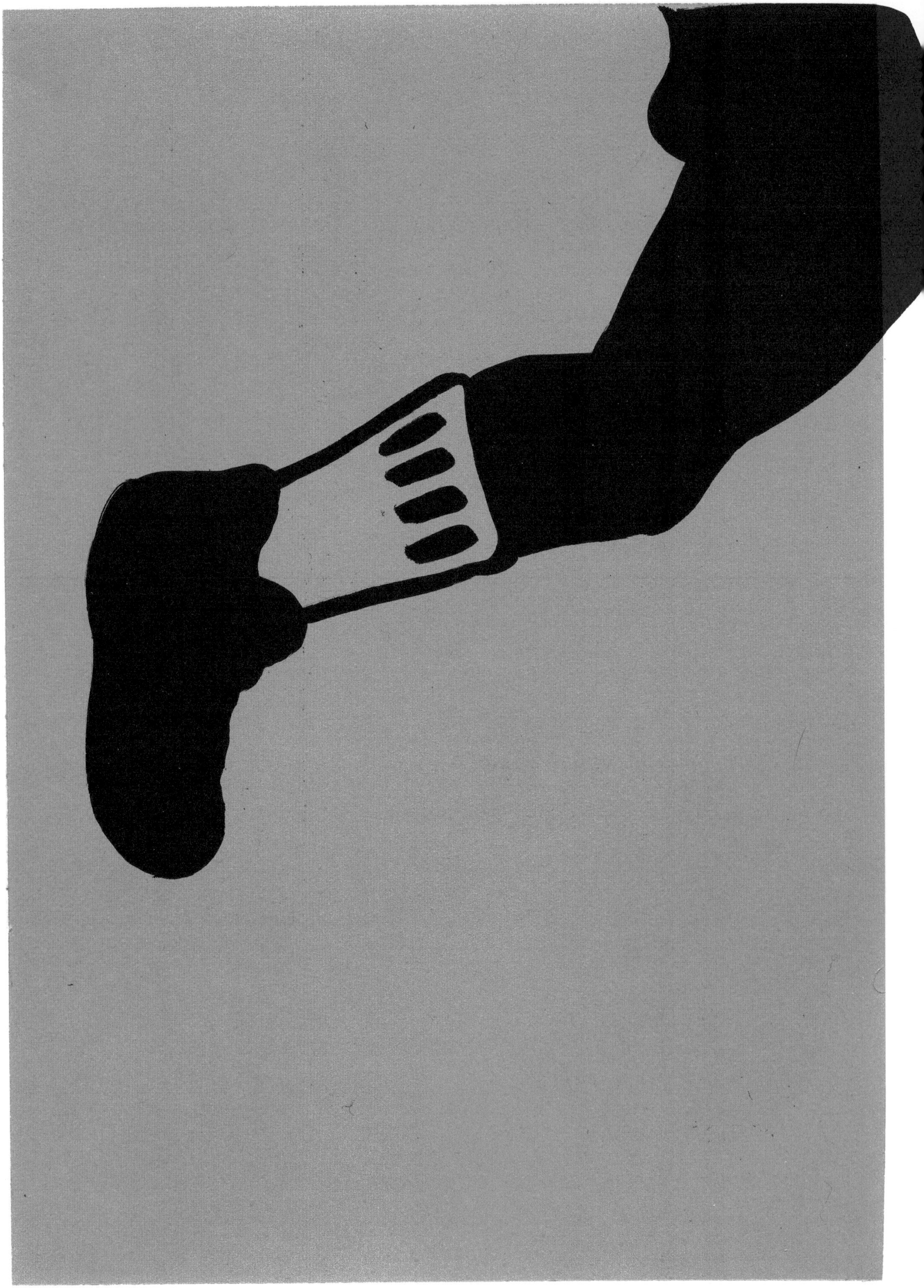

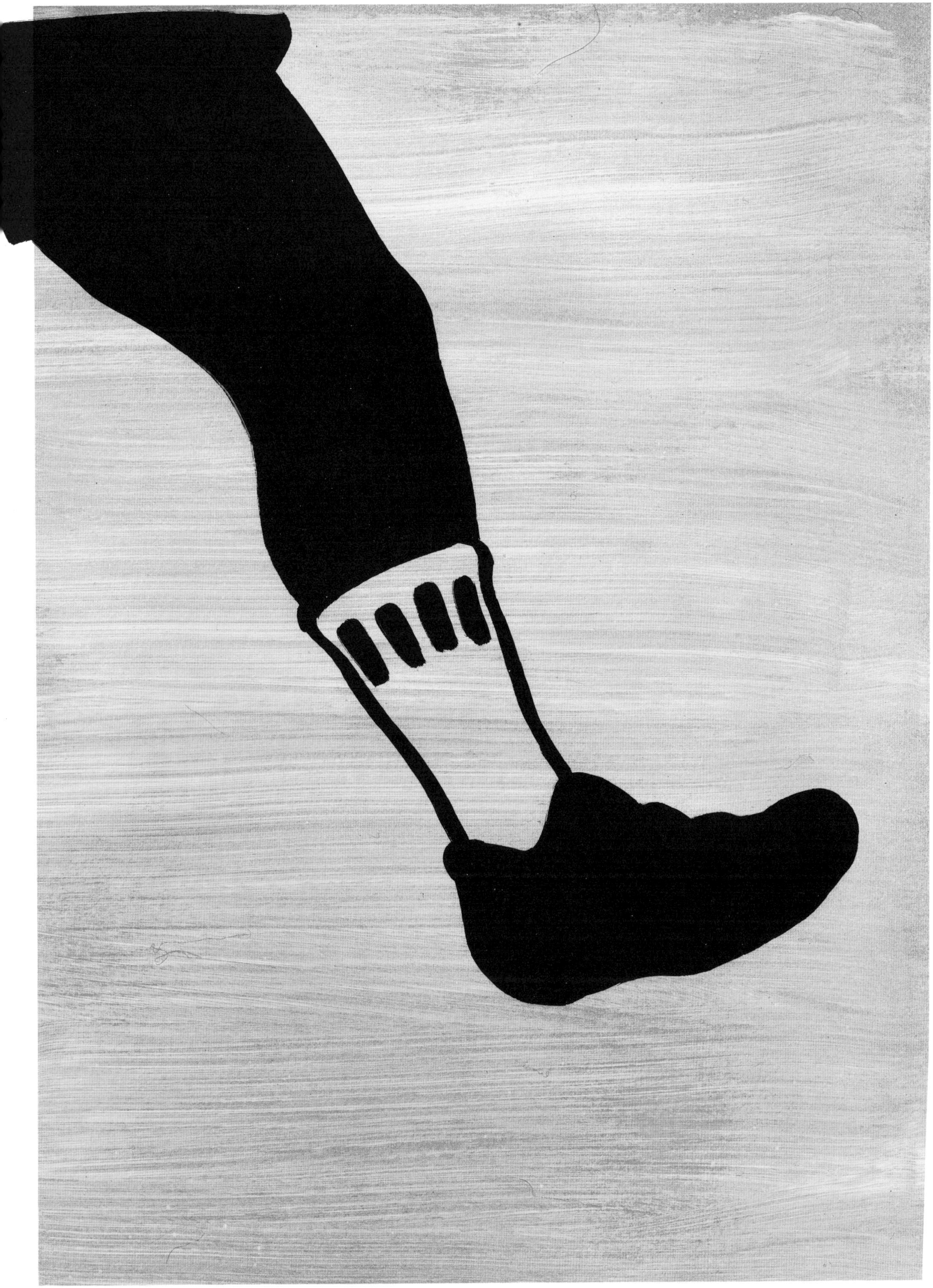

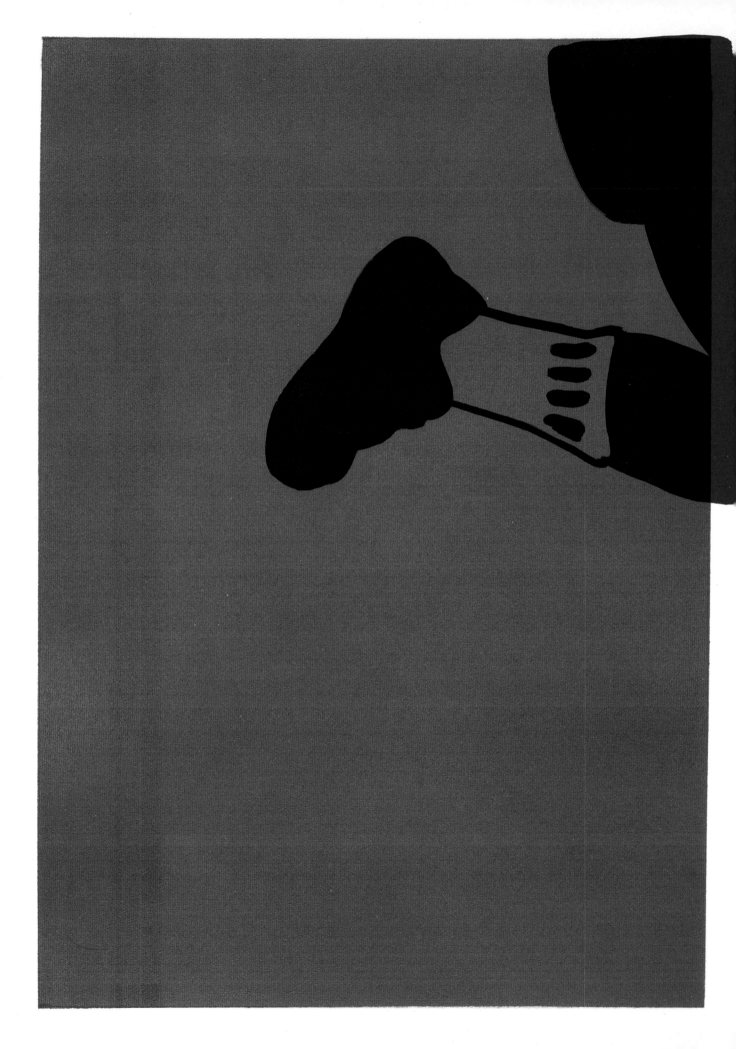

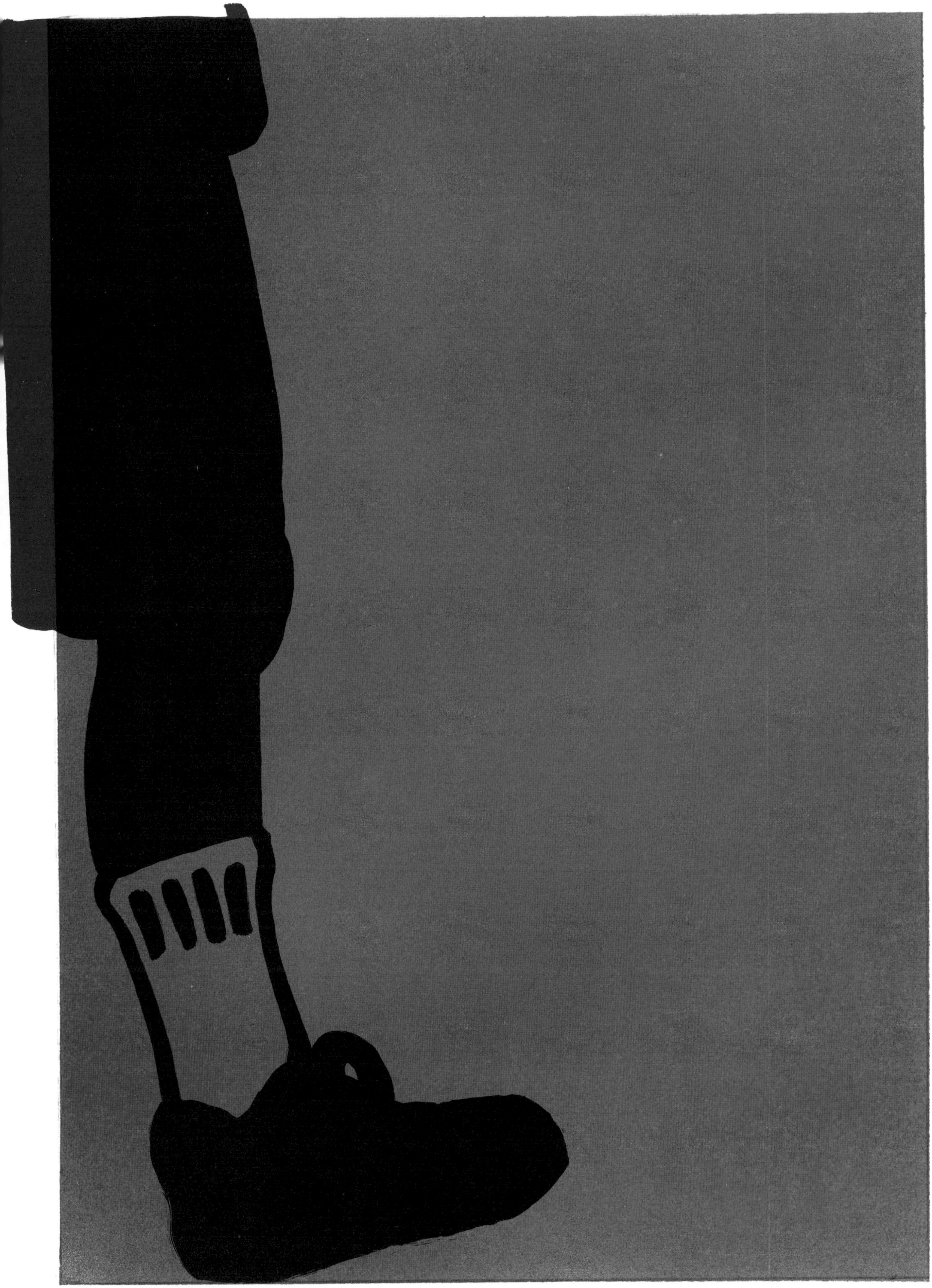

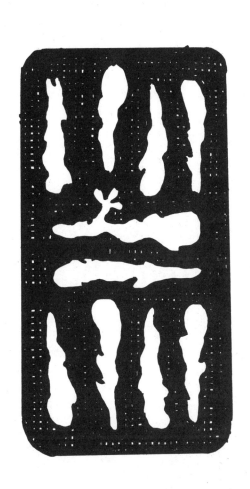

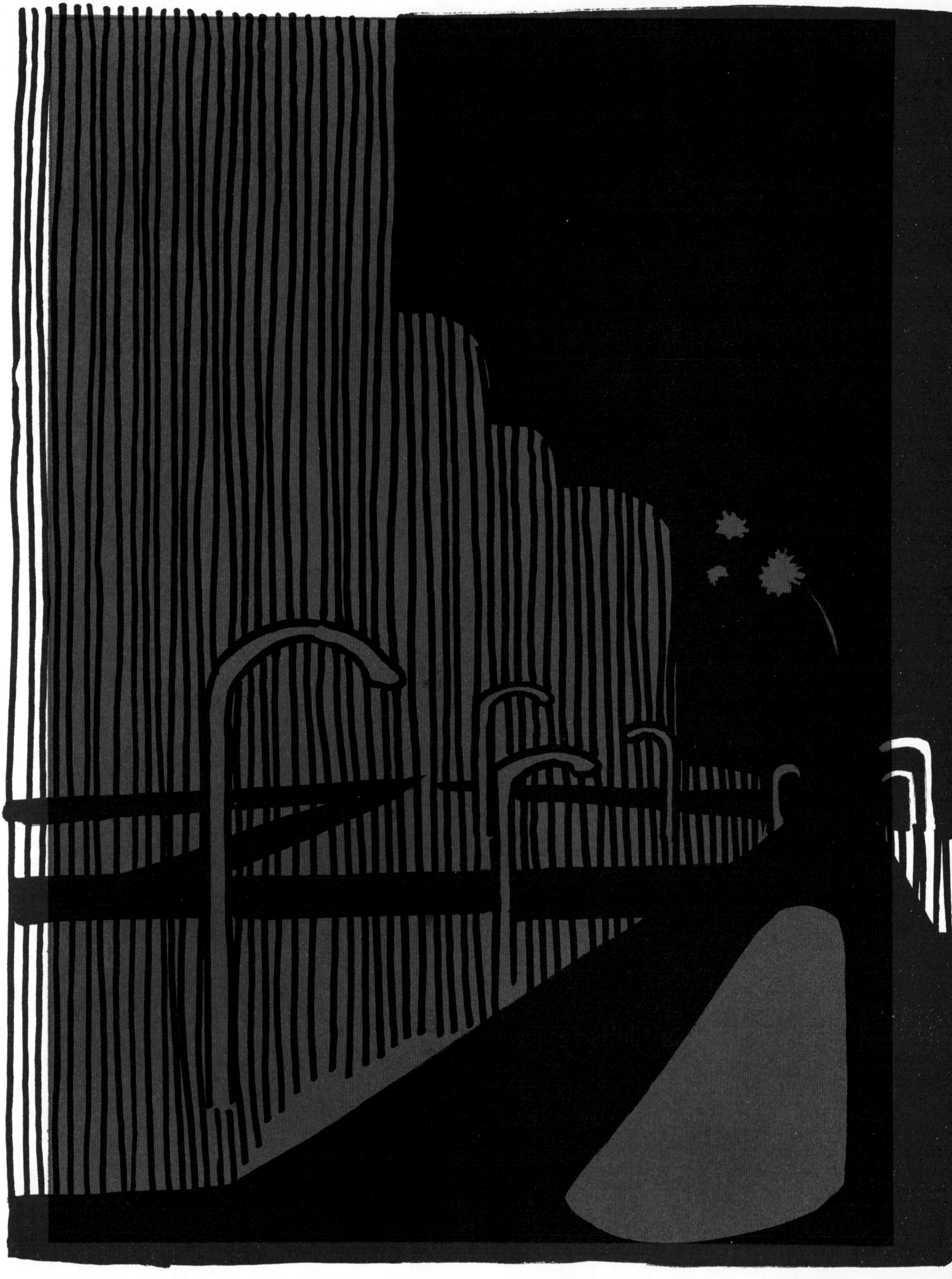

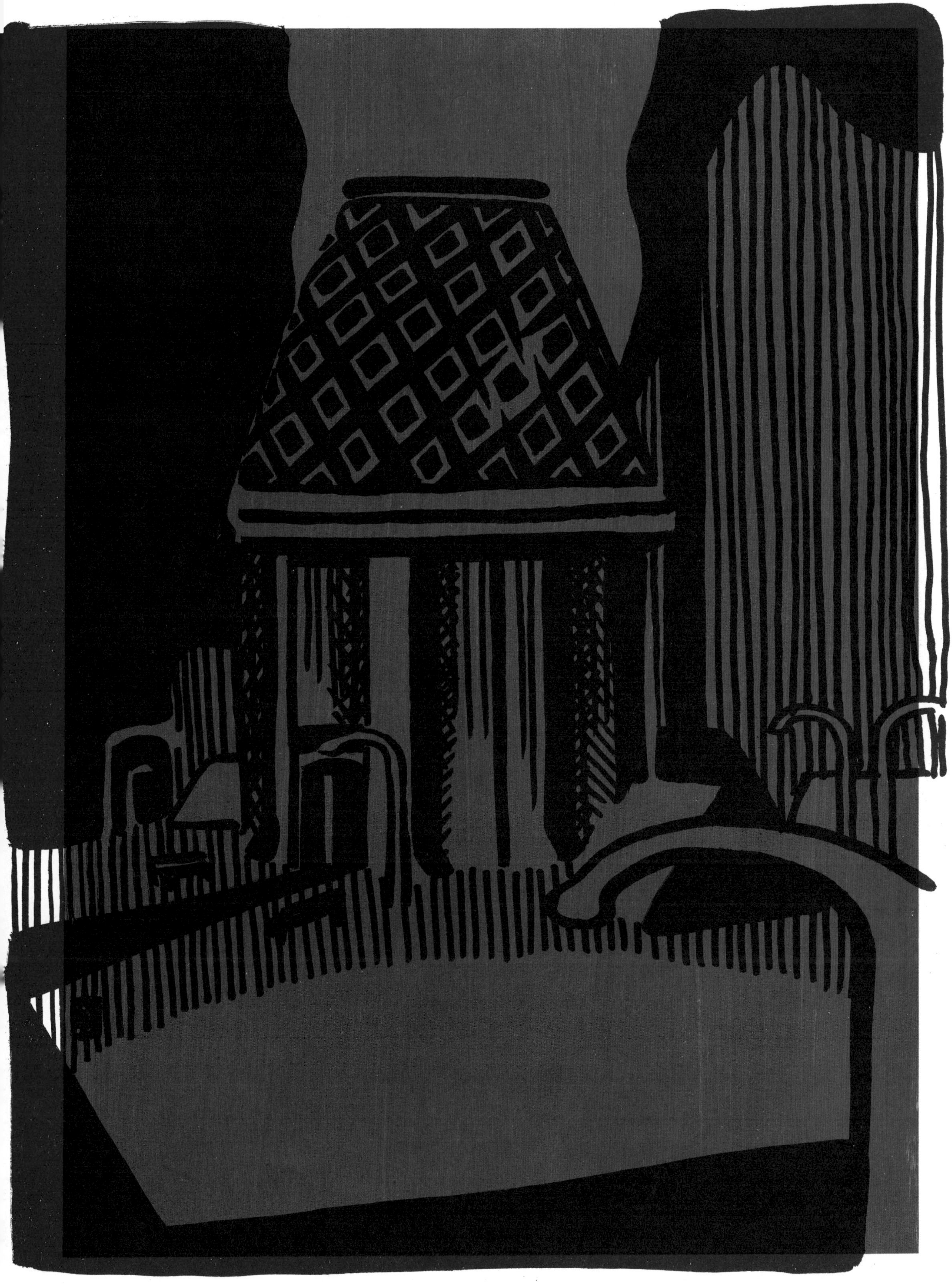

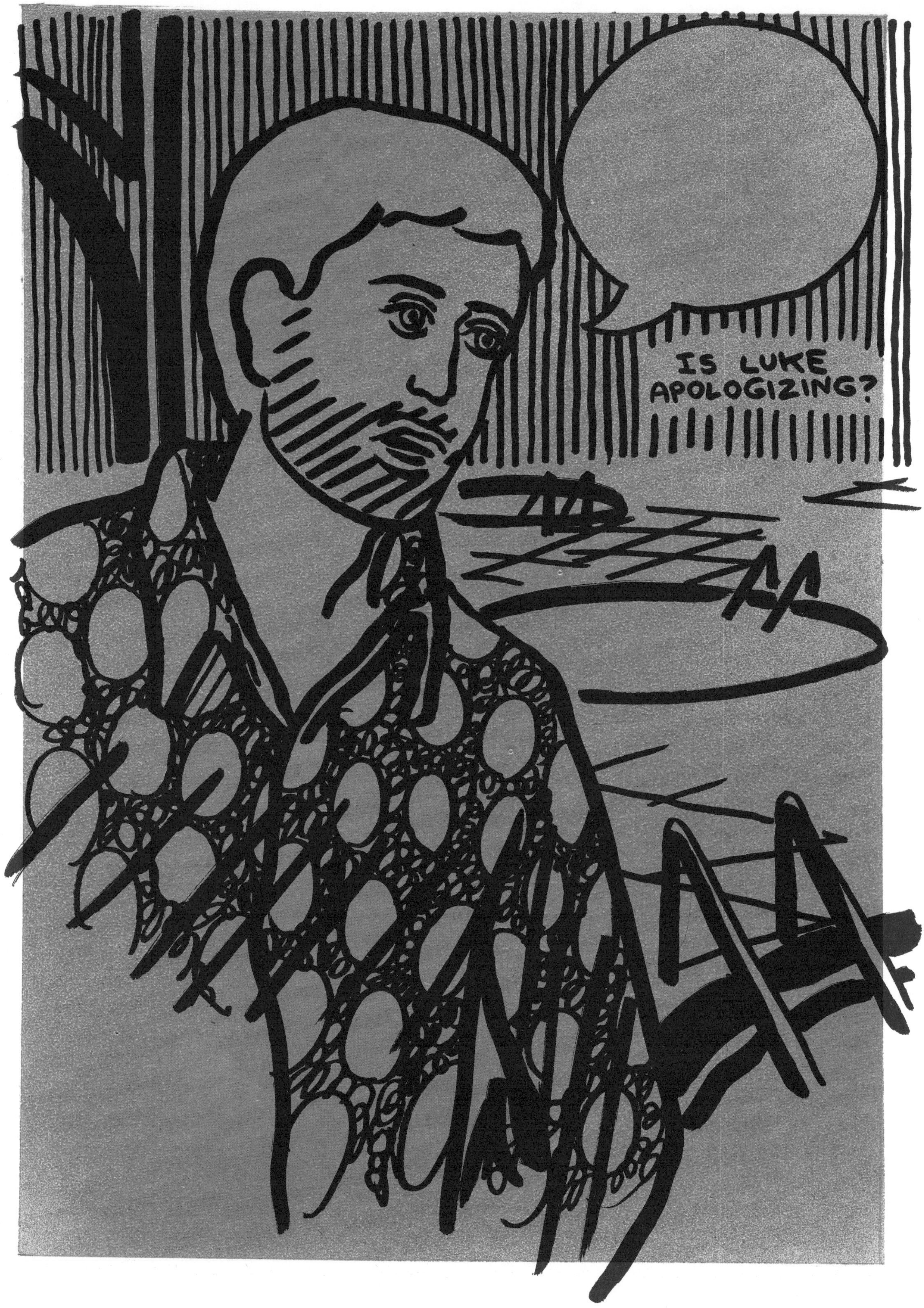
IS LUKE
APOLOGIZING?

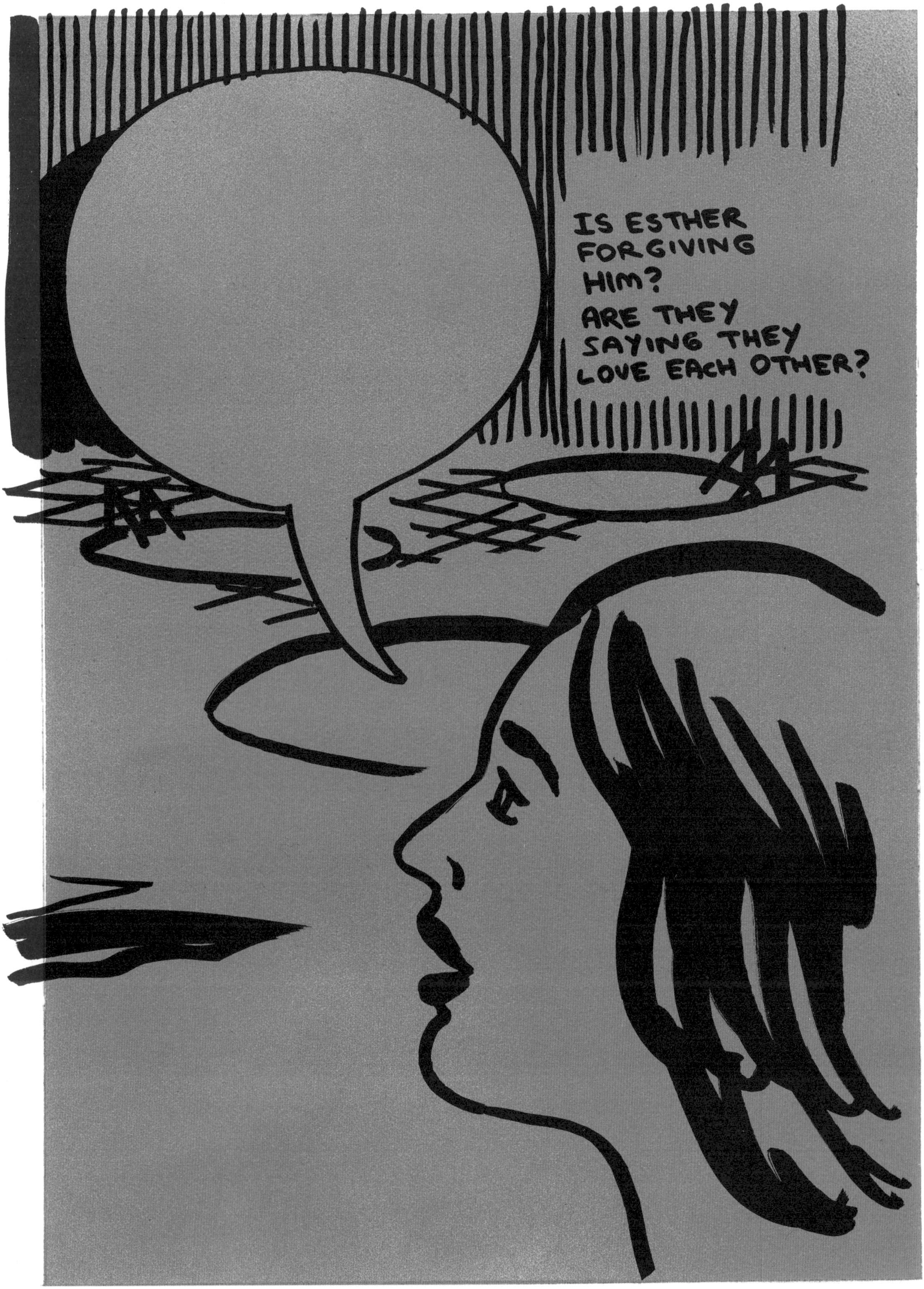
IS ESTHER FORGIVING HIM? ARE THEY SAYING THEY LOVE EACH OTHER?

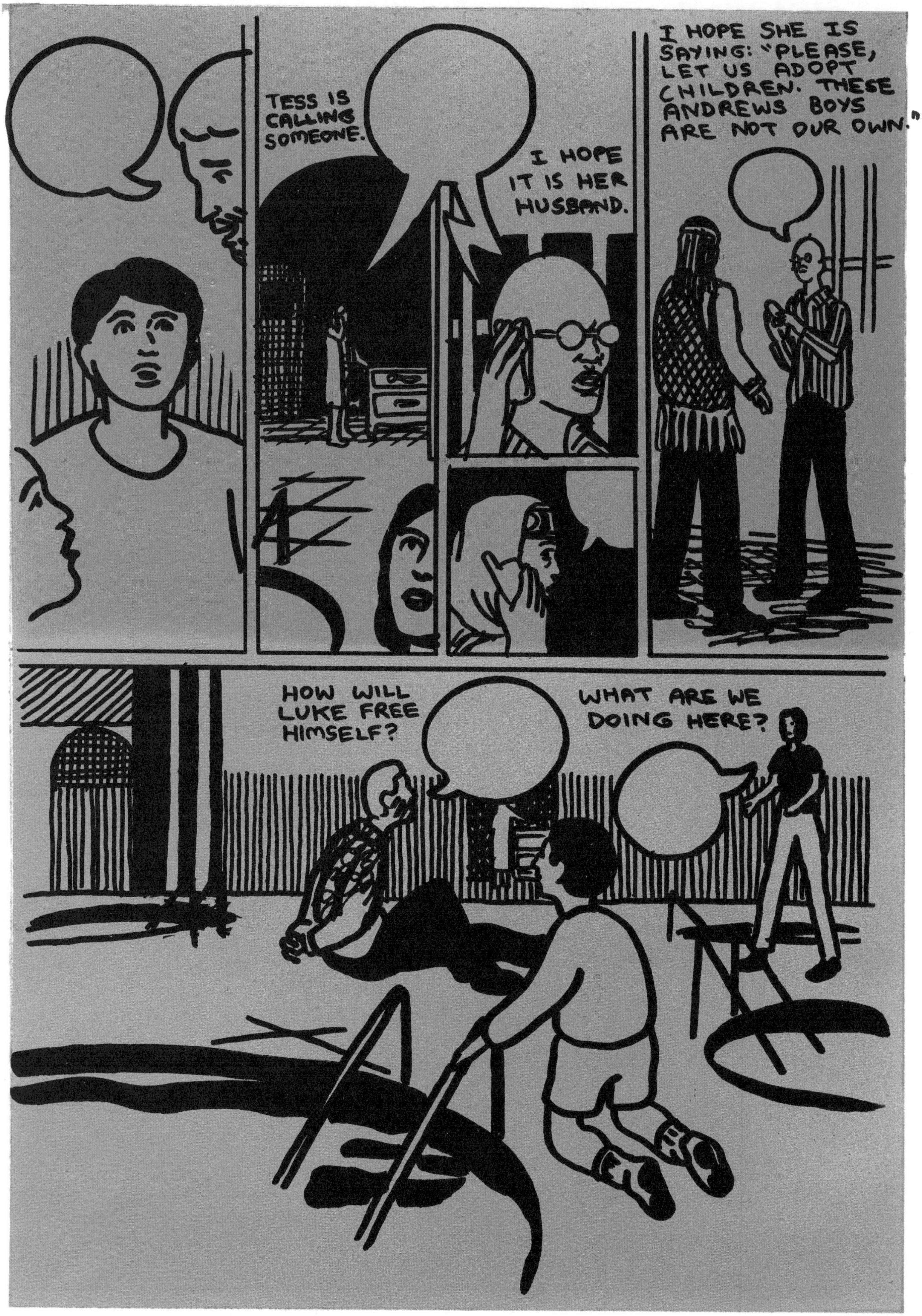
TESS IS CALLING SOMEONE.
I HOPE IT IS HER HUSBAND.
I HOPE SHE IS SAYING: "PLEASE, LET US ADOPT CHILDREN. THESE ANDREWS BOYS ARE NOT OUR OWN."
HOW WILL LUKE FREE HIMSELF?
WHAT ARE WE DOING HERE?

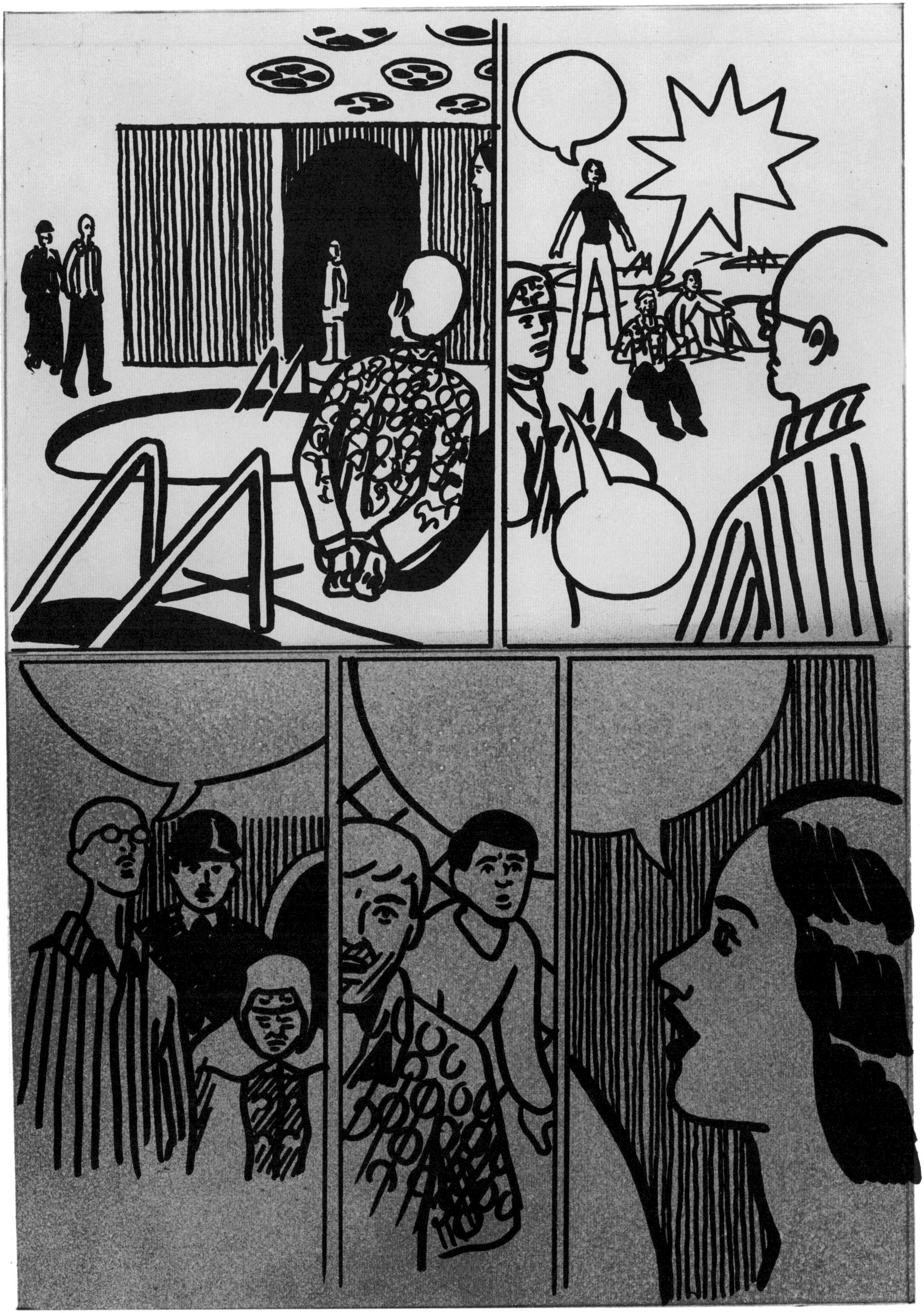

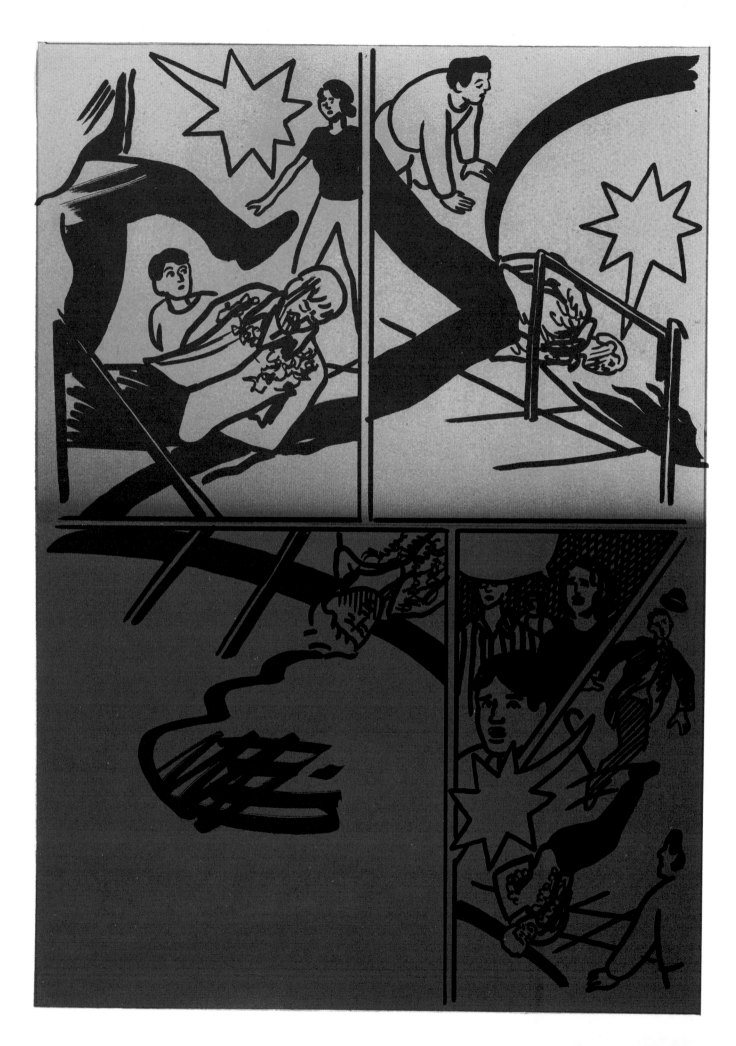

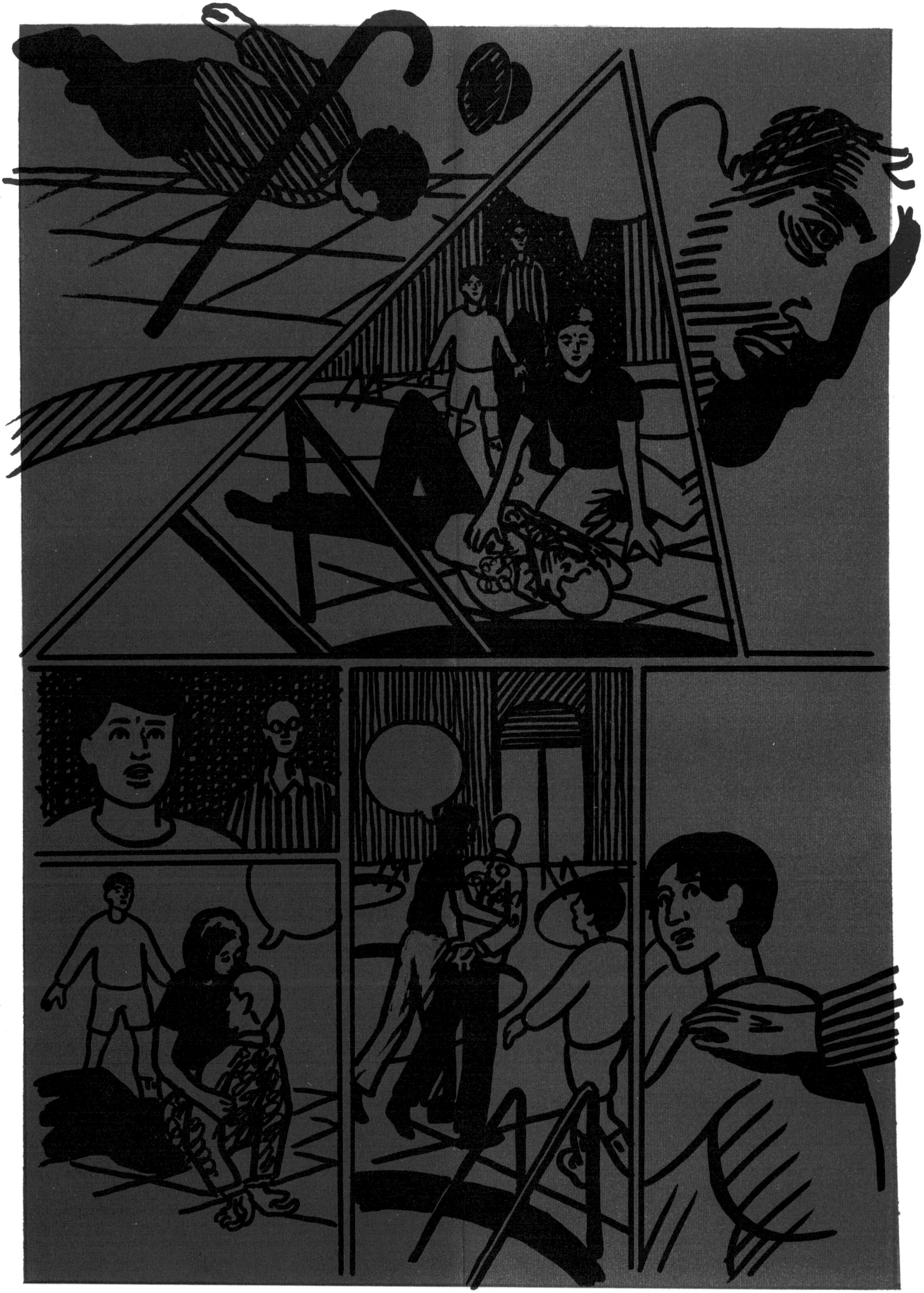

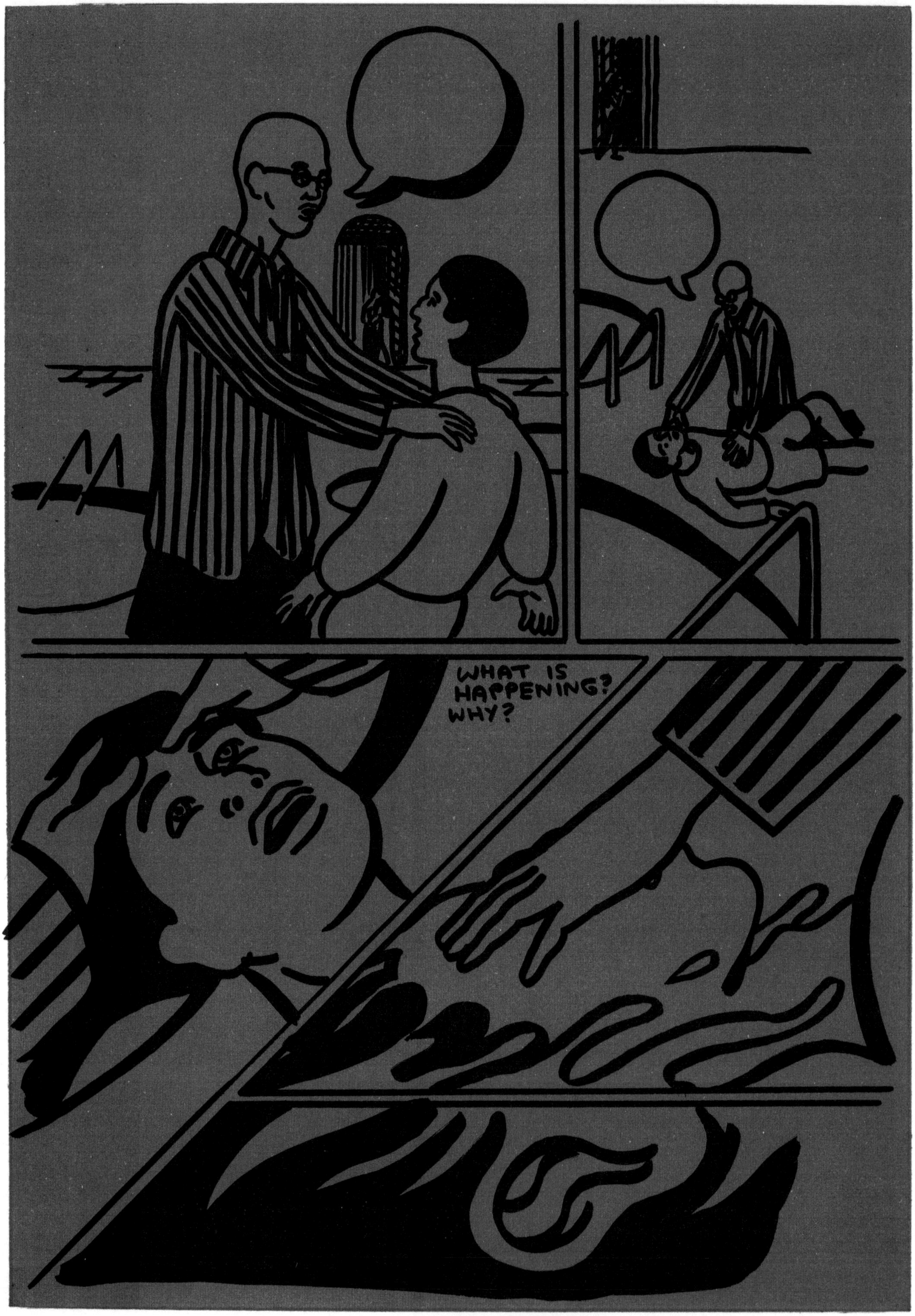
WHAT IS
HAPPENING?
WHY?

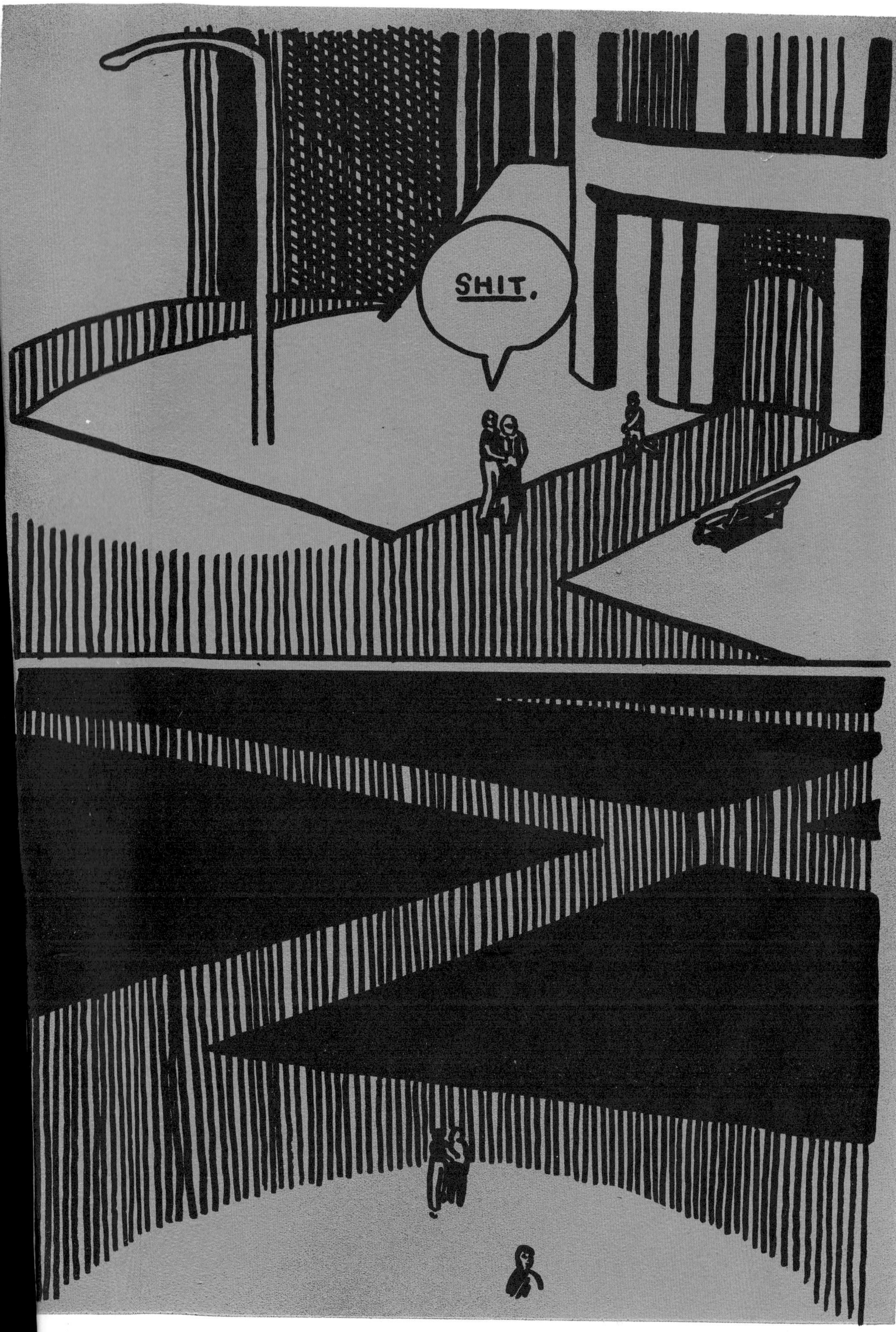
SHIT.

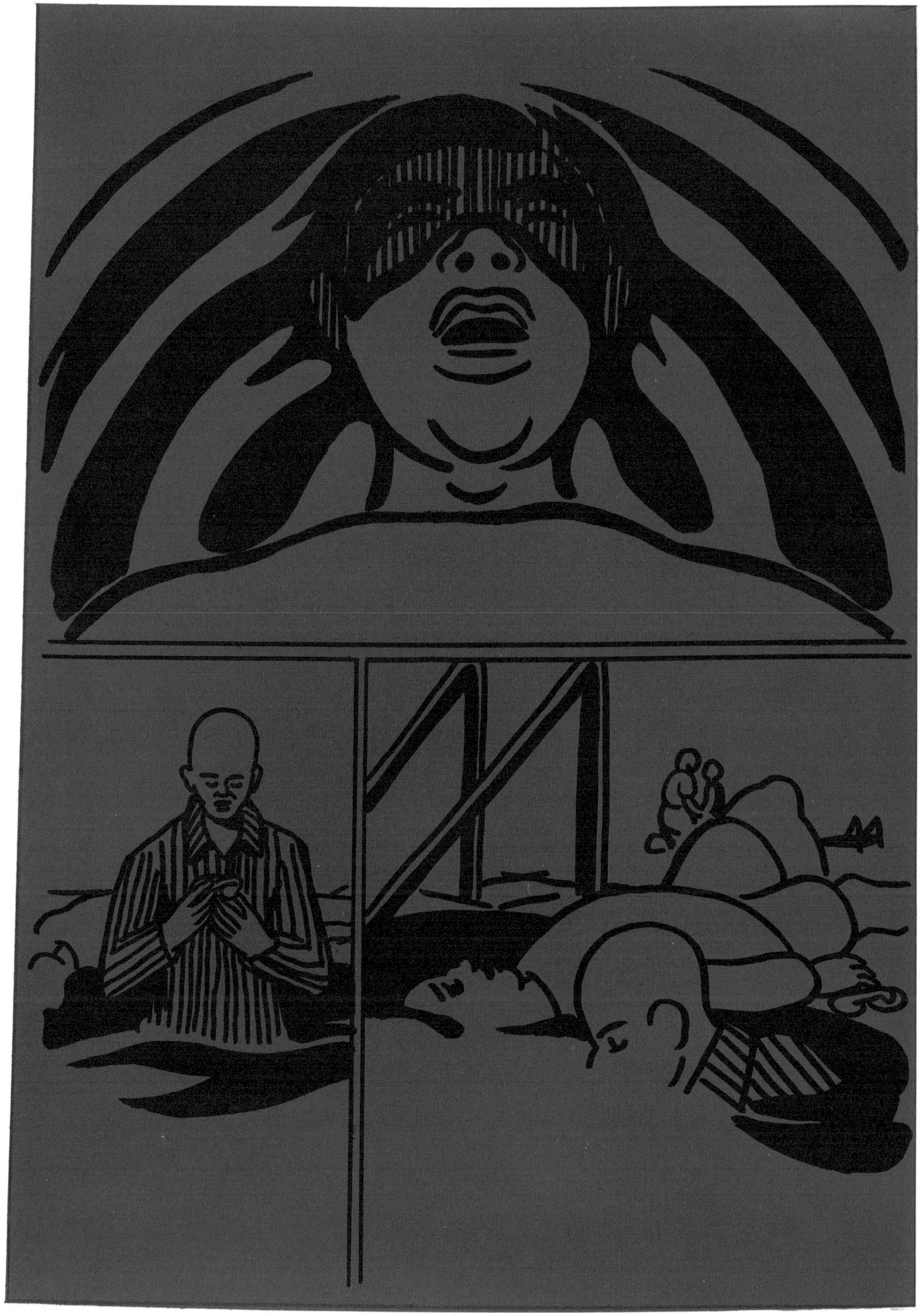

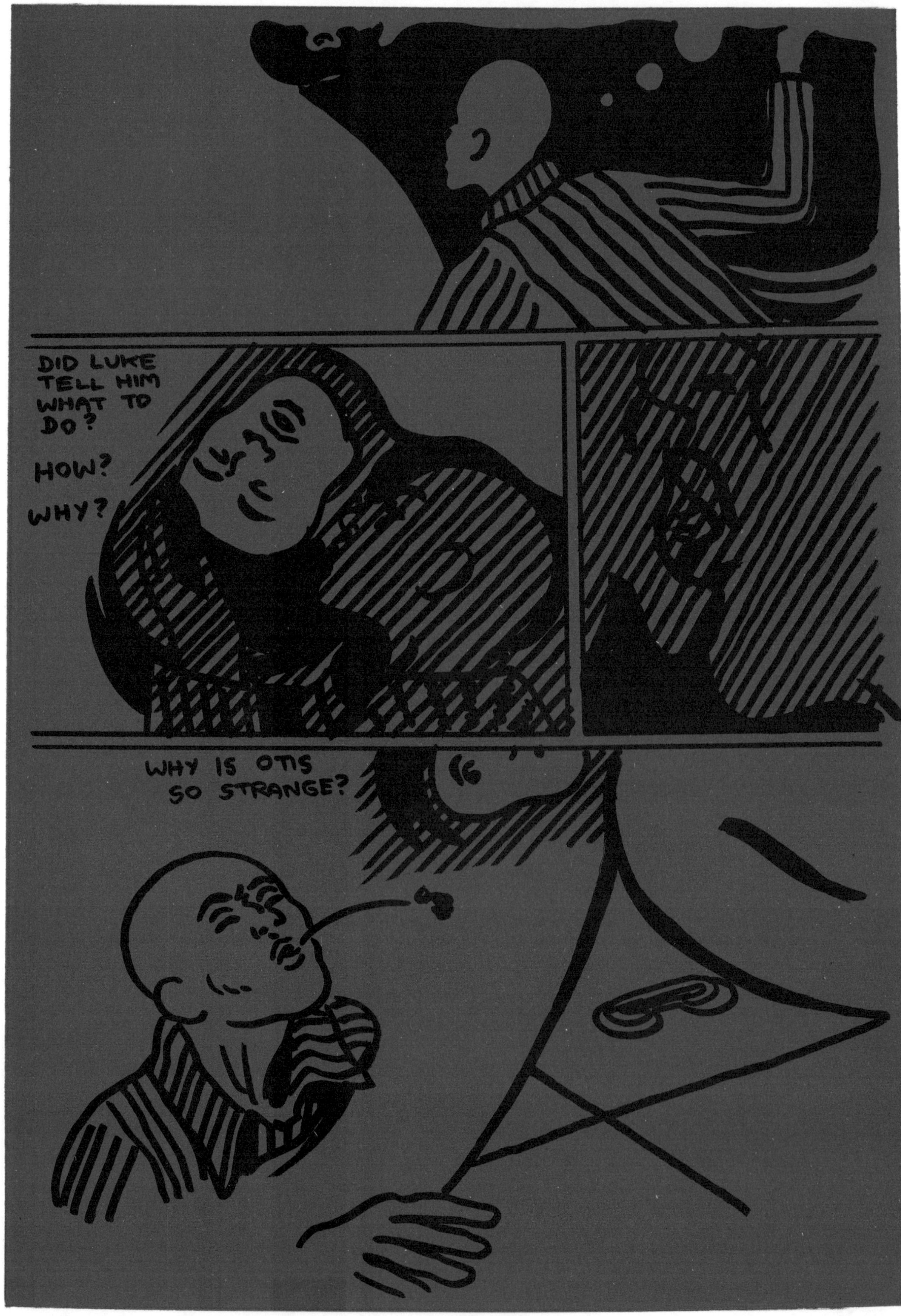
DID LUKE TELL HIM WHAT TO DO?
HOW?
WHY?
WHY IS OTIS SO STRANGE?

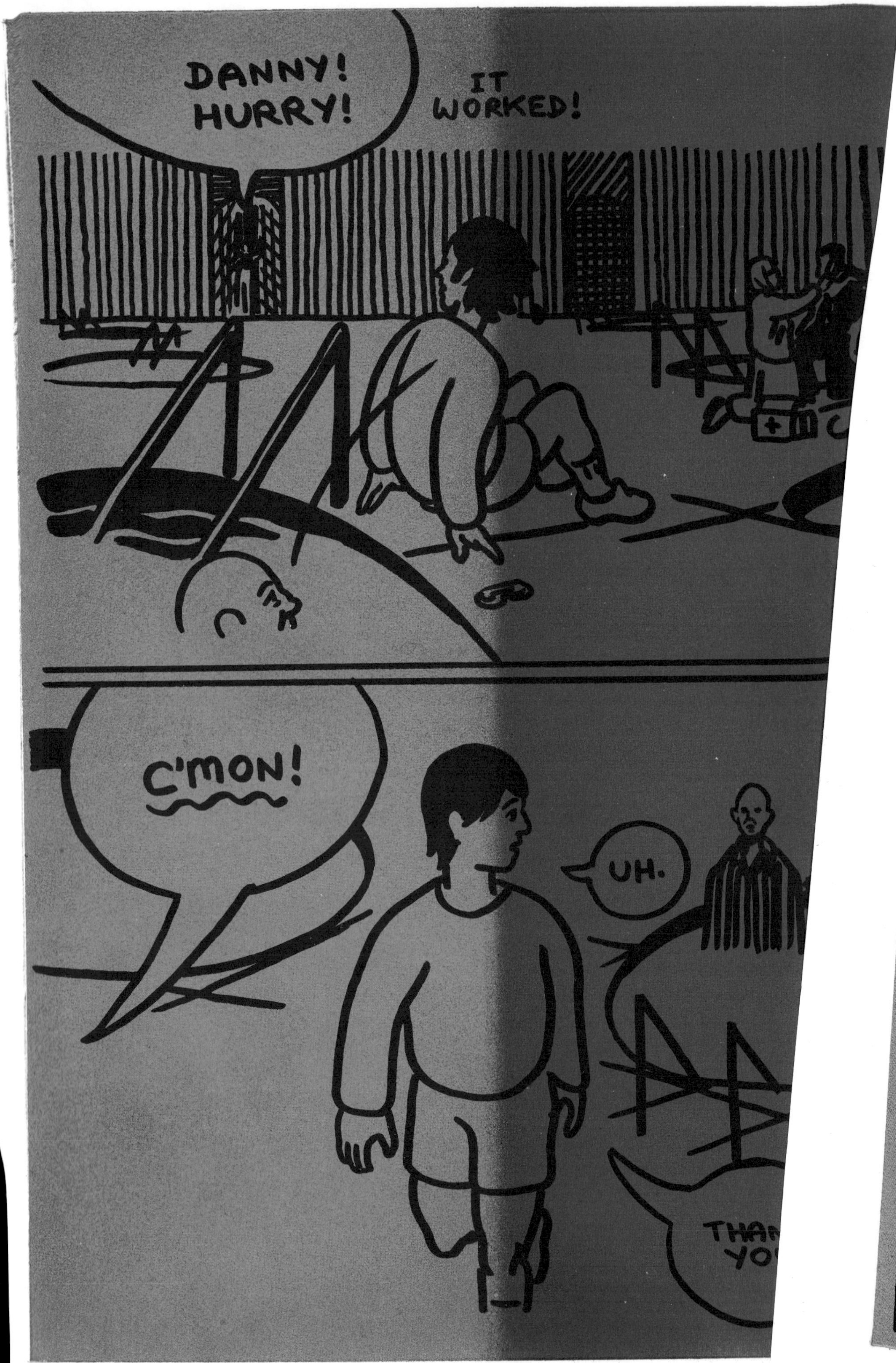
DANNY! HURRY!
IT WORKED!
C'MON!
UH.

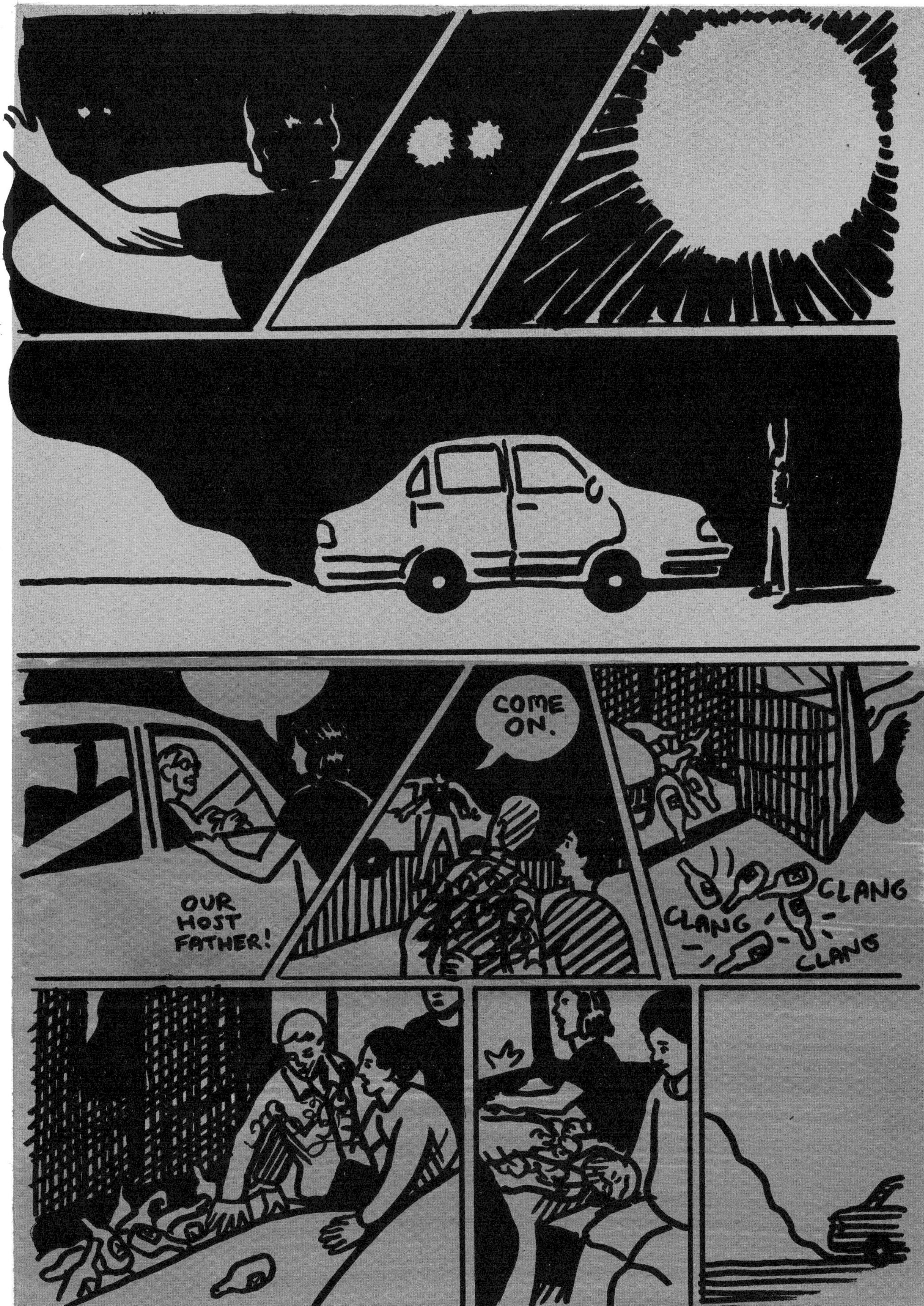
COME ON.
OUR HOST FATHER!
CLANG
CLANG
CLANG

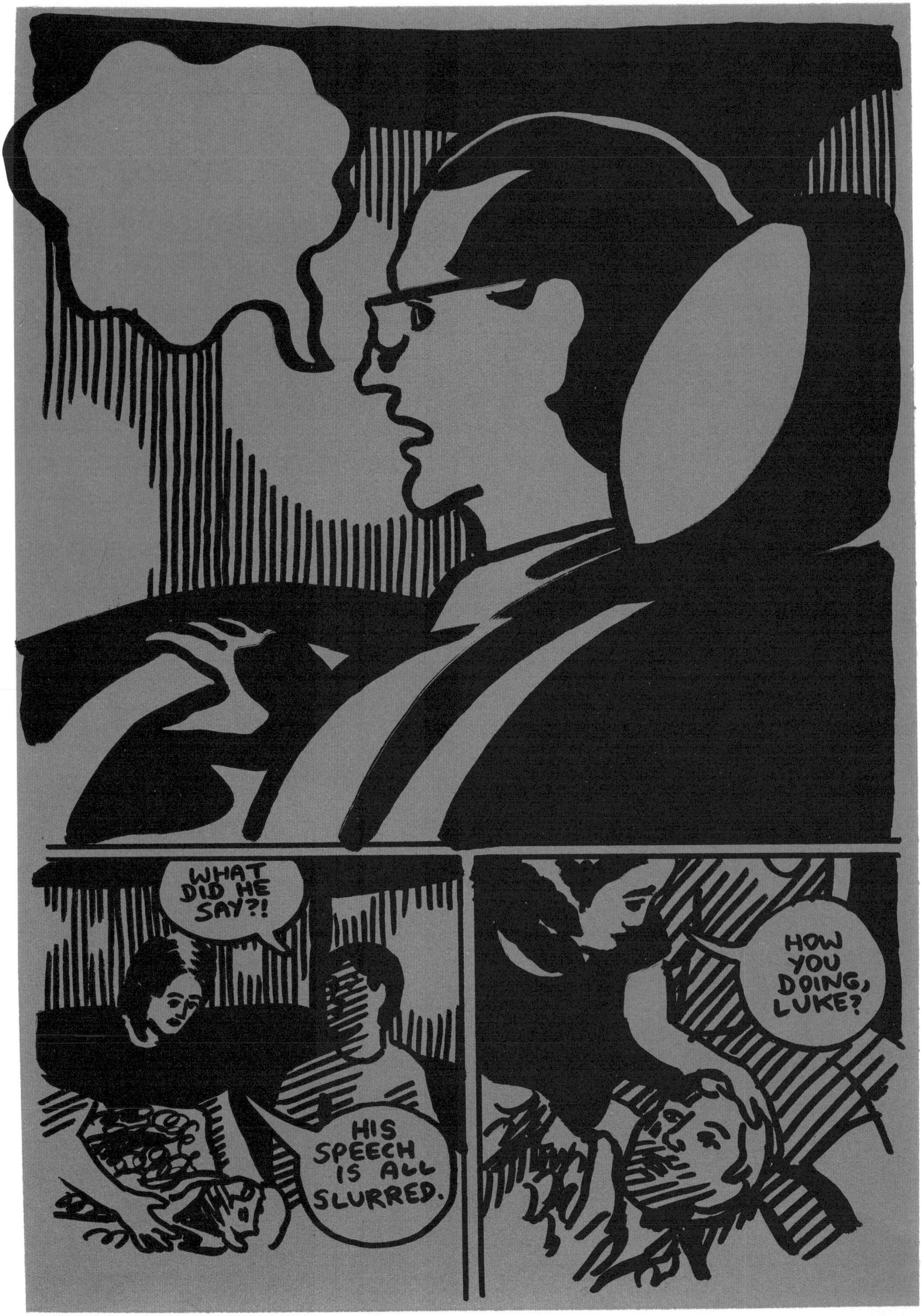
WHAT DID HE SAY?!
HIS SPEECH IS ALL SLURRED.
HOW YOU DOING, LUKE?

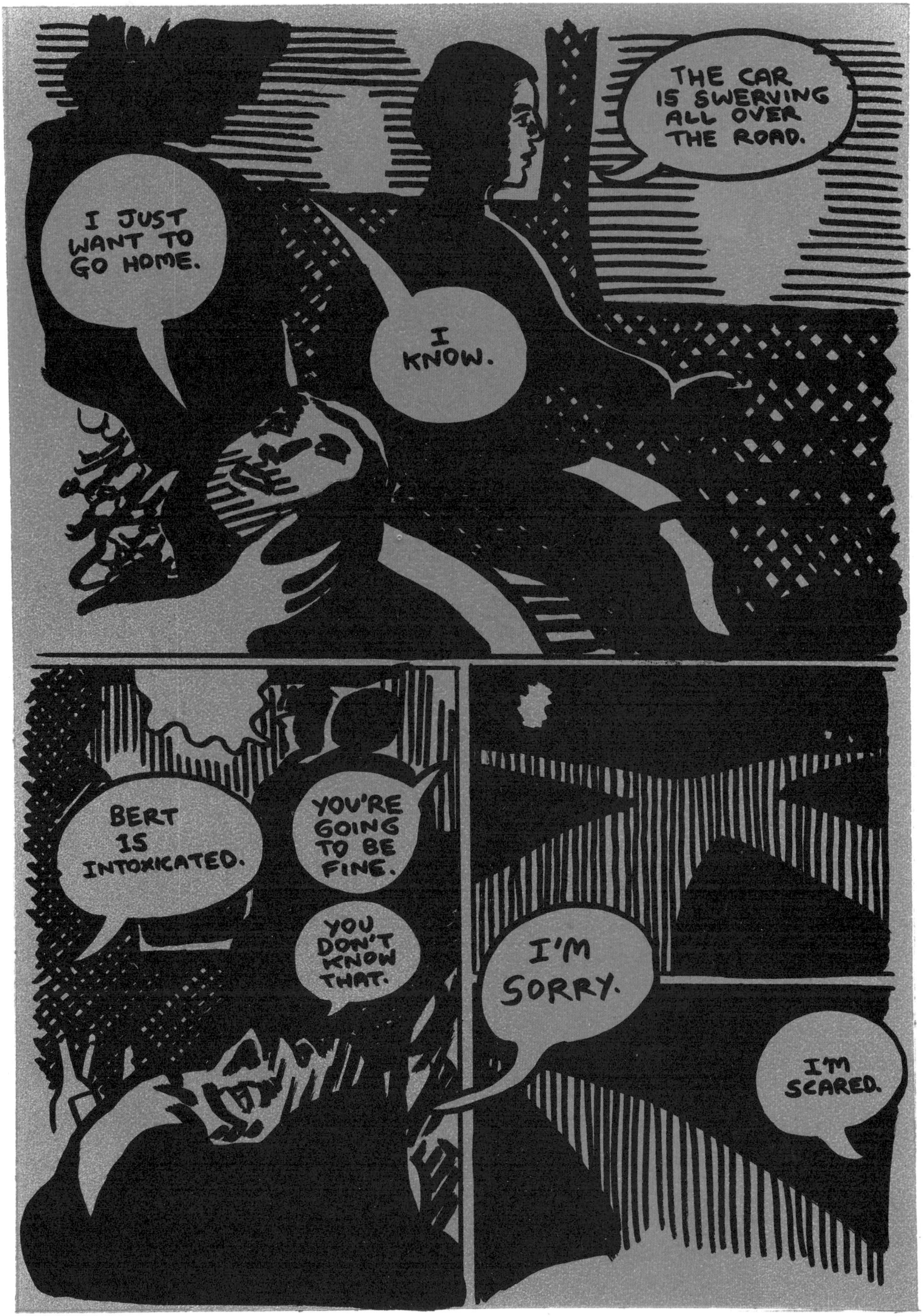
THE CAR IS SWERVING ALL OVER THE ROAD.
I JUST WANT TO GO HOME.
I KNOW.
BERT IS INTOXICATED.
YOU'RE GOING TO BE FINE.
YOU DON'T KNOW THAT.
I'M SORRY.
I'M SCARED.

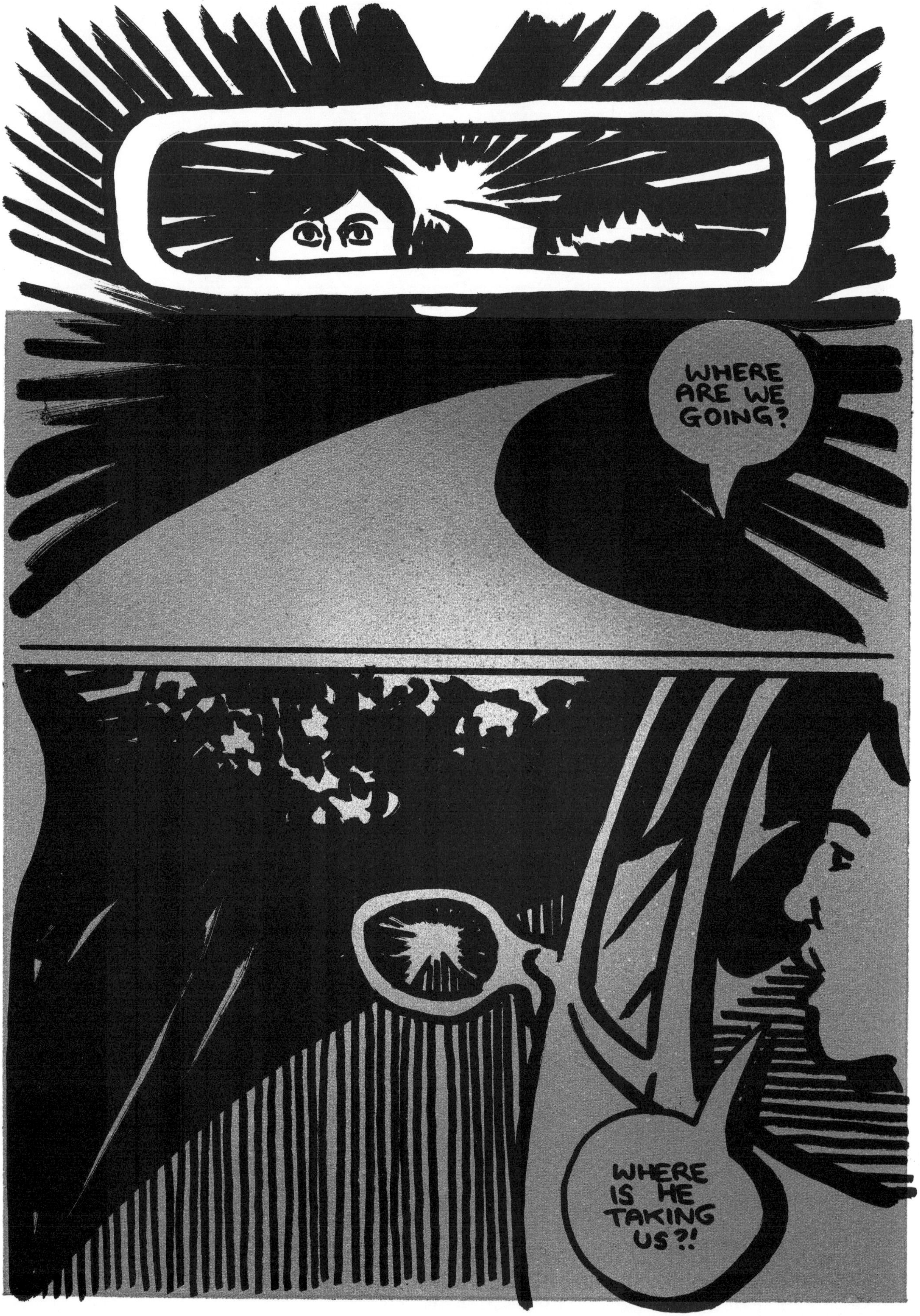
WHERE ARE WE GOING?
WHERE IS HE TAKING US?!

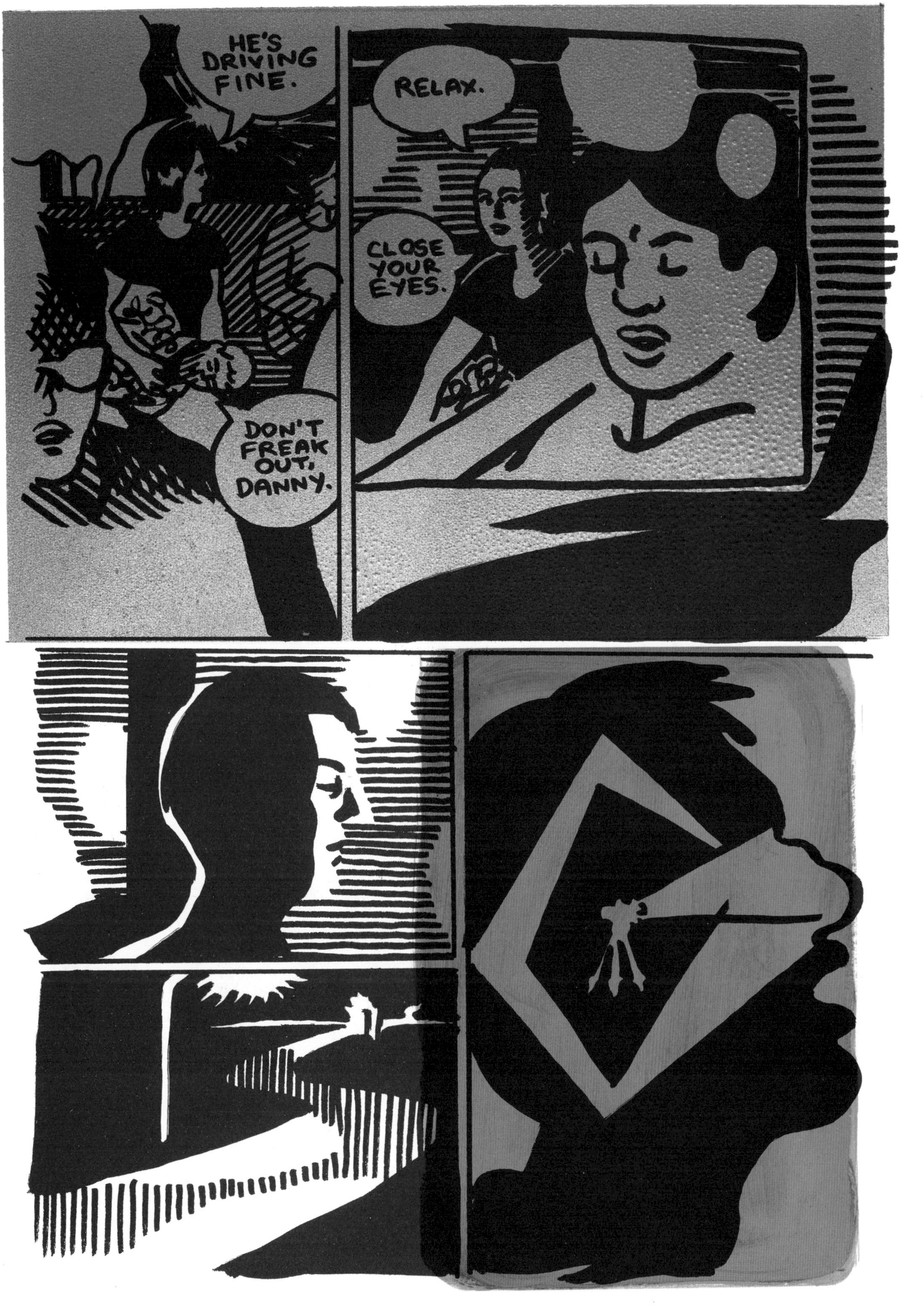
HE'S DRIVING FINE.
DON'T FREAK OUT, DANNY.
RELAX.
CLOSE YOUR EYES.

I SEE THE FUTURE.

LUKE AND I RETURN TO NEW JERSEY.

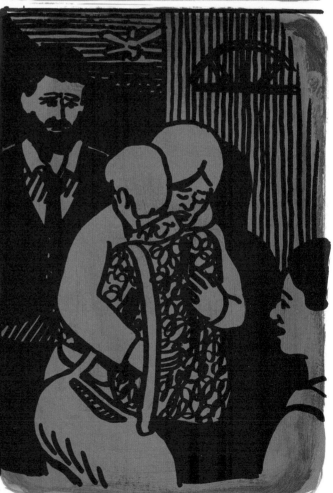

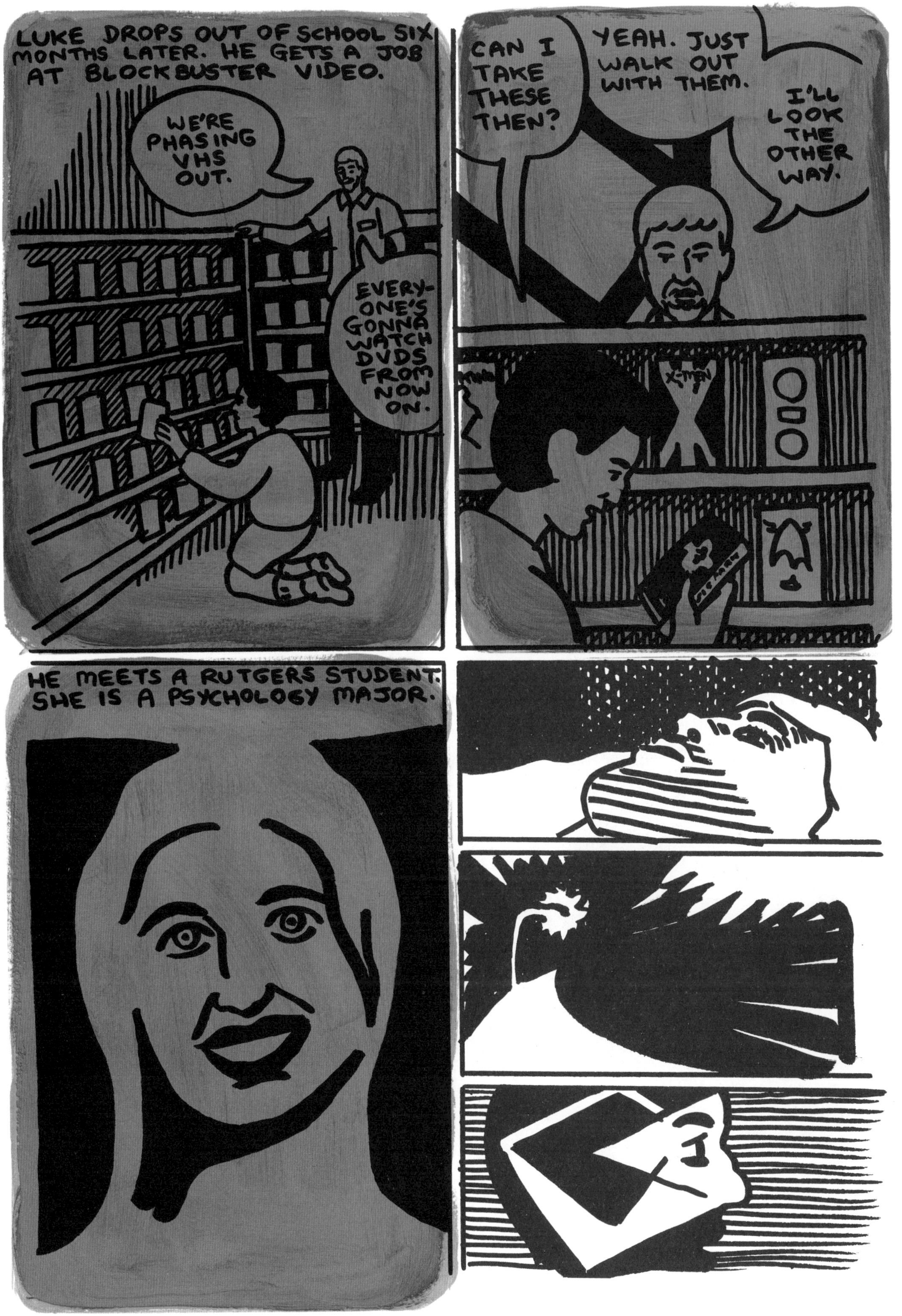
LUKE DROPS OUT OF SCHOOL SIX MONTHS LATER. HE GETS A JOB AT BLOCKBUSTER VIDEO.
WE'RE PHASING VHS OUT.
EVERY-ONE'S GONNA WATCH DVDS FROM NOW ON.
CAN I TAKE THESE THEN?
YEAH. JUST WALK OUT WITH THEM.
I'LL LOOK THE OTHER WAY.
X-MEN
HE MEETS A RUTGERS STUDENT. SHE IS A PSYCHOLOGY MAJOR.

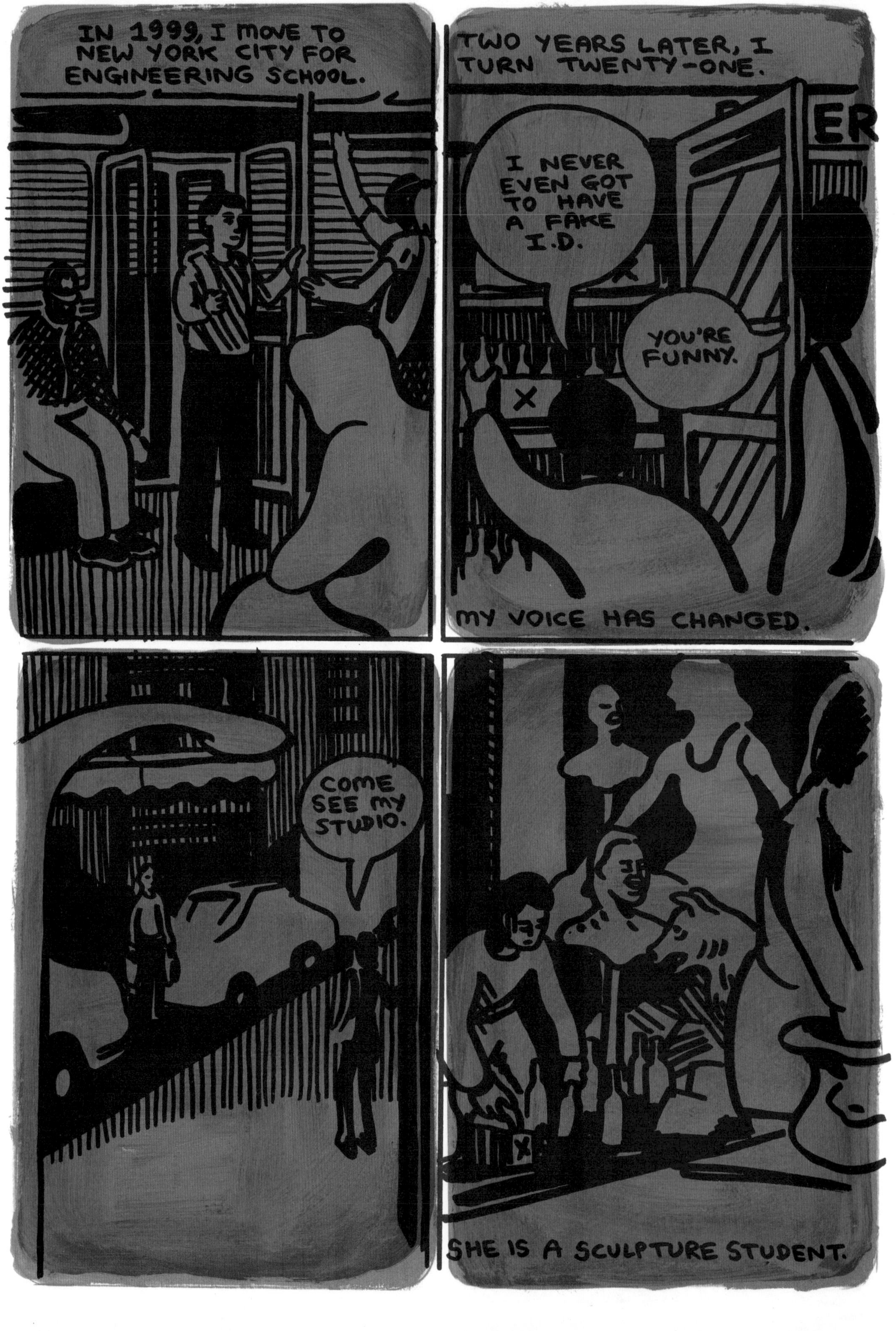
IN 1999, I MOVE TO NEW YORK CITY FOR ENGINEERING SCHOOL.
TWO YEARS LATER, I TURN TWENTY-ONE.
I NEVER EVEN GOT TO HAVE A FAKE I.D.
YOU'RE FUNNY.
MY VOICE HAS CHANGED.
COME SEE MY STUDIO.
SHE IS A SCULPTURE STUDENT.

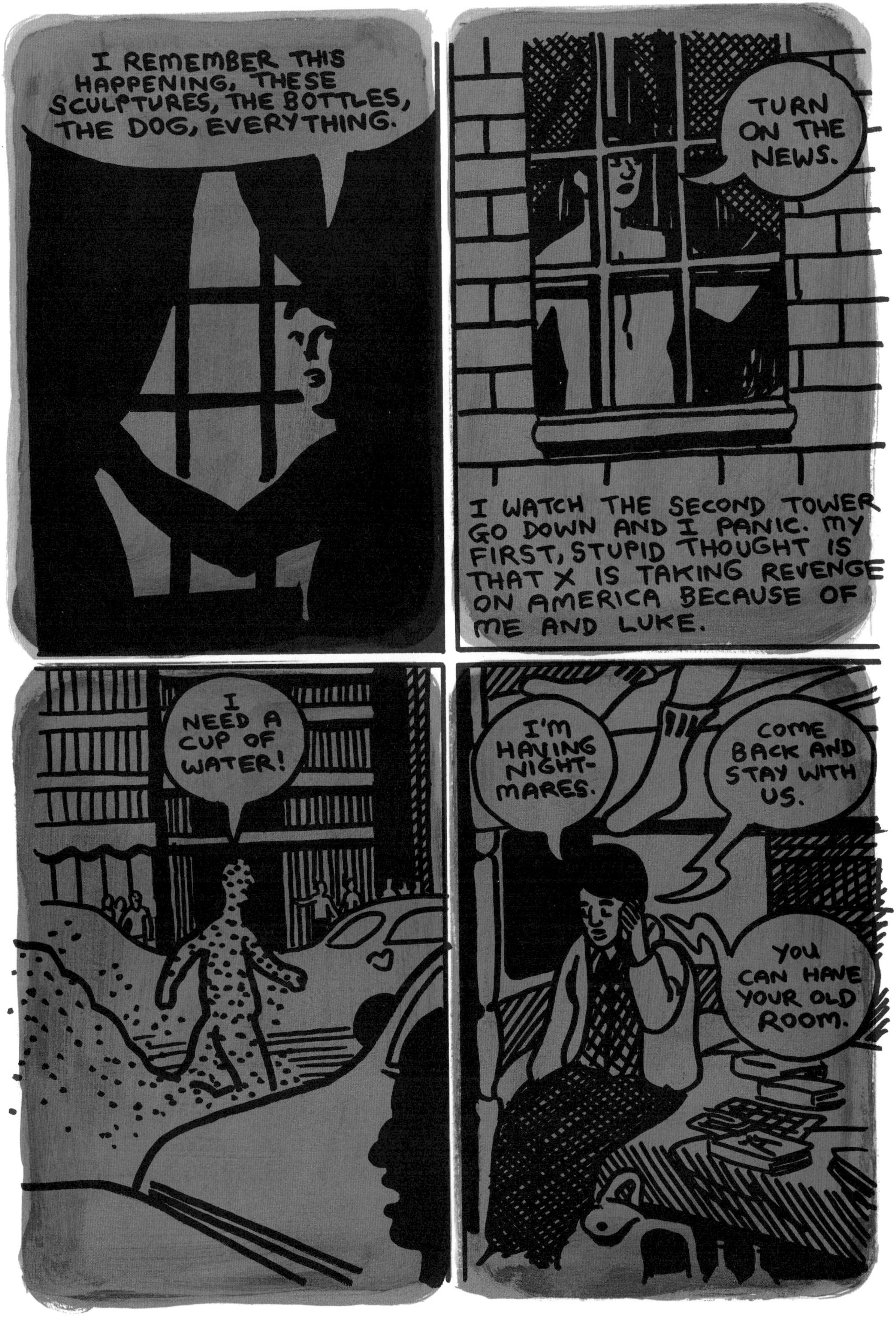
I REMEMBER THIS HAPPENING, THESE SCULPTURES, THE BOTTLES, THE DOG, EVERYTHING.
TURN ON THE NEWS.
I WATCH THE SECOND TOWER GO DOWN AND I PANIC. MY FIRST, STUPID THOUGHT IS THAT X IS TAKING REVENGE ON AMERICA BECAUSE OF ME AND LUKE.
I NEED A CUP OF WATER!
I'M HAVING NIGHT-MARES.
COME BACK AND STAY WITH US.
YOU CAN HAVE YOUR OLD ROOM.

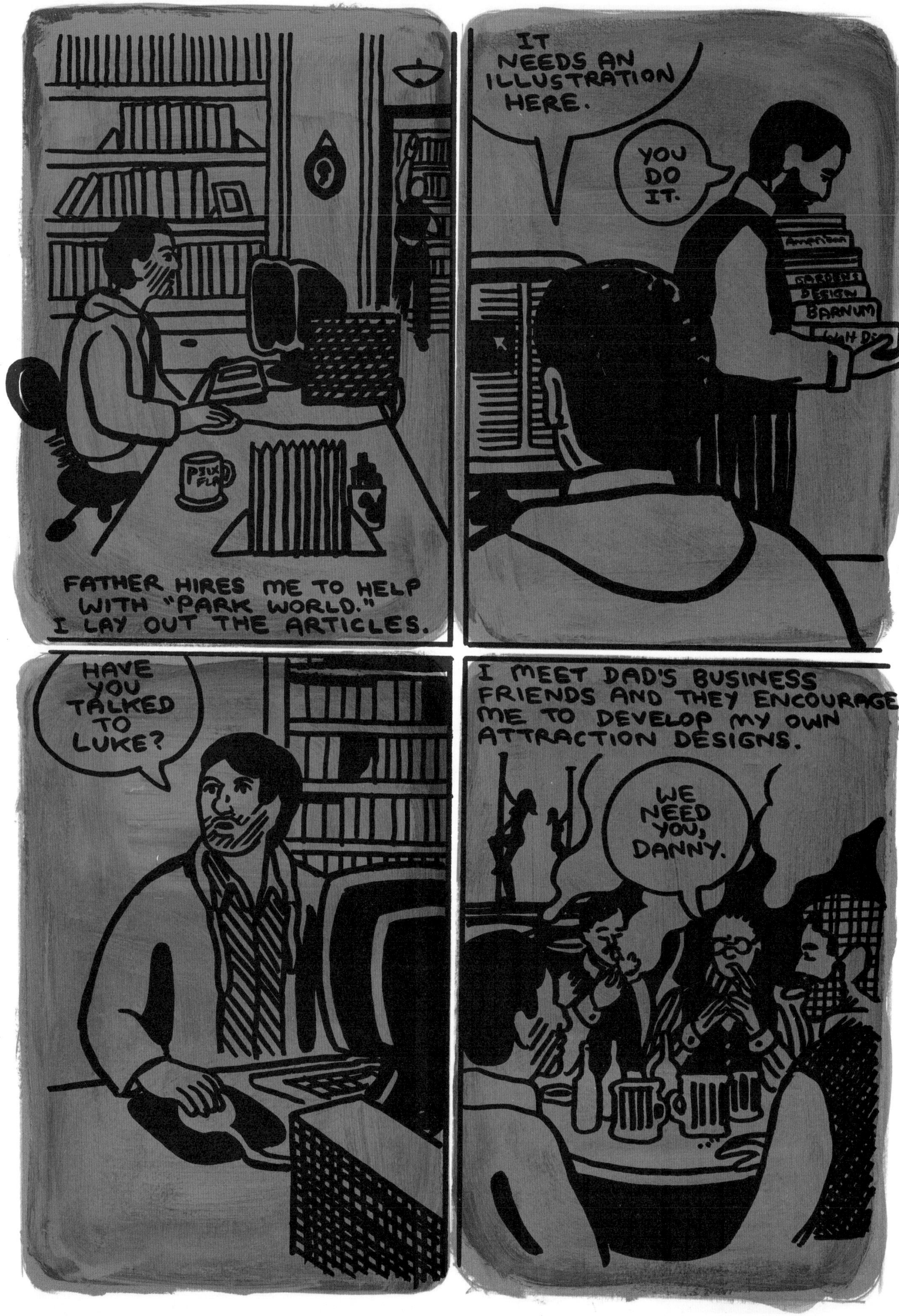
FATHER HIRES ME TO HELP WITH "PARK WORLD." I LAY OUT THE ARTICLES.
IT NEEDS AN ILLUSTRATION HERE.
YOU DO IT.
BARNUM
HAVE YOU TALKED TO LUKE?
I MEET DAD'S BUSINESS FRIENDS AND THEY ENCOURAGE ME TO DEVELOP MY OWN ATTRACTION DESIGNS.
WE NEED YOU, DANNY.

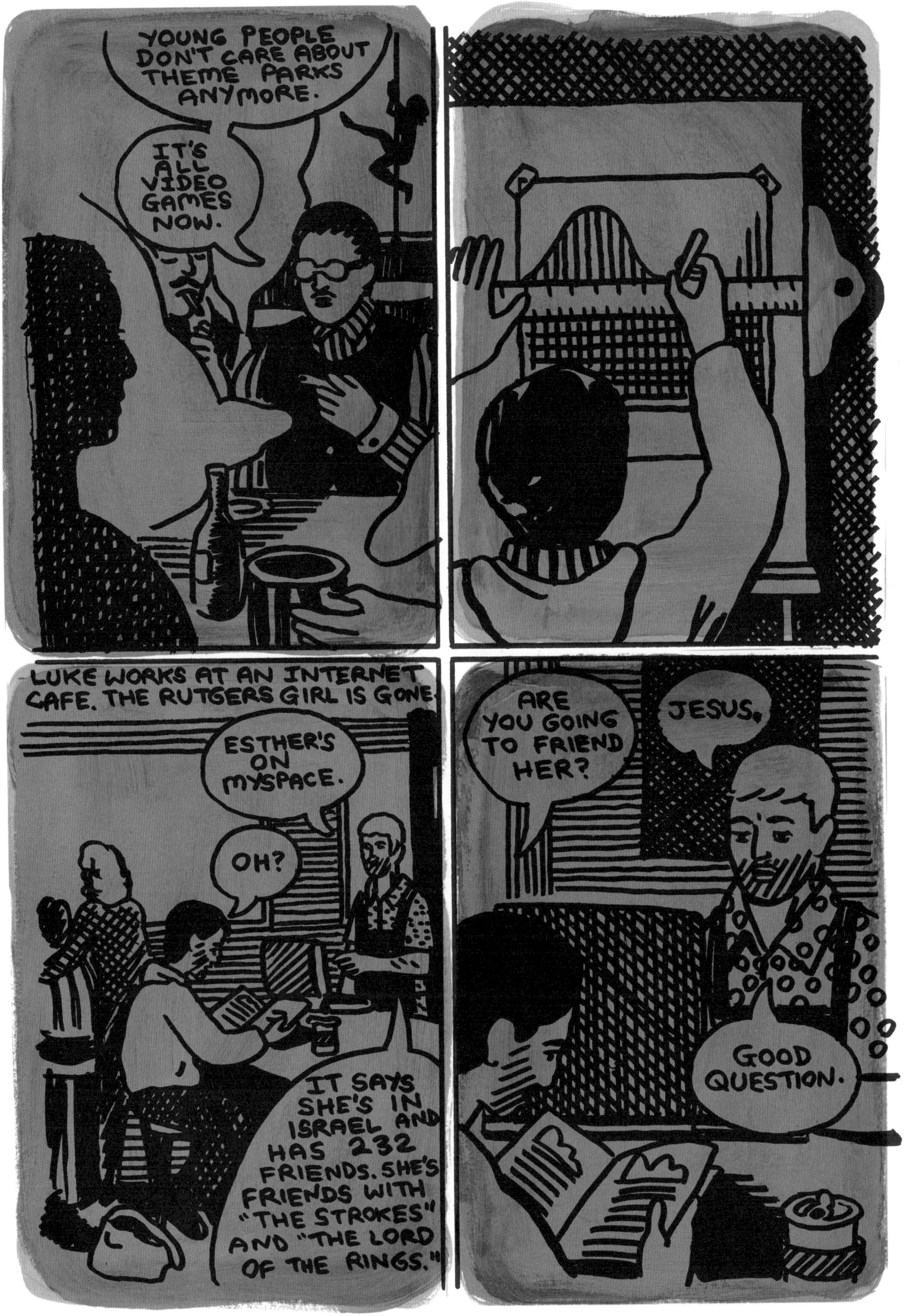
YOUNG PEOPLE DON'T CARE ABOUT THEME PARKS ANYMORE.
IT'S ALL VIDEO GAMES NOW.
LUKE WORKS AT AN INTERNET CAFE. THE RUTGERS GIRL IS GONE.
ESTHER'S ON MYSPACE.
OH?
IT SAYS SHE'S IN ISRAEL AND HAS 232 FRIENDS. SHE'S FRIENDS WITH "THE STROKES" AND "THE LORD OF THE RINGS."
ARE YOU GOING TO FRIEND HER?
JESUS.
GOOD QUESTION.

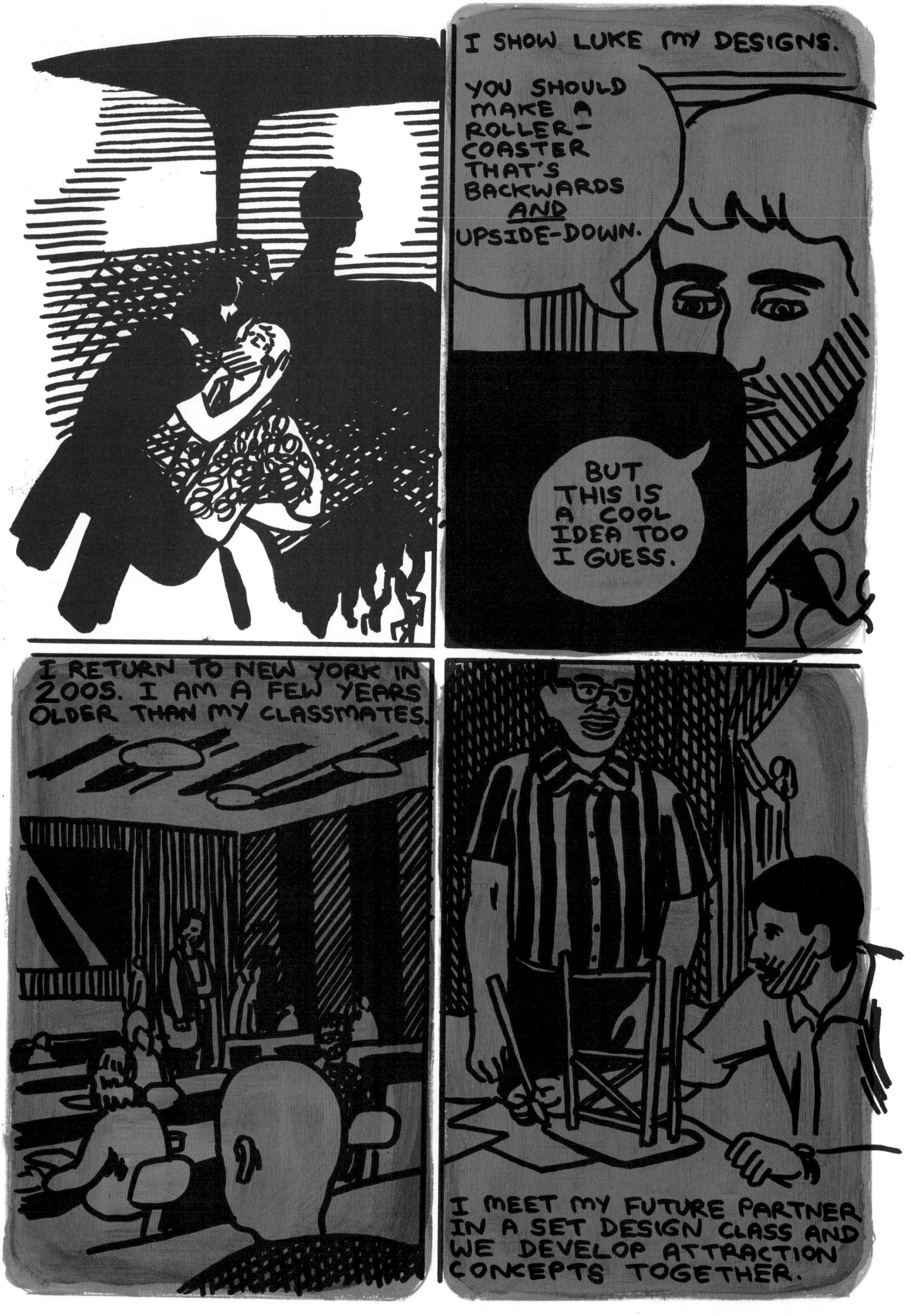
I SHOW LUKE MY DESIGNS.
YOU SHOULD MAKE A ROLLER-COASTER THAT'S BACKWARDS AND UPSIDE-DOWN.
BUT THIS IS A COOL IDEA TOO I GUESS.
I RETURN TO NEW YORK IN 2005. I AM A FEW YEARS OLDER THAN MY CLASSMATES.
I MEET MY FUTURE PARTNER IN A SET DESIGN CLASS AND WE DEVELOP ATTRACTION CONCEPTS TOGETHER.

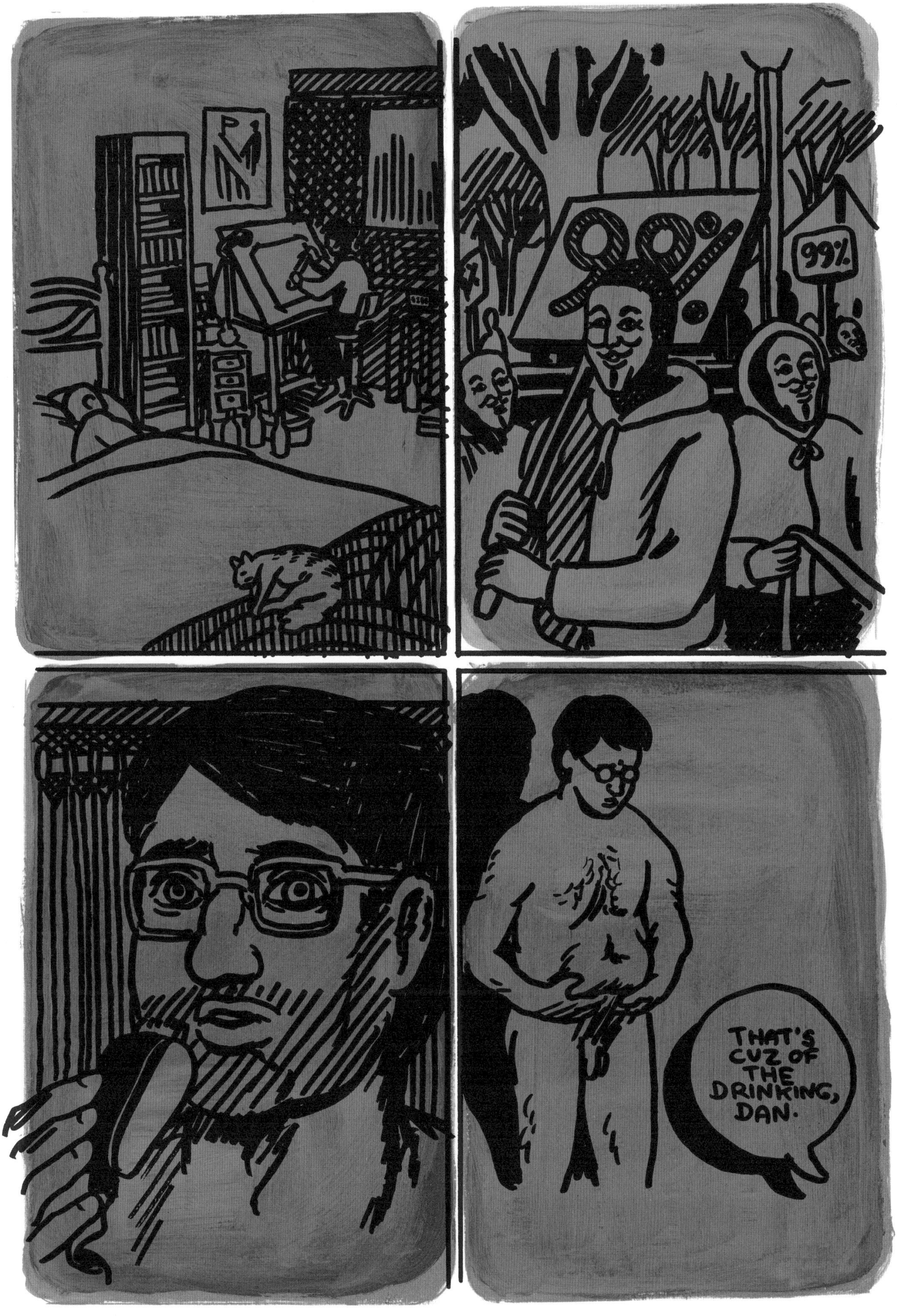
99%
99%
THAT'S CUZ OF THE DRINKING, DAN.

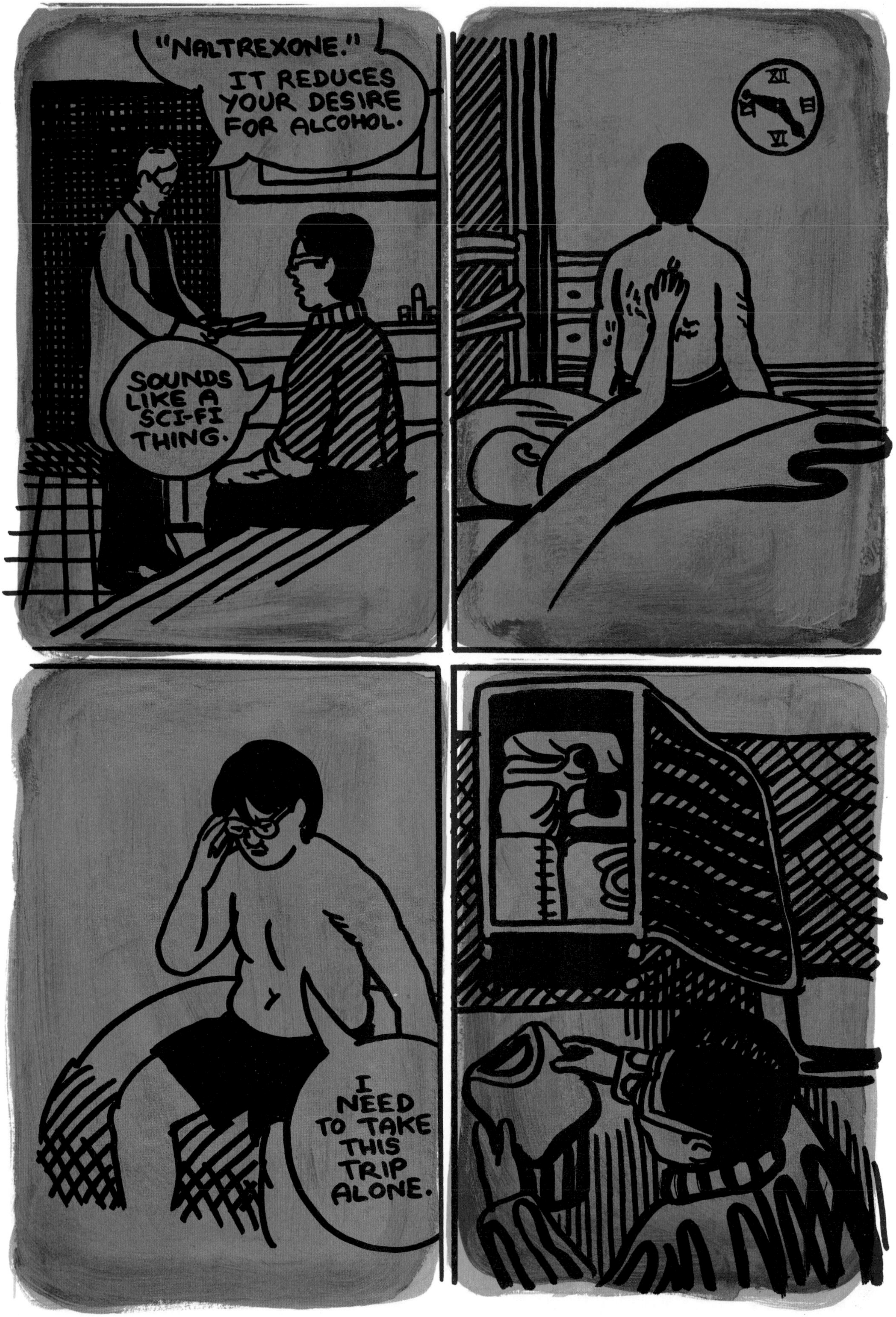
"NALTREXONE."
IT REDUCES YOUR DESIRE FOR ALCOHOL.
SOUNDS LIKE A SCI-FI THING.
I NEED TO TAKE THIS TRIP ALONE.

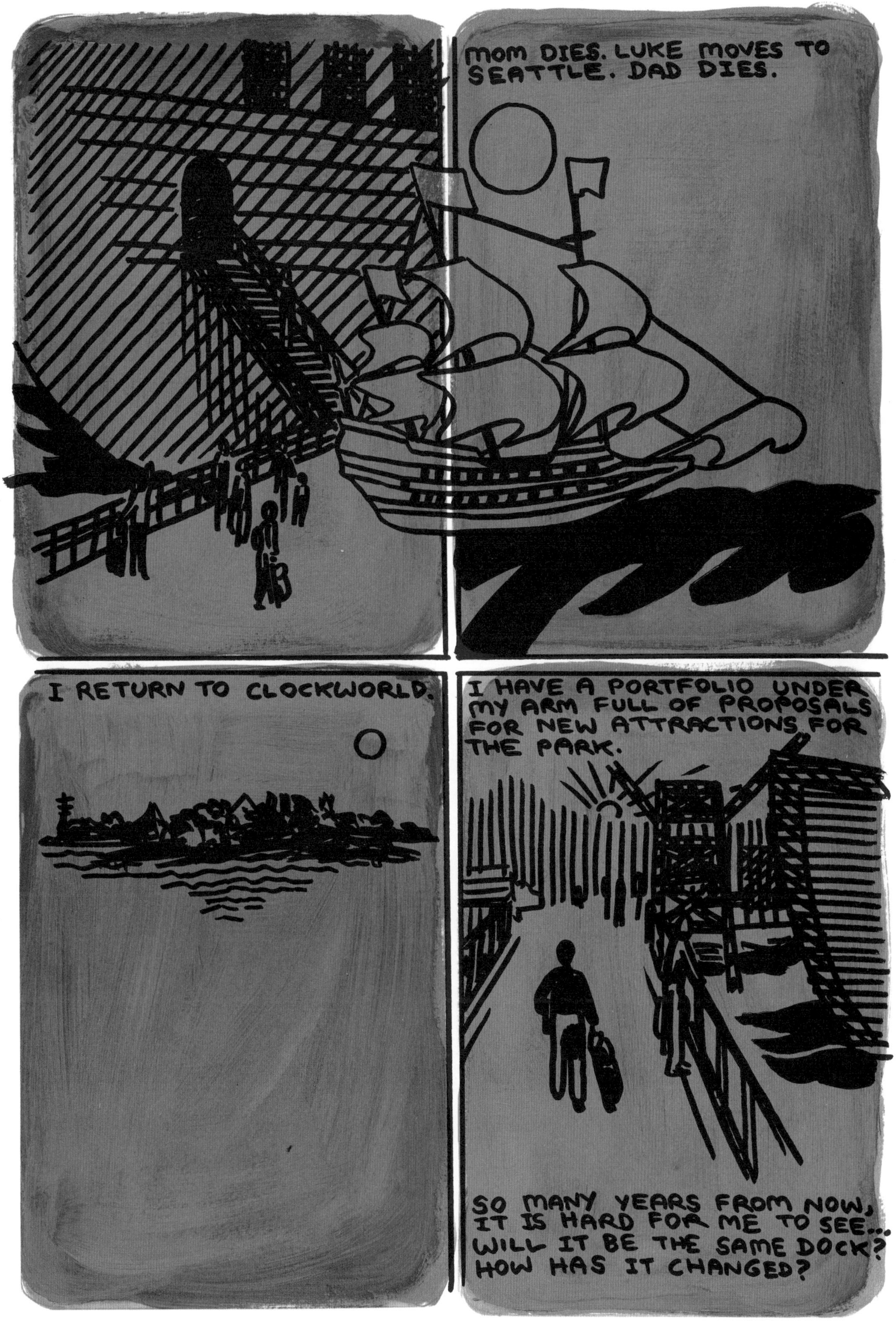
MOM DIES. LUKE MOVES TO SEATTLE. DAD DIES.
I RETURN TO CLOCKWORLD.
I HAVE A PORTFOLIO UNDER MY ARM FULL OF PROPOSALS FOR NEW ATTRACTIONS FOR THE PARK.
SO MANY YEARS FROM NOW, IT IS HARD FOR ME TO SEE... WILL IT BE THE SAME DOCK? HOW HAS IT CHANGED?

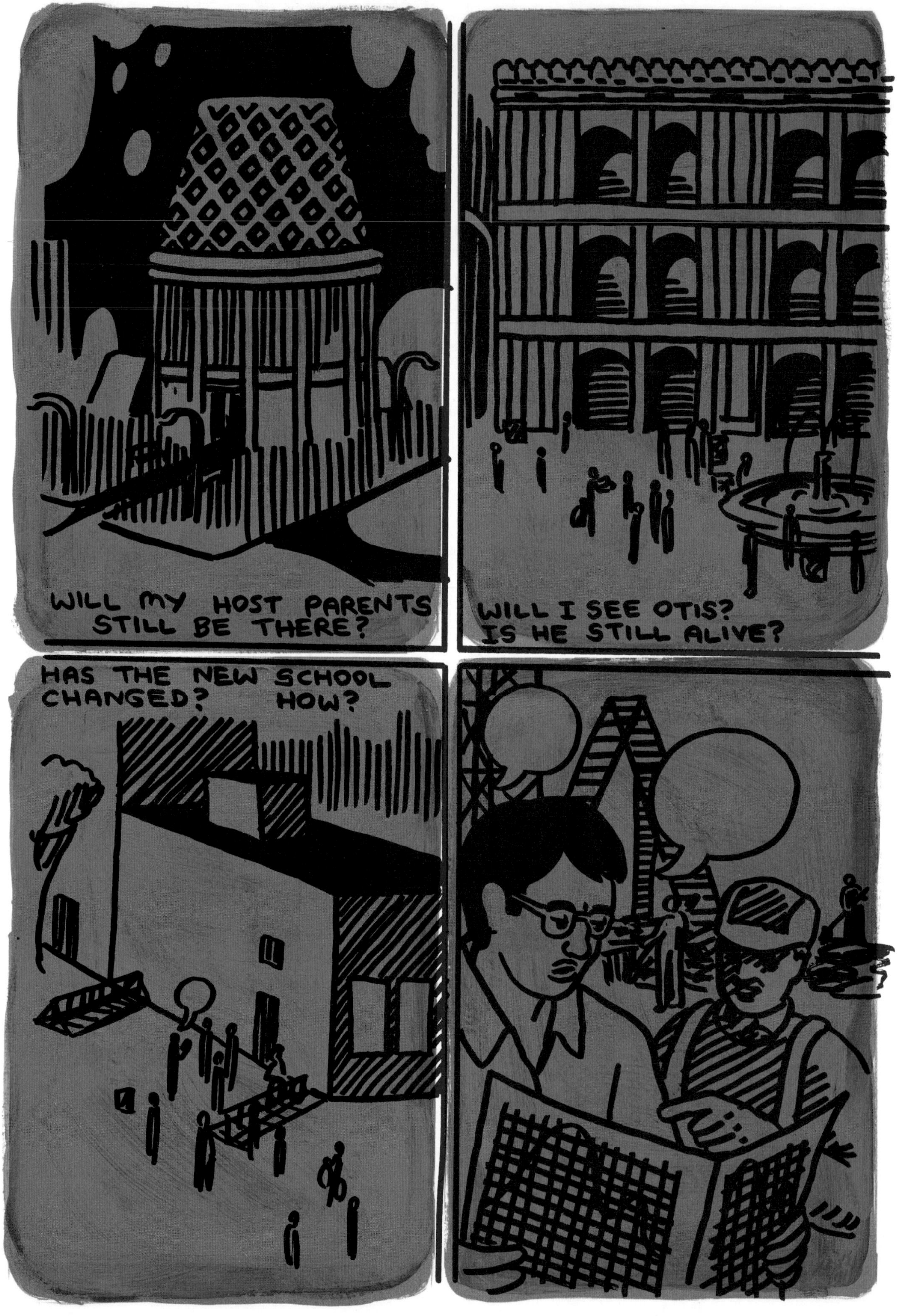

WILL MY HOST PARENTS STILL BE THERE?
WILL I SEE OTIS? IS HE STILL ALIVE?
HAS THE NEW SCHOOL CHANGED? HOW?

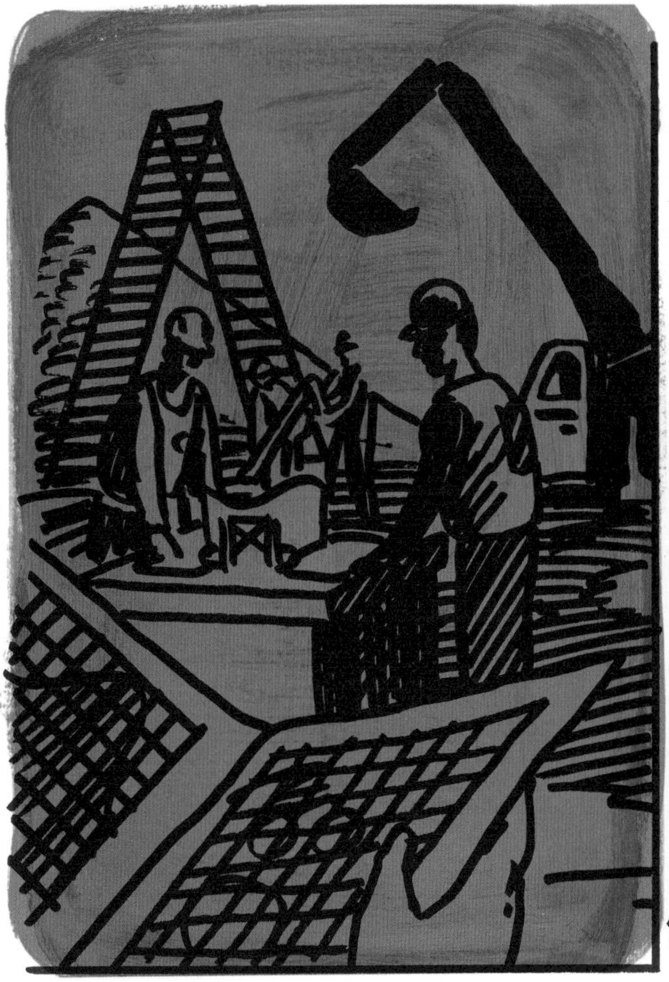

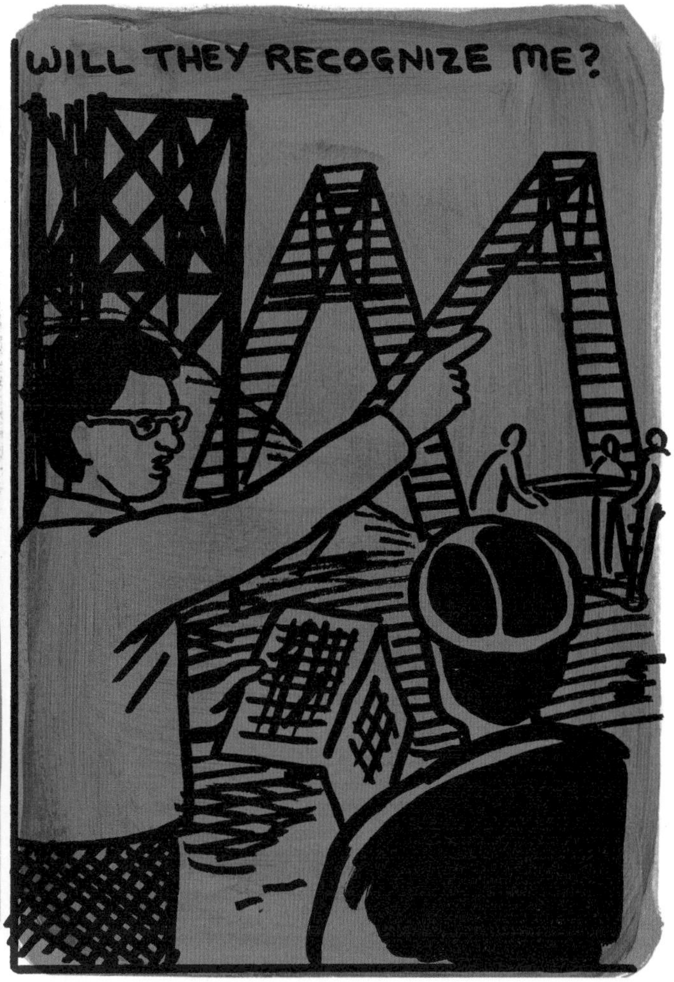
WILL THEY RECOGNIZE ME?

THE END

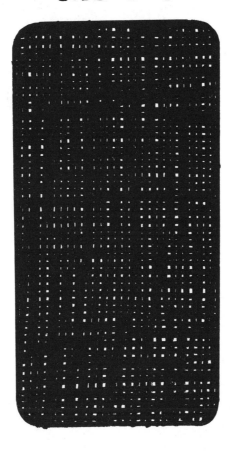

Also by Dash Shaw:

Comics:

3 New Stories
BodyWorld
The Unclothed Man in the 35th Century A.D.
Bottomless Belly Button

Cartoons:

Seraph (Sigur Ros video)
Wheel of Fortune
Blind Date 4
Unclothed Man (IFC series)

dashshaw.tumblr.com